D1200750

# TRADE, STABILITY, AND MACROECONOMICS

## *Essays in Honor of Lloyd A. Metzler*

Portrait by Fabian Bachrach

# TRADE, STABILITY, AND MACROECONOMICS

## Essays in Honor of Lloyd A. Metzler

*Edited by*

*GEORGE HORWICH* and *PAUL A. SAMUELSON*

*Department of Economics*
*Purdue University*
*West Lafayette, Indiana*

*Department of Economics*
*Massachusetts Institute*
*of Technology*
*Cambridge, Massachusetts*

1974

ACADEMIC PRESS New York and London
A Subsidiary of Harcourt Brace Jovanovich, Publishers

# ECONOMIC THEORY AND MATHEMATICAL ECONOMICS

## Consulting Editor: Karl Shell

UNIVERSITY OF PENNSYLVANIA
PHILADELPHIA, PENNSYLVANIA

*Franklin M. Fisher and Karl Shell.* The Economic Theory of Price Indices: *Two Essays on the Effects of Taste, Quality, and Technological Change*

*Luis Eugenio Di Marco (Ed.).* International Economics and Development: *Essays in Honor of Raúl Presbisch*

*Erwin Klein.* Mathematical Methods in Theoretical Economics: *Topological and Vector Space Foundations of Equilibrium Analysis*

*Paul Zarembka (Ed.).* Frontiers in Econometrics

*George Horwich and Paul A. Samuelson (Eds.).* Trade, Stability, and Macroeconomics: *Essays in Honor of Lloyd A. Metzler*

ACADEMIC PRESS, INC.
111 Fifth Avenue, New York, New York 10003

*United Kingdom Edition published by*
ACADEMIC PRESS, INC. (LONDON) LTD.
24/28 Oval Road, London NW1

LIBRARY OF CONGRESS CATALOG CARD NUMBER: 73-9426

PRINTED IN THE UNITED STATES OF AMERICA

# CONTENTS

## The Welfare Economics of Reversed International Transfers
*Harry G. Johnson*

## Some Problems of Stabilization Policy under Floating Exchange Rates
*M. June Flanders*

## Devaluation and the Balance of Trade under Flexible Wages
*Joanne Salop*

## On the Analytical Framework of Tariffs and Trade Policy
*Akira Takayama*

# PART II   MATHEMATICAL ECONOMICS

## Stability Independent of Adjustment Speed
### Kenneth J. Arrow

## A Class of Generalized Metzlerian Matrices                      203
### James P. Quirk

## Hysteresis of Long-Run Equilibrium from Realistic Adjustment Costs
### Murray C. Kemp and Henry Y. Wan, Jr.

## Stability in an Economy with Production
### Anjan Mukherji

## PART III   INVENTORY FLUCTUATIONS

## Monetary Policy and the Inventory Cycle
### Michael C. Lovell

## PART IV    MACROMONETARY THEORY

## IS–LM as a Dynamic Framework
### Patric H. Hendershott and George Horwich

## The Dynamics of Interest Rate Adjustment in a Keynesian Macroeconomic Model
### Wayne F. Perg

**The Theory of Money and Income Consistent with Orthodox Value Theory**
*Earl A. Thompson*

**Monetary Theory and Economic Consolidations**
*Gerrit Bilkes and Edward Ames*

# PART V   GROWTH

**Money, Growth, and the Propensity to Save: An Iconoclastic View**
*Ronald I. McKinnon*

**Economic Growth and Stages of the Balance of Payments: A Theoretical Model**
*Stanley Fischer and Jacob A. Frenkel*

## On the Dynamic Stability of Economic Growth: The Neoclassical versus Keynesian Approaches
*Hirofumi Uzawa*

# LIST OF CONTRIBUTORS

Numbers in parentheses indicate the pages on which the authors' contributions begin.

EDWARD AMES (455), Department of Economics, State University of New York, Stony Brook, Long Island, New York

KENNETH J. ARROW (181), Department of Economics, Harvard University, Cambridge, Massachusetts

GERRIT BILKES* (455), Department of Economics, State University of New York, Stony Book, Long Island, New York

JOHN A. CARLSON (311), Krannert Graduate School of Industrial Administration, Purdue University, West Lafayette, Indiana

GERALD L. CHILDS (333), Department of Economics, Rutgers University, New Brunswick, New Jersey

JOHN S. CHIPMAN† (19), Center for Advanced Study in the Behavioral Sciences, Stanford University, Stanford, California

STANLEY FISCHER‡ (503), Department of Economics, University of Chicago, Chicago, Illinois

M. JUNE FLANDERS (111), Department of Economics, Tel-Aviv University, Ramat-Aviv, Tel-Aviv, Israel

JACOB A. FRENKEL (503), Department of Economics, University of Chicago, Chicago, Illinois,§ and Tel-Aviv University, Tel-Aviv, Israel

PATRIC H. HENDERSHOTT (375), Krannert Graduate School of Industrial Administration, Purdue University, West Lafayette, Indiana

* Present address: Laurentian University, Sudbury, Ontario, Canada.
† Present address: Department of Economics, University of Minnesota, Minneapolis, Minnesota.
‡ Present address: Department of Economics, Massachusetts Institute of Technology, Cambridge, Massachusetts.
§ Present address.

GEORGE HORWICH (375), Department of Economics, Purdue University, West Lafayette, Indiana

HARRY G. JOHNSON (79), Department of Economics, University of Chicago, Chicago, Illinois and The London School of Economics, London, England

RONALD W. JONES (3), Department of Economics, University of Rochester, Rochester, New York

MURRAY C. KEMP (221), School of Economics, University of New South Wales, Kensington, New South Wales, Australia

MICHAEL C. LOVELL (355), Department of Economics, Wesleyan University, Middletown, Connecticut

RONALD I. McKINNON (487), Department of Economics, Stanford University, Stanford, California

ANJAN MUKHERJI (243), Department of Economics, University of Rochester, Rochester, New York and School of Social Sciences, Jawaharlal Nehru University, New Delhi, India

TAKASHI NEGISHI (259), Faculty of Economics, University of Tokyo, Bunkyoku, Tokyo, Japan

WAYNE F. PERG* (401), Division of Research and Statistics, Board of Governors of the Federal Reserve System, Washington, D.C.

JAMES P. QUIRK (203), Humanities and Social Sciences Department, California Institute of Technology, Pasadena, California

JOANNE SALOP (129), Division of International Finance, Board of Governors of the Federal Reserve System, Washington, D.C.

PAUL A. SAMUELSON (269), Department of Economics, Massachusetts Institute of Technology, Cambridge, Massachusetts

AKIRA TAKAYAMA (153), Krannert Graduate School of Industrial Administration, Purdue University, West Lafayette, Indiana

EARL A. THOMPSON (427), Department of Economics, University of California, Los Angeles, California

HIROFUMI UZAWA (523), Faculty of Economics, University of Tokyo, Tokyo, Japan

HENRY Y. WAN, JR. (221), Department of Economics, Cornell University, Ithaca, New York and Academia Sinica, Taipei, Taiwan

WILLIAM E. WEHRS (311), Department of Economics, University of Wisconsin, La Crosse, Wisconsin

* Present address: Department of Finance, Bowling Green State University, Bowling Green, Ohio.

# INTRODUCTION

Lloyd Metzler arrived in Cambridge in 1937 just as Harvard's Golden Age in economics was getting under way. He was one of a long line of Kansas economists sent East by John Ise: Edward Mason, John Lintner, Challis Hall—their names are legion. Already on the scene in the graduate school were the Sweezys, Musgrave, Stolper, Vandermeulen, Bergson, Alexander, Bourneuf, and Bain. Still to come were Dunlop, Tobin, Bishop, Fels, Higgins, Domar, Ruggles, Laursen, Wallich, and Goodwin. If every Camelot must have its Galahad, surely Metzler was the knight without reproach. Indeeed, he was Galahad and Lancelot rolled into one.

Being so able a man, he was naturally put into the basement galleys, assisting Professor Frickey in the statistics and accounting courses. In an era when Schumpeter's depreciation of the currency of grades was notorious— the A+'s showered down in great abundance, blessing him who gave and those who received—the academic records of a Metzler or a Paul Sweezy still stood out as Pareto–Levy outliers: whether on the flat plains of industrial organization or on the peaks of E. B. Wilson's lectures in pure theory and statistics, Metzler's quality was quickly recognized. It is harder for the brightest boy in the class to be popular than it is for rich men to pass through the eye of a needle; but, since people are liked in inverse proportion for their ability to thrive in the struggle for existence, Metzler was enormously loved. The only time he drew anger was on a historic occasion when the informal graduate-students' seminar took up Schumpeter's two-volume *Business Cycles*. This was at the prompting of Metzler, who thought it a shame that the brilliance of Keynes' *General Theory* had so completely eclipsed the Schumpeter work as to cause it to be ignored. Metzler led the discussion, with Schumpeter graciously agreeing to participate. Quite without guile, Metzler pointed out some of the manifest weaknesses of the work. It is asking much of graciousness to expect an author to enjoy criticism, however merited, and for once the Viennese veneer showed cracks. Galahad was genuinely startled that he had seemed to give offense.

Was Metzler perfect? Yes, in all things. Well, in *almost* all things. It is true he had a propensity to lose in zero-sum poker games. But most of his colleagues considered that a venial fault and they never ruled him out of the game on that account. Then too, perhaps some of the parties in his tutor's room at Winthrop House may have interrupted the studying of a future President. However, in the hierarchal days of the sweet *ancien regime*, rank had its privileges; and the times have long since evened the score.

When Metzler left Cambridge for wartime Washington, he never left home. He remained a don. (His famous researches on market stability were done there.) Indeed when called to Yale after the war, he seriously wondered why one should leave the excellent research and secretarial facilities of a government office for the committee meetings of academic life. An anthropologist visiting Washington in the immediate post-Roosevelt era reported that he had found only two happy economists in Washington: Lloyd Metzler, and another person who had his bags packed for Williams College. Yet the vintage papers that came from Metzler's pen in the years following his return to university life demonstrate that the preference he revealed was wise if not consistent.

After only a year at Yale, the Midwest beckoned and Metzler arrived at Chicago in 1947 just as *its* Golden Age was unfolding. The towering figures of Lange and Viner had moved on, and Henry Simons had died, but Frank Knight was flourishing, as were Jacob Marschak and Tjalling Koopmans, who were the senior staff of the Cowles Commission, T. W. Schultz, Paul Douglas, who had just returned from the wars, the historians Earl Hamilton and John Nef, Lloyd Mints, and the younger faculty: Milton Friedman, who had arrived the year before, D. Gale Johnson, H. Gregg Lewis, and William H. Nicholls. Within the next three years the following were also among those present at Chicago either as faculty or postdoctoral fellows: Kenneth Arrow, O. H. Brownlee, John Chipman, Evsey Domar, Richard Goode, Leo Hurwicz, Franco Modigliani, Don Patinkin, and Albert Rees.

Metzler was the man for all seasons. He succeeded Viner as the department's primary resource in international trade, but he was soon teaching pure theory, including monetary theory. Not only did he provide a link with Viner, with whom he frequently corresponded, but he related his own work, particularly in capital theory, to that of his distinguished colleague Knight. Thus while one took for granted his Keynesianism, Metzler communicated with all points of view. Perhaps uniquely among economists in the late 1940's, he was equally at home with Keynesian and neoclassical economics.

His classes were well attended—by economics students as well as a steady contingent of those in international relations. The pace was often determined by the students (frequently the noneconomists), for no question was too trivial to be ignored. And, generalist that he was, his teaching employed the whole gamut of expository tools—verbal, mathematical, numerical, and graphical. Metzler offered something to everyone (including, in his first year, a Schumpeterian grading policy which the department quietly discouraged!).

His rapport with students became legendary. A visit to Metzler in his office or his home—where Edith added her considerable charm and wit—was an ego trip. Nowhere else in the innovative and exciting, but often bruising atmosphere of the Chicago department, was a student more likely to emerge with the assurance that he was ten feet tall. It was not unusual for a seemingly casual conversation to lead to an acknowledgment in a footnote or even the text of one of Metzler's continuing stream of papers in the *Journal of Political Economy*. It was entirely in character that a meeting of the Political Economy Club, the graduate students' organization, was the first forum (in October, 1950) for the presentation of his classic paper, "Wealth, Saving, and the Rate of Interest."

Never before or after, a former colleague remarked in characterizing Metzler, has such brilliance and gentleness been combined in the same individual.

\* \* \*

The following essays in Metzler's honor, occasioned by his sixtieth birthday in 1973, cover the broad range of fields to which he himself has contributed. Our coverage more or less parallels his own *Collected Papers*, published earlier this year by the Harvard University Press. His remarkable collection, most of which was produced in little over a ten-year period, is divided into the theory of international trade; money, interest, and prices; business cycles and economic fluctuations; and mathematical economics and statistics. This present volume reorders the topics slightly and classifies the macro-material somewhat differently. Growth theory, to which Metzler has not specifically addressed himself, appears as a separate category, one to which his contributions in monetary theory are readily applied.

The papers in international trade extend Metzler's "tariff paradox" to include nontraded and intermediate commodities (Jones); restate and significantly generalize the transfer problem (Chipman), including "reverse" transfers, whereby a country alternates as payer and receiver of the transfer (Johnson); analyze the coordination of stabilization policies with floating exchange rates under conditions of capital mobility and price flexibility (Flanders); examine devaluation in an improved macromodel under a regime of flexible wage rates (Salop); and synthesize the analytical framework of tariffs and trade policy (Takayama).

The section on mathematical economics offers, among other things, a significant extension of the field of stability analysis. The conditions for stability independent of adjustment speed are derived (Arrow); a broader class of Metzlerian matrices is identified (Quirk); the dynamic adjustment of an entire economy of firms is analyzed (Kemp and Wan); and more general stability conditions for a production economy (Mukherji) and for markets for local public goods (Negishi) are provided. The contributions of Marx to general equilibrium and modern growth theory are explored in an essay in the history of thought (Samuelson).

Three papers on inventory fluctuations evaluate the empirical plausibility of recent inventory–investment models in terms of an explicit optimizing model (Carlson and Wehrs), extend the uses of the generalized accelerator model (Childs), and introduce monetary policy and the rate of interest into the Metzler inventory-cycle model (Lovell).

In the macromonetary area, dynamic analyses based on financial underpinnings stressed by Metzler are offered of the Hicks IS–LM framework (Hendershott and Horwich) and of a Keynesian nontâtonnement model containing separate Walras' laws for stocks and flows (Perg). Metzler's challenge to classical monetary theory evokes a precise model of money and income that embodies neoclassical value theory (Thompson), and the role of alternative sectoral consolidations in macroeconomic models is subjected to a searching examination (Bilkes and Ames).

The essays in growth analyze the Metzlerian saving–wealth relation under conditions of equilibrium growth (McKinnon); derive and classify the stages of the balance of payments for a growing economy (Fischer and Frenkel); and reinterpret and contrast the stability properties of the neoclassical and Keynesian growth models (Uzawa).

The authors represented in the volume are Metzler's colleagues, past and present, former students, and economists throughout the world whose work has reflected his influence. Several of the latter group have never met Metzler —they are young economists whose contributions are drawn from their recently completed dissertations: Joanne Salop, Anjan Mukherji, and Wayne F. Perg. We felt it was particularly appropriate that a volume honoring Lloyd Metzler should include essays by young as yet unknown economists.

GEORGE HORWICH          PAUL A. SAMUELSON
*West Lafayette, Indiana   Cambridge, Massachusetts*

*Part I*

# INTERNATIONAL TRADE THEORY

# THE METZLER TARIFF PARADOX

## Extensions to Nontraded and Intermediate Commodities

*Ronald W. Jones*

*University of Rochester*

## Introduction

Two of Metzler's classic papers on the theory of international trade deal with the effect of a tariff or export tax on domestic prices [1]. Whereas it seemed natural to assume that a duty levied on imports would be "protective" in the sense of raising the domestic relative price of imports, Metzler pointed out that the tariff could lower the relative *world* price of imports by an amount exceeding the height of the tariff, so that consumers and producers behind the tariff wall actually face lower relative prices for imports.[1] This result can also be phrased for the case of export taxes: A country levying an export tax may succeed in raising the relative domestic price of exports.

The argument needed to establish the Metzler result is briefly sketched in Section I. The hallmark of the model is the assumption that all commodities are internationally traded consumer goods. The purpose of this chapter is to extend the argument to a simple model where some commodities are not traded internationally because of high transport costs and one of the commodities is a pure intermediate good. Section II examines the home country

---

[1] This possibility has recently been challenged by Södersten and Vind [2]. For a reply defending the Metzler results see R. Jones [3].

3

reaction to the tariff or tax, whereas Section III investigates the sign of the foreign country's elasticity of demand for imports. In both respects the Metzler argument is changed; the possibility of a paradoxical result reemerges for somewhat different reasons. Section IV provides some concluding remarks. The Appendix is included to supply a formal expression for the elasticity of the foreign country's offer curve.

A variation of the model developed here has recently been applied to a problem in economic history [4]. In the antebellum period did the American South suffer from protectionist policies pushed by the North? This is a question that Metzler raised in his classic papers in suggesting the possibility that the relative domestic price of cotton exported from the South may not have been depressed by the duties on textile imports imposed in the antebellum period. This historical case conveniently provides the setting for this paper's simple model with nontraded and intermediate goods.

## I. The Metzler Analysis in the Traditional Case

If commodity markets are stable, the direction of price changes can be inferred from the sign of excess demands at initial prices. This procedure provides the key to the Metzler paradox while avoiding a complete comparative statics analysis of the model. Suppose two countries are initially engaged in the production and unimpeded exchange of two consumer goods. Let the home country levy a tariff on its imports or, equivalently, levy a tax on its exports. Our concern is with the effect of this tariff or tax on domestic prices in the home country, and this can be ascertained by asking whether *at the initial domestic prices for traded goods* there exists an excess world demand for the home country's imports and excess supply of its exports. If so, the relative domestic price of imports must rise and the tariff is protective.

The assumption that domestic prices are initially constant makes the analysis of the home country's response to the tariff simple. There are no substitution effects, either in home demand or home production. But there is an income effect, triggered by the necessary improvement in the home country's terms of trade. (At given domestic prices the tariff or export tax must raise the relative price of the home country's exports on world markets.) With only two traded goods being consumed, part of this increase in real income will spill over to increase the home country's demand for imports (as shown by $m$, the home country's marginal propensity to import) and part will increase the home country's demand for its export commodity (shown by $1 - m$).

The terms of trade have deteriorated for the foreign country, causing its demand for the home country's export commodity to fall along the foreign offer curve. Both income and substitution effects combine to reduce foreign demand for imports. This reduction is captured by $\varepsilon^*$, the elasticity of the foreign offer curve (defined so as to be positive). The foreign supply of exports is also reduced if $\varepsilon^*$ exceeds unity.

The state of world excess demands and supplies involves the summation of home and foreign responses to the tariff or tax at initial domestic prices. In terms of the home country's export commodity, world excess demand is positive if the home country's increased demand, as represented by $(1 - m)$, exceeds the foreign country's reduced demand, as represented by $\varepsilon^*$:

$$1 - m > \varepsilon^*. \tag{1}$$

If (1) is satisfied the tariff or export tax must, paradoxically, raise the domestic relative price of the home country's exports. In terms of the home country's import commodity, home demand has increased, as represented by the marginal propensity to import, $m$. However, foreign supply is also increased if $1 - \varepsilon^*$ is positive, and this supply increase will outweigh the home country's increased demand if condition (2) is satisfied:

$$1 - \varepsilon^* > m. \tag{2}$$

Obviously conditions (1) and (2) are the same, and represent the Metzler criterion for a tariff or export tax paradoxically to raise the relative domestic price of exports.

In what follows I shall reexamine the logic of this argument in the case in which both countries produce a nontraded commodity, whose price must adjust to clear local markets, and in which the home country exports a pure intermediate good. With reference to condition (1) or (2) I shall show (i) that the home country's response at initial domestic prices for traded goods is not given by $m$, but by some higher value, but (ii) that the foreign import demand elasticity $\varepsilon^*$ may be negative.

## II. Nontraded Goods: The Home Country Reaction

Think of the home country as the United States and the foreign country as Great Britain. The United States produces two commodities: cotton and food. Food is assumed to be nontraded so that equilibrium in the food market must match American demand and supply. On the other hand, cotton is a pure traded intermediate good, which enters into the production of textiles abroad but not into any commodity at home.[2] Thus the pattern of trade involves the export of raw cotton from the United States in exchange for cotton textiles from Great Britain. Two commodities are consumed locally: food and textiles.

---

[2] Although the nomenclature suggests the antebellum picture, note that for simplicity I have assumed away the existence of a local cotton textile industry.

Suppose the United States levies an export tax on cotton. Examine the impact of this tax on American demand for imports of cotton textiles at the initial *domestic prices of traded goods* (cotton and textiles). The tax raises the world (British) price of cotton, which represents an improvement in the United States terms of trade and thus real incomes. Part of this spills over into an increased American import demand for textiles. In the traditional Metzler model, discussed in Section I, this was the end of the story. But in this model part of the real income increase goes into food. The price of nontraded goods, food, must adjust to clear the local food market, and it is clear which way the adjustment must run. With real incomes greater in the United States, the demand for food rises, and this drives up the price of food. This increase in the price of the nontraded good relative to imports triggers a substitution effect in demand toward imports and away from food. Thus $m$, the marginal propensity to import in conditions (1) and (2), becomes an underestimate of the increased United States demand for imports. The rest of this section is devoted to developing an explicit expression for the increased United States import demand at initial domestic prices for traded goods.

Let $M$ denote the quantity of American imports, which is the total American demand for textiles. Thus

$$M = D_T(p_T/p_F, y) \tag{3}$$

where $p_T$ (assumed constant) is the local price of textiles, $p_F$ the local price of nontraded food, and $y$ the real income, measured in units of food. Two behavior parameters capture the response of demand to a change in the terms of trade. Let $\bar{\eta}$ be defined as the elasticity of demand for textiles with real income held constant:

$$\bar{\eta} \equiv -\left.\frac{\hat{M}}{\hat{p}_T/p_F}\right|_{\bar{y}}.$$

[A caret ($\hat{\ }$) over a variable represents a relative change, e.g., $\hat{M}$ is $dM/M$.] This must be positive. Similarly,

$$m \equiv (p_T/p_F)(\partial M/\partial y),$$

defined to be a pure number, is the marginal propensity to import. Therefore the relative change in imports, derived by differentiating Eq. (3), can be written as

$$\hat{M} = \bar{\eta}\hat{p}_F + (p_F/p_T M)m \, dy \tag{4}$$

since the domestic price of traded textiles is being held constant by assumption.

Two tasks remain. The first is to link the change in real income $dy$ to the improvement in the terms of trade. The second is to solve for the change in the price of the nontraded good that will clear the food market. Taking these in order, the change in real income in food units is defined by

$$dy = dD_F + (p_T/p_F)\, dD_T$$

which is the change in demands evaluated at initial domestic prices. The budget constraint links aggregate demand to the value of aggregate production *at world prices* for traded goods:

$$D_F + (p_T{}^*/p_F)D_T = x_F + (p_C{}^*/p_F)x_C.$$

The $x$'s denote production and world prices are indicated by an asterisk. Differentiate this, and make use of the definition of the change in real incomes, to obtain

$$dy = -M\, d(p_T{}^*/p_F) + x_C\, d(p_C{}^*/p_F) + \{dx_F + (p_C{}^*/p_F)\, dx_C\}.$$

Further simplification follows if the initial value of the export tax is zero, which I assume. This implies that the expression in braces equals

$$\{dx_F + (p_C/p_F)\, dx_C\},$$

which must vanish if the domestic relative price of cotton is equated to the slope of the transformation schedule. In addition the value of exports, $p_C{}^*x_C$, must equal the value of imports, $p_T{}^*M$, by the balance of payments (or budget) constraint. Therefore expression (5) emerges as the link between the change in the terms of trade and the consequent change in real income at home:

$$dy = -(p_T{}^*M/p_F)(\hat{p}_T{}^* - \hat{p}_C{}^*) = (p_T{}^*M/p_F)\hat{p}_C{}^* \tag{5}$$

since the world price of textiles equals the domestic price, which is constant by assumption. Substitute this expression into (4) to obtain

$$\hat{M} = \{m + \bar{\eta}(\hat{p}_F/\hat{p}_C{}^*)\}\hat{p}_C{}^*. \tag{6}$$

This expression confirms that a given improvement in the world terms of trade at initial domestic prices of *traded* goods, $p_T$ and $p_C$, affects imports not only through the marginal propensity to import, $m$, but also via a substitution effect if the home price of nontraded food, $p_F$, is disturbed.

The equilibrium condition in the nontraded food market is

$$D_F(p_T/p_F, y) = x_F(p_C/p_F). \tag{7}$$

Demand depends on the relative price of the two commodities consumed locally and real income, and production along the transformation schedule depends only on the domestic relative price of the two commodities locally produced. The change in demand reflects both a substitution effect and an income effect. The substitution term, $\partial D_F/\partial(p_T/p_F)$, can be related to the substitution elasticity of demand for imports, $\bar{\eta}$, by making use of the definition for $dy$ and noting that $y$ is being held constant in this term. The income term, $\partial D_F/\partial y$, is merely $(1 - m)$. Therefore the change in demand for food can be expressed as

$$dD_F = - (p_T M/p_F)\bar{\eta}\hat{p}_F + (1 - m)\, dy.$$

On the supply side it becomes convenient to define the elasticity of *export* supply $e$ as

$$e \equiv \hat{x}_C/(\hat{p}_C/p_F)$$

and to relate the change in production of food to $e$ by virtue of the fact that $\{dx_F + (p_C/p_F)\, dx_C\}$ is zero for small movements along the transformation schedule. Thus

$$dx_F = (p_T M/p_F)e\hat{p}_F.$$

The change in the price of food required to clear the market at initial prices for traded goods is obtained by equating $dD_F$ and $dx_F$. After making use of expression (5) for the change in real incomes, the solution for $\hat{p}_F$ can be written as

$$\hat{p}_F = [(1 - m)/(\bar{\eta} + e)]\hat{p}_C^*. \tag{8}$$

The improvement in the home country's terms of trade ($\hat{p}_C^* > 0$) must drive up the local price of food.

This result is illustrated in Fig. 1. Since the local prices of traded cotton and cotton textiles are assumed constant, both demand (for given real income) and

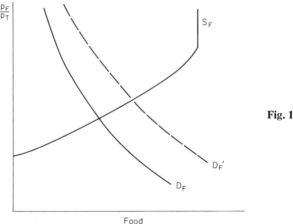

Fig. 1

supply of United States food depend only on the price of food. However, an export tax on cotton which raises the world price of cotton by the same amount and therefore increases real incomes shifts the demand curve $D_F$ to the right (to $D_F'$). The shift is captured by the $(1 - m)$ term, whereas the elasticities $\bar{\eta} + e$ determine the extent of the rise in food's price.

The solution for $\hat{p}_F$ shown in (8) can be substituted into (6):

$$\hat{M} = \{m + \bar{\eta}[(1 - m)/(\bar{\eta} + e)]\}\hat{p}_C.$$

The expression in braces must exceed the marginal propensity to import, $m$. It must, however, still be a fraction, as can be seen by rewriting $\hat{M}$ as

$$\hat{M} = \left\{\frac{e}{\bar{\eta} + e} \cdot m + \frac{\bar{\eta}}{\bar{\eta} + e} \cdot 1\right\}\hat{p}_C^*. \tag{9}$$

This shows the effect of an improvement in the terms of trade on import demand to be a positively weighted average of the marginal propensity to import and unity.[3]

The Metzler criterion for the paradoxical case in which an export tax raises the local relative price of the exported good can be obtained by replacing "$m$" in inequality (2) by the braced term in (9). Thus the inequality

$$\varepsilon^* + \left\{\frac{e}{\bar{\eta} + e} m + \frac{\bar{\eta}}{\bar{\eta} + e} \cdot 1\right\} < 1 \tag{10}$$

becomes the criterion for the paradox. Although the inclusion of nontraded goods at home seems to make this criterion less likely to be satisfied, I show in Section III that the value of $\varepsilon^*$ need no longer be positive if the foreign country produces a nontraded good and imports cotton, a pure intermediate good.

## III. Nontraded and Intermediate Goods: The Elasticity of the Foreign Offer Curve

If a country imports a final consumer good and its terms of trade worsen, the demand for that good falls. Both substitution and income effects conspire to produce this result.[4] Thus in the Metzler criterion (1) or (2), $\varepsilon^*$, the elasticity of the foreign offer curve, is positive. If a country imports an intermediate good which does not directly enter utility functions, this argument fails to

---

[3] I have shown elsewhere [5] that this weighted average expresses the effect of a transfer payment on import demand in a model with nontraded goods. The real income gain for the home country from the export tax is the equivalent of a transfer payment.

[4] This assumes the consumer good is "normal."

apply. In its place it is necessary to investigate the impact of a change in the terms of trade on production, especially of that commodity making use of the intermediate good.

This is the kind of setting I assume for the foreign country (Britain). It produces cotton textiles, partly for its own consumption and partly for export in order to obtain the necessary inputs of raw cotton from the home country (the United States). Britain produces no raw cotton of its own, but does produce a nontraded commodity, food. To make matters simple, I assume that a fixed quantity of cotton $a_{CT}^*$ is required per unit output of textiles.

British imports of cotton $M^*$ thus equal $a_{CT}^* x_T^*$. In terms of relative changes, $\hat{M}^* = \hat{x}_T^*$. This implies that the *direction* of change of British imports depends exclusively on whether gross output of British cotton textile production is depressed by the adverse movement in British terms of trade. Assuming full employment of primary factors in Britain, gross outputs of cotton textiles and food are located on the gross production-possibilities schedule $T^*T^*$ illustrated in Fig. 2.

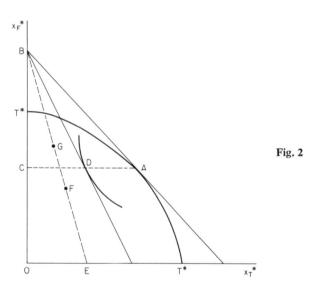

Fig. 2

As is familiar from the theory of effective protection (e.g., see Ruffin [6]), the slope of this transformation schedule is *not* given by the commodity price ratio $p_T^*/p_F^*$. Instead, the slope indicates the ratio of *effective* prices,

$$(p_T^* - a_{CT}^* p_C^*)/p_F^*,$$

and it is this price ratio that guides production. From the price of textiles must be subtracted the payment made to the United States for imports of raw cotton per unit textile production.[5] When the United States levies an export tax on cotton, the British effective price of textiles is lowered, and this would suggest that the production of textiles (and therefore the import of raw cotton) would fall. But the price of nontraded food in Great Britain will be depressed by the fall in British real incomes. If this falls sufficiently, the *relative* effective price of textiles could rise and, with it, British imports of raw cotton. In such a case $\varepsilon^*$ would be negative.

In developing an explicit formula for $\varepsilon^*$ in the Appendix, I shall return to the condition specified earlier that the American prices of traded goods are kept at their initial values while the export tax raises the British price of raw cotton. Recall that this assumption was made in order to analyze the net change in demands and supplies that would indicate which way the United States prices of traded goods would ultimately have to change to clear world markets. In describing heuristically the condition that would lead to a negative $\varepsilon^*$, I shall adopt the spirit of this procedure by asking whether at the initial British *relative effective prices* (of textiles and food) there exists an excess British demand or supply of food. If there exists an excess supply of food, its relative effective price would have to fall, textile production would expand and, paradoxically, so would British demand for imports.

The argument centers on Fig. 2. To show the initial British equilibrium, before the export tax on raw cotton is levied by the United States, it is necessary to locate the budget line faced by British consumers. Consider the vertical intercept $OB$. This is the sum of food production $OC$ and the product of gross textile production $CA$ times the slope of line $BA$, which is the relative effective price of textiles $(p_T^* - a_{CT}^* p_C^*)/p_F^*$. That is, distance $OB$ equals

$$(1/p_F^*)\{p_F^* x_F^* + p_T^* x_T^* - p_C^* a_{CT}^* x_T^*\}.$$

---

[5] This can be proved in the following manner. Gross production in Britain, $p_F^* x_F^* + p_T^* x_T^*$, must, in a competitive equilibrium, be equal to total factor payments for primary factors plus payments for any imported intermediate goods, $w^* L^* + r^* K^* + p^* a_{CT}^* x_T^*$. Therefore the total changes must be equal as well:

$$\{x_F^* \, dp_F^* + x_T^* \, dp_T^*\} + \{p_F^* \, dx_F^* + p_T^* \, dx_T^*\}$$
$$= \{L^* \, dw^* + K^* \, dr^* + a_{CT}^* x_T^* \, dp_C^*\} + \{w^* \, dL^* + r^* \, dK^* + p_C^* a_{CT}^* \, dx_T^*\}.$$

From the competitive profit conditions the first brace on the left-hand side must equal the first brace on the right-hand side. (For example, check the case of pure inflation in which no output changes occur.) Furthermore, along the gross transformation curve labor and capital endowments are constant. Therefore

$$p_F^* \, dx_F^* + p_T^* \, dx_T^* = p_C^* a_{CT}^* \, dx_T^*.$$

From this it follows that the slope of the gross transformation curve, $dx_F^*/dx_T^*$, is given by the ratio of effective prices.

Because food is nontraded, the value of food production $p_F^* x_F^*$ equals the value of food consumption $p_F^* D_F^*$. Furthermore, $p_C^* a_{CT}^* x_T^*$ represents the value of British imports of raw cotton, which equals the value of British exports of cotton textiles. Therefore the difference between this term and the gross value of textile output $p_T^* x_T^*$ must reflect the value of British demand for textiles $p_T^* D_T^*$. That is,

$$OB = (1/p_F^*)\{p_F^* D_F^* + p_T^* D_T^*\}.$$

The vertical intercept $OB$ shows the value of aggregate British demand in food units.

The budget line facing consumers in Britain has a vertical intercept $OB$, but must be steeper than line $BA$ tangent to the gross transformation schedule. Consumers face the price ratio $p_T^*/p_F^*$, whereas producers respond to the *effective* price ratio $(p_T^* - a_{CT}^* p_C^*)/p_F^*$. Line $BD$ extended is the budget line. The initial consumption point is $D$, with the British food market cleared and the difference between gross and retained output of textiles represented by $DA$.

Now consider the following exercise: (i) Keep the British price of food $p_F^*$ constant (e.g. by treating food as the numéraire); (ii) let the United States levy an export tax on cotton so that $p_C^*$ rises; (iii) raise $p_T^*$ just enough so that the *effective* price of textiles is kept unaltered. That is, let

$$\widehat{p_T^* - a_{CT}^* p_C^*} = (\hat{p}_T^* - \theta_{CT}^* \hat{p}_C^*)/(1 - \theta_{CT}^*) = 0$$

where $\theta_{CT}^*$ denotes the share of revenue earned in textiles that must be paid for cotton imports. The required rise in $p_T^*$ equals a fraction $\theta_{CT}^*$ of the assumed increase in $p_C^*$ so that the British terms of trade have worsened. This is illustrated in Fig. 2. Production remains at $A$ since the effective relative price ratio is, by construction, unchanged. Therefore the vertical intercept of the new budget line remains at $OB$. But the budget line becomes steeper ($p_T^*$ has risen and $p_F^*$ is assumed constant), swinging to line $BE$. What is the new consumption point? If textiles are not inferior in British taste patterns, the demand for textiles must fall. If the uncompensated demand in Biitain for textiles is elastic, the new consumption is at a point such as $G$. However, if the uncompensated demand elasticity is less than unity, a greater total outlay must be made on textiles as $p_T^*$ rises, indicating a lower outlay on food (and reduced $D_F^*$ as $p_F^*$ is constant) such as at point $F$. In the latter case there would exist an excess British supply of nontraded food at the initial effective price ratio. Hence, in order to clear the food market, the production point would move southeast of $A$ along $T^*T^*$, the production of textiles would rise, as would cotton imports.

As this argument shows, the possibility of British imports rising as the British terms of trade deteriorate cannot be ruled out if imports are an intermediate good such as cotton. The only condition required for a negative $\varepsilon^*$ is that the uncompensated elasticity of demand in Britain for cotton textiles be less than unity. If it is, then the Metzler paradox *must* hold. As condition (10) suggests, even if British demand for textiles is elastic (a positive $\varepsilon^*$), the Metzler paradox is still possible. The Appendix provides a formal analysis of the value of $\varepsilon^*$.

## IV. Concluding Remarks

Both nontraded goods and an intermediate good have been introduced in a simple model to examine the Metzler tariff paradox. Is it possible to disentangle the effect of each separately on the modifications required in the Metzler criterion?

Suppose, first, that raw cotton is *not* an intermediate good, but enters directly into the foreign (British) utility function. To keep matters simple suppose the United States, as before, consumes only textiles and its nontraded commodity (food), and produces only cotton, its export commodity, and food. Similarly, with cotton now entering British utility functions, simplify by assuming the British consume no textiles. In this way each country consumes only two commodities.

The role of nontraded goods in this altered model is unambiguously to make the Metzler paradox less likely. The reaction in the home country is precisely as described in Section II: the marginal propensity to import understates the impact on United States demand for imports at initial domestic prices of traded goods. Account must be taken of the fact that the price of nontraded goods is bid up by the improvement in the world terms of trade, and this encourages a substitution away from nontraded goods to imports. The corrected response of import demand, as shown by the braced term in Eq. (9), is a weighted average of $m$ and unity. A somewhat similar story can be told in the foreign country. Suppose initially the foreign price of nontraded goods is kept constant as the price of cotton imports (now a consumer good) rises. The foreign elasticity of demand for imports could be expressed as $(\bar{\eta}^* + m^*)$, a combination of a substitution effect and income effect on demand. For the Metzler paradox to be at all possible, this must be less than unity. I have shown elsewhere that in this case the foreign elasticity of import demand $\varepsilon^*$ must exceed $(\bar{\eta}^* + m^*)$ once account is taken of the fact that the price of nontraded goods abroad will fall. Indeed, $\varepsilon^*$ is a weighted average of $(\bar{\eta}^* + m^*)$ and unity, the weights being precisely the foreign equivalents of the domestic weights shown in (9). (See Jones [5].) What emerges is the conclusion that if the Metzler paradox is possible when price changes for nontraded goods are ignored, it is still possible, but less likely, when these price changes are allowed to react back upon the demand for imports in each country.

The existence of a pure intermediate good in the model thus seems to be crucial in making the Metzler paradox more likely. But this must be qualified. If the foreign country's production of food traded freely on world markets, so that at initial domestic (United States) prices its price was constant, the foreign (British) *relative* effective price of textiles would have to decrease as the price of raw cotton rises. That is, $\varepsilon^*$ would have to be positive. To introduce the possibility that $\varepsilon^*$ is negative, as was done in Section III, it is necessary to *combine* the fact that cotton imports are an intermediate good with the existence of a nontraded sector abroad. Only in this way is it possible that the commodity produced abroad which has suffered a reduction in effective protection (textiles as the price of cotton input rises) can nonetheless expand (because food prices have fallen relatively more).

In concluding, note that the form which Metzler's condition (1) and (2) provides can be interpreted in a generally valid way. It was Metzler's contribution to point out that the paradox involved a value smaller than unity for the sum of (i) the home country's increased spending on imports as of constant domestic prices for *traded* goods (per unit increase in income) and (ii) the foreign elasticity of demand for imports. This form of the criterion has not been challenged here. Instead, the values which (i) and (ii) may take in the presence of nontraded and intermediate goods have been reinterpreted.[6]

## Appendix

As suggested in Section III, British imports of raw cotton will rise as the relative British price of raw cotton rises if and only if the production of cotton textiles $x_T^*$ is increased. With a fixed input–output coefficient, $\hat{M}^*$ equals $\hat{x}_T^*$. The terms of trade (relative import price) for Britain is $p_C^*/p_T^*$. The United States prices of traded goods ($p_T$ and $p_C$) are held constant throughout. The United States levies an export tax on cotton so that $p_C^*$ rises. With no interference in the textile market directly, $p_T^*$ remains equal to $p_T$ and is thus constant. Therefore, by definition

$$\varepsilon^* \equiv -\hat{M}^*/(\hat{p}_C^* - \hat{p}_T^*) = -\hat{x}_T^*/\hat{p}_C^*. \tag{A.1}$$

Let $E_T^*$ be defined as the elasticity of supply of textiles along the gross transformation schedule. That is,

$$\hat{x}_T^* \equiv E_T^* \hat{q}^* \tag{A.2}$$

where $q^*$ indicates the relative effective price of textiles:

$$q^* \equiv (p_T^* - a_{CT}^* p_C^*)/p_F^*. \tag{A.3}$$

[6] For earlier examples in the literature of the Metzler paradox in models in which variable labor supply and/or income redistribution arguments are used to establish a negative $\varepsilon^*$, see Kemp and Jones [7] and Bhagwati and Johnson [8].

It follows that

$$\hat{q}^* \equiv [(\hat{p}_T{}^* - \theta_{CT}^* \hat{p}_C{}^*)/(1 - \theta_{CT}^*)] - \hat{p}_F{}^*.$$

Since the price of textiles is being held constant, this can be simplified as

$$\hat{q}^* = -\{[\theta_{CT}^*/(1 - \theta_{CT}^*)]\hat{p}_C{}^* + \hat{p}_F{}^*\}. \tag{A.4}$$

The conflict is apparent. The export tax raises $p_C{}^*$, worsens British terms of trade and therefore real incomes, and causes a reduction in the demand for nontraded food. The $p_F{}^*$ falls, perhaps sufficiently actually to raise $q^*$, textile's *relative effective price*.

The formal analysis can proceed exactly as in the discussion of American demand behavior in Section II. The conditions of equilibrium in the non-traded food sector determine the response of the price of food $p_F{}^*$ to the initiating rise in the price of imports $p_C{}^*$. Thus

$$D_F{}^*(p_T{}^*/p_F{}^*, y^*) = x_F{}^*(q^*). \tag{A.5}$$

As illustrated in Section II, with only two commodities being consumed or produced, the reaction of demand and supply for nontraded food can be related to behavior parameters for traded cotton textiles.

First consider foreign demand. Let $\gamma_T{}^*$ represent the *compensated* (real incomes constant) elasticity of demand for textiles in Britain, defined so as to be positive:

$$\gamma_T{}^* \equiv - \left. \frac{\hat{D}_T{}^*}{\hat{p}_T{}^* - \hat{p}_F{}^*} \right|_{\bar{y}^*}.$$

Similarly, let $\alpha_T{}^*$ indicate the British marginal propensity to consume textiles:

$$\alpha_T{}^* \equiv (p_T{}^*/p_F{}^*)\partial D_T{}^*/\partial y^*.$$

By definition of the change in British real incomes expressed in units of non-traded food,

$$dy^* \equiv dD_F{}^* + (p_T{}^*/p_F{}^*)\, dD_T{}^*,$$

the substitution term $(dy^* = 0)$ in the demand for food can be linked to $\gamma_T{}^*$:

$$\partial D_F{}^*/\partial(p_T{}^*/p_F{}^*) = D_T{}^*\gamma_T{}^*.$$

In addition, $\partial D_F{}^*/\partial y^* = (1 - \alpha_T{}^*)$. The total change in food demand is thus[7]

$$dD_F{}^* = -(p_T{}^* D_T{}^*/p_F{}^*)\gamma_T{}^*\hat{p}_F{}^* + (1 - \alpha_T{}^*)\, dy^*. \tag{A.6}$$

---

[7] Again note that $p_T{}^*$ is held constant.

British real incomes are depressed by the rise in $p_C^*$. An expression for $dy^*$ can be obtained as in the derivation for $dy$ shown in Eq. (5). Thus

$$dy^* = -(p_C^* M^*/p_F^*)\hat{p}_C^*. \tag{A.7}$$

Substitute this into (A.6) to obtain

$$dD_F^* = -(p_T^* D_T^*/p_F^*)\{\gamma_T^* \hat{p}_F^* + (p_C^* M^*/p_T^* D_T^*) \cdot (1 - \alpha_T^*)\hat{p}_C^*\}.$$

Note that the value of British demand for textiles $p_T^* D_T^*$ expresses the difference between the value of gross production $p_T^* x_T^*$ and the value of exports of textiles (equal at world prices to $p_C^* M^*$). Therefore,

$$p_C^* M^*/p_T^* D_T^* = p_C^* M^*/(p_T^* x_T^* - p_C^* M^*) = \theta_{CT}^*/(1 - \theta_{CT}^*).$$

The final expression for the change in British food demand is

$$dD_F^* = -(p_T^* D_T^*/p_F^*)\{\gamma_T^* \hat{p}_F^* + [\theta_{CT}^*/(1 - \theta_{CT}^*)](1 - \alpha_T^*)\hat{p}_F^*\}. \tag{A.8}$$

As Eq. (A.5) suggests, changes in British food supply are linked to changes in the relative effective price of textiles. Indeed, along the gross transformation schedule,

$$dx_F^* + q^* dx_T^* = 0.$$

Therefore by (A.2) the change in British food production is explained by the textile supply elasticity $E_T^*$ and the extent of the change in the relative effective price of textiles $\hat{q}^*$, which is given by (A.4). Thus

$$dx_F^* = (p_T^* D_T^*/p_F^*)E_T^*\{[\theta_{CT}^*/(1 - \theta_{CT}^*)]\hat{p}_C^* + \hat{p}_F^*\}. \tag{A.9}$$

If the price of food adjusts in Britain to clear the British food market, $dD_F^*$ in (A.8) must equal $dx_F^*$ in (A.9). The change in $p_F^*$ required is

$$\hat{p}_F^* = -[\theta_{CT}^*/(1 - \theta_{CT}^*)]\{[E_T^* + (1 - \alpha_T^*)]/(E_T^* + \gamma_T^*)\}\hat{p}_C^*. \tag{A.10}$$

This verifies that the price of food falls in Britain.

The sign of $\varepsilon^*$ depends on the extent of this fall in $p_F^*$ compared with the fall in the effective price of textiles. The change in the *relative* effective price of textiles is given by substituting $\hat{p}_F^*$ from (A.10) into (A.4). Thus

$$\hat{q}^* = -[\theta_{CT}^*/(1 - \theta_{CT}^*)]\{(\gamma_T^* + \alpha_T^* - 1)/(E_T^* + \gamma_T^*)\}\hat{p}_C^*. \tag{A.11}$$

By using (A.1) and (A.2), the elasticity of the British offer curve is

$$\varepsilon^* = [\theta_{CT}^*/(1 - \theta_{CT}^*)][E_T^*/(E_T^* + \gamma_T^*)][\gamma_T^* + \alpha_T^* - 1]. \tag{A.12}$$

This is the expression required in the Metzler criterion (10). The term

$$(\gamma_T^* + \alpha_T^*),$$

the sum of the substitution elasticity of demand for textiles and the marginal propensity to consume textiles, is the uncompensated elasticity of demand for textiles. An inelastic British demand for textiles requires an increased demand for cotton imports as the price of cotton rises.

In Section II a simple supply–demand diagram (Fig. 1) was used to illustrate the adjustment in the home country's market for nontraded food

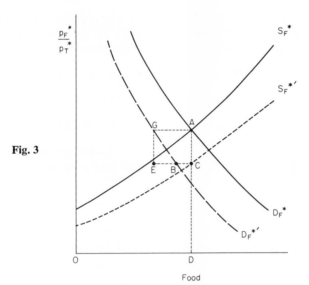

**Fig. 3**

required by the export tax on cotton. A similar kind of diagram can illustrate the changes required in the British food sector. In Fig. 3 the initial equilibrium price and quantity of food is shown by point $A$. The $D_F^*$ curve is drawn under the assumption of a given terms of trade (or given $p_C^*$ since $p_T^*$ is being held constant in any case) and, therefore, as of a given real income. The $S_F^*$ curve also assumes a given value for $p_T^*$ and $p_C^*$ since production depends on the effective relative price $q^*$.

Keeping $p_T^*$ constant, consider the impact of a rise in the British price of cotton $p_C^*$: (i) The demand curve shifts to the left to $D_F^{*\prime}$ because real income has been reduced. For a small deterioration in the terms of trade the extent of this shift ($GA$ at constant $p_F^*$) is shown by (A.8):

$$GA = (p_T^* D_T^*/p_F^*)[\theta_{CT}^*/(1 - \theta_{CT}^*)](1 - \alpha_T^*)\hat{p}_C^*.$$

(ii) The supply curve shifts downwards to $S_F^{*\prime}$. The extent of the downward shift ($AC$ in Fig. 3) is shown by (A.4) since if the price of food falls by

$$d(p_F^*/p_T^*) = -(p_F^*/p_T^*)[\theta_{CT}^*/(1 - \theta_{CT}^*)]\hat{p}_C^*,$$

the relative effective price $q^*$ is kept constant (thereby ensuring the same production of food). Figure 3 illustrates that the price of food must fall. The crucial question concerns the output of food. This is shown to fall in Fig. 3, since at relative price $DC$ there is an excess supply of food. This implies that the leftward shift in the demand curve ($GA$, equal to $EC$) exceeds the amount by which demand for food would increase along the demand curve as a consequence of a drop in food's relative price from $AD$ to $CD$. This increase in food demand $EB$ can be shown by (A.6), setting real income constant (as it is along the compensated demand curve) and substituting for $\hat{p}_F^*$ that value [shown by (A.4)] that would keep $q^*$ constant (as it is in going from $AD$ to $CD$). Thus

$$EB = (p_T^* D_T^*/p_F^*)[\theta_{CT}^*/(1 - \theta_{CT}^*)]\gamma_T^* \hat{p}_C^*.$$

The existence of an excess supply of food at price $CD$ means that distance $EB$ falls short of $GA$ (equal to $EC$). Alternatively it means that

$$\gamma_T^* < (1 - \alpha_T^*)$$

or that the uncompensated demand curve in Britain for traded cotton textiles is inelastic.

## ACKNOWLEDGMENTS

I have benefited from discussions of this material with Clayne Pope and Rudiger Dornbusch.

## REFERENCES

1. Metzler, L., "Tariffs, the Terms of Trade, and the Distribution of National Income," *The Journal of Political Economy* **57** (February 1949), 1–29; "Tariffs, International Demand and Domestic Prices," *ibid.* (August 1949), 345–351.
2. Södersten, B., and Vind, K., "Tariffs and Trade in General Equilibrium," *American Economic Review* **58** (June 1968), 394–408.
3. Jones, R. W., "Tariffs and Trade in General Equilibrium: Comment, "*American Economic Review* **59** (June 1969), 418–424.
4. Pope, C., "The Impact of the Ante-Bellum Tariff on Income Distribution " *Explorations in Economic History* **9** (Summer 1972), 375–421.
5. Jones, R. W., "Trade with Non-Traded Goods: The Anatomy of Interconnected Markets." Unpublished.
6. Ruffin, R., "Trade, Intermediate Goods, and Domestic Protection," *American Economic Review* **59** (June 1969), 261–269.
7. Kemp, M. C., and Jones, R. W., "Variable Labor Supply and the Theory of International Trade," *Journal of Political Economy* **70** (February 1962), 30–36.
8. Bhagwati, J. N., and Johnson, H. G., "A Generalized Theory of the Effect of Tariffs on the Terms of Trade," *Oxford Economic Papers* **13** (October 1961), 225–253.

# THE TRANSFER PROBLEM ONCE AGAIN

*John S. Chipman**

*Stanford University*

## I. Introduction

In the century and a half that has gone by since the science of economics began, few topics have been so vigorously and inconclusively debated as the Transfer Problem. Hundreds of pages have been devoted to theoretical controversy, empirical analysis, and summaries of both;[1] and yet the outcome, in terms of positive results and basic understanding of the issues, has been astonishingly meagre.

Mill's flat statement [46, pp. 41–43; 47, Book III, Ch. XXI, §4] that a transfer of funds from one country to another would worsen the paying country's terms of trade, thereby creating a secondary burden, was accompanied by virtually no explanation; and subsequent elaborations of this view—which Ohlin [50] conveniently described as the " orthodox " doctrine—by Taussig [66, 67], Viner [70], Keynes [34, 35], and others, have provided few additional clues as to the underlying "real" relationships as opposed to the monetary mechanisms of adjustment.

In what was probably the first rigorous formal treatment of the problem, Pigou [55] formulated it in terms of a model of pure exchange between representative citizens in the two counties. However, the meaning of his criterion

---

* Present affiliation: University of Minnesota.
[1] Valuable surveys are those of Iversen [31], Elliott [16], Haberler [27], Viner [70, 71], and Rostow [57].

for a change in the terms of trade was obscured by his assumption of independent utilities, and, more seriously, he was forced to appeal to considerations lying outside his formal model (production, transport costs) in order to
justify his belief that the paying country's terms of trade would deteriorate.
The first of these deficiencies was completely overcome in Samuelson's
masterly treatment [60], in which Pigou's criterion was generalized and
restated in terms of propensities to consume. The second deficiency was also
overcome—at least in a formal sense—by means of the device adopted by
Samuelson [61] of assuming a certain proportion of each good to be lost in
transit. However, the startling conclusion was reached that under Pigou's
assumptions of independent and linear marginal utilities and with identical
tastes, the "antiorthodox" result would follow; only in the case of artificial
tariff barriers did Samuelson find a presumption in favor of the orthodox
thesis.

The question is obviously a delicate one, the results depending quite
sensitively on the particular idealization chosen to represent transport costs
or other impediments to trade.[2] In this chapter I shall adopt an idealization
that goes back to Taussig [65, 66] and which formed the basis for Ohlin's
analysis of the transfer problem [50, 51].[3] This consists in the assumption that

---

[2] In a remarkable paper, Wicksell [72] pointed out that since a transfer would result in
a larger volume of goods being shipped from the paying to the receiving country, it would
raise freight rates from the paying to the receiving country but lower them for goods moving
in the opposite direction, on account of the additional ballast traffic. The result would be
a rise in the price spread between the two countries with respect to commodities moving
from the paying to the receiving country and a fall in the price spread for commodities
moving in the opposite direction. According to Wicksell, this would entail a rise in the prices
of *both* import and export goods in the receiving country and a fall of both of these prices
in the paying country, with no presumption as to the effects on the terms of trade. While
Wicksell's analysis is extremely suggestive, it is also very incomplete, as any attempt to make
it precise will show. In order to calculate equilibrium prices one would need to know the
production transformation relations among exportables, importables, and transportation
services—and such an analysis would require another lengthy paper.

In a little-known tract, Torrens [69, p. 33] argued that a result of a transfer would be an
increase in the price spread between countries for corresponding commodities in direct
relation to their transport costs, those prices rising highest in the receiving country and
falling lowest in the paying country which had the highest transport costs. In terms of the
constructs of the present chapter this would correspond to a rise in the ratio of the price
of the receiving country's domestic commodity to that of the paying country (see Appendix
B).

[3] See also Viner [70, p. 210; 71, pp. 348–349], Graham [23; 25, p. 298; 26], Wilson [73],
Samuelson [60, pp. 302–303; 61, p. 289], and more recently, Pearce [53; 54, pp. 78–117].
The first formal analysis of the role of nontraded goods within the general framework of the
Heckscher–Ohlin–Lerner–Samuelson model appears to be that of Komiya [37], who did
not, however, concern himself with the transfer problem. On the other hand, McDougall
[39] has analyzed the transfer problem in a model involving nontraded goods, but not

there are two classes of commodities: "international commodities" which are freely tradable internationally at zero transport costs, and "domestic commodities" ("home-market goods" in Ohlin's terminology) which are not tradable between countries, i.e., have infinite transport costs. Ohlin's contention was that in the short run a transfer would raise prices of domestic goods relative to international goods in the receiving country, and lower prices of domestic goods relative to international goods in the paying country, with no presumption as to the relative prices of import and export goods; and that in the long run, resources would move from international to domestic industries in the receiving country, and from domestic to international industries in the paying country, mitigating the original price changes but, again, with no presumption as to the ultimate effect on the terms of trade.

My purpose here is to carry out the above type of analysis in precise form. It will be assumed that there are two international commodities, and one domestic commodity in each country. First, a short-run model with no variation in production (formally a pure exchange model) will be analyzed in Section IV, and a condition obtained for a transfer to leave the terms of trade unchanged (Theorem 2). This condition—which was actually stated in essence by Samuelson [60, p. 303], without proof—is that the conditional Engel curves (income–consumption curves) of the two countries—tracing out the consumption of the two international commodities when incomes vary, the terms of trade are fixed, and the consumption of each domestic commodity is fixed at any level—should be linear with the same slopes (as between countries and for each level of consumption of the respective domestic commodities) at each fixed price ratio of international commodities. This is a generalization of a well-known aggregation criterion of Gorman [20], and is valid so long as the consumption of the two commodities remains positive. The condition will be assumed to hold in the ensuing analysis which takes account of production adjustments, and will be called the Hypothesis of Neutral Tastes.[4] In particular (Theorem 3) it will be fulfilled if the two countries have demand functions which are generated by utility functions which

----

[4] The justification of this assumption is that provided by Viner [71, p. 343]: "The assumption of 'similarity' of the utility functions is a reasonable one, not because 'similarity' is in fact probable, but because in the absence of specific information the 'dissimilarity' which is likely to exist is, *a priori*, as likely to be in one direction as in the other." It may thus be considered as a prelude to a more general treatment in which probability distributions are specified over utility functions, production functions, and even (cf. Jones [32]) endowments.

----

within the HOLS framework. The fact that more definite results have been obtained in the present study may be attributed to its exploitation of the HOLS structure underlying the transformation relations [as exemplified by formula (48)], combined with the formulation and exploitation of the Hypothesis of Neutral Tastes.

are separable as between domestic and international commodities, and such that the subutility functions corresponding to the international commodities fulfill the Gorman condition of yielding linear Engel curves which are parallel as betweeen countries for each set of prices of international commodities (a sufficient condition for which is of course that the subutility functions be identical and homogeneous). It is also assumed throughout that the domestic commodities are "regular," i.e., strongly superior and weakly Hicks substitutable in the tastes of the respective consumers. These assumptions— regularity and, above all, the Hypothesis of Neutral Tastes—make it possible to separate out the production effects, and provide the key to the analysis of production adjustments which forms the remainder of the chapter (Section V).

The treatment of production adjustments is formulated in terms of the standard Lerner–Samuelson model with two factors of production in each country and no factor intensity reversal as between any two industries. (A limited treatment of the three-factor case is taken up in Appendix A.) It is assumed that country 1 (the paying country) is relatively well endowed with factor 1, and country 2 (the receiving country) with factor 2; that in both countries, industry 1 uses factor 1 more intensively relatively to factor 2 than industry 2; and that the paying country exports commodity 1 to the receiving country and imports commodity 2. The conclusions may be summarized as follows.

(i)   If both countries specialize in the production of their domestic (non-traded) and export goods (i.e., the paying country in commodities 1 and 3, and the receiving country in commodities 2 and 3), the "orthodox" result holds (Theorem 4). This is consistent with the positions of Mill[5] and Taussig,[6] and

---

[5] Mill's position was stated in the following words [46, p. 42]: "When a nation has regular payments to make in a foreign country, for which it is not to receive any return, its exports must annually exceed its imports by the amount of the payments which it is bound so to make. In order to force a demand for its exports greater than its imports will suffice to pay for, it must offer them at a rate of interchange more favorable to the foreign country, and less so to itself, than if it had no payments to make beyond the value of its imports." This position was criticized by Bastable [3, pp. 14–17] and others as involving a fallacy— of failing to take account of the fact that the receiving country could buy up the paying country's export surplus out of its increased purchasing power. The alternative explanation presented here takes full account of shifts in purchasing power and is also in accord with the classical presumption that countries tend to specialize. Of course, there is no way of knowing whether it was the true explanation in the back of Mill's mind.

[6] Cf. Taussig [67, pp. 109–117, 358–362], where the examples chosen to illustrate his arguments (in which the United States produces a commodity such as wheat or cotton, and Great Britain one such as linen or steel), as well as the detailed descriptions of the illustrative adjustment processes, leave one no choice but to conclude that he implicitly assumed that these countries did not produce any import-competing goods (see also Taussig [67, p. 352]). One will also find the implicit assumption of specialization contained in the writings of

possibly that of Keynes.[7] The explanation is extremely simple: in the receiving country, resources move out of the export industry into the domestic industry, lowering world output of the paying country's import good; and in the paying country, resources move out of the domestic industry into the export industry, raising the world output of its export good. Given the assumptions concerning consumers' tastes, this must lower the paying country's terms of trade.

[7] Keynes appears to have rested his case entirely on the following brief and difficult argument [*A Treatise on Money*, Vol. I, New York: Harcourt, 1930, pp. 333–334]: "If. . . the new investment goods in *A* [the receiving country] have to be produced by factors of production in *A*, which factors are made available by being released from producing goods hitherto exported to *B* [the paying country] or henceforth imported from *B*, then the presumption is. . . " in favor of a deterioration in the paying country's terms of trade, "for it is unlikely that *A* would have previously exported the goods in question to *B* or refrained from importing them unless there was some gain in doing so." If "henceforth imported from *B*" implies a withdrawal of resources from import-competing industries into "domestic-trade industries" [35, Vol. I, p. 334], then this argument seems to be a *non sequitur*. An alternative interpretation is that Keynes had in mind a switch in comparative advantage following the transfer, and specialization in export and domestic industries before the transfer. Whatever be the correct interpretation, Keynes' explicit expression of approval of Taussig's treatment places him firmly in the orthodox camp. As Ellis and Metzler expressed it [17, pp. x–xi]: "The paradoxical aspect of the controversy [with Ohlin [51]] is that Keynes, who later laid the groundwork for the modern theory, adopted an extremely classical view in his discussion of German reparations."

other upholders of the orthodox thesis, e.g., Viner [70, p. 228] and Bresciani–Turroni [4, pp. 77–79]. Curiously enough, this implicit assumption is also contained in an early analysis by Graham [24, p. 213], who not only rejected the orthodox thesis but in later years quoted his 1925 article [25, p. 188] as evidence that he had previously provided the same analysis as that subsequently furnished by Ohlin [50]. In his earlier article [24], Graham had spoken about Germany's export industries drawing labor and capital out of her domestic industries, but had not mentioned the possibility of Germany's import-competing industries doing the same. Ohlin's argument, which Graham quoted [25, pp. 188–189], made specific mention of this other possibility, and yet Graham appeared not to notice this crucial difference between the two arguments. Graham used his 1925 reasoning to argue that a new equilibrium would be established automatically, apparently not realizing that under his premises this would entail a deterioration in the paying country's terms of trade (a thesis which Graham had accepted in an earlier paper [23]). In response to a similar, but less analytically reasoned, claim by Rueff [58, p. 396] that "equilibrium in the balance of payments has always been restored, whatever the extent of the initial disturbance and however arbitrary it may have been," Keynes [34, p. 406] had retorted that the fact that adjustment took place did not "prove that economic readjustments are as easy as shelling peas!" To complete the story, Ohlin in his later writings seems himself at one point [52, p. 403] to have forgotten all about the import-competing industries (which he called "the semi-international industries" [52, p. 410n]) and presented essentially the explanation given in the text for a deterioration in the paying country's terms of trade.

(ii)   If each country produces both international commodities as well as its domestic commodity, sufficient conditions for a deterioration (resp. improvement) in the paying country's terms of trade can be stated in the following terms (Theorem 6, formula (144) (resp. (146)): that the share of factor 2 in the outlay on the domestic commodity be less (resp. greater), in the paying country, and greater (resp. less) in the receiving country, than a certain weighted average of the shares of factor 2 in the outlays of the international commodities, the weights being quantities which can be interpreted—in the case in which utility functions are separable as between international and domestic commodities—as "average subpropensities to consume the international commodities" out of the income allotted to these commodities.[8] A special case is of very great interest, and has already been stated by Samuelson [63] (Theorem 5): if the domestic commodities in the two countries are (physically) identical, and if production functions are identical as between the two countries and preferences are identical and homothetic, and if factor prices are initially equalized (a sufficient condition for which being that there be no reversal of factor intensity as between the international industries), then a transfer will leave all prices, and hence the terms of trade, unchanged.[9]

---

[8] In particular this implies that if the domestic industry in the paying country uses a higher ratio of factor 1 to factor 2 than either of the international industries, and the domestic industry in the receiving country uses a higher ratio of factor 2 to factor 1 than either of the international industries, the terms of trade of the paying country will deteriorate. This result is based essentially on the well-known Rybczynski theorem: as resources move out of the domestic industry in the paying country, a larger proportion of the paying country's relatively abundant factor is released for employment in the international industries than of its relatively scarce factor, so that output of its exportables rises and of its importables falls; and a similar phenomenon takes place in the receiving country. If the relative factor intensity in the domestic industry is, in each country, intermediate between those of the export and import-competing industries, we can expect the change in the terms of trade to be relatively slight and that it could go in either direction. It is interesting to note that this line of argument can be found in Iversen [31, pp. 481–482], and it is puzzling that it was apparently never picked up during the three decades that followed the publication of this stimulating work. See also the remarks of Ohlin [52, pp. 424–425].

[9] It is of some interest to observe that this result is in accord with a late statement by Cassel of his Purchasing Power Party doctrine, to be found in a little known tract [8, pp. 19–22]. In his early writings Cassel [5] had implied that relative commodity prices in and between countries tend to remain invariant with respect to disturbances, the exchange rate reflecting only changes in nominal prices, i.e., different rates of inflation as between countries. When the Purchasing Power Parity theory was first presented as such [6], Cassel introduced a qualification to the effect that quantitative restrictions on exports or imports could alter these relative prices, or in his words, "if the trade between the two countries is hampered more severely in one direction than in the other the rate of exchange will deviate from its purchasing power parity" [6, p. 413]. Further exceptions were added to the list of qualifications in a later presentation [7, pp. 39–43], including tariffs and (apparently) short-term capital movements. At any rate, these earlier statements of the doctrine contain nothing in

Again, the explanation is extremely simple: under the given assumptions, factor prices and the prices of the two countries' domestic commodities must be equalized; hence factors must be employed in the same proportions as between countries in each industry; consequently, the changes in outputs of the three commodities in the receiving country resulting from the movement of resources to its domestic industry must be exactly counterbalanced by the changes in the corresponding outputs in the paying country resulting from the movement of resources out of its domestic industry, since the movements take place along linear and parallel Rybczynski paths (cf. Chipman [11, p. 214]). World outputs of the international commodities, as well as the sum of the outputs of the two countries' domestic commodities, remain unchanged, so their prices (owing to the demand assumptions) remain unchanged.

(iii)   If one country specializes in the production of domestic and export commodities and the other country diversifies, i.e., produces all three commodities, the following results are obtained (Theorem 7): a *sufficient* condition for deterioration of the paying country's terms of trade is that the share of the diversifying country's relatively abundant factor in the output of its domestic commodity be greater than a weighted average of the share of this factor in the outputs of the international commodities (the weights being subpropensities to consume, as above). In particular this will hold if, in the diversifying country, the domestic industry uses the relatively abundant factor relatively more intensively than either of the international industries. The explanation is as follows: if the receiving country diversifies, then—since by hypothesis its domestic industry uses factor 2 more intensively than either international

---

common with the analysis described in the text. Subsequent writers who have made use of purchasing power parity calculations (notably Metzler [44, p. 19]) have tended to specifically exempt capital movements on the grounds that a capital outflow would (at least in the short run) depreciate a country's exchange rate below the parity rate; in terms of the analysis of this paper this would correspond to a fall in the price of the paying country's domestic commodity relative to the price of the receiving country's domestic commodity (see Appendix B). Houthakker [30, p. 294] has restricted this qualification to autonomous, as opposed to accommodating, capital movements. In his last and most illuminating statement of the Purchasing Power Parity theory, however (cf. [8, pp. 14–23]), Cassel specifically allowed for autonomous capital transfers such as reparations payments, presenting an argument that was virtually indistinguishable from the argument subsequently put forward by Ohlin [50] to support his thesis that reparations would have little or no effect on the terms of trade. Nevertheless, Ohlin [52, p. 546] vigorously criticized the Purchasing Power Parity theory, calling it "absurd." Perhaps, in retrospect, we can say that he sensed better than Cassel that stronger hypotheses than those of our Theorem 6 were needed to obtain the conclusions of Theorem 5. A position essentially the same as Cassel's, but without the theoretical underpinnings, was taken by Rueff [58, p. 389], who described it by the rather amusing phrase "the principle of the conservation of purchasing power."

industry—as resources move out of its international into its domestic industries the production of its exportables will fall and of its importables rise (by a generalization of the Rybczynski theorem); hence world output of commodity 1 rises and of commodity 2 falls. Likewise if the paying country diversifies, since by hypothesis its domestic industry uses factor 1 more intensively than either of the international industries, as resources move out of the latter into the former the production of its exportables will rise and of its importables fall, leading to the same result.

If the above inequalities are reversed, we obtain only *necessary* rather than sufficient conditions for an improvement in the terms of trade of the paying country; however, if the stronger assumption is imposed that utility functions in the two countries are of identical Millian (" Cobb–Douglas ") type, then a *sufficient* condition for improvement of the paying country's terms of trade is that, in the diversifying country, the domestic industry should use the country's relatively abundant factor relatively less intensively than either of the international industries (Theorem 8). Perhaps a still more interesting result is that if both utility functions and production functions are of identical Cobb–Douglas type (the respective domestic commodities being treated as identical for purposes of this comparison), then under conditions which guarantee that a transfer will leave the terms of trade unchanged when both countries diversify [formula (164)], a transfer necessarily worsens the paying country's terms of trade when one of the countries specializes. This creates a decided *a priori* presumption that a transfer can generally be expected to worsen the paying country's terms of trade. A limited treatment of the three-factor case in Appendix A suggests that the same conclusion tends to hold there as well.[10]

As the above summary indicates, the approach adopted here is the "classical" one in which full employment is assumed to be maintained in both countries, rather than the approach of post-Keynesian employment theory which was fully and definitively treated by Metzler [42, 45]. This difference in

---

[10] One interesting generalization that seems to emerge from this analysis is that the combined action of transport costs and specialization (or more broadly than specialization, the production conditions that give rise to countries' positions of comparative advantage) tend to produce a presumption in favor of the orthodox thesis. In the absence of domestic commodities, it is easy to show (and is implicit in the treatment of Mundell [49]) that Samuelson's criterion for a change in the terms of trade is unaffected by the introduction of production adjustments, so the combined action of both domestic commodities and production adjustments is needed. The relevance of specialization to the orthodox conclusion was singled out by Joan Robinson [56, p. 163]; and in a forthcoming paper I shall argue that the " elasticity " concepts she used in order to reach this conclusion require for their validity the existence of domestic (nontraded) goods. A recent contribution by Samuelson [63] in terms of classical partial equilibrium models appears to give rise to similar conclusions—with leisure taking the place of domestic commodities.

approach obviously reflects changed economic conditions; but, from a broader scientific point of view it will be apparent to the reader that the analysis presented here rests heavily on the comparative static method developed by Samuelson [59], Mosak [48], and Metzler [43], and to which Metzler made so many other important contributions.

## II. General Formulation

### A. THE BASIC MODEL

The model will first be set up in a form general enough to cover all cases to be taken up subsequently, including that of pure exchange. Let there be two countries, country 1 (which will be the paying country) and country 2 (the receiving country), each having endowments

$$l^k = (l_1{}^k, l_2{}^k, l_3{}^k) \geqq 0 \qquad (k = 1, 2) \tag{1}$$

of three factors of production, assumed freely allocable among industries within each country but immobile as between countries. (A superscript will always indicate the country.) Assume that they are used in the production of three commodities, of which the first two (the *international commodities*) are freely tradable internationally at zero transport costs, and the third (the *domestic commodity*) is not internationally tradable, in accordance with the production functions:

$$y_i{}^k = f_i{}^k(l_{i1}^k, l_{i2}^k, l_{i3}^k) \qquad (k = 1, 2; \quad i = 1, 2, 3) \tag{2}$$

which are assumed to be continuous, nondecreasing in each argument, concave, and positively homogeneous of degree 1. (In Section V it will occasionally be assumed that production functions are identical between countries, i.e., $f_i^1 = f_i^2 = f_i$, $i = 1, 2, 3$.) The production possibility sets $\mathscr{Y}^k(l^k)$ of the respective countries (denoted simply $\mathscr{Y}(l^k)$ in the case of identical production functions) are defined, as usual, as the sets of commodity bundles

$$y^k = (y_1{}^k, y_2{}^k, y_3{}^k) \geqq 0 \qquad (k = 1, 2) \tag{3}$$

satisfying (2) and

$$\sum_{i=1}^{3} l_{ij}^k \leqq l_j^k \qquad (j = 1, 2, 3; \quad k = 1, 2). \tag{4}$$

Given a vector of positive prices[11]

$$p^k = (p_1, p_2, p_3{}^k) > 0 \qquad (k = 1, 2) \tag{5}$$

---

[11] The symbols $>0$ and $\geqq 0$ for vectors indicate that the components of the vector are respectively all positive or all nonnegative.

we define the *national product functions*[12]

$$\Pi^k(p^k, l^k) = \max\{p^k \cdot y : y \in \mathscr{Y}^k(l^k)\} \qquad (k = 1, 2). \qquad (6)$$

It is assumed that production is carried out efficiently, i.e., that the quantities $y^k$ supplied satisfy

$$p^k \cdot y^k = \Pi^k(p^k, l^k) \qquad (k = 1, 2). \qquad (7)$$

Country 1 is assumed to collect amounts

$$\gamma_1 \tau, \quad \gamma_2 \tau \qquad (\gamma_i \geq 0, \quad \gamma_1 + \gamma_2 = 1) \qquad (8)$$

of the two tradable commodities from its citizens per unit of time, and transfer them to the receiving country. Here, $\gamma_1$ and $\gamma_2$ are considered as fixed parameters, and $\tau \geq 0$ measures parametrically the amount or intensity of the transfer. Disposable incomes in the two countries are then determined, respectively, by

$$I^1 = \Phi^1(p^1, l^1, \tau) \equiv \Pi^1(p^1, l^1) - (p_1\gamma_1 + p_2\gamma_2)\tau$$
$$I^2 = \Phi^2(p^2, l^2, \tau) \equiv \Pi^2(p^2, l^2) + (p_1\gamma_1 + p_2\gamma_2)\tau. \qquad (9)$$

These may be identified with Ohlin's "purchasing power" [50] or "buying power" [52, pp. 61n, 378].

It will be assumed that the respective countries have aggregate demand functions

$$x_i^k = h_i^k(p^k, I^k) \qquad (i = 1, 2, 3; \quad k = 1, 2) \qquad (10)$$

which are single-valued and continuously differentiable and generated by aggregate utility functions[13]

$$U^k(x_1^k, x_2^k, x_3^k) \qquad (k = 1, 2) \qquad (11)$$

---

[12] In [12] I described this function as a "production function for foreign exchange," since the emphasis was on the dependence on $l$ with fixed $p$; here the emphasis will instead be on the dependence on $p$ with fixed $l$. When production functions are identical between countries, these functions will of course be denoted $\Pi(p^k, l^k)$. As usual, $p \cdot y$ denotes the inner product $\sum_{i=1}^{3} p_i y_i$.

[13] This can be interpreted to mean either (1) that consumers in each country have, for each set of prices, linear and parallel Engel curves (cf. Gorman [20]) or (2) that the government in each country implements an income distribution policy assigning for each set of prices and aggregate income an income distribution which maximizes a social welfare function (cf. Chipman and Moore[14]). (As pointed out by Samuelson [62], conditions (1) are the conditions under which a transfer of these internally tradable commodities among individuals will leave prices unchanged.) It is important to stress that interpretation (1) does not permit one to interpret $U^k$ as a measure of country $k$'s welfare, at least not without further qualification (see Section II. C).

which are assumed to be twice continuously differentiable, strongly increasing in each argument, and strictly quasi concave.[14] From the monotonicity it follows that the demand functions (10) satisfy the budget identity

$$p^k \cdot h^k(p^k, I^k) = I^k \qquad \text{for all} \quad p^k > 0, \quad I^k \geqq 0 \qquad (k = 1, 2) \qquad (12)$$

where $h^k = (h_1{}^k, h_2{}^k, h_3{}^k)$.

The model is closed by postulating the equality of demand and supply:

$$x_i{}^1 + x_i{}^2 = y_i{}^1 + y_i{}^2 \quad (i = 1, 2); \qquad x_3{}^1 = y_3{}^1; \qquad x_3{}^2 = y_3{}^2. \qquad (13)$$

The system is homogeneous of degree 0 in the four prices $p_1, p_2, p_3{}^1, p_3{}^2$, which will be normalized in the following analysis by holding $p_1$ constant; and since the conditions are not independent (in view of (7) and (12)), we shall in the subsequent analysis suppress the first equation of (13) (for $i = 1$).

Defining country $k$'s *national demand function* $X^k = (X_1{}^k, X_2{}^k, X_3{}^k)$ by

$$X_i{}^k(p^k, I^k, \tau) = h_i{}^k[p^k, \Phi^k(p^k, I^k, \tau)] \qquad (i = 1, 2, 3; \quad k = 1, 2) \qquad (14)$$

and its *national supply correspondence* $Y^k$ by

$$Y^k(p^k, I^k) = \{y^k \in \mathscr{Y}^k(I^k): p^k \cdot y^k = \Pi^k(p^k, I^k)\} \qquad (k = 1, 2), \qquad (15)$$

standard arguments can be used to show that there exist positive prices $p_1$, $p_2$, $p_3{}^1$, $p_3{}^2$ and national supplies $y^k \in Y^k(p^k, I^k)$ such that (13) holds, where $x_i{}^k = X_i{}^k(p^k, I^k, \tau)$ and $\tau = 0$.[15] It will be assumed that this solution is

---

[14] For a monotone, strictly quasi-concave $C^2$ utility function to generate a $C^1$ demand function it is necessary and sufficient that the bordered Hessian of the utility function (cf. Section IV.B) be nonvanishing (cf. Debreu [15], Katzner [33], Fenchel [18]). As an example of a $C^2$ utility function which does not generate a $C^1$ demand function we may take, following Katzner [33, p. 54], the function $U(x_1, x_2) = (x_1{}^3 x_2 + x_1 x_2{}^3)^{1/4}$; this function is homogeneous of degree 1, concave, and strictly quasi concave, but its bordered Hessian vanishes for $x_1 = x_2$. A strictly quasi-concave utility function $U^k$ whose bordered Hessian is everywhere nonvanishing will be called *strongly quasi-concave*.[18] Likewise, in saying that $U^k$ is "strongly increasing in each argument" we mean that $U_i{}^k = \partial U^k/\partial x_i > 0$ for $i = 1, 2, 3$ and at all points of the domain of $U^k$.

[15] Denote $\xi^1 = (X_1{}^1, X_2{}^1, X_3{}^1, 0)$, $\xi^2 = (X_1{}^2, X_2{}^2, 0, X_3{}^2)$, and define

$$\eta^1(p^1, I^1) = \{(y_1{}^1, y_2{}^1, y_3{}^1, 0) : (y_1{}^1, y_2{}^1, y_3{}^1) \in \mathscr{Y}^1(I^1), p^1 \cdot y^1 = \Pi^1(p^1, I^1)\}$$
$$\eta^2(p^2, I^2) = \{(y_1{}^2, y_2{}^2, 0, y_3{}^2) : (y_1{}^2, y_2{}^2, y_3{}^2) \in \mathscr{Y}^2(I^2), p^2 \cdot y^2 = \Pi^2(p^2, I^2)\}.$$

The correspondence

$$\zeta(p_1, p_2, p_3{}^1, p_3{}^2) = \{\xi^1(p^1; I^1, 0) + \xi^2(p^2; I^2, 0)\} - \eta^1(p^1; I^1) - \eta^2(p^2; I^2)$$

is convex-valued and upper semicontinuous; hence (since the $\hat{U}^k$ are monotone) there exist $(p_1, p_2, p_3{}^1, p_3{}^2) > 0$ such that $(0, 0, 0, 0) \in \zeta(p_1, p_2, p_3{}^1, p_3{}^2)$ (see, for instance, Chipman and Moore [14, p. 166]). If $\tau \neq 0$ there is the further problem of ensuring $I^k \geqq 0$ in (9).

isolated;[16] then in some interval $\tau_0 \le \tau \le \tau_1$ we can express equilibrium prices and quantities as functions of $\tau$, to be denoted

$$\tilde{p}^k(\tau) = (p_1, \tilde{p}_2(\tau), \tilde{p}_3{}^k(\tau)); \qquad \tilde{y}^k(\tau) = (\tilde{y}_1{}^k(\tau), \tilde{y}_2{}^k(\tau), \tilde{y}_3{}^k(\tau)). \qquad (16)$$

B. CLASSIFICATION OF CASES

Throughout the rest of this chapter we shall deal with various special cases of the above model.

1. *Pure Exchange* (Section IV)

This case is handled formally by giving the production functions the special form $f_i^k(l_{i1}^k, l_{i2}^k, l_{i3}^k) = l_{ii}^k$. The amounts $l_i^k$ then correspond to the endowments of commodities. It is more illuminating, however, to think of this case as one of short-run adjustment, in which factors of production are temporarily immobile between industries and production is carried out at a fixed rate per unit of time. The corresponding production possibility set $\mathcal{Y}^k(l^k)$ has the shape of a box (cf. Haberler [28]).

2. *Two-Factor Case* (Section V)

In this case we have $l_3^k = 0$ for $k = 1, 2$, and it will be assumed that the production functions are strongly increasing and strongly quasi concave in their first two arguments,[17] and they will be denoted $f_i^k(l_{i1}^k, l_{i2}^k)$. As is well known, the production possibility surfaces will be ruled, and for prices at which all three commodities can be efficiently produced, $Y^k$ is a multivalued correspondence, i.e., the supplies $y^k$ satisfying (7) are not unique; in more old-fashioned terminology this is described by saying that the supply of exports is infinitely elastic. If each country specializes in its domestic commodity and one international commodity, however, then the supplies (under conditions that will be assumed to hold) will be single-valued functions of prices.

3. *Three-Factor Case* (Appendix A)

If both countries have positive endowments of all three factors, we shall assume that the production functions (2) are strongly increasing in each argument and strongly quasi concave.[17] It will be assumed, furthermore, that in each country the production possibility surface $\hat{\mathcal{Y}}^k(l^k)$ (the boundary of $\mathcal{Y}^k(l^k)$ relative to the nonnegative octant) is strongly concave to the origin[17] and that all three commodities are produced.

---

[16] More specifically, it will be assumed below that the equilibrium is perfectly stable in the Hicksian sense.

[17] See footnotes 14 and 18 for definitions of strong monotonicity and strong quasi concavity and concavity to the origin, and the discussion in Section III.A.

For technical reasons we shall first take up (in Section III) the case in which $Y^k$ is single-valued, i.e., $Y^k(p^k, l^k)$ is a one-element set for given values of the arguments; we shall in this case treat $Y^k$ as an ordinary single-valued function. This case will cover the case of pure exchange, the two-factor case with specialization, and the three-factor case. Special methods will be introduced in Section V.B to take care of the two-factor case with diversification.

## III. The Case of Single-Valued Supply Functions: Some General Results

### A. NATIONAL SUPPLY FUNCTIONS

Consider a given country's production possibility set $\mathcal{Y}(l)$—for convenience we shall temporarily drop the country superscript. We have defined the *frontier* (or *outer boundary*) $\hat{\mathcal{Y}}(l)$ of $\mathcal{Y}(l)$ as its boundary relative to the non-negative octant. It will be convenient to define the *efficient frontier* $\hat{\mathcal{Y}}_P(l)$ of $\mathcal{Y}(l)$ relative to a convex set $P$ of prices $p = (p_1, p_2, p_3) > 0$, as the set

$$\hat{\mathcal{Y}}_P(l) = \{y \in \mathcal{Y}(l): (\exists p \in P)p \cdot y = \Pi(p, l)\}. \tag{17}$$

$\hat{\mathcal{Y}}_P(l)$ is called *strictly concave to the origin* if, for all $y \in \hat{\mathcal{Y}}_P(l)$, there is a $p \in P$ such that $p \cdot y = \Pi(p, l)$ and $p \cdot y' < \Pi(p, l)$ for all $y' \in \mathcal{Y}(l)$ such that $y' \neq y$. (Cf. Chipman [12], Khang [36].)

If $\hat{\mathcal{Y}}_P(l)$ is strictly concave to the origin, for every $p \in P$ there is a unique $y$ such that $p \cdot y = \Pi(p, l)$; this defines the single-valued function $y = Y(p, l)$ with components $y_i = Y_i(p, l)$, $i = 1, 2, 3$. Now suppose that $P$ is such that for each $i = 1, 2, 3$, either $Y_i(p, l) > 0$ for all $p \in P$, or $Y_i(p, l) = 0$ for all $p \in P$, the inequality holding for at least two of the three commodities. In other words, at least two of the three commodities are produced, and there is no switching from specialization to diversification as prices vary over the set $P$. Then we shall say that $\hat{\mathcal{Y}}_P(l)$ is *strongly concave to the origin* if (i) it is strictly concave to the origin, and (ii) the functions $Y_i(p, l)$ are continuously differentiable at $(p, l)$ for all $p \in P$. We shall assume throughout the remainder of the section that $\hat{\mathcal{Y}}_P(l)$ is strongly concave to the origin for the relevant set of prices $P$.[18]

---

[18] This assumption is designed to rule out the following troublesome kind of case. Adapting an example of Katzner [33, p. 54], suppose that just two commodities are produced, and let the production possibility frontier be given by

$$\hat{\mathcal{Y}} = \{(y_1, y_2) \geq 0 : (y_1 - b)^3(y_2 - b) + (y_1 - b)(y_2 - b)^3 = c, y_i < b\}$$

where $b$ and $c$ are both positive constants. $\hat{\mathcal{Y}}$ is strictly concave to the origin but not strongly concave to the origin, since the functions $Y_1(p_1, p_2)$ and $Y_2(p_1, p_2)$ are not differentiable at $p_1 = p_2$, where $y_1 = y_2$. $Y_1(p_1, p_2)$ is a strictly increasing function of $p_1$ for each fixed $p_2$ but has an infinite derivative at $p_1 = p_2$. This results from the fact that $\hat{\mathcal{Y}}$ is extremely flat at $y_1 = y_2$, i.e., has zero Gaussian curvature there (cf. Debreu [15]).

Sufficient conditions for $\hat{\mathcal{Y}}_P(l)$ to be strongly concave to the origin can be obtained as

Under these conditions we can write the national product function in the form

$$\Pi(p, l) = p_1 Y_1(p, l) + p_2 Y_2(p, l) + p_3 Y_3(p, l), \tag{18}$$

and thus $\Pi$ is continuously differentiable. From the assumed properties of the production functions it follows further that[19]

$$p_1 \, \partial Y_1/\partial p_i + p_2 \, \partial Y_2/\partial p_i + p_3 \, \partial Y_3/\partial p_i = 0 \qquad (i = 1, 2) \tag{19}$$

so that

$$\partial \Pi/\partial p_i = Y_i, \tag{20}$$

whence $\Pi$ is twice continuously differentiable. Since by the definition (6), $\Pi(\cdot, l)$ is the support function of $\mathscr{Y}(l)$, which is convex, it follows that $\Pi(\cdot, l)$ is convex (cf. Fenchel [18, pp. 67–68]). Thus, the Hessian matrix of $\Pi$ is symmetric and positive semidefinite. Defining the *transformation terms* $t_{ij}$ by

$$t_{ij} = \partial Y_i/\partial p_j = \partial^2 \Pi/\partial p_i \, \partial p_j, \tag{21}$$

---

[19] Cf. Chipman [12, p. 221]. Unfortunately the statement of Theorem 3 in that paper was not quite correct; "any neighborhood" should have read "almost any neighborhood," i.e., the set of price vectors for which the proposition is false (such as the price vector with $p_1 = p_2$ in the example of footnote 18) has zero Lebesgue measure. The argument presented here provides the required correction.

---

follows, for the case in which the number of commodities produced is equal to the number of factors; I shall state the argument for the general case of $n$ commodities and factors. Since the production functions $f_i$ are twice continuously differentiable, homogeneous, increasing, strongly quasi concave, and concave (so that the isoquants of $f_i$ are strongly convex to the origin (see footnote 14)), the demand for the $j$th factor per unit of the $i$th product is a continuously differentiable function $b_{ij}(w)$ of the factor prices $w = (w_1, w_2, \ldots, w_n)$; hence the minimum-unit-cost functions $g_i(w) = \sum_{k=1}^n w_k b_{ik}(w)$ are continuously differentiable and $\partial g_i/\partial w_j = b_{ij}$ by the envelope theorem of production theory (this is proved by differentiating the identity

$$f_i[b_{i1}(w), b_{i2}(w), \ldots, b_{in}(w)] = 1$$

through with respect to $w_j$ and noting that $\partial f_i/\partial l_j = w_j/p_i$). We then have a mapping $p = g(w)$ from factor prices to commodity prices whose Jacobian matrix is $B(w) = [b_{ij}(w)] = \partial g/\partial w$. If it is nonsingular at $w^0$, then it has an inverse in a neighborhood of $p^0 = g(w^0)$ (if the principal minors of $B$ are all positive, then by the Gale–Nikaido theorem [19], $g$ is globally univalent), and we have (locally) an inverse mapping $w = g^{-1}(p)$ with Jacobian matrix denoted $B^{-1}(p) = [b^{ij}(p)] = \partial g^{-1}/\partial p$. Our *sufficient condition is that $g^{-1}$ be twice continuously differentiable*; for, the full employment condition $yB = l$ implies that the function $Y(p, l)$ satisfies $Y(p, l) = l B^{-1}(p) = l [\partial g^{-1}/\partial p]$ (locally), and this is $C^1$ if $g^{-1}$ is $C^2$.

It would, of course, be desirable to try to obtain sufficient conditions in terms of the functions $g_i$ themselves, or better still in terms of the production functions $f_i$, but this will not be pursued here. It will suffice to remark that the sufficient condition always holds for CES production functions with the same elasticity of substitution $\sigma$, since the cost functions then have the CES form with elasticity of substitution $1/\sigma$ (cf. Chipman [9, pp. 59–60]).

the *transformation matrix* $T$ is defined as the Hessian of $\Pi$:

$$T = \begin{bmatrix} t_{11} & t_{12} & t_{13} \\ t_{21} & t_{22} & t_{23} \\ t_{31} & t_{32} & t_{33} \end{bmatrix}. \tag{22}$$

In view of (19) it satisfies

$$Tp = 0; \tag{23}$$

hence $T$ has rank at most 2.

## B. NATIONAL DEMAND FUNCTIONS AND EXCESS DEMAND FUNCTIONS

Given a country's aggregate demand function $h(p, I)$ we define the Slutsky *substitution terms* $s_{ij}$ and the *income coefficients* $m_i$ by

$$s_{ij} = \partial h_i/\partial p_j + (\partial h_i/\partial I) h_j; \qquad m_i = \partial h_i/\partial I, \tag{24}$$

and the *Slutsky matrix* (or *substitution matrix*) $S$ by

$$S = \begin{bmatrix} s_{11} & s_{12} & s_{13} \\ s_{21} & s_{22} & s_{23} \\ s_{31} & s_{32} & s_{33} \end{bmatrix}. \tag{25}$$

As is well known, $S$ is symmetric and negative semidefinite and, owing to the assumption of strong quasi concavity of $U$, of rank 2 (cf. e.g., Katzner [33, p. 48]), and it satisfies

$$Sp = 0. \tag{26}$$

Attaching country superscripts to these expressions, we shall define the composed functions $\bar{s}_{ij}^k$ and $\bar{m}_i^k$ by

$$\bar{s}_{ij}^k(p^k, l^k, \tau) = s_{ij}^k[p^k, \Phi^k(p^k, l^k, \tau)]$$
$$\bar{m}_i^k(p^k, l^k, \tau) = m_i^k[p^k, \Phi^k(p^k, l^k, \tau)], \tag{27}$$

and the composed substitution matrix will be denoted

$$\bar{S}^k = [\bar{s}_{ij}^k]. \tag{28}$$

In terms of this notation we have $\bar{h}_i^k = X_i^k$ as defined in (14). From these definitions we find readily, making use of (9) and (14), that

$$\partial X_i^1/\partial p_j^1 = \bar{s}_{ij}^1 - \bar{m}_i^1(X_j^1 - Y_j^1 + \gamma_j\tau)$$
$$\partial X_i^2/\partial p_j^2 = \bar{s}_{ij}^2 - \bar{m}_i^2(X_j^2 - Y_j^2 - \gamma_j\tau) \tag{29}$$

and

$$\partial X_i^1/\partial\tau = -(p_1\gamma_1 + p_2\gamma_2)\bar{m}_i^1; \qquad \partial X_i^2/\partial\tau = (p_1\gamma_1 + p_2\gamma_2)\bar{m}_i^2. \tag{30}$$

Country $k$'s *excess demand function* $Z_i^k$ for commodity $i$ is defined by

$$Z_i^k(p^k, l^k, \tau) = X_i^k(p^k, l^k, \tau) - Y_i^k(p^k, l^k). \tag{31}$$

It will be convenient also to introduce the notation[20]

$$\zeta_i^1 = Z_i^1 + \gamma_i \tau, \qquad \zeta_i^2 = Z_i^2 - \gamma_i \tau, \tag{32}$$

as well as to define the function $\beta_1$ (the "primary burden" per unit of transfer) by

$$\beta_1(p) = p_1 \gamma_1 + p_2 \gamma_2. \tag{33}$$

Then we may express the partial derivatives of the excess demand functions (31), from (29) and (21), by

$$\partial Z_i^1/\partial p_j{}^1 = \bar{s}_{ij}^1 - t_{ij}^1 - \bar{m}_i^1 \zeta_j^1; \qquad \partial Z_i^1/\partial \tau = -\beta_1 \bar{m}_i^1$$
$$\partial Z_i^2/\partial p_j{}^2 = \bar{s}_{ij}^2 - t_{ij}^2 - \bar{m}_i^2 \zeta_j^2; \qquad \partial Z_i^2/\partial \tau = \beta_1 \bar{m}_i^2. \tag{34}$$

Finally, we define the *total substitution terms* $\hat{s}_{ij}^k$ by

$$\hat{s}_{ij}^k = \bar{s}_{ij}^k - t_{ij}^k \tag{35}$$

and the *total substitution matrix* for country $k$ by

$$\hat{S}^k = \bar{S}^k - T^k. \tag{36}$$

$\hat{S}^k$ is symmetric and negative semidefinite of rank 2, and satisfies $\hat{S}p = 0$ in view of (26) and (23).[21]

---

[20] Excess demand $z_i{}^k$ may be interpreted as country $k$'s exports of commodity $i$, if negative, and imports of commodity $i$, if positive. However, if we interpret the transfer as permanently changing the countries' production possibility sets to $\mathcal{Y}^1(l^1) - \{(\gamma_1, \gamma_2, 0)\}$ and $\mathcal{Y}^2(l^2) + \{(\gamma_1, \gamma_2, 0)\}$, respectively, then we may consider $\zeta_i^k$ to represent country $k$'s exports, if negative, and imports, if positive. The substantive results do not, of course, depend in any way on which interpretation is chosen. In the ensuing analysis it may be helpful to think of country 1 (the paying country) as exporting commodity 1 and importing commodity 2, though the analysis does not depend on this assumption.

[21] If, following Meade [41], we define a country's "trade utility function" $\hat{U}$ by

$$\hat{U}(z_1, z_2, z_3; l) = \max\{U(x_1, x_2, x_3) : (x_1, x_2, x_3) - (z_1, z_2, z_3) \in \mathcal{Y}(l)\},$$

and the corresponding "trade demand function" $\hat{h}(p_1, p_2, p_3, d; l)$ as the function whose value $(z_1, z_2, z_3)$ maximizes $\hat{U}$ subject to $p_1 z_1 + p_2 z_2 + p_3 z_3 \leqq d$, where $d$ is the deficit in the balance of payments on current account, then it can be shown that

$$\hat{h}(p, d; l) = h[p, \Pi(p, l) + d] - Y(p, l)$$

and that consequently

$$\hat{s}_{ij} = \partial \hat{h}_i/\partial p_j + (\partial \hat{h}_i/\partial d) \hat{h}_j, \qquad \bar{m}_i = \partial \hat{h}_i/\partial d.$$

## C. COMPARATIVE STATICS OF THE TRANSFER PROBLEM

From the budget equalities (7) and (12) the excess demand functions (31) satisfy

$$p^1 \cdot Z^1(p^1, l^1, \tau) = -\tau(p_1\gamma_1 + p_2\gamma_2) = -p^2 \cdot Z^2(p^2, l^2, \tau) \qquad (37)$$

identically, so conditions (13) yield the system of three independent equations

$$Z_2^1(p_1, p_2, p_3^1, l^1, \tau) + Z_2^2(p_1, p_2, p_3^2, l^2, \tau) = 0$$
$$Z_3^1(p_1, p_2, p_3^1, l^1, \tau) \qquad\qquad\qquad\quad = 0 \qquad (38)$$
$$Z_3^2(p_1, p_2, p_3^2, l^2, \tau) = 0$$

in the three variables $p_2, p_3^1, p_3^2$, where $p_1$ and $l^1, l^2$ are fixed and $\tau$ is a parameter.

Since the first equation of (38) implies that $\zeta_i^2 = -\zeta_i^1$ in (32), we can express the Jacobian matrix of (38) with the aid of (34) as

$$J = \begin{bmatrix} \partial Z_2^1/\partial p_2 + \partial Z_2^2/\partial p_2 & \partial Z_2^1/\partial p_3^1 & \partial Z_2^2/\partial p_3^2 \\ \partial Z_3^1/\partial p_2 & \partial Z_3^1/\partial p_3^1 & 0 \\ \partial Z_3^2/\partial p_2 & 0 & \partial Z_3^2/\partial p_3^2 \end{bmatrix}$$

$$= \begin{bmatrix} \hat{s}_{22}^1 + \hat{s}_{22}^2 - (\overline{m}_2^1 - \overline{m}_2^2)\zeta_2^1 & \hat{s}_{23}^1 & \hat{s}_{23}^2 \\ \hat{s}_{32}^1 - \overline{m}_3^1\zeta_2^1 & \hat{s}_{33}^1 & 0 \\ \hat{s}_{32}^2 + \overline{m}_3^2\zeta_2^1 & 0 & \hat{s}_{33}^2 \end{bmatrix}. \qquad (39)$$

It will be assumed that $J$ is *Hicksian*, i.e., that its principal minors are alternately negative and positive. One way to justify this is to postulate the Samuelson dynamic process of adjustment:

$$\dot{p}_2 = \kappa_2\{Z_2^1(p_1, p_2, p_3^1, l^1, \tau) + Z_2^2(p_1, p_2, p_3^2, l^2, \tau)\}$$
$$\dot{p}_3^1 = \kappa_3^1 Z_3^1(p_1, p_2, p_3^1, l^1, \tau) \qquad\qquad\qquad (40)$$
$$\dot{p}_3^2 = \kappa_3^2 Z_3^2(p_1, p_2, p_3^2, l^2, \tau)$$

where $\dot{p}_i^k = dp_i^k/dt$ and the $\kappa_i^k$'s are constant positive speeds of adjustment. It was shown by Metzler [43, pp. 282–283] that the Hicks conditions are necessary for the system (40) to be locally stable for all speeds of adjustment.

---

Thus, the total substitution terms are the Slutsky substitution terms of the trade utility function. $\hat{U}$ also has the interesting property that the marginal conditions

$$\frac{\partial\hat{U}/\partial z_i}{\partial\hat{U}/\partial z_j} = \frac{p_i}{p_j} \quad \text{and} \quad \frac{\partial\hat{U}/\partial l_i}{\partial\hat{U}/\partial l_j} = \frac{w_i}{w_j}$$

hold in equilibrium.

Since we may assume that the initial equilibrium is stable, these necessary conditions are sufficient for our purposes, at least as far as the adjustment process (40) is concerned.[22] In particular, therefore, we shall assume that

$$|J| < 0. \tag{41}$$

Since from (34) we have

$$(\partial Z_2{}^1/\partial\tau + \partial Z_2{}^2/\partial\tau, \; \partial Z_3{}^1/\partial\tau, \; \partial Z_3{}^2/\partial\tau) = -\beta_1(\overline{m}_2{}^1 - \overline{m}_2{}^2, \; -\overline{m}_3{}^1, \overline{m}_3{}^2), \tag{42}$$

we obtain from (38) the system

$$\begin{bmatrix} \hat{s}_{22}^1 + \hat{s}_{22}^2 - (\overline{m}_2{}^1 - \overline{m}_2{}^2)\zeta_2{}^1 & \hat{s}_{23}^1 & \hat{s}_{23}^2 \\ \hat{s}_{32}^1 - \overline{m}_3{}^1\zeta_2{}^1 & \hat{s}_{33}^1 & 0 \\ \hat{s}_{32}^2 + \overline{m}_3{}^2\zeta_2{}^1 & 0 & \hat{s}_{33}^2 \end{bmatrix} \begin{bmatrix} d\tilde{p}_2/d\tau \\ d\tilde{p}_3{}^1/d\tau \\ d\tilde{p}_3{}^2/d\tau \end{bmatrix} = \beta_1 \begin{bmatrix} \overline{m}_2{}^1 - \overline{m}_2{}^2 \\ \overline{m}_3{}^1 \\ -\overline{m}_3{}^2 \end{bmatrix}. \tag{43}$$

## D. Effect of a Transfer on Prices of Domestic Relative to International Commodities

Use of Cramer's rule and straightforward computations yield the following expressions from (43):

$$\frac{d\tilde{p}_2}{d\tau} = \frac{\beta_1 \hat{s}_{33}^1 \hat{s}_{33}^2}{|J|} \left\{ \begin{vmatrix} \overline{m}_2{}^1 & \hat{s}_{23}^1 \\ \overline{m}_3{}^1 & \hat{s}_{33}^1 \end{vmatrix} - \begin{vmatrix} \overline{m}_2{}^2 & \hat{s}_{23}^2 \\ \overline{m}_3{}^2 & \hat{s}_{33}^2 \end{vmatrix} \right\}; \tag{44a}$$

$$\frac{d\tilde{p}_3{}^k}{d\tau} = -(-1)^k \frac{\beta_1 \hat{s}_{33}^i}{|J|} \left\{ \overline{m}_3{}^k \frac{\begin{vmatrix} \hat{s}_{22}^i & \hat{s}_{23}^i \\ \hat{s}_{32}^i & \hat{s}_{33}^i \end{vmatrix}}{\hat{s}_{33}^i} + \hat{s}_{32}^k \frac{\begin{vmatrix} \overline{m}_2{}^i & \hat{s}_{23}^i \\ \overline{m}_3{}^i & \hat{s}_{33}^i \end{vmatrix}}{\hat{s}_{33}^i} - \begin{vmatrix} \overline{m}_2{}^k & \hat{s}_{22}^k \\ \overline{m}_3{}^k & \hat{s}_{32}^k \end{vmatrix} \right\} \tag{44b}$$

$$(i \neq k = 1, 2).$$

---

[22] If $J$ is a Metzler matrix, i.e., if its off-diagonal elements are nonpositive, then as Metzler showed [43], the Hicks conditions are also sufficient for stability of the process (40). However, even if $\hat{S}$ is a Metzler matrix (as is reasonable to assume), $J$ need not be. It should be added that a deeper analysis would require investigation of nontâtonnement production adjustment processes—not one, but several, e.g.: the gold standard process, the flexible exchange rate process, the Bretton Woods process, etc.; but this is beyond the scope of this chapter. In the meantime, the general results of McFadden [40, p. 335] may be appealed to as providing additional justification for relying on the Hicks conditions.

These also give, of course, the effects of a transfer on the prices $p_2, p_3^1$, $p_3^2$ relative to $p_1$. To find the effect on $p_3^1$ and $p_3^2$ relative to $p_2$ we obtain from (44)

$$\frac{d\tilde{p}_3^k}{d\tau} - \frac{p_3^k}{p_2}\frac{d\tilde{p}_2}{d\tau}$$

$$= -(-1)^k \frac{\beta_1 \hat{s}_{33}^i}{|J|}\left(\overline{m}_3^k \frac{\begin{vmatrix} \hat{s}_{22}^i & \hat{s}_{23}^i \\ \hat{s}_{32}^i & \hat{s}_{33}^i \end{vmatrix}}{\hat{s}_{33}^i} - \frac{p_1 \hat{s}_{31}^k}{p_2}\frac{\begin{vmatrix} \overline{m}_2^i & \hat{s}_{23}^i \\ \overline{m}_3^i & \hat{s}_{33}^i \end{vmatrix}}{\hat{s}_{33}^i} + \frac{p_1}{p_2}\begin{vmatrix} \overline{m}_2^k & \hat{s}_{21}^k \\ \overline{m}_3^k & \hat{s}_{31}^k \end{vmatrix}\right)$$

$$(i \neq k = 1, 2), \quad (45)$$

where use has been made of the fact that the total substitution terms satisfy $\sum_{i=1}^3 \hat{s}_{ij}p_j^k = 0$, from (26) and (23).

Country $k$'s domestic commodity will be called

(i) *strongly superior*, if $m_3^k > 0$; and
(ii) *weakly totally substitutable with both international commodities*, if $\hat{s}_{i3}^k \geq 0$ for $i = 1, 2$.

Country $k$'s domestic commodity will be called *totally regular* if (i) and (ii) both hold, and simply *regular* if (i) holds and $s_{i3}^k \geq 0$ for $i = 1, 2$.

A sufficient condition for (ii) to hold is of course that $s_{i3}^k \geq 0$ for $i = 1, 2$ (international commodities are weak Hicksian substitutes of the domestic commodity) and $t_{i3}^k \leq 0$ (they are weakly substitutable with the domestic commodity in production). Since these conditions will be used in the ensuing discussion, let us show that they are not vacuous.

We shall say that a $3 \times 3$ matrix is a Metzler (or Mosak–Metzler—cf. [48, 43]), block Metzler, or semi-Metzler matrix according as it has the sign pattern

$$\begin{bmatrix} - & + & + \\ + & - & + \\ + & + & - \end{bmatrix} \text{ or } \begin{bmatrix} - & - & + \\ - & - & + \\ + & + & - \end{bmatrix} \text{ or } \begin{bmatrix} - & ? & + \\ ? & - & + \\ + & + & - \end{bmatrix}, \quad (46)$$

and a Leontief (or Minkowski–Leontief), block Leontief (or Morishima), or semi-Leontief matrix according as it has the opposite sign pattern

$$\begin{bmatrix} + & - & - \\ - & + & - \\ - & - & + \end{bmatrix} \text{ or } \begin{bmatrix} + & + & - \\ + & + & - \\ - & - & + \end{bmatrix} \text{ or } \begin{bmatrix} + & ? & - \\ ? & + & - \\ - & - & + \end{bmatrix}, \quad (47)$$

where $+$ means $\geq 0$ and $-$ means $\leq 0$.

That a Slutsky matrix can be a Metzler matrix is clear; in fact, the property is less restrictive than it might appear, since it holds in the case of CES utility functions with any positive elasticity of substitution, even arbitrarily close to 0.[23]

If $\mathscr{Y}(l)$ is box-shaped (the case of "pure exchange"), $T = 0$; hence the condition trivially holds. Let us consider the case in which a country produces three commodities with three factors, and in which the minimum-unit-cost mapping $g(w) = p$ from factor prices to commodity prices is locally univalent, and all three commodities are produced in positive amounts. Then the Stolper–Samuelson mapping $W(p, l) = w$ (cf. Chipman [12]) is locally independent of $l$ and coincident with the local inverse branch of the mapping $g$, which we may denote $g^{-1}(p)$, i.e., $W(p, l) = g^{-1}(p)$, independently of $l$ and for a set of prices $p \in P$ for which all three commodities are actually produced. Denoting the Hessian matrix of $W_k(p, l)$ by $H_k = [\partial^2 W_k / \partial p_i \, \partial p_j]$, then it follows from the analysis of footnote 18 that

$$T = \sum_{k=1}^{3} l_k H_k, \qquad t_{ij} = \sum_{k=1}^{3} l_k \frac{\partial^2 W_k}{\partial p_i \, \partial p_j}. \tag{48}$$

If the production functions are of Cobb–Douglas type, so are the minimum-unit-cost functions (which are therefore globally univalent) and we have, say, for $p \in P$,

$$p_1 = g_1(w) = v_1 w_1^{\beta_{11}} w_2^{\beta_{12}} w_3^{\beta_{13}}; \qquad w_1 = W_1(p, l) = \alpha_1 p_1^{\beta^{11}} p_2^{\beta^{12}} p_3^{\beta^{13}};$$

$$p_2 = g_2(w) = v_2 w_1^{\beta_{21}} w_2^{\beta_{22}} w_3^{\beta_{23}}; \qquad w_2 = W_2(p, l) = \alpha_2 p_1^{\beta^{21}} p_2^{\beta^{22}} p_3^{\beta^{23}}; \tag{49}$$

$$p_3 = g_3(w) = v_3 w_1^{\beta_{31}} w_2^{\beta_{32}} w_3^{\beta_{33}}; \qquad w_3 = W_3(p, l) = \alpha_3 p_1^{\beta^{31}} p_2^{\beta^{32}} p_3^{\beta^{33}};$$

where $B = [\beta_{ij}]$ and $B^{-1} = [\beta^{ij}]$, and $\beta_{ij} > 0$, $\sum_{j=1}^{3} \beta_{ij} = 1$; hence $\sum_{j=1}^{3} \beta^{ij} = 1$ (cf. Chipman [10]). Now if the Stolper–Samuelson matrix $B^{-1}$ has the block Leontief sign pattern, then it is easily verified that the Hessian $H_k$ of each Stolper–Samuelson function $W_k$ is also block Leontief, as must therefore be the transformation matrix $T$. If also the Slutsky matrix $S$ is semi-Metzler, so is the total substitution matrix $\hat{S} = S - T$.

---

[23] The CES utility function has the form

$$U(x_1, x_2, x_3) = [\theta_1 x_1^{(\sigma-1)/\sigma} + \theta_2 x_2^{(\sigma-1)/\sigma} + \theta_3 x_3^{(\sigma-1)/\sigma}]^{\sigma/(\sigma-1)} \qquad \left(\theta_i > 0, \ \sum_{i=1}^{3} \theta_i = 1\right)$$

and we have

$$m_i = \frac{\eta_i}{p_i}, \qquad s_{ij} = \frac{\eta_i(\eta_j - \delta_{ij})}{p_i p_j} \sigma I, \qquad \text{where } \eta_i = \frac{\theta_i^\sigma p_i^{1-\sigma}}{\sum_{j=1}^{3} \theta_j^\sigma p_j^{1-\sigma}}$$

and $\delta_{ij}$ is the Kronecker delta. Thus $S$ is a Metzler matrix.

A simple analysis (see Section V.A) shows that in the two-factor case when country 1 specializes in commodities 1 and 3 and country 2 in commodities 2 and 3, the transformation matrices have the sign patterns

$$T^1 \in \begin{bmatrix} + & 0 & - \\ 0 & 0 & 0 \\ - & 0 & + \end{bmatrix}, \qquad T^2 \in \begin{bmatrix} 0 & 0 & 0 \\ 0 & + & - \\ 0 & - & + \end{bmatrix}, \tag{50}$$

so that $\hat{S}^1$ and $\hat{S}^2$ are Metzler matrices whenever $S^1$ and $S^2$ are.

We can now state our first, rather weak, result. (For a stronger result, requiring stronger assumptions, see Appendix B.)

***Theorem 1*** Let the Hicksian stability condition (41) hold. Then:

(a) If the domestic commodity in the paying country is totally regular, a transfer will lower its price relative to the price of at least one of the international commodities.

(b) If the domestic commodity in the receiving country is totally regular, a transfer will raise its price relative to the price of at least one of the international commodities.

*Proof* We prove only (a), the proof of (b) being similar. Suppose $d\tilde{p}_2/d\tau \leqq 0$; then the expression in braces in (44a) is $\geqq 0$ ($\hat{s}^1_{33}$ and $\hat{s}^2_{33}$ being of course negative); hence substitution of this inequality in (44b) and use of the condition $\hat{s}^1_{23} \geqq 0$ yields

$$\frac{d\tilde{p}_3{}^1}{d\tau} \leqq \frac{\beta_1 \bar{m}_3{}^1 \hat{s}^2_{33}}{|J|} \left( \frac{\begin{vmatrix} \hat{s}^1_{22} & \hat{s}^1_{23} \\ \hat{s}^1_{32} & \hat{s}^1_{33} \end{vmatrix}}{\hat{s}^1_{33}} + \frac{\begin{vmatrix} \hat{s}^2_{22} & \hat{s}^2_{23} \\ \hat{s}^2_{32} & \hat{s}^2_{33} \end{vmatrix}}{\hat{s}^2_{33}} \right) < 0, \tag{51}$$

the last inequality following from $\bar{m}_3{}^1 > 0$ and the fact that the matrices $\hat{S}^k$ are negative semidefinite of rank 2. Thus, $p_3{}^1$ falls relative to $p_1$. Conversely, if $d\tilde{p}_2/d\tau \geqq 0$ then from (45a) we find, making use of the fact that $\hat{s}^1_{31} \geqq 0$ and $\bar{m}_3{}^1 > 0$, that the middle expression in (51) is also an upper bound to $d\tilde{p}_3{}^1/d\tau - (p_3{}^1/p_2)\, d\tilde{p}_2/d\tau$. In this case, $p_3{}^1$ falls relative to $p_2$. Q.E.D.

Of course, if the transfer leaves the terms of trade unaffected (i.e., $d\tilde{p}_2/d\tau = 0$) then $p_3{}^1$ and $p_3{}^2$ will respectively fall and rise relative to *both* $p_1$ and $p_2$, and the expression for $d\tilde{p}_3{}^1/d\tau$ coincides with the middle term of (51). In this case, the expression for $d\tilde{p}_3{}^2/d\tau$ is identical except for the replacement of $\bar{m}_3{}^1 \hat{s}^2_{33}$ by $-\bar{m}_3{}^2 \hat{s}^1_{33}$.

## E. PRIMARY AND SECONDARY BURDEN

Let us first of all suppose, as is usually (but generally only implicitly) done, that the functions $U^k$ of (11) are social utility functions in Samuelson's sense [62], so that they may be treated as indicators of the two countries' welfare.

Then, given the national demand functions (14) and the solution functions (16), we may express country $k$'s welfare as a function of the rate of transfer as follows:

$$\tilde{U}^k(\tau) = U^k[X_1^k(\tilde{p}^k(\tau), l^k, \tau), X_2^k(\tilde{p}^k(\tau), l^k, \tau), X_3^k(\tilde{p}^k(\tau), l^k, \tau)]. \tag{52}$$

Since equilibrium entails

$$\partial U^k/\partial x_1^k = \mu^k p_i^k \qquad (k = 1, 2; \quad i = 1, 2, 3), \tag{53}$$

where $\mu^k$ is country $k$'s marginal utility of income $\partial U^k[h^k(p^k, I^k)]/\partial I^k$, we find upon making use of (26), (25), and the condition $p^k \cdot m^k = 1$, that

$$d\tilde{U}^1/d\tau = -\mu^1\{\beta_1 + \zeta_2^1 \, d\tilde{p}_2/d\tau\}; \qquad d\tilde{U}^2/d\tau = \mu^2\{\beta_1 + \zeta_2^1 \, d\tilde{p}_2/d\tau\}. \tag{54}$$

The burden on the paying country is thus decomposed into two parts (both of which are factors of the marginal utility of the paying country's income, $\mu^1$), of which the first, $\beta_1$, is the value of a unit transfer (see (33)), or "primary burden," and the second is

$$\beta_2 = \zeta_2^1 \, d\tilde{p}_2/d\tau, \tag{55}$$

which may be defined as the "secondary burden" per unit of transfer. It is positive (an additional burden on the paying country) if the paying country imports commodity 2 and its terms of trade deteriorate.[24] It is worth stressing that $\beta_2$ is not "secondary" in the mathematical sense of a "second-order term"; it is part of the first-order effect, and could very well outweigh the primary burden in magnitude.

If the functions $U^k$ of (11) are aggregative utility functions in the purely behavioral sense (interpretation (1) of footnote 13), then use of formula (54) would not be legitimate. One would have to, say, determine the effects of the transfer on individual incomes (or at least on factor incomes) and measure welfare in terms of some social welfare function. However, if the distribution of income was considered to be optimal (in terms of some social welfare function) before the transfer, then (54) would still provide a measure of the minimum burden of the transfer on the paying country—since there would still be an additional "tertiary burden" resulting from failure to redistribute the new incomes optimally.

---

[24] This is readily generalized to the $n$-commodity case, where it is more illuminating to choose a domestic commodity as numéraire and the secondary burden then becomes

$$\beta_2 = \sum_{i=1}^{n_1} \zeta_i^1 \frac{d\tilde{p}_i}{d\tau}$$

where $n_1$ is the number of traded commodities. Cf. Samuelson [61, p. 288]; see also the discussion in Pearce [54, p. 155].

## IV. The Case of Pure Exchange

### A. CRITERION FOR A DETERIORATION IN THE TERMS OF TRADE

It will be assumed that at the initial equilibrium, country 1 (the paying country) exports commodity 1 and imports commodity 2; $p_1$ being fixed (by convention), a deterioration in the paying country's terms of trade is equivalent to a rise in $p_2$.[25] From (44a), in order that $d\tilde{p}_2/d\tau > 0$ it is necessary and sufficient (in the case of pure exchange[26]) that

$$\hat{m}_2{}^1 \equiv \frac{\begin{vmatrix} m_2{}^1 & s_{23}^1 \\ m_3{}^1 & s_{33}^1 \end{vmatrix}}{s_{33}^1} < \frac{\begin{vmatrix} m_2{}^2 & s_{23}^2 \\ m_3{}^2 & s_{33}^2 \end{vmatrix}}{s_{33}^2} \equiv \hat{m}_2{}^2, \tag{56}$$

which defines the functions $\hat{m}_2{}^k(p_1, p_2, p_3{}^k, I^k)$, where these (and therefore the functions $m_i^k$, $s_{ij}^k$) are understood to be evaluated at the prices $p_1{}^*$, $p_2{}^*$, $p_3^{1*}$, $p_3^{2*}$ and incomes $I^{1*}$, $I^{2*}$ prevailing in the initial equilibrium.

From the assumptions made in Section II.A concerning utility and demand functions (see footnote 14), the bordered Hessian

$$\Upsilon = \begin{bmatrix} 0 & U_1 & U_2 & U_3 \\ U_1 & U_{11} & U_{12} & U_{13} \\ U_2 & U_{21} & U_{22} & U_{23} \\ U_3 & U_{31} & U_{32} & U_{33} \end{bmatrix} \tag{57}$$

of $U$, where $U_i = \partial U/\partial x_i > 0$ and $U_{ij} = \partial^2 U/\partial x_i \, \partial x_j$, is nonsingular (we drop country superscripts temporarily). Let us define the indirect utility function $V$ and the marginal utility of income $\mu$ by

$$V(p, I) = U[h(p, I)], \qquad \mu(p, I) = \partial V(p, I)/\partial I \tag{58}$$

[25] Thus, the terms of trade deteriorate locally if and only if $\tilde{p}_2$ is a strictly increasing function of $\tau$ at the initial rate of transfer. This is not the same as $d\tilde{p}_2/d\tau > 0$, since a strictly increasing function can have zero derivatives at isolated points; nevertheless, $d\tilde{p}_2/d\tau > 0$ will have to hold within an arbitrarily small neighborhood of the initial transfer rate. For convenience we shall say that the paying country's terms of trade "deteriorate strongly" if $d\tilde{p}_2/d\tau > 0$.

[26] In fact, in the general case this can be done in terms of the "trade utility functions" of footnote 21, by expressing the total substitution terms as functions of the prices and the deficit in the balance of payments on current account. The ensuing analysis can be given this interpretation if desired. However, while it is natural to assume "neutral tastes" as between countries (see below), such an assumption would not in general be warranted with respect to trade utility functions.

where $p = (p_1, p_2, p_3)$, and likewise let us denote

$$V_i(p, I) = U_i[h(p, I)], \qquad V_{ij}(p, I) = U_{ij}[h(p, I)]. \tag{59}$$

(Note that $V_i$ and $V_{ij}$ are composed functions and not partial derivatives.) Then by the standard procedure for deriving the Slutsky equation (see, e.g., Samuelson [59, p. 101]) we verify that

$$
\begin{bmatrix}
0 & V_1 & V_2 & V_3 \\
V_1 & V_{11} & V_{12} & V_{13} \\
V_2 & V_{21} & V_{22} & V_{23} \\
V_3 & V_{31} & V_{32} & V_{33}
\end{bmatrix}^{-1}
= \frac{1}{\mu}
\begin{bmatrix}
a & m_1 & m_2 & m_3 \\
m_1 & s_{11} & s_{12} & s_{13} \\
m_2 & s_{21} & s_{22} & s_{23} \\
m_3 & s_{31} & s_{32} & s_{33}
\end{bmatrix}
\tag{60}
$$

where

$$a = \mu \Delta_{00}/\Delta, \qquad \Delta(p, I) = | \Upsilon[h(p, I)]|, \tag{61}$$

and $\Delta_{ij}(p, I)$ denotes the cofactor of the element in the $i$th row and $j$th column of $\Upsilon[h(p, I)]$. We thus have

$$
\begin{bmatrix}
a & m_1 & m_2 & m_3 \\
m_1 & s_{11} & s_{12} & s_{13} \\
m_2 & s_{21} & s_{22} & s_{23} \\
m_3 & s_{31} & s_{32} & s_{33}
\end{bmatrix}
= \frac{\mu}{\Delta}
\begin{bmatrix}
\Delta_{00} & \Delta_{01} & \Delta_{02} & \Delta_{03} \\
\Delta_{10} & \Delta_{11} & \Delta_{12} & \Delta_{13} \\
\Delta_{20} & \Delta_{21} & \Delta_{22} & \Delta_{23} \\
\Delta_{30} & \Delta_{31} & \Delta_{32} & \Delta_{33}
\end{bmatrix}.
\tag{62}
$$

From Jacobi's theorem (cf. Aitken [1, p. 98]) it now follows that

$$
\begin{vmatrix}
m_2 & s_{23} \\
m_3 & s_{33}
\end{vmatrix}
= \frac{\mu^2}{\Delta^2}
\begin{vmatrix}
\Delta_{20} & \Delta_{23} \\
\Delta_{30} & \Delta_{33}
\end{vmatrix}
= \frac{\mu^2}{\Delta}
\begin{vmatrix}
V_1 & V_2 \\
V_{11} & V_{12}
\end{vmatrix}
\tag{63}
$$

and likewise

$$
s_{33} = \frac{\mu}{\Delta} \Delta_{33} = \frac{\mu}{\Delta}
\begin{bmatrix}
0 & V_1 & V_2 \\
V_1 & V_{11} & V_{12} \\
V_2 & V_{21} & V_{22}
\end{bmatrix}.
\tag{64}
$$

Our required expression is then

$$
\hat{m}_2 = \frac{
\begin{vmatrix}
m_2 & s_{23} \\
m_3 & s_{33}
\end{vmatrix}
}{s_{33}}
= \frac{
\mu
\begin{vmatrix}
V_1 & V_2 \\
V_{11} & V_{12}
\end{vmatrix}
}{
\begin{vmatrix}
0 & V_1 & V_2 \\
V_1 & V_{11} & V_{12} \\
V_2 & V_{21} & V_{22}
\end{vmatrix}
}.
\tag{65}
$$

Making use of the equilibrium condition $V_i = \mu p_i$ this may be expressed as

$$\hat{m}_2 = \frac{\begin{vmatrix} m_2 & s_{23} \\ m_3 & s_{33} \end{vmatrix}}{s_{33}} = \frac{\begin{vmatrix} p_1 & p_2 \\ V_{11} & V_{12} \end{vmatrix}}{\begin{vmatrix} 0 & p_1 & p_2 \\ p_1 & V_{11} & V_{12} \\ p_2 & V_{21} & V_{22} \end{vmatrix}} = \left[ p_2 - p_1 \frac{\begin{vmatrix} V_1 & V_2 \\ V_{21} & V_{22} \end{vmatrix}}{\begin{vmatrix} V_1 & V_2 \\ V_{11} & V_{12} \end{vmatrix}} \right]^{-1}. \tag{66}$$

Let us now define the *marginal rate of substitution function R* by

$$R(x_1, x_2, x_3) = \frac{U_1(x_1, x_2, x_3)}{U_2(x_1, x_2, x_3)}. \tag{67}$$

Let us also assume that all three commodities are strongly superior, i.e., $m_i > 0$ for $i = 1$, 2, 3, and that the international commodities are weak Hicksian substitutes of the domestic commodity, i.e., $s_{i3} \geqq 0$ for $i = 1$, 2. Define

$$R_i = \partial R / \partial x_i; \qquad Q_i(p, I) = R_i[h(p, I)]. \tag{68}$$

(Again, note that $Q_i$ is a composed function and not a partial derivative.) By Jacobi's theorem we have

$$Q_1 = -\frac{\begin{vmatrix} V_1 & V_2 \\ V_{11} & V_{12} \end{vmatrix}}{V_2^2} = -\frac{\Delta}{\mu^2 V_2^2} \begin{vmatrix} m_2 & s_{23} \\ m_3 & s_{33} \end{vmatrix} < 0 \tag{69a}$$

and

$$Q_2 = -\frac{\begin{vmatrix} V_1 & V_2 \\ V_{21} & V_{22} \end{vmatrix}}{V_2^2} = \frac{\Delta}{\mu^2 V_2^2} \begin{vmatrix} m_1 & s_{13} \\ m_3 & s_{33} \end{vmatrix} > 0, \tag{69b}$$

and (66) can now be written in the form

$$\hat{m}_2 = \frac{\begin{vmatrix} m_2 & s_{23} \\ m_3 & s_{33} \end{vmatrix}}{s_{33}} = \left( p_2 - p_1 \frac{Q_2}{Q_1} \right)^{-1} > 0. \tag{70}$$

Now let the *conditional Engel function E* be defined implicitly by

$$R[x_1, E(x_1, x_3, r), x_3] = r. \tag{71}$$

$E$ is well defined, since $\partial R / \partial x_2 > 0$ from (69b). For any $x_3$ and $r = p_1/p_2$ this defines a curve in the $x_1 x_2$ plane whose slope is

$$E_1(x_1, x_3, r) = \frac{\partial E(x_1, x_3, r)}{\partial x_1} = -\frac{R_1[x_1, E(x_1, x_3, r), x_3]}{R_2[x_1, E(x_1, x_3, r), x_3]}. \tag{72}$$

The criterion (56) can now be stated in terms of the slopes of these Engel curves. Let $p_i^{k*}$, $I^{k*}$, $x_i^{k*}$ denote equilibrium prices, incomes, and quantities consumed in country $k$, and $r^* = p_1/p_2^*$. Attaching country superscripts to all the above functions and denoting $E_i^{k*} = E_i^k(x_1^{k*}, x_3^{k*}, r^*)$, $Q_i^{k*} = Q_i^k(p_1, p_2^*, p_3^{k*}, I^{k*})$, and $R_i^{k*} = R_i^k(x_1^{k*}, x_2^{k*}, x_3^{k*})$, we see immediately from (70) that (56) is equivalent to $Q_2^{1*}/Q_1^{1*} < Q_2^{2*}/Q_1^{2*}$, which is in turn equivalent, in view of (68) and (72), to

$$E_1^{1*} = -R_1^{1*}/R_2^{1*} < -R_1^{2*}/R_2^{2*} = E_1^{2*}. \tag{73}$$

In words, this states that the paying country's terms of trade deteriorate (strongly) if and only if its conditional Engel curve is flatter at the equilibrium point than the receiving country's conditional Engel curve.[27] This is a straight-forward generalization of Samuelson's criterion [60, p. 287; 61, p. 278]; in fact this generalization was already stated by Samuelson, without proof (cf. [60, p. 303]).[28]

[27] They can also deteriorate provided the Engel curves cross at a point of tangency; see footnote 25.

[28] The criterion (73) can also be restated in terms of concepts borrowed from the theory of rationing (cf. Tobin and Houthakker [68]). Let a country's conditional demand function given $x_3 = q_3$, denoted $\tilde{h} = (\tilde{h}_1, \tilde{h}_2)$, be defined by the property that

$$(x_1, x_2) = \tilde{h}(p_1, p_2, \tilde{I}; q_3) \quad \text{maximizes} \quad U(x_1, x_2, q_3) \tag{F.28.1}$$

$$\text{subject to } p_1 x_1 + p_2 x_2 = \tilde{I} = I - p_3 q_3.$$

Then, defining

$$\tilde{V}_{ij}(p_1, p_2, \tilde{I}; q_3) = U_{ij}[\tilde{h}_1(p_1, p_2, \tilde{I}; q_3), \tilde{h}_2(p_1, p_2, \tilde{I}; q_3), q_3] \tag{F.28.2}$$

we see immediately that

$$\tilde{m}_2 \equiv \frac{\partial \tilde{h}_2}{\partial \tilde{I}} = \frac{\begin{vmatrix} p_1 & p_2 \\ \tilde{V}_{11} & \tilde{V}_{12} \end{vmatrix}}{\begin{vmatrix} 0 & p_1 & p_2 \\ p_1 & \tilde{V}_{11} & \tilde{V}_{12} \\ p_2 & \tilde{V}_{21} & \tilde{V}_{22} \end{vmatrix}}. \tag{F.28.3}$$

By analogy with the theory of rationing, if we choose the ration $q_3$ to be precisely the amount that would be chosen voluntarily at the given prices and income, then it follows from the definitions that

$$\tilde{h}_i[p_1, p_2, I - p_3 h_3(p_1, p_2, p_3, I); h_3(p_1, p_2, p_3, I)] = h_i(p_1, p_2, p_3, I) \quad (i = 1, 2) \tag{F.28.4}$$

and

$$\tilde{V}_{ij}[p_1, p_2, I - p_3 h_3(p_1, p_2, q_3, I); h_3(p_1, p_2, p_3, I)] = V_{ij}(p_1, p_2, p_3, I) \quad (i, j = 1, 2). \tag{F.28.5}$$

Thus, combining (F.28.3), (F.28.5), and (66), and defining

$$\hat{m}_2(p_1, p_2, p_3, I) = \tilde{m}_2[p_1, p_2, I - p_3 h_3(p_1, p_2, p_3, I); h_3(p_1, p_2, p_3, I)] \tag{F.28.6}$$

B. Conditions for Unchanging Terms of Trade

For $d\tilde{p}_2/d\tau = 0$ to hold at the equilibrium position, it is clearly necessary and sufficient that

$$\hat{m}_2^{\,1}(p_1, p_2{}^*, p_3^{1*}, I^{1*}) = \hat{m}_2^{\,2}(p_1, p_2{}^*, p_3^{2*}, I^{2*}), \qquad (74)$$

where $p_2{}^*$, $p_3^{1*}$, $p_3^{2*}$ and $I^{1*}$, $I^{2*}$ are the equilibrium prices and incomes. However, this is just a local condition; it is of greater interest to obtain a global condition for unchanging terms of trade.

A *sufficient* condition that a finite transfer should leave the terms of trade unchanged is clearly that the functions $\hat{m}_2^{\,1}$ and $\hat{m}_2^{\,2}$ should be identical with each other and independent of their third and fourth arguments; i.e., that $\hat{m}_2^{\,1} = \hat{m}_2^{\,2} = \hat{m}_2$ where $\hat{m}_2$ depends only on $p_1$ and $p_2$. I shall call this the *Hypothesis of Neutral Tastes*.

If, as is certainly reasonable, we require that the condition that a transfer leave the terms of trade unaffected be invariant with respect to the countries' initial endowments $l_i^{\,k}$, then it may be conjectured that the above condition is also *necessary*. By fixing $l_1^{\,1}$, say, we may for any level of $\tau$ express the equilibrium prices and incomes $p_2{}^*$, $p_3^{1*}$, $p_3^{2*}$, $I^{1*}$, $I^{2*}$ as functions of $l_2^{\,1}$, $l_3^{\,1}$, $l_1^{\,2}$, $l_2^{\,2}$, $l_3^{\,2}$. If the Jacobian of this transformation (which is readily computed) is nonvanishing—which can certainly be expected to be the case—then in some convex neighborhood of the initial equilibrium the equilibrium prices and incomes can be made to vary independently by suitably choosing the endowments. The result then follows (in this neighborhood) from classical theorems on functional dependence. The global result would follow if the mapping from endowments to equilibrium prices and incomes could be shown to be globally univalent with a convex range. A detailed pursuit of this question is, however, beyond the scope of the present investigation.[29]

---

[29] See Gorman [20] for closely related arguments; the question at issue is, of course, intimately bound up with the question of the existence of aggregate utility functions.

---

we have immediately

$$\hat{m}_2 = \frac{\begin{vmatrix} m_2 & s_{23} \\ m_3 & s_{33} \end{vmatrix}}{s_{33}}. \qquad \text{(F.28.7)}$$

Consequently, in order that $d\tilde{p}_2/d\tau > 0$ in the model of pure exchange, it is necessary and sufficient that $\hat{m}_2^{1*} < \hat{m}_2^{2*}$, where $\hat{m}_2^{k*} = \hat{m}_2^{\,k}(p_1, p_2{}^*, p_3^{k*}, I^{k*})$ is country $k$'s conditional income coefficient for commodity 2, defined by (F.28.3) and (F.28.6), evaluated at the prices and income prevailing at the initial equilibrium.

Needless to say, the criterion could also be stated in terms of "conditional marginal propensities to consume," in the form $p_2{}^*\hat{m}_2^{1*} < p_2{}^*\hat{m}_2^{2*}$.

It is readily seen that the function $\hat{m}_2\,(p_1, p_2, p_3, I)$ is homogeneous of degree $-1$ in its four arguments. It follows from (70) that $Q_1/Q_2$ is homogeneous of degree $0$ in its four arguments. If the Hypothesis of Neutral Tastes holds, then $Q_1^1/Q_2^1 = Q_1^2/Q_2^2 = Q_1/Q_2$ and $Q_1/Q_2$ depends only on $p_1/p_2$, i.e.,

$$-\frac{Q_1^k(p_1, p_2, p_3^k, I^k)}{Q_2^k(p_1, p_2, p_3^k, I^k)} = \varphi\left(\frac{p_1}{p_2}\right) \qquad (k = 1, 2) \tag{75}$$

identically in $p_2$, $p_3^k$, $I^k$, for some continuous function $\varphi$. Now

$$R^k[h^k(p^k, I^k)] = p_1/p_2$$

and $h^k$ is invertible (owing to the assumptions of Section II.A), that is, it establishes for fixed $p_1$ a one-to-one correspondence between bundles $(x_1^k, x_2^k, x_3^k)$ and triples $(p_2, p_3^k, I^k)$. Thus, (75) goes over into the condition that

$$-\frac{R_1^k(x_1^k, x_2^k, x_3^k)}{R_2^k(x_1^k, x_2^k, x_3^k)} = \varphi[R^k(x_1^k, x_2^k, x_3^k)] \qquad (k = 1, 2) \tag{76}$$

identically in $x_1^k$, $x_2^k$, $x_3^k$. It follows that country $k$'s conditional Engel function $E^k$ [defined by (71) in terms of $R^k$] must satisfy

$$\frac{\partial E^k(x_1^k, x_3^k, r)}{\partial x_1^k} = \varphi(r) \tag{77}$$

identically in $x_1^k$, $x_3^k$, $r$. Integrating (77) we obtain

$$E^k(x_1^k, x_3^k, r) = \varphi(r) \cdot x_1^k + \psi^k(x_3^k, r) \qquad (k = 1, 2). \tag{78}$$

Conversely, let $E^k$ have the form (78). Then from (71) we obtain (76), which goes over into (75). Thus we have proved the following theorem.

**Theorem 2** A necessary and sufficient condition for the Hypothesis of Neutral Tastes to hold, i.e., for the functions $\hat{m}_2^k = m_2^k - m_3^k s_{23}^k/s_{33}^k$ to be identical with each other for $k = 1, 2$ and to be independent of $p_3^k$ and $I^k$, is that the two countries' conditional Engel functions should be of the form (78).

What (78) states is that for any $x_3^k$'s and any $r$, the two countries' conditional Engel curves are parallel straight lines in the $x_1 x_2$ plane. This generalizes a well-known condition (expressed in terms of unconditional Engel curves) obtained by Gorman [20] for the existence of community utility functions. It is perhaps worth remarking that for (78) to be plausible there is no need to interpret commodity 3 in the respective countries as being the "same commodity."

Some examples of utility functions satisfying (78) are given in Appendix C. As these examples show, such utility functions need be neither separable (as between international and domestic commodities) nor homogeneous. Nevertheless, the Hypothesis of Neutral Tastes takes on a particularly plausible and natural form when separability as between international and domestic commodities is assumed. We shall therefore discuss this case briefly in Section C.

## C. The Separable Case

We shall now consider the special case in which the utility function (11) is separable as between international and domestic commodities, i.e., can be expressed as

$$U(x_1, x_2, x_3) = F[\overline{U}(x_1, x_2), x_3] \tag{79}$$

(dropping country superscripts for convenience). This implies that $R$ is independent of $x_3$; hence

$$\begin{vmatrix} U_1 & U_2 \\ U_{13} & U_{23} \end{vmatrix} = 0, \tag{80}$$

and, as Leontief [38] showed, (80) is both necessary and sufficient for (79). By Jacobi's theorem, (80) is equivalent to the condition

$$\begin{vmatrix} m_1 & s_{13} \\ m_2 & s_{23} \end{vmatrix} = 0. \tag{81}$$

It has been shown by Gorman [21] (see also Strotz [64]) that if (79) holds with $\overline{U}$ homogeneous, then, and only then, the demand function $h$ can be decomposed into subfunctions such that, once the expenditures allotted to international and domestic commodities are given (as functions of prices and total income), the demand for each international commodity depends only on the income allotted to the international commodities and their prices, and likewise the demand for the domestic commodity depends (and in this case obviously in a unique way) on the income allotted to it and its price.[30]

The following related result does not require assuming homogeneity of $\overline{U}$.

**Lemma 1**   For all $p_i > 0$ $(i = 1, 2, 3)$, $I > 0$, the condition

$$m_i - m_3 s_{i3}/s_{33} = - s_{i3}/(p_3 s_{33}) \qquad (i = 1, 2) \tag{82}$$

holds if and only if (81) holds, and, provided $m_3 \neq 0$, the condition

$$m_i - m_3 s_{i3}/s_{33} = m_i/(p_1 m_1 + p_2 m_2) \qquad (i = 1, 2) \tag{83}$$

holds if and only if (82) holds. Thus, when $m_3 \neq 0$, the three conditions (81), (82), and (83) are equivalent.

---

[30] I.e., $h_i(p_1, p_2, p_3, I) = \overline{h}_i[p_1, p_2, \Psi(p_1, p_2, p_3, I)]$ for $i = 1, 2$, and $h_3(p_1, p_2, p_3, I) = [I - \Psi(p_1, p_2, p_3, I)]/p_3$, where $\overline{h} = (\overline{h}_1, \overline{h}_2)$ is the demand function generated by $\overline{U}(x_1, x_2)$.

The proof is obtained by straightforward manipulations, making use of the identities $\sum_{i=1}^{3} p_i m_i = 1$ and $\sum_{i=1}^{3} p_i s_{i3} = 0$, and is omitted.

For later convenience we shall define the weights

$$c_i = -(p_i s_{i3})/(p_3 s_{33}) \qquad (i = 1, 2) \tag{84}$$

which sum to one and are nonnegative if both international commodities are Hicksian substitutes of the domestic commodity. These weights will play an interesting role in the analysis of Section V.

Defining $\hat{m}_1$ analogously to $\hat{m}_2$ in (56), an analysis similar to the one leading up to (70) shows that

$$\hat{m}_1 = \frac{\begin{vmatrix} m_1 & s_{13} \\ m_3 & s_{33} \end{vmatrix}}{s_{33}} = \left( p_1 - p_2 \frac{Q_1}{Q_2} \right)^{-1}, \tag{85}$$

and we verify directly that $p_1 \hat{m}_1 + p_2 \hat{m}_2 = 1$. From Lemma 1 it follows that whenever (79) holds, we have

$$c_i = p_i \hat{m}_i = p_i m_i / (p_1 m_1 + p_2 m_2) \qquad (i = 1, 2), \tag{86}$$

so that the weight $c_i$ may be described as the "average subpropensity to consume the $i$th international commodity." It may be noted that when $\bar{U}$ is homogeneous, $m_i/(p_1 m_1 + p_2 m_2)$ is the income coefficient of the Strotz–Gorman subdemand function for the $i$th international commodity—that is, its derivative with respect to the income allotted to international commodities, or the "marginal subpropensity to consume the $i$th international commodity."

When (79) holds it is clear from (67) that $R = \bar{U}_1/\bar{U}_2 \equiv \bar{R}$, where $\bar{R}$ is independent of $x_3$; hence, analogously to (71) we may define the sub-Engel function $\bar{E}$ by $\bar{R}[x_1, \bar{E}(x_2, r)] = r$. In place of Theorem 2 we then have the following result.[31]

**Theorem 3**  Let each country's utility function be of the separable form (79), i.e., $U^k(x_1{}^k, x_2{}^k, x_3{}^k) = F^k[\bar{U}^k(x_1{}^k, x_2{}^k), x_3{}^k]$. Then a necessary and sufficient condition for the Hypothesis of Neutral Tastes to hold is that the two countries' subutility functions $\bar{U}^k$ should yield sub-Engel functions $\bar{E}^k$ of the form

$$\bar{E}^k(x^k, r) = \varphi(r) \cdot x_1{}^k + \psi^k(r) \qquad (k = 1, 2). \tag{87}$$

---

[31] This result makes it possible to simplify the analysis of footnote 28, since, when (79) holds, the conditional income term $\tilde{m}_2$ of (F.28.3) [which is the same as (88) after making the appropriate substitutions, i.e., is the same as $\bar{m}_2 = \partial \bar{h}_2/\partial \bar{I}$] no longer depends on $q_3$. This remark applies to the theory of rationing generally, since the validity of the formulas in this theory is limited to the case in which the ration coincides with the amount that would voluntarily be consumed at the given prices and income, unless it is assumed that the utility function is separable as between rationed and unrationed commodities.

*Proof*  We verify readily from (79) and the condition $U_i = F' \cdot \bar{U}_i = \mu p_i$
that

$$
\mu \frac{\begin{vmatrix} U_1 & U_2 \\ U_{11} & U_{12} \end{vmatrix}}{\begin{vmatrix} 0 & U_1 & U_2 \\ U_1 & U_{11} & U_{12} \\ U_2 & U_{21} & U_{22} \end{vmatrix}} = \frac{\begin{vmatrix} p_1 & p_2 \\ \bar{U}_{11} & \bar{U}_{12} \end{vmatrix}}{\begin{vmatrix} 0 & p_1 & p_2 \\ p_1 & \bar{U}_{11} & \bar{U}_{12} \\ p_2 & \bar{U}_{21} & \bar{U}_{22} \end{vmatrix}}. \tag{88}
$$

Defining $\bar{h}(p_1, p_2, \bar{I})$ as the demand function generated by the subutility
function $\bar{U}(x_1, x_2)$, and defining the composed functions $\bar{V}_i(p_1, p_2, \bar{I}) = \bar{U}_i[\bar{h}(p_1, p_2, \bar{I})]$, $\bar{V}_{ij}(p_1, p_2, \bar{I}) = \bar{U}_{ij}[\bar{h}(p_1, p_2, \bar{I})]$, and $\bar{Q}_i(p_1, p_2, \bar{I}) = \bar{R}_i[\bar{h}(p_1, p_2, \bar{I})]$, $i = 1, 2$, the argument proceeds exactly as in Section IV.A.
                                                                    Q.E.D.

Clearly, (87) always holds if the subutility functions $\bar{U}^k$ are identical and
homogeneous. Thus, the Hypothesis of Neutral Tastes is a fairly natural
assumption to make when the separability condition (79) holds.


## V. The Transfer Problem with Production

### A. THE TWO-FACTOR CASE: GENERAL CONSIDERATIONS

Throughout this section we shall assume that each country is endowed with
two factors of production. The production functions in the two countries—
which need not be identical—will be of the form $f_i^k(l_{i1}^k, l_{i2}^k)$, $i = 1, 2, 3$ and
$k = 1, 2$, and be assumed to have isoquants strongly convex to the origin
(see footnote 18); their dual minimum-unit-cost functions (cf. Chipman [10])
will be denoted $g_i^k(w_1^k, w_2^k)$.

Under these circumstances, each country's production possibility frontier
will be a ruled surface (cf. Chipman [12]), and the national supply correspondences (15) will be multivalued at those prices for which it is profitable for
all three commodities to be produced. At prices for which it is only profitable
to produce one domestic and one international commodity, equilibrium
outputs will be restricted to an edge of the surface and, under assumptions
that we shall make, this edge—which is the efficient frontier corresponding
to those prices—will be strongly convex to the origin, and the analysis of
Section III.A can be used. This is no longer possible in the case of prices for
which the supply correspondence is multivalued—or, to use the old-fashioned
terminology, for which "the supply function is infinitely elastic." In that case
we shall instead, in Section V.B, define the supply of the international commodities as a function of their prices and of the output of the domestic
commodity; this is possible because under our assumptions, the cross section

of the production possibility surface corresponding to any fixed amount of the domestic commodity will be strictly concave to the origin of the plane of this cross section.

After developing the necessary technique we shall consider the four cases corresponding to the possible combinations in which the respective countries either specialize (in the domestic and one international commodity) or diversify (i.e., produce all three commodities).

## B. The Case of Diversification

Consider a country which produces all three commodities with its two, fully employed, factors. We consider the mapping (assumed twice continuously differentiable) from factor prices to the prices of the two internationally traded commodities, along with its Jacobian matrix (dropping country subscripts for convenience):

$$
\begin{aligned}
p_1 &= g_1(w_1, w_2); \\
p_2 &= g_2(w_1, w_2);
\end{aligned}
\qquad
B = \begin{bmatrix} b_{11} & b_{12} \\ b_{21} & b_{22} \end{bmatrix} = \begin{bmatrix} \partial g_1/\partial w_1 & \partial g_1/\partial w_2 \\ \partial g_2/\partial w_1 & \partial g_2/\partial w_2 \end{bmatrix}.
\tag{89}
$$

We shall assume that

$$
|B| = b_{11}b_{21}(b_{22}/b_{21} - b_{12}/b_{11}) > 0
\tag{90}
$$

for all $w_1, w_2 > 0$, i.e., that commodity 2 uses factor 2 relatively more intensively than factor 1 in comparison with commodity 1, and there is therefore no factor intensity reversal as between the two international industries. We may then define the inverse mapping (which will also be assumed to be twice continuously differentiable) along with its Jacobian matrix:

$$
\begin{aligned}
w_1 &= \tilde{W}_1(p_1, p_2); \\
w_2 &= \tilde{W}_2(p_1, p_2);
\end{aligned}
\qquad
\tilde{B}^{-1} = \begin{bmatrix} \tilde{b}^{11} & \tilde{b}^{12} \\ \tilde{b}^{21} & \tilde{b}^{22} \end{bmatrix} = \begin{bmatrix} \partial \tilde{W}_1/\partial p_1 & \partial \tilde{W}_1/\partial p_2 \\ \partial \tilde{W}_2/\partial p_1 & \partial \tilde{W}_2/\partial p_2 \end{bmatrix}.
\tag{91}
$$

Note that the $\tilde{b}^{ij}$'s are functions of $p_1$ and $p_2$. In order for all three commodities to be produced, the price of the domestic commodity must satisfy

$$
p_3 = \tilde{P}_3(p_1, p_2) \equiv g_3[\tilde{W}_1(p_1, p_2), \tilde{W}_2(p_1, p_2)].
\tag{92}
$$

Defining the matrix $[b^{ij}(w)] = B(w)^{-1}$, the functions $\tilde{b}^{ij}$ of (91) satisfy

$$
\tilde{b}^{ij}(p_1, p_2) = b^{ij}[\tilde{W}_1(p_1, p_2), \tilde{W}_2(p_1, p_2)] \qquad (i, j = 1, 2),
\tag{93}
$$

and we define analogously the composed functions

$$
\tilde{b}_{ij}(p_1, p_2) = b_{ij}[\tilde{W}_1(p_1, p_2), \tilde{W}_2(p_1, p_2)] \qquad (i = 1, 2, 3; \; j = 1, 2)
\tag{94}
$$

where $b_{3j} = \partial g_3/\partial w_j$. Likewise we define

$$
\tilde{B} = \begin{bmatrix} \tilde{b}_{11} & \tilde{b}_{12} \\ \tilde{b}_{21} & \tilde{b}_{22} \end{bmatrix}.
\tag{95}
$$

The demand for factor $j$ in industry $i$ is determined by

$$l_{ij} = y_i b_{ij}(w_1, w_2) \qquad (i = 1, 2, 3; \quad j = 1, 2) \tag{96}$$

and from the full employment condition[32] $\sum_{i=1}^{3} l_{ij} = l_j$ we obtain

$$b_{11}y_1 + b_{21}y_2 = -b_{31}y_3 + l_1; \qquad b_{12}y_1 + b_{22}y_2 = -b_{32}y_3 + l_2. \tag{97}$$

Inverting (97) and using (91) and (95) we obtain

$$\begin{bmatrix} y_1 \\ y_2 \end{bmatrix} = -\begin{bmatrix} \tilde{b}^{11} & \tilde{b}^{21} \\ \tilde{b}^{12} & \tilde{b}^{22} \end{bmatrix}\begin{bmatrix} \tilde{b}_{31} \\ \tilde{b}_{32} \end{bmatrix} y_3 + \begin{bmatrix} \tilde{b}^{11} & \tilde{b}^{21} \\ \tilde{b}^{12} & \tilde{b}^{22} \end{bmatrix}\begin{bmatrix} l_1 \\ l_2 \end{bmatrix} \tag{98}$$

so that we may define the *modified national supply function* for commodity $j$, $j = 1, 2$, by

$$\tilde{Y}_j(p_1, p_2, y_3; l_1, l_2) = -[\tilde{b}^{1j}(p_1, p_2)\tilde{b}_{31}(p_1, p_2) + \tilde{b}^{2j}(p_1, p_2)\tilde{b}_{32}(p_1, p_2)]y_3$$
$$+ \tilde{b}^{1j}(p_1, p_2)l_1 + \tilde{b}^{2j}(p_1, p_2)l_2. \tag{99}$$

Thus we have

$$\frac{\partial \tilde{Y}_1}{\partial y_3} = \frac{\begin{vmatrix} \tilde{b}_{21} & \tilde{b}_{22} \\ \tilde{b}_{31} & \tilde{b}_{32} \end{vmatrix}}{\begin{vmatrix} \tilde{b}_{11} & \tilde{b}_{12} \\ \tilde{b}_{21} & \tilde{b}_{22} \end{vmatrix}} = \frac{\tilde{b}_{21}\tilde{b}_{31}}{|\tilde{B}|}\left(\frac{\tilde{b}_{32}}{\tilde{b}_{31}} - \frac{\tilde{b}_{22}}{\tilde{b}_{21}}\right) \tag{100a}$$

and

$$\frac{\partial \tilde{Y}_2}{\partial y_3} = -\frac{\begin{vmatrix} \tilde{b}_{11} & \tilde{b}_{12} \\ \tilde{b}_{31} & \tilde{b}_{32} \end{vmatrix}}{\begin{vmatrix} \tilde{b}_{11} & \tilde{b}_{12} \\ \tilde{b}_{21} & \tilde{b}_{22} \end{vmatrix}} = \frac{\tilde{b}_{11}\tilde{b}_{31}}{|\tilde{B}|}\left(\frac{\tilde{b}_{12}}{\tilde{b}_{11}} - \frac{\tilde{b}_{32}}{\tilde{b}_{31}}\right). \tag{100b}$$

Given assumption (90), that industry 2 is relatively more intensive than industry 1 in its use of factor 2 relative to factor 1, (100a) implies that $\partial \tilde{Y}_1/\partial y_3 < 0$ (a rise in the output of commodity 3, with fixed world prices of commodities 1 and 2, will have to be at least partly at the expense of commodity 1) if and only if $b_{22}/b_{21} > b_{32}/b_{31}$, i.e., industry 2 is relatively more intensive than industry 3 in the use of factor 2 relative to factor 1. Likewise, (100b) implies that $\partial \tilde{Y}_2/\partial y_3 < 0$ (a rise in the output of commodity 3 at fixed world prices of commodities 1 and 2 will have to be at least partly at the expense of commodity 2) if and only if $b_{32}/b_{31} > b_{12}/b_{11}$, i.e., industry 3 is relatively more intensive than industry 1 in its use of factor 2 relative to factor 1. Thus, at

---

[32] Full employment necessarily holds under the assumptions of the model; cf. Chipman [12, p. 217].

given world prices $p_1$, $p_2$, a rise in the output of the domestic commodity gives rise to a fall in the outputs of both international commodities *if and only if* the domestic commodity is intermediate in its factor intensity between the two international commodities.

Since the functions $\tilde{Y}_j$ express the $y_j$'s as single-valued functions of the prices $p_1$, $p_2$ for each fixed $y_3$, it follows that the cross section of the production possibility frontier $\mathscr{Y}(l)$ by the plane $y_3 = \bar{y}_3$ is strictly concave to the origin of that plane. From the assumptions that the functions $g_i$ and $\tilde{W}_i$ are twice continuously differentiable it follows moreover that the $\tilde{Y}_j$'s are continuously differentiable with respect to $p_1$ and $p_2$ as well as $y_3$ (see footnote 18).

The functions $\tilde{Y}_j$ and $\tilde{P}_3$ satisfy some interesting duality relationships. From (92) and (99) it follows at once that

$$\partial \tilde{P}_3/\partial p_j = \tilde{b}_{31}\tilde{b}^{1j} + \tilde{b}_{32}\tilde{b}^{2j} = -\partial \tilde{Y}_j/\partial y_3. \tag{101}$$

Further, since the functions $g_i$ are homogeneous of degree 1 we have from Euler's theorem and (89), (92)

$$p_1 = g_1(w_1, w_2) = (\partial g_1/\partial w_1)w_1 + (\partial g_1/\partial w_2)w_2 = b_{11}w_1 + b_{12}w_2$$

$$p_2 = g_2(w_1, w_2) = (\partial g_2/\partial w_1)w_1 + (\partial g_2/\partial w_2)w_2 = b_{21}w_1 + b_{22}w_2 \tag{102}$$

$$p_3 = g_3(w_1, w_2) = (\partial g_3/\partial w_1)w_1 + (\partial g_3/\partial w_2)w_2 = b_{31}w_1 + b_{32}w_2;$$

or equivalently,

$$\begin{bmatrix} p_1 & b_{11} & b_{12} \\ p_2 & b_{21} & b_{22} \\ p_3 & b_{31} & b_{32} \end{bmatrix} \begin{bmatrix} 1 \\ -w_1 \\ -w_2 \end{bmatrix} = \begin{bmatrix} 0 \\ 0 \\ 0 \end{bmatrix}. \tag{103}$$

Thus, the determinant of the matrix in (103) must vanish. Expanding it down the first column and making use of (100) and (92), we obtain

$$\tilde{P}_3 = -p_1 \, \partial \tilde{Y}_1/\partial y_3 - p_2 \, \partial \tilde{Y}_2/\partial y_3. \tag{104}$$

This of course leads back to (101).

Using the techniques of nonlinear programming, it may readily be shown (as in Chipman [12]) that if we define

$$\tilde{\Pi}(p_1, p_2, y_3; l_1, l_2) = \max_{y_1, y_2} \{p_1 y_1 + p_2 y_2 + \tilde{P}_3(p_1, p_2)y_3 : y \in \mathscr{Y}(l)\}, \tag{105}$$

then the functions (99) are those that solve the maximization problem (105) for given $p_1$, $p_2$, $y_3$, and thus

$$\tilde{\Pi}(p_1, p_2, y_3; l_1, l_2) = p_1 \tilde{Y}_1(p_1, p_2, y_3; l_1, l_2)$$
$$+ p_2 \tilde{Y}_2(p_1, p_2, y_3; l_1, l_2) + \tilde{P}_3(p_1, p_2)y_3. \tag{106}$$

It is readily shown that[33]

$$p_1 \, \partial \tilde{Y}_1 / \partial p_j + p_2 \, \partial \tilde{Y}_2 / \partial p_j = 0 \qquad (j = 1, 2). \tag{107}$$

Consequently, from (106), (107), (101), and (104) we have

$$\partial \tilde{\Pi} / \partial p_j = \tilde{Y}_j - y_3 \, \partial \tilde{Y}_j / \partial y_3 \quad (j = 1, 2); \qquad \partial \tilde{\Pi} / \partial y_3 = 0. \tag{108}$$

We shall define the *conditional transformation terms* $\tilde{\imath}_{ij}(p_1, p_2, y_3; l_1, l_2)$ by

$$\tilde{\imath}_{ij} = \partial \tilde{Y}_i / \partial p_j = \partial^2 \tilde{\Pi} / \partial p_i \, \partial p_j. \tag{109}$$

We may now define the modified national demand functions. Attaching country superscripts $k$ to all the relevant expressions, we define the *modified purchasing power functions* $\tilde{\Phi}^k$ by

$$\begin{aligned} &\tilde{\Phi}^k(p_1, p_2, y_3{}^k; l_1{}^k, l_2{}^k; \tau) \\ &= \tilde{\Pi}^k(p_1, p_2, y_3{}^k; l_1{}^k, l_2{}^k) + (-1)^k(p_1 \gamma_1 + p_2 \gamma_2)\tau \quad (k = 1, 2) \end{aligned} \tag{110}$$

and the *modified national demand functions* $\tilde{X}_i{}^k$ by

$$\begin{aligned} &\tilde{X}_i{}^k(p_1, p_2, y_3{}^k, l_1{}^k, l_2{}^k; \tau) \\ &= h_i{}^k[p_1, p_2, \tilde{P}_3{}^k(p_1, p_2), \tilde{\Phi}^k(p_1, p_2, y_3{}^k; l_1{}^k, l_2{}^k; \tau)] \quad (i, k = 1, 2) \end{aligned} \tag{111}$$

The *modified excess demand functions* $\tilde{Z}_i{}^k$ are defined by

$$\begin{aligned} &\tilde{Z}_i{}^k(p_1, p_2, y_3{}^k; l_1{}^k, l_2{}^k; \tau) \\ &= \tilde{X}_i{}^k(p_1, p_2, y_3{}^k; l_1{}^k, l_2{}^k; \tau) - \tilde{Y}_i{}^k(p_1, p_2, y_3{}^k; l_1{}^k, l_2{}^k) \\ &\hspace{6cm} (i = 1, 2, 3; \quad k = 1, 2) \end{aligned} \tag{112}$$

where of course

$$\tilde{Y}_3{}^k(p_1, p_2, y_3{}^k; l_1, l_2) = y_3{}^k, \tag{113}$$

---

[33] Define the functions $l_{ij} = \tilde{L}_{ij}(p_1, p_2, y_3; l_1, l_2)$ as those which solve the programming problem. The functions (99) are then given by $\tilde{Y}_i = f_i(\tilde{L}_{i1}, \tilde{L}_{i2})$, $i = 1, 2$. Differentiating these with respect to $p_j$, one obtains, upon using the fact that $\partial f_i / \partial l_{ij} = w_j / p_i$,

$$p_1 \frac{\partial \tilde{Y}_1}{\partial p_j} + p_2 \frac{\partial \tilde{Y}_2}{\partial p_j} = w_1 \left( \frac{\partial \tilde{L}_{11}}{\partial p_j} + \frac{\partial \tilde{L}_{21}}{\partial p_j} \right) + w_2 \left( \frac{\partial \tilde{L}_{12}}{\partial p_j} + \frac{\partial \tilde{L}_{22}}{\partial p_j} \right). \tag{F.33.1}$$

Differentiating the identity $y_3 = f_3[\tilde{L}_{31}(p_1, p_2, y_3; l_1, l_2), \tilde{L}_{32}(p_1, p_2, y_3; l_1, l_2)]$ through with respect to $p_j$, we obtain similarly

$$w_1 \frac{\partial \tilde{L}_{31}}{\partial p_j} + w_2 \frac{\partial \tilde{L}_{32}}{\partial p_j} = 0. \tag{F.33.2}$$

Combining (F.30.1) and (F.30.2) with the full employment condition $\sum_{i=1}^{3} \partial \tilde{L}_{ik} / \partial p_j = 0$ $(j, k = 1, 2)$, we obtain (107).

and for convenience we define, as in (32),

$$\zeta_i^{\ k} = \tilde{Z}_i^{\ k} - (-1)^k \gamma_i \tau \qquad (i = 1, 2, 3; \quad k = 1, 2) \tag{114}$$

and[34]

$$\begin{aligned}
&\tilde{s}_{ij}^k(p_1, p_2, y_3^{\ k}; l_1^{\ k}, l_2^{\ k}; \tau) \\
&\quad = s_{ij}^k[p_1, p_2, \tilde{P}_3^{\ k}(p_1, p_2), \tilde{\Phi}^k(p_1, p_2, y_3^{\ k}; l_1^{\ k}, l_2^{\ k}, \tau)] \\
&\tilde{m}_i^{\ k}(p_1, p_2, y_3^{\ k}; l_1^{\ k}, l_2^{\ k}, \tau) \\
&\quad = m_i^{\ k}[p_1, p_2, \tilde{P}_3^{\ k}(p_1, p_2), \tilde{\Phi}^k(p_1, p_2, y_3^{\ k}; l_1^{\ k}, l_2^{\ k}; \tau)].
\end{aligned} \tag{115}$$

It is now easy to verify from (111) with the aid of (101), (104), and (108) that [recalling (33) and (114)]

$$\frac{\partial \tilde{X}_i^{\ k}}{\partial p_j} = \tilde{s}_{ij}^k - \tilde{s}_{i3}^k \frac{\partial \tilde{Y}_j^{\ k}}{\partial y_3^{\ k}} - \tilde{m}_i^{\ k} \zeta_j^{\ k}; \qquad \frac{\partial \tilde{X}_i^{\ k}}{\partial y_3^{\ k}} = 0; \qquad \frac{\partial \tilde{X}_i^{\ k}}{\partial \tau} = (-1)^k \beta_1 \tilde{m}_i^{\ k}$$

$$(i = 1, 2, 3; \quad j = 1, 2; \quad k = 1, 2), \tag{116}$$

so that from (109) and (112),

$$\frac{\partial \tilde{Z}_i^{\ k}}{\partial p_j} = \tilde{s}_{ij}^k - \tilde{t}_{ij}^k - \tilde{s}_{i3}^k \frac{\partial \tilde{Y}_j^{\ k}}{\partial y_3^{\ k}} - \tilde{m}_i^{\ k} \zeta_j^{\ k}; \qquad \frac{\partial \tilde{Z}_i^{\ k}}{\partial \tau} = (-1)^k \beta_1 \tilde{m}_i^{\ k}$$

$$(i = 1, 2, 3; \quad j = 1, 2; \quad k = 1, 2) \tag{117}$$

and from (113),

$$\frac{\partial \tilde{Z}_i^{\ k}}{\partial y_3^{\ k}} = -\frac{\partial \tilde{Y}_i^{\ k}}{\partial y_3^{\ k}} \quad (i = 1, 2); \qquad \frac{\partial \tilde{Z}_3^{\ k}}{\partial y_3^{\ k}} = -1, \tag{118}$$

where the expressions for $\partial \tilde{Y}_i^k / \partial y_3^{\ k}$ are given by (100) with appropriate country suffixes attached.

We may finally verify without difficulty that upon substituting the modified national demand functions (111) into the utility function (11) and differentiating the composed function totally with respect to $\tau$, we again get the expression (54) for the primary and secondary burden of a transfer.

## C. The Case of Specialization

We shall take up cases in which a country specializes in the production of its domestic commodity and one of the two international commodities, and continues to do so when it is subjected to sufficiently small disturbances. We shall assume that country 1 (the paying country) is always an exporter of commodity 1 to, and an importer of commodity 2 from, country 2 (the

---

[34] The function $\tilde{m}_i^k$ of course bears no relation to the function (F.28.3) of footnote 28.

receiving country). Thus, if country 1 specializes, it produces commodities 1 and 3, if country 2 specializes, it produces commodities 2 and 3.

In that case, the dual minimum-unit-cost functions respectively (but not necessarily simultaneously) satisfy the relations

$$
\begin{aligned}
p_1 &= g_1^{1}(w_1^{1}, w_2^{1}), & p_1 &< g_1^{2}(w_1^{2}, w_2^{2}) \\
p_2 &< g_2^{1}(w_1^{1}, w_2^{1}), & p_2 &= g_2^{2}(w_1^{2}, w_2^{2}), \\
p_3 &= g_3^{1}(w_1^{1}, w_2^{1}), & p_3^{2} &= g_3^{2}(w_1^{2}, w_2^{2});
\end{aligned}
\tag{119}
$$

in equilibrium. For the respective equalities on the left and right in (119) we obtain, assuming the Jacobians $\partial(g_1^{1}, g_3^{1})/\partial(w_1, w_2)$ and $\partial(g_2^{2}, g_3^{2})/\partial(w_1, w_2)$ to be nonvanishing for all factor prices $(w_1, w_2) > 0$ (i.e., that there is no factor intensity reversal as between the respective countries' export and domestic industries), the inverse mappings

$$
\begin{aligned}
w_1^{1} &= \overline{W}_1^{1}(p_1, p_3^{1}), & w_1^{2} &= \overline{W}_1^{2}(p_2, p_3^{2}) \\
w_2^{1} &= \overline{W}_2^{1}(p_1, p_3^{1}), & w_2^{2} &= \overline{W}_2^{2}(p_2, p_3^{2}).
\end{aligned}
\tag{120}
$$

These are defined, respectively, for the prices $p^1 = (p_1, p_2, p_3^{1}) > 0$ and $p^2 = (p_1, p_2, p_3^{2}) > 0$ for which the relations (119) hold; let these sets of prices be denoted $P^1$ and $P^2$, respectively. We shall assume that the functions $\overline{W}_i^{k}$ are twice continuously differentiable for $p^k \in P^k$; it follows (see footnote 18) that the national product functions $Y_i^{k}(p^k, l^k)$ are defined and continuously differentiable for $p^k \in P^k$, $k = 1, 2$ and $i = 1, 2, 3$ (where of course $Y_2^{1} = 0$ and $Y_1^{2} = 0$, respectively). The transformation matrices then have the forms

$$
T^1 = \begin{bmatrix} t_{11}^{1} & 0 & t_{13}^{1} \\ 0 & 0 & 0 \\ t_{31}^{1} & 0 & t_{33}^{1} \end{bmatrix}, \qquad
T^2 = \begin{bmatrix} 0 & 0 & 0 \\ 0 & t_{22}^{2} & t_{23}^{2} \\ 0 & t_{32}^{2} & t_{33}^{2} \end{bmatrix},
\tag{121}
$$

respectively. Since the efficient frontiers $\mathcal{Y}_{pk}(l^k)$ are strongly concave to the origin, these matrices have rank 1 and, being symmetric and positive semi-definite and satisfying (23), their elements respectively satisfy

$$
t_{kk}^{k} = -\frac{p_3^{k}}{p_k} t_{k3}^{k} > 0, \qquad t_{33}^{k} = -\frac{p_k}{p_3^{k}} t_{3k}^{k} > 0 \qquad (k = 1, 2),
\tag{122}
$$

the prices being necessarily positive in equilibrium on account of the monotonicity assumption concerning (11).

Let us define the function $\varphi_i^{k}(p_1, p_2, p_3^{k}, I^k)$ by

$$
\varphi_i^{k} = \frac{\begin{vmatrix} m_i^{k} & s_{i3}^{k} \\ m_3^{k} & s_{33}^{k} \end{vmatrix}}{s_{33}^{k}} - \frac{\begin{vmatrix} m_i^{k} & s_{i3}^{k} - t_{i3}^{k} \\ m_3^{k} & s_{33}^{k} - t_{33}^{k} \end{vmatrix}}{s_{33}^{k} - t_{33}^{k}}.
\tag{123}
$$

(Intuitively, this function nets out the consumption effect and may be considered as expressing the conditional income effect on country $k$'s supply of commodity $i$.) Then we may state the following very simple result.

**Lemma 2**   If country $k$ specializes in commodities $k$ and 3 and its domestic commodity is regular (see Section III.D), then

$$\varphi_1{}^1 \leqq 0 \qquad \text{and} \qquad \varphi_2{}^1 \geqq 0, \tag{124a}$$

with strict inequality if and only if $s_{23}^1 > 0$; and

$$\varphi_2{}^2 \leqq 0 \qquad \text{and} \qquad \varphi_1{}^2 \geqq 0, \tag{124b}$$

with strict inequality if and only if $s_{13}^2 > 0$.

*Proof*   We have from (123)

$$\varphi_i{}^k = m_3{}^k \frac{s_{i3}^k t_{33}^k - s_{33}^k t_{i3}^k}{s_{33}^k(s_{33}^k - t_{33}^k)} \qquad (i, k = 1, 2). \tag{125}$$

It follows from (121) that if $i \neq k$, then $t_{i3}^k = 0$; hence from (125), clearly $\varphi_i{}^k \geqq 0$, with strict inequality if and only if $s_{i3}^k > 0$. On the other hand, if $i = k$, then from (122) and (26) we have

$$s_{13}^1 t_{33}^1 - s_{33}^1 t_{13}^1 = -\frac{t_{13}^1}{p_3{}^1}(p_1 s_{13}^1 + p_3 s_{33}^1) = \frac{t_{13}^1}{p_3{}^1} p_2 s_{23}^1 \leqq 0$$

$$s_{23}^2 t_{33}^2 - s_{33}^2 t_{23}^2 = -\frac{t_{23}^2}{p_3{}^2}(p_2 s_{23}^2 + p_3 s_{33}^2) = \frac{t_{23}^2}{p_3{}^2} p_1 s_{13}^2 \leqq 0 \tag{126}$$

with strict inequalities holding, respectively, if and only if $s_{23}^1 > 0$ and $s_{13}^2 > 0$.   Q.E.D.

## D. SPECIALIZATION IN BOTH COUNTRIES

If both countries specialize, we have the following immediate consequence of Lemma 2:

**Theorem 4**   In the two-factor model, suppose each country specializes in its export and domestic commodities, and assume further that
    (i) the domestic commodity in each country is regular (see Section III.D), and moreover is a strong Hicksian substitute of its import commodity;
    (ii) the Hypothesis of Neutral Tastes holds (see Section IV.C);
    (iii) the Hicksian stability condition (41) holds.
Then a transfer worsens the paying country's terms of trade.

*Proof* From (i), (ii), and Lemma 2 we have immediately

$$\frac{\begin{vmatrix} m_2{}^1 & s_{23}^1 \\ m_3{}^1 & s_{33}^1 - t_{33}^1 \end{vmatrix}}{s_{33}^1 - t_{33}^1} < \frac{\begin{vmatrix} m_2{}^1 & s_{23}^1 \\ m_3{}^1 & s_{33}^1 \end{vmatrix}}{s_{33}^1} = \frac{\begin{vmatrix} m_2{}^2 & s_{23}^2 \\ m_3{}^2 & s_{33}^2 \end{vmatrix}}{s_{33}^2}$$

$$< \frac{\begin{vmatrix} m_2{}^2 & s_{23}^2 - t_{23}^2 \\ m_3{}^2 & s_{33}^2 - t_{33}^2 \end{vmatrix}}{s_{33}^2 - t_{33}^2}, \tag{127}$$

whence the conclusion follows from (iii) and (44a). Q.E.D.

It is easy to see that the conclusions of Theorem 4 will be precisely reversed if either (a) the domestic commodity is strongly superior in both countries and a strong Hicksian complement of the country's import commodity, or (b) the domestic commodity is strongly inferior in both countries and a strong Hicksian substitute of the import commodity. However, (a) is rather unlikely a priori; if, for example, tastes are identical in the two countries then (a) would entail that the function $s_{23}(=s_{23}^1 = s_{23}^2)$ satisfy

$$s_{23}(p_1, p_2{}^*, p_3^{1*}, I^{1*}) < 0 \quad \text{and} \quad s_{23}(p_1, p_2{}^*, p_3^{2*}, I^{2*}) > 0$$

at two different points of its domain (corresponding to the equilibrium prices and incomes in the respective countries); i.e., commodities 2 and 3 would switch from being Hicksian complements to Hicksian substitutes at different values of $p_3$ and $I$. Thus, while the possibility of a local improvement in the terms of trade is not excluded, the possibility does not hold globally. On the other hand, Theorem 4 is a global result.

### E. Diversification in Both Countries

When both countries produce all three commodities, which entails that their production possibility frontiers have interior points with common slopes

$$\frac{\partial \tilde{Y}_2{}^1(p_1, p_2, y_3{}^1; l_1{}^1, l_2{}^1)/\partial p_2}{\partial \tilde{Y}_1{}^1(p_1, p_2, y_3{}^1; l_1{}^1, l_2{}^1)/\partial p_2} = \frac{\partial \tilde{Y}_2{}^2(p_1, p_2, y_3{}^2; l_1{}^2, l_2{}^2)/\partial p_2}{\partial \tilde{Y}_1{}^2(p_1, p_2, y_3{}^2; l_1{}^2, l_2{}^2)/\partial p_2}, \tag{128}$$

given by (107), in the respective cross sections $y_3 = y_3{}^1$, $y_3 = y_3{}^2$, then the equilibrium conditions (13) give rise to the system of three independent equations

$$\tilde{Z}_2{}^1(p_1, p_2, y_3{}^1; l_1{}^1, l_2{}^1; \tau) + \tilde{Z}_2{}^2(p_1, p_2, y_3{}^2; l_1{}^2, l_2{}^2; \tau) = 0$$

$$\tilde{Z}_3{}^1(p_1, p_2, y_3{}^1; l_1{}^1, l_2{}^1; \tau) \qquad\qquad\qquad\qquad = 0 \tag{129}$$

$$\tilde{Z}_3{}^2(p_1, p_2, y_3{}^2; l_1{}^2, l_2{}^2; \tau) = 0$$

in the three variables $p_2$, $y_3{}^1$, $y_3{}^2$ ($p_1$ being fixed), in place of the system (38), where the functions $\tilde{Z}_i{}^k$ are defined by (112). Its Jacobian matrix

$$J = \begin{bmatrix} \partial \tilde{Z}_2{}^1/\partial p_2 + \partial \tilde{Z}_2{}^2/\partial p_2 & \partial \tilde{Z}_2{}^1/\partial y_3{}^1 & \partial \tilde{Z}_2{}^2/\partial y_3{}^2 \\ \partial \tilde{Z}_3{}^1/\partial p_2 & \partial \tilde{Z}_3{}^1/\partial y_3{}^1 & 0 \\ \partial \tilde{Z}_3{}^2/\partial p_2 & 0 & \partial \tilde{Z}_3{}^2/\partial y_3{}^2 \end{bmatrix} \tag{130}$$

will be assumed to be Hicksian, a reasonable, even if makeshift, justification for which is that by Metzler's [43] result, this is a necessary condition for the local stability, at all positive speeds of adjustment $\tilde{\kappa}_2$, $\tilde{\kappa}_3{}^1$, $\tilde{\kappa}_3{}^2$, of the dynamic system

$$\dot{p}_2 = \tilde{\kappa}_2\{\tilde{Z}_2{}^1(p_1, p_2, y_3{}^1; l_1{}^1, l_2{}^1; \tau) + \tilde{Z}_2{}^2(p_1, p_2, y_3{}^2; l_1{}^2, l_2{}^2; \tau)\}$$

$$\dot{y}_3{}^1 = \tilde{\kappa}_3{}^1 \tilde{Z}_3{}^1(p_1, p_2, y_3{}^1; l_1{}^1, l_2{}^1; \tau) \tag{131}$$

$$\dot{y}_3{}^2 = \tilde{\kappa}_3{}^2 \tilde{Z}_3{}^2(p_1, p_2, y_3{}^2; l_1{}^2, l_2{}^2; \tau).$$

Then with the aid of (117) and (118), we obtain, by applying the implicit function theorem to (129) [analogously to the development leading up to (43)],

$$\frac{\partial \tilde{p}_2}{d\tau} = \frac{\beta_1}{|J|} \begin{vmatrix} \tilde{m}_2{}^1 - \tilde{m}_2{}^2 & -\partial \tilde{Y}_2{}^1/\partial y_3{}^1 & -\partial \tilde{Y}_2{}^2/\partial y_3{}^2 \\ \tilde{m}_3{}^1 & -1 & 0 \\ -\tilde{m}_3{}^2 & 0 & -1 \end{vmatrix}$$

$$= \frac{\beta_1}{|J|} \left\{ \begin{vmatrix} \tilde{m}_2{}^1 & \partial \tilde{Y}_2{}^1/\partial y_3{}^1 \\ \tilde{m}_3{}^1 & 1 \end{vmatrix} - \begin{vmatrix} \tilde{m}_2{}^2 & \partial \tilde{Y}_2{}^2/\partial y_3{}^2 \\ \tilde{m}_3{}^2 & 1 \end{vmatrix} \right\}. \tag{132}$$

The following theorem has already been stated by Samuelson [63, p. 351].

**Theorem 5**  In the two-factor model, suppose each country diversifies, i.e., produces positive amounts of all three commodities, and continues to do so when subjected to sufficiently small disturbances; and assume further that (the domestic commodities being identified as the same)

(i)   production functions are identical as between countries;

(ii)   utility functions are homogeneous and identical as between countries;[35] and

---

[35] Of course, it is only required that preferences be identical and homothetic, but if this is the case it is always possible (under our assumptions) to represent them by identical homogeneous utility functions. Actually, assumption (ii) is stronger than necessary and can be replaced by Gorman's [20] condition that the (unconditional) Engel curves be parallel straight lines for each set of prices ($p_1$, $p_2$, $p_3$), as is certainly the case with identical functions of the type (C.7) of Appendix C.

(iii)   factor prices are initially equalized between countries.[36]
Then a transfer leaves all prices, and hence the terms of trade, unaffected.

*Proof*   Since the production functions $f_i^k$ are identical [from (i)] so are the cost functions $g_i^k$, i.e., $g_i^1 = g_i^2$ for $i = 1, 2$; and from (iii), so are the Stolper–Samuelson functions $W_i^k$ in the relevant range of prices, and therefore [from (92) and (101)] so are the functions $\partial \tilde{Y}_2^k / \partial y_3^k = -\partial \tilde{P}_3^k / \partial p_2$ which, furthermore [as is clear from (92)], are independent of $y_3^k$ and $\tau$. Thus, $\partial \tilde{Y}_2^1 / \partial y_3^1 = \partial \tilde{Y}_2^2 / \partial y_3^2$ for all $p_1, p_2$, and independently of $y_3^1, y_3^2$, and $\tau$. The homogeneity of the utility functions implies that the functions $m_i^k$ of (24) are independent of $I^k$ (see for instance Chipman [13]); hence the functions $\tilde{m}_2^k$ of (115) are independent of $y_3^k$ and $\tau$; and they are identical for $k = 1, 2$ since the utility functions are identical, from (ii). Thus, the functions $\tilde{m}_2^k - \tilde{m}_3^k \, \partial \tilde{Y}_2^k / \partial y_3^k$ of (132) depend only on $p_1$ and $p_2$, and are identical for $k = 1, 2$; and since $p_1$ and $p_2$ are the same in the two countries, $d\tilde{p}_2 / d\tau = 0$ for all $\tau$ such that the hypothesis that both countries diversify holds.   Q.E.D.

It should be noted that this is a global result, valid for all finite transfers provided they are not so large as to force a country to switch from diversification to specialization.

Before proceeding to the next theorem, we shall develop a number of useful relationships. Just as, from $\sum_{i=1}^3 p_i^k m_i^k = 1$ and $\sum_{i=1}^3 p_i^k (s_{i3}^k - t_{i3}^k) = 0$, we have

$$p_1 \left( m_1^k - m_3^k \frac{s_{13}^k - t_{13}^k}{s_{33}^k - t_{33}^k} \right) + p_2 \left( m_2^k - m_3^k \frac{s_{23}^k - t_{23}^k}{s_{33}^k - t_{33}^k} \right) = 1 \qquad (133)$$

(i.e., $p_1 \hat{m}_1^k + p_2 \hat{m}_2^k = 1$ in the notation of Section IV. B), we have from $\sum_{i=1}^3 p_i^k m_i^k = 1$ and (104) the relation

$$p_1 \left( m_1^k - m_3^k \frac{\partial \tilde{Y}_1^k}{\partial y_3^k} \right) + p_2 \left( m_2^k - m_3^k \frac{\partial \tilde{Y}_2^k}{\partial y_3^k} \right) = 1. \qquad (134)$$

---

[36] A sufficient condition for this is that there should be no reversal of factor intensity as between industries 1 and 2, i.e., that condition (90) should hold. However, it is enough to assume that the factor endowment vectors of the two countries should lie within the same "diversification cone" (cf. Chipman [9]) spanned by the points of tangency of the common tangents to the isoquants corresponding to a dollar's worth of each of the international commodities. In fact, even this condition is stronger than necessary, since it would require a very pathological relationship among the three production isoquants for it to be possible for them to give rise to two diversification cones in each of which all three commodities are produced [9, p. 32, Fig. 3.6]. In other words, if we specified absolutely continuous a priori probability distributions over the space of production functions for the three commodities (assuming them to be identical as between countries), we could "almost" dispense with hypothesis (iii) in the technically rigorous sense that it is implied with probability 1 by the remaining assumptions of Theorem 5 (namely, hypothesis (i) and the assumption that all three commodities are produced).

Likewise, using (104) and $\sum_{i=1}^{3} p_i{}^k s_{i3}^k = 0$ we obtain

$$p_1\left(\frac{\partial \tilde{Y}_1{}^k}{\partial y_3{}^k} - \frac{s_{13}^k}{s_{33}^k}\right) + p_2\left(\frac{\partial \tilde{Y}_2{}^k}{\partial y_3{}^k} - \frac{s_{23}^k}{s_{33}^k}\right) = 0. \tag{135}$$

From (104) and (101), or directly from the fact that $\tilde{P}_3{}^k$ in (92) is homogeneous of degree 1, we have

$$\frac{p_1}{\tilde{P}_3{}^k}\frac{\partial \tilde{P}_3{}^k}{\partial p_1} + \frac{p_2}{\tilde{P}_3{}^k}\frac{\partial \tilde{P}_3{}^k}{\partial p_2} = 1, \tag{136}$$

and defining $c_i{}^k = -p_i s_{i3}^k/p_3{}^k s_{33}^k$ for $i = 1, 2$ as in (84), (135) together with (101) is equivalent to

$$c_1{}^k - \frac{p_1}{\tilde{P}_3{}^k}\frac{\partial \tilde{P}_3{}^k}{\partial p_1} + c_2{}^k - \frac{p_2}{\tilde{P}_3{}^k}\frac{\partial \tilde{P}_3{}^k}{\partial p_2} = 0. \tag{137}$$

Now let the elasticity of the unit cost of production of commodity $i$ with respect to the rental of factor $j$ be denoted

$$\beta_{ij}^k = \frac{w_j{}^k}{g_i{}^k}\frac{\partial g_i{}^k}{\partial w_j{}^k} = \frac{w_j{}^k}{g_i{}^k} b_{ij}^k. \tag{138}$$

This is, of course, the same as the relative share of factor $j$ in the costs of industry $i$. Define the composed function $\tilde{\beta}_{ij}^k(p_1, p_2, p_3{}^k)$ by

$$\tilde{\beta}_{ij}^k = \frac{\tilde{W}_j{}^k}{p_i{}^k}\tilde{b}_{ij}^k \quad (i = 1, 2), \qquad \tilde{\beta}_{3j}^k = \frac{\tilde{W}_j{}^k}{\tilde{P}_3{}^k}\tilde{b}_{ij}^k \quad (j = 1, 2, \quad k = 1, 2). \tag{139}$$

Since $g_i{}^k$ is homogeneous of degree 1 we have $\tilde{\beta}_{i1}^k + \tilde{\beta}_{i2}^k = 1$; hence from (100) and (101) we obtain

$$\frac{p_1}{\tilde{P}_3{}^k}\frac{\partial \tilde{P}_3{}^k}{\partial p_1} = \frac{\tilde{\beta}_{22}^k - \tilde{\beta}_{32}^k}{\tilde{\beta}_{22}^k - \tilde{\beta}_{12}^k}, \qquad \frac{p_2}{\tilde{P}_3{}^k}\frac{\partial \tilde{P}_3{}^k}{\partial p_2} = \frac{\tilde{\beta}_{32}^k - \tilde{\beta}_{12}^k}{\tilde{\beta}_{22}^k - \tilde{\beta}_{12}^k}, \tag{140}$$

the denominators being positive from (90). Thus we have

$$\frac{p_1}{\tilde{P}_3{}^k}\left(\frac{\partial \tilde{Y}_1{}^k}{\partial y_3{}^k} - \frac{s_{13}^k}{s_{33}^k}\right) = c_1{}^k - \frac{p_1}{\tilde{P}_3{}^k}\frac{\partial \tilde{P}_3{}^k}{\partial p_1} = \frac{\tilde{\beta}_{32}^k - (c_1{}^k\tilde{\beta}_{12}^k + c_2{}^k\tilde{\beta}_{22}^k)}{\tilde{\beta}_{22}^k - \tilde{\beta}_{12}^k} \tag{141a}$$

and

$$\frac{p_2}{\tilde{P}_3{}^k}\left(\frac{\partial \tilde{Y}_2{}^k}{\partial y_3{}^k} - \frac{s_{23}^k}{s_{33}^k}\right) = c_2{}^k - \frac{p_2}{\tilde{P}_3{}^k}\frac{\partial \tilde{P}_3{}^k}{\partial p_2} = -\frac{\tilde{\beta}_{32}^k - (c_1{}^k\tilde{\beta}_{12}^k + c_2{}^k\tilde{\beta}_{22}^k)}{\tilde{\beta}_{22}^k - \tilde{\beta}_{12}^k}. \tag{141b}$$

Let us finally define the function $\psi_i^k(p_1, p_2, p_3^k, I^k)$ by

$$\psi_i^k = \begin{vmatrix} m_i^k & \partial \tilde{Y}_i^k / \partial y_3^k \\ m_3^k & 1 \end{vmatrix} - \frac{\begin{vmatrix} m_i^k & s_{i3}^k \\ m_3^k & s_{33}^k \end{vmatrix}}{s_{33}^k} = m_3^k \left( \frac{s_{i3}^k}{s_{33}^k} - \frac{\partial \tilde{Y}_i^k}{\partial y_3^k} \right). \tag{142}$$

From (141b) we then have

$$\psi_2^k = \frac{p_3 m_3^k}{p_2} \left( \frac{p_2}{\tilde{P}_3^k} \frac{\partial \tilde{P}_3^k}{\partial p_2} - c_2^k \right) = \frac{p_3^k m_3^k}{p_2} \frac{\tilde{\beta}_{32}^k - (c_1^k \tilde{\beta}_{12}^k + c_2^k \tilde{\beta}_{22}^k)}{\tilde{\beta}_{22}^k - \tilde{\beta}_{12}^k}. \tag{143}$$

We may now state:

***Theorem 6*** In the two-factor model, suppose that each country produces all three commodities, and that in each country industry 1 uses factor 1 more intensively relative to factor 2 than industry 2 [i.e., (90) holds]. Suppose further that
(i) the domestic commodity in each country is regular;
(ii) the Hypothesis of Neutral Tastes holds;
(iii) the stability condition $|\tilde{J}| < 0$ holds.
Then
(1) A sufficient condition for a deterioration in the paying country's terms of trade is that

$$\tilde{\beta}_{32}^1 < c_1^1 \tilde{\beta}_{12}^1 + c_2^1 \tilde{\beta}_{22}^1 \quad \text{and} \quad \tilde{\beta}_{32}^2 > c_1^2 \tilde{\beta}_{12}^2 + c_2^2 \tilde{\beta}_{22}^2 \tag{144}$$

for all $p_1, p_2, p_3^1, p_3^2$, where $\tilde{\beta}_{ij}^k$ and $c_i^k$ are defined by (138) and (84), respectively. In particular, (144) will hold if $\beta_{22}^1 > \beta_{12}^1 > \beta_{32}^1$ and $\beta_{32}^2 > \beta_{22}^2 > \beta_{12}^2$, i.e., if

$$\frac{b_{22}^1}{b_{21}^1} > \frac{b_{12}^1}{b_{11}^1} > \frac{b_{32}^1}{b_{31}^1} \quad \text{and} \quad \frac{b_{32}^2}{b_{31}^2} > \frac{b_{22}^2}{b_{21}^2} > \frac{b_{12}^2}{b_{11}^2} \tag{145}$$

for all $(w_1^1, w_2^1)$ and $(w_1^2, w_2^2)$.
(2) A sufficient condition for an improvement in the paying country's terms of trade is that

$$\tilde{\beta}_{32}^1 > c_1^1 \tilde{\beta}_{12}^1 + c_2^1 \tilde{\beta}_{22}^1 \quad \text{and} \quad \tilde{\beta}_{32}^2 < c_1^2 \tilde{\beta}_{12}^2 + c_2^2 \tilde{\beta}_{22}^2 \tag{146}$$

for all $p_1, p_2, p_3^1, p_3^2$. In particular, (146) will hold if $\beta_{32}^1 > \beta_{22}^1 > \beta_{12}^1$ and $\beta_{22}^2 > \beta_{12}^2 > \beta_{32}^2$, i.e., if

$$\frac{b_{32}^1}{b_{31}^1} > \frac{b_{22}^1}{b_{21}^1} > \frac{b_{12}^1}{b_{11}^1} \quad \text{and} \quad \frac{b_{22}^2}{b_{21}^2} > \frac{b_{12}^2}{b_{11}^2} > \frac{b_{32}^2}{b_{31}^2} \tag{147}$$

for all $(w_1^1, w_2^1)$ and $(w_1^2, w_2^2)$.

(3)   A sufficient condition for a transfer to leave the terms of trade unchanged is that production functions be of the Cobb–Douglas type

$$f_i^k(l_{i1}, l_{i2}) = \alpha_i^k l_{i1}^{\beta_{i1}^k} l_{i2}^{\beta_{i2}^k} \qquad (\beta_{ij}^k > 0, \quad \beta_{i1}^k + \beta_{i2}^k = 1) \qquad (148)$$

(where $\beta_{ij}^k$ = constant), and utility functions likewise of the type

$$U^k(x_1, x_2, x_3) = x_1^{\theta_1^k} x_2^{\theta_2^k} x_3^{\theta_3^k} \qquad (\theta_i^k > 0, \quad \theta_1^k + \theta_2^k + \theta_3^k = 1), \qquad (149)$$

and that

$$\beta_{32}^k = c_1^k \beta_{12}^k + c_2^k \beta_{22}^k \qquad (k = 1, 2), \qquad (150)$$

where $c_i^k = \theta_i^k/(\theta_1^k + \theta_2^k)$.

*Proof*   In view of (145) and (ii), (132) may be written in the form

$$\frac{d\tilde{p}_2}{d\tau} = \frac{\beta_1}{|\tilde{J}|}\{\psi_2^1 - \psi_2^2\} \qquad (151)$$

where the functions $\psi_2^k$ are evaluated at the equilibrium values of their arguments. From (iii), a sufficient condition for $d\tilde{p}_2/d\tau > 0$ is then $\psi_2^1 < 0$ and $\psi_2^2 > 0$, which, on account of (143), is equivalent to (144). From (i) and (84) the $c_i^k$'s are nonnegative; hence (145) follows. This proves (1), and a similar argument proves (2). Since (148) implies that $g_i^k$ is also of the Cobb–Douglas type, (3) readily follows.   Q.E.D.

## F.  Mixed Cases

If the paying country specializes (in commodities 1 and 3) and the receiving country diversifies, the systems (38) or (129) are replaced by the system of independent equations

$$Z_2^1(p_1, p_2, p_3^1; l_1^1, l_2^1; \tau) + \tilde{Z}_2^2(p_1, p_2, y_3^2; l_1^2, l_2^2; \tau) = 0$$
$$Z_3^1(p_1, p_2, p_3^1; l_1^1, l_2^1; \tau) \qquad\qquad\qquad = 0 \qquad (152)$$
$$\tilde{Z}_3^2(p_1, p_2, y_3^2; l_1^2, l_2^2; \tau) = 0$$

in the three variables $p_2, p_3^1, y_3^2$ ($p_1$ being assumed fixed). Likewise, if the paying country diversifies and the receiving country specializes (in commodities 2 and 3), then in place of (152) we have the system of equations

$$\tilde{Z}_2^1(p_1, p_2, y_3^1; l_1^1, l_2^1; \tau) + Z_2^2(p_1, p_2, p_3^2; l_1^2, l_2^2; \tau) = 0$$
$$\tilde{Z}_3^1(p_1, p_2, y_3^1; l_1^1, l_2^1; \tau) \qquad\qquad\qquad = 0 \qquad (153)$$
$$Z_3^2(p_1, p_2, p_3^2; l_1^2, l_2^2; \tau) = 0$$

in the three variables $p_2, y_3^1, p_3^2$. As counterparts to (40) and (131) we may postulate the obvious dynamic adjustment processes in terms of $\dot{p}_2, \dot{p}_3^1$,

$\dot{y}_3{}^2$ for (152) and $\dot{p}_2$, $\dot{y}_3{}^1$, $\dot{p}_3{}^2$ for (153), to justify the assumption, which we shall make, that the Jacobian matrices of (152) and (153), which we shall denote $\tilde{J}_1$ and $\tilde{J}_2$, respectively, are Hicksian.

For the system (152) we then obtain

$$
\frac{d\tilde{p}_2}{d\tau} = \frac{\beta_1}{|\tilde{J}_1|}
\begin{vmatrix}
\bar{m}_2{}^1 - \tilde{m}_2{}^2 & \bar{s}_{23}^1 & -\partial \tilde{Y}_2{}^2/\partial y_3{}^2 \\
\bar{m}_3{}^1 & \bar{s}_{33}^1 - t_{33}^1 & 0 \\
-\tilde{m}_3{}^2 & 0 & -1
\end{vmatrix}
$$

$$
= \frac{\beta_1(\bar{s}_{33}^1 - t_{33}^1)}{|\tilde{J}_1|} \left\{
\begin{vmatrix}
\tilde{m}_2{}^2 & \partial \tilde{Y}_2{}^2/\partial y_3{}^2 \\
\tilde{m}_3{}^2 & 1
\end{vmatrix}
- \frac{\begin{vmatrix} \tilde{m}_2{}^1 & \bar{s}_{23}^1 \\ \tilde{m}_3{}^1 & \bar{s}_{33}^1 - t_{33}^1 \end{vmatrix}}{\bar{s}_{33}^1 - t_{33}^1}
\right\} \quad (154)
$$

which, in view of (133) and (134), may be written in the equivalent form

$$
\frac{d\tilde{p}_2}{d\tau} = \frac{\beta_1(\bar{s}_{33}^1 - t_{33}^1)}{|\tilde{J}_1|} \frac{p_1}{p_2} \left(
\frac{\begin{vmatrix} \bar{m}_1{}^1 & \bar{s}_{13}^1 - t_{13}^1 \\ \bar{m}_3{}^1 & \bar{s}_{33}^1 - t_{33}^1 \end{vmatrix}}{\bar{s}_{33}^1 - t_{33}^1}
- \begin{vmatrix} \tilde{m}_1{}^2 & \partial \tilde{Y}_1{}^2/\partial y_3{}^2 \\ \tilde{m}_3{}^2 & 1 \end{vmatrix}
\right). \quad (154')
$$

For the system (153) we obtain

$$
\frac{d\tilde{p}_2}{d\tau} = \frac{\beta_1}{|\tilde{J}_2|}
\begin{vmatrix}
\tilde{m}_2{}^1 - \bar{m}_2{}^2 & -\partial \tilde{Y}_2{}^1/\partial y_3{}^1 & \bar{s}_{23}^2 - t_{23}^2 \\
\tilde{m}_3{}^1 & -1 & 0 \\
-\bar{m}_3{}^2 & 0 & \bar{s}_{33}^2 - t_{33}^2
\end{vmatrix}
$$

$$
= \frac{\beta_1(\bar{s}_{33}^2 - t_{33}^2)}{|\tilde{J}_2|} \left(
\frac{\begin{vmatrix} \bar{m}_2{}^2 & \bar{s}_{23}^2 - t_{23}^2 \\ \bar{m}_3{}^2 & \bar{s}_{33}^2 - t_{33}^2 \end{vmatrix}}{\bar{s}_{33}^2 - t_{33}^2}
- \begin{vmatrix} \tilde{m}_2{}^1 & \partial \tilde{Y}_2{}^1/\partial y_3{}^1 \\ \tilde{m}_3{}^1 & 1 \end{vmatrix}
\right) \quad (155)
$$

which likewise may be written as

$$
\frac{d\tilde{p}_2}{d\tau} = \frac{\beta_1(\bar{s}_{33}^2 - t_{33}^2)}{|\tilde{J}_2|} \frac{p_1}{p_2} \left(
\begin{vmatrix} \tilde{m}_1{}^1 & \partial \tilde{Y}_1{}^1/\partial y_3{}^1 \\ \tilde{m}_3{}^1 & 1 \end{vmatrix}
- \frac{\begin{vmatrix} \bar{m}_1{}^2 & \bar{s}_{13}^2 \\ \bar{m}_3{}^2 & \bar{s}_{33}^2 - t_{33}^2 \end{vmatrix}}{\bar{s}_{33}^2 - t_{33}^2}
\right). \quad (155')
$$

**Theorem 7** In the two-factor model, assume that industry 1 in each country uses factor 1 more intensively relatively to factor 2 than industry 2 [i.e., (90) holds]. Assume further that

(i)   the domestic commodity in each country is regular;

(ii)   the Hypothesis of Neutral Tastes holds;

(iii)   the Hicksian stability condition holds; specifically, the Jacobians of (152) and (153) satisfy $|\tilde{J}_1| < 0$ and $|\tilde{J}_2| < 0$, respectively.

Then:

(1)   If the paying country specializes in commodities 1 and 3 and the

receiving country produces all three commodities, (a) a *sufficient* condition for a deterioration in the paying country's terms of trade is that

$$\tilde{\beta}_{32}^2 > c_1{}^2\tilde{\beta}_{12}^2 + c_2{}^2\tilde{\beta}_{22}^2 \qquad \text{(i.e., } \tilde{\beta}_{31}^2 < c_1{}^2\tilde{\beta}_{11}^2 + c_2{}^2\tilde{\beta}_{21}^2\text{)} \qquad (156)$$

(where the $\tilde{\beta}_{ij}^k$ and $c_i{}^k$ are defined by (139) and (84) respectively); in particular, (156) will hold if

$$b_{32}^2/b_{31}^2 > b_{22}^2/b_{21}^2 > b_{12}^2/b_{11}^2, \qquad (157)$$

i.e., if the domestic industry in the receiving country uses factor 2 more intensively relatively to factor 1 than either of the international industries. And (b) a *necessary* condition for an improvement in the paying country's terms of trade is that

$$\tilde{\beta}_{32}^2 < c_1{}^2\tilde{\beta}_{12}^2 + c_2{}^2\tilde{\beta}_{22}^2 \qquad \text{(i.e., } \tilde{\beta}_{31}^2 > c_1{}^2\tilde{\beta}_{11}^2 + c_2{}^2\tilde{\beta}_{21}^2\text{)}. \qquad (158)$$

(2)   If the receiving country specializes in commodities 2 and 3 and the paying country produces all three commodities, (a) a *sufficient* condition for a deterioration in the paying country's terms of trade is that

$$\tilde{\beta}_{32}^1 < c_1{}^1\tilde{\beta}_{12}^1 + c_2{}^1\tilde{\beta}_{22}^1 \qquad \text{(i.e., } \tilde{\beta}_{31}^1 > c_1{}^1\tilde{\beta}_{11}^1 + c_2{}^1\tilde{\beta}_{21}^1\text{)}; \qquad (159)$$

in particular, (159) will hold if

$$b_{22}^1/b_{21}^1 > b_{12}^1/b_{11}^1 > b_{32}^1/b_{31}^1, \qquad (160)$$

i.e., if the domestic industry in the paying country uses factor 1 more intensively relatively to factor 2 than either of the international industries. And (b) a *necessary* condition for an improvement in the paying country's terms of trade is that

$$\tilde{\beta}_{32}^1 > c_1{}^1\tilde{\beta}_{12}^1 + c_2{}^1\tilde{\beta}_{22}^1 \qquad \text{(i.e., } \tilde{\beta}_{31}^1 < c_1{}^1\tilde{\beta}_{11}^1 + c_2{}^1\tilde{\beta}_{21}^1\text{)}. \qquad (161)$$

*Proof*   In case (1), from (ii) we may write (154) in the form

$$\frac{d\tilde{p}_2}{d\tau} = \frac{\beta_1(s_{33}^1 - t_{33}^1)}{|\tilde{J}_1|}\{\psi_2{}^2 + \varphi_2{}^1\}, \qquad (162)$$

where $\psi_i{}^k$ and $\varphi_i{}^k$ are defined by (142) and (123), respectively, and the functions are evaluated at equilibrium values of their arguments. From (i) and Lemma 1 we have $\varphi_2{}^1 \geqq 0$, hence from (iii) a sufficient condition $d\tilde{p}_2/d\tau > 0$ is $\psi_2{}^2 > 0$, which is equivalent to (156) in view of (143) and (i). Condition (157) is [from (138)] equivalent to $\beta_{32}^2 > \beta_{22}^2 > \beta_{12}^2$, which obviously implies (156) since the $c_i{}^2$ are $\geqq 0$ from (i). This proves (a). For $d\tilde{p}_2/d\tau < 0$ it is clearly necessary that $\psi_2{}^2 < -\varphi_2{}^1 \leqq 0$, and this gives (158) from (5.5.16) and (i), proving (b).

In case (2) we have similarly

$$\frac{d\tilde{p}_2}{d\tau} = -\frac{\beta_1(s_{33}^2 - t_{33}^2)}{|J_2|}\{\varphi_2{}^2 + \psi_2{}^1\}, \tag{163}$$

and $\varphi_2{}^2 \leqq 0$ from (i) and Lemma 1, so a sufficient condition for $d\tilde{p}_2/d\tau > 0$ is $\psi_2{}^1 < 0$, which, in view of (143) and (i), is the same as (159). The remainder of the proof proceeds as in case (1). Q.E.D.

It is worth observing that if condition (i) of Theorem 7 is strengthened to require that the domestic commodity in each country be a strong Hicksian substitute of both international commodities, i.e., $s_{i3}^k > 0$ for $i$, $k = 1$, 2, then the strict inequalities in (156) and (159) may be replaced by the corresponding weak inequalities. This has an interesting application: Suppose that utility functions in both countries are separable as between domestic and international commodities (see Section IV. C), so that (ii) implies that $c_i{}^1 = c_i{}^2$ for $i = 1$, 2; and suppose further that the production functions in the two countries are of identical Cobb–Douglas type (147), with $\beta_{ij}^1 = \beta_{ij}^2 = \beta_{ij}$, where the $\beta_{ij}$'s are constants. Then it follows from Theorem 7 that a sufficient condition for the paying country's terms of trade to deteriorate, given that one of the countries specializes and the other diversifies, is that

$$\beta_{32} = c_1\beta_{12} + c_2\beta_{22}. \tag{164}$$

This is a local condition. To obtain a global one, suppose further that utility functions are of Cobb–Douglas type (149) with $\theta_i{}^1 = \theta_i{}^2$ for $i = 1$, 2, 3; then (164) becomes a global condition, with $c_i = \theta_i/(\theta_1 + \theta_2)$. Under these same conditions, Theorem 6 guarantees [by condition (150)] that if both countries diversify, the terms of trade will remain unchanged. This brings out sharply the crucial importance of the assumption in Theorem 6 that both countries produce all three commodities; under the special conditions assumed in this paragraph, it is enough for either one of the countries (or of course both) to specialize in order that the "orthodox" presumption of a deterioration in the paying country's terms of trade should be valid. And (164) is a very neutral condition stating that the factor intensity of the domestic commodity should be a weighted average of the factor intensities of the two international commodities (factor intensities being expressed in terms of shares in outlays), the weights being the marginal subpropensities to consume the respective international commodities.

Under considerably more stringent conditions than those of Theorem 7, although not as stringent as those of the preceding paragraph, we may obtain a converse to conditions (157) and (160) of Theorem 7, as follows:

**Theorem 8**   Let the hypotheses of Theorem 7 hold, and assume furthermore that utility functions in the two countries are of identical Millian ("Cobb–Douglas") type (149). Then

(1)   If the paying country specializes in commodities 1 and 3 and the receiving country produces all three commodities, a sufficient condition for the paying country's terms of trade to improve is that

$$b_{22}^2/b_{21}^2 > b_{12}^2/b_{11}^2 > b_{32}^2/b_{31}^2. \tag{165}$$

(2)   If the receiving country specializes in commodities 2 and 3 and the paying country produces all three commodities, a sufficient condition for the paying country's terms of trade to improve is that

$$b_{32}^1/b_{31}^1 > b_{22}^1/b_{21}^1 > b_{12}^1/b_{11}^1. \tag{166}$$

*Proof*   If utility functions are as indicated, then $m_i^k = \theta_i/p_i$ for $i, k = 1, 2$. From (154) we then obtain

$$\frac{d\tilde{p}_2}{d\tau} = \frac{\beta_1(s_{33}^1 - t_{33}^1)}{|\tilde{J}_1|} \left\{ m_3^{\ 1} \frac{s_{23}^1}{s_{33}^1 - t_{33}^1} - m_3^{\ 2} \frac{\partial \tilde{Y}_2^2}{\partial y_3^2} \right\}, \tag{167}$$

all functions being evaluated at equilibrium values of their arguments. A sufficient condition for $d\tilde{p}_2/d\tau < 0$ is clearly $\partial \tilde{Y}_2^2/dy_3^2 > 0$, which is equivalent to (165) in view of (100b) and (90). This proves (1). Likewise, from (155') we obtain

$$\frac{d\tilde{p}_2}{d\tau} = \frac{\beta_1(s_{33}^2 - t_{33}^2)}{|\tilde{J}_2|} \frac{p_1}{p_2} \left\{ m_3^{\ 2} \frac{s_{13}^2}{s_{33}^2 - t_{33}^2} - m_3^{\ 1} \frac{\partial \tilde{Y}_1^1}{\partial y_3^1} \right\}, \tag{168}$$

and this time a sufficient condition for $d\tilde{p}_2/d\tau < 0$ is $\partial \tilde{Y}_1^1/\partial y_3^1 > 0$, which is equivalent to (166) in view of (100a) and (90), proving (2).   Q.E.D.

## G.   The Question of Probabilities

On the basis of the above results, it would not be difficult to carry out some formal calculations to show that, in a perfectly rigorous sense, the a priori probability that the paying country's terms of trade will deteriorate is greater than one half, so long as stability, regularity, and the Hypothesis of Neutral Taste hold.[37] The following sketch will suffice, based on the approach described in Chipman [11] in which a priori probability distributions are defined

---

[37] The qualification that the Hypothesis of Neutral Tastes holds is essential. If it does not hold, then by Jones's ingenious argument [32] it can be demonstrated in the case of pure exchange that the probability of an improvement in the paying country's terms of trade exceeds $\frac{1}{2}$. The outcome in the general case would then be unpredictable.

over the spaces of production functions, utility functions, and factor endowments. From the symmetry of the conditions of Theorem 6 we can conclude that when both countries diversify, the terms of trade of the paying country are just as likely to move in one direction as the other; hence the conditional probability of deterioration, given that both countries diversify, is $\frac{1}{2}$. From the fact that more stringent conditions are needed to obtain the conclusions of Theorem 8 than those of Theorem 7, and from the discussion following the latter, we can conclude that the conditional probability of deterioration exceeds $\frac{1}{2}$, given that one of the countries specializes and the other diversifies. From Theorem 4, the conditional probability is 1, given that both countries specialize. It follows at once that the unconditional probability that the paying country's terms of trade will deteriorate exceeds $\frac{1}{2}$.

## Appendix A. The Three-Factor Case

It will be evident from the analysis that follows that the question of whether a transfer will improve, leave unchanged, or worsen the paying country's terms of trade is a much more delicate one in the three-factor than in the two-factor case. I shall confine myself to the very special case in which both production functions and utility functions are of identical Cobb–Douglas type in the two countries; even then, only very limited results will be obtained. It will be assumed that both countries diversify, i.e., produce positive amounts of all three commodities.

In each country we have

$$y_i^k = \mu_i l_{i1}^{\beta_{i1}} l_{i2}^{\beta_{i2}} l_{i3}^{\beta_{i3}}, \qquad \sum_{i=1}^{3} l_{ij} = l_j^k \qquad (i, j = 1, 2, 3; \quad k = 1, 2), \quad \text{(A.1)}$$

where $\beta_{ij} > 0$ and $\sum_{j=1}^{3} \beta_{ij} = 1$. The corresponding minimum-unit-cost functions $g_i(w_1, w_2, w_3)$ are given by (49), where

$$v_i = \mu_i^{-1} \beta_{i1}^{-\beta_{i1}} \beta_{i2}^{-\beta_{i2}} \beta_{i3}^{-\beta_{i3}} \qquad (i = 1, 2, 3). \quad \text{(A.2)}$$

The following extremely stringent conditions will be imposed, to confer complete symmetry and at the same time satisfy the "total regularity" property of Section III.D:

$$\mu_1 = \mu_2, \qquad \beta_{11} = \beta_{22}, \qquad \beta_{21} = \beta_{12} \qquad \text{(A.3a)}$$

$$\beta_{13} = \beta_{23}, \qquad \beta_{31} = \beta_{32} \qquad \text{(A.3b)}$$

$$\beta_{32}/\beta_{33} \geq \beta_{12}/\beta_{13} \qquad \text{(A.3c)}$$

$$\beta_{jj} > \beta_{ij} \qquad \text{for} \quad i \neq j, \quad j = 1, 2, 3. \qquad \text{(A.3d)}$$

Condition (A.3d) implies (cf. Chipman [10]) that the matrix $B = [\beta_{ij}]$ has positive principal minors; hence the inverse matrix $B^{-1} = [\beta^{ij}]$ exists and from (A.2), (A.3), and (49) we readily verify that

$$v_1 = v_2, \qquad \alpha_1 = \alpha_2 \tag{A.4a}$$

$$\beta^{11} = \beta^{22} > \beta^{21} = \beta^{12} \geq 0 \tag{A.4b}$$

$$\beta^{13} = \beta^{23} < 0, \qquad \beta^{31} = \beta^{32} < 0. \tag{A.4c}$$

In particular, the Stolper–Samuelson matrix $B^{-1}$ is of block Leontief type (cf. Section III.D). As examples of matrices $B$ and their inverses $B^{-1}$ satisfying (A.3) and (A.4) we have

$$B = \begin{bmatrix} 0.5 & 0.1 & 0.4 \\ 0.1 & 0.5 & 0.4 \\ 0.2 & 0.2 & 0.6 \end{bmatrix}, \qquad B^{-1} = \begin{bmatrix} 2.75 & 0.25 & -2 \\ 0.25 & 2.75 & -2 \\ -1 & -1 & 3 \end{bmatrix} \tag{A.5a}$$

and

$$B = \begin{bmatrix} \frac{5}{8} & \frac{1}{8} & \frac{1}{4} \\ \frac{1}{8} & \frac{5}{8} & \frac{1}{4} \\ \frac{1}{4} & \frac{1}{4} & \frac{1}{2} \end{bmatrix}, \qquad B^{-1} = \begin{bmatrix} 2 & 0 & -1 \\ 0 & 2 & -1 \\ -1 & -1 & 3 \end{bmatrix}. \tag{A.5b}$$

Since the mappings (49) are of log-linear form, they are infinitely continuously differentiable; thus, for all prices such that country $k$ produces all three commodities, its efficient frontier is strongly concave to the origin.

The following extemely strong symmetry condition will be imposed on the factor endowments:

$$l_1^1 = l_2^2 > l_2^1 = l_1^2; \qquad l_3^1 = l_3^2. \tag{A.6}$$

Finally, we assume that utility functions in the two countries are of the identical Cobb–Douglas type

$$U^k(x_1, x_2, x_3) = x_1^{\theta_1} x_2^{\theta_2} x_3^{\theta_3} \qquad (\theta_i > 0, \quad \theta_1 + \theta_2 + \theta_3 = 1) \tag{A.7}$$

with the strong symmetry condition

$$\theta_1 = \theta_2 = \theta_3. \tag{A.8}$$

Under these conditions, we obtain the following result:

**Proposition** If the production functions (2) are of the form (A.1) and the utility functions (11) of the form (A.7), and if conditions (A.3), (A.6), and (A.8) hold, then starting from an initial equilibrium with $\tau = 0$, for sufficiently small $\tau > 0$ a transfer will worsen the paying country's terms of trade.

*Proof* We have for (14)

$$X_j^k(p^k, l^k, \tau) = \frac{\theta_j}{p_j^k} \left\{ \sum_{i=1}^3 l_i^k W_i(p^k, l^k) + (-1)^k(p_1\gamma_1 + p_2\gamma_2)\tau \right\} \quad \text{(A.9)}$$

where the functions $W_i$ are independent of $l^k$ for those prices $p^k$ for which all three commodities are produced, and are given by (49). Since $\Pi(p^k, l^k) = \sum_{i=1}^3 l_i^k W_i(p^k, l^k)$, we have from (20) and (49)

$$Y_j(p^k, l^k) = \sum_{i=1}^3 l_i^k \frac{\partial W_i(p^k, l^k)}{\partial p_j^k} = \frac{1}{p_j^k} \left\{ \sum_{i=1}^3 l_i^k \beta^{ij} W_i(p^k, l^k) \right\}, \quad \text{(A.10)}$$

whence the equilibrium conditions (38) become

$$\sum_{i=1}^3 (\theta_2 - \beta^{i2})\alpha_i p_1^{\beta^{i1}} p_2^{\beta^{i2}} [l_i^1 (p_3^1)^{\beta^{i3}} + l_i^2(p_3^2)^{\beta^{i3}}] = 0$$

$$\sum_{i=1}^3 (\theta_3 - \beta^{i3})l_i^1 \alpha_i p_1^{\beta^{i1}} p_2^{\beta^{i2}} (p_3^1)^{\beta^{i3}} - \theta_3(p_1\gamma_1 + p_2\gamma_2)\tau = 0 \quad \text{(A.11)}$$

$$\sum_{i=1}^3 (\theta_3 - \beta^{i3})l_i^2 \alpha_i p_1^{\beta^{i1}} p_2^{\beta^{i2}} (p_3^2)^{\beta^{i3}} + \theta_3(p_1\gamma_1 + p_2\gamma_2)\tau = 0.$$

Differentiating the last two functions of (A.11) with respect to $p_2$ and noting that $(\theta_3 - \beta^{i3})\beta^{i2} \geqq 0$ ($i = 1, 2, 3$) from (A.3), we see that

$$\partial Z_3^k(p^k, l^k, 0)/\partial p_2 \geqq 0$$

for $k = 1, 2$. Since $m_2^k = \theta_2/p_2$ for $k = 1, 2$, we see directly from (39) that $\partial Z_2^1/\partial p_2 + \partial Z_2^2/\partial p_2 < 0$. Thus, $J$ is a Metzler matrix at $\tau = 0$. It follows by a well-known result of Arrow *et al.* [2, p. 89, Lemma 4] that for $\tau = 0$ and $p_1$ fixed, (A.11) has a unique solution $p_2^* > 0$, $p_3^{1*} > 0$, $p_3^{2*} > 0$. We shall now show that this solution has the property $p_2^* = p_1$ and $p_3^{1*} = p_3^{2*}$. Because of the uniqueness, it will suffice to show that an equilibrium with this property exists. Indeed, we may verify directly that such a solution is

$$p_1 = p_2^* = 1; \quad p_3^{1*} = p_3^{2*} = \left[ \frac{\theta_3 - \beta^{13}}{\beta^{33} - \theta_3} \frac{\alpha_1(l_1^1 + l_2^1)}{\alpha_3 l_3^1} \right]^{1/(\beta^{33} - \beta^{13})}. \quad \text{(A.12)}$$

Now, since (A.7) implies that the Hypothesis of Neutral Tastes holds, the expression for the effect of a transfer on the terms of trade is given by, according to (44a),

$$\frac{d\tilde{p}_2}{d\tau} = \frac{\beta_1(\bar{s}_{33}^1 - t_{33}^1)(\bar{s}_{33}^2 - t_{33}^2)}{|J|} \{\varphi_2^2 - \varphi_2^1\}, \quad \text{(A.13)}$$

where $\varphi_2^k$ is defined by (123). We shall show that $\varphi_2^2 < 0$ and $\varphi_2^1 > 0$ at equilibrium with $\tau = 0$, i.e., in view of (125), that

$$\text{sign}(\bar{s}_{23}^k t_{33}^k - \bar{s}_{33}^k t_{23}^k) = -(-1)^k \quad (k = 1, 2) \quad \text{(A.14)}$$

for $\tau = 0$, $p_1 = p_2$, and $p_3^1 = p_3^2$. Since $J$ is symmetric and negative semi-definite at $\tau = 0$ (being the sum of two symmetric negative semidefinite matrices), the Hicks conditions hold; hence $|J| < 0$ at $\tau = 0$. The proposition will then follow from (A.14) and (A.13).

From (24), (27), and (48), we have in the present case

$$\bar{s}_{j3}^k(p^k, l^k, 0) = \frac{(\theta_j - \delta_{j3})\theta_3}{p_j p_3^{\ k}} \Phi^k(p^k, l^k, 0) \tag{A.15}$$

where $\Phi^k(p^k, l^k, 0) = \sum_{i=1}^3 l_i^k W_i(p^k, l^k)$, and

$$t_{j3}^k(p^k, l^k) = \frac{1}{p_j p_3^{\ k}} \sum_{i=1}^3 (\beta^{ij} - \delta_{ij})\beta^{i3} l_i^k W_i(p^k, l^k) \tag{A.16}$$

where $\delta_{ij}$ is the Kronecker delta. Thus we obtain[38]

$$\bar{s}_{23}^k t_{33}^k - \bar{s}_{33}^k t_{23}^k = \frac{\theta_3 \Phi^k}{p_2(p_3^{\ k})^3} \left\{ \sum_{i=1}^3 (\theta_1 \beta^{i2} - \theta_2 \beta^{i1})\beta^{i3} l_i^k W_i \right\}. \tag{A.17}$$

Applying (A.12), (A.4), (A.6), and (A.8), we obtain in equilibrium at $\tau = 0$

$$\bar{s}_{23}^k t_{33}^k - \bar{s}_{33}^k t_{23}^k = \tfrac{1}{3}(\beta^{12} - \beta^{11})\beta^{13}\alpha_1 p_3^{*\beta^{13}}(l_1^{\ k} - l_2^{\ k}), \tag{A.18}$$

which has the sign of $l_1^k - l_2^k$. In view of (A.6), this immediately implies (A.14).   Q.E.D.

## Appendix B. The Effect of a Transfer on the Relative Prices of the Two Domestic Commodities

The question was left open in Theorem 1, Section III.D, as to whether a transfer would raise the price of the domestic commodity in the receiving country relative to the price of the domestic commodity in the paying country. Since this price ratio may be identified in many contexts with the exchange rate between the two countries' currencies (the prices of the domestic commodities being supposed fixed in terms of the respective currencies), this question is of obvious interest. Sufficient conditions for this result will now be obtained; the problem will be formulated in terms of the pure exchange model, but can obviously be reformulated for the general case in terms of the trade utility functions of footnote 21.

---

[38] Equation (A.17) can be used to show why we cannot expect in the three-factor case to get a result corresponding to Theorem 5. For if (A.17) is to vanish identically in the $l_i^k$'s, the first two columns of $B^{-1}$ must be proportional to one another, which of course is impossible.

Commodity $i$ will be said to be (*weakly*) *relatively substitutable with commodity* $j$ *in relation to commodity* 3, in the tastes of the consumers of country $k$, if

$$\frac{\partial}{\partial x_j^{\ k}}\left(\frac{U_i^{\ k}}{U_3^{\ k}}\right) \leqq 0, \tag{B.1}$$

i.e., if an increase in the consumption of commodity $j$ lowers or leaves unchanged the marginal rate of substitution of commodity $i$ for commodity 3. This definition is similar to one of the definitions of substitutability given by Hicks [29, pp. 14, 20].

***Theorem 1'*** In the model of pure exchange, let the domestic commodities in the two countries be regular and let the stability condition (41) hold. Then a sufficient condition for a transfer to lower the price of the domestic commodity in the paying country relative to the price of the domestic commodity in the receiving country is that, in *both* countries, *either* (a) commodity 2 is weakly relatively substitutable with commodity 1 in relation to commodity 3 (the domestic commodity), *or* (b) commodity 1 is weakly relatively substitutable with commodity 2 in relation to commodity 3.

*Proof* From (45) and Jacobi's theorem it is clear that sufficient conditions for $p_3^{\ 1}$ to fall relatively to $p_2$, and for $p_3^{\ 2}$ to rise relatively to $p_2$, are given by

$$\begin{vmatrix} m_2^{\ k} & s_{21}^k \\ m_3^{\ k} & s_{31}^k \end{vmatrix} = \frac{\mu_k^{\ 2}}{\Delta_k}\begin{vmatrix} V_2^{\ k} & V_3^{\ k} \\ V_{12}^k & V_{13}^k \end{vmatrix} \leqq 0 \tag{B.2}$$

for $k = 1, 2$, respectively (where the suffix $k$ refers to country $k$). Since $\Delta_k < 0$ (by strong quasi concavity of $U^k$) and

$$\frac{\partial}{\partial x_j^{\ k}}\left(\frac{U_i^{\ k}}{U_3^{\ k}}\right) = -\frac{\begin{vmatrix} U_i^{\ k} & U_3^{\ k} \\ U_{ji}^k & U_{j3}^k \end{vmatrix}}{(U_3^{\ k})^2}, \tag{B.3}$$

it follows that (B.1) implies (B.2) for $i = 2$ and $j = 1$, proving (a). To prove (b) we note that by using the relations $\sum_{i=1}^{3} p_i^{\ k} m_i^{\ k} = 1$ and $\sum_{i=1}^{3} p_i^{\ k} s_{ij}^k = 0$, we can rewrite (44b) in the form

$$\frac{d\tilde{p}_3^{\ k}}{d\tau} = (-1)^k \frac{p_1}{p_2}\frac{\beta_1}{|J|}\left\{\bar{m}_3^{\ k}\begin{vmatrix} \hat{s}_{21}^i & \hat{s}_{23}^i \\ \hat{s}_{31}^i & \hat{s}_{33}^i \end{vmatrix} + \hat{s}_{32}^k\begin{vmatrix} \bar{m}_1^{\ i} & \hat{s}_{13}^i \\ \bar{m}_3^{\ i} & \hat{s}_{33}^i \end{vmatrix}\right.$$

$$\left. - \hat{s}_{33}^i\begin{vmatrix} \bar{m}_1^{\ k} & \hat{s}_{12}^k \\ \bar{m}_3^{\ k} & \hat{s}_{32}^k \end{vmatrix}\right\} \qquad (i \neq k = 1, 2). \tag{B.4}$$

Sufficient conditions for $p_3^1$ to fall (relative to $p_1$) and for $p_3^2$ to rise (relative to $p_1$) are then given by

$$\begin{vmatrix} m_1^k & s_{12}^k \\ m_3^k & s_{32}^k \end{vmatrix} = \frac{\mu_k^2}{\Delta_k} \begin{vmatrix} V_1^k & V_3^k \\ V_{21}^k & V_{23}^k \end{vmatrix} \leqq 0 \qquad (B.5)$$

for $k = 1$, 2, respectively. From (B.3) it follows that (B.1) implies (B.5) for $i = 1$ and $j = 2$, proving (b).   Q.E.D.

We may note that the hypotheses of Theorem 1' are satisfied in particular if the utility functions are additively separable, i.e., expressible in the form

$$U^k(x_1^k, x_2^k, x_3^k) = \Phi^k[\varphi_1(x_1^k) + \varphi_2(x_2^k) + \varphi_3(x_3^k)], \qquad (B.6)$$

giving rise to equality in (B.1).

### Appendix C. Classes of Utility Functions That Satisfy the Hypothesis of Neutral Tastes

To grasp the meaning of the necessary and sufficient condition (78) that the respective countries' utility functions must satisfy in order to conform to the Hypothesis of Neutral Tastes, it may be helpful to consider some examples. Unfortunately, it is not possible without imposing additional restrictions to obtain an explicit expression for the general solution of the partial differential equation (76) for $R^k$, and therefore it is not possible to find an explicit expression for the general solution of the partial differential equation (67) for $U^k$. However, there are two cases in which an explicit solution of (76) is possible, and the corresponding expressions are given respectively by (C.3) and (C.10); in these cases, explicit solutions of (67) can also be obtained, and these are given, respectively, by (C.6) and (C.16). Examples of such solutions are given, respectively, by (C.7) and (C.17).

We may consider the following two alternative properties of the function $\varphi$ of (76): (i) $\varphi(r)$ is a positive constant; (ii) $\varphi$ is one-to-one. Locally, it is evident that any continuous function $\varphi$ must fall into one of these two categories.

*Case* (i)   Let $\varphi(r) = c > 0$. Then from (76), $R^k$ satisfies the partial differential equation

$$\frac{\partial R^k}{\partial x_1} + c \frac{\partial R^k}{\partial x_2} + 0 \frac{\partial R^k}{\partial x_3} = 0, \qquad (C.1)$$

which is equivalent to the system of ordinary differential equations

$$\frac{dx_1}{1} = \frac{dx_2}{c} = \frac{dx_3}{0} \qquad (C.2)$$

(cf., e.g., Goursat [22, pp. 74–76]) whose general solution is

$$R^k(x_1, x_2, x_3) = G^k(x_2 - cx_1, x_3).$$ (C.3)

From (67) $U^k$ satisfies the partial differential equation

$$\frac{\partial U^k}{\partial x_1} - G^k(x_2 - cx_1, x_3)\frac{\partial U^k}{\partial x_2} + 0\frac{\partial U^k}{\partial x_3} = 0,$$ (C.4)

which is equivalent to

$$\frac{dx_1}{1} = \frac{dx_2}{-G^k(x_2 - cx_1, x_3)} = \frac{dx_3}{0},$$ (C.5)

which has the general solution

$$U^k(x_1, x_2, x_3) = F[x_1 + f^k(x_2 - cx_1), x_3],$$ (C.6)

where $f^k(y) = \int_0^y [c + G^k(\eta, x_3)]^{-1}\, d\eta$.

As an illustration, suppose $G^k$ has the special form $G^k(y, x_3) = \rho_k e^{\lambda_k y}$. Then

$$f^k(y) = \frac{1}{c\lambda_k}\left[\log\frac{e^{\lambda_k y}}{c + \rho_k e^{\lambda_k y}}\right],$$

and substituting $y = x_2 - cx_1$ we find that

$$x_1 + f^k(x_2 - cx_1) = -\frac{1}{c\lambda_k}\log\left[\frac{\rho_k e^{-c\lambda_k x_1} + ce^{-\lambda_k x_2}}{c + \rho_k}\right].$$

Choosing $F$ to be of the form

$$F(w, x_3) = -(c + \rho_k)e^{-c\lambda_k w} - \mu_k e^{-\nu_k x_3},$$

(C.6) becomes

$$U^k(x_1, x_2, x_3) = -\rho_k e^{-c\lambda_k x_1} - ce^{-\lambda_k x_2} - \mu_k e^{-\nu_k x_3},$$

which may be written in the more symmetric form

$$U^k(x_1, x_2, x_3) = -\alpha_1^k \exp(-\beta_1^k x_1) - \alpha_2^k \exp(-\beta_2^k x_2) - \alpha_3^k \exp(-\beta_3^k x_3)$$ (C.7)

where $\beta_1^k/\beta_2^k = c$ for $k = 1, 2$.

*Case* (*ii*)   In this case, explicit solutions are not in general possible. However, if we take the special case in which (78) has the form

$$E^k(x_1, x_3, r) = \varphi(r)(x_1 + \psi_1^k(x_3)) - \psi_2^k(x_3),$$ (C.8)

i.e., $\psi^k(x_3, r) = \varphi(r)\psi_1{}^k(x_3) - \psi_2{}^k(x_3)$, then we have

$$\frac{x_2 + \psi_2{}^k(x_3)}{x_1 + \psi_1{}^k(x_3)} = \varphi(r); \tag{C.9}$$

hence

$$R^k(x_1, x_2, x_3) = \varphi^{-1}\left(\frac{x_2 + \psi_2{}^k(x_3)}{x_1 + \psi_1{}^k(x_3)}\right). \tag{C.10}$$

Thus, $U^k$ must satisfy

$$\frac{\partial U^k}{\partial x_1} - \varphi^{-1}\left(\frac{x_2 + \psi_2{}^k(x_3)}{x_1 + \psi_1{}^k(x_3)}\right)\frac{\partial U^k}{\partial x_2} + 0\frac{\partial U^k}{\partial x_3} = 0, \tag{C.11}$$

which is equivalent to the system

$$\frac{dx_1}{1} = -\frac{dx_2}{\varphi^{-1}} = \frac{dx_3}{0}. \tag{C.12}$$

The first equation of (C.12) may be written

$$\frac{dx_2}{dx_1} = -\varphi^{-1}\left(\frac{x_2 + \psi_2{}^k(x_3)}{x_1 + \psi_1{}^k(x_3)}\right). \tag{C.13}$$

Introducing the transformation of variables $y_i = x_i + \psi_i{}^k(x_3)$, $i = 1, 2$, (C.13) becomes

$$\frac{dy_2}{dy_1} = -\varphi^{-1}\left(\frac{y_2}{y_1}\right), \tag{C.14}$$

which has the well-known solution (cf. Goursat [22, p. 8])

$$y_1 = C \exp\left\{-\int_a^{y_2/y_1} \frac{du}{\varphi^{-1}(u) + u}\right\} = Af(y_2/y_1). \tag{C.15}$$

Thus we can write the general solution of (C.11) in the form

$$U^k(x_1, x_2, x_3) = F\left[(x_1 + \psi_1{}^k(x_3))/f\left(\frac{x_2 + \psi_2{}^k(x_3)}{x_1 + \psi_1{}^k(x_3)}\right), x_3\right]. \tag{C16}$$

As an illustration, let $\varphi(r) = \alpha r$ $(\alpha > 0)$. Then we obtain $f(u) = u^{-\alpha/(1+\alpha)}$; hence if we set $\alpha = \theta_2/\theta_1$, we have

$$y_1/f(y_2/y_1) = y_1^{\theta_1/(\theta_1 + \theta_2)} y_2^{\theta_2/(\theta_1 + \theta_2)}.$$

Choosing $F$ to be of the form $F(w, x_3) = w^{\theta_1 + \theta_2}x_3^{\theta_3}$ $(\theta_3 > 0)$, we obtain

$$U^k(x_1, x_2, x_3) = [x_1 + \psi_1{}^k(x_3)]^{\theta_1}[x_2 + \psi_2{}^k(x_3)]^{\theta_2}x_3^{\theta_3}. \tag{C.17}$$

If $\theta_1 + \theta_2 + \theta_3 \leq 1$ and each $\psi_i^k$ is increasing and concave and satisfies $\psi_i^k(0) = 0$, then $U^k$ is increasing and concave. As observed in the text, in general $U^k$ is neither homogeneous nor separable as between its first two and its third arguments.

## ACKNOWLEDGMENTS

This paper was written while the author was a Fellow at the Center for Advanced Study in the Behavioral Sciences at Stanford. The support and facilities of the Center are gratefully acknowledged. I am indebted to Lionel W. McKenzie and Paul A. Samuelson for valuable comments on an earlier draft.

## REFERENCES

1. Aitken, A. C., *Determinants and Matrices*. Edinburgh: Oliver and Boyd, 1948.
2. Arrow, K. J., Block, H. D., and Hurwicz, L., "On the Stability of the Competitive Equilibrium, II," *Econometrica* **27** (January 1959), 82–109.
3. Bastable, C. F., "On Some Applications of the Theory of International Trade," *Quarterly Journal of Economics* **4** (October 1889), 1–17.
4. Bresciani-Turroni, C., *Inductive Verification of the Theory of International Payments*. Cairo: Publications of the Faculty of Law, No. 1, Egyptian University, undated (ca. 1930).
5. Cassel, G., "The Present Situation of the Foreign Exchanges," *Economic Journal* **26** (March, September 1916), 62–65, 319–323.
6. Cassel, G. "Abnormal Deviations in the International Exchanges," *Economic Journal* **28** (December 1918), 413–415.
7. Cassel, G., *The World's Monetary Problems: Two Memoranda*. London: Constable, 1921.
8. Cassel, G., "The International Movements of Capital," in G. Cassel et al., *Foreign Investments*. pp. 1–93. Chicago: Univ. of Chicago Press, 1928.
9. Chipman, J. S., "A Survey of the Theory of International Trade: Part 3, The Modern Theory," *Econometrica* **34** (January 1966), 18–76.
10. Chipman, J. S., "Factor Price Equalization and the Stolper-Samuelson Theorem," *International Economic Review* **10** (October 1969), 399–406.
11. Chipman, J. S., "International Trade with Factor Mobility: A Substitution Theorem," in *Trade, Balance of Payments, and Growth: Papers in International Economics in Honor of Charles P. Kindleberger* (J. N. Bhagwati, R. W. Jones, R. A. Mundell, and J. Vanek, eds.), pp. 201–237. Amsterdam: North-Holland Publ., 1971.
12. Chipman, J. S., "The Theory of Exploitative Trade and Investment Policies: A Reformulation and Synthesis," in *International Economics and Development: Essays in Honor of Raúl Prebisch* (L. E. Di Marco, ed.), pp. 209–244. New York: Academic Press, 1972.
13. Chipman, J. S., "Homothetic Preferences and Aggregation," *Journal of Economic Theory* (to be published).
14. Chipman, J. S., and Moore, J. C., "Social Utility and the Gains from Trade," *Journal of International Economics* **2** (May 1972), 157–172.
15. Debreu, G., "Smooth Preferences," *Econometrica* **40** (July 1972), 603–615.
16. Elliott, G. A., "Transfer of Means-of-Payment and the Terms of International Trade," *Canadian Journal of Economics and Political Science* **2** (November 1936), 481–492.

17. Ellis, H. S., and Metzler, L. A., "Introduction," in *Readings in the Theory of International Trade* (H. S. Ellis and L. A. Metzler eds.), pp. v–xiv. Philadelphia: Blakiston, 1950.
18. Fenchel, W., *Convex Cones, Sets, and Functions* (mimeographed). Princeton, New Jersey: Princeton Univ., Department of Mathematics, Logistics Research Project, September 1953.
19. Gale, D., and Nikaido, H., "The Jacobian Matrix and Global Univalence of Mappings," *Mathematische Annalen* **159** (1965), 81–93.
20. Gorman, W. M., "Community Preference Fields," *Econometrica* **21** (January 1953), 63–80.
21. Gorman, W. M., "Separable Utility and Aggregation," *Econometrica* **27** (July 1959), 469–481.
22. Goursat, E., *A Course in Mathematical Analysis*, Volume II, Part Two: *Differential Equations*. New York: Dover, 1959.
23. Graham, F. D., "International Trade under Depreciated Paper. The United States, 1862–79," *Quarterly Journal of Economics* **36** (February 1922), 220–273.
24. Graham, F. D., "Germany's Capacity to Pay and the Reparation Plan," *American Economic Review* **25** (June 1925), 209–227.
25. Graham, F. D., *The Theory of International Values*. Princeton, New Jersey: Princeton Univ. Press, 1948.
26. Graham, F. D., "The Cause and Cure of 'Dollar Shortage,'" *Essays in International Finance*, No. 10. Princeton, New Jersey: Princeton Univ., International Finance Section, January 1949.
27. Haberler, G., *The Theory of International Trade, with its Applications to Commercial Policy*. New York: Macmillan, 1936.
28. Haberler, G., "Some Problems in the Pure Theory of International Trade," *Economic Journal* **60** (June 1950), 223–240.
29. Hicks, J. R., *Value and Capital*. London and New York: Oxford Univ. (Clarendon) Press, 1939.
30. Houthakker, H. S., "Exchange Rate Adjustment," in *Factors Affecting the United States Balance of Payments*. Compilation of Studies prepared for the Subcommittee on International Exchange and Payments of the Joint Economic Committee, Congress of the United States, pp. 287–304. Washington, D.C.: U.S. Government Printing Office, 1962.
31. Iversen, C., *Aspects of the Theory of International Capital Movements*. Copenhagen: Levin & Munksgaard, 1936.
32. Jones, R. W., "The Transfer Problem Revisited," *Economica*, N.S. **37** (May 1970), 178–184.
33. Katzner, D. W., *Static Demand Theory*. New York: Macmillan, 1970.
34. Keynes, J. M., "The German Transfer Problem," *Economic Journal* **30** (March 1929), 1–7; "The Reparations Problem: A Discussion. II. A Rejoinder," *ibid.* **39** (June 1929), 179–182; "Mr. Keynes' Views on the Transfer Problem. III. A Reply," *ibid.* **39** (September 1929), 404–408.
35. Keynes, J. M., *A Treatise on Money*, in two volumes. New York: Harcourt, 1930.
36. Khang, C., "The Strict Convexity of the Transformation Surface in Case of Linear Homogeneous Production Functions: A General Case," *Econometrica* **39** (September 1971), 857–859.
37. Komiya, R., "Non-Traded Goods and the Pure Theory of International Trade," *International Economic Review* **8** (June 1967), 132–152.
38. Leontief, W., "A Note on the Interrelation of Subsets of Independent Variables of a Continuous Function with Continuous First Derivatives," *Bulletin of the American Mathematical Society* **53** (April 1947), 343–350.

39. McDougall, I. A., "Non-Traded Goods and the Transfer Problem," *Review of Economic Studies* **32** (January 1965), 67–84.
40. McFadden, D., "On Hicksian Stability," in *Value, Capital and Growth, Papers in honour of Sir John Hicks* (J. N. Wolfe, ed.), pp. 329–351, Edinburgh: Edinburgh Univ. Press, 1968.
41. Meade, J. E., *A Geometry of International Trade*. London: Allen and Unwin, 1952.
42. Metzler, L. A., "The Transfer Problem Reconsidered," *Journal of Political Economy* **50** (June 1942), 397–414.
43. Metzler, L. A., "Stability of Multiple Markets: The Hicks Conditions," *Econometrica* **13** (October 1945), 277–292.
44. Metzler, L. A., "Exchange Rates and the International Monetary Fund," in L. A. Metzler, R. Triffin, and G. Haberler, *International Monetary Policies*, pp. 1–45. Washington, D.C.: Board of Governors of the Federal Reserve System, Postwar Economic Studies, No. 7, September 1947.
45. Metzler, L. A., "A Multiple-Country Theory of Income Transfers," *Journal of Political Economy* **59** (February 1951), 14–29.
46. Mill, J. S., *Essays on Some Unsettled Questions of Political Economy*. London: Parker, 1844.
47. Mill, J. S., *Principles of Political Economy*, in two volumes. London: Parker, 1848.
48. Mosak, J. L., *General Equilibrium Theory in International Trade*. Bloomington, Indiana: The Principia Press, 1944.
49. Mundell, R. A., "The Pure Theory of International Trade," *American Economic Review* **50** (March 1960), 67–110.
50. Ohlin, B., "The Reparations Problem," *Index (Svenska Handelsbanken, Stockholm)*, No. 28 (April 1928), 2–33.
51. Ohlin, B., "The Reparations Problem: A Discussion. I. Transfer Difficulties, Real and Imagined," *Economic Journal* **39** (June 1929), 172–178; "Mr. Keynes' Views on the Transfer Problem. II. A Rejoinder," *ibid.* **39** (September 1929), 400–404.
52. Ohlin, B., *Interregional and International Trade*. Cambridge, Massachusetts: Harvard Univ. Press, 1933.
53. Pearce, I. F., "The Problem of the Balance of Payments," *International Economic Review* **2** (January 1961), 1–28.
54. Pearce, I. F., *International Trade*. New York: Norton, 1970.
55. Pigou, A. C., "The Effect of Reparations on the Real Ratio of International Interchange," *Economic Journal* **42** (December 1932), 532–543.
56. Robinson, J., "Beggar-my-Neighbour Remedies for Unemployment," in J. Robinson, *Essays in the Theory of Employment*, 2nd ed., pp. 156–170. Oxford: Basil Blackwell, 1947.
57. Rostow, W. W., "The Terms of Trade in Theory and Practice," *Economic History Review* **3** (No. 1, 1950), 1–20; **4** (No. 1, 1951), 53–76. Reprinted with minor modifications in W. W. Rostow, *The Process of Economic Growth*, pp. 167–217. New York: Norton, 1952.
58. Rueff, J., "Mr. Keynes' Views on the Transfer Problem. I. A Criticism," *Economic Journal* **39** (September 1929), 388–399.
59. Samuelson, P. A., *Foundations of Economic Analysis*. Cambridge, Massachusetts: Harvard Univ. Press, 1947.
60. Samuelson, P. A., "The Transfer Problem and Transport Costs: The Terms of Trade When Impediments Are Absent," *Economic Journal* **62** (June 1952), 278–304.
61. Samuelson, P. A., "The Transfer Problem and Transport Costs, II: Analysis of Effects of Trade Impediments," *Economic Journal* **64** (June 1954), 264–289.

62. Samuelson, P. A., "Social Indifference Curves," *Quarterly Journal of Economics* **70** (February 1956), 1–22.
63. Samuelson, P. A., "On the Trail of Conventional Beliefs about the Transfer Problem," in *Trade, Balance of Payments, and Growth: Papers in International Economics in Honor of Charles P. Kindleberger* (J. N. Bhagwati, R. W. Jones, R. A. Mundell, and J. Vanek, eds.), pp. 327–351. Amsterdam: North-Holland Publ., 1971.
64. Strotz, R. H., "The Empirical Implications of a Utility Tree," *Econometrica* **25** (April 1957), 269–280.
65. Taussig, F. W., "Wages and Prices in Relation to International Trade," *Quarterly Journal of Economics* **20** (August 1906), 497–522.
66. Taussig, F. W., "International Trade under Depreciated Paper: A Contribution to Theory," *Quarterly Journal of Economics* **31** (May 1917), 380–403.
67. Taussig, F. W., *International Trade*. New York: Macmillan, 1927.
68. Tobin, J., and H. S. Houthakker, "The Effects of Rationing on Demand Elasticities," *Review of Economic Studies* **18** (No. 3, 1950–1951), 140–153.
69. Torrens, R., *A Comparative Estimate of the Effects which a Continuance and a Removal of the Restriction upon Cash Payments are Respectively Calculated to Produce: with Strictures on Mr. Ricardo's Proposal for Obtaining a Secure and Economical Currency*. London: Printed for R. Hunter, Successor to Mr. Johnson, 1819.
70. Viner, J., *Canada's Balance of International Indebtedness, 1900–1913*. Cambridge, Massachusetts: Harvard Univ. Press, 1924.
71. Viner, J., *Studies in the Theory of International Trade*. New York: Harper, 1937.
72. Wicksell, K., "International Freights and Prices," *Quarterly Journal of Economics* **32** (February 1918), 404–410.
73. Wilson, R., *Capital Imports and the Terms of Trade*. Melbourne: Melbourne Univ. Press, in association with Macmillan, 1931.

NOTE ADDED IN PROOF. In his contribution to this volume K. J. Arrow remarks, with respect to Metzler's theorem that the Hicks conditions are necessary for stability to hold independently of speeds of adjustment, that Metzler's proof actually established only weak rather than strict inequalities in the signs of the principal minors of the Jacobian matrix, e.g., of (39) above. Nevertheless, the condition (41) still follows from the assumption made in Section II.A that the solution to (38) is isolated. Furthermore, it may be conjectured that Metzler's proposition can be shown to be true by use of Arrow's methods in conjunction with earlier results of M. Fiedler and V. Pták, "On Matrices with Non-Positive Off-Diagonal Elements and Positive Principal Minors," *Czechoslovak Mathematical Journal* **12** (1962), 382–400, Theorem 3.3, p. 385; or at least that it is true for "almost all economies."

# THE WELFARE ECONOMICS OF REVERSED INTERNATIONAL TRANSFERS

*Harry G. Johnson**

*University of Chicago*
  *and*
*The London School of Economics*

## Introduction

Among Metzler's many important contributions to the development of contemporary economic theory, three have been particularly important to the development of my own understanding of and work on international trade theory. These were his work on the transfer problem in a Keynesian setting, on which we spent a number of sessions of William C. Hood's graduate international trade seminar at the University of Toronto in 1946–1947 [1]; his work in extending the Stolper–Samuelson analysis of the effects of protection on the distribution of income, to take account of changes in the terms of trade, which Gottfried Haberler previewed for us in his graduate course at Harvard in 1948 [2]; and his joint article with Laursen on the effects of

* Visiting Irving Fisher Professor of Economics, Yale University, Fall 1972 and Winter 1973.

floating exchange rates on domestic employment [3], which I read in my early days as a Lecturer at Cambridge and which helped to shape my critical review of Meade's first volume on the theory of international economic policy, on the balance of payments [4]. All three were concerned in a broad sense, not all that obvious at the time, with the economics of international transfers.[1]

The standard transfer problem is concerned with a continuing transfer from one country to another, such that the transfer has to be effected by the development of a current account (basically, merchandise trade) surplus by the country making the transfer, and specifically with the question of whether the generation of the trade surplus requires a worsening or involves an improvement in the terms of trade of the country making the transfer. In the former case there is said to be a "secondary burden" of the transfer—and the famous Keynes–Ohlin controversy over German reparations after World War I was essentially concerned with whether the secondary burden might be so large as to make the transfer itself economically impossible [5]. In the latter case, there is a "secondary gain" which reduces the burden of the transfer; this secondary gain cannot, however, be great enough for the transferring country to gain a net benefit from the transfer, assuming the initial equilibrium to be unique.[2] As Samuelson has pointed out [6], however,

---

[1] This is obvious in the case of Metzler's article on the transfer problem. The Metzler exception to the standard case of a tariff improving a country's terms of trade but raising the domestic relative price of importable goods—an improvement in the terms of trade great enough to reduce the relative domestic price of importables and hence give "anti-protection" to the industry apparently favored by the tariff—rests on a "transfer" or "income-redistribution" effect such that, at a constant domestic relative price ratio between exportables and importables, the income gain for the tariff-imposing country leads to a smaller increase in that country's demand for imports than the increase in the supply of imports resulting on net from the positive income effect and negative substitution effect on that supply due to the income loss and worsened terms of trade imposed on the foreign country by the imposition of the tariff. (Necessary conditions are, first, an inelastic foreign demand for the tariff-imposing country's exports, second, a relatively higher marginal propensity of each country to consume its own exportable good as compared with the importable good, i.e., a marginal preference of each country for its own exportable good.) The Metzler–Laursen article introduces the effect on aggregate spending of the transfer implicit in the change in the terms of trade consequent on a change in foreign income combined with the preservation of international equilibrium by an exchange rate adjustment.

[2] The limiting case of a transfer that left the utility of the transferor unchanged is obviously impossible, since it would require two tangency points of the pretransfer domestic indifference curve with a foreign indifference curve within the Edgeworth–Bowley contract box, and hence violate the usual assumption of convexity of both sets of indifference curves toward the origin. Samuelson [6, p. 284, note 1] asserts but does not prove that a transfer

the question of secondary gain or loss is semantic or artificial, or else it involves "externalities" of a kind that one would expect governments engaged in negotiating reparations payments to take into account.[3] To be precise, one would expect that governments would be smart enough not to do their calculations at pretransfer price ratios, but instead to calculate the burdens and benefits of international transfers with due regard to the effects of the transfers on relative prices and hence on economic welfare. This argument, however, typically does not apply to international transfers (such as foreign private investment) effected by private choices made by atomistic competitors in competitive markets, whose choices may be assumed to treat prices, returns, etc., as determined parametrically. (An externality of this kind constitutes the essence of the optimum tariff argument, which has recently been extended to include the optimum tax on foreign investment and the optimum combination of taxes on international trade and taxes on international investment [7].)

While the standard problem of transfer theory is a "real" problem, involving the effects on relative prices and economic welfare of a continuing

---

[3] The analysis of the welfare effects of a reversed transfer to be presented shows that, contrary to Samuelson's (accurate) contention for the usual transfer problem, it does make a difference whether the transfer is specified in domestic or foreign goods. Samuelson of course recognized that it does make a difference to the real burden of a transfer on the transferor whether the amount of the transfer is specified (at pretransfer prices) in one good or the other.

---

that improves the welfare of the transferor requires conditions of multiple and unstable equilibrium. The point can be proved rigorously, though with considerable geometrical or algebraical labor. The essence of it is that even though a country might gain utility from a small outward transfer, it must lose utility from a large enough outward transfer; and correspondingly, even though it might lose utility from a small inward transfer, it must gain utility from a large enough inward transfer. Hence there must be three price ratios (at a minimum) representing three levels of utility, consistent with a zero transfer—the case of multiple equilibrium with the middle one unstable. Consider an Edgeworth–Bowley contract box, with the sides corresponding to the amounts of the two goods produced by the two (completely specialized) countries, and some initial no-transfer equilibrium price ratio. A movement toward more utility for country 1 may involve a change in the price ratio so favorable that country 1 makes a transfer to country 2, as compared with the initial no-transfer situation; but a large enough increase in country 1's utility must require receipt of a transfer from country 2, so that in between there must be a price ratio entailing no transfer; and correspondingly, for a movement toward less utility for country 1. The initial equilibrium price ratio must therefore be the middle, and unstable, equilibrium point without transfers for an outward transfer to produce a gain in utility for the country making it.

transfer from one country to another,[4, 5] there is no reason to confine real transfer theory to the standard case of a continuing transfer. (In fact, the assumption of permanence is primarily a device for clearing the possibility of effecting the transfer by transfers of international monetary assets out of the way of real equilibrium analysis.) An alternative interesting and practically relevant case is that of the reversed transfer; that is, a transfer made at a certain rate for a certain period from one country to another, followed by a transfer of the same amount in the reverse direction from the second country to the first, which leaves both countries eventually back where they started. The most obvious example in the contemporary world is development assistance loans. A less obvious but perhaps more practically important case is the financing of temporary balance-of-payments deficits and surpluses by the running down and subsequent running up of foreign exchange reserves.

The equivalence of the maintenance of disequilibrium exchange rates with reversed transfers was first noticed by Hause [11], who applied the analytics of welfare cost analysis to determining the welfare losses involved in maintaining disequilibrium exchange rates. Two subsequent papers of mine, based on Hause's work [12], attempted to improve on that work by introducing the primary impact effects of the transfer, operating through the marginal propensities to import, on demands for goods at the pretransfer terms of trade, with the predictable result that the welfare effects of a reversed transfer depend on the classical sum-of-marginal-propensities-to-import-minus-one

---

[4] Metzler's main contribution in this context was to show that a transfer will be "undereffected" at constant international prices, requiring some further adjustment to eliminate the residual deficit, if both countries are "stable in isolation," i.e., have positive marginal net propensities to save, and "overeffected" if one is "unstable in isolation," though his work is important also from the technical point of view in its explicit treatment of the dynamics of the system. Meade [8] arrived at the classical sum-of-marginal-propensities-to-import-minus-unity criterion for a transfer to be undereffected or overeffected in the Keynesian case; the difference in results was due to the fact that Meade assumed that expenditure in each country initially was changed by the amount of the transfer, whereas Metzler assumed that disposable income was so changed and hence that part of the transfer came from and went into savings in the two countries involved.

In my essay on "The Transfer Problem and Exchange Stability" [9], I expressed a criticism of Metzler's formulation of the problem. I should like to take this opportunity to retract that criticism, which rested on a confusion on my part between output and disposable income.

[5] The problem can be treated without difficulty as a "monetary" problem, i.e., the effects of a continuing transfer fixed in monetary terms, by making due allowance for the effects of the transfer of expenditure from one country to another in raising or lowering the world money price level according as the transferee or the transferor has the higher velocity of circulation. A rise in the world price level reduces the real value of a transfer fixed in monetary terms, by comparison with its initial real value, and so constitutes a "secondary gain" to the transferor, and vice versa. On this, see Viner [10].

criterion, which determines whether the terms of trade turn in favor of or against a country making a transfer, and hence whether a country making a reversed transfer first gains and then loses on its terms of trade or vice versa.

All these previous contributions, however, have employed the welfare-cost analysis technique of approximating the welfare effects of small changes about an initial equilibrium point rather than employing a full general equilibrium analysis including an explicit utility function. Accordingly, this chapter seeks to round out previous analysis by tackling the problem of reversed transfers with the use of Cobb–Douglas utility functions. Such functions have the restrictive disadvantage of entailing unitary price and income elasticities of demand; unfortunately, the more flexible CES function does not yield a manageable functional relation between the amount of the transfer and the terms of trade.

Before proceeding to the analysis, it is important to note certain difficulties in the analogy between reversed transfers and exchange rate stabilization. Essentially, exchange rate stabilization involves the holding of buffer stocks of international money, and the use of these stocks for stabilization may have inflationary or deflationary consequences for world prices which should be taken into account in the analysis, as should the monetary behavior that gives rise to the balance-of-payments disturbances that necessitated the exchange rate stabilization activity [13]. The transfers implicit in current account deficits and surpluses are the outcome of a general equilibrium process in a system incorporating money and monetary behavior. The analysis of reversed transfers presented here, on the other hand, pertains to a "real" model without money and takes the transfers as having been planned in amount and effected by reductions and increases in consumption relative to full employment productive capacity.

## I. The Cobb–Douglas Utility Function

Assume that the national social utility function is of the Cobb–Douglas form

$$U' = AX^{\alpha}Y^{1-\alpha}$$

where $X$ and $Y$ are quantities of two goods consumed (one of which will subsequently be assumed to be an export good, and the other an import good). Let $p$ be the price of $X$ in terms of $Y$.

Utility maximization under competition requires that

$$\frac{U_x'}{U_y'} = \frac{\alpha U'/X}{(1-\alpha)U'/Y} = \frac{\alpha}{1-\alpha}\frac{Y}{X} = p.$$

Hence

$$Y/X = [(1 - \alpha)/\alpha]p, \qquad Y/pX = (1 - \alpha)/\alpha,$$

and, letting $M \equiv Y + pX$ represent income,

$$Y/M = 1 - \alpha, \qquad pX/M = \alpha, \qquad \text{and} \qquad X/M = \alpha/p.$$

Hence, utility

$$U' = A(\alpha/p)^{\alpha}(1 - \alpha)^{1-\alpha}M.$$

For simplicity, and for the purpose of permitting comparison and summation of the effects of changes in the welfares of two countries engaged in international trade resulting from temporary transfers, it is convenient to measure utility in units such that the marginal utility of an increment of income, when the price of $X$ in terms of $Y$ is unity, is itself unity. By setting $A = (\alpha)^{-\alpha}(1 - \alpha)^{\alpha-1}$, $U'$ is transformed into

$$U = (1/p)^{\alpha}M.$$

Henceforth, subscripts 1 and 2 on $\alpha$, $M$, and $U$ denote the value of these two parameters and variables for the two countries.

It is assumed in what follows that country 1 produces only $Y$ and country 2 produces only $X$, each country producing a fixed amount of its national commodity $\overline{Y}$ and $\overline{X}$, respectively.

In order to have $p = 1$ in the absence of a transfer, we must have $\alpha_1 \overline{Y} = (1 - \alpha_2)\overline{X}$ or $\overline{X} = [\alpha_1/(1 - \alpha_2)]\overline{Y}$ (i.e., outputs and incomes in the absence of a transfer are such that trade balances at a unitary price). It is convenient to normalize by setting $\overline{Y}$ equal to unity, whence $\overline{X} = \alpha_1/(1 - \alpha_2)$. This permits the use of $t$ to symbolize the ratio of the transfer to country 1's productive capacity at the pretransfer price ratio.

The transfer, which is assumed to take place from country 1 to country 2 in the first period and to be reversed in the second period, can be specified in terms of either commodity $X$ or $Y$. This yields the following specification of the countries' incomes in the two periods.

*Case 1*   Transfer specified in terms of $Y$.

Period one:   country 1 income   $1 - t$

country 2 income   $p_1 \dfrac{\alpha_1}{1 - \alpha_2} + t.$

Period two:   country 1 income   $1 + t$

country 2 income   $p_2 \dfrac{\alpha_1}{1 - \alpha_2} - t.$

*Case 2*  Transfer specified in terms of $X$.

Period one:  country 1 income  $1 - p_1' t$

country 2 income  $p_1'\left(\dfrac{\alpha_1}{1 - \alpha_2} + t\right).$

Period two:  country 1 income  $1 + p_2' t$

country 2 income  $p_2'\left(\dfrac{\alpha_1}{1 - \alpha_2} - t\right).$

To determine $p$, the price of $X$ in terms of $Y$, we use the international equilibrium condition that the value of country 1's imports of $X$ in terms of $Y$, plus the transfer from country 1 to country 2, or minus the transfer from country 2 to country 1, be equal to the value of country 2's imports of $Y$.

*Case 1*

Period one:  $\alpha_1(1 - t) + t = (1 - \alpha_2)\left(p_1 \dfrac{\alpha_1}{1 - \alpha_2} + t\right).$

Period two:  $\alpha_1(1 + t) - t = (1 - \alpha_2)\left(p_2 \dfrac{\alpha_1}{1 - \alpha_2} - t\right).$

Thus

$$p_1 = 1 + \frac{\alpha_2 - \alpha_1}{\alpha_1} t, \qquad p_2 = 1 - \frac{\alpha_2 - \alpha_1}{\alpha_1} t.$$

*Case 2*

Period one:  $\alpha_1(1 - p_1' t) + p_1' t = (1 - \alpha_2)p_1'\left(\dfrac{\alpha_1}{1 - \alpha_2} + t\right).$

Period two:  $\alpha_2(1 + p_2' t) - p_2' t = (1 - \alpha_2)p_2'\left(\dfrac{\alpha_1}{1 - \alpha_2} - t\right).$

Thus

$$p_1' = \left(1 + \frac{\alpha_1 - \alpha_2}{\alpha_1} t\right)^{-1}, \qquad p_2' = \left(1 - \frac{\alpha_1 - \alpha_2}{\alpha_1} t\right)^{-1}.$$

Note that in both cases, the terms of trade turn against the transferor country if its (marginal and average) propensity to spend on its import good is less than the marginal propensity of the transferee country to spend on its export good (the same good), and vice versa. This is of course standard theory.

In the absence of the reversed transfer, the utility levels of the two countries are $U_{10} = 1$ and $U_{20} = \alpha_1/(1 - \alpha_2)$, respectively, in each period.

In the presence of the reversed transfer, for Case 1 (transfer specified in $Y$) the utility levels are, for the successive periods denoted by the second subscripts,

$$U_{11} = \left(1 + \frac{\alpha_2 - \alpha_1}{\alpha_1} t\right)^{-\alpha_1} (1 - t)$$

$$U_{21} = \left(1 + \frac{\alpha_2 - \alpha_1}{\alpha_1} t\right)^{-\alpha_2} \left(\frac{\alpha_1 + (1 - \alpha_1)t}{1 - \alpha_2}\right)$$

$$U_{12} = \left(1 - \frac{\alpha_2 - \alpha_1}{\alpha_1} t\right)^{-\alpha_1} (1 + t)$$

$$U_{22} = \left(1 - \frac{\alpha_2 - \alpha_1}{\alpha_1} t\right)^{-\alpha_2} \left(\frac{\alpha_1 - (1 - \alpha_1)t}{1 - \alpha_2}\right).$$

For Case 2 (transfer specified in $X$), they are

$$U_{11} = \left(1 + \frac{\alpha_1 - \alpha_2}{\alpha_1} t\right)^{\alpha_1 - 1} \left(1 - \frac{\alpha_2}{\alpha_1} t\right)$$

$$U_{21} = \left(1 + \frac{\alpha_1 - \alpha_2}{\alpha_1} t\right)^{\alpha_2 - 1} \left(\frac{\alpha_1}{1 - \alpha_2} + t\right)$$

$$U_{12} = \left(1 - \frac{\alpha_1 - \alpha_2}{\alpha_1} t\right)^{\alpha_1 - 1} \left(1 + \frac{\alpha_2}{\alpha_1} t\right)$$

$$U_{22} = \left(1 - \frac{\alpha_1 - \alpha_2}{\alpha_1} t\right)^{\alpha_2 - 1} \left(\frac{\alpha_1}{1 - \alpha_2} - t\right).$$

Note, in passing, the reversal of signs of the influence of $\alpha_2 - \alpha_1$ in the denominators of the utility expressions in the two cases, even though the influence of this term on the effect of a transfer on the terms of trade is identical. Also note with reference to the classical Keynes–Ohlin controversy over reparations, that if the transfer is specified in terms of domestic output, it can be increased to the extent of the transferor's total national output before the utility level of the transferor becomes zero, whereas if it is specified in terms of foreign goods the zero-utility limit of the transfer-to-output ratio is $t = \alpha_1/\alpha_2$, i.e., the ratio of the (marginal and average) propensity to spend on foreign goods of the transferor country to that of the transferee. Assuming a bias in each country toward consumption of its own domestic goods, this sets a limit to the transfer ratio which may be considerably less than unity. A fuller treatment of this particular problem would set a minimum (survival) level of utility in the reparations-paying country, and hence (on the same assumption of bias in import propensities) restrict the feasible transfer ratio still further. (Mathematically, one would solve for $t$ by setting $U_{11}$ in Case 2 equal to $U_{1S}$, the survival level of utility.)

We now turn to the effects of reversed transfers on the welfare of the individual countries concerned and the world system as a whole. In this context, note that we have simplified the problem of world welfare by assuming that the marginal utility of income is constant and the same for both countries in the no-transfer situation.[6] Clearly, a difference in the marginal utilities of income between countries, as judged according to some world social welfare function, would indicate the desirability of a permanent income transfer from one country to another; and the optimal level of this transfer would be limited to something short of the whole national income of one or the other country only if (as a necessary but not sufficient condition) the marginal world social utility of income for any country diminished as its income rose. The problem under consideration, however, is reversed transfers; and while differences in the world marginal social utility of individual countries' incomes and diminishing marginal world social utilities of those incomes could make a difference to the results, the problem is complex enough without the introduction of these complications. In any case, the qualitative nature of the effects of introducing these complications follows straightforwardly from the existing literature on utility maximization in the face of uncertainty. As Friedman and Savage [14], Tobin [15], and others have shown, any equal deviation of income to both sides of its average will reduce utility below the utility derived from the average received with certainty, if the marginal utility of income is diminishing. Hence, in the simplest case of identical marginal propensities of both countries to spend on each good (in which case the reversed transfer does not affect relative commodity prices), a reversed transfer must produce a welfare loss for both countries and hence for the world as a whole. In more complex cases involving a change in the terms of trade resultant on the transfer, the real income changes consequent on a reversed transfer are unequal in magnitude, so that this simple conclusion no longer holds. There is some sort of presumption that a reversed transfer may raise world welfare if it involves a net utility gain for the country to whose utility a higher world welfare function weight is attached, but this possibility remains to be explored in detail.

On the assumptions made, the utility of country 1 is changed as a result of a reversed transfer by

$$\Delta U_1 = U_{11} + U_{12} - 2U_{10},$$

---

[6] I am grateful to Rudiger Dornbusch and Michael Mussa for calling my attention to the implications of abandoning this assumption.

that of country 2 by

$$\Delta U_2 = U_{21} + U_{22} - 2U_{20},$$

and that of the world as a whole by

$$\Delta U_w = \Delta U_1 + \Delta U_2.$$

## II. Reversed Transfer, Case 1: Transfer Specified in Domestic Product

By using the Taylor expansion we obtain

$$U_{11} \approx (1 - t)[1 - (\alpha_2 - \alpha_1)t]$$

$$U_{12} \approx (1 + t)[1 + (\alpha_2 - \alpha_1)t]$$

$$U_{21} \approx \left(\frac{\alpha_1 + (1 - \alpha_1)t}{1 - \alpha_2}\right)\left(1 - \frac{\alpha_2}{\alpha_1}(\alpha_2 - \alpha_1)t\right)$$

$$U_{22} \approx \left(\frac{\alpha_1 - (1 - \alpha_1)t}{1 - \alpha_2}\right)\left(1 + \frac{\alpha_2}{\alpha_1}(\alpha_2 - \alpha_1)t\right)$$

$$\Delta U_1 \approx 2t^2(\alpha_2 - \alpha_1)$$

$$\Delta U_2 \approx -2t^2 \frac{\alpha_2(1 - \alpha_1)}{\alpha_1(1 - \alpha_2)}(\alpha_2 - \alpha_1)$$

$$\Delta U_w \approx \frac{-2t^2(\alpha_2 - \alpha_1)^2}{\alpha_1(1 - \alpha_2)}.$$

It follows that the world economy as a whole must lose from a reversed transfer. However, one of the countries involved will gain in welfare and the other lose, depending on the relative magnitudes of $\alpha_1$ and $\alpha_2$. Specifically, country 1 will gain if $\alpha_2 > \alpha_1$, and country 2 will gain if $\alpha_2 < \alpha_1$. The criterion $\alpha_2 - \alpha_1 \gtrless 0$ can be transformed into the more familiar transfer problem criterion $1 \gtrless \alpha_1 + (1 - \alpha_2)$, i.e., whether the sum of the marginal propensities to spend on imports of the two countries is less than or greater than unity. Country 1 gains and country 2 loses if the familiar "classical presumption" that the sum of the marginal propensities to spend on imports is less than unity holds true, and vice versa.

In order to understand these latter intuitively somewhat surprising results, it is useful to notice (a) that in the absence of price changes there would be no net effect on the welfare of either country or of the world as a whole of a reversed transfer; (b) that the Cobb–Douglas utility functions make the price changes a linear function of the amount of the transfer; and (c) that consequently, the welfare effects of a reversed transfer, by comparison with no transfer, can be analyzed in terms of the effects of equal changes of prices below and above the no-reversed-transfer equilibrium level, income being held constant.[7] As will be seen from the formula $U = (1/p)^{\alpha}M$, the utility level as a function of $p$ is a hyperbola; and since $p = 1 + [(\alpha_2 - \alpha_1)/\alpha_1]t$ where $t$ can now take either sign, $p$ increases or decreases with $t$ according to whether $\alpha_2 - \alpha_1$ is positive or negative. Hence the average utility received from a reversed transfer will be higher than the average utility received in the absence of a transfer if $\alpha_2 - \alpha_1 > 0$ and $p$ increases with $t$, and vice versa. An alternative way of understanding the same conclusion is to note that utility is the product of a linear function of $t$ and a hyperbolic function of $t$, and that the utility curve as a function of $t$ will accordingly be convex or concave to the horizontal axis depending on whether $\alpha_2$ is greater or less than $\alpha_1$. The two possibilities are illustrated graphically in Figs. 1a and 1b;

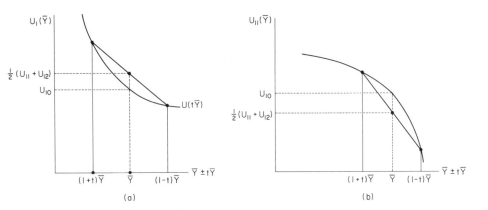

**Fig. 1.** (a) $\alpha_2 > \alpha_1$; (b) $\alpha_2 < \alpha_1$.

Fig. 1a represents the case $\alpha_2 > \alpha_1$ and Fig. 1b the opposite case. In each case $\frac{1}{2}(U_{11} + U_{12})$ is the average utility per period with the reversed transfer, and $U_{10}$ the average (constant) utility per period in the absence of the transfer. While Figs. 1a and 1b refer only to country 1 (the reversed-transfer-imposing country), the logic can easily be extended to country 2, as this requires only a reversal of the conditions required for each of the two curves.

[7] I am indebted to extensive comments by Rudiger Dornbusch and Michael Mussa for the following explanation, and also for the stimulus to develop the general geometrical explanation of the algebraic results to be presented. The explanation presented here has also, I hope, benefitted considerably in clarity through rewriting in response to referee's comments received from R. W. Jones.

For those who prefer a more explicitly mathematical proof, not relying on the Taylor expansion, differentiation of

$$U = \left(1 + \frac{\alpha_2 - \alpha_1}{\alpha_1} t\right)^{-\alpha_1} (1 - t)$$

yields

$$\frac{dU}{dt} = \frac{\alpha_2 - \alpha_1}{\alpha_1} \left(1 + \frac{\alpha_2 - \alpha_1}{\alpha_1} t\right)^{-\alpha_1 - 1} \left(\frac{\alpha_2}{\alpha_1} t (1 + \alpha_2 - \alpha_1)(1 - t)\right)$$

which must necessarily be negative. (This incidentally proves, for this specific case, that a country can never gain from a transfer to another country no matter how much the transfer turns the terms of trade in its favor, and conversely a country can never lose by receipt of a transfer from the other, no matter how much the transfer turns its terms of trade against it.)

Similarly,

$$\frac{d^2U}{dt^2} = \frac{\alpha_2 - \alpha_1}{\alpha_1} \left(1 + \frac{\alpha_2 - \alpha_1}{\alpha_1} t\right)^{-\alpha_1 - 2} [\alpha_2(1 + \alpha_1 + t(1 - \alpha_1))$$
$$+ \alpha_1(1 - \alpha_1)(1 - t)].$$

Since the expressions in parentheses and brackets must be positive, the sign of $d^2U/dt^2$ will be positive or negative according as $\alpha_2 \gtrless \alpha_1$. If $\alpha_2 > \alpha_1$, utility decreases at a decreasing rate as the outward transfer increases (increases at an increasing rate as the inward transfer increases) and vice versa. (These are the two cases depicted in Figs. 1a and 1b.)

### III. Reversed Transfer, Case 2: Transfer Specified in Foreign Product

Since the assumption of no discounting of second-period utility as compared with first-period utility permits the periods to be reversed and the transaction envisaged as a reversed transfer from country 2 to country 1 denominated in country 1's commodity, it follows immediately that a reversed transfer expressed in the foreign commodity must reduce world welfare, and reduce or increase the welfare of the country making the transfer according as an outward transfer turns the terms of trade against it or in its favor, i.e., according to whether the sum of the marginal propensities to spend on imports is less than or greater than unity. However, it seems worthwhile to work the case out explicitly.

Again using the Taylor expansion, or differentiating with respect to $t$ and setting $t = 0$ initially and $dt = t$, we obtain

$$\Delta U_1 \approx -2 \frac{1 - \alpha_1}{\alpha_1} \frac{\alpha_2}{\alpha_1} (\alpha_2 - \alpha_1)t^2$$

$$\Delta U_2 \approx +2 \frac{1 - \alpha_2}{\alpha_1} (\alpha_2 - \alpha_1)t^2$$

$$\Delta U_w \approx -2 \frac{1}{\alpha_1{}^2} (\alpha_2 - \alpha_1)^2 t^2.$$

Again, the world as a whole must lose from the reversed transfer, and one country gains and the other loses. The criterion for which country gains out of the world loss is the same as before, $\alpha_2 \gtrless \alpha_1$. But in this case country 1 loses if $\alpha_2 > \alpha_1$, i.e., the transfer to country 2 turns its terms of trade against it, and vice versa if $\alpha_2 < \alpha_1$ and a transfer turns the terms of trade in its favor.

The intuitive explanation of these results, which could be illustrated by diagrams similar to Figs. 1a and 1b, is that if $\alpha_2 > \alpha_1$, then country 1's utility curve as a function of $t$ will be concave to the horizontal axis, and hence the average utility enjoyed over the two periods of the reversed transfer will be less than it would be if no reversed transfer occurred; and conversely, if $\alpha_2 < \alpha_1$, then the utility curve as a function of $t$ will be convex to the horizontal axis and average utility will be greater with than without the reversed transfer. The same logic applies, as noted previously, to country 2.

## IV. Summary of Results

Assuming initially equal marginal utilities of income in the two countries involved, the world economy as a whole must lose from a reversed transfer. The country initiating the reversed transfer will gain *either if* the transfer is specified in terms of its domestic output *and* the traditional criterion for an outward transfer to turn its terms of trade against it holds (the sum of the marginal propensities to spend on imports is less than unity) *or if* the transfer is specified in terms of foreign output *and* the traditional criterion for an outward transfer to turn the terms of trade in its favor is fulfilled. Thus the operation of the traditional criterion for a transfer to be over-effected or undereffected at constant terms of trade has to be used in conjunction with the specification of the national output in which the transfer is denominated in order to determine the effects of a reversed transfer on the welfare levels of the two countries.[8]

The finding that a reversed transfer must reduce world welfare is congruent with the findings of earlier work by others that destabilizing speculation must lead to a welfare loss for the community as a whole, and more recent work showing that uncertainty of prices will have the same effect. The rather more puzzling finding that there is a welfare gain for one country and a loss for the other, whose statement can be boiled down to the proposition that a country gains from a reversed transfer if the outward transfer reduces and the inward transfer increases the price of the good in terms of which the transfer is denominated, and vice versa, can be understood heuristically in terms of the presumption that, if one gives and receives back a gift, one will gain if what one receives is more valuable than what one gives, and lose in the opposite eventuality.

## V. Time Preference and Reversed Transfers

Since the foregoing results rest on the assumption that each country's and the world's utility in the two periods is additive without discounting, it makes no difference whether country 1 is assumed (as in the analysis) to make the transfer to the other country in the first period and reverse it in the second, or vice versa. In either case, the world as a whole loses from a reversed transfer, while one country gains and the other loses. If, however, as is customary, it is assumed that countries have a rate of time preference between present and future income, these simple conclusions have to be modified.

If the transfer is made by country 1 in period 1 and reversed in period 2, country 1 is a lender in period one and a borrower (debt reclaimer) in period two, and vice versa for country 2. If country 1 is a net loser of utility measured additively without discounting, it must have a negative rate of time preference (a preference for future over present consumption) to be better off as a result; conversely, country 2 must have a positive rate of time preference not to be better off as a result. If instead the transfer is made by country 2 to country 1 in period 1 and reversed in period 2, country 1 is a borrower in period 1 and a lender (debt repayer) in period 2. If it is a net loser of utility measured additively without discounting, it must have a positive rate of time preference to be as well off as it would have been in the absence of the reversed transfer. Conversely, if it is a net gainer of utility so measured (which

---

[8] In the two papers cited in reference [12], I assumed without question that the transfer had to be specified in terms of the foreign commodity. This is obviously not necessarily true, and the present analysis makes good the error of a priori judgment.

implies that country 2 must be a net loser), country 2 must have a negative rate of time preference to be as well off in the presence as in the absence of the reversed transfer. From the point of view of world welfare, a reversed transfer can only constitute an improvement (instead of a loss as measured by the total utility of the two countries evaluated without discounting) if the rate of time preference of the country receiving the transfer in the first period is higher than that of the country making the transfer in that period.

By way of illustration for Case 1, with an initial transfer from country 1 to country 2, the rate of time preference $r_1$ in country 1 that would make $U_{11} + [U_{12}/(1 + r_1)] = U_{10} + [U_{10}/(1 + r_1)]$ is

$$r_1 = \frac{U_{12} - U_{10}}{U_{10} - U_{11}} - 1 \approx \frac{2t(\alpha_2 - \alpha_1)}{1 + (\alpha_2 - \alpha_1)(1 - t)},$$

and for the same case, the rate of time preference $r_2$ in country 2 that would make $U_{21} + [U_{22}/(1 + r_2)] = U_{20} + [U_{20}/(1 + r_2)]$ is

$$r_2 = \frac{U_{20} - U_{22}}{U_{21} - U_{20}} - 1 \approx \frac{2t(\alpha_2 - \alpha_1)}{(\alpha_1/\alpha_2) - (\alpha_2 - \alpha_1)[t + \alpha_1/(1 - \alpha_1)]},$$

where the denominator must be positive by the nature of the problem. For $\alpha_2 > \alpha_1$, the traditional case, both $r_1$ and $r_2$ must be positive for each country to be exactly as well off with the reversed transfer as without it, and vice versa for $\alpha_2 < \alpha_1$. It is easily shown that

$$r_1 - r_2 = - \frac{2t(\alpha_2 - \alpha_1)^2(1 + \alpha_2 - \alpha_1)}{\alpha_2(1 - \alpha_1)[1 + (\alpha_2 - \alpha_1)(1 - t)]} \times [(\alpha_1/a_2) - (\alpha_2 - \alpha_1)(t + \alpha_1/(1 - \alpha_1))]$$

which must be negative; that is, for each country to be exactly as well off in the presence as in the absence of reversed transfers, the algebraic value of the rate of time preference of the country initiating the transfer must be greater than that of the other country. This is, of course, a consequence of the fact that the world economy as a whole must use undiscounted utility from the reversed transfer. We know from the preceding analysis that

$$U_{11} + U_{21} < U_{10} + U_{20}, \qquad U_{12} + U_{22} < U_{10} + U_{20}$$

(that is, given initial equalities of marginal social utilities of national incomes, any transfer must reduce world welfare). Assuming given (positive) rates of time preference in the two countries, in place of finding the rates that would leave each country indifferent between no transfer and a reversed transfer, the effect of a reversed transfer on world welfare is

$$\Delta U_w = U_{11} + U_{21} - U_{10} - U_{20} + \frac{U_{12} - U_{10}}{1 + r_1} - \frac{U_{20} - U_{22}}{1 + r_2}$$

$$= (U_{11} + U_{21} - U_{10} - U_{20}) + \frac{U_{12} + U_{22} - U_{10} - U_{20}}{(1 + r_1)(1 + r_2)}$$

$$+ \frac{r_2(U_{12} - U_{10}) - r_1(U_{20} - U_{22})}{(1 + r_1)(1 + r_2)}.$$

The first two terms must be negative; and since $U_{20} - U_{22}$ must be greater than $U_{12} - U_{10}$, the necessary but not sufficient condition for world welfare to be increased by the reversed transfer is $r_1 < r_2$; i.e., the country initiating the reversed transfer must have a lower rate of time preference than the other country.

## VI. A Geometrical Explanation and Extension of the Results

The results just presented derive from two strong properties of the Cobb–Douglas utility functions assumed: the linear homogeneity of utility in terms of the two commodities, and the fact that the relative price of the commodity in terms of which the transfer is specified, in terms of the other commodity, is a linear function of the amount of the transfer, which is equal in the two directions of transfer and reversal of transfer, so that the price changes are equal and opposite. This means, heuristically, that the country initiating the reversed transfer must gain utility from the reversed transfer if the reversed transfer first lowers and then raises the price of the commodity in terms of which the transfer is expressed—because the loss from a lower price applies to a smaller income base than the gain from a higher price.

This simple explanation of the results is illustrated in Figs. 2a and 2b, where the reversed transfer is assumed to be specified alternatively in country 1's product (the transfer fraction being $t$) and in country 2's product (the transfer fraction again being $t$)[9] and conditions are assumed to be such that the price ratio turns first against and then in favor of the commodity in terms of which the transfer is fixed ($Y$ in Fig. 1a, $X$ in Fig. 1b). The $OC$ in

---

[9] This represents a departure from the mathematics of the Cobb–Douglas case presented in previous sections, in which the transfer is specified in terms of the fraction of domestic output of the reversed-transfer-initiating country it represents. It should be easily appreciated, however, that since there is assumed to be zero discounting of utility, so that utility in each period counts the same, a reversed transfer expressed in foreign output is simply the negative of a reversed transfer by the foreign country expressed in its own output.

each case is country 1's income-expansion line for consumption of the two goods at the no-transfer price ratio (standardized at unity by the 45° slope of the budget lines). If the reversed transfer had no effect on the terms of trade $(\alpha_2 = \alpha_1), P_{+t} - P_0 = P_0 - P_{-t}$ and the transfer would have no effect on country 1's total utility over the two periods. (Note the dependence of the result on the assumption of constant returns to scale in utility; with diminishing marginal utility of income there would be a welfare loss.) If the transfer and its reversal first turn the terms of trade against the commodity in terms of which the transfer is denominated, and then in favor of that commodity, and by the same amount, country 1's budget lines with the transfer and after the transfer has been reversed are respectively $\overline{Y}(1 - t)$, $X'_{-t}$ and $\overline{Y}(1 + t)$, $X'_{+t}$ in Fig. 2a, and $\overline{X}(1 - t)$, $Y'_{-t}$ and $\overline{X}(1 + t)$, $Y'_{+t}$ in Fig. 2b, where the

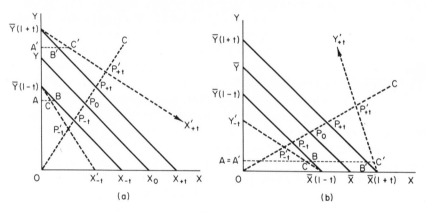

**Fig. 2**

second coordinate in each of the four cases represents purchasing power over the other commodity than the one in which the transfer is specified. The slopes of the two budget lines in each case are related through the equality of the price changes in each direction from the no-transfer budget line, $BC/AB = B'C'/A'B'$. The equilibrium consumption points for country 1 at the two post-transfer prices must lie on indifference curves that cut $OC$ to the right of the two points $P'_{-t}$ and $P'_{+t}$. It is obvious from the construction that $P_{-t} - P'_{-t}$ must be smaller than $P'_{+t} - P_{+t}$; hence the loss of utility from the initial transfer must be less than the gain of utility from the reversal of the transfer.

Since it may be assumed that the proportional price changes induced by the making and reversal of a transfer will be approximately equal for a wider variety of utility functions than the Cobb–Douglas, the analysis may be interpreted as holding as a more general proposition than has been presented here. However, the analysis still rests on the assumption of constant and equal marginal utility of income. If diminishing marginal utility of income is assumed, the condition that the terms of trade initially turn against, and then turn in favor, of the commodity in terms of which the reversed transfer is specified becomes a necessary but not a sufficient condition for the country making the reversed transfer to gain in terms of utility. In diagrammatic terms (see Figs. 2a and 2b), the fact that $P'_{+t} - P_{+t}$ is greater in distance than $P_{-t} - P'_{-t}$ does not necessarily mean that $U(P'_{+t}) - U(P_{+t})$ is greater than $U(P_{-t}) - U(P'_{-t})$. If the marginal social utilities of the nontransfer incomes differ, there is a case for a permanent transfer from one country to the other, its amount depending on the behavior of the marginal social utility of individual countries' incomes and being determined by equalization of those marginal social utilities.

It remains to be shown that, on the assumptions of equal and constant marginal utilities of income, there must be a world welfare loss from a reversed transfer. The proof follows obviously from the production side of the standard theory of the two-sector model of general equilibrium [16]. Interpret the fixed outputs of the two commodities $\overline{Y}$ and $\overline{X}$ as factor endowments, and the social utility functions of the two countries as (utility) production functions. Then, so long as the (linear homogeneous) production functions differ in factor intensity, the transformation frontier between the utilities of the two countries must be concave toward the origin (in the limiting case of identical preferences, the transformation frontier is a straight line). With a transformation curve concave to the origin, any reversed redistribution of income between the two countries, regardless of whether the utility gains and losses by comparison with the levels of utility prevailing in the absence of reversed income redistribution are equal for one country or not, must reduce the average level of utility enjoyed by the two countries together, on the assumption of equal and constant marginal utilities of income. This is illustrated in Fig. 3, where $P$ represents the no-transfer utility-level points and the slope of the 45° line tangent to the utility transformation curve at $P$ represents the assumption of equal social marginal utilities of income, $P_1$ and $P_2$ represent the first-period and second-period utility levels of the two countries, and $P$ (which could lie southeast or northwest of $P$) the average utilities of the two countries obtained by a reversed transfer. It is obvious that $\overline{P}$ must lie between the tangent to $P$ and the origin, i.e., total utility must be reduced. (To make this clearer, the tangent at $P$ could be interpreted as the world utility-maximizing member of a set of budget lines with a 45° slope representing the equality of the world marginal utilities of the two countries' incomes.) The construction also proves that if some other point on the world-utility-transformation curve is deemed socially superior to $P$, it can never be achieved by a reversed transfer; the only way to achieve it is by a permanent redistribution of income, via a continuing transfer, from one country to the other. Finally, if permanent income redistributions via continuing transfers are ruled out, but $P$ is deemed to be a suboptimization point from the viewpoint of world welfare (i.e., a contour of the Bergsonian world welfare function is not tangent to the utility transformation curve at $P$ but intersects it from above or below) and if $\bar{P}$ lies correspondingly either northwest or southeast of $P$, the point $\bar{P}$, even though it lies inside the utility transformation curve, may represent a higher level of world welfare than the point $P$. This possibility is illustrated in Fig. 3 by points $P_1'$, $P_2'$, and $\bar{P}'$

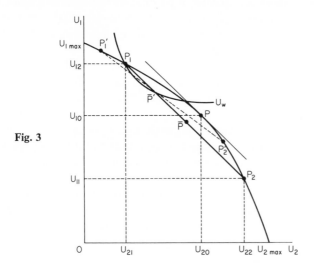

**Fig. 3**

representing the utility-redistribution effects of a reversed transfer, and the world social indifference curve $U_w U_w$, which passes through $\bar{P}'$ and to the northeast of $P$.

Note that the foregoing argument requires no restrictions on the form of the utility functions other than the usual international trade assumptions of diminishing marginal rate of substitution between goods in consumption and nonidentical homotheticity of utility functions coupled with the additional assumptions that returns to scale in utility are nonincreasing (diminishing returns to scale in utility would make the utility transformation curve still more concave to the origin) and that there is a diminishing marginal rate of substitution between countries' utility levels in the world welfare function. The use of the specific form of the Cobb–Douglas utility function adds the information that with such a specification of the utility function the point $\bar{P}$ must lie either northeast or southwest of the point $P$ within the utility transformation curve: i.e., one or the other country must gain in average (undiscounted) utility while the other must lose sufficiently to impose a loss on average. The key point in the proof is that the price of the commodity in terms of which the transfer is specified is a linear function of the amount of the transfer; hence a reversed transfer produces equal price changes around the no-reversed-transfer equilibrium price. Since a far wider class of utility functions than the Cobb–Douglas may be expected to yield an approximately linear functional relationship between the equilibrium price and the amount of the transfer, the result that one country must gain, the other lose, and the world as a whole lose from a reversed transfer by comparison with the no-transfer situation may be taken as a generally valid result.[10,11]

### Appendix I. Some Numerical Results

The purpose of using explicit utility functions is not merely to check on the accuracy of the use of linear approximations to changes in the immediate neighborhood of an initial equilibrium position, but to permit calculation and assessment of the magnitude of welfare gains and losses. Tables 1–4 present the results of computation of domestic, foreign, and world welfare gains or losses, for transfers denominated alternatively in the domestic and the foreign product, for values of $\alpha_1$ and $\alpha_2$ ranging from 0.1 to 0.9 by intervals of 0.1 and for transfers ranging from 0.05 to 0.20 by intervals of 0.05.

One of the most striking results of the computations is a confirmation of the classical transfer-problem-analysis hypothesis that it may be impossible to effect a transfer of apparently reasonable size. See Tables 3 and 4, where transfers of 0.15 and 0.20 of country 1's national product at no-transfer equilibrium prices cannot be effected for $\alpha_1 = 0.1$, $\alpha_2 = 0.8$ and 0.9, and $\alpha_1 = 0.1$, $\alpha_2 = 0.6$, 0.7, 0.8, and 0.9, respectively. (It might be impossible to effect smaller transfers, or the same transfers with a smaller difference between $\alpha_1$ and $\alpha_2$, because each of the net welfare gains or losses is the sum of a positive and a negative element, and the negative element might exceed 100% of pretransfer national income.)

---

[10] "World loss," of course, must be interpreted on the assumption either that the marginal social utilities of national incomes are equal in the no-transfer equilibrium situation, or that permanent transfers are being made to secure this result, and the reversed-transfer analysis starts from this permanent-transfer equilibrium.

[11] Since this chapter was written, I have come across an unpublished paper by Pazner and Razin [17] which attempts to demonstrate that exchange rate uncertainty is welfare-beneficial. If one interprets exchange rate uncertainty in the full general equilibrium sense of reversed transfers, which they purport to do but do not in fact do, the analysis of the present paper indicates that exchange-rate uncertainty will benefit one country, but involve a welfare loss for the other country and the world as a whole.

Another striking result is that the welfare gains or losses for the individual countries are not a monotonically increasing function of the difference between $\alpha_1$ and $\alpha_2$, i.e., of the difference in marginal propensities to spend on imports between the two countries, as might be expected from the formula for the change in the terms of trade consequent on the transfer. Instead, the welfare change tends first to rise and then to fall as the difference between the marginal propensities to spend on imports increases.

TABLE 1

PERCENTAGE GAINS OR LOSSES OF WELFARE, REVERSED TRANSFER OF 5% FROM COUNTRY 1 TO COUNTRY 2, VARYING VALUES OF $\alpha_1$ AND $\alpha_2$

(a) Transfer Denominated in Country 1's Good

| $\alpha_2$ | $\alpha_1$ | | | | | | | | |
|---|---|---|---|---|---|---|---|---|---|
| | 0.1 | 0.2 | 0.3 | 0.4 | 0.5 | 0.6 | 0.7 | 0.8 | 0.9 |

(i) Domestic welfare

| $\alpha_2$ | 0.1 | 0.2 | 0.3 | 0.4 | 0.5 | 0.6 | 0.7 | 0.8 | 0.9 |
|---|---|---|---|---|---|---|---|---|---|
| 0.1 | 0 | −0.02 | −0.03 | −0.035 | −0.04 | −0.04 | −0.04 | −0.035 | −0.03 |
| 0.2 | +0.04 | 0 | −0.04 | −0.035 | −0.04 | −0.045 | −0.05 | −0.05 | −0.045 |
| 0.3 | +0.105 | +0.03 | 0 | −0.02 | −0.035 | −0.045 | −0.05 | −0.055 | −0.055 |
| 0.4 | +0.20 | +0.08 | +0.03 | 0 | −0.02 | −0.035 | −0.05 | −0.055 | −0.06 |
| 0.5 | +0.325 | +0.145 | +0.07 | +0.03 | 0 | −0.02 | −0.04 | −0.05 | −0.06 |
| 0.6 | +0.485 | +0.22 | +0.125 | +0.065 | +0.03 | 0 | −0.02 | −0.04 | −0.05 |
| 0.7 | +0.675 | +0.315 | +0.185 | +0.115 | +0.065 | +0.03 | 0 | −0.02 | −0.04 |
| 0.8 | +0.905 | +0.425 | +0.26 | +0.17 | +0.11 | +0.065 | +0.03 | 0 | −0.02 |
| 0.9 | +1.18 | +0.55 | +0.345 | +0.235 | +0.16 | +0.105 | +0.06 | +0.03 | 0 |

(ii) Foreign welfare

| $\alpha_2$ | 0.1 | 0.2 | 0.3 | 0.4 | 0.5 | 0.6 | 0.7 | 0.8 | 0.9 |
|---|---|---|---|---|---|---|---|---|---|
| 0.1 | 0 | +0.055 | +0.045 | +0.035 | +0.03 | +0.025 | +0.02 | +0.015 | +0.015 |
| 0.2 | −0.42 | 0 | +0.04 | +0.045 | +0.04 | +0.035 | +0.03 | +0.025 | +0.02 |
| 0.3 | −1.16 | −0.14 | 0 | +0.03 | +0.04 | +0.035 | +0.035 | +0.03 | +0.025 |
| 0.4 | −2.095 | −0.33 | −0.07 | 0 | +0.025 | +0.03 | +0.03 | +0.03 | +0.03 |
| 0.5 | −3.07 | −0.54 | −0.155 | −0.04 | 0 | +0.015 | +0.025 | +0.025 | +0.025 |
| 0.6 | −3.905 | −0.725 | −0.23 | −0.085 | −0.025 | 0 | +0.01 | +0.015 | +0.02 |
| 0.7 | −4.365 | −0.83 | −0.28 | −0.115 | −0.045 | 0.015 | 0 | +0.01 | +0.01 |
| 0.8 | −4.16 | −0.795 | −0.28 | −0.12 | −0.055 | −0.025 | −0.01 | 0 | +0.005 |
| 0.9 | −2.89 | −0.545 | −0.185 | −0.09 | −0.045 | −0.04 | −0.01 | −0.005 | 0 |

(iii) World welfare

| $\alpha_2$ | 0.1 | 0.2 | 0.3 | 0.4 | 0.5 | 0.6 | 0.7 | 0.8 | 0.9 |
|---|---|---|---|---|---|---|---|---|---|
| 0.1 | 0 | −0.005 | −0.01 | −0.015 | −0.015 | −0.015 | −0.015 | −0.01 | −0.01 |
| 0.2 | −0.02 | 0 | −0.005 | −0.005 | −0.01 | −0.01 | −0.01 | −0.01 | −0.01 |
| 0.3 | −0.055 | −0.005 | 0 | 0 | −0.005 | −0.005 | −0.01 | −0.01 | −0.01 |
| 0.4 | −0.125 | −0.025 | −0.005 | 0 | 0 | −0.005 | −0.005 | −0.005 | −0.005 |
| 0.5 | −0.24 | −0.055 | −0.015 | 0 | 0 | 0 | 0 | −0.005 | −0.005 |
| 0.6 | −0.395 | −0.095 | −0.03 | −0.01 | 0 | 0 | 0 | 0 | −0.005 |
| 0.7 | −0.585 | −0.145 | −0.045 | −0.015 | −0.005 | 0 | 0 | 0 | 0 |
| 0.8 | −0.78 | −0.185 | −0.065 | −0.025 | −0.01 | −0.005 | 0 | 0 | 0 |
| 0.9 | −0.855 | −0.18 | −0.06 | −0.025 | −0.01 | −0.005 | 0 | 0 | 0 |

Table 1 (continued)

### (b) Transfer Denominated in Country 2's Good

| $\alpha_2$ | $\alpha_1$ | | | | | | | | |
|---|---|---|---|---|---|---|---|---|---|
| | 0.1 | 0.2 | 0.3 | 0.4 | 0.5 | 0.6 | 0.7 | 0.8 | 0.9 |

#### (i) Domestic welfare

| $\alpha_2$ | 0.1 | 0.2 | 0.3 | 0.4 | 0.5 | 0.6 | 0.7 | 0.8 | 0.9 |
|---|---|---|---|---|---|---|---|---|---|
| 0.1 | 0 | +0.095 | +0.105 | +0.095 | +0.08 | +0.065 | +0.045 | +0.03 | +0.015 |
| 0.2 | −0.235 | 0 | +0.055 | +0.065 | +0.065 | +0.055 | +0.04 | +0.025 | +0.015 |
| 0.3 | −0.50 | −0.105 | 0 | +0.035 | +0.045 | +0.04 | +0.035 | +0.025 | +0.01 |
| 0.4 | −0.79 | −0.22 | −0.06 | 0 | +0.025 | +0.03 | +0.025 | +0.02 | +0.01 |
| 0.5 | −1.12 | −0.345 | −0.13 | −0.04 | 0 | +0.015 | +0.02 | +0.015 | +0.01 |
| 0.6 | −1.485 | −0.485 | −0.20 | −0.085 | −0.025 | 0 | +0.01 | +0.01 | +0.005 |
| 0.7 | −1.895 | −0.635 | −0.28 | −0.13 | −0.055 | −0.02 | 0 | +0.005 | +0.005 |
| 0.8 | −2.36 | −0.795 | −0.365 | −0.18 | −0.085 | −0.035 | −0.01 | 0 | +0.005 |
| 0.9 | −2.89 | −0.865 | −0.46 | −0.235 | −0.12 | −0.06 | −0.025 | −0.005 | 0 |

#### (ii) Foreign welfare

| $\alpha_2$ | 0.1 | 0.2 | 0.3 | 0.4 | 0.5 | 0.6 | 0.7 | 0.8 | 0.9 |
|---|---|---|---|---|---|---|---|---|---|
| 0.1 | 0 | −0.455 | −0.355 | −0.26 | −0.19 | −0.135 | −0.09 | −0.06 | −0.03 |
| 0.2 | +1.785 | 0 | −0.16 | −0.155 | −0.125 | −0.10 | −0.07 | −0.05 | −0.03 |
| 0.3 | +3.07 | +0.345 | 0 | −0.065 | −0.075 | −0.065 | −0.05 | −0.04 | −0.025 |
| 0.4 | +3.84 | +0.57 | +0.115 | 0 | −0.03 | −0.035 | −0.035 | −0.025 | −0.02 |
| 0.5 | +4.11 | +0.68 | +0.18 | +0.045 | 0 | −0.015 | −0.02 | −0.015 | −0.01 |
| 0.6 | +3.90 | +0.685 | +0.205 | +0.065 | +0.02 | 0 | −0.005 | −0.01 | −0.005 |
| 0.7 | +3.275 | +0.59 | +0.185 | +0.07 | +0.025 | +0.01 | 0 | −0.005 | −0.005 |
| 0.8 | +2.325 | +0.425 | +0.14 | +0.055 | +0.025 | +0.01 | +0.005 | 0 | 0 |
| 0.9 | +1.18 | +0.215 | +0.07 | +0.03 | +0.015 | +0.005 | 0 | 0 | 0 |

#### (iii) World welfare

| $\alpha_2$ | 0.1 | 0.2 | 0.3 | 0.4 | 0.5 | 0.6 | 0.7 | 0.8 | 0.9 |
|---|---|---|---|---|---|---|---|---|---|
| 0.1 | 0 | −0.005 | −0.01 | −0.015 | −0.15 | −0.015 | −0.015 | −0.01 | −0.01 |
| 0.2 | −0.01 | 0 | −0.005 | −0.005 | −0.01 | −0.01 | −0.01 | −0.01 | −0.01 |
| 0.3 | −0.055 | −0.005 | 0 | 0 | −0.005 | −0.005 | −0.01 | −0.01 | −0.01 |
| 0.4 | −0.13 | −0.025 | −0.005 | 0 | 0 | −0.005 | −0.005 | −0.005 | −0.005 |
| 0.5 | −0.245 | −0.055 | −0.015 | 0 | 0 | 0 | 0 | −0.005 | −0.005 |
| 0.6 | −0.405 | −0.095 | −0.03 | −0.01 | 0 | 0 | 0 | 0 | −0.005 |
| 0.7 | −0.60 | −0.145 | −0.045 | −0.015 | −0.005 | 0 | 0 | 0 | 0 |
| 0.8 | −0.80 | −0.185 | −0.065 | −0.025 | −0.01 | −0.005 | 0 | 0 | 0 |
| 0.9 | −0.855 | −0.18 | −0.06 | −0.025 | −0.01 | −0.005 | 0 | 0 | 0 |

TABLE 2

PERCENTAGE GAINS OR LOSSES OF WELFARE, REVERSED TRANSFER OF 10% FROM COUNTRY 1 TO COUNTRY 2, VARYING VALUES OF $\alpha_1$ AND $\alpha_2$

(a)   Transfer Denominated in Country 1's Good

| $\alpha_2$ | $\alpha_1$ | | | | | | | | |
|---|---|---|---|---|---|---|---|---|---|
| | 0.1 | 0.2 | 0.3 | 0.4 | 0.5 | 0.6 | 0.7 | 0.8 | 0.9 |
| | | | | (i)   Domestic welfare | | | | | |
| 0.1 | 0 | −0.07 | −0.115 | −0.145 | −0.16 | −0.165 | −0.165 | −0.15 | −0.125 |
| 0.2 | +0.155 | 0 | −0.08 | −0.13 | −0.165 | −0.185 | −0.195 | −0.195 | −0.185 |
| 0.3 | +0.43 | +0.13 | 0 | −0.085 | −0.14 | −0.18 | −0.205 | −0.22 | −0.22 |
| 0.4 | +0.83 | +0.32 | +0.12 | 0 | −0.085 | −0.145 | −0.19 | −0.22 | −0.235 |
| 0.5 | +1.395 | +0.575 | +0.285 | +0.115 | 0 | −0.085 | −0.15 | −0.20 | −0.23 |
| 0.6 | +2.16 | +0.90 | +0.50 | +0.27 | +0.115 | 0 | −0.09 | −0.155 | −0.205 |
| 0.7 | +3.21 | +1.295 | +0.755 | +0.46 | +0.26 | +0.115 | 0 | −0.09 | −0.16 |
| 0.8 | +4.71 | +1.765 | +1.06 | +0.685 | +0.435 | +0.255 | +0.11 | 0 | −0.09 |
| 0.9 | +7.035 | +2.325 | +1.415 | +0.945 | +0.645 | +0.42 | +0.25 | +0.11 | 0 |
| | | | | (ii)   Foreign welfare | | | | | |
| 0.1 | 0 | +0.215 | +0.18 | +0.145 | +0.115 | +0.095 | +0.075 | +0.065 | +0.055 |
| 0.2 | −1.685 | 0 | +0.17 | +0.18 | +0.165 | +0.14 | +0.125 | +0.105 | +0.09 |
| 0.3 | −4.71 | −0.55 | 0 | +0.125 | +0.15 | +0.15 | +0.135 | +0.125 | +0.11 |
| 0.4 | −8.70 | −1.325 | −0.28 | 0 | +0.09 | +0.12 | +0.125 | +0.12 | +0.11 |
| 0.5 | −13.255 | −2.185 | −0.615 | −0.165 | 0 | +0.065 | +0.09 | +0.10 | +0.10 |
| 0.6 | −17.935 | −2.955 | −0.925 | −0.33 | −0.10 | 0 | +0.045 | +0.065 | +0.075 |
| 0.7 | −22.14 | −3.43 | −1.135 | −0.455 | −0.185 | −0.06 | 0 | +0.03 | +0.045 |
| 0.8 | −24.76 | −3.345 | −1.135 | −0.485 | −0.22 | −0.10 | −0.035 | 0 | +0.02 |
| 0.9 | −22.745 | −2.36 | −0.805 | −0.355 | −0.175 | −0.085 | −0.04 | −0.015 | 0 |
| | | | | (iii)   World welfare | | | | | |
| 0.1 | 0 | −0.02 | −0.04 | −0.055 | −0.06 | −0.065 | −0.06 | −0.05 | −0.035 |
| 0.2 | −0.05 | 0 | −0.01 | −0.025 | −0.04 | −0.045 | −0.05 | −0.045 | −0.04 |
| 0.3 | −0.215 | −0.02 | 0 | −0.005 | −0.02 | −0.03 | −0.035 | −0.035 | −0.035 |
| 0.4 | −0.53 | −0.09 | −0.01 | 0 | −0.005 | −0.015 | −0.02 | −0.025 | −0.03 |
| 0.5 | −1.05 | −0.21 | −0.05 | −0.01 | 0 | −0.005 | −0.01 | −0.015 | −0.02 |
| 0.6 | −1.86 | −0.385 | −0.11 | −0.03 | −0.005 | 0 | 0 | −0.005 | −0.01 |
| 0.7 | −3.125 | −0.595 | −0.19 | −0.065 | −0.02 | −0.005 | 0 | 0 | −0.005 |
| 0.8 | −5.115 | −0.79 | −0.26 | −0.095 | −0.035 | −0.01 | 0 | 0 | 0 |
| 0.9 | −7.855 | −0.80 | −0.25 | −0.095 | −0.04 | −0.015 | −0.005 | 0 | 0 |

Table 2 (continued)

(b) Transfer Denominated in Country 2's Good

| $\alpha_2$ | $\alpha_1$ | | | | | | | | |
|---|---|---|---|---|---|---|---|---|---|
| | 0.1 | 0.2 | 0.3 | 0.4 | 0.5 | 0.6 | 0.7 | 0.8 | 0.9 |

(i) Domestic welfare

| $\alpha_2$ | 0.1 | 0.2 | 0.3 | 0.4 | 0.5 | 0.6 | 0.7 | 0.8 | 0.9 |
|---|---|---|---|---|---|---|---|---|---|
| 0.1 | 0 | +0.38 | +0.42 | +0.385 | +0.32 | +0.25 | +0.18 | +0.115 | +0.055 |
| 0.2 | −0.955 | 0 | +0.22 | +0.27 | +0.255 | +0.215 | +0.16 | +0.105 | +0.05 |
| 0.3 | −2.05 | −0.42 | 0 | +0.14 | +0.18 | +0.17 | +0.135 | +0.095 | +0.045 |
| 0.4 | −3.365 | −0.895 | −0.245 | 0 | +0.095 | +0.12 | +0.11 | +0.08 | +0.04 |
| 0.5 | −5.005 | −1.405 | −0.515 | −0.16 | 0 | +0.065 | +0.075 | +0.065 | +0.035 |
| 0.6 | −7.14 | −1.98 | −0.81 | −0.33 | −0.105 | 0 | +0.04 | +0.045 | +0.03 |
| 0.7 | −10.10 | −2.625 | −1.135 | −0.52 | −0.22 | −0.07 | 0 | +0.025 | +0.02 |
| 0.8 | −14.62 | −3.345 | −1.485 | −0.725 | −0.345 | −0.145 | −0.045 | 0 | +0.01 |
| 0.9 | −22.745 | −4.16 | −1.87 | −0.945 | −0.48 | −0.23 | −0.095 | −0.025 | 0 |

(ii) Foreign welfare

| $\alpha_2$ | 0.1 | 0.2 | 0.3 | 0.4 | 0.5 | 0.6 | 0.7 | 0.8 | 0.9 |
|---|---|---|---|---|---|---|---|---|---|
| 0.1 | 0 | −1.815 | −1.425 | −1.045 | −0.755 | −0.535 | −0.365 | −0.235 | −0.125 |
| 0.2 | +7.18 | 0 | −0.63 | −0.62 | −0.51 | −0.395 | −0.285 | −0.195 | −0.12 |
| 0.3 | +12.575 | +1.375 | 0 | −0.27 | −0.295 | −0.26 | −0.205 | −0.15 | −0.10 |
| 0.4 | +16.175 | +2.295 | +0.455 | 0 | −0.125 | −0.145 | −0.135 | −0.105 | −0.075 |
| 0.5 | +17.955 | +2.76 | +0.725 | +0.18 | 0 | −0.06 | −0.07 | −0.065 | −0.05 |
| 0.6 | +17.875 | +2.79 | +0.82 | +0.27 | +0.075 | 0 | −0.025 | −0.035 | −0.03 |
| 0.7 | +15.96 | +2.43 | +0.755 | +0.28 | +0.105 | +0.03 | 0 | −0.01 | −0.015 |
| 0.8 | +12.31 | +1.765 | +0.565 | +0.22 | +0.09 | +0.035 | +0.01 | 0 | −0.005 |
| 0.9 | +7.035 | +0.905 | +0.295 | +0.12 | +0.05 | +0.02 | +0.01 | 0 | 0 |

(iii) World welfare

| $\alpha_2$ | 0.1 | 0.2 | 0.3 | 0.4 | 0.5 | 0.6 | 0.7 | 0.8 | 0.9 |
|---|---|---|---|---|---|---|---|---|---|
| 0.1 | 0 | −0.02 | −0.04 | −0.055 | −0.06 | −0.065 | −0.06 | −0.05 | −0.035 |
| 0.2 | −0.05 | 0 | −0.01 | −0.025 | −0.04 | −0.045 | −0.05 | −0.045 | −0.04 |
| 0.3 | −0.225 | −0.02 | 0 | −0.005 | −0.02 | −0.03 | −0.035 | −0.035 | −0.035 |
| 0.4 | −0.575 | −0.09 | −0.01 | 0 | −0.005 | −0.015 | −0.02 | −0.025 | −0.03 |
| 0.5 | −1.18 | −0.215 | −0.05 | −0.01 | 0 | −0.005 | −0.01 | −0.015 | −0.02 |
| 0.6 | −2.135 | −0.39 | −0.115 | −0.03 | −0.005 | 0 | 0 | −0.005 | −0.01 |
| 0.7 | −3.585 | −0.655 | −0.19 | −0.065 | −0.02 | −0.005 | 0 | 0 | −0.005 |
| 0.8 | −5.645 | −0.79 | −0.255 | −0.095 | −0.035 | −0.01 | 0 | 0 | 0 |
| 0.9 | −7.855 | −0.78 | −0.25 | −0.095 | −0.04 | −0.15 | −0.005 | 0 | 0 |

TABLE 3

PERCENTAGE GAINS OR LOSSES OF WELFARE, REVERSED TRANSFER OF 15% FROM COUNTRY 1 TO COUNTRY 2, VARYING VALUES OF $\alpha_1$ AND $\alpha_2$

(a)  Transfer Denominated in Country 1's Good

| $\alpha_2$ | $\alpha_1$ | | | | | | | | |
|---|---|---|---|---|---|---|---|---|---|
| | 0.1 | 0.2 | 0.3 | 0.4 | 0.5 | 0.6 | 0.7 | 0.8 | 0.9 |

(i)  Domestic welfare

| $\alpha_2$ | 0.1 | 0.2 | 0.3 | 0.4 | 0.5 | 0.6 | 0.7 | 0.8 | 0.9 |
|---|---|---|---|---|---|---|---|---|---|
| 0.1 | 0 | −0.16 | −0.255 | −0.32 | −0.36 | −0.38 | −0.37 | −0.34 | −0.285 |
| 0.2 | +0.35 | 0 | −0.175 | −0.295 | −0.375 | −0.425 | −0.445 | −0.445 | −0.415 |
| 0.3 | +0.985 | +0.295 | 0 | −0.185 | −0.315 | −0.405 | −0.465 | −0.495 | −0.50 |
| 0.4 | +1.99 | +0.73 | +0.275 | 0 | −0.19 | −0.33 | −0.43 | −0.495 | −0.535 |
| 0.5 | +3.565 | +1.315 | +0.65 | +0.265 | 0 | −0.195 | −0.34 | −0.45 | −0.52 |
| 0.6 | +6.235 | +2.08 | +1.13 | +0.61 | +0.26 | 0 | −0.20 | −0.35 | −0.46 |
| 0.7 | +12.245 | +3.045 | +1.72 | +1.035 | +0.585 | +0.255 | 0 | −0.20 | −0.355 |
| 0.8 | — | +4.26 | +2.43 | +1.55 | +0.985 | +0.57 | +0.25 | 0 | −0.20 |
| 0.9 | — | +5.79 | +3.275 | +2.155 | +1.455 | +0.95 | +0.56 | +0.25 | 0 |

(ii)  Foreign welfare

| $\alpha_2$ | 0.1 | 0.2 | 0.3 | 0.4 | 0.5 | 0.6 | 0.7 | 0.8 | 0.9 |
|---|---|---|---|---|---|---|---|---|---|
| 0.1 | 0 | +0.48 | +0.405 | +0.325 | +0.26 | +0.21 | +0.175 | +0.145 | +0.12 |
| 0.2 | −3.815 | 0 | +0.38 | +0.405 | +0.37 | +0.32 | +0.275 | +0.24 | +0.205 |
| 0.3 | −10.87 | −1.245 | 0 | +0.28 | +0.34 | +0.335 | +0.31 | +0.28 | +0.245 |
| 0.4 | −20.955 | −3.005 | −0.63 | 0 | +0.205 | +0.27 | +0.28 | +0.27 | +0.25 |
| 0.5 | −34.78 | −5.00 | −1.385 | −0.37 | 0 | +0.15 | +0.205 | +0.225 | +0.225 |
| 0.6 | −56.216 | −6.88 | −2.10 | −0.745 | −0.225 | 0 | +0.105 | +0.15 | +0.17 |
| 0.7 | −112.733 | −8.195 | −2.595 | −1.03 | −0.415 | −0.14 | 0 | +0.07 | +0.105 |
| 0.8 | — | −8.305 | −2.625 | −1.10 | −0.50 | −0.22 | −0.075 | 0 | +0.04 |
| 0.9 | — | −6.195 | −1.895 | −0.815 | −0.395 | −0.195 | −0.09 | −0.035 | 0 |

(iii)  World welfare

| $\alpha_2$ | 0.1 | 0.2 | 0.3 | 0.4 | 0.5 | 0.6 | 0.7 | 0.8 | 0.9 |
|---|---|---|---|---|---|---|---|---|---|
| 0.1 | 0 | −0.04 | −0.09 | −0.125 | −0.14 | −0.14 | −0.13 | −0.11 | −0.08 |
| 0.2 | −0.11 | 0 | −0.025 | −0.06 | −0.09 | −0.105 | −0.11 | −0.105 | −0.09 |
| 0.3 | −0.495 | −0.05 | 0 | −0.015 | −0.04 | −0.065 | −0.08 | −0.085 | −0.08 |
| 0.4 | −1.285 | −0.205 | −0.03 | 0 | −0.01 | −0.03 | −0.045 | −0.06 | −0.065 |
| 0.5 | −2.825 | −0.49 | −0.115 | −0.015 | 0 | −0.01 | −0.02 | −0.035 | −0.045 |
| 0.6 | −6.255 | −0.905 | −0.255 | −0.07 | −0.01 | 0 | −0.005 | −0.015 | −0.025 |
| 0.7 | −19.00 | −1.45 | −0.435 | −0.145 | −0.04 | −0.005 | 0 | −0.005 | −0.01 |
| 0.8 | — | −2.025 | −0.605 | −0.215 | −0.075 | −0.025 | −0.005 | 0 | 0 |
| 0.9 | — | −2.20 | −0.600 | −0.22 | −0.085 | −0.03 | −0.01 | 0 | 0 |

Table 3 (continued)

(b) Transfer Denominated in Country 2's Good

| $\alpha_2$ | $\alpha_1$ | | | | | | | | |
|---|---|---|---|---|---|---|---|---|---|
| | 0.1 | 0.2 | 0.3 | 0.4 | 0.5 | 0.6 | 0.7 | 0.8 | 0.9 |

(i) Domestic welfare

| $\alpha_2$ | 0.1 | 0.2 | 0.3 | 0.4 | 0.5 | 0.6 | 0.7 | 0.8 | 0.9 |
|---|---|---|---|---|---|---|---|---|---|
| 0.1 | 0 | +0.86 | +0.951 | +0.087 | +0.725 | +0.57 | +0.41 | +0.26 | +0.12 |
| 0.2 | −2.17 | 0 | +0.50 | +0.061 | +0.575 | +0.485 | +0.365 | +0.24 | +0.115 |
| 0.3 | −4.84 | −0.95 | 0 | +0.032 | +0.405 | +0.385 | +0.31 | +0.21 | +0.105 |
| 0.4 | −8.485 | −2.015 | −0.55 | 0 | +0.215 | +0.27 | +0.245 | +0.18 | +0.095 |
| 0.5 | −14.165 | −3.235 | −1.165 | −0.355 | 0 | +0.14 | +0.175 | +0.145 | +0.08 |
| 0.6 | −25.18 | −4.645 | −1.84 | −0.745 | −0.235 | 0 | +0.09 | +0.10 | +0.065 |
| 0.7 | −62.335 | −6.31 | −2.595 | −1.175 | −0.495 | −0.16 | 0 | +0.055 | +0.045 |
| 0.8 | — | −8.305 | −3.43 | −1.645 | −0.78 | −0.33 | −0.10 | 0 | +0.025 |
| 0.9 | — | −10.77 | −4.365 | −2.155 | −1.09 | −0.52 | −0.21 | −0.06 | 0 |

(ii) Foreign welfare

| $\alpha_2$ | 0.1 | 0.2 | 0.3 | 0.4 | 0.5 | 0.6 | 0.7 | 0.8 | 0.9 |
|---|---|---|---|---|---|---|---|---|---|
| 0.1 | 0 | −4.095 | −3.225 | −2.36 | −1.705 | −1.21 | −0.83 | −0.53 | −0.285 |
| 0.2 | +16.33 | 0 | −1.425 | −1.40 | −1.155 | −0.885 | −0.65 | −0.445 | −0.265 |
| 0.3 | +29.49 | +3.105 | 0 | −0.605 | −0.67 | −0.585 | −0.465 | −0.34 | −0.225 |
| 0.4 | +39.99 | +5.215 | +1.02 | 0 | −0.28 | −0.33 | −0.30 | −0.235 | −0.165 |
| 0.5 | +48.23 | +6.33 | +1.635 | +0.405 | 0 | −0.135 | −0.16 | −0.145 | −0.11 |
| 0.6 | +55.275 | +6.48 | +1.855 | +0.61 | +0.17 | 0 | −0.06 | −0.075 | −0.065 |
| 0.7 | +67.34 | +5.745 | +1.72 | +0.63 | +0.235 | +0.07 | 0 | −0.025 | −0.03 |
| 0.8 | — | +4.26 | +1.295 | +0.50 | +0.205 | +0.08 | +0.025 | 0 | −0.01 |
| 0.9 | — | +2.245 | +0.675 | +0.27 | +0.115 | +0.05 | +0.02 | +0.005 | 0 |

(iii) World welfare

| $\alpha_2$ | 0.1 | 0.2 | 0.3 | 0.4 | 0.5 | 0.6 | 0.7 | 0.8 | 0.9 |
|---|---|---|---|---|---|---|---|---|---|
| 0.1 | 0 | −0.04 | −0.09 | −0.125 | −0.14 | −0.145 | −0.135 | −0.11 | −0.08 |
| 0.2 | −0.115 | 0 | −0.025 | −0.06 | −0.09 | −0.105 | −0.11 | −0.105 | −0.085 |
| 0.3 | −0.55 | −0.05 | 0 | −0.015 | −0.04 | −0.065 | −0.08 | −0.085 | −0.08 |
| 0.4 | −1.56 | −0.21 | −0.03 | 0 | −0.01 | −0.03 | −0.045 | −0.06 | −0.065 |
| 0.5 | −3.765 | −0.50 | −0.115 | −0.015 | 0 | −0.01 | −0.02 | −0.035 | −0.045 |
| 0.6 | −9.09 | −0.935 | −0.255 | −0.07 | −0.01 | 0 | −0.005 | −0.015 | −0.025 |
| 0.7 | −29.915 | −1.485 | −0.435 | −0.145 | −0.04 | −0.005 | 0 | −0.005 | −0.01 |
| 0.8 | — | −2.025 | −0.595 | −0.215 | −0.075 | −0.025 | −0.005 | 0 | 0 |
| 0.9 | — | −2.095 | −0.585 | −0.215 | −0.085 | −0.03 | −0.01 | 0 | 0 |

TABLE 4

PERCENTAGE GAINS OR LOSSES OF WELFARE, REVERSED TRANSFER OF 20% FROM COUNTRY 1 TO COUNTRY 2, VARYING VALUES OF $\alpha_1$ AND $\alpha_2$

(a)   Transfer Denominated in Country 1's Good

| $\alpha_2$ | $\alpha_1$ | | | | | | | | |
|---|---|---|---|---|---|---|---|---|---|
| | 0.1 | 0.2 | 0.3 | 0.4 | 0.5 | 0.6 | 0.7 | 0.8 | 0.9 |

(i)   Domestic welfare

| $\alpha_2$ | | | | | | | | | |
|---|---|---|---|---|---|---|---|---|---|
| 0.1 | 0 | −0.28 | −0.455 | −0.575 | −0.65 | −0.675 | −0.665 | −0.605 | −0.51 |
| 0.2 | +0.63 | 0 | −0.315 | −0.525 | −0.665 | −0.755 | −0.795 | −0.795 | −0.745 |
| 0.3 | +1.82 | +0.52 | 0 | −0.33 | −0.56 | −0.725 | −0.83 | −0.885 | −0.895 |
| 0.4 | +3.92 | +1.305 | +0.49 | 0 | −0.34 | −0.59 | −0.765 | −0.885 | −0.955 |
| 0.5 | +8.195 | +2.39 | +1.16 | +0.47 | 0 | −0.345 | −0.605 | −0.80 | −0.93 |
| 0.6 | +186.485 | +3.85 | +2.025 | +1.085 | +0.46 | 0 | −0.35 | −0.62 | −0.825 |
| 0.7 | — | +5.805 | +3.11 | +1.855 | +1.045 | +0.455 | 0 | −0.355 | −0.63 |
| 0.8 | — | +8.48 | +4.455 | +2.79 | +1.755 | +1.015 | +0.45 | 0 | −0.36 |
| 0.9 | — | +12.31 | +6.095 | +3.90 | +2.605 | +1.69 | +0.995 | +0.445 | 0 |

(ii)   Foreign welfare

| $\alpha_2$ | | | | | | | | | |
|---|---|---|---|---|---|---|---|---|---|
| 0.1 | 0 | +0.86 | +0.725 | +0.58 | +0.465 | +0.38 | +0.315 | +0.26 | +0.215 |
| 0.2 | −6.84 | 0 | +0.675 | +0.725 | +0.655 | +0.575 | +0.495 | +0.425 | +0.365 |
| 0.3 | −20.065 | −2.215 | 0 | +0.50 | +0.605 | +0.60 | +0.555 | +0.495 | +0.44 |
| 0.4 | −41.70 | −5.395 | −1.125 | 0 | +0.365 | +0.48 | +0.50 | +0.485 | +0.50 |
| 0.5 | −85.093 | −9.115 | −2.47 | −0.655 | 0 | +0.265 | +0.37 | +0.40 | +0.395 |
| 0.6 | −2045.5 | −12.865 | −3.78 | −1.33 | −0.405 | 0 | +0.185 | +0.27 | +0.305 |
| 0.7 | — | −15.995 | −4.74 | −1.84 | −0.745 | −0.245 | 0 | +0.125 | +0.185 |
| 0.8 | — | −17.39 | −4.86 | −1.88 | −0.895 | −0.395 | −0.135 | 0 | +0.075 |
| 0.9 | — | −14.62 | −3.595 | −1.485 | −0.705 | −0.35 | −0.16 | −0.06 | 0 |

(iii)   World welfare

| $\alpha_2$ | | | | | | | | | |
|---|---|---|---|---|---|---|---|---|---|
| 0.1 | 0 | −0.075 | −0.16 | −0.22 | −0.25 | −0.255 | −0.235 | −0.20 | −0.145 |
| 0.2 | −0.20 | 0 | −0.045 | −0.105 | −0.155 | −0.185 | −0.185 | −0.185 | −0.16 |
| 0.3 | −0.915 | −0.085 | 0 | −0.03 | −0.075 | −0.115 | −0.14 | −0.15 | −0.145 |
| 0.4 | −2.595 | −0.37 | −0.05 | 0 | −0.02 | −0.055 | −0.085 | −0.105 | −0.115 |
| 0.5 | −7.355 | −0.895 | −0.205 | −0.03 | 0 | −0.015 | −0.04 | −0.06 | −0.075 |
| 0.6 | −408.805 | −1.72 | −0.46 | −0.12 | −0.02 | 0 | −0.01 | −0.025 | −0.045 |
| 0.7 | — | −2.915 | −0.805 | −0.255 | −0.075 | −0.01 | 0 | −0.005 | −0.02 |
| 0.8 | — | −4.455 | −1.135 | −0.39 | −0.135 | −0.04 | −0.005 | 0 | −0.005 |
| 0.9 | — | −5.645 | −1.175 | −0.405 | −0.155 | −0.055 | −0.015 | −0.005 | 0 |

Table 4 (continued)

(b) Transfer Denominated in Country 2's Good

| $\alpha_2$ | $\alpha_1$ | | | | | | | | |
|---|---|---|---|---|---|---|---|---|---|
| | 0.1 | 0.2 | 0.3 | 0.4 | 0.5 | 0.6 | 0.7 | 0.8 | 0.9 |

(i) Domestic welfare

| $\alpha_2$ | 0.1 | 0.2 | 0.3 | 0.4 | 0.5 | 0.6 | 0.7 | 0.8 | 0.9 |
|---|---|---|---|---|---|---|---|---|---|
| 0.1 | 0 | +1.535 | +1.705 | +1.555 | +1.305 | +1.02 | +0.735 | +0.465 | +0.215 |
| 0.2 | −3.92 | 0 | +0.89 | +1.09 | +1.03 | +0.865 | +0.65 | +0.425 | +0.205 |
| 0.3 | −9.23 | −1.695 | 0 | +0.57 | +0.725 | +0.685 | +0.555 | +0.38 | +0.19 |
| 0.4 | −18.23 | −3.635 | −0.985 | 0 | +0.38 | +0.48 | +0.44 | +0.32 | +0.17 |
| 0.5 | −41.08 | −5.945 | −2.08 | −0.63 | 0 | +0.255 | +0.31 | +0.255 | +0.145 |
| 0.6 | −36728 | −8.785 | −3.315 | −1.33 | −0.42 | 0 | +0.165 | +0.18 | +0.115 |
| 0.7 | — | −12.43 | −4.72 | −2.10 | −0.885 | −0.28 | 0 | +0.095 | +0.08 |
| 0.8 | — | −17.39 | −6.325 | −2.955 | −1.39 | −0.59 | −0.18 | 0 | +0.04 |
| 0.9 | — | −24.76 | −8.19 | −3.905 | −1.95 | −0.925 | −0.38 | −0.105 | 0 |

(ii) Foreign welfare

| $\alpha_2$ | 0.1 | 0.2 | 0.3 | 0.4 | 0.5 | 0.6 | 0.7 | 0.8 | 0.9 |
|---|---|---|---|---|---|---|---|---|---|
| 0.1 | 0 | −7.31 | −5.775 | −4.24 | −3.065 | −2.18 | −1.495 | −0.85 | −0.51 |
| 0.2 | +29.48 | 0 | −2.535 | −2.50 | −2.06 | −1.585 | −1.16 | −0.795 | −0.48 |
| 0.3 | +55.78 | +5.54 | 0 | −1.08 | −1.195 | −1.045 | −0.83 | −0.61 | −0.40 |
| 0.4 | +83.07 | +9.39 | +1.82 | 0 | −0.50 | −0.59 | −0.53 | −0.425 | −0.30 |
| 0.5 | +123.605 | +11.57 | +2.925 | +0.72 | 0 | −0.235 | −0.285 | −0.26 | −0.20 |
| 0.6 | +266.73 | +12.09 | +3.335 | +1.085 | +0.30 | 0 | −0.11 | −0.13 | −0.115 |
| 0.7 | — | +11.015 | +3.11 | +1.13 | +0.415 | +0.12 | 0 | −0.045 | −0.05 |
| 0.8 | — | +8.48 | +2.365 | +0.90 | +0.365 | +0.14 | +0.04 | 0 | −0.015 |
| 0.9 | — | +4.71 | +1.25 | +0.485 | +0.205 | +0.09 | +0.035 | +0.01 | 0 |

(iii) World welfare

| $\alpha_2$ | 0.1 | 0.2 | 0.3 | 0.4 | 0.5 | 0.6 | 0.7 | 0.8 | 0.9 |
|---|---|---|---|---|---|---|---|---|---|
| 0.1 | 0 | −0.075 | −0.165 | −0.225 | −0.255 | −0.26 | −0.24 | −0.20 | −0.145 |
| 0.2 | −0.21 | 0 | −0.045 | −0.11 | −0.16 | −0.185 | −0.195 | −0.185 | −0.155 |
| 0.3 | −1.10 | −0.085 | 0 | −0.03 | −0.75 | −0.115 | −0.14 | −0.15 | −0.14 |
| 0.4 | −3.76 | −0.38 | −0.05 | 0 | −0.02 | −0.055 | −0.085 | −0.105 | −0.11 |
| 0.5 | −13.635 | −0.94 | −0.205 | −0.03 | 0 | −0.015 | −0.04 | −0.06 | −0.075 |
| 0.6 | −19327 | −1.825 | −0.465 | −0.12 | −0.02 | 0 | −0.01 | −0.025 | −0.045 |
| 0.7 | — | −3.05 | −0.805 | −0.255 | −0.07 | −0.01 | 0 | −0.005 | −0.02 |
| 0.8 | — | −4.455 | −1.11 | −0.385 | −0.135 | −0.04 | −0.005 | 0 | −0.005 |
| 0.9 | — | −5.115 | −1.11 | −0.395 | −0.15 | −0.055 | −0.015 | −0.005 | 0 |

**Appendix II. A Postscript**

It should be obvious from general considerations that the normalization $p = 1$ and the assumption of complete specialization of endowments used in the text could be relaxed without altering the conclusion that one country must gain and the other lose from a reversed international transfer. (For that matter, the geometrical analysis suggests that substitutability in production could be introduced without altering the result in most plausible cases.) However, in correspondence that occurred too close to the publication deadline to permit a full-scale rewriting of the paper, Rudiger Dornbusch and R. W. Jones have urged the desirability of a more general proof for an incompletely specialized exchange economy. This postscript presents a modified version of a proof provided by Dornbusch.

We have

$$U = AX^{\alpha}Y^{1-\alpha}, \qquad A^{-1} = \alpha^{\alpha}(1-\alpha)^{1-\alpha}, \qquad M = \overline{Y} - T + p\overline{X}.$$

Utility maximization yields the demand functions

$$X = \alpha(M/p), \qquad Y = (1-\alpha)M$$

and utility as a function of $p$,

$$U = Mp^{-\alpha}.$$

Setting $X_1 + X_2 = \overline{X}_1 + \overline{X}_2$ to determine the equilibrium price, we have

$$p = \frac{\alpha_1 \overline{Y}_1 + \alpha_2 \overline{Y}_2 + (\alpha_2 - \alpha_1)T}{(1-\alpha_1)\overline{X}_1 + (1-\alpha_2)\overline{X}_2},$$

whence

$$\frac{dp}{dT} = p' = \frac{\alpha_2 - \alpha_1}{(1-\alpha_1)\overline{X}_1 + (1-\alpha_2)\overline{X}_2}.$$

Define the indirect utility function (utility as a function of $T$)

$$V_1 = U_1 = M_1 p^{-\alpha_1} = V_1(T).$$

Differentiating, we obtain

$$\frac{dV_1}{dt} = -p^{-\alpha_1}\left[1 + \left(\alpha_1 \frac{M_1}{p} - \overline{X}_1\right)p'\right]$$

$$\frac{d^2V_1}{dT^2} = \alpha_1 p' p^{-(1+\alpha_1)}\left\{\alpha + p'\left[(1+\alpha_1)\frac{\overline{Y}_1 - T}{p} - (1-\alpha_1)\overline{X}_1\right]\right\}.$$

The term in braces is equal to

$$(1 + \alpha_1)[1 + p'/p(\overline{Y}_1 - T)] + (1 - \alpha_1)(1 - p'\overline{X}_1)$$

$$= (1 + \alpha_1)\left(1 + \frac{(\alpha_2 - \alpha_1)(\overline{Y}_1 - T)}{\alpha_1 \overline{Y}_1 + \alpha_2 \overline{Y}_2 + (\alpha_2 - \alpha_1)T}\right)$$

$$+ (1 - \alpha_1)\left(1 - \frac{(\alpha_2 - \alpha_1)\overline{X}_1}{(1 - \alpha_1)\overline{X}_1 + (1 - \alpha_2)\overline{X}_2}\right)$$

$$= \frac{(1 + \alpha_1)\alpha_2(\overline{Y}_1 + \overline{Y}_2)}{\alpha_1 \overline{Y}_1 + \alpha_2 \overline{Y}_2 + (\alpha_2 - \alpha_1)T} + \frac{(1 - \alpha_1)(1 - \alpha_2)(\overline{X}_1 + \overline{X}_2)}{(1 - \alpha_1)\overline{X}_1 + (1 - \alpha_2)\overline{X}_2}.$$

Since the denominator of the first expression is positive by the assumption that the equilibrium price $p$ is positive, $d^2 V_1/dT^2$ is positive or negative according as $p'$ is positive or negative; that is, according as $\alpha_2$ is greater or less than $\alpha_1$. This establishes the general result of this chapter, that in an international exchange economy with Cobb–Douglas utility functions, a country must gain from a reversed transfer if the price of the commodity in terms of which the transfer is denominated falls when the transfer is made and rises when the transfer is reversed, and vice versa. (Note that the price fall in the general case is consistent with either an improvement or a worsening of the terms of trade, since either denominator good may be either an export or an import good for the country undertaking the reversed transfer, depending on the relationship between countries' relative endowments and relative preferences.) The conclusion that the world as a whole loses in welfare from a reversed transfer follows simply from the concavity of the utility possibility locus to the origin when preferences differ.

## REFERENCES

1. Metzler, L. A., " The Transfer Problem Reconsidered," *The Journal of Political Economy* **50**, No. 3 (June 1942), 397–414. Reprinted in AEA *Readings in the Theory of International Trade*. Philadelphia: Blakiston, 1949.
2. Metzler, L. A., "Tariffs, the Terms of Trade, and the Distribution of the National Income," *The Journal of Political Economy* **57**, No. 1 (February 1949), 1–29.
3. Laursen, S., and Metzler, L. A., "Flexible Exchange Rates and the Theory of Employment," *Review of Economics and Statistics* **32**, No. 4 (November 1950), 281–299.
4. Johnson, H. G., "The Taxonomic Approach to Economic Policy," *The Economic Journal* **61**, No. 254 (December 1951), 812–832.
5. Keynes, J. M., "The German Transfer Problem," and Ohlin, B., "The Reparation Problem: A Discussion," in AEA *Readings in the Theory of International Trade*, Chapters 6 and 7, pp. 161–178, respectively. Philadelphia: Blakiston, 1949.
6. Samuelson, P. A., "The Transfer Problem and Transport Costs: The Terms of Trade When Impediments Are Absent," *The Economic Journal* **62**, No. 246 (June 1952), 278–304, especially p. 283.

7. Jones, R. W., "International Capital Movements and the Theory of Tariffs and Trade," *The Quarterly Journal of Economics* **81**, No. 1 (February 1967), 1–38.

8. Meade, J. E., *The Balance of Payments*. London and New York: Oxford Univ. Press, 1951.

9. Johnson, H. G., "The Transfer Problem and Exchange Stability," *The Journal of Political Economy* **64**, No. 3 (June 1956), 212–225. Reprinted in Johnson, H. G., *International Trade and Economic Growth*, Chapter VII, pp. 169–195. London: Allen and Unwin, 1958.

10. Viner, J., *Studies in the Theory of International Trade*, Chapter VI, pp. 290–387, especially Section XII, pp. 365–374. New York: Harper, 1937.

11. Hause, J. C., "The Welfare Costs of Disequilibrium Exchange Rates," *The Journal of Political Economy* **74**, No. 4 (August 1966), 333–352.

12. Johnson, H. G., "The Welfare Costs of Exchange Rate Stabilization," *The Journal of Political Economy* **74**, No. 5 (October 1966), 312–318, reprinted in Johnson, H. G., *Further Essays in Monetary Economics*. London: Allen and Unwin, 1972; "Notes on the Welfare Cost of Exchange Rate Stabilization," *The Philippine Economic Journal* **5**, No. 10 (2nd Semester 1966), 227–238.

13. Johnson, H. G., "The Monetary Approach to Balance-of-Payments Theory," *Economic Notes*, Economic Review of Monte dei Paschi di Siena **1**, No. 1 (January–April 1972), 20–39. Reprinted in Johnson, H. G., *Further Essays in Monetary Economics*. London: Allen and Unwin, 1972.

14. Friedman, M., and Savage, L. J., "The Expected Utility Hypothesis and the Measurability of Utility," *The Journal of Political Economy* **60**, No. 6 (December 1952), 463–474.

15. Tobin, J., "Liquidity Preference as Behavior towards Risk," *The Review of Economic Studies* **25**, No. 2 (February 1958), 65–86.

16. Johnson, H. G., "The Standard Theory of Tariffs," *Canadian Journal of Economics* **2**, No. 3 (August 1969), 333–352; also *The Two-Sector Model of General Equilibrium*, Chapter 1. London: Allen and Unwin, 1971.

17. Pazner, E., and Razin, A., "The Analytical Case for Exchange Rate Uncertainty." Tel-Aviv Univ. Unpublished (April 1972).

# SOME PROBLEMS OF STABILIZATION POLICY
# UNDER FLOATING EXCHANGE RATES

*M. June Flanders*

*Tel-Aviv University*

## I. Introduction

The theory of internal–external balance, or the assignment problem as related to macroeconomic policy in an open economy, has two roots.

First, Tinbergen [22] developed the general theory of economic policy in the book by that name and Meade [12] applied it specifically to the question of policy in an open economy. The Meade application, unfortunately, is based heavily on the use of policy tools which the economists of the developed, industrialized, market economies have eschewed, even if the policy makers have clung to them. These include commercial policy (changes in tariffs, quotas, subsidies, and the like) and incomes policy (wage and price controls).

Metzler [14] in his seminal paper read at the Econometrics Society meeting in December, 1960, opened the way for the second approach. What he did in that paper was essentially to consolidate the explanations of the nineteenth century gold standard and bring them up to date: the automaticity of the gold standard is preserved in that imbalances in international payments lead to continuing changes in the money supply (as long as the central bank does not act to offset them). At the same time, it is a " Keynesian " model (not in the sense of rigid prices and wages—on the contrary) in that the quantity of money and the rate of interest are related. And finally, the balance of payments and monetary policy are linked through the capital account as described, and prescribed, by Bagehot [2].

As is frequently the case, there seems to have been a connection between the history of economics and economic history (*pace* Stigler [21]). From 1914 until the late 1950's nobody thought seriously of building a model in which international adjustment depended significantly on interest-sensitive capital movements between countries. The exchange controls and restrictions of the war and postwar years greatly hindered the international movement of capital. And as far as short-term financial capital movements at any rate were concerned, after the experience of the interwar years, their demise was generally regarded with approval. There was little nostalgia in the memories of the hot money movements of the 1930's, often politically motivated, generally exacerbating an already chaotic and disorderly situation (*vide*, e.g. Nurkse [17], passim).

During the 1960's there have been other developments of thought on the subject of policy for external and internal balance, developments which followed two separate and almost parallel tracks. On one, the models were honed and refined and made ever more sophisticated. But they continued to be aimed basically at the same question: How, if at all, can the monetary authorities achieve internal and external balance simultaneously, under alternative exchange rate regimes? External balance was defined, with cheerful indifference, as either a zero (sometimes, a given) rate of change in the level of international reserves, in the case of pegged exchange rates, or a zero (sometimes, a given) rate of change in the exchange rate, under flexible rates. In this format, the models could be solved to show which policy mixes would be effective and which not. But there was nothing within the models as built and exercised which gave any presumption toward a preference of one type of exchange-rate regime over the other.[1]

On the parallel track, advocacy of a system of flexible exchange rates was growing and strengthening among professional and academic economists. Starting with Friedman [5] through Meade [13] and Haberler [6] and up to Sohmen [20], the idea has gained strength and adherents. And recently, it has been spreading outside the confines of the profession. In a desire to meet the politicians halfway, economists have been talking increasingly about limited flexibility rather than totally free floating.[2] That is, many current advocates of reforms involving sliding and widening and crawling would really prefer floating, but refrain from advocacy thereof in the belief that the " real world " is not yet ready to take the plunge.

---

[1] For an excellent survey of this literature, see Whitman [23]. A major addition to the literature, which appeared after this survey, is that of Claassen and Salin [4].

[2] The Bürgenstock Papers (Halm [7]) constitute a fine example of this trend.

I propose here to remain in the ivory tower of freely floating exchange rates, but yet to look out onto the real world. I ask what benefits that world might expect to derive from a system of freely and cleanly floating exchange rates, and what problems it might expect to face.[3]

The pros and cons of floating exchange rates have been discussed in two conceptually distinct frameworks. On the one hand, there is the question of whether (government intervention aside) such a system is possible, that is, whether the foreign exchange markets are likely to be stable. On the other hand, we have the question of whether the operations of a stable foreign exchange market lead to desirable results compared to either permanently fixed rates or frequently adjusted pegs.

I shall not deal here with the stability problem, either in terms of the "elasticity pessimism" which is aimed at the shape of the demand and supply functions of traders, or in terms of the separate question of the effects of speculation.[4] I shall assume simply both that there is a stable equilibrium in the foreign exchange market and that speculation will be stabilizing.

The question of the desirability of floating exchange rates, as distinct from their possibility, can again be broken into categories, roughly the real and the monetary. The argument on the real side is whether the advantages of adjustment to structural changes (in tastes or in technology or in factor endowments) outweigh the costs of frequent fluctuation, or the costs of insuring against such fluctuations, or the cost of excessive frequency of adjustment and movements of resources in response to what prove to be temporary disturbances.[5] This question too I ignore.

The monetary argument for exchange rate flexibility is that it is easier, in such a system, to execute a policy program directed at internal balance and to insulate oneself from the events in other countries (whether these be due to different policy goals abroad or to the clumsiness of foreign policy makers and their inability to achieve their desired goals). Furthermore, it is generally understood that a floating exchange rate regime avoids the redundancy problem and the related questions of the consistency of the several desired rates of exchange of the individual countries. These are the issues I propose to deal with. That is, I shall be concerned with short-run stabilization policy (hence

---

[3] I shall use the term "floating" to distinguish the case of nonintervention in the foreign exchange market from that of either a frequently adjusted adjustable peg, or a "float" in which the authorities are generally believed, correctly, to be intervening. For the problems of defining such a case unambiguously, see McKinnon [11].

[4] For an excellent and detailed discussion of both of these issues, extensively annotated, the reader is referred to Chapters I and III, respectively, of Sohmen [20].

[5] See the discussion by Lanyi [8]. For a novel defense of the benefits of fluctuations per se, see Pazner and Razin [18].

with disequilibrium situations) in a world characterized by flexible exchange rates, Phillips curves, and mobile international capital.

That capital is in fact highly mobile between the important money markets of the world is hardly to be disputed. The close integration of these markets is viewed as a mixed blessing. It is obvious that in the current system of the adjustable peg, speculative capital movements play a highly destabilizing role. And movements of capital in response to interest rate differentials are alleged frequently to frustrate the stabilization programs of the authorities. Yet it is not obvious that under a flexible rate system, even without destabilizing speculation, there would not be serious problems stemming from the international mobility of short-term capital.

In fact, the effect of a high degree of capital mobility may be more serious in a flexible than in a pegged rate system (if one ignores for the moment the major problem of speculation in the expectation of a large change in an adjustable peg). The reason is as follows. In a system of perfectly mobile capital, the interest rate is identical throughout the world. In a pegged rate system, the rationale for the system is that there is—or there should be—a high degree of coordination and a similarity between countries with respect to growth rates and rates of price level change. The fact that capital movements tend to bring interest rates closer together (in the limiting case, to make them identical) helps to bring rates of investment, of saving, of growth, and levels of income, closer together. Furthermore, if changes are temporary and short-lived, capital flows finance imbalances and avert the need for basic structural adjustments.

On the other hand, the prime advantage of flexibility in exchange rates is that it recognizes the desire (if not the desirability) of countries to pursue independent policies and to insulate themselves from one another. Any change in a single economy, including a change in the growth rate, which depends on there being a change in the rate of interest, and hence may depend on the rate of interest in that economy being different from that in the rest of the world, becomes difficult (in the limiting case, impossible).

In short, one can say that international mobility of capital strengthens the purported advantages of a fixed rate system (to wit, interdependence of countries) but weakens the argument in favor of flexibility (that is to say, independence).

## II. Policy Considerations for a Single Country

Consider now a world of floating exchange rates. The authorities do not intervene in either the spot or the forward markets for foreign exchange. Assume that speculation is stabilizing, in the sense of tending to bring the exchange rates toward their equilibrium values.

Assume that commercial policy is given and unchanging, and that restrictions on exchange movements and direct controls, if they exist at all, are unchanging.

Policy tools are the level of government spending (or the rate of taxation), and operations on the open market for domestic securities. (Under a floating exchange rate regime, the authorities do not operate in the foreign exchange market.) Open market operations affect the quantity of money; to the extent that capital is not perfectly mobile, they also affect the rate of interest. If capital is perfectly mobile internationally, the rate of interest is exogenously determined.

Policy goals include something which for the moment can be labeled very generally "internal balance." Other goals may include the growth rate,[6] the public–private expenditure mix, determined by various welfare and by non-economic considerations; the consumption–investment mix, which may be a final goal or an intermediate goal influenced by the target growth rate; the size of the trade surplus. This last may be a final goal as well as an intermediate goal. There are a number of considerations here. One is the irrational but (to me) undeniable streak of mercantilism that seems to run through all policy makers. Another is the fact that in the short run a surplus on trade account implies a decrease in resources available for home use, since it involves lending abroad. Attitudes toward a surplus, then, will be closely related to the rate of time preference in the social welfare function. Additionally, the export surplus is a major intermediate policy tool, as we shall see.

Consider first the case of *a small country*, and consider the now-standard Mundellian analysis of the assignment problem, in which there is excess capacity and *prices are rigid*.

## A. FISCAL POLICY

In such a world, an increase in government spending creates excess demand in the commodity market and also in the money market. The resulting upward pressure on the rate of interest induces an inflow of capital.[7]

With exchange rates flexible, the capital inflow bids up the price of domestic currency on the foreign exchange market, which stimulates net imports, offsetting the expansionary effect on employment of the initial increase in expenditures. With the interest rate exogenously determined, total expenditures

---

[6] This is not inconsistent with the earlier statement that this is a short-run, disequilibrium model. A country may be (in general will be) in disequilibrium most of the time. That does not mean that the authorities, in determining their macropolicy programs, will ignore the impact of alternative programs on the rate of growth.

[7] In the pegged exchange rate system, this capital inflow implies a surplus in the balance of payments and an open market operation in the foreign exchange market. The public holdings of domestic money increase, as does the central bank's holding of foreign currency. There has thus been a passive, involuntary monetary policy accompanying the fiscal policy.

can increase, of course, only if the real quantity of money also increases. In the case of pegged exchange rates, the monetary authorities are forced, by the very act of pegging the rate, to expand the domestic money supply. With floating rates, this imperative is lacking and the money supply (by assumption) is unchanged. Expenditures are therefore affected only to the extent that real balances increase (due to the fall in price of traded goods, that is, the fall in the price of foreign currency). Aside from this effect, there is an increase in government spending offset by a decrease in net exports. On the production side, there is a shift from traded goods in the direction of those things which the government buys.

If, on the other hand, the central bank finances the increase in government spending, then on the "first round" there is an increase in total expenditures. Neither the interest rate nor foreign holdings of domestic securities will change, and the exchange rate will *depreciate* by an extent depending on the net marginal propensity to import and the elasticities of demand and supply of traded and nontraded goods.

## B. MONETARY POLICY

An expansion in the quantity of money results in downward pressure on the rate of interest, a capital outflow, and upward pressure on the price of foreign exchange.[8] The price of foreign currency rises, net imports fall, and the demand for domestic output increases. Monetary policy alone is thus highly effective.[9]

To summarize. If capital is perfectly mobile, then under a pegged rate regime, the authorities have no control over the quantity of money. They can increase the level of output only by increasing government spending (or decreasing taxes). This will be financed by domestic money creation as the central bank trades domestic bank deposits either for foreign currency (if it is pursuing a passive monetary policy) or for domestic securities (in the case of an active monetary policy).

---

[8] With pegged exchange rates, the activities of the monetary authorities in the foreign exchange market involve a decrease in the public holding of domestic money, wiping out the initial increase.

[9] Caves and Reuber [3, pp. 49–50], indicate that this is a no-lose system, having flexible exchange rates and monetary tools. By this they mean that if capital is mobile, the effect of monetary policy is through external influences (the balance of trade) and if capital is immobile, monetary tools work through the conventional internal channels. My point, however, is that the authorities are not likely to be indifferent for long as between the two types of stimulus, because in the "real world" it may matter to a country whether it increases investment by lending abroad or by engaging in real capital formation at home.

Under floating exchange rates, the authorities have a choice. And here precisely is the extra degree of freedom about which we hear so much.[10] They can raise the level of total expenditures by increasing government spending (or decreasing taxes), but if this is unaccompanied by an increase in the money supply it works only through the real balances effect. Or they can increase government spending and expand the money supply at the same time. Alternatively, they can increase employment by monetary policy alone, which essentially means that they are engaging in foreign lending to the extent of the size of the multiplicand (since the injection in this case is the export surplus). In the short run, a "selfish" or "short-sighted" country would presumably prefer to increase its spending domestically. In the long run one needs to compare the relative rates of return on government spending, private domestic spending, and foreign investment.[11]

There may, of course, be various motivations of political convenience and expedience which make it easier for the authorities to use the foreign trade sector as the valve for making frequent adjustments. In our neomercantilist world, it may be less controversial to take action which expands exports than to increase government expenditures or to cut taxes, with the danger that one may have to raise them again in the (near) future. However, the choice is not an all-or-nothing one. As long as one tool is sufficient for achieving internal balance, presently defined as a certain level of employment, we can think of using monetary policy to achieve this and fiscal policy to achieve the desired domestic–foreign spending mix, or the desired public–private spending mix. The structural question of where the increased spending is likely to do the most good in terms of eliminating unemployment most directly may well play an important role in the decision. For instance, if unemployment is particularly heavy in the construction industry, an increase in government spending accompanied by an increase in the money supply may be an efficient policy program. In other situations, the direct stimulus to the traded goods sector caused by monetary policy alone may be more effective as a stimulant to employment. Note, however, that the way the fiscal–monetary mix affects the structure of the economy is precisely through the rate of exchange; that is, every combination of fiscal and monetary policy which yields the same level of output implies a different exchange rate. In this sense there is no such thing

---

[10] The analog under pegged rates is the ability to determine the size of the debt to foreigners, relative to the size of the internal debt.

[11] If private domestic spending means private domestic investment, the rate of return on this is presumably the same as on foreign investment in a world of perfect capital mobility. If the comparison is with private domestic consumption, the relevant comparison is with the domestic rate of social time preference. In long-run equilibrium, of course, these rates are all identical.

as a really clean float, even if there is no intervention in the foreign exchange market and the authorities do not view the exchange rate as a policy goal.

Now instead of rigid prices, consider the world of the *Phillips curve*, in which both the price level and employment are variable. (Without entering into the debate over the existence of the Phillips curve, particularly as a long-run phenomenon, I simply point to the fact of the simultaneous existence of unemployment and inflation in many countries.) The policy goal, in such a world, may be to achieve a particular point on a Phillips curve. An alternative, or an additional, goal may be to shift, or twist, the curve.

In its simplest version, a Phillips curve is a single-valued relationship between the level of unemployment and the rate of inflation. If the level of expenditures is changed—either by the use of monetary policy, which affects the rate of interest, or by fiscal policy—the level of unemployment and the rate of inflation will both change. Additions to the money supply serve to enlarge "transactions balances" (where they both "finance" higher prices and enlarge real balances, if output is expanding) and to increase the demand for securities (which, in a closed economy, influences the rate of interest and hence expenditures).

However, if the authorities wish to attain a combination of inflation and unemployment which is not on the existing Phillips curve this will be possible, if at all, only if both fiscal and monetary tools are applied to this end.

In an open economy with mobile capital, the interest rate is not an endogenous variable. If exchange rates are fixed, the money supply is endogenous, but it is not a policy tool. Thus, shifting the Phillips curve may be impossible; that is, it may be impossible to achieve any combination of unemployment and inflation which is not on the existing curve.

But with flexible exchange rates and mobile capital, it may also be impossible to shift the Phillips curve. In this world, we can think of additions to the money supply as finding their way into the goods market and into the foreign exchange market (rather than the domestic securities market) where they feed back into the goods market through changes in the exchange rate, leaving the Phillips curve unaffected.

Alternatively, it may be that the Phillips curve itself varies with the rate of exchange, in which case there may be more than one rate of inflation corresponding to each level of unemployment, depending on how the corresponding level of output is attained. Whether or not this is the case depends very much on the wage bargaining mechanism, on the extent of openness of the economy, and on the structure of trade: whether, for example, traded goods tend to be wages goods (or inputs in general), so that every increase in the price of foreign exchange leads to wage increases and increases in the price of nontraded goods as well.[12] If this is the case, the mix of fiscal and monetary policy required to achieve a desired level of employment may be determined by this feedback effect. Specifically, the authorities may need to use more fiscal stimulus instead of monetary expansion in order to increase employment; more, that is, than in the case in which the Phillips curve was invariant with respect to the exchange rate. Every combination of fiscal and monetary policy yields a different exchange rate, so here again there is no such thing as a really clean float.

In a rigid price world, a small country with a pegged exchange rate can choose the composition of the central bank's portfolio (as between domestic and foreign debt); whereas a small country under flexible rates has the freedom to determine something perhaps more important: the composition of expenditures as between the public and the private sectors. In a Phillips curve world, this freedom may be lost, since both monetary and fiscal policy may be required to achieve a predetermined combination of unemployment and inflation.[13]

## C. The Independence of the Rate of Inflation

We turn now to the question of the freedom of an individual (small) country to choose its rate of inflation. That is, can a single country have a rate of inflation different from that of its trading partners?

Suppose that a particular country has an unusually "far out" Phillips curve and/or suppose that the authorities are particularly averse to unemployment, so that "internal balance" implies a higher rate of inflation than the rest of the world. (We can, of course, phrase the question from the opposite normative point of view: Can a "sensible" country protect itself from the inflationary excesses of its partners, on the one hand, or the pathological anti-inflationary bias of other countries, on the other?)

With pegged exchange rates and capital immobile, an above-average rate of inflation can be sustained only as long as foreign exchange reserves last. This is, of course, the standard argument *in favor of* fixed exchange rates— the imposition of "discipline" on the profligate treasuries of the world. Or

---

[12] This last, fairly mechanistic, relationship between retail prices and the prices of traded goods inputs, has been noted more often by British than by American writers, for fairly obvious reasons. A good example of a Phillips curve model involving such a relationship is that of Lipsey and Parkin [9].

[13] Mundell [16] has argued recently that monetary and fiscal policy are both needed, as independent tools, to achieve a given set of price level and unemployment goals, even in the context of fixed exchange rates.

else it is the standard argument *against* fixed rates—the lack of freedom to engage in one's own internal policy.

With pegged rates and mobile capital, the inflationary pressure tends to push up nominal interest rates and attract foreign capital. This prevents (or retards) the depletion of the foreign exchange reserves and provides the domestic money to finance the inflation. It will continue until either the inflow of capital is matched by the interest and amortization payments plus the growing balance of trade deficit (as the exchange rate gets more and more "out of line") or until the country has attracted so much capital that it becomes a monopsonist in world securities markets and capital is no longer infinitely mobile. Correcting the balance of payments deficit then requires generating ever higher domestic interest rates, which in turn will offset the expansionary effect of the fiscal policy and make it increasingly difficult to pursue the existing policy without altering the exchange rate. Such a system, then, is workable only if it is temporary. That is, any country can undertake an expansionary policy, involving more-than-average inflation, and finance this policy by borrowing from abroad, but no country can do this indefinitely.

If the country with "excess inflation" is not always the same country (if there is no country with chronic "excess inflation") then the system is viable.

The ability to sustain, indefinitely, a rate of inflation different from that in one's trading partners is a major advantage claimed for floating exchange rates. We can think of a steady state with nominal interest rates higher than the real rate by the amount of inflation. With tastes given, the spot rate will change at the same rate, and the forward discount (equal to the rate of "excess inflation" over the rest of the world) will reflect the expectation of the decline in the spot rate and will prevent the capital movements which would otherwise exert additional pressure on the spot rate. The price ratio of traded and nontraded goods does not change, and the process can continue indefinitely.

### III. The "$n-1$" Problem

Thus far, I have dealt with the problems of a small country and have not been concerned with either the policy responses or the endogenous feedback resulting from any change in the home country.[14]

---

[14] This is the world, for example, envisaged by Sohmen when he writes as follows: "Under flexible exchange rates, employment rises . . . because exports rise relatively to imports. It might be objected that this effect occurs at the expense of a fall of employment in the rest of the world. . . .When other countries experience a "worsening". . .of their trade balance under. . .a system of *flexible* exchange rates, . . .this never imposes the slightest need for unwarranted contraction on them. . . .[T]hey are always perfectly free to adopt whatever expansionary policies they consider appropriate—in contrast with a system of

I turn now to the question of interactions between countries. Assume that there are $n$ countries, where $n$ is small enough so that we have to worry about what is happening in other countries, and large enough so that we can continue to assume that capital movements are highly (infinitely) mobile over some significant range.

In the earlier literature, the fact that $n$ countries can have only $n - 1$ exchange rates between them was referred to as the "redundancy problem," and the discussions generally gave it a benign air. Thus, to quote Mundell [15, p. 379]: "Only $n - 1$ independent balance-of-payments instruments are needed in an $n$-country world because equilibrium in the balances of $n - 1$ countries implies equilibrium in the balance of the $n$th country. The *redundancy problem* is the problem of deciding how to utilize the extra degree of freedom." This is a perfectly correct statement, but the problem as defined here has an air of gentility which may not be justified. It is, of course, true that if all countries want to attain zero balances of payments, then one country need not be concerned about its balance of payments, and the question then is how to choose the lucky country and to decide what it is to be allowed to do with its free policy tool. But one can also state the problem as follows, making it sound more sinister, albeit technically equivalent: In a world of $n$ countries, if the balance-of-payments goals are not all zero balance, then there must be one country which *cannot* decide what its balance of payments will be; one country, that is, which cannot achieve its goal. If the several countries wish to change the levels of their foreign exchange reserves, then the goals of the individual countries will be consistent with one another only by accident.

Consider, as before, a world of pegged exchange rates, mobile capital, and rigid prices. The authorities in all countries rely on fiscal policy to determine the level of employment and use monetary policy to determine the level of reserves and the level of foreign indebtedness. The more money is issued domestically during a period of expansionary fiscal policy, the less the inflow of foreign capital, and the lower both the level of foreign exchange reserves and the level of debt to foreigners. There is no mechanism which tends to equate the surpluses and deficits that would emerge from such decision making. Only if there is at least one country which is really indifferent to its balance of payments (and level of foreign exchange reserves)—only then is there no redundancy problem, and only if there is some way for it to absorb the surplus or finance the deficit implied by satisfying the goals of the other $n - 1$ countries—only then is there no liquidity problem.

---

fixed rates, in which their freedom of action may be seriously impaired [from E. Sohmen, *Flexible Exchange Rates*. Chicago: Univ. of Chicago, 1969; copyright 1969 by the University of Chicago.]"

The last point is important. It is not unreasonable to argue that the picture drawn here describes the world of the 1960's (cf. McKinnon [10, pp. 30–31]). Two essential requirements were satisfied. There was one country, the United States, which did not really care about its balance of payments and was willing to permit the deficit which matched the desired surplus of the rest of the world. And at the same time, the United States was able to finance its deficit with an asset which the surplus countries wanted to acquire.[15] When this last was no longer true and the deficit ran into conflict with the conditions for maintaining the "quality" of international money, we witnessed the emergence of the "confidence problem," culminating in the crises of 1971. Those who today advocate a fixed exchange rate system with "reforms" are essentially seeking a device for changing the amount of international liquidity regularly, without compromising its quality, so that the quantity (the supply) should conform to the "needs" (the demand?) of the world. This involves either somehow restoring the unlimited acceptability of the dollar, or establishing either an outside agency, or a set of rules, for adding to (or subtracting from) the world's reserves, in accordance with the net desired deficit (or surplus).

Consider, alternatively, a situation in which there are not two independent tools, or in which another goal has been added. This means using both monetary and fiscal policy to achieve internal balance, as Meade suggested. Again, we can express this most conveniently in terms of the need for two tools because the authorities want to shift the Phillips curve. In this case, the authorities pursue a fiscal policy designed to attain a certain level of employment, and they will try to change the money supply more or less than required to sustain the prevailing rate of inflation (as recommended by Mundell [16]). The level of employment and the rate of price level increase will determine the "natural balance of trade." The rate of domestic credit creation will determine the "natural balance on capital account,"[16] which is the capital inflow required to peg the interest rate at the world level. Together these will establish the "natural balance of payments" on official account, and there is no reason for these to sum to zero for the world as a whole. Some authority (or authorities) will be frustrated in trying to carry about the domestic policy program. Thus, from a redundancy of tools we have come, quickly, to an "inadequacy problem."

Now consider a world of floating exchange rates. What is the problem analogous to that of "redundancy"? As before, I maintain the assumption of mobile capital.

In order to attain a predetermined point on a given Phillips curve, we

---

[15] *Vide* Aliber [1] for a statement of this "demand theory" of the balance of payments.
[16] The use of this term here is an easy extension of the concept as defined by Metzler [14].

require a particular level of real expenditure and a given quantity of money available to the goods market. Both the real expenditures and the supply of money (to the goods market) are functions, *inter alia*, of the rate of interest, but in a world of perfect international capital mobility this is given, so real expenditures depend on the government deficit and the foreign trade deficit.

As already described, an increase in the money supply influences both the goods market, where it stimulates output and price increases; and the securities market, where it affects the exchange rate. At least part of the multiplicand in the expansion process, then, is the export surplus, the size of which depends on the various relevant elasticities: the response of expenditures to the increased money supply and the effect of this on the net demand for imports; the response of prices to the rise in output (and increased cash balances), which influences the exchange rate directly. Now, a simultaneous fiscal expansion will shift the public–private spending mix and will also decrease the foreign trade surplus. That is, it substitutes some public spending for exports as the multiplicand. The point is that the same point on the Phillips curve can be achieved by a variety of fiscal–monetary policy combinations, each one implying a different rate of exchange. Again, as stated earlier, there is no really clean float. The authorities affect the exchange rate through their macropolicies whether they want to or not.

Now, if the authorities care about the exchange rate, or if they care about the public–private spending mix, or if they care about the output mix of traded and nontraded goods, or if they care about the amount of foreign lending, they will combine their fiscal and monetary actions in a way to attempt to achieve their goals in these respects; and there is no reason for these domestic policy programs to be consistent with one another for the world as a whole.

If, on the other hand, the authorities are indifferent to all of the above-mentioned variables (including, I repeat, the size of the public sector, which is a strong assumption indeed), then there exists a set of equilibrium exchange rates, but I am unable to formulate a set of rules for the several authorities which will achieve that constellation of rates. Essentially, a set of rules for this purpose would involve estimating the level of capital exports appropriate to the given interest rate and differences in the marginal productivity of capital. This would yield a set of current account surpluses which would sum to zero for the world as a whole; it would yield, that is to say, consistency. The authorities in each country would then be instructed to use monetary policy to achieve the desired level of employment (which implies a certain rate of inflation) and to use fiscal policy in order to maintain balance in the basic balance of payments. This is, of course, not operational, due to the impossibility of establishing, by objective criteria, what the "appropriate" amount of capital transfer should be.

Furthermore, when we recognize, as in the previous discussion, that the position of the Phillips curve may not be invariant with respect to the exchange rate, this hard-earned consistency again disappears, and we are back in the "inadequacy problem," because the attainment of a certain combination of unemployment and inflation requires a particular mix of monetary and fiscal policies—the mix that will give the "correct" level of effective demand and "correct" exchange rate for the desired rate of inflation. There is no reason to expect the "correct" exchange rates, thus defined, to be consistent with one another.

When capital is completely immobile, these problems do not arise. Here we have the traditional case for flexible exchange rates. With capital immobile, the authorities direct monetary and fiscal policy at achieving whatever they consider to be internal balance, and the exchange rate clears the foreign exchange market. The exchange rate can be affected, in such a system, only by changes in expenditure or by the imposition of direct controls. The interaction between the exchange rate and the Phillips curve relationship may, of course, make the life of the policy maker more difficult, but it does not affect the existence of equilibrium in the world's foreign exchange markets, except in the case in which prices and wages rise by the full amount of the price of foreign exchange. (In that case, there can never be any change in the price relationship of traded and nontraded goods; the exchange rate then ceases to have any influence on the relative price structure and hence on the trade pattern. Stated differently, in such a case the "real" exchange rate could never change and hence would have no allocative or market-clearing power.)

In a world of mobile capital, on the other hand, it is not only true that, as McKinnon [11] and others have pointed out, the actions of the monetary authorities influence domestic monetary variables whether the action is in the open market for domestic securities or in the market for foreign exchange; the other side of the coin is that any actions of the monetary authorities, whether in the securities market or in the foreign exchange market, influences the exchange rate; again, clean floating is simply impossible.[17] The

[17] This is implied in the following statement by Plumptre: "...since any exchange rate, whether floating or pegged, is affected by monetary, fiscal, and other economic policies, a country with a floating rate must expect to expose and discuss its whole range of such policies with others in the international community. The consultations that take place. . .do not become irrelevant or unnecessary merely because one exchange-rate policy is substituted for another. It may in fact be argued that the need for consultations. . .may be even greater under a floating than under a fixed rate. The rules of the game, the codes of acceptable behavior are of course different; but rules and codes there must be if economic warfare is to be prevented and if economic peace is to prevail [from A. F. W. Plumptre, *Exchange Rate Policy: Experience with Canada's Floating Rate*. Princeton, New Jersey: Princeton Univ., Internat. Finance Section, Essays in International Finance No. 81, 1970]."

exchange rate, in such a system, is not merely the price which equates demand and supply for traded goods once macroeconomic equilibrium has been established. The exchange rate becomes, rather, a major intermediate tool of stabilization policy, whether used deliberately to that end or not; whether influenced by operations in the foreign exchange market or by operations in the "domestic" money markets.

## IV. Conclusion

What, in sum, can we say about policy recommendations? This is not intended as a tract against flexible exchange rates. It is intended, however, to serve as a caveat against overselling the advantages of exchange rate flexibility, lest we be too sorely disappointed by the results. Some of the problems which we have encountered in recent years on the international monetary front have arisen from the rigidity of exchange rates; others from the high degree of international capital mobility; others still from the inherent difficulty of managing an effective macroeconomic stabilization policy. Not all of these difficulties will be eliminated by a movement to highly or completely flexible exchange rates.

Nor am I suggesting adoption of restrictions and controls on capital movements. It is difficult, if not impossible, to eliminate only the "undesirable" and maintain the "desirable" capital movements, those that do increase world efficiency. Furthermore, controls are both difficult and costly to apply, and imperfectly successful at best. The close interaction between trade transactions and short-term capital movements implies that either many speculative movements would get through the net of controls, or that much "legitimate" trade would be discouraged.

The real world presents problems less tractable than the capital-movement-free world of Milton Friedman of 1953 and more difficult than the price-less world of Mundell of the early 1960's. But floating exchange rates would clear the foreign exchange markets; they would minimize the structural upheavals brought on by monetary disturbances; and they would (or might) prevent stubborn finance ministers from going to great and painful lengths to defend inappropriate exchange rates. If they accomplished only this we should have gained much.

### ACKNOWLEDGMENTS

My thanks in general to my colleagues who commented on various versions of this chapter. Very particular thanks to Jacob Frenkel, Elchanan Helpman, Elisha Pazner, and Yoram Weiss; also to the Foerder Institute for Economic Research for assistance in preparation of the manuscript.

REFERENCES

1. Aliber, R. Z., "Choices for the Dollar," Washington, D.C.: Planning Pamphlets No. 127, Nat. Planning Assoc., 1969.
2. Bagehot, W., *Lombard Street, A Description of the Money Market*. Homewood, Illinois: Irwin, 1962. Reprinted from Scribner Armstrong, New York, 1873.
3. Caves, R. E., and Reuber, G. L., *Capital Transfers and Economic Policy: Canada, 1951–1962*. Cambridge, Massachusetts: Harvard Univ. Press, 1971.
4. Claassen, E., and Salin, P., eds., *Stabilization Policies in Interdependent Economies*. Amsterdam: North-Holland Publ., 1972.
5. Friedman, M., "The Case for Flexible Exchange Rates," in *Essays in Positive Economics*. Chicago: Univ. of Chicago Press, 1953.
6. Haberler, G., *Currency Convertibility*. Washington, D.C.: American Enterprise Association, 1954.
7. Halm, G. N., *Approaches to Greater Flexibility of Exchange Rates: The Bürgenstock Papers* (arranged by C. F. Bergsten, G. N. Halm, F. Machlup, and R. V. Roosa). Princeton, New Jersey: Princeton Univ. Press, 1970.
8. Lanyi, A., *The Case for Floating Exchange Rates Reconsidered*. Princeton, New Jersey: Princeton Univ., Internat. Finance Section, Essays in Internat. Finance No. 72, 1969.
9. Lipsey, R. G., and Parkin, J. M., "Incomes Policy: A Re-appraisal," *Economica* **37** (1970), 115–137.
10. McKinnon, R., *Private and Official International Money: The Case for the Dollar*. Princeton, New Jersey: Princeton Univ., Internat. Finance Section, Essays in International Finance No. 74, 1969.
11. McKinnon, R. I., *Monetary Theory and Controlled Flexibility in the Foreign Exchanges*. Princeton, New Jersey: Princeton Univ., Internat. Finance Section, Essays in International Finance No. 84, 1971.
12. Meade, J. E., *The Balance of Payments*. London and New York: Oxford Univ. Press, 1951.
13. Meade, J. E., "The Case for Variable Exchange Rates," *Three Banks Review* (1955), 3–27.
14. Metzler, L. A., "The Process of International Adjustment under Conditions of Full Employment: A Keynesian View," in *Readings in International Economics* (R. E. Caves and H. G. Johnson, eds.). Amer. Econ. Assoc. and Homewood, Illinois: Irwin, 1968.
15. Mundell, R. A., "The Redundancy Problem and the World Price Level," in *Monetary Problems of the International Economy* (R. A. Mundell and A. K. Swoboda, eds.). Chicago: Univ. of Chicago Press, 1969.
16. Mundell, R. A., *The Dollar and the Policy Mix: 1971*. Princeton, New Jersey: Princeton Univ. Internat. Finance Section, Essays in International Finance No. 85, 1971.
17. [Nurkse, R.], *International Currency Experience, Lessons of the Inter-War Period*. League of Nations, Economic, Financial and Transit Dept. 1944.
18. Pazner, E., and Razin, A., "The Analytical Case for Exchange Rate Uncertainty." Tel-Aviv Univ. Unpublished. (April 1972).
19. Plumptre, A. F. W., *Exchange Rate Policy: Experience with Canada's Floating Rate*. Princeton, New Jersey: Princeton Univ. Internat. Finance Section, Essays in International Finance No. 81, 1970.
20. Sohmen, E., *Flexible Exchange Rates* (rev. ed.). Chicago: Univ. of Chicago Press, 1969.

21. Stigler, G. J., "The Influence of Events and Policies on Economic Theory," *American Economic Review* **50** (1960), 36–45. Reprinted in *Essays in the History of Economics.* Chicago: Univ. of Chicago Press, 1965.
22. Tinbergen, J., *On the Theory of Economic Policy*, 3rd ed. Amsterdam: North-Holland Publ., 1963.
23. Whitman, M. vN., *Policies for Internal and External Balance.* Princeton, New Jersey: Princeton Univ., Internat. Finance Section, Special Papers in International Economics No. 9, 1970.

# DEVALUATION AND THE BALANCE OF TRADE UNDER FLEXIBLE WAGES

*Joanne Salop*

*Board of Governors*
 *of the Federal Reserve System*

## Introduction

The current revival of interest in devaluation among policy makers makes this an appropriate time for reconsidering our conclusions about the effects of exchange rate changes. To this end this chapter presents a general macroeconomic model of the open economy and analyzes the effects of devaluation on the trade balance, output, and employment. Crucial to the analysis is the endogeneity of domestic prices, for a devaluation which leads to a rise in domestic prices is really a net devaluation of smaller magnitude. In fact, if domestic prices rise by the same percentage as the devaluation, then the relative prices of imports and exports are unchanged, leaving the trade balance unimproved.

The prevailing theory of balance of payments adjustments assumes that domestic prices do not rise on devaluation as long as the economy is less than fully employed. However, when there is full employment, lowering the exchange rate causes prices to be bid up as the increased level of aggregate demand pushes against the constant aggregate supply of output. In the context of the full employment model, Meade [4] showed that domestic

129

prices would rise by the full percentage of the devaluation if the interest rate were pegged by the monetary authorities. Since both income and the interest rate are fixed, a change in the exchange rate can result only in a change in prices, so that devaluation is unsuccessful in improving the balance. This is easily explained in terms of Alexander's [1] theory in which a reduction in domestic absorption is a necessary condition for the balance of trade of a fully employed economy to improve on devaluation. In Meade's model, constant income implies constant consumption, and constant interest rate implies constant investment. Since it does not reduce absorption, devaluation is unsuccessful in improving the balance and instead causes prices to rise to eliminate the excess demand it initiates.

In amending Meade's and Alexander's work, Tsiang [9] showed the following. If the monetary authorities were to hold constant the nominal supply of money rather than the interest rate, devaluation, even at full employment, would improve the balance. As prices begin to rise from the initial increase in demand, the real supply of money falls, thereby raising the interest rate. This causes investment to fall from its predevaluation level, allowing the difference between the two investment levels to be directed toward the foreign sector. As exports increase and imports are displaced by domestic products, the balance improves; however, for this to occur, domestic goods must become relatively cheaper. Hence prices must rise by less than the devaluation; the reduction in absorption allows the trade balance to improve at full employment.

While this analysis recognizes that prices rise on devaluation, it assumes they rise only in response to excess demand. All feedback from the labor market onto prices is ignored by assuming that the supply of labor is perfectly elastic at the current nominal wage up to the point of full employment and perfectly inelastic thereafter. Thus the nominal wage is affected only when labor is fully employed and then the change is dictated solely by demand conditions. Consequently, these models are inappropriate for analyzing devaluations in which labor, either through unions or the classical mechanism, is successful in raising money wages and domestic prices. In order to incorporate these wage-push price increases into the analysis and capture more fully the effects of devaluation on prices, this paper replaces the Keynesian supply assumption of the Meade–Tsiang model with the classical assumption that labor supply is positively related to the real wage. We find that the conclusions about the effects of devaluation are extremely sensitive to this assumption.

In Section I we present the model and indicate that devaluation at full employment improves the trade balance, but reduces output and employment levels. In order to explain this result and provide a graphical framework for analyzing related questions, Section II solves the model for the macroeconomic equilibrium using IS–LM and aggregate supply and demand analysis. Using the same tools Section III analyzes the effects of devaluation and clarifies the role of the classical labor supply assumption in determining our conclusions. Section IV examines the Meade–Tsiang model and introduces unemployment into our classical analysis. Section V presents our conclusions.

## Symbols

| | |
|---|---|
| $r$ | Interest rate |
| $Y$ | Output |
| $F$ | Exogenous price of foreign good in foreign currency |
| $\rho$ | Exchange rate, expressed in units of foreign currency per unit of domestic currency |
| $D$ | Selling price of domestically produced good in local currency |
| $R$ | Terms of trade; $R = D/(F/\rho)$ |
| $Y_b$ | Exogenous foreign income |
| $L$ | Exogenous nominal supply of money |
| $P$ | Consumers' price index |
| $DY/P$ | Real income |
| $N$ | Employment |
| $w$ | Money wage |
| $N^d$ | Quantity of labor demanded |
| $N^s$ | Quantity of labor supplied |
| $B$ | Balance of trade: exports minus imports (in domestic output terms) |
| $X$ | Exports |
| $M$ | Imports |

## I. A Macromodel of an Open Economy

In this section a simple macroeconomic model[1] of an open economy is developed to analyze the effects of devaluation on income, employment, and the balance of trade. The economy consists of markets for labor services, money, and goods, which simultaneously interact in the determination of the aggregate level of income and the price level. Starting from a point of macroeconomic equilibrium in which it is assumed that the balance of trade is zero, the exchange rate is lowered and the effect of this change on the markets is analyzed.

We consider the economy at a moment of time and treat wealth and the capital stock as exogenous. Although saving and investment are occurring, there are flows which do not affect the current stocks of wealth and physical capital. For the same reason, we ignore the effect of trade surpluses and deficits on the stock of money. Since we assume there are no capital flows,

---

[1] This is an extension of the conventional aggregate demand and supply analysis. For an exposition of the closed-economy case see Tobin [8].

a trade surplus (deficit) is reflected in an increase (decrease) in the domestic money supply. However, these changes are flows, and while they affect the future level, do not affect the current money stock which is also treated as exogenous.

It is assumed that one good is produced at home with one variable factor, labor, and that this good is both consumed domestically and exported. It is produced according to perfectly competitive conditions and its price is set to equate demand and supply. The home country is not "small"—that is, there exists a demand curve for this good which is less than perfectly elastic. Producers determine the quantity of labor they wish to hire according to the price of the good and the nominal wage. And, in contrast to Meade and Tsiang who assume that the supply of labor is invariant to the price of consumer goods, we assume that laborers determine the quantity of labor they wish to sell according to the prices of the domestic good and the imported consumer good and the nominal wage. The fact that labor supply is a function of three prices, while labor demand is a function of two, provides the basic asymmetry in the labor market which this chapter exploits.

Unless Pigou effects are considered, the closed-economy IS schedule describes a relation between real variables and is invariant to the price level. However, in the open economy the IS relation includes the demands for imports and exports, which depend on the relative price of domestic and foreign goods. Holding foreign prices constant, changes in domestic prices affect the demands for imports and exports and thereby the IS relation. In its simplest form the IS equation of the open economy is

$$I(r) - S(DY/P) = (1/R)M(R, DY/P) - X(R, Y_b) \tag{1}$$

such that $I_r < 0$, $S_y > 0$, $X_R < 0$, $M_R > 0$, $M_y > 0$.[2] The explanation for this equation follows. Investment $I$ is a function of the interest rate. Real saving $S$ is a function of real income, where real income to consumers is the total value of output divided by the consumers' price index $DY/P$. Demand for imports is a function of the terms of trade, $R = D/(F/\rho)$, which denote the price of domestic output relative to the price of the import, and of real income. To keep imports in the same units as the other components of IS, multiply the quantity of imports $M$ by $F/\rho$, which gives the domestic value of imports, and then divide by $D$ to bring it into real terms—or simply divide by $R$. Real exports $X$ are a function of the terms of trade $R$ and foreign income $Y_b$. Both foreign income and foreign prices $F$ are held constant throughout the analysis.

The LM relation equates the supply and demand for real balances:

$$\bar{L}/P = L(r, DY/P) \quad \text{such that} \quad L_r < 0, \quad L_y > 0. \tag{2}$$

[2] The subscript $y$ denotes the derivative with respect to $DY/P$.

$\bar{L}$ is the exogenous nominal money supply; thus, deflating by $P$, we have the real stock of money $\bar{L}/P$. Demand for real balances is a function of the interest rate, representing the opportunity cost of holding money, and of real income, which determines the transactions demand for money. Payments imbalances, which affect the flow supply of money and next period's money stock, are omitted from Eq. (2), which is a relation between current stock demands and supplies.

Income earners consume two goods—a domestic good priced at $D$ at home or $D\rho$ abroad, and an import which sells for $F/\rho$ in domestic markets. $P$, the consumers' price index, is a composite of these two prices, and it is related to $D$, the producers' price index, in the following way:

$$P = f(D, F/\rho) \qquad \text{where} \quad f_1 > 0, \quad f_2 > 0.^3 \tag{3}$$

It is assumed that $P$ is homogeneous of degree one in $D$ and $F/\rho$; thus a doubling of both $D$ and $F/\rho$ leads to a doubling of $P$.[4]

On the supply side it is assumed that there is an aggregate production function. Output $Y$ is a function of employment $N$ and the supply of capital $\bar{K}$, which is fixed in the current period:

$$Y = \phi(N, \bar{K}), \qquad \phi_N > 0. \tag{4}$$

Demand for labor is derived from the aggregate production function, as producers set marginal revenue product equal to the money wage:

$$D \cdot \phi_N = w. \tag{4a}$$

In inverse form, demand for labor $N^d$ is a function of the money wage $w$ divided by the producers' price index $D$:

$$N^d = \psi(w/D), \qquad \psi' < 0. \tag{5}$$

The supply of labor is a function of the real wage, where the relevant price index to labor is the consumers' price index of all goods, $P$. Hence,

$$N^s = N(w/P), \qquad N' \gtreqqless 0. \tag{6}$$

---

[3] As $D$ rises, the bundle of goods originally desired can no longer be purchased because one of the prices is now higher; since the original assortment was purchased when the new mix was also feasible, the first bundle must have been preferred. Thus an increase in $D$ with other prices held constant constitutes a lower utility level. Since a price index is an abstraction whose function is to capture changes in utility wrought by changes in the price components, a good price index increases when one of its components rises, reflecting the decline in utility, and it decreases when a price falls, reflecting the increase in potential utility. Thus we assume $f_1 > 0$ and $f_2 > 0$.

[4] One specific formulation of the index is $P = aD + (1 - a)F/\rho$, where $a$ is the proportion of expenditure directed toward the domestic good and is a function of the terms of trade, i.e., $a = a(R)$.

And in equilibrium the demand for labor equals the supply of labor:

$$N^s = N^d \equiv N. \tag{7}$$

In summary, the IS relation of Eq. (1) assures that the supply of goods equals the demand for goods. Equation (2), the LM relation, indicates that the supply and demand for the stock of real balances are equal. Equation (7) equates the demand for and supply of labor services. Finally, since this is a system with fixed exchange rates, exports need not equal imports, and the trade balance $B$ is defined in local output terms as

$$B = X(R, Y_b) - (1/R)M(R, D\,Y/P). \tag{8}$$

For given values of the rate of exchange $\rho$, the nominal money supply $\bar{L}$, and foreign income $Y_b$ and prices $F$, this economy is described by the preceding system of eight equations. The system can be solved for the eight endogenous variables $Y$, $r$, $D$, $P$, $N^s$, $N^d$, $w$, and $B$ if a solution exists. We may ask what the effect of a devaluation is on this solution. Totally differentiating the system, we find that $dB/d\rho \leqq 0$.[5] When the nominal money supply, foreign income, and foreign prices are held constant, devaluation improves the trade balance, even when domestic price increases are included. Using the same technique we find that $dY/d\rho \geqq 0$;[6] that is, contrary to the conclusions of the Meade–Tsiang model, devaluation leads to a fall in output and employment. In the following sections we explore the reasoning behind this result.

## II. The Component Markets

We first consider the markets separately and then solve the total system using aggregate supply and demand analysis. For given levels of the rate of exchange, nominal money supply, and foreign prices ($\rho$, $\bar{L}$, and $F$), the aggregate demand curve indicates the locus of points $\{Y, D\}$ which simultaneously clear the goods (IS) and the money (LM) markets, while the

[5] $$\frac{dB}{d\rho} = \left\{ (L_r S_y + I_r L_y)\frac{MF}{\rho^2}\left(\frac{-X_R R^2}{M} + \frac{M_R R}{M} - 1\right)\right.$$
$$\left. + I_r M_y \frac{f_2 LDF}{RP\rho^2}\left(1 - \frac{L_y}{L}\frac{DY}{P} + \frac{1}{LP}\right)\right\} \bigg/ \frac{\phi_N N'\psi' f_2 w}{DP^2}\left(L_y I_r + I_r S_y + \frac{L_r M_y}{R}\right) \leqq 0.$$

[6] $$\frac{dY}{d\rho} = \left\{ I_r f_2 \frac{FL}{\rho^2}\left(\frac{L_y}{L}\frac{DY}{P} - 1\right) - \frac{L_r PMF}{D\rho^2}\left(\frac{-X_R R^2}{M} + \frac{M_R R}{M} - 1\right)\right.$$
$$\left. + \frac{L_y f_2 FDY}{\rho^2 P}\left(S_y + \frac{M_y}{R}\right)\right\} \bigg/ \frac{\phi_N N'\psi' f_2 w}{DP^2}\left(L_y I_r + I_r S_y + \frac{L_r M_y}{R}\right) \geqq 0.$$

aggregate supply curve indicates the locus of points $\{Y, D\}$ which clear the labor market. These two relationships may be combined to determine the single point $\{Y^*, D^*\}$ which clears all the markets; this is the macroeconomic equilibrium. One demand curve and one supply curve can be constructed for each value of $\rho$; by varying $\rho$ and examining the change in the equilibrium $\{Y^*, D^*\}$, the effect of devaluation on the equilibrium values of income, prices, the terms of trade, and the balance of trade may be determined.

## A. DERIVATION OF THE AGGREGATE DEMAND CURVE (ADC)

Holding $\rho$ constant in Eq. (1), there exists one IS curve for each value of $D$. An increase in $D$ shifts the IS curve down and to the left if the General Elasticity Condition (GEC) is satisfied; that is, if

$$(-X_R R^2/M) + (M_R R/M) - 1 > 0. \qquad (9)$$

The GEC is a generalization of the Marshall–Lerner Condition (MLC);[7] satisfying it assures that the balance (measured in domestic currency) deteriorates as the terms of trade rise.[8] As $D$ rises, demand for imports rises, while demand for domestic products, both for export and domestic consumption, falls as consumers substitute foreign goods for the now more expensive domestic goods. Algebraically, the shift in the IS curve may be calculated by totally differentiating Eq. (1). Holding the interest rate constant we have

$$\left.\frac{dY}{dD}\right|_{\text{IS}, r=\bar{r}}$$

$$= \frac{-\dfrac{PM}{RD}\left(\dfrac{-X_R R^2}{M} + \dfrac{M_R R}{M} - 1\right) + \left(S_y Y + \dfrac{M_y Y}{R}\right)\left(f_1 \dfrac{D}{P} - 1\right)}{\left(S_y + \dfrac{1}{R} M_y\right)} < 0; \qquad (10)$$

$dY/dD$ is negative as long as the GEC holds and $f_1(D/P)$ is less than one. We assume the former and verify the latter by using the homogeneity

---

[7] The MLC says the following: $(-X_R R/X) + (M_R R/M) - 1 > 0$. When $B = 0$, $X = M/R$ and the GEC is equivalent to the MLC.

[8] The GEC is a sufficient condition for $\partial B/\partial R < 0$:

$$\frac{\partial B}{\partial R} = \frac{-M}{R^2}\left(\frac{-X_R R^2}{M} + \frac{M_R R}{M} - 1\right) - 2M_y \frac{F/\rho^2 f_2}{RP^2 \rho^2}$$

where $f_2 > 0$ from Eq. (3). The second term represents the Laursen–Metzler [3] effect, which suggests that an increase in the terms of trade raises real income and worsens the trade balance.

property. Since a $1\%$ rise in $D$ and in $F/\rho$ results in a $1\%$ rise in $P$, we can write, from Eq. (3),

$$f_1(D/P) + f_2[(F/\rho)/P] = 1. \tag{11}$$

It is clear that $f_1(D/P)$ is less than one since $f_2$ is positive. The effect on the IS curve of a rise in $D$ is depicted in Fig. 1.

In the same manner, holding $\rho$ and $\bar{L}$ constant, one LM curve can be drawn for each value of $D$. A rise in $D$ reduces the real money supply and shifts the LM curve up and to the left, as shown in Fig. 1. Algebraically the

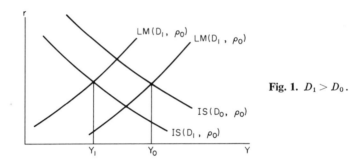

Fig. 1. $D_1 > D_0$.

shift in LM is described by differentiating Eq. (2) totally; holding the interest rate constant we have

$$\left.\frac{dY}{dD}\right|_{\text{LM},r=\bar{r}} = \frac{-Lf_1 - L_y\, Y(1 - f_1(D/P))}{L_y\, D} < 0. \tag{12}$$

The aggregate demand curve (ADC) can be derived graphically from Fig. 1. We have two points on the ADC: $\{Y_0, D_0\}$ and $\{Y_1, D_1\}$; the remaining points are determined similarly by varying $D$ and finding the value of $Y$ consistent with both the IS and LM relations. The ADC for given $\rho = \rho_0$ is shown in Fig. 2. It is downward sloping because a rise in $D$ both reduces the real money

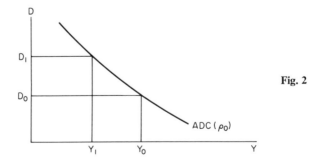

Fig. 2

supply, which raises the interest rate and decreases investment, and makes foreign goods relatively cheaper, which reduces demand for domestic output. Algebraically the slope is derived by solving Eqs. (1)–(3) and totally differentiating the system:

$$\frac{dY}{dD}\bigg|_{ADC,\,\rho=\bar{\rho}} = \left\{ L_r \frac{MP}{DR}\left(\frac{-X_R R^2}{M} + \frac{M_R R}{M} - 1\right)\right.$$

$$+ I_r f_1 L + f_2 \frac{F/\rho}{P}$$

$$\left. \times \left(L_r S_y Y + I_r L_y Y + \frac{L_r M_y Y}{R}\right)\right\} \bigg/ \left(-I_r L_y D - S_y L_r D - L_r M_y \frac{D}{R}\right) < 0;$$

(13)

$dY/dD < 0$ because $I_r < 0$, $L_r < 0$, $L_y > 0$, $S_y > 0$, $M_y > 0$, $f_1 > 0$, $f_2 > 0$, and $(-X_R R^2/M) + (M_R R/M) - 1 > 0$.

## B. DERIVATION OF THE AGGREGATE SUPPLY CURVE (ASC)

In a similar manner we derive the Aggregate Supply Curve (ASC) from Eqs. (4)–(7). Starting from a point of equilibrium in the labor market and holding the exchange rate fixed, consider a 1% rise in $D$ from $D_0$ to $D_1$. In order to maintain equilibrium in the labor market, $w/D$ must fall and $w/P$ rise, with employment rising. This can be verified by studying Fig. 3. If $P$ also were to rise by 1%, then a 1% rise in $w$, the nominal wage, would leave $w/D$, $w/P$, and employment unchanged. However, with reference to Eq. (11), we can see that a 1% rise in $D$ leads to a less than 1% rise in $P$, given that $F/\rho$ is constant. Thus there would be excess supply of labor if $w$ were to rise by 1%, since the demand for labor is homogeneous of degree zero in $w$ and $D$, while the supply of labor is homogeneous of degree zero in $w$ and $P$.

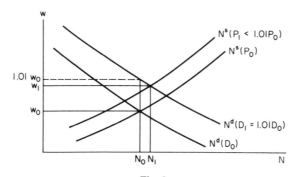

Fig. 3

Some increase in $w$ smaller than $1\%$ again equates supply and demand for labor. But since $w/D$ is lower than originally, employment is higher. Therefore $w$ must have increased by a percentage greater than the increase in $P$, raising $w/P$, in order to increase the quantity of labor supplied. Employment is now $N_1 > N_0$ corresponding to $D_1 > D_0$, and the aggregate production function (4) converts this into a positive supply relationship between $D$ and $Y$ as illustrated in Fig. 4. It should be emphasized that every point on the ASC is a point of labor market equilibrium, denoting full employment. Algebraically, differentiating Eqs. (4)–(7) totally we have the slope of the ASC,

$$\frac{dY}{dD}\bigg|_{\text{ASC}, \rho = \bar{\rho}} = \frac{\phi_N \psi' N' w (f_2 F/\rho)}{D^2 P^2 (N'/P - \psi'/D)} > 0; \tag{14}$$

$dY/dD > 0$ because $\phi_N > 0$, $\psi' < 0$, $N' > 0$, $f_2 > 0$.

Combining the ADC and the ASC in Fig. 5, we find the equilibrium pair $\{Y^*, D^*\}$ which is determined for the given value of $\rho$. Hence the terms of trade $R^* = D^*/(F/\rho)$ are known, which, along with $Y^*$, determine the level of the balance of trade $B^*$ [Eq. (8)].

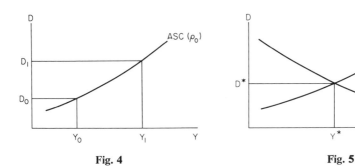

Fig. 4                                                                          Fig. 5

## III. Devaluation

In the first instance devaluation results in a rise in the domestic price of foreign goods, which disturbs the equilibrium in each of the three markets. In the goods market devaluation raises the demand for domestic production at every price, and is equivalent to an exogenous increase in the demand for exports and a decrease in the demand for imports. Another effect of the increase in the price of imports is to increase the consumers' price index (CPI). This reduces the real wage of labor and leads to a reduction in the quantity of labor supplied at each nominal wage. In addition, the increase in the CPI, given a constant nominal money supply, reduces the supply of real balances. Whether devaluation leads to a rise or fall in the equilibrium level of real income and employment depends on the relative strength of the expansionary impact of devaluation on the market for domestic production compared to the contractionary impact on the markets for money and labor.

We may now examine the effect on the equilibrium system of a change in the exchange rate. As before, the markets are treated separately in partial equilibrium and then combined to see the effects on the general equilibrium. Turning first to the labor market, we determine the effects on the aggregate supply curve of a decrease in the exchange rate.

## A. THE EFFECTS OF DEVALUATION ON THE ASC

Since demand for labor depends only on $w/D$, it is initially unaffected by the devaluation. On the other hand, since supply of labor depends on $w/P$, it is immediately decreased by the increase in the price of imports; for every nominal wage, the supply of labor declines with the resulting rise in $\rho$. This is pictured in Fig. 6. The leftward shift in the labor supply curve causes the ASC to shift up and to the left, as depicted in Fig. 7, where $\rho$ is entered as a parameter of the schedule. This shift can be seen algebraically in Eq. (15). Totally differentiating Eqs. (4)–(7), and holding $D$ constant, we have

$$\frac{dY}{d\rho}\bigg|_{D=\bar{D}} = \frac{-\phi_N \psi' N' wF(f_2)}{\rho^2 DP^2(N'/P - \psi'/D)} > 0. \tag{15}$$

We may ascertain exactly how much the ASC shifts by calculating the percentage rise in $D$ that is needed to keep employment (and the supply of output) constant when $\rho$ is cut by 1%. Denoting this relationship, or elasticity, by $E$ we have

$$E \equiv (-\rho/D)(dD/d\rho)\bigg|_{Y=\bar{Y}}. \tag{16}$$

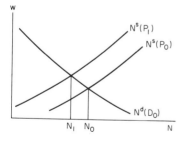

**Fig. 6.** $P_1 > P_0$.

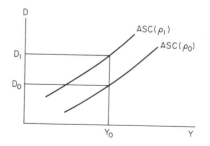

**Fig. 7.** $\rho_1 < \rho_0$.

In terms of Fig. 7, $E$ states the percentage that $D$ must rise when $\rho$ is cut by 1% (from $\rho_0$ to $\rho_1$) if $Y$ is to remain at $Y_0$. Calculating the value of $E$ from the aggregate supply equations (4)–(7), it is easy to verify that $E = 1$.[9] That is, a 1% devaluation entails a 1% rise in producers' prices and a 1% rise in the general price level in order to keep real output supplied constant. Intuitively, this results from the basic asymmetry in the labor market mentioned previously. In order for output to remain constant after devaluation, employment must remain constant; this requires that $w/D$, the real cost of labor to producers, and $w/P$, the real wage to labor, must both be unchanged. When $\rho$ falls by 1%, raising $F/\rho$ by 1%, $w$, $D$, and $P$ must each rise by 1% in order to leave both $w/D$ and $w/P$ unchanged. Therefore, for a given level of output, a 1% devaluation necessitates a 1% rise in domestic producers' prices and the general price level.

If output remains constant on devaluation, the rise in domestic prices negates the effect of the fall in $\rho$ because macroequilibrium requires the economy to be on its aggregate supply curve. This leaves the terms of trade, $R = D/(F/\rho)$, unchanged. That this eradicates any improvement in the trade balance which devaluation may have initiated can be substantiated by examining Eq. (8):

$$B = X(R, Y_b) - (1/R)M(R, DY/P). \tag{8}$$

Since both $D$ and $P$ rise by equal percentages and $Y$ and $R$ are unchanged, $B$, the real trade balance, is also unchanged. Moreover, if output rises from devaluation, the balance deteriorates. Along any ASC, $D$ and $Y$ rise together; likewise for $R$ and $Y$ and $D/P$ and $Y$. Furthermore, the balance of trade moves inversely with each of these variables *ceteris paribus*; and when all three rise simultaneously, as they are constrained to do by the aggregate supply relation, the trade balance deteriorates *a fortiori*. This analysis leads us to the following proposition:

**Proposition 1** For devaluation to improve the balance of trade, real income and output must fall.

Moreover, if output does fall, the balance improves. Totally differentiating Eq. (8) with respect to $R$ we have

$$\frac{dB}{dR} = \frac{\partial B}{\partial R} + \frac{\partial B}{\partial(DY/P)}\left[\frac{D}{P}\frac{dY}{dR} + \frac{F^2 Yf_2}{\rho^2 P^2}\right] < 0. \tag{17}$$

[9] $\dfrac{dD}{d\rho} = -\dfrac{dY/d\rho}{dY/dD} = \dfrac{\phi_N\psi'N'wFf_2/\rho^2 DP^2(N'/P - \psi'/D)}{\phi_N\psi'N'wFf_2/\rho D^2P^2(N'/P - \psi'/D)} = -\dfrac{D}{\rho}$ or $E \equiv -\dfrac{dD}{d\rho}\dfrac{\rho}{D} = 1.$

This is negative for the following reasons. As demonstrated in Eq. (9) the GEC is sufficient for $\partial B/\partial R < 0$, and we assume that imports rise with real income; thus $\partial B/\partial(DY/P) < 0$. That $dY/dR$ is $> 0$ depends on the positive slope of the ASC and the fact that $E = 1$. Finally, $f_2 > 0$ by assumption. Because of the unique supply relation between the terms of trade and output, if devaluation leads to a fall in output then it also reduces the terms of trade, and improves the trade balance. Thus we have:

**Proposition 2**  If the GEC holds and devaluation results in a decline in real income and output, then the balance of trade improves.

Thus in conjunction with the GEC, a decline in output is a necessary and sufficient condition for devaluation to improve the trade balance. However, in order to ascertain what actually happens to output and the trade balance, we must determine how devaluation affects the ADC.

## B. THE EFFECTS OF DEVALUATION ON THE ADC

The IS curve shifts up and to the right on devaluation if the GEC holds, since demand for exports increases and domestic goods replace some import demand at constant domestic prices. Algebraically, totally differentiating Eq. (1), we have

$$\frac{dY}{d\rho}\bigg|_{IS, r=\bar{r}, D=\bar{D}} = \frac{f_2 \dfrac{D}{P^2} Y\left(S_y + \dfrac{M_y}{R}\right) + \dfrac{FM}{D\rho^2}\left(\dfrac{-X_R R^2}{M} + \dfrac{M_R R}{M} - 1\right)}{-\dfrac{D}{P}\left(S_y + \dfrac{M_y}{R}\right)} < 0.$$

(18)

The LM curve shifts up and to the left at constant domestic prices, since the stock of real money falls with the decrease in $\rho$. Differentiating Eq. (2) totally we have

$$\frac{dY}{d\rho}\bigg|_{LM, r=\bar{r}, D=\bar{D}} = \frac{Lf_2\left(1 - \dfrac{L_y}{L}\dfrac{DY}{P}\right)}{DL_y} > 0$$

(19)

which is positive, assuming the income elasticity of the demand for money is less than one.

The ADC shifts to the left or right depending on whether the expansionary IS effect or the contractionary LM effect dominates. The former case is illustrated in Fig. 8. Looking at it algebraically, the two forces which determine the direction of the shift in the ADC are apparent in Eq. (20):

$$\frac{dY}{d\rho}\bigg|_{\text{ADC, } D=\bar{D}} = \frac{LI_r f_2\left[1 - \frac{L_y}{L}\frac{DY}{P}\right] - L_r P\left[S_y \frac{DY}{P^2}f_2 + M_y \frac{DY}{RP^2}f_2 + \frac{FM}{D\rho^2}\left(\frac{-X_R R^2}{M} + \frac{M_R R}{M} - 1\right)\right]}{DL_r \frac{M_y}{R} + DL_r S_y + DL_y I_r}; \quad (20)$$

$dY/d\rho$ is negative if the IS effect, given by the second term in the numerator, dominates; but positive if the LM effect, given by the first term in the numerator, dominates.

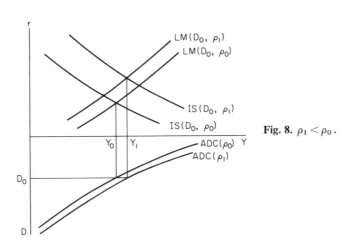

Fig. 8. $\rho_1 < \rho_0$.

## C. The Effects of Devaluation on the Complete System

If the ADC shifts to the left, then output falls, as is obvious from inspection of Fig. 9. Furthermore, the trade balance improves in accordance with Proposition 2. Moreover, even if the ADC shifts to the right, output falls and the balance improves if the monetary authorities hold the nominal money supply constant. We demonstrate this by examining the equations for IS (1) and LM (2) subject to the aggregate supply relation, and showing that they are consistent with a reduced exchange rate only if output is simultaneously reduced. The outcome in the aggregate markets is illustrated in Fig. 10.

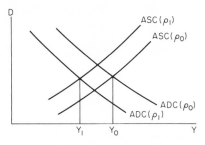

Fig. 9. $\rho_1 < \rho_0$.

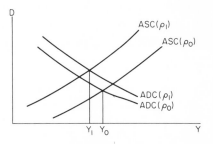

Fig. 10. $\rho_1 < \rho_0$.

We begin by rewriting Eqs. (1) and (2):

$$I(r) - S(DY/P) = (1/R)M(R, DY/P) - X(R, Y_b) \tag{1}$$

$$\bar{L}/P = L(r, DY/P). \tag{2}$$

Furthermore, $Y$ and $R$ are uniquely related by the aggregate supply relation, which we can collapse into the following single equation:

$$R = g(Y) \qquad \text{where} \quad g' > 0. \tag{21}$$

In addition, since $P$ is homogeneous of degree one in $D$ and $F/\rho$, we can write $D/P$ as a function of $R$ alone. Thus

$$D/P = h(R) \qquad \text{where} \quad h' = 2F^2 f_2 /P^2 \rho^2 > 0. \tag{22}$$

If output remains constant when the exchange rate is reduced, $R$ and $D/P$ remain constant, by Eqs. (21) and (22), keeping saving, imports, and exports constant. Thus investment and its determinant, the interest rate, must also be constant to satisfy Eq. (1). However, the interest rate rises according to Eq. (2) in order to reduce the demand for real balances concomitantly with supply, which falls as $P$ rises with $D$ and $F/\rho$. This inconsistency with respect to the interest rate implies that output cannot stay constant when the nominal stock of money is fixed on devaluation. Neither can output rise under these conditions, since in this case, Eq. (1) requires a decrease and Eq. (2) an increase in the interest rate. Only if output falls can Eqs. (1) and (2) be simultaneously satisfied. Therefore we have the following proposition:

**Proposition 3** When the nominal money supply is fixed, devaluation results in a fall in output and an improvement in the balance, assuming the GEC holds.

If, instead, the monetary authorities follow a policy of holding the interest rate constant, Eqs. (1) and (2) can be and are satisfied with constant output.

Real balances ($\bar{L}/P$) are also constant and prices rise by the full amount of the devaluation. This leaves the terms of trade unchanged and the balance unimproved.

## D. WEALTH EFFECTS

Proposition 1 does not hold if consumption demand varies directly with wealth. Letting $W$ denote wealth, which equals the sum of the real value of money $\bar{L}/P$ plus the real value of bonds $\bar{Z}/P$ plus other forms of wealth $V$, we have

$$W = (\bar{L}/P) + (\bar{Z}/P) + V. \tag{23}$$

Rewriting IS to indicate that consumption and import demand rise with wealth, we have

$$I(r) - S(D\,Y/P, W) = (1/R)M(R, D\,Y/P, W) - X(R, Y_b) \tag{24}$$

where $S_W < 0$ and $M_W > 0$.[10] Devaluation lowers wealth by reducing the real value of outside monetary assets, $\bar{L}/P$ and $\bar{Z}/P$, inducing wealth holders to save more to restore their wealth to its previous level. Thus, unlike Proposition 1, a devaluation accompanied by policies which leave the terms of trade and output unchanged improves the trade balance, since the concomitant fall in wealth induces a fall in consumption. This decrease in absorption releases resources which can be directed to production in the foreign sector, improving the trade balance.

When wealth effects are ignored, the balance of trade is homogeneous of degree zero in $D$ and $F/\rho$ because of the unique supply relation between $R$ and $Y$ [Eq. (21)]. Inclusion of wealth effects eliminates this homogeneity and makes the trade balance dependent on the actual price level. Since wealth is an argument in the demand for imports and $\partial W/\partial\rho < 0$, the balance of trade improves on devaluation even if all prices change by the same percentage and output remains constant.

## IV. Comparison and Synthesis

### A. THE MEADE–TSIANG MODEL

In Section III we demonstrated that a successful devaluation causes a fall in employment and output. This contradicts the conclusion of Meade [4] and Tsiang [9] that devaluation improves the trade balance and increases

---

[10] See Metzler [6] for a statement of the saving-wealth relation and, in particular, for the first post-Keynesian theoretical treatment of the role of nonmonetary, as well as, monetary assets.

employment. However, this discrepancy arises from the differences in the labor market postulated by these models. In our model we make the classical assumptions that the supply of labor varies directly with the real wage and that a flexible nominal wage rate clears the labor market. Thus our conclusions apply only to devaluation at full employment, for which the accompanying reduction in output is also a reduction in its *full employment* level. On the other hand, the Meade-Tsiang model makes the Keynesian assumptions that labor is supplied inelastically and that wages exhibit downward rigidity. Thus the labor market does not necessarily clear and unemployment may result.

The differences between the two models are clearly seen algebraically. In the Meade–Tsiang model Eqs. (25) and (26) replace our Eqs. (6) and (7). The supply of labor is inelastic, such that

$$N^s \equiv N_{FE} \quad \text{for all} \quad w \tag{25}$$

where $N_{FE}$ denotes the fixed and exogenous level of full employment, while wage rigidity implies

$$N = N^d \leq N^s \quad \text{for} \quad w = \bar{w}, \qquad N = N^d = N^s \quad \text{for} \quad w > \bar{w} \tag{26}$$

where $\bar{w}$ is the initial (inflexible downward) wage rate. Since prices do not affect the labor supply decision in this framework, devaluation does not directly affect either the supply of or the demand for labor; hence the ASC does not shift. However, the ADC shifts to the right on devaluation because Meade holds the interest rate constant and Tsiang has the demand for money depending on $D$ rather than $P$.[11]

As a result, if output and employment are initially below their full employment levels, output and employment rise on devaluation. This is illustrated in Fig. 11. Moreover, in contrast to the classical model's Proposition 1, if devaluation is accompanied by aggregate demand policies which keep output constant, the terms of trade, $R = D/(F/\rho)$, fall and the trade balance improves.

On the other hand, if output is initially at the full employment level, then devaluation results solely in an increase in prices, as illustrated in Fig. 12. If the monetary authority holds the nominal money supply constant (Tsiang's Orthodox Neutral Monetary Policy), the price rise is insufficient to eradicate the competitive edge that devaluation gains for domestic products, and the trade balance improves. The mechanism is as follows. The devaluation raises prices, thereby reducing the real money supply and increasing the rate of interest. This, in turn, reduces investment and allows the trade balance to improve. Alternatively, if the monetary authority follows

---

[11] Tsiang has $\bar{L}/D = L(r, Y)$. Differentiating, we have $(dY/d\rho)|_{LM, r=\bar{r}, D=\bar{D}} = 0$.

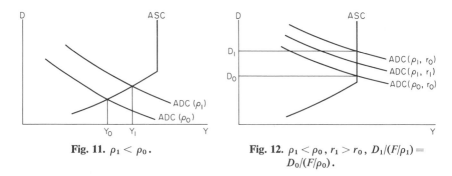

Fig. 11. $\rho_1 < \rho_0$.                Fig. 12. $\rho_1 < \rho_0$, $r_1 > r_0$, $D_1/(F/\rho_1) =$
                                                           $D_0/(F/\rho_0)$.

Meade's constant-rate-of-interest policy, rather than a constant nominal money supply, investment is not reduced and the resulting domestic price rise completely eliminates the increase in demand initiated by the devaluation. In other words, unless domestic absorption is reduced, the price rise continues until the initial terms of trade are restored. These cases are illustrated in Fig. 12. The lowest ADC labeled $(\rho_0, r_0)$ is the predevaluation schedule, the middle ADC labeled $(\rho_1, r_1)$ corresponds to the constant-nominal-money-supply policy, and the upper ADC labeled $(\rho_1, r_0)$ represents the constant-interest-rate policy.

### B. Devaluation and Unemployment

In the preceding Meade–Tsiang model the concept of full employment is obviously different from the classical notion embodied here. In the former model, the level of full employment is exogenous and there is unemployment if the demand for labor falls short of this level at the minimum nominal wage $\bar{w}$. Given this initial situation, devaluation increases employment (and reduces unemployment) by generating an increase in aggregate demand, making it profitable for producers to hire more workers at the fixed money wage. In our model the full employment level varies directly with the real wage. Independently of its effect on domestic demand, devaluation alters the real wage and hence the level of full employment. There can be no unemployment in our model because a perfectly flexible nominal wage rate ensures that both labor demand and supply are always satisfied. Thus our analysis and conclusions are relevant only to devaluations undertaken by fully employed economies. However, by retaining our variable labor supply function, but replacing the assumption of perfect wage flexibility with the Meade–Tsiang view that money wages are rigid downward, we can introduce unemployment into our framework and achieve a synthesis of the two models. Such a synthesis gives devaluation a direct impact on the labor market while allowing unemployment to exist.

In place of the Meade–Tsiang inelastic labor supply, we repeat our Eq. (6), the classical supply of labor:

$$N^s = N(w/P), \qquad N' \geqq 0. \tag{27}$$

Instead of assuming that the labor market always clears, we assume downward wage rigidity, as in Eq. (26):

$$N = N^d \leqq N^s \quad \text{for} \quad w = \bar{w}, \qquad N = N^d = N^s \quad \text{for} \quad w > \bar{w}. \tag{28}$$

As usual, if the rigid wage constraint is binding at $\bar{w}$, then at wage levels below $\bar{w}$ employment is determined by the demand for labor, and involuntary unemployment $(U)$ results:

$$\begin{aligned} U = N^s - N^d &\geqq 0 \qquad \text{for} \quad w = \bar{w} \\ &= 0 \qquad \text{for} \quad w > \bar{w}. \end{aligned} \tag{29}$$

The synthesized model is represented by Eqs. (1)–(5), (8), and (27)–(29) with endogenous variables $Y$, $r$, $D$, $P$, $N^s$, $N^d$, $w$, $B$, and $U$. The initial wage level $\bar{w}$ is exogenous.

We derive the ASC for this model as follows. Consider first a classical labor market of the sort analyzed in Sections II and III with flexible wages and prices and initial price levels $\bar{D}$ and $\bar{P}$. The market clears at a nominal wage $\bar{w}$ and employment $\bar{N}$. As $D$ and $P$ vary, the supply of and demand for labor shift, leading to an upward-sloping ASC (see Section II.B). The labor market is pictured in Fig. 13 and the corresponding ASC is the curve $GEB$ in Fig. 14. However, suppose that when $D$ and $P$ fall to $D_0$ and $P_0$, respectively, the wage rate is unable to fall below $\bar{w}$; that is, let $\bar{w}$ be the rigid money wage constraint. Hence, rather than employment falling to $N_0$ and the wage to $w_0$, employment is determined by the demand for labor at the wage $\bar{w}$. Thus employment is given by $N_0{}^d$ and unemployment by $U_0 = N_0{}^s - N_0{}^d$. In this situation $GEB$ does not describe the constrained ASC. Instead, when $D$ falls to $D_0$, output falls below $Y_0$ to $Y_0{}^d$ (corresponding to $N_0$ and $N_0{}^d$, respectively); thus the constrained ASC is given by $CE$. Along $CE$ the labor

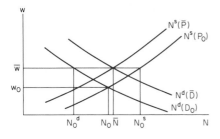

Fig. 13.  $D_0 < \bar{D}$, $P_0 < \bar{P}$.

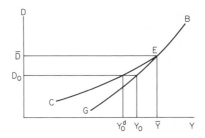

Fig. 14

market does not clear, and employment and output are determined by the demand for labor at the minimum wage $\bar{w}$. For increases in $D$ and $P$ above $\bar{D}$ and $\bar{P}$, the rigid wage constraint is not binding and the classical ASC obtains. Hence, when the rigid wage is $\bar{w}$, the full ASC in the synthesized model is given by $CEB$ is Fig. 14.

The unconstrained ASC is identical to the classical ASC derived in Section II.B; therefore, it shifts on devaluation in accordance with the principles developed in Section III. Referring to Fig. 15, when the exchange rate falls

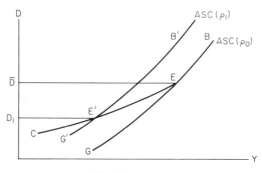

**Fig. 15.** $\rho_1 < \rho_0$.

from $\rho_0$ to $\rho_1$ the ASC curve $GEB$ shifts up to $G'E'B'$. Analogously the constrained ASC, like the ASC of the Meade–Tsiang rigid wage model, does not shift on devaluation. Thus the synthesized ASC shifts from $CEB$ to $CE'B'$.

Note that the price level at which the wage constraint becomes binding falls from $\bar{D}$ to $D_1$. The explanation for this is straightforward. For any domestic price level and wage rate, devaluation raises import prices and reduces the supply of labor. The resulting excess demand for labor can be eliminated by an increase in the real wage. In particular, at the rigid money wage $\bar{w}$, the excess demand for labor is eliminated by a decrease in the price of output from $\bar{D}$ to $D_1$. With the new exchange rate, for all $D > D_1$ the labor market clears at a nominal wage rate above $\bar{w}$. Thus the money wage constraint is not binding and the constrained ASC is relevant only for the region in which $D \leqq D_1$.

Since the addition of the money wage constraint does not affect the ADC, we may now analyze the effects of devaluation on the total economy. We first consider devaluation from a point of full employment. Suppose that the economy is initially in equilibrium at $(Y_0, D_0)$ with the exchange rate $\rho_0$, as pictured in Fig. 16. Lowering the exchange rate shifts the synthesized ASC from $CEB$ to $CE'B'$. As demonstrated in Section III, the ADC shifts to the right if devaluation's expansionary impact on the goods market dominates its contradictory impact on the money market; it shifts to the left

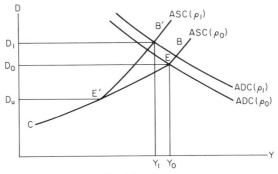

**Fig. 16.** $\rho_1 < \rho_0$.

if the converse holds. The former case is illustrated in Fig. 16, in which the postdevaluation equilibrium is given by $(Y_1, D_1)$. This is identical to the classical case. The conclusions of Section III are unaffected by the addition of the constraint, since it is never binding. In the unlikely case in which the contractionary influence of devaluation on the real money supply is not only strong enough to shift the ADC to the left, but also powerful enough to force the price level below $D_u$, unemployment results. However, the monetary authority could easily remedy this result by increasing the nominal money supply in order to shift ADC back up to the right.

The case in which the money wage constraint is binding both before and after devaluation, and the economy moves from one point of unemployment to another, occurs if both ADC curves in Fig. 16 intersect ASC over the range $CE'$. Then, on devaluation, output and employment rise and unemployment falls. In addition, the trade balance improves if the GEC holds and the interest rate does not decrease. In the event that ADC were to shift to the left on devaluation, output could be reduced, unemployment increased, and the trade balance improved.

This case corresponds to the pure Meade–Tsiang model. Since there is excess supply of labor both before and after the devaluation, the analysis is unaffected by the addition of the variable (full employment) labor supply function.

Finally, we consider the case in which an initial unemployment situation is eliminated by the devaluation. This analysis involves elements of both the classical and the Meade–Tsiang models. Although devaluation eliminates the involuntary unemployment, the level of output and employment may rise or fall, depending on the strength of the aggregate demand shift relative to that of supply. We analyze the expansionary case in Fig. 17.

Suppose the economy is initially at the equilibrium $(Y_0, D_0)$, characterized by some involuntary unemployment. The exchange rate is lowered from

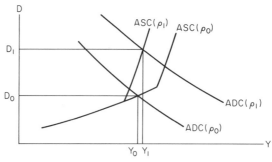

**Fig. 17.** $\rho_1 < \rho_0$.

$\rho_0$ to $\rho_1$. As usual, ASC shifts to the left. Again we assume that ADC shifts to the right and output rises. The new equilibrium $(Y_1, D_1)$ is on the unconstrained ASC and therefore is a point of full employment. In addition, if the monetary authorities prevent the interest rate from falling, the trade balance improves. This may be compared to the pure classical model of Section III in which an increase in the interest rate is a necessary and sufficient condition for devaluation to improve the trade balance (see pages 142 and 143).

In each of these cases an increase in the interest rate is sufficient for devaluation to improve the trade balance if the GEC holds. However, the qualitative impact of devaluation on the level of output depends critically on the particular labor-market assumptions made.

## V. Summary and Conclusions

We have analyzed the effects of devaluation on employment, output, and the balance of trade. We have done so by extending aggregate supply and demand analysis to the open economy. This general framework is useful for the study of a wide variety of questions arising in international trade, particularly because it stresses the endogeneity of the domestic price level, a variable of crucial importance in determining the trade balance.

When the supply of labor is positively related to the real wage and the labor market clears, there exists a unique relation between the terms of trade and the level of output which is invariant to the rate of exchange. This is due to the asymmetric effect which foreign prices have on the demand for and supply of labor. As a result, a successful devaluation reduces the terms of trade, output, and employment. Since the labor market clears, there is always full employment before and after the devaluation. Furthermore, any policy which reduces output, such as a reduction in the nominal money supply, likewise reduces the terms of trade and improves the trade balance.

Again, because of wage and price flexibility, full employment prevails before and after the disturbance.

In this classical model, devaluation is thus not alone in its ability to improve the balance of trade without raising unemployment. However, when downward rigidity of money wages is introduced, the role of the exchange rate as a policy instrument increases. If initially there is unemployment because of wage rigidity, devaluation raises prices and increases the demand for labor, just as other expansionary policies do. But the other policies simultaneously increase the terms of trade and worsen the trade balance, while devaluation decreases the terms of trade and improves the trade balance. Moreover, although contractionary monetary policy improves the balance of trade, it simultaneously increases the level of unemployment (or initiates unemployment if previously there was full employment).

In general, devaluation improves the trade balance regardless of the assumptions made about the labor market. Its importance as a policy instrument rests on its unique ability to reduce the relative price of domestic goods and improve the trade balance at the same time that it increases domestic prices and reduces unemployment.

## ACKNOWLEDGMENTS

This article is based on a chapter of my doctoral dissertation [7] presented to Columbia University, for which financial support was provided by the Woodrow Wilson Fellowship Foundation. I would like to express my gratitude to R. Findlay, G. Horwich, P. Kenen, D. Mathieson, and S. Salop for comments and suggestions on earlier drafts. The views expressed in this paper do not necessarily reflect those of the Board of Governors of the Federal Reserve System.

## REFERENCES

1. Alexander, S. S., "Effects of a Devaluation on a Trade Balance," *IMF Staff Papers* **2**, (April 1952), 263–278.
2. Alexander, S. S., "Effects of a Devaluation: A Simplified Synthesis of Elasticities and Absorption Approaches," *American Economic Review* **49** (March 1959), 22–42.
3. Laursen, S., and Metzler, L. A., "Flexible Exchange Rates and the Theory of Employment," *Review of Economics and Statistics* **32** (November 1950), 281–299.
4. Meade, J. E., *The Balance of Payments*. London and New York: Oxford Univ. Press, 1951.
5. Meade, J. E., *The Balance of Payments, Mathematical Supplement*. London and New York: Oxford Univ. Press, 1951.
6. Metzler, L. A., "Wealth, Saving, and the Rate of Interest," *Journal of Political Economy* **59** (April 1951), 93–116.
7. Salop, J. K, *The Exchange Rate and the Terms of Trade: Aspects of Devaluation Theory*. Unpublished Manuscript, Columbia Univ., 1973.
8. Tobin, J., "Aggregative Models: Keynesian, Classical, and Variants." Mimeograph.
9. Tsiang, S. C., "The Role of Money in Trade-Balance Stability," *American Economic Review* **51** (December 1961), 912–936.

# ON THE ANALYTICAL FRAMEWORK OF
# TARIFFS AND TRADE POLICY

*Akira Takayama*

*Purdue University*

## I. Introduction

One of the exciting and eye-opening experiences for students of international trade is the discovery that the imposition of an import duty does not necessarily increase the domestic price of the import-competing commodity vis à vis the export commodity—the famous thesis expounded by Metzler [20, 21]. This thesis is exciting not because it provides an example based on some pathological cases, but because it teaches us the importance of having a clear analytical framework and the pitfalls of partial equilibrium analysis.

This has been well recognized by international trade theorists by now, and many neoclassical theories of tariffs, unilateral transfers, domestic taxes and subsidies, and so on are discussed under a unified general equilibrium framework.[1] In this connection, it may be pointed out that trade theorists are lucky in inheriting a powerful diagrammatical tool of general equilibrium analysis, the Mill–Marshall offer curve.

---

[1] For this, it may suffice to quote an excellent treatise by Mundell [22]. See also Chapter 8 of ref. [28]. The extension to the model with "nontraded commodities" is given by Mc-Dougall [18].

As is well known, this tool is not only very useful for obtaining comparative statics results as summarized by Mundell [22], but also for obtaining the optimality conditions as exemplified in the age-old optimal tariff argument by Bickerdike, Edgeworth, Kaldor, Graaf, and others.

Since many policy questions can be handled either by the comparative statics procedure in which policy tools are taken as shift parameters of the equilibrium system *or* by obtaining the conditions for certain optimization problems, the success of the offer-curve analysis is quite remarkable. However, this tool also has weaknesses which are common in many geometric analyses: (a) the basic assumption and logical steps in the analysis are often concealed in the "usual" manner that the curves are drawn, and (b) it is hard to extend the analysis to situations which are more complicated than the analytical framework incorporated in the usual offer curve technique. For the latter point, it may suffice to point out the difficulties involved in analyzing such questions as domestic distortions and nontraded commodities by means of the offer curve.

Thus many trade theorists are led to build a specific mathematical model of general equilibrium which would fit the particular analysis that the researcher intends to pursue. Each of these models is important and shows considerable ingenuity. But the students of international trade theory are often confused by the many diversified models. This is rather unfortunate, for these models in essence have many points in common, and above all they are based on a more or less similar framework. In fact, most of them are, at least mathematically, simple extensions of the traditional discussions in terms of the offer curve technique.

The purpose of this chapter is to point out the common analytical framework which exists in the recent literature on international trade policy. Needless to say, some results presented here are known, but our purpose is not to obtain these results, but to clarify the common analytical framework involved in them so that we can find additional useful results in a systematic manner. In the course of our discussion, we shall find that the compensated demand functions obtained through the minimum-expenditure approach play a very useful role, especially in simplifying the analysis.

After having clarified the basic analytical structure and obtained the major traditional results in Section II, Sections III and IV will pick up two recently debated problems in trade theory, that of domestic distortions and of nontraded commodities. These two problems will be analyzed as simple extensions of the traditional results based on the analytical framework developed in Section II. Not only do we get some new results, but we also hope to illustrate the importance of the basic analytical framework by these examples. Once the framework is established, the extensions and the discussion of new results are often very simple (at least analytically), although these extensions may provide some important insights into "real world" problems.[2]

## II. Basic Model

### A. WALRAS' LAW AND EQUILIBRIUM

Consider the trading world of two countries (I and II) and two commodities ($X$ and $Y$). Let $p$ and $q$ denote the relative price of $X$ in terms of $Y$ in countries I and II, respectively.[3] Let $C_{xi}$ and $C_{yi}$, respectively, denote the consumption of $X$ and $Y$ in country $i$ ($i = 1, 2$). Let $X_i$ and $Y_i$, respectively, denote the output of $X$ and $Y$ in country $i$ ($i = 1, 2$). The excess demand for each commodity in country $i$ is defined by

$$E_{xi} \equiv C_{xi} - X_i \quad \text{and} \quad E_{yi} \equiv C_{yi} - Y_i, \quad i = 1, 2. \quad (1)$$

To describe the model, it is necessary to specify the policy variables in the system. The usual policy variables which are considered are import and export tariffs and subsidies, unilateral transfer payments, domestic consumption, and production taxes and subsidies. If we introduce all these variables into our model at the same time, the model becomes quite complicated. On the other hand, if we consider only one policy variable and ignore the rest, it will be sufficient to characterize the basic analytical framework. Hence we consider one policy variable alone, an import tariff.

Assume that country I imports $Y$ from country II in equilibrium,[4] where I imposes an import tariff whose *ad valorem* rate $t - 1$ on her import of $Y$ from II. Then the basic equilibrium model of the trading world is described by the following five equations:

$$pE_{x1} + E_{y1} \equiv [(t - 1)/t]E_{y1} \quad \text{(budget of I)}[5] \quad (2)$$

---

[2] As a further extension of the present chapter, the reader may wish to carry out the analysis of domestic distortions in the model which involves nontraded commodities. The result thus obtained will be new in the literature, but the analysis is a simple extension of the one developed in Sections III and IV.

[3] Let $p_x$ and $p_y$ denote the prices of $X$ and $Y$, respectively, in country I. Then $p \equiv p_x/p_y$. Similarly $q \equiv q_x/q_y$.

[4] Then $E_{y1}$ signifies country I's volume of import of $Y$, and $-E_{x1}(=E_{x2}$ in equilibrium) signifies country I's volume of export of $X$.

[5] It is assumed here that the tariff proceeds are reimbursed to the home consumers in the form of lump-sum subsidies. To understand (2), write the budget condition of I as

$$p_x E_{x1} + p_y E_{y1} = (t - 1)eq_y E_{y1}$$

where $e$ denotes the exchange rate (the price of II's currency in terms of I's). The right-hand side of this equation signifies the tariff revenue. Then noting that $p_y = teq_y$, we obtain (2).

$$qE_{x2} + E_{y2} \equiv 0 \qquad \text{(budget of II)} \tag{3}$$

$$E_{x1} + E_{x2} = 0 \qquad \text{(equilibrium of } X) \tag{4}$$

$$E_{y1} + E_{y2} = 0 \qquad \text{(equilibrium of } Y) \tag{5}$$

$$p = q/t \qquad \text{(trade with tariff)}^6 \tag{6}$$

where $t = 1 + \tau$ ($\tau = $ *ad valorem* rate of tariff). Equation (2) can equivalently be written as

$$qE_{x1} + E_{y1} \equiv 0, \tag{2'}$$

using (6). Then combining (2') and (3), we obtain

$$q(E_{x1} + E_{x2}) + (E_{y1} + E_{y2}) \equiv 0. \tag{7}$$

Equation (7) is the *Walras law* of the present model.

In view of (7), one of the equilibrium relations, (4) or (5), is not independent. That is, either (4) *or* (5) is sufficient to describe the equilibrium of the system. Conditions (3) and (5) are combined to yield

$$qE_{x2} - E_{y1} = 0. \tag{8}$$

On the other hand, when (8) holds, the equilibrium condition (5) holds in view of the identity (3). Therefore (8) can be used as the equilibrium condition of the system *instead of* (4) or (5).

Denote the "balance of payments" of I in terms of II's currency by $\tilde{B}_1$.[7] Then

$$\tilde{B}_1 \equiv q_x E_{x2} - q_y E_{y1} \tag{9}$$

where $q_x$ and $q_y$, respectively, denote the price of $X$ and $Y$ in country II. Equation (9) can equivalently be rewritten as

$$B_1 \equiv qE_{x2} - E_{y1} \qquad \text{where} \quad B_1 \equiv \tilde{B}_1/q_y. \tag{9'}$$

Clearly $B_1 = 0$ if and only if $\tilde{B}_1 = 0$. Also $B_1 = 0$ if and only if (8) holds. Therefore the equilibrium condition (8) is interpreted in the literature as the "balance of payments equilibrium."

---

[6] This is in essence the international arbitrage condition. In the following analysis, this condition holds all the time. Hence, in practice, it can be treated as an identity.

[7] Since there is no explicit treatment of money in the model, words such as "balance of payments" and "currency" are, strictly speaking, illegitimate [28, Chapter 9]. However, the use of such words in the present context is often seen in the literature and is quite convenient. Under certain circumstances, we may consider the present model as a submodel of a more general system in which money is explicitly introduced.

Similarly, (2) and (4) are combined to yield

$$pE_{x2} - E_{y1} + [(t-1)/t]E_{y1} = 0. \tag{10}$$

When (10) holds, (4) holds in view of the identity (2). Therefore (10) can also be used as the equilibrium condition of the system. We can see easily that (10) is equivalent to the "balance of payments equilibrium" in country I in terms of country I's currency. The third term of the LHS of (10) signifies the tariff revenue.

From the above observations, we can conclude that the *full* equilibrium of the system can be described by any *one* of the four equilibrium conditions [that is, (4) for commodity $X$, (5) for commodity $Y$, (8) for the balance of payments of I in terms of her foreign currency, and (10) for the balance of payments of I in terms of her domestic currency]. In the literature one of these conditions is chosen arbitrarily. Since there is no uniform framework discussed, this is very confusing; that is, one often wonders which is the correct equilibrium condition. The above analysis provides the basis for the fact that it does not make any difference which one we choose.

As another illustration, let us consider a unilateral transfer from II to I (by the amount of $T$ in II's currency). For the sake of simplicity, assume away all the other policy variables. In this case, the model can be described by (4), (5), and[8]

$$pE_{x1} + E_{y1} \equiv eT/p_y \qquad \text{(budget of I)} \tag{11}$$

$$qE_{x2} + E_{y2} \equiv -T/q_y \qquad \text{(budget of II)} \tag{12}$$

$$p = q \qquad \text{(free trade)} \tag{13}$$

where $e$ denotes the exchange rate (the price of II's currency in terms of I's currency). From (11)–(13), we obtain Eq. (7) by noting that $p_y = eq_y$. That is, Eq. (7) is again the *Walras law* of the system.

Note that either (4) or (5) describes the full equilibrium of the system in view of (7).

Next note that the balance of payments equilibrium of I in terms of II's currency holds if and only if

$$qE_{x2} - E_{y1} + T/q_y = 0, \tag{14}$$

or

$$q_x E_{x2} - q_y E_{y1} + T = 0. \tag{14'}$$

---

[8] We assume that the government of the transferee redistributes the amount of the transfer to its citizens in the form of income subsidies, and that the government of the transferer collects the amount of the transfer in the form of income taxes.

In view of identity (12), we can easily see that (14) [or (14′)] holds if and only if (5) holds.

The balance of payments equilibrium of I in terms of I's currency holds if and only if

$$pE_{x2} - E_{y1} + eT/p_y = 0. \tag{15}$$

In view of identity (11), we can easily see that (15) holds if and only if (4) holds.

From the above observations, we can conclude that the full equilibrium of the system can be described by any *one* of (4), (5), (14), (14′), and (15). That is, the above analysis provides the framework for what determines the equilibrium.

Finally, we have to mention a very common assumption in international trade theory, which is the *small country assumption*. This means that the country in question is small enough compared to the rest of the world so that the country takes the world terms of trade as a given constant. Let country I be such a small country. Then the small country assumption simply means that $q$ is a given constant to country I.

In this case, not only do we ignore the budget equation for II [such as (3) and (12)], but also we ignore the equilibrium conditions (4) and (5). For the case of a tariff, we have Eq. (2) or (2′), where $q$ is now a given constant. Country I can trade as much as she can within the bound imposed by such an equation. Similarly for the transfer problem, Eq. (11) or its equivalent form

$$qE_{x1} + E_{y1} \equiv T/q_y \tag{11′}$$

becomes the key equation. Here $q$, $q_x$, and $q_y$ are given constants to country I.

## B. Offer Curve

When the levels of the policy variables are exogenously given, we obtain the values of consumption and production of (and hence the excess demand for) each commodity in each country as functions of the commodity price ratio. The diagrammatical representation of the excess demand functions is known as the "offer curve." Here we shall illustrate this concept, again using a simple example in which the only policy variable is country I's import tariff. Since we focus our attention on one country (I) here, we omit the subscript 1.

Assume that the people in this country behave as though the following utility function is maximized:

$$u = u(C_x, C_y) \tag{16}$$

where any monotone transformation of $u$, $U = U(u)$, $U'(u) > 0$ for all $u$, also serves as a valid index of welfare.

As before, the budget condition can be given by

$$pE_x + E_y \equiv [(t - 1)/t]E_y, \tag{17}$$

which can also be written as

$$pE_x \equiv -E_y/t \tag{17'}$$

where $E_x \equiv C_x - X$ and $E_y \equiv C_y - Y$. Consumers' equilibrium under perfect competition is described by (17) and

$$p = v(C_x, C_y) \tag{18}$$

where

$$v \equiv u_x/u_y, \tag{19}$$

and $u_x$ and $u_y$ are defined by $u_x \equiv \partial u/\partial C_x$ and $u_y \equiv \partial u/\partial C_y$, which are assumed to be positive. Needless to say, (18) is invariant even if $U(u)$ is chosen instead of $u$.

It is certainly possible to describe the demand functions from (17) and (18) in the usual Hicks–Slutsky manner. However, as I found [28], it is often convenient to write them directly as[9]

$$C_x = C_x(p, u) \quad \text{and} \quad C_y = C_y(p, u) \tag{20}$$

which can be obtained directly from the problem of minimizing the expenditure $pC_x + C_y$ subject to $u = u(C_x, C_y)$ where $p$ and $u$ are taken to be the parameters. Needless to say, the solution of such a problem will yield the same solution as the one which is obtained in the Hicks–Slutsky fashion.[10] Indeed, the functional form of (20) can readily be interpreted by the substitution effect and the income effect in the Hicks–Slutsky equation.

The output of each commodity is determined from the production transformation curve by the tangency condition, once the price ratio is given. Thus

$$X = X(p) \quad \text{and} \quad Y = Y(p) \tag{21}$$

---

[9] See, for example, Chapters 8, 12, and 13 of ref. [28]. See also Ohyama [24].

[10] The Hicks–Slutsky equation is usually obtained from the condition of maximizing utility subject to the budget constraint. The meaning of the so-called substitution term of the H–S equation is then not obvious, as it stands. That is, we need a further consideration to obtain the economic meaning of the term in order to justify the name, the substitution term. On the other hand, we can also obtain the H–S equation from the above minimum expenditure approach, and then the meaning of the substitution term is obvious, as can be seen from (20). For a rigorous treatment of the minimum expenditure approach and the structure of demand theory, see McKenzie [19] and Hurwicz and Uzawa [8]. We call the demand function in the form of (20) the "compensated demand function," because of its obvious implications when $u$ is held constant.

where we assume[11]

$$X' > 0 \quad \text{and} \quad Y' < 0. \tag{22}$$

The tangency condition is written as

$$pX' + Y' = 0. \tag{23}$$

From (20) and (21), we obtain

$$E_x = E_x(p, u) \equiv C_x(p, u) - X(p) \quad \text{and} \quad E_y = E_y(p, u) \equiv C_y(p, u) - Y(p) \tag{24}$$

which signifies the equation for the "offer curve."[12] Since $dE_y = (\partial E_y/\partial p)\, dp + (\partial E_y/\partial u)\, du$, etc., we have to know $du$, the change in real income, to determine the shape of the offer curve. For this purpose, observe that

$$du/u_y = (u_x/u_y)\, dC_x + dC_y = (p\, dE_x + dE_y) + (p\, dX + dY) \tag{25}$$

from (16) and (18), so that

$$du/u_y = p\, dE_x + dE_y \tag{26}$$

from (23). Needless to say, $du/u_y$ is invariant when $u$ is replaced by $U(u)$. Differentiating both sides of (17) and utilizing (17'), we obtain

$$p\, dE_x + dE_y = (1 - 1/t)\, dE_y + (E_y/t)\hat{q} \tag{27}$$

where $\hat{q} \equiv dq/q$ and $q = tp$. The symbol $q$ signifies the foreign price ratio under the present tariff scheme [recall Eq. (6)]. Hence, combining (26) and (27), we obtain

$$du/u_y = \{[(t - 1)/t]\hat{E}_y + (\hat{q}/t)\}E_y \tag{28}$$

where $\hat{E}_y \equiv dE_y/E_y$.[13]

---

[11] $X'$ and $Y'$, respectively, denote $dX/dp$ and $dY/dp$. Here we are assuming that both commodities are produced (incomplete specialization). In the case of complete specialization, (21) is replaced by $[X = \bar{X}, Y = 0]$ or $[X = 0, Y = \bar{Y}]$. Since the analysis for such cases is analogous to the subsequent one, we shall omit it.

[12] Alternatively, write (17') as $p[C_x - X(p)] = -[C_y - Y(p)]/t$. Assume, then, that for a given value of $t$, this equation and (18) determine the values of $C_x$ and $C_y$ as $C_x = C_x(p, t)$ and $C_y = C_y(p, t)$, from which we obtain the more common expression of the offer curve,

$$E_x = E_x(p, t) \equiv C_x(p, t) - X(p) \quad \text{and} \quad E_y = E_y(p, t) \equiv C_y(p, t) - Y(p).$$

This is a little harder to use, for we have to determine the signs of $\partial C_x/\partial p$ and $\partial C_y/\partial p$.

[13] Assume $t = 1$ and $u_y = 1$. Then (28) is reduced to $du = E_y\hat{q}$. A simple derivation of this formula is presented by Takayama [28, p. 231]. The justification for $u_y = 1$ will be discussed shortly.

With this preparation, differentiating $E_y = C_y(p, u) - Y(p)$, we obtain[14]

$$\alpha \hat{E}_y = (\eta + \varepsilon/t)(\hat{q} - \hat{\imath}) + mu_y \hat{q}/t \tag{29}$$

where

$$\alpha \equiv 1 - mu_y(1 - 1/t), \qquad \hat{\imath} \equiv dt/t \tag{30}$$

and

$$\eta \equiv (\partial C_y/\partial p)(p/E_y), \quad m \equiv \partial C_y/\partial u, \quad \text{and} \quad \varepsilon \equiv [dX/dp][p/(-E_x)]. \tag{31}$$

Note that $mu_y$ is invariant when $u$ is replaced by $U(u)$. Note also that $\alpha = 1$ if and only if $t = 1$. Assuming that $Y$ is the imported commodity for the country, $\eta$, $m$, and $\varepsilon$ are, respectively, interpreted as the "elasticity of substitution of the imported commodity," the "marginal propensity to consume of the imported commodity," and the "elasticity of export supply."[15]

The "elasticity of the offer curve" (denoted by $\eta_d$) is defined by $\eta_d \equiv \hat{E}_y/\hat{p}$ with $\hat{\imath} = 0$. Therefore, from (29), we obtain

$$\eta_d \equiv [\eta + (mu_y + \varepsilon)/t]/\alpha, \tag{32}$$

which is simplified as

$$\eta_d = \eta + m + \varepsilon \tag{32'}$$

when $u_y = 1$ and $t = 1$ (initial free trade). Equation (32′) is the famous decomposition of the elasticity of the offer curve by Jones [10].

Although the assumption of $u_y = 1$ cannot in general be justified for all values of $(C_x, C_y)$, it can be justified for a particular value of $(C_x, C_y)$, say the "equilibrium value" $(C_x^*, C_y^*)$, by choosing a monotone transformation $U$ of the utility function properly.[16] In other words, $u_y = 1$ can be justified in the comparative statics analysis, which is concerned with a small change from the equilibrium point.

In view of (32), (29) is also written as

$$\hat{E}_y = \eta_d \hat{q} - \hat{\imath}(\eta + \varepsilon/t)/\alpha. \tag{29'}$$

If we let $\hat{q} = 0$ in (29′), we obtain

$$\hat{E}_y < 0 \qquad \text{when} \quad \hat{\imath} > 0 \tag{33}$$

---

[14] By (23), $X' = -Y'/p$. Also from (2′) and (6) we have $-E_x = E_y/q = E_y/(pt)$. Substituting these relations into the definition of $\varepsilon$ in (31) we obtain $\varepsilon = -tpY'/E_y$. Hence, $-pY'/E_y = \varepsilon/t$. This relation is used to obtain (29).

[15] See Jones [10] and Takayama [28, pp. 232–233]. The $\eta$ and $\varepsilon$ are always positive, but $m$ is negative if $Y$ is an inferior commodity.

[16] Choose $U$ such that $U'u_y = 1$ at $(C_x^*, C_y^*)$. Often in the literature, "real income" is measured in terms of one of the commodities, say $Y$ (the imported commodity). This amounts to setting $u_y = 1$ for *all* values of $(C_x, C_y)$.

provided $\alpha > 0$. Condition (33) is the traditional result that a rise in the rate of import tariff will cause an inward shift of the tariff-ridden offer curve. If the initial state is free trade ($t = 1$), then $\alpha = 1$. Also, if none of the two commodities is inferior, then $0 < mu_y < 1$,[17] which in turn implies that $\alpha$ is *always* positive.

## C. WORLD EQUILIBRIUM—COMPARATIVE STATICS AND OPTIMAL TARIFF[18]

We now introduce the other country and consider the world trade equilibrium. For the sake of illustration, we again assume that the only policy variable is the import tariff of country I. Assume again that country I imports $Y$ and exports $X$, and suppose that country I is not "small."

As mentioned earlier, any one of (4), (5), (8), and (10) describes the full equilibrium. Here we choose (8):

$$qE_{x2} - E_{y1} = 0 \tag{8}$$

from which we obtain

$$\hat{q} + \hat{E}_{x2} = \hat{E}_{y1} \tag{34}$$

where $\hat{E}_{x2} \equiv dE_{x2}/E_{x2}$. Since country II, by assumption, imposes no tariff, her offer curve can simply be written as[19]

$$E_{x2} = E_{x2}(q). \tag{35}$$

Hence defining $\eta_f$, the elasticity of II's offer curve, by

$$\eta_f \equiv -\hat{E}_{x2}/\hat{q}, \tag{36}$$

we obtain from (34)

$$\hat{E}_{y1} = (1 - \eta_f)\hat{q}. \tag{37}$$

First we consider the comparative statics. For this purpose, we denote the equilibrium value of $(C_{x1}, C_{y1})$ determined by (8) as $(C_{x1}^*, C_{y1}^*)$, and let $u_{y1}(C_{x1}^*, C_{y1}^*) = 1$, where $u_{y1} \equiv \partial u_1/\partial C_{y1}$, by a suitable choice of a monotone transformation $U_1$. With this simplification, combine (29′) with (37) to yield

$$\alpha_1 \Omega \hat{q} = (\eta_1 + \varepsilon_1/t)\hat{t} \tag{38}$$

---

[17] Partially differentiate both sides of $u = u[C_x(p, u), C_y(p, u)]$ with respect to $u$. Then we obtain $u_x \, \partial C_x/\partial u + u_y \, \partial C_y/\partial u = 1$. Hence, if $\partial C_x/\partial u > 0$ and $m \equiv \partial C_y/\partial u > 0$, we must have $0 < mu_y < 1$.

[18] For the references to the traditional comparative statics analysis of trade policy, see ref. [28, pp. 248–250]. For the references to the traditional optimal tariff argument, see ref. [28, pp. 460–461].

[19] If we write $E_{x1} = E_{y1}(p, t)$ following footnote 12, we can, from (8), summarize the full equilibrium relation for a given value of $t$ by $qE_{x2}(q) = E_{y1}(p, t)$, where $p = q/t$.

where

$$\Omega \equiv \eta_d + \eta_f - 1 \tag{39}$$

and

$$\eta_d = [\eta_1 + (m_1 + \varepsilon_1)/t]/\alpha_1 \quad \text{and} \quad \alpha_1 \equiv 1 - m_1(1 - 1/t). \tag{40}$$

If $t > 1$ and $0 < m_1 < 1$, then $0 < \alpha_1 < 1$, and $\alpha_1 = 1$ if and only if $t = 1$ (initial free trade). Hence assuming $\alpha_1 > 0$,

$$\hat{q}/\hat{t} > 0 \tag{41}$$

provided that

$$\Omega > 0. \tag{42}$$

It can be easily shown that (42) is a sufficient condition for local stability.[20] That is, under such a situation an increase in the tariff rate will usually improve the terms of trade for country I.

When the initial rate of tariff is zero (that is, $t = 1$), condition (42) is reduced to the familiar *Marshall–Lerner condition*

$$\eta_d + \eta_f - 1 > 0$$

where $\eta_d = \eta_1 + m_1 + \varepsilon_1$. Also, when $t = 1$, condition (41) is written in the better-known traditional form [28, p. 243, Eq. (8-74)]:

$$\hat{q}/\hat{t} = (\eta_1 + \varepsilon_1)/\Omega > 0. \tag{41'}$$

The effect of a change in the tariff rate on the domestic price ratio is obtained easily from (38)

$$\hat{p}/\hat{t} < 0 \quad \text{if and only if} \quad m_1/t + \alpha_1(\eta_f - 1) > 0 \tag{43}$$

by noticing that $\hat{p} = \hat{q} - \hat{t}$, and assuming the stability condition $\Omega > 0$. When $t = 1$ (initial free trade), (43) is reduced to the well-known *Metzler condition* [20; 21; 28, p. 243],

$$\hat{p}/\hat{t} < 0 \quad \text{if and only if} \quad m_1 + \eta_f - 1 > 0. \tag{43'}$$

When country I is "small," we do not have the usual equilibrium relations such as (8), (4), and (5), as remarked earlier. In this case, the volume of exports

---

[20] A sufficient condition for local stability is $d(E_{y1} + E_{y2})/dq > 0$, where the derivative is evaluated at the equilibrium point. Then recalling $qE_{x2} \equiv E_{y2}$ (II's budget), and (36), we obtain from (29')

$$d(E_{y1} + E_{y2})/dq = (\eta_d + \eta_f - 1)E_{y1}/q,$$

by setting $\hat{t} = 0$. From this, (42) follows easily. For an exposition of the Marshall–Lerner condition, see Takayama [28, Chapter 8].

and imports, that is, $-E_{x1}$ and $E_{y1}$, are determined once $t$ is given, since $q$ is a given constant. Note that $dq/dt = 0$ directly from the small country assumption, and that $\hat{p}/\hat{t} < 0$ follows trivially from $p = q/t$ or $\hat{p} = \hat{q} - \hat{t} = -\hat{t}$. Also in view of (29), the volume of imports $E_{y1}$ (hence, also the volume of exports, $-E_{x1}$) decreases as the tariff rate increases, provided that $\alpha > 0$. Also note from (28) that $du_1 < 0$ if the volume of imports decreases ($\hat{E}_{y1} < 0$), as long as $\hat{q} = 0$. When $t = 1$ (initial free trade), then $\alpha = 1$, so that this conclusion always holds.

Now turn to the optimal tariff problem. Here we do not let $t$ be exogenously given. Instead, $t$ is chosen so as to maximize country I's utility $u_1$. We do not assume that country I is small. The first-order condition for optimality requires

$$du_1/dt = 0 \qquad \text{or} \qquad du_1/\hat{t} = 0. \qquad (44)$$

Hence, from (28), we immediately obtain

$$(t - 1)\hat{E}_{y1}/\hat{t} + \hat{q}/\hat{t} = 0. \qquad (45)$$

Then using (37) and noting that $\hat{q}/\hat{t} \neq 0$, we obtain at once the age-old optimal tariff formula

$$\tau = 1/(\eta_f - 1) \qquad (46)$$

where $\tau \equiv t - 1$, the *ad valorem* rate of tariff.

When the country is small, set $\hat{q} = 0$ in (28) and (29), and obtain

$$du_1/u_{y1} = -[(t - 1)/\alpha_1 t](\eta_1 + \varepsilon_1/t)E_{y1}\hat{t} \qquad (28')$$

assuming $\alpha_1 \neq 0$. Therefore the first-order condition, $du_1/dt = 0$, requires that $t = 1$.[21] In other words, free trade is optimal for the small country, which again is a well-known result in traditional trade theory.

## III. Domestic Distortions

Consider a country which has two productive sectors, agriculture and industry. Assume that there is "friction" in the mobility of labor from agriculture to industry so that the industrial workers enjoy a higher wage rate than the agricultural workers ("domestic distortions"). Assume that the country exports agricultural goods and imports the industrial goods, and assume also that the country is small enough so that the world terms of trade is a given constant to her. Hagen [6] argues that under such circumstances complete protection (say, by a prohibitively high rate of tariff) is better for the country than free trade. Then Bhagwati and Ramaswami [1] show that

---

[21] This result is the same as the one which is obtained by letting $\eta_f \to \infty$ in (46).

Hagen's conclusion is not necessarily true. They go on to say, "it is impossible to find any level of tariff (or trade subsidy) that is superior to free trade" [1, p. 49]. Kemp and Negishi [14] and Negishi [23] argue that this is not true and conclude "there exists a tariff superior to free trade" [23, p. 164].

Needless to say, all in the above controversy admit that the truly best solution is to remove the domestic distortions (say by some suitable tax-cum-subsidy policy). Therefore the above controversy is concerned with the "second-best" solution *given* the domestic distortions.[22] In this section, we obtain the explicit formula for the optimal tariff as well as the critical evaluation of the controversy as a simple extension of the analytical framework developed above. We then extend our analysis by dropping the small country assumption which underlies the discussion.

The key outcome of the "domestic distortions"—that the wage rate is not equalized between the two sectors—may be expressed as

$$dY_1/dX_1 = -\delta p, \qquad \delta > 0 \tag{47}$$

where we assume that country I is the country in question. In other words, the price line is no longer tangent to the production transformation curve. We then assume away all the other complications associated with domestic distortions such as a nonconvex production possibility set.[23] For the sake of simplicity, we assume $\delta$ is a constant. Then, given $\delta$, the output of each commodity is determined, once the domestic price ratio is given. In other words, we can still write

$$X_1 = X_1(p) \qquad \text{and} \qquad Y_1 = Y_1(p), \tag{48}$$

although we no longer have the tangency condition $pX_1' + Y_1' = 0$. Instead we can easily compute[24]

$$pX_1' + Y_1' = \varepsilon_1(1 - \delta)E_{y1}/q \tag{49}$$

---

[22] An excellent summary of the above controversy is offered by Negishi [23, Chapter 11]. A further consideration of this problem is undertaken by Ohyama [24], to whom we are indebted in some of the discussions of this section.

[23] The nonconvex production possibility set and further complications arising from domestic distortions have recently been discussed extensively in the literature. See Johnson [9], Herberg and Kemp [7], Bhagwati and Srinivasan [3], and Jones [12]. However, if labor is the only shiftable factor—that is, all the other factors such as capital and land are specific to each sector and not shiftable between the two sectors—then we can show that the production transformation curve has the usual strictly concave shape under a set of plausible assumptions, such as the law of diminishing returns. See Negishi [23, Chapter 11, Section 4].

[24] Note that $pX_1' + Y_1' = pX_1'(1 - \delta) = \varepsilon_1(\delta - 1)E_{x1}$. Then observe $E_{x1} \equiv -E_{y1}/q$ from (2'). Recall footnote 14, in which $\delta = 1$.

where $\varepsilon_1$ is defined in (31) and signifies the "elasticity of export supply" if country I exports $X$. Substituting (49) and (27) into (25), we obtain[25]

$$du_1/u_{y1} = [\varepsilon_1(1 - \delta)(\hat{q} - \hat{t}) + \{(t - 1)\hat{E}_{y1} + \hat{q}\}](E_{y1}/t). \tag{50}$$

When there are no domestic distortions ($\delta = 1$), (50) is reduced to (28).

Next, differentiating $E_{y1} = C_{y1}(p, u_1) - Y_1(p)$, and recalling the definitions of $\eta$, $m$, and $\varepsilon$ in (31), we obtain[26]

$$\hat{E}_{y1} = (\eta_1 + \delta\varepsilon_1/t)(\hat{q} - \hat{t}) + m_1(du_1/E_{y1}). \tag{51}$$

Then combining (50) and (51), we obtain the following basic formula for domestic distortions:

$$du_1[1/u_{y1} - m_1(1 - 1/t)]t/E_{y1} = (\hat{q} - \hat{t})[\eta_1(t - 1) + \varepsilon_1(1 - \delta/t)] + \hat{q}. \tag{52}$$

The Hagen–Bhagwati–Ramaswami–Kemp–Negishi problem of domestic distortions is simply the problem of choosing $t$ (or $\tau$) so as to maximize $u_1$ for a given value of $\delta$, assuming $\hat{q} = 0$ (small country).[27] We thus set $\hat{q} = 0$ in (52) and note that the first-order condition for an optimum requires $du_1/dt = 0$. Then we obtain from (52),

$$\eta_1(t - 1) + \varepsilon_1(1 - \delta/t) = 0. \tag{53}$$

That is,

$$\tau(\eta_1 t + \varepsilon_1) = \varepsilon_1(\delta - 1). \tag{54}$$

If there are no domestic distortions ($\delta = 1$), we can at once conclude from (54) that free trade ($\tau = 0$) is best for the country, which is the conclusion mentioned earlier.

When domestic distortions are present, we have $\delta > 1$, since country I exports $X$ in the present context and the wage rate in $X$ is lower than that in $Y$. Since $t > 0$, $\tau$ is unambiguously positive in view of (54).[28] This seems to be the basis of the proposition of Kemp–Negishi [14] that some protection is better than free trade for the small country. An interesting observation one can make in this connection is that if $\delta < 1$, then we have $\tau < 0$ in view of

---

[25] Note that $dp = (\hat{q} - \hat{t})q/t$. Needless to say, the expression for $du_1/u_{y1}$ for the small country can be obtained by setting $\hat{q} = 0$ in (50).

[26] Note that $\varepsilon_1 \equiv -pX_1'/E_{x1}$ can be rewritten as $\varepsilon_1 = -(tpY_1')/(\delta E_{y1})$, by recalling (47) and (2').

[27] Since $X$ is agriculture and $Y$ is industry, the higher wage rate in industry compared to agriculture means that $|dY_1/dX_1| > p$, i.e., the marginal rate of transformation between $Y$ and $X$ exceeds $p$. If the country exports $X$ and imports $Y$, then $\delta > 1$.

[28] Since we require $p > 0$, $q > 0$ and $p = q/t$, $t$ must be positive. Also $t > 0$ implies $\eta_1 t + \varepsilon_1 > 0$, which guarantees $\tau = 0$ from (54) when $\delta = 1$.

(54).[29] That is, an import subsidy is required for an optimum. Needless to say, $\delta < 1$ if the wage rate in the exporting industry (here $X$) is higher than that in the import competing industry, which also is a quite plausible case.

We can also conclude from (54) that free trade ($\tau = 0$) is hardly an optimal solution under domestic distortions whether or not $t > 0$. Hence the Bhagwati–Ramaswami conclusion is in general false. As explained by Negishi [23], their famous diagrammatical analysis only shows an example that free trade is better than *complete* protection. What they should have compared with free trade is *some*, rather than complete, protection.

Let us now obtain the expression for the optimal tariff rate. To do this, simply regard (54) as a quadratic equation in $\tau$ and solve it for $\tau$. Thus

$$\tau = (2\eta_1)^{-1}\{-(\eta_1 + \varepsilon_1) \pm [(\eta_1 + \varepsilon_1)^2 + 4\eta_1\varepsilon_1(\delta - 1)]^{1/2}\},$$

so that

$$t \equiv 1 + \tau = (2\eta_1)^{-1}\{(\eta_1 - \varepsilon_1) \pm [(\eta_1 - \varepsilon_1)^2 + 4\eta_1\varepsilon_1\delta]^{1/2}\}.$$

Then, one of the two values of $t$ is positive and the other is negative. However, only the positive one is permitted since $t$ must be positive. Hence the optimal tariff rate is unambiguously and explicitly obtained as

$$\tau = (2\eta_1)^{-1}\{-(\eta_1 + \varepsilon_1) + [(\eta_1 + \varepsilon_1)^2 + 4\eta_1\varepsilon_1(\delta - 1)]^{1/2}\}. \tag{55}$$

If $\delta < 1$, then $\tau < 0$. On the other hand, if $\delta > 1$, the case of the Hagen–Bhagwati–Ramaswami–Kemp–Negishi controversy, $\tau$ is clearly positive, confirming the Kemp–Negishi conclusion. Note that if the elasticities $\eta_1$ and $\varepsilon_1$ are not affected by $\delta$, then the optimal tariff rate $\tau$ is greater, the greater is the distortion parameter $\delta$ (when $\delta > 1$). Note also that (55) gives $\tau = 0$ when $\delta = 1$, thus incorporating the case of no domestic distortions.

We now drop the small country assumption (that is, $\hat{q} = 0$) which is common in the literature on the above controversy. We assume instead that country I faces a constant foreign offer curve, $E_{x2} = E_{x2}(q)$. We again assume, for the sake of simplicity, that country II imposes no tariff and that it has no domestic distortions. First observe from (37) that

$$(t - 1)\hat{E}_{y1} = -\tau(\eta_f - 1)\hat{q}. \tag{56}$$

Then, combining (50) with (56), we obtain

$$(t/E_{y1})(du_1/u_{y1}) = [\varepsilon_1(1 - \delta) + \{1 - \tau(\eta_f - 1)\}]\hat{q} - \varepsilon_1(1 - \delta)\hat{t}. \tag{57}$$

The first-order condition for an optimal tariff requires $du_1/dt = 0$; that is,

$$[\varepsilon_1(1 - \delta) + \{1 - \tau(\eta_f - 1)\}]\hat{q} = \varepsilon_1(1 - \delta)\hat{t}. \tag{58}$$

---

[29] Since $t = 1 + \tau > 0$, we have $0 > \tau > -1$.

If there are no domestic distortions, so that $\delta = 1$, then (58) is reduced to

$$1 - \tau(\eta_f - 1) = 0 \qquad \text{or} \qquad \tau = 1/(\eta_f - 1)$$

which is the famous optimal tariff formula. When domestic distortions are present, the conclusion depends on the sign of $\hat{q}/\hat{\imath}$. Here we consider the usual case in which $\hat{q}/\hat{\imath} > 0$; that is, an increase in the tariff rate moves the terms of trade in favor of the tariff imposing country. Then from (58) we obtain

$$\tau(\eta_f - 1) > 1 + \varepsilon_1(1 - \delta) \tag{59}$$

assuming $\delta > 1$. Note that $\tau$ can be either positive or negative; that is, protection may not be desirable for the country under domestic distortions.[30]

## IV. Nontraded Commodities[31]

### A. INTRODUCTION

Looking into the "real world," it is obvious that there is a bulk of goods, notably service goods such as "haircuts," which are not traded internationally. The traditional trade theory tends to avoid these commodities, probably because of the hardship involved in carrying out the analysis in the two-dimensional diagram. However, as long as the mathematical structure of the analytics is clear for the two-commodity world (as it should be from the discussion in Section II), the extension of the analysis to the world which involves nontraded commodities is an easy, but rather tedious mathematical exercise. Thus, the "real world" concern has excited a number of mathematical theorists to produce interesting works on nontraded commodities.[32] Here, confining ourselves to the comparative statics analysis, we obtain the major results with nontraded commodities in a systematic and the easiest possible

[30] When $\eta_f > 0$, we can rewrite (59) as $\tau(1 - 1/\eta_f) > [1 + \varepsilon_1(1 - \delta)]/\eta_f$. Hence in the limit of $\eta_f \to \infty$, we have $\tau > 0$. This again confirms the Kemp–Negishi conclusion for the small country case.

[31] For a brief description of the history of the discussion on this topic, see McDougall [18, p. 158].

[32] See, for example, Pearce [26], Komiya [15], McDougall [16–18]. Among them, McDougall [18] probably gives the most systematic discussion on the comparative statics analysis of the model with nontraded commodities. However, his analysis is unduly complex and quite tedious; the relation to the traditional discussion is sometimes not clear. We shall simplify the analysis by using the approach in the previous sections via the compensating demand functions. All the discussions here require no knowledge of matrix algebra. Although we shall confine our discussion to the effect of an import tariff, the extension to the other standard topics (such as unilateral transfer payments, domestic taxes and subsidies, and productivity changes) should be straightforward to the reader with the usual background in trade theory.

way. Once again the compensated demand function plays a useful role in simplifying the analysis, as Eq. (20) did in the previous sections.

## B. WALRAS' LAW AND EQUILIBRIUM

Let $Z_i$ and $C_{zi}$, respectively, be the output and the consumption of the nontraded commodity in country $i$ ($i = 1, 2$). Then the equilibrium condition for the nontraded commodity is obviously

$$E_{zi} = C_{zi} - Z_i = 0, \qquad i = 1, 2. \tag{60}$$

Assume again that country I imports $Y$ from country II in equilibrium, where I imposes an import tariff whose *ad valorem* rate is $t - 1$. Assume that country II imposes no tariffs. The budget conditions of countries I and II, (2) and (3), can be rewritten as

$$pE_{x1} + E_{y1} + p_{zy}E_{z1} \equiv [(t - 1)/t]E_{y1} \tag{61}$$

$$qE_{x2} + E_{y2} + q_{zy}E_{z2} \equiv 0 \tag{62}$$

where $p_{zy}$ and $q_{zy}$, respectively, denote the price of $Z$ in terms of the price of $Y$ in countries I and II (that is, $p_{zy} \equiv p_z/p_y$ and $q_{zy} \equiv q_z/q_y$). The equilibrium conditions (4) and (5) hold as they are. The international trade arbitrage condition (6) holds as it is.

Equation (61) can equivalently be written as

$$qE_{x1} + E_{y1} + tp_{zy}E_{z1} \equiv 0. \tag{63}$$

Hence combining (62) and (63), we obtain

$$q(E_{x1} + E_{x2}) + (E_{y1} + E_{y2}) + tp_{zy}E_{z1} + q_{zy}E_{z2} \equiv 0, \tag{64}$$

which is the *Walras law* of the present system. Therefore one of the four equilibrium conditions, (4), (5), and (60), is not independent. Notice that we now need three equations to describe the equilibrium, while we needed only one equation in the model without the nontraded commodities.

If we adopt (60) as two of the three equilibrium conditions, then any one of (4), (5) and

$$qE_{x2} - E_{y1} = 0 \tag{8}$$

will completely describe the equilibrium together with (60). Equation (8) is now obtained from (62), (5), and $E_{z2} = 0$. Obviously, (8) and $E_{z2} = 0$ also imply (5) in view of (62).

Finally, it may be worthwhile to notice that (61) and (62) are, respectively, reduced to

$$pE_{x1} + E_{y1} = [(t - 1)/t]E_{y1} \qquad (\text{or} \quad qE_{x1} + E_{y1} = 0) \tag{65}$$

and

$$qE_{x2} + E_{y2} = 0, \tag{66}$$

if we assume $E_{zi} = 0$, $i = 1, 2$. Unlike (2) and (3), conditions (65) and (66) are not identities. However, if we assume that the markets for the nontraded commodities are *always* held in equilibrium, then (65) and (66), as well as (60), may be treated as identities.

## C. OFFER CURVE

Since we focus our discussion on country I, we omit the subscript 1 to ease the notation. The utility function (16) under the present model should be rewritten as

$$u = u(C_x, C_y, C_z) \qquad (67)$$

where, again, any monotone transformation of $u$, $u = U(u)$, $U'(u) > 0$ for all $u$, can also serve as a valid index of welfare.

The tangency conditions which describe the consumers' equilibrium are

$$p_x/p_y = u_x/u_y \qquad \text{and} \qquad p_z/p_y = u_z/u_y \qquad (68)$$

where $u_x \equiv \partial u/\partial C_x$, $u_y \equiv \partial u/\partial C_y$, and $u_z \equiv \partial u/\partial C_z$, all of which we assume to be positive. Obviously, $u_x/u_y$ and $u_z/u_y$ are both functions of $C_x$, $C_y$, and $C_z$, as is $u$. Condition (68) implies

$$p_y/p_x = u_y/u_x \qquad \text{and} \qquad p_z/p_x = u_z/u_x. \qquad (69)$$

All the relations in (68) and (69) are invariant when $U(u)$ is chosen instead of $u$. Equation (20) should be rewritten as

$$C_x = C_x(p_x, p_y, p_z, u)$$
$$C_y = C_y(p_x, p_y, p_z, u) \qquad (70)$$
$$C_z = C_z(p_x, p_y, p_z, u).$$

Also, (21) is rewritten as

$$X = X(p_x, p_y, p_z), \qquad Y = Y(p_x, p_y, p_z), \qquad Z = Z(p_x, p_y, p_z). \qquad (71)$$

The functions $C_x$, $C_y$, $C_z$, $X$, $Y$, and $Z$ are all homogeneous of degree zero in $p_x$, $p_y$, and $p_z$. The tangency condition for production is written as follows, assuming away the "domestic distortions": [33]

$$p_x \, dX + p_y \, dY + p_z \, dZ = 0. \qquad (72)$$

The functions $E_x$, $E_y$, and $E_z$ can be obtained from (70) and (71); that is,

$$E_x = E_x(p_x, p_y, p_z, u) \equiv C_x(p_x, p_y, p_z, u) - X(p_x, p_y, p_z) \qquad (73a)$$

$$E_y = E_y(p_x, p_y, p_z, u) \equiv C_y(p_x, p_y, p_z, u) - Y(p_x, p_y, p_z) \qquad (73b)$$

$$E_z = E_z(p_x, p_y, p_z, u) \equiv C_z(p_x, p_y, p_z, u) - Z(p_x, p_y, p_z). \qquad (73c)$$

---

[33] The reader should be able to extend our analysis easily to the case in which domestic distortions are involved. As we did in Section III, it only amounts to modifying Eq. (72) by using an equation such as (47).

We now obtain the change in real income. For this purpose, observe that

$$du/u_y = (u_x/u_y) \, dC_x + dC_y + (u_z/u_y) \, dC_z$$
$$= (p \, dE_x + dE_y + p_{zy} \, dE_z) + (p \, dX + dY + p_{zy} \, dZ)$$
$$= p \, dE_x + dE_y + p_{zy} \, dE_z, \tag{74}$$

using (68) and (72), where $p \equiv p_x/p_y$ and $p_{zy} \equiv p_z/p_y$. Assume that equilibrium in the nontraded commodity is maintained, so that we have $dE_z = 0$ as well as $E_z = 0$. Then (74) is reduced to (26); that is,

$$du/u_y = p \, dE_x + dE_y. \tag{26}$$

Also, in view of (65), we obtain the same equation as (27). Hence combining (26) and (27) as before, we again obtain (28):[34]

$$du/u_y = \{[(t-1)/t]\hat{E}_y + (\hat{q}/t)\}E_y; \tag{28}$$

that is, the presence of the nontraded commodity does not cause any change in the formula for the change in real income.

With this preparation, we differentiate both sides of (73a) and (73b) and obtain

$$\hat{E}_x = (\eta_{xx} - \varepsilon_{xx})\hat{p}_x + (\eta_{xy} - \varepsilon_{xy})\hat{p}_y + (\eta_{xz} - \varepsilon_{xz})\hat{p}_z + m_x(du/E_x) \tag{75a}$$

$$\hat{E}_y = (\eta_{yx} - \varepsilon_{yx})\hat{p}_x + (\eta_{yy} - \varepsilon_{yy})\hat{p}_y + (\eta_{yz} - \varepsilon_{yz})\hat{p}_z + m_y(du/E_y) \tag{75b}$$

where

$$\eta_{ij} \equiv (\partial C_i/\partial p_j) \, (p_j/E_i), \qquad i = x, y \quad \text{and} \quad j = x, y, z, \tag{76}$$

$$\varepsilon_{xj} \equiv (\partial X/\partial p_j) \, (p_j/E_x), \qquad \varepsilon_{yj} \equiv (\partial Y/\partial p_j) \, (p_j/E_y), \qquad j = x, y, z, \tag{77}$$

$$m_x \equiv \partial C_x/\partial u, \qquad m_y \equiv \partial C_y/\partial u. \tag{78}$$

Because of the homogeneity, we have (use Euler's equation)

$$\eta_{xx} + \eta_{xy} + \eta_{xz} = 0, \qquad \eta_{yx} + \eta_{yy} + \eta_{yz} = 0 \tag{79}$$

$$\varepsilon_{xx} + \varepsilon_{xy} + \varepsilon_{xz} = 0, \qquad \varepsilon_{yx} + \varepsilon_{yy} + \varepsilon_{yz} = 0. \tag{80}$$

We may assume that[35]

$$\varepsilon_{xx} > 0, \qquad \varepsilon_{xy} < 0, \qquad \text{and} \qquad \varepsilon_{xz} < 0 \qquad \text{if} \quad E_x > 0, \tag{81a}$$

$$\varepsilon_{yx} < 0, \qquad \varepsilon_{yy} > 0, \qquad \text{and} \qquad \varepsilon_{yz} < 0 \qquad \text{if} \quad E_y > 0. \tag{81b}$$

---

[34] As before, we are here assuming that the country in question (i.e., country I) imports $Y$ in equilibrium and imposes a duty on $Y$, whose *ad valorem* rate is $(t-1)$.

[35] Depending on the number of factors, it is possible for the production transformation surface to have "linear segments," so that these supply elasticities may become zero. See Otani [25]. This possibility will not alter the subsequent discussions.

Assume that $E_i > 0$ ($i = x$ or $y$).[36] Then from the theory of consumer's choice, we have $\eta_{ii} < 0$, and for $i = x$, $y$, and $j = x$, $y$, $z$,[37]

$$\eta_{ij} > 0, \qquad i \neq j, \qquad \text{if } i \text{ and } j \text{ are substitutes} \tag{82a}$$

and

$$\eta_{ij} < 0, \qquad i \neq j, \qquad \text{if } i \text{ and } j \text{ are complements.} \tag{82b}$$

In the two-commodity world, there is no possibility of complementarity. In the three-commodity world with nontraded commodities, an important complication arises because of possible complementarities.

Note that, in view of (79) and (80), (75) is rewritten as

$$\hat{E}_x = -a_{xy}(\hat{p}_x - \hat{p}_y) + a_{xz}(\hat{p}_z - \hat{p}_x) + m_x(du/E_x) \tag{83a}$$

$$\hat{E}_y = a_{yx}(\hat{p}_x - \hat{p}_y) + a_{yz}(\hat{p}_z - \hat{p}_y) + m_y(du/E_y) \tag{83b}$$

where

$$a_{xy} \equiv \eta_{xy} - \varepsilon_{xy}, \qquad a_{xz} \equiv \eta_{xz} - \varepsilon_{xz} \tag{84a}$$

$$a_{yx} \equiv \eta_{yx} - \varepsilon_{yx}, \qquad a_{yz} \equiv \eta_{yz} - \varepsilon_{yz}. \tag{84b}$$

Suppose that $X$, $Y$, and $Z$ are all substitutes. Then $a_{xy}$ and $a_{xz}$ are both positive if $E_x > 0$; also $a_{yx}$ and $a_{yz}$ are both positive if $E_y > 0$ [recall (81b) and (82a)]. If some of the commodities are complements, then some of these coefficients can be negative.[38]

Assume that the country in question (that is, I) imports $Y$ in equilibrium, so that we focus our attention on $E_y$. Combining (83b) with (28) and noting that $\hat{q} = \hat{p} + \hat{t} = (\hat{p}_x - \hat{p}_y) + \hat{t}$, we have

$$\alpha_y \hat{E}_y = (a_{yx} + m_y u_y/t)(\hat{p}_x - \hat{p}_y) + a_{yz}(\hat{p}_z - \hat{p}_y) + m_y u_y(\hat{t}/t) \tag{85}$$

where $\alpha_y$ is the same as the $\alpha$ defined in (30), or more precisely,

$$\alpha_y \equiv 1 - m_y u_y(1 - 1/t). \tag{30''}$$

[36] We cannot, of course, assume $E_x > 0$ *and* $E_y > 0$. The expressions which involve $E_x$ will be used later to obtain the necessary relations for country II (which will be assumed to import $X$ in equilibrium so that $E_{x2} > 0$). The basic relations (75a) and (75b) obtained here do not depend on whether the country imports $X$ or $Y$ in equilibrium.

[37] One of the strengths of our approach via the compensated demand functions (70) is that the signs of the $\eta_{ij}$'s are obvious from the definition of substitutes and complements.

[38] We are not saying that some of these commodities are actually complements in the "real world." We are only pointing out a theoretical possibility. In a model of highly aggregated commodities such as the present one, it is probably plausible to assume that all commodities are substitutes.

If none of the three commodities is inferior, then we have $0 < m_y u_y < 1$, so that $\alpha_y > 0$ always. If there is no tariff ($t = 1$, $\hat{t} = 0$), we obtain

$$\hat{E}_y = (\eta_{yx} + m_y u_y - \varepsilon_{yx})\hat{p} + (\eta_{yz} - \varepsilon_{yz})\hat{p}_{zy}. \tag{86}$$

When $p_{zy} = \text{constant}$ (i.e., $\hat{p}_{zy} = 0$), then $\hat{E}_y$ reduces to the Jones formula (32′) with $u_y = 1$.

Let us now obtain the expression corresponding to (75) and (83) for the nontraded commodity. Differentiating both sides of (73c) and noting the homogeneity conditions (79) and (80), we obtain

$$0 = \left(\frac{\partial C_z}{\partial p_x}p_x - \frac{\partial Z}{\alpha p_x}p_x\right)(\hat{p}_x - \hat{p}_y) + \left(\frac{\partial C_z}{\partial p_z}p_z - \frac{\partial Z}{\partial p_z}p_z\right)(\hat{p}_z - \hat{p}_y) + m_z\,du \tag{87}$$

where $m_z \equiv \partial C_z/\partial u$. Here, as we may recall, the equilibrium for the nontraded commodity requires $dE_z = 0$ as well as $E_z = 0$. Using (28), we may rewrite (87) as

$$0 = (a_{zx} + m_z u_y/t)\hat{p} - a_{zz}\hat{p}_{zy} + m_z u_y\{[t - 1/t]\hat{E}_y + (\hat{t}/t)\} \tag{88}$$

where $p \equiv p_x/p_y$, $p_{zy} \equiv p_z/p_y$, and

$$a_{zx} \equiv \left(\frac{\partial C_z}{\partial p_x}p_x - \frac{\partial Z}{\partial p_x}p_x\right)\bigg/E_y, \qquad a_{zz} \equiv -\left(\frac{\partial C_z}{\partial p_z}p_z - \frac{\partial Z}{\partial p_z}p_z\right)\bigg/E_y. \tag{89}$$

Note that the denominator of $a_{zx}$ and $a_{zz}$ is $E_y$ instead of $E_z$, which avoids division by zero. Also note that $a_{zz} > 0$ always, if $E_y > 0$.

Combining (85) and (88), we obtain

$$\beta_y\hat{E}_y = b\hat{p} + c\hat{t} \tag{90}$$

where

$$\beta_y \equiv 1 - (m_y + m_z a_{yz}/a_{zz})u_y(1 - 1/t) \tag{91}$$

$$b \equiv (a_{yx} + a_{zx}a_{yz}/a_{zz}) + (m_y + m_z a_{yz}/a_{zz})u_y/t \tag{92}$$

$$c \equiv (m_y + m_z a_{yz}/a_{zz})u_y/t. \tag{93}$$

Observe that $\beta_y = 1$ if $t = 1$ (initial free trade). It is probably plausible to assume that $1 > (p_y a_{yz})/(p_z a_{zz})$ [ $= (u_y a_{yz})/(u_z a_{zz})$].[39] Then, noting that $(m_y + m_z a_{yz}/a_{zz})u_y = m_y u_y + m_z u_z(u_y a_{yz})/(u_z a_{zz})$, we obtain $\beta_y > 0$ for all $t > 1$, if none of the commodities is inferior (so that $0 < m_y u_y + m_z u_z < 1$). Note also that $b/\beta_y$ can be considered as the elasticity of the offer curve (when the nontraded commodity is held in equilibrium). Hence we may write

$$\eta_d \equiv b/\beta_y. \tag{94}$$

---

[39] When $Y$ and $Z$ are substitutes ($\eta_{yz} > 0$), $a_{yz} > 0$. $1 > (p_y a_{yz})/(p_z a_{zz})$ ($>0$) says that the "own" (price) effect is larger than a "cross" (price) effect. If $a_{yz} < 0$, then we always have $\beta_y \geqslant 0$ for all $t > 1$, if none of the commodities is inferior.

When the nontraded commodity does not exist *or* when commodities $Y$ and $Z$ are not "related" (i.e., $a_{yz} = 0$), $b/\beta_y$ reduces to the usual form—that is, Eq. (32),[40]

$$\eta_d = [\eta + (mu_y + \varepsilon)/t]/\alpha \tag{32}$$

which in turn reduces to the Jones decomposition formula (32′) if $t = 1$ (initial free trade) and $u_y = 1$. In other words, (94) can be considered as an extension of the Jones decomposition formula when the nontraded commodity is present and when initial free trade is *not* assumed.

The traditional offer curve is concerned with the relation between $E_y$ and $p$. If $b/\beta_y > 0$, then the volume of imports $E_y$ increases as the relative price of $X$ vis à vis $Y$ (i.e., $p$) increases; that is, the offer curve has the "usual" shape. Notice that if all commodities are substitutes for each other (i.e., $a_{yx} > 0$, $a_{zx} > 0$, and $a_{yz} > 0$) and if none of the commodities is inferior with the property that $(p_y a_{yz})/(p_z a_{zz}) < 1$ (so that $0 < (m_y + m_z a_{yz}/a_{zz})u_y < 1$), then we have $b > 0$ as well as $\beta_y > 0$. Hence we have $b/\beta_y > 0$: the offer curve has the usual shape.

On the other hand, if these conditions do not hold, then the offer curve may not have the usual shape. For example, even with $\beta_y > 0$, $b/\beta_y$ can be negative if $X$ and $Y$ are complements, a possibility which never arises in the traditional two-commodity world.

So much for country I. Let us now briefly turn to country II. Assume that II imports $X$ in equilibrium; we are now interested in $E_{x2}$. Assuming that II imposes no import tariffs and, dropping subscript 2 to ease the notation, we obtain the following equation for the change in real income in the manner we obtained (28):[41]

$$du/u_x = -E_x \hat{q}. \tag{95}$$

Combining this with (83a), we obtain

$$\hat{E}_x = -(a_{xy} + m_x u_x)\hat{q} + a_{xz} \hat{q}_{zx} \tag{96}$$

where $q_{zy} \equiv q_z/q_x$. In the manner we obtained (88); we also obtain

$$0 = -(a'_{zy} + m_z u_x)\hat{q} - a'_{zz} \hat{q}_{zx} \tag{97}$$

---

[40] When the nontraded commodity does not exist or $a_{yz} = 0$, $-\varepsilon_{yx}$ corresponds to $\varepsilon/t$ in (32). Recall foonote 14.

[41] Since we are talking about country II, replace $q$ by $p$. Then from (26), we obtain $du/u_x = (du/u_y)/q = (q\, dE_x + dE_y)/q$. But from (66), we obtain $q\, dE_x + dE_y = -E_x\, dq$. Combining these two, we obtain (95).

where

$$a'_{zy} \equiv \left( \frac{\partial C_z}{\partial p_y} p_y - \frac{\partial Z}{\partial p_y} p_y \right) \Big/ E_x, \qquad a'_{zz} \equiv - \left( \frac{\partial C_z}{\partial p_z} p_z - \frac{\partial Z}{\partial p_z} p_z \right) \Big/ E_x,$$

$$m_z \equiv \frac{\partial C_z}{\partial u}. \tag{98}$$

Note that $E_y$ in (89) is replaced by $E_x$ in (98).

Combining (96) and (97), we obtain

$$\hat{E}_x = - \eta_f \hat{q} \tag{99}$$

where

$$\eta_f \equiv (a_{xy} + a'_{zy} a_{xz}/a'_{zz}) + (m_x + m_z a_{xz}/a'_{zz})u_x. \tag{100}$$

When $a_{xz} = 0$, then $\eta_f$ reduces to the usual elasticity of the foreign offer curve defined in (36), which justifies the use of the notation $\eta_f$. In other words, $\eta_f$ as defined in (100), like (94), gives the decomposition of the elasticity of the generalized offer curve with the nontraded commodity. It is possible for either $a_{xy}$ or $a_{xz}$ to be negative, thus causing the possibility of a negative $\eta_f$ even with the noninferiority of any commodities.

## D. World Equilibrium—Comparative Statics and Optimal Tariff

As remarked earlier, the world equilibrium can be completely described by the following three equations:

$$qE_{x2} - E_{y1} = 0 \tag{8}$$

$$E_{z1} = 0 \qquad \text{and} \qquad E_{z2} = 0. \tag{60}$$

From (8) we obtain (34),

$$\hat{q} + \hat{E}_{x2} = \hat{E}_{y1}. \tag{34}$$

Substituting (90) and (99) into (34), we at once obtain[42]

$$\hat{q}(\eta_d + \eta_f - 1) = \hat{t}(a^1_{yz} + a^1_{zx} a^1_{yz}/a^1_{zz})/\beta_y^1 \tag{101}$$

by recalling (94), and then (92) and (93), where superscript 1 refers to country I.

Therefore if $\beta_y^1 > 0$ and if none of the commodities are complements (i.e., $a^1_{yx} > 0$ and $a^1_{yz} > 0$), then we have the traditional result

$$\hat{q}/\hat{t} > 0 \tag{102}$$

provided

$$\eta_d + \eta_f - 1 > 0. \tag{103}$$

[42] The parameters in (100) are, of course, all for country II. Hence, in general, they are different from the corresponding ones in country I which appear in (91), (92), and (93).

It can again be shown easily that (103) is a sufficient condition for local stability, provided the markets for the nontraded commodities are held in equilibrium [i.e., Eq. (60) holds].[43] In other words, (103) generalizes the Marshall–Lerner condition to the world with nontraded commodities.

Assuming that condition (103) holds, the necessary and sufficient condition for $\hat{q}/\hat{t} > 0$ to hold is

$$(a_{yx}^1 + a_{zx}^1 a_{yz}^1/a_{zz}^1)/\beta_y^1 > 0. \tag{104}$$

When $\beta_y^1 > 0$, this is simplified as

$$a_{yx}^1 + a_{zx}^1 a_{yz}^1/a_{zz}^1 > 0. \tag{105}$$

Needless to say, neither (104) nor (105) is automatically satisfied. That is, the traditional result, $\hat{q}/\hat{t} > 0$, does not hold automatically.

Next, the effect of a change in the tariff rate on the domestic price ratio between $X$ and $Y$ (i.e., $p$) can be obtained immediately from (101) as

$$(\eta_d + \eta_f - 1)\hat{p} = -\hat{t}(c^1/\beta_y^1 + \eta_f - 1) \tag{106}$$

by noting that $\hat{q} = \hat{p} + \hat{t}$. Here $c$ is defined in (93). Therefore, the necessary and sufficient condition for an increase in the tariff rate to increase the domestic price of $Y$ vis à vis $X$ (that is $\hat{p}/\hat{t} < 0$) is

$$(m_y^1 + m_z^1 a_{yz}^1/a_{zz}^1)/(t\beta_y^1) + \eta_f - 1 > 0 \tag{107}$$

where we set $u_y = 1$ by the choice of $U$. This generalizes the famous Metzler condition for the world with nontraded commodities. The reader may at once realize the complications due to the presence of the nontraded commodities, that is, due to the possibility of a negative $a_{yz}^1$ and a negative $\eta_f$.

Finally, we obtain the optimal tariff formula. That is, we obtain the value of $t$ which maximizes country I's utility, $u_1$. Recall that this requires $du_1/dt = 0$, and that formula (28) for the change in real income still holds under the present circumstance (with the nontraded commodities). Then again (45) is the optimality condition. Note that (37) still holds with a new interpretation of $\eta_f$ in terms of (100). Therefore the age-old formula (46), $\tau = 1/(\eta_f - 1)$, still holds with the new interpretation of $\eta_f$.

---

[43] Assuming equilibrium in the markets for the nontraded commodities, the only market equilibrium condition to be considered is any one of (4), (5), and (8). We choose (5). Then a sufficient condition for local stability is $d(E_{y1} + E_{y2})/dq > 0$, where the derivative is evaluated at the equilibrium point. Then recalling (66), (99), and (94), we obtain from (90)

$$d(E_{y1} + E_{y2})/dq = [\eta_d + \eta_f - 1]E_{y1}/q$$

with $\hat{t} = 0$. From this, (103) follows easily.

ACKNOWLEDGMENTS

I am grateful to Sheng Cheng Hu, Yuji Kubo, John Z. Drabicki, and the referee for useful comments.

REFERENCES

1. Bhagwati, J. N., and Ramaswami, V. K., "Domestic Distortions, Tariffs, and the Theory of Optimum Subsidy," *Journal of Political Economy* **71** (February 1963), 44–50.
2. Bhagwati, J. N., Ramaswami, V. K., and Srinivasan, T. N., "Domestic Distortions, Tariffs, and the Theory of Optimum Subsidy: Further Results," *Journal of Political Economy* **77** (November/December 1969), 1005–1010.
3. Bhagwati, J. N., and Srinivasan, T. N., "The Theory of Wage Differentials: Production Response and Factor Price Equalization," *Journal of International Economics* **1** (February 1971), 19–36.
4. Fishlow, A., and David, P. A., "Optimal Resource Allocation in an Imperfect Market Setting," *Journal of Political Economy* **69** (December 1961), 529–546.
5. Haberler, G., "Some Problems in the Pure Theory of International Trade," *Economic Journal* **60** (June 1950), 223–240.
6. Hagen, E. E., "An Economic Justification of Protectionism," *Quarterly Journal of Economics* **72** (November 1958), 496–514.
7. Herberg, H., and Kemp, M. C., "Factor Market Distortions, the Shape of the Locus of Competitive Outputs, and the Relation between Product Prices and Equilibrium Outputs," in *Trade, Balance of Payments, and Growth, Papers in Honor of Charles P. Kindleberger* (J. Bhagwati *et al.*, eds.), pp. 22–48. Amsterdam: North-Holland Publ., 1971.
8. Hurwicz, L., and Uzawa, H., "On the Integrability of Demand Functions," in *Preferences, Utility, and Demand, A Minnesota Symposium* (J. S. Chipman, L. Hurwicz, M. K. Richter, and H. F. Sonnenschein, eds.), pp. 114–148. New York: Harcourt, 1971.
9. Johnson, H. G., "Factor Market Distortions and the Shape of the Transformation Curve," *Econometrica* **34** (July 1966), 686–698.
10. Jones, R. W., "Stability Conditions in International Trade: A General Equilibrium Analysis," *International Economic Review* **2** (May 1961), 199–209.
11. Jones, R. W., "Tariffs and Trade in General Equilibrium: Comment," *American Economic Review* **59** (June 1969), 418–424.
12. Jones, R. W., "Distortions in Factor Markets and the General Equilibrium Theory of Production," *Journal of Political Economy* **79** (May/June 1971), 437–459.
13. Kemp, M. C., *The Pure Theory of International Trade and Investment*. Englewood Cliffs, New Jersey: Prentice-Hall, 1969.
14. Kemp, M. C., and Negishi, T., "Domestic Distortions, Tariffs, and the Theory of Optimum Subsidy," *Journal of Political Economy* **77** (November/December 1969), 1011–1013.
15. Komiya, R., "Non-Traded Goods and the Pure Theory of International Trade," *International Economic Review* **8** (June 1967), 132–152.
16. McDougall, I. A., "Non-Traded Goods and the Transfer Problem," *Review of Economic Studies* **32** (January 1965) 67–84.
17. McDougall, I. A., "Tariffs and Relative Prices," *Economic Record* **42** (June 1966), 219–243.

18. McDougall, I. A., "Non-traded Commodities and the Pure Theory of International Trade," in *Studies in International Economics, Monash Conference Papers* (I. A. McDougall and R. H. Snape, eds.), pp. 157–192. Amsterdam: North-Holland Publ., 1970,
19. McKenzie, L. W., "Demand Theory without a Utility Index," *Review of Economic Studies* 24 (June 1957), 185–189.
20. Metzler, L. A., "Tariffs, the Terms of Trade, and the Distribution of National Income," *Journal of Political Economy* 57 (February 1949), 1–29.
21. Metzler, L. A., "Tariffs, International Demand, and Domestic Prices," *Journal of Political Economy* 57 (August 1949), 345–351.
22. Mundell, R. A., "The Pure Theory of International Trade," *American Economic Review* 50 (March 1960), 67–110.
23. Negishi, T., *General Equilibrium Theory and International Trade*. Amsterdam: North-Holland Publ., 1972.
24. Ohyama, M., "Domestic Distortions and the Theory of Tariffs," Univ. of Rochester, January 1972.
25. Otani, Y., "Neo-Classical Technology Sets and Properties of Production Possibility Sets," *Econometrica* 41 (March 1973).
26. Pearce, I. F., *International Trade*. New York: Norton, 1970.
27. Södersten, B., and Vind, K., "Tariffs and Trade in General Equilibrium," *American Economic Review* 58 (June 1968), 394–408.
28. Takayama, A., *International Trade—An Approach to the Theory*. New York: Holt, 1972.

*Part II*

# MATHEMATICAL ECONOMICS

# STABILITY INDEPENDENT OF ADJUSTMENT SPEED

*Kenneth J. Arrow*

*Harvard University*

## I. Introduction

In his classic work, Hicks [5] introduced for serious consideration by economists the problem of analyzing stability in multiple markets. He defined a concept of *perfect stability*, in which one market was singled out and the remaining markets were divided into two sets: in one, all prices were held fixed at their equilibrium values, while, as the singled-out price varied, all prices in the second set were continuously adjusted to keep supply and demand on all the markets in that set constant. Under these conditions, excess demand was defined as a function of the singled-out price. If the resulting function was downward sloping for all ways of singling out a price and all ways of dividing the remaining markets into two sets as indicated, then the economy was said to be *perfectly stable*. It was demonstrated that a necessary and sufficient condition for perfect stability was that the Jacobian matrix of the excess demand functions (omitting one commodity and one price, chosen as numéraire) have the property that the principal minors of odd order have negative determinants and those of even order have positive determinants.

Matrices with this property have continued to be of great interest. The negative of such a matrix has the property that all its principal minors have positive determinants; such matrices have become known as *P matrices* (for this name, see Gale and Nikaidô [4]).

Samuelson [8] insisted that the definition of stability must be grounded in an explicit dynamic system, specifically,

$$dp_i/dt = H[z_i(p)] \qquad (i = 1, \ldots, n) \tag{1}$$

where $i$ runs over the nonnuméraire commodities, $p_i$ is the price of the $i$th commodity, $z_i$ the excess demand for the $i$th commodity, $p$ the vector of (nonnuméraire) prices, and $H$ an increasing function, with $H(0) = 0$. (Local) stability requires that every solution of the system of differential equations (1) whose starting point lies in some neighborhood of the equilibrium point $p^0$, defined by $z(p^0) = 0$ (where $z$ is the vector of excess demands), converge to $p^0$. By well-known theorems, the stability of equilibrium is equivalent (apart from borderline cases) to the condition that the characteristic roots of the Jacobian of the right-hand side of (1) have negative real parts. A matrix with this property will be termed *stable*.

The function $H$ indicates the adjustment of price to excess demand. The imposed conditions imply that a price rises if the corresponding excess demand is positive and falls otherwise. The derivative $H'(0)$ can be regarded as the speed of adjustment in the neighborhood of equilibrium.

There is no reason for the function $H$ to be the same for all commodities; indeed, simple dimensional considerations show that this cannot be true in general. For suppose the units in which commodity $i$ is measured are changed, for example each unit is twice as large. Then the measured excess demand is half as much, while the price is twice as great. The rate of change of price per unit time is also doubled; hence, the speed of adjustment of that commodity is quadrupled, while leaving the speeds of adjustment of other commodities unchanged. Thus equal speeds of adjustment on all markets can hold only for one particular choice of units.

If one assumes a single speed of adjustment, then the Jacobian of the right-hand sides of (1) can be written simply $H'(0)X$, where $X$ is the Jacobian of the excess demand functions. The characteristic roots of $H'(0)X$ are simply those of $X$ multiplied by the positive scalar $H'(0)$, and hence the stability of the dynamic system (1) depends only on the properties of the excess demand functions. Here, Samuelson noted that the condition that $X$ be the negative of a $P$ matrix was not necessary for the stability of (1); and later [9], he gave an example due to W. Hurewicz which showed that this condition was not sufficient either.

Meanwhile Lange [6, pp. 94–97] first explicitly stated that the adjustment functions might differ from one commodity to another. Then (1) is generalized to

$$dp_i/dt = H_i[z_i(p)] \qquad (i = 1, \ldots, n) \tag{2}$$

where $H_i(0) = 0$, $H_i' > 0$. The Jacobian of the right-hand sides of (2) can be written as $DX$, where $D$ is a diagonal matrix with $d_{ii} = H_i'(0) > 0$. In general, then, stability depends not only on the properties of the excess demand functions but also on the speeds of adjustment.

It is against this background that the brilliant and exciting paper of Metzler [7] appeared. Metzler accomplished two rehabilitations of the Hicks conditions. The second of his propositions [7, p. 285] has had the greatest impact; if one confines oneself to what have become known as *Metzler matrices*, that is, matrices with nonnegative off-diagonal elements, then a matrix $X$ is stable if and only if its negative is a $P$ matrix. But the first of his two propositions has been much less remarked. He noted that Hicks' definition of perfect stability could be thought of as dealing with varying speeds of adjustment. On some markets adjustment is infinitely rapid, on others infinitely slow; the criterion of perfect stability is that stability hold no matter how the markets are divided into these two classes. This suggests the following question: Under what conditions is the stability of the system independent of the speeds of adjustment? In mathematical terms, we are asking when a matrix $X$ has the property that $DX$ is stable for all positive diagonal matrices $D$. We will call this property $D$ stability. Metzler showed [7, pp. 280–283] that a *necessary* condition for $D$ stability is that $-X$ be a $P$ matrix.

As to why this question is economically interesting, one can do no better than to quote Metzler's own statement:

> Two answers may be given. . . . First, the extent to which the stability of a group of markets depends upon speeds of adjustment is a question of considerable interest. It is important to know, for example, whether the inflexibility of certain prices is a stabilizing factor or whether the markets would be stable even if all prices were responsive to discrepancies between supply and demand. If the Hicks conditions of perfect stability are not satisfied, stability of the system clearly depends upon a relative inflexibility of certain prices. Second, and more important, the conditions which govern price responsiveness are much more obscure than are the static supply and demand conditions in individual markets. Economists are usually more confident of their knowledge of supply and demand conditions than of their knowledge of such dynamic factors as speeds of adjustment. If possible, it is therefore desirable to describe market systems in terms which are independent of speeds of adjustment [p. 284].*

Metzler's first theorem, in turn, opens up two questions, with which this paper is concerned. (1) The property that $X$ is $D$ stable is a statement about the characteristic roots of the family of matrices $DX$, with $X$ fixed and $D$ varying over the positive diagonal matrices. As we have seen, stability and *a fortiori*, $D$ stability, is stronger than being the negative of a $P$ matrix. Is there some other statement about the characteristic roots of the family $DX$ which

* From L. A. Metzler, "Stability of Multiple Markets: The Hicks Conditions," *Econometrica* **13** (1945), 277–292.

is exactly equivalent to being the negative of a $P$ matrix? It is shown in Section II that roughly speaking, $X$ is a $P$ matrix if and only if, for every positive diagonal matrix $D$, every *real* characteristic root of $DX$ is positive. (Hence, if $X$ is the *negative* of a $P$ matrix, every real characteristic root of $DX$ is negative.) A more exact statement is to be found below. It is interesting to note that Metzler's example [7, pp. 284–285] to show that one can have a negative of a $P$ matrix whose stability depends upon speed of adjustment illustrates this property; it is the *complex* roots which can have positive real parts for suitably chosen adjustment speeds, but the real roots are always negative, as Metzler explicitly notes.

(2) Another question is that of sufficient conditions for $D$ stability. Some answers have been given in earlier papers (Enthoven and Arrow [2], Arrow and McManus [1]). There was some resemblance among the proofs of these apparently diverse theorems. In Sections III–VI, I develop a general theoretical structure from which the previous results (somewhat generalized) can easily be deduced. Actually, as already seen implicitly in the article by Enthoven and Arrow [2], these methods can yield more information. It is sometimes economically meaningful to consider the stability of matrices $DX$ where $D$ is diagonal but the diagonal elements are not necessarily positive. We actually find sufficient conditions on $X$ that the number of characteristic roots of $DX$ with positive, zero, and negative real parts, be equal respectively to the number of diagonal elements of $D$ which are positive, zero, and negative. (In particular, then, when these conditions hold, $-X$ is stable when $D$ is positive diagonal, for then every characteristic root of $X$ has a positive real part, or, equivalently, every characteristic root of $-X$ has a negative real part.)

## II. Real Characteristic Roots of Products of Positive Diagonal and $P$ Matrices

As can be seen from the sometimes tortured language used above, it is easier to reverse the signs of the usual stability criteria. It is linguistically easier to talk about matrices with positive or nonnegative principal minors than about matrices whose principal minors have alternating signs. Hence, throughout this chapter we shall be concerned with criteria for characteristic roots to have *positive* real parts or to be positive reals. Of course, any result found here has an obvious counterpart by simply reversing the sign of the matrix and therewith of all its characteristic roots.

In this section we will therefore be concerned with conditions on $X$ which ensure that the real characteristic roots of $DX$ be nonnegative for all positive diagonal $D$. It is necessary to shift from positive to nonnegative to achieve definite results. A careful reading of Metzler's first proposition and its proof will reveal that, strictly speaking, what he showed was that if the characteristic roots of $DX$ have nonnegative real parts for all positive diagonal $D$, then the principal minors of $X$ have nonnegative determinants. He states the result with the signs reversed, with the word "positive" instead of "nonnegative" in both places, but the proof involves a passage to a limit in which the determinants might approach zero. A counterexample to the stronger assertion is

$$X = \begin{pmatrix} 1 & 1 \\ -1 & 0 \end{pmatrix};$$

it is easy to calculate that the two characteristic roots of $DX$ are real and positive if $4d_{22} \leqq d_{11}$, and complex conjugate with real part $d_{11}/2 > 0$ if $4d_{22} > d_{11}$. Thus $X$ is $D$ stable but has a principal minor which is zero. The same example shows that Theorem 1(c) below is no longer valid if "$P_0$ matrix" is replaced by "$P$ matrix" and "nonnegative" by "positive."

***Definition 1***   $X$ is a $P$ matrix if every principal minor has a positive determinant.

***Definition 2***   $X$ is a $P_0$ matrix if every principal minor has a nonnegative determinant.

***Notation 1***   If $x$ is a vector with $n$ components and $S$ a subset of the integers $1, \ldots, n$, then $x_S$ is the vector with components $x_i$ $(i \in S)$.

***Notation 2***   If $A$ is a square matrix of order $n$ and $S$ and $T$ are subsets of the integers $1, \ldots, n$, then $A_{ST}$ is the matrix with elements $a_{ij}$ $(i \in S, j \in T)$.

***Notation 3***   If $x$ and $y$ are vectors, then $x \geqq y$ means $x_i \geqq y_i$, all $i$; $x > y$ means $x_i \geqq y_i$, all $i$, $x_i > y_i$, at least one $i$; $x \gg y$ means $x_i > y_i$, all $i$.

***Notation 4***   If $x$ is a vector, $\hat{x}$ is the diagonal matrix defined by $\hat{x}_{ii} = x_i$, $\hat{x}_{ij} = 0$ for $i \neq j$.

***Notation 5***   The vector $e$ is defined by $e_i = 1$, all $i$.

From Notations 4 and 5, we note immediately that $\hat{x}e = x$.
We now state the basic result of this section.

***Theorem 1***   Each of the following conditions is necessary and sufficient that $X$ be a $P_0$ matrix.
   (a)   $X + D$ is a $P$ matrix for all positive diagonal $D$.
   (b)   If $x \neq 0$ and $y = Xx$, then there exists $i$ such that $x_i \neq 0$, $x_i y_i \geqq 0$.
   (c)   For all positive diagonal matrices $D$, every real root of $DX$ is nonnegative.

*Note*   The new result established here is Theorem 1(c). Theorem 1(b) is part of Theorem 1.3 of Fiedler and Pták [3, p. 164] and Theorem 1(a) is implicit in their proof. The parallel results for $P$ matrices had also been obtained by Gale and Nikaidô [4]. We reprove these results here to make the exposition self-contained.

*Proof* $X$ is a $P_0$ matrix if and only if (a): Use the notation $A^{ii}$ to mean the minor obtained by deleting the $i$th row and column. Then,

$$\partial \det(X + D)/\partial d_{ii} = \det(X + D)^{ii}.$$

We proceed by induction on the order of $X$. Clearly the equivalence holds if $n = 1$; suppose it is true for matrices of order $n - 1$. If $X$ is a $P_0$ matrix, then so is $X^{ii}$; hence by induction $(X + D)^{ii} = X^{ii} + D^{ii}$ is a $P$ matrix and, in particular, $\det(X + D)^{ii} > 0$. Thus $\det(X + D)$ is a strictly increasing function of the $d_{ii}$'s in the region where all are positive. It immediately follows that $\det(X + D) > \det X \geq 0$ if $X$ is a $P_0$ matrix. Conversely, if $X + D$ is a $P$ matrix for all positive $D$, $\det(X + D) > 0$ for all such $D$; by continuity, $\det X \geq 0$. But for any $S$ which is a proper subset of the integers $1, \ldots, n$, $X_{SS} + D_{SS}$ is a $P$ matrix for all positive diagonal $D_{SS}$; by the induction hypothesis, $X_{SS}$ is a $P_0$ matrix and in particular $\det X_{SS} \geq 0$.

Before proceeding with the proof of the theorem, we prove the following lemma, based on the result just proved.

**Lemma 1** If $X$ is a $P_0$ matrix and $y = Xe$, then $y_i \geq 0$, for some $i$.

*Proof of Lemma 1* By assumption, $Xe = \hat{y}e$, so that

$$(X - \hat{y})e = 0;$$

$X - \hat{y}$ is singular and cannot be a $P$ matrix. By Theorem 1(a), $-\hat{y}$ cannot be a positive diagonal matrix, which means that $\hat{y}$ has at least one nonnegative diagonal element, or $y_i \geq 0$, some $i$.

We now return to the proof of Theorem 1.

$X$ a $P_0$ matrix implies (b): Note that since $\hat{x}$ is a diagonal matrix

$$(\hat{x}X\hat{x})_{SS} = \hat{x}_S X_{SS} \hat{x}_S,$$

nd therefore $\det(\hat{x}X\hat{x})_{SS} = (\det \hat{x}_S)^2 \det X_{SS} \geq 0$ for all $S$, so that $\hat{x}X\hat{x}$ is also $P_0$ matrix. Since any principal minor of a $P_0$ matrix is trivially a $P_0$ matrix, $X\hat{x})_{SS} = \hat{x}_S X_{SS} \hat{x}_S$ is a $P_0$ matrix. Let

$$z_S = \hat{x}_S X_{SS} x_S = (\hat{x}_S X_{SS} \hat{x}_S)e_S.$$

mma 1, we must have $z_i \geq 0$ for some $i \in S$. Choose now $S = \{i \mid x_i \neq 0\}$. $v = Xx$. Then,

$$y_S = X_{SS} x_S + X_{S\bar{S}} x_{\bar{S}} = X_{SS} x_S$$

where $\tilde{S}$ is the set of indices $i$ not in $S$; by construction, $x_{\tilde{S}} = 0$. Since $z_S = \hat{x}_S y_S$, $z_i = x_i y_i$ for $i \in S$. It has been shown that $x_i y_i \geq 0$ for some $i$ for which $x_i \neq 0$, by the definition of $S$.

(b) implies (c): For any positive diagonal $D$, let $\lambda$ be a real characteristic root of $DX$ and $x$ a corresponding real characteristic vector:

$$DXx = \lambda x, \qquad x \neq 0,$$

so that

$$y = Xx = \lambda D^{-1}x.$$

Since $y_i = \lambda x_i/d_{ii}$, it follows from (b) that $\lambda x_i^2/d_{ii} \geq 0$ for some $i$ for which $x_i \neq 0$. As $x_i^2/d_{ii} > 0$, it must be that $\lambda \geq 0$.

(c) implies that $X$ is a $P_0$ matrix: For any fixed $S$, we seek to show that $\det X_{SS} \geq 0$. If $\det X_{SS} = 0$, the result is true, so assume that $\det X_{SS} \neq 0$. Then no characteristic root of $X_{SS}$ is zero. Define, for each $t > 0$, the positive diagonal matrix,

$$D(t) = \begin{pmatrix} I_{SS} & 0 \\ 0 & tI_{\tilde{S}\tilde{S}} \end{pmatrix}$$

where $I$ is the identity matrix with appropriate indices. The characteristic roots of $D(t)X$ are continuous functions of $t$, Since

$$D(0)X = \begin{pmatrix} X_{SS} & X_{S\tilde{S}} \\ 0 & 0 \end{pmatrix},$$

its nonzero characteristic roots are precisely the characteristic roots of $X_{SS}$, with the same multiplicities. Choose $\varepsilon$ to be greater than 0 and less than the smallest absolute value of a characteristic root of $X_{SS}$. Then as $t$ approaches 0, some of the characteristic roots of $D(t)X$ approach those of $X_{SS}$, while the remainder approach 0; for $t$ sufficiently small those approaching the roots of $X_{SS}$ will be above $\varepsilon$ in absolute value while the remainder are below. Call the first set the *large* roots. Since the conjugate of a complex number has the same absolute value and since the complex roots of $D(t)X$ come in conjugate pairs, the product of the complex large roots must be positive. By hypothesis, the real roots of $D(t)X$ are nonnegative for $t > 0$. Hence, the product of the large roots is nonnegative for $t > 0$. Since the large roots approach the roots of $X_{SS}$, the product of the characteristic roots of $X_{SS}$ must be nonnegative. But this product is equal to $\det X_{SS}$.

We have now shown that if $X$ is a $P_0$ matrix, then (b) holds; if (b) holds, then (c) holds; and if (c) holds, $X$ is a $P_0$ matrix. Hence, the three conditions are equivalent, as was to be proved.

For a linear system or within the linear approximation around equilibrium to a nonlinear system, the motion of the system can be expressed as a sum of monotonic motions, corresponding to the real characteristic roots, and oscillatory motions, corresponding to the complex roots. What is established here is that the Hicksian conditions tell us about the stability of monotonic motions. This result therefore makes clear the extent to which the Hicksian conditions are useful in stability analysis.

## III. Some Notes on Connected Sets

We digress here to introduce a mathematical concept which may seem unrelated. Let $K$ be a subset of a finite-dimensional space.

**Definition 3**   $N$ is a *neighborhood relative to* $K$ if it is the nonnull intersection of a neighborhood with $K$, i.e., if $N$ is nonempty and if $N$ can be written as $N = N' \cap K$, where $N'$ is a neighborhood in the usual sense.

**Definition 4**   $C$ is *open relative to* $K$ if $C$ is a subset of $K$ such that for every element $x \in C$, there is a neighborhood $N$ relative to $K$ such that $x \in N \subset C$.

**Definition 5**   A sequence $\{x^v\}$ *converges to* $x^0$ *relative to* $K$ if, for every neighborhood $N$ relative to $K$ and containing $x^0$, $x^v \in N$ for all $v$ sufficiently large.

**Definition 6**   The subset $C$ of $K$ is *closed relative to* $K$ if it contains all $x^0$ to which sequences in $C$ converge relative to $K$.

To illustrate, the half-open interval $[0, 1)$ is open relative to the nonnegative reals; for the neighborhoods of 0 relative to the nonnegative reals are the half-open intervals $[0, \varepsilon)$.

For later use, also remark that if a set $C$ is closed (respectively, open) relative to $K$ and if $K' \subset K$, then $C \cap K'$ is closed (respectively, open) relative to $K'$.

Now consider the set $K$ made of the two closed intervals $[0, 1]$ and $[2, 3]$. is easy to verify that $[0, 1]$ is both open and closed relative to $K$. This fact clearly related to the observation that $K$ is made up of two distinct parts. s example leads to the formal definition:

**Definition 7**   A set $K$ is said to be *connected* if it does not contain any r nonempty subset which is both open and closed relative to $K$. (A subset is one that does not contain every member of the set.)

' sequel, we will be concerned with connected sets of matrices; the atrices of any given order clearly constitute a finite-dimensional

(All the preceding definitions can be stated more abstractly and are in standard works on analysis. But only the preceding definitions are needed here.)

An obvious restatement of the definition is contained in the following lemma.

**Lemma 2** $K$ is connected if and only if it cannot be partitioned into a family containing two or more open nonnull subsets

*Proof* If $K$ is not connected, it contains a nonnull proper subset $C$ which is both open and closed in $K$. Hence $C$ is open in $K$, and $K \sim C$ (the set-theoretic difference between $K$ and $C$, i.e., the set of all elements of $K$ not in $C$) is open in $K$, since the complement of a closed set relative to $K$ is open relative to $K$. These two sets constitute a partition into two nonnull subsets open relative to $K$.

Conversely, if such a partition exists, let $C$ be any member of the partition and $C'$, the union of all other members. Both are nonnull; since $C'$ is a union of open sets, it is open. Hence, $C$ is the complement of an open set and therefore closed; it is also proper, since its complement is nonnull.

We state first of all a theorem about connected sets which will be used subsequently.

**Theorem 2** Let $f$ be a function from a connected set $K$ to any range. If $f^{-1}(y)$ is open for every $y$ in the range of $f$, then $f$ is a constant.

**Notation 6** If $f$ is a function, $f(K) = \{y \mid y = f(x) \text{ for some } x \in K\}, f^{-1}(y) = \{x \mid f(x) = y\}$.

*Proof* Since $f$ is a function, $f(x)$ is single-valued; hence the family of sets $f^{-1}(y)$ as $y$ varies over $f(K)$ is a partition of $K$ (that is, every element of $K$ is in one and only one member of the family). If each set is open, it follows from Lemma 2 and the connectedness of $K$ that the partition can have but one member.

We also need some method of establishing whether a set is connected. First, note that the interval $[0, 1]$ is connected. For suppose it contained a proper nonnull subset $C$ both closed and open in $[0, 1]$. Since $C$ has 1 as an upper bound, it possesses a supremum, say $M$. If $M < 1$, the open intervals $(M - \varepsilon, M + \varepsilon)$ are neighborhoods relative to $[0, 1]$ for $\varepsilon$ sufficiently small; if $M = 1$, then the half-open intervals $(1 - \varepsilon, 1]$ are neighborhoods relative to $[0, 1]$. In either case, by definition of a supremum, each such neighborhood must contain a point of $C$; since $C$ is closed, $M \in C$. But since $C$ is open, if $M < 1$, then some neighborhood of $M$ is included in $C$, which means that $C$ contains an element greater than $M$, in contradiction to the definition of a supremum. Therefore, $M = 1$, and $1 \in C$. But the complement of $C$ in $[0, 1]$ is also open and closed in $[0, 1]$ and therefore also contains 1, a contradiction since the two sets are disjoint.

Second we note:

**Lemma 3** If $f$ is a continuous function and $K$ is connected, then $f(K)$ is connected.

*Proof* Suppose $f(K)$ were the union of two disjoint sets $Y$ and $Y'$, each nonnull and open in $f(K)$. Then $K$ would be the union of $f^{-1}(Y)$ and $f^{-1}(Y')$. If $y_0 \in Y$, then there is a neighborhood $N$ of $y_0$ relative to $f(K)$ contained in $Y$. Let $y_0 = f(x_0)$; then for $x$ sufficiently close to $x_0$, $f(x) \in N$, since $f$ is continuous. Then $f(x) \in Y$, or $x \in f^{-1}(Y)$, for those $x$. Hence, $f^{-1}(Y)$ is open relative to $K$; so would be $f^{-1}(Y')$, in contradiction to the connectedness of $K$.

A *line segment* $[x^0, x^1]$ in some finite-dimensional space consists of all points $x = (1 - t)x^0 + tx^1$ for some $t$, $0 \leq t \leq 1$. If we write $f(t) = (1 - t)x^0 + tx^1$, we can say that $[x^0, x^1]$ is the image of $[0, 1]$ under the continuous function $f(t)$; since $[0, 1]$ is connected, so is every line segment.

We now state a general condition by which we can prove that many sets are connected, given that we know that some, like line segments, are.

**Definition 8** A family $F$ of sets is said to be a *connected family* if, for every proper nonnull subfamily $F'$, there is at least one set $S \in F'$ and one set $T \in F \sim F'$ such that $S \cap T$ is nonnull.

**Notation 7** If $F$ is a family of sets, then $U(F)$ is the union of all the sets in $F$, i.e., the set consisting of all elements which belong to at least one member of $F$.

**Theorem 3** The union of a connected family of connected sets is a connected set.

*Proof* Let $F$ be the connected family of connected sets. Suppose $U(F)$ is not connected; then it possesses a proper nonnull subset $L$ which is both open and closed in $U(F)$. If $K \in F$, $K \subset U(F)$; as remarked earlier, $K \cap L$ is both open and closed in $K$. But $K$ is connected so that $K \cap L$ cannot be a proper nonnull subset of $K$ for each $K \in F$: either $K \cap L$ is null or $K \cap L = K$. Let $F'$ be the subfamily of $F$ for which the latter condition holds; it is equivalent to the statement $K \subset L$. Notice that if $K \cap L$ were null for all $K \in F$, $L$ would have to be null, while if $K \subset L$, all $K \in F$, $U(F) \subset L$, and $L$ would not be a proper subset of $U(F)$, both contrary to assumption. Hence, $F'$ is a proper nonnull subfamily of $F$.

But now, any set belonging to $F'$ is included in $L$ while any set belonging to $F \sim F'$ is disjoint from $L$, so that their intersection must be null, contrary to the definition of a connected family. Hence the supposition $U(F)$ not connected has led to a contradiction.

**Corollary 3**   A convex set is connected.

*Proof*   If $C$ is a convex set, let $F$ be the family of all line segments joining any pair of elements of $C$. As already noted, every member of $F$ is a connected set. Further, any set in $F$ is a subset of $C$ by the definition of a convex set, so that $U(F) \subset C$; but every member of $C$ belongs to at least one member of $F$, so that $C \subset U(F)$. Hence, $C = U(F)$. By Theorem 3, it suffices to show that $F$ is a connected family.

Let $F'$ be any proper nonnull subfamily of $F$, $L'$ any line segment belonging to $F'$, and $L''$ any line segment belonging to $F \sim F'$. Choose any points $x' \in L'$ and $x'' \in L''$; both are members of $C$. Finally, let $L$ be the line segment $[x', x'']$; it belongs to $F$. If $L \in F'$, note that $L \cap L''$ contains the point $x''$ and is therefore nonnull; if $L \in F \sim F'$, then note that $L \cap L'$ contains the point $x'$ and is nonnull. In either case, there is a set belonging to $F'$ which intersects a set belonging to $F \sim F'$, and therefore $F$ is a connected family.

## IV. Location of Characteristic Roots of Matrices

From now on, it will be more convenient to deal with complex matrices even though the intended application is to real matrices.

*Notation 8*   For any complex number $\lambda$ and any matrix $X$, $\mu(X, \lambda)$ is the algebraic multiplicity of $\lambda$ as a characteristic root of $X$. (If $\lambda$ is not a characteristic root of $X$, this value is 0.)

*Notation 9*   For any set $C$ of complex numbers and any matrix $X$, $\mu(X, C)$ is the sum of the multiplicities of all the characteristic roots of $X$ which lie in the set $C$.

(We are going to be interested in such sets as those with positive or negative real parts.)

In what follows we will have occasion to use the continuity of the characteristic roots as a function of the matrix. We may enumerate the $n$ roots of a matrix of order $n$ as, say, $\lambda_1, \ldots, \lambda_n$, where each multiple root appears the number of times given by its multiplicity. But of course the order of the roots has no significance; in particular, a permutation of them would be no difference at all. Hence, the distance between two sets of roots $\lambda_1, \ldots, \lambda_n$ and $\lambda_1', \ldots, \lambda_n'$ has to be defined in a way which is invariant under permutation. We can define the distance in some conventional way provided we first permute the subscripts so as to make the measure of distance as small as possible.

***Definition 9***   Let $\lambda$ and $\lambda'$ be two $n$-tuples of complex numbers. The distance between them will be defined as

$$\rho(\lambda, \lambda') = \min_{\pi} \left[ \sum_{i=1}^{n} |\lambda_i - \lambda'_{\pi(i)}|^2 \right]^{1/2}$$

where $\pi$ varies over all permutations of the integers $1, \ldots, n$ into themselves.

Then the characteristic roots of $X$ are continuous functions of $X$ in the sense that as $X$ approaches a fixed matrix $X_0$, the distance between the $n$-tuple of characteristic roots of $X$ and that of $X_0$ approaches 0, when distance is understood in the sense of Definition 9.

We now discuss the behavior of $\mu(X, \lambda)$ and $\mu(X, C)$, as $X$ varies locally.

Suppose $\mu(X_0, \lambda_0) = m$. Let $N$ be a neighborhood of $\lambda_0$ sufficiently small to exclude any other characteristic roots. Then $\mu(X_0, N) = m$. Now let $X$ vary in a neighborhood of $X_0$. Clearly $m$ of the roots have to remain near $\lambda_0$, i.e., in $N$. It is not excluded, however, that additional roots may enter the neighborhood $N$:

$$\mu(X, N) \geqq \mu(X_0, N) = m \qquad \text{for } X \text{ close to } X_0.$$

Now consider an open set $C$ with several distinct roots $\lambda_i$ $(i = 1, \ldots, p)$ of $X_0$. We can find a neighborhood $N_i$ for each $\lambda_i$ which is entirely contained in $C$ and so that the neighborhoods $N_i$ are disjoint.

By definition,

$$\mu(X, C) \geqq \sum_{i=1}^{p} \mu(X, N_i),$$

while from the previous remark, we have, for $X$ sufficiently close to $X_0$,

$$\mu(X, N_i) \geqq m_i,$$

the multiplicity of $\lambda_i$ as a root of $X_0$. Hence, for $X$ sufficiently close to $X_0$,

$$\mu(X, C) \geqq \sum_{i=1}^{p} m_i = \mu(X_0, C).$$

Now consider a partition of the complex numbers into sets, all but one of which is open (the application we make is into the sets of complex numbers with positive real parts, negative real parts, and zero real parts). Let the sets be $C_j$ $(j = 0, \ldots, m)$, with $C_j$ open for $j \geqq 1$. Further, we will let $X$ vary over a connected set $K$, and we will assume that $\mu(X, C_0)$ is constant over $K$. Since the sum of the multiplicities of the characteristic roots is $n$, we must have

$$\sum_{j=0}^{m} \mu(X, C_j) = n.$$

If $\mu(X, C_0)$ is constant, then

$$\sum_{j=1}^{m} \mu(X, C_j) \qquad \text{is constant for} \quad X \in K.$$

But as we have just seen,

$$\mu(X, C_j) \geq \mu(X_0, C_j) \qquad (j = 1, \ldots, m)$$

for $X$ sufficiently close to $X_0$. If we combine these two remarks, we see that, as $X$ varies over a neighborhood of $X_0$ relative to $K$,

$$\mu(X, C_j) = \mu(X_0, C_j) \qquad (j = 1, \ldots, m).$$

Let $\mu(X)$ be the function of $X$ defined as the vector of nonnegative integers with components $\mu(X, C_j)$ $(j = 1, \ldots, m)$, and let $r = (r_1, \ldots, r_m)$ be any realized value of this vector. We have shown that if $\mu(X_0) = r$, then $\mu(X) = r$ for all $X$ in a neighborhood of $X_0$ relative to $K$, that is, we have shown that $\mu^{-1}(r)$ is open relative to $K$ for each $r$. But now Theorem 2 immediately assures us that $\mu(X)$ must be a constant, that is, $\mu(X, C_j)$ is a constant on $K$ for each $j$.

***Theorem 4*** If $C_j$ $(j = 0, \ldots, m)$ is a partition of the complex numbers, with $C_j$ open for $j \geq 1$ and if $\mu(X, C_0)$ is constant as $X$ varies over a connected set of matrices $K$, then $\mu(X, C_j)$ is constant on $K$ for all $j$.

The point of this result is that the constancy of the numbers of characteristic roots in each set follows from the constancy on the single set which, so to speak, separates all the others.

## V. Constancy of the Inertia of a Matrix

As already indicated, we now specialize to partitions defined by the real parts of characteristic roots of matrices.

***Notation 10*** $R(\lambda)$ is the real part of $\lambda$.

***Notation 11***

$$C^+ = \{\lambda \,|\, R(\lambda) > 0\}, \qquad C^0 = \{\lambda \,|\, R(\lambda) = 0\}, \qquad C^- = \{\lambda \,|\, R(\lambda) < 0\}.$$

***Notation 12*** $v^k(X) = \mu(X, C^k)$ $(k = +, 0, -)$.

***Definition 10*** The *inertia* of a matrix $X$ (denoted by in $X$) is the triple $v^+(X), v^0(X), v^-(X)$.

(This is a standard definition in matrix theory.)

With this definition Theorem 4 specializes as follows:

***Corollary 4*** If $v^0(X)$ is constant for $X$ on a connected set $K$, then in $X$ is constant on that set.

This corollary could itself be the basis of ordinary stability proofs. Suppose that $K$ contains at least one stable member, so that in $X = (0, 0, n)$ for that matrix. Then if we can show that $v^0(X)$ is always 0 on $K$, that is, no $X \in K$ is singular or has purely imaginary roots, we have shown that all members of $K$ are stable. We will not pursue this matter here but consider instead the application of this corollary to $D$ stability and related matters.

Let $D$ be any fixed matrix (we will in the sequel assume it to be a real diagonal matrix, but for the moment that is unnecessary). If $X$ varies over a connected set $K$, $DX$ varies over a connected set, so that on such a set the constancy of $v^0(DX)$ implies that of in $DX$. If in particular $I \in K$, where $I$ is the identity matrix, then the constancy of $v^0(DX)$ is the same as the statement that $v^0(DX) = v^0(D)$, and similarly with the constancy of in $DX$. Finally, if the statement that $v^0(DX) = v^0(D)$ holds for all $D$ in some class $A$ as well as for all $X \in K$, then the conclusion in $DX =$ in $D$ holds for the same range of $D$ and $X$.

***Theorem 5*** If $K$ is a connected set of matrices, with $I \in K$, and if $v^0(DX) = v^0(D)$ for all $D$ in some set $A$ and all $X \in K$, then in $DX =$ in $D$ for all $D \in A$ and $X \in K$.

If we consider $A$ to be the class of positive diagonal matrices, then in $D = (n, 0, 0)$, and $v^0(D) = 0$. Then Theorem 5 tells us that if $DX$ has no zero or purely imaginary roots for all $X \in K$ and all positive diagonal $D$, then the characteristic roots of $DX$ have positive real parts for all $X \in K$ and all positive diagonal $D$. That is, the negatives of the members of $K$ are $D$ stable.

If instead we take $A$ to be the set of *all* diagonal matrices, and if the hypotheses hold, then we have identified a class of matrices such that the number of characteristic roots of $DX$ whose real parts have given signs is the same as the numbers of diagonal elements of $D$ with those signs. In particular, it means that stability fails to hold when the diagonal matrix is not positive (if the sign of $X$ is reversed).

Just how important economically is the stronger question of the last paragraph is hard to answer. The problem was raised in the Enthoven–Arrow model on the basis of an expectational model which is perhaps none too satisfactory. Assume that excess demand for a commodity is made up of two parts, the ordinary excess demand which depends on current prices as usual, and a speculative demand which depends only on the rate of change of the price of that commodity. Then excess demand for commodity $i$ can be written

$$z_i(p_1, \ldots, p_n) + w_i(dp_i/dt),$$

or, to a linear approximation,

$$\sum_{i=1}^{n} X_{ij}(p_j - \bar{p}_j) + w_i'(0)(dp_i/dt)$$

where $X_{ij} = \partial z_i/\partial p_j$, and $(\bar{p}_1, \ldots, \bar{p}_n)$ is the equilibrium. As before, let $H_i'(0)$ be the speed of adjustment on the $i$th market in the neighborhood of equilibrium, so the linear approximation to the dynamic system is

$$dp_i/dt = H_i'(0)\left[\sum_{j=1}^{n} X_{ij}(p_j - \bar{p}_j) + w_i'(0)(dp_i/dt)\right],$$

or

$$[1 - H_i'(0)w_i'(0)] \, dp_i/dt = H_i'(0) \sum_{j=1}^{n} X_{ij}(p_i - \bar{p}_j),$$

so that the stability of the system is determined by the matrix $DX$, where now $D$ is a diagonal matrix with the $i$th diagonal element being

$$H_i'(0)/[1 - H_i'(0)w_i'(0)].$$

As can be seen, if the speculative demand is sufficiently responsive, i.e., $w_i'(0)$ large enough, some of the diagonal elements can be negative. It is interesting to conclude that not only is there stability when the $d_{ii}$'s are all positive but that it fails when $d_{ii} < 0$ for some $i$.

## VI. Conditions That $DX$ and $D$ Have the Same Number of Characteristic Roots with Zero Real Part

In view of Theorem 5, it is useful to characterize matrices $X$ for which $v^0(DX) = v^0(D)$ for all $D$ in some set $A$. If we can find the class of matrices $X$ with that property, we then will seek a connected subset $K$ which also contains $I$; $K$ will then satisfy the conclusions of the theorem.

We will first take the case where $A$ is the set of all diagonal matrices. Of course, conditions sufficient for this case are sufficient for any other set $A$, though one might hope to find weaker conditions valid for smaller sets. While such weaker conditions are stated, it has so far not been found possible to make effective use of them.

Consider then first the condition on a matrix $X$ that the property which I will denote by (A) holds:

$$v^0(DX) = v^0(D) \qquad \text{for all real diagonal } D. \tag{A}$$

In what follows, the phrase "real diagonal matrix" will be abbreviated to "rdm," to avoid offensive repetition. For any such matrix, we define:

*Notation 13* $\Sigma(D) = \{i \, | \, d_{ii} \neq 0\}$.

$\Sigma(D)$ is a function defined on matrices whose values are sets of integers; hence the notation $\Sigma^{-1}(S)$ means the set of diagonal matrices whose diagonal elements are nonzero precisely for $i \in S$.

If $S = \Sigma(D)$, then we can write

$$DX = \begin{pmatrix} D_{SS} & 0 \\ 0 & 0 \end{pmatrix} \begin{pmatrix} X_{SS} & X_{S\bar{S}} \\ X_{\bar{S}S} & X_{\bar{S}\bar{S}} \end{pmatrix} = \begin{pmatrix} D_{SS} X_{SS} & D_{SS} X_{S\bar{S}} \\ 0 & 0 \end{pmatrix},$$

so that

$$\det(DX - \lambda I) = \det\begin{pmatrix} D_{SS} X_{SS} - \lambda I_{SS} & D_{SS} X_{S\bar{S}} \\ 0 & -\lambda I_{\bar{S}\bar{S}} \end{pmatrix}$$

$$= (-\lambda)^{n - \#S} \det(D_{SS} X_{SS} - \lambda I_{SS})$$

where we use:

**Notation 14**   $\#S$ is the number of elements in the set $S$.

Clearly, if $\lambda \neq 0$, then $\mu(DX, \lambda) = \mu(D_{SS} X_{SS}, \lambda)$, while $\mu(DX, 0) = \mu(D_{SS} X_{SS}, 0) + n - \#S$. If we sum over all characteristic roots with zero real parts, we have

$$v^0(DX) = v^0(D_{SS} X_{SS}) + n - \#S.$$

By construction $D_{SS}$ is nonsingular, so that it does not have zero as a characteristic root, while, being real diagonal, it has no purely imaginary roots. That is, $v^0(D_{SS}) = 0$. If we set $X = I$ in the above equation, we have

$$v^0(D) = v^0(D_{SS}) + n - \#S = n - \#S,$$

so that

$$v^0(DX) = v^0(D_{SS} X_{SS}) + v^0(D).$$

Thus, for rdm's in $\Sigma^{-1}(S)$, condition (A) is equivalent to the condition that $v^0(D_{SS} X_{SS}) = 0$. Note that by varying $D$ over all members of $\Sigma^{-1}(S)$, we can make $D_{SS}$ any nonsingular rdm of order $\#S$. Write the condition

$$v^0(DX) = 0 \qquad \text{for all nonsingular rdm's } D. \tag{B}$$

Then it has been shown that (A) holds for a matrix $X$ if and only if (B) holds for all principal minors of $X$. Let us then examine the conditions for (B) to hold.

Note that $v^0(DX) = 0$ if and only if both $\mu(DX, 0) = 0$ and $\mu(DX, ia) = 0$ for every real $a \neq 0$. The first condition is the same as the nonsingularity of $DX$; for $D$ nonsingular, this is equivalent to the nonsingularity of $X$. The second condition is that of the nonsingularity of $DX - iaI$. Since $D$ is nonsingular, we can write

$$DX - iaI = D(X - iaD^{-1}),$$

and nonsingularity of this matrix is equivalent to that of $X - iaD^{-1}$. But as $a$ varies over nonzero reals and $D$ over nonsingular rdm's, $-aD^{-1}$ varies over all nonsingular rdm's. Thus (B) holds if and only if both $X$ is nonsingular and $X + iE$ is nonsingular for all nonsingular rdm's $E$. This yields the following condition for (A).

**Theorem 6** A necessary and sufficient condition that $v^0(DX) = v^0(D)$ for all rdm's $D$ is that both $X_{SS}$ be nonsingular for all $S$ and $X_{SS} + iE_{SS}$ be nonsingular for all $S$ and all nonsingular rdm's $E_{SS}$ of order $\# S$.

For completeness, we state the criterion that $v^0(DX) = v^0(D)$ for all rdm's $D$ in some arbitrary set $A$ and sketch the proof which uses the same reasoning as the foregoing.

For any given $A$, $A \cap \Sigma^{-1}(S)$ is the subset of $A$ for which $d_{ii} \neq 0$ for precisely the members of $S$. For $D$ in this set, $D_{SS}$ is nonsingular.

**Notation 15** $A_S$ is the image of $A \cap \Sigma^{-1}(S)$ under the mapping $D \rightarrow D_{SS}$.

**Notation 16** If $B$ is a set of nonsingular matrices, $B^{-1}$ is the image of $B$ under the operation of taking the inverse of the matrix.

**Notation 17** If $B$ is any set of matrices, define the double cone spanned by $B$ as

$$dk(B) = \{X \mid X = tY \text{ for some real } t \text{ and some } Y \text{ in } B\}.$$

Then the condition $v^0(DX) = v^0(D)$ for all $D \in A$ becomes, following the preceding reasoning,

$$v^0(DX_{SS}) = 0 \qquad \text{for all} \quad D \in A \cap \Sigma^{-1}(S).$$

But this means $DX_{SS} - iaI_{SS}$ is nonsingular for all real $a$, or, since $D$ is nonsingular, that

$$X_{SS} - iaD^{-1} \qquad \text{is nonsingular for all real } a \text{ and all } D \text{ in } A \cap \Sigma^{-1}(S),$$

that is, that $X_{SS} + iE$ is nonsingular for all $E \in dk(A_S^{-1})$.

**Theorem 7** A necessary and sufficient condition that $v^0(DX) = v^0(D)$ for all $D \in A$ is that $X_{SS} + iE$ is nonsingular for every $S$ and $E$ for which $E \in dk(A_S^{-1})$.

To illustrate this theorem, we may consider the problem of $D$ stability in its original form, where we simply ask that $DX$ be stable (with reversal of sign, so that we seek that all roots have positive real parts) for all positive rdm's. In this case, $A$ is the set of positive rdm's. Then $\Sigma(D)$ is the entire set of integers $1, \ldots, n$ for all $D$, and therefore $\Sigma^{-1}(S)$ is null for $S$ a proper subset of them. When $S$ is the entire set of integers, $A \cap \Sigma^{-1}(S) = A$; $A^{-1}$ is again the set of positive rdm's, and $dk(A^{-1})$ is the set of all one-signed rdm's (i.e., those for which either all diagonal elements are positive, all are negative, or all are zero). In this case, of course, $v^0(D) = 0$ for all $D \in A$.

*Corollary 7*   A necessary and sufficient condition that $v^0(DX) = 0$ for all positive rdm's is that $X + iE$ be nonsingular for all one-signed rdm's $E$.

## VII. A General Class of Matrices for Which the Inertia of $DX$ Is Equal to That of $D$

In this section, we draw together Theorems 5 and 6 to find a very broad class $K$ with the property that in $DX =$ in $D$ for all rdm's $D$ and all $X \in K$. Finally, we show that some earlier results actually identified subsets of this class.

*Theorem 8*   Let $X$ have the property that, for every real $a \geqq 0$, every principal minor of $X + aI$ is nonsingular, and for any nonsingular rdm $E$ every principal minor of $X + iE + aI$ is nonsingular. Then in $DX =$ in $D$ for all rdm's $D$.

*Proof*   The hypothesis can be restated: For every real $a \geqq 0$ and every rdm $E = 0$ or nonsingular, every principal minor of $X + iE + aI$ is nonsingular. Let $K$ be the class of all such matrices. The hypothesis, for $a = 0$, implies, according to Theorem 6, that $v^0(DX) = v^0(D)$ for all rdm's and all $X \in K$.

If $X = I$, $X + iE + aI = (1 + a)I + iE$, a diagonal matrix. Since the real part of every diagonal element is $1 + a \geqq 1 > 0$, every principal minor is certainly nonsingular; hence, $I \in K$.

By Theorem 5, it suffices to show that $K$ is connected. For each $X$ in $K$, consider the line segment $[X, I]$. Let $F$ be the family of such line segments. Each member of the family is convex and therefore connected, by Corollary 3.1. Any two members of the family have the element $I$ in common; hence, no matter how $F$ is partitioned into two nonnull subfamilies, every member of one intersects every member of the other, and, by Definition 8, $F$ is a connected family. By Theorem 3, the union of $F$ is a connected set; we need only show that $K = U(F)$.

Since $X \in [X, I]$, every member of $K$ belongs to at least one member of $F$, so that $K \subset U(F)$. We need therefore only show that $[X, I] \subset K$ for each $X \in K$, for then the union of all those segments must also be included in $K$; since $K \subset U(F)$, $K$ would equal $U(F)$.

We already know that $I \in K$. Consider any member of $[X, I]$ other than $I$, say $Y = (1 - t)X + tI$, $0 \leqq t < 1$. For any rdm $E = 0$ or nonsingular,

$$Y + iE + aI = (1 - t)X + iE + (a + t)I = (1 - t)(X + iE' + bI)$$

where

$$E' = E/(1 - t), \qquad b = (a + t)/(1 - t).$$

Clearly, $E'$ is again a rdm and $b \geqq 0$; further $E' = 0$ if $E = 0$ and is nonsingular if $E$ is nonsingular. Since $X \in K$, every principal minor of $X + iE' + bI$ is nonsingular, and this property remains valid when the matrix is premultiplied by the positive scalar $1 - t$. Hence $Y$ satisfies the defining characteristic of $K$.

We now give two classes of matrices which will be shown to be subsets of the class defined by Theorem 8.

**Notation 18** If $X$ is a matrix, $X'$ is its transpose and $\overline{X}$ its conjugate (formed by taking the conjugate of each element).

**Notation 19** $X^* = X + \overline{X}'$.

**Definition 11** $X$ is *Hermitian* if $X^*$ is real positive definite symmetric.

We will show that Hermitian matrices are included in the set defined by Theorem 8. If we restrict ourselves to real matrices, as one would in economic theory, this class contains those for which $X + X'$ is positive definite, i.e., the class sometimes called *positive quasidefinite*.

It is obvious from the definition that any principal minor of a Hermitian matrix is Hermitian. It is also well known that Hermitian matrices are non-singular. To see this, consider any vector $x$ for which

$$Xx = 0.$$

Multiply on the right by $\overline{x}'$; then $\overline{x}'Xx = 0$. This expression is a real scalar and therefore equal to its conjugate transpose, which can be written

$$\overline{X}'\overline{X}'x = 0.$$

Adding these last two equations, we have $\overline{x}'X^*x = 0$. Since $X^*$ is real and positive definite, this is possible only if $x = 0$, so we have shown that $Xx = 0$ implies $x = 0$, i.e., $X$ is nonsingular.

From these remarks, it is obvious that every principal minor of a Hermitian matrix is nonsingular. To show that every Hermitian matrix satisfies the conditions of Theorem 9, it suffices then to show that if $X$ is Hermitian, then $Y = X + iE + aI$ is also. But

$$Y^* = X^* + (iE)^* + aI = X^* + aI,$$

which is certainly real positive definite and symmetric if $X^*$ is.

**Corollary 8.1** If $X$ is positive Hermitian, then in $DX = $ in $D$ for all rdm's $D$.

This generalizes the result of Arrow and McManus [1] in one direction. It is weaker in another, because the result was found there to be true for all symmetric matrices, not merely for diagonal matrices.

This generalization is, however, an implication of Corollary 8.1. Note the following facts: If $R$ is a real orthogonal matrix, then (a) $RXR'$ has the same characteristic roots as $X$ and therefore in $X =$ in $RXR'$, and (b) if $X$ is positive Hermitian, then so is $RXR'$. Further, if $M$ is real symmetric, then we can find real orthogonal $R$ and real diagonal $D$ such that $RMR' = D$. Then,

$$\text{in } MX = \text{in } RMXR' = \text{in } RMR'RXR' \geqq \text{in } D(RXR').$$

If $X$ is positive Hermitian, then so is $RXR'$, and by Corollary 8.1,

$$\text{in } D(RXR') = \text{in } D = \text{in } R'DR = \text{in } M.$$

**Corollary 8.2**  If $X$ is positive Hermitian, then in $MX =$ in $M$ for all real symmetric $M$.

We now consider a class of matrices which have dominant diagonals.

**Definition 12**  $X$ has a (weighted) dominant diagonal if there exist positive numbers $w_1, \ldots, w_n$ such that, for each $i$, $w_i |X_{ii}| > \sum_{i \neq j} w_j |X_{ij}|$.

It is, of course, very well known that any principal minor of a dominant diagonal matrix has a dominant diagonal and that dominant diagonal matrices are nonsingular.

**Notation 20**  For any matrix $X$, we define $X^{**}$ to be obtained by replacing the diagonal element $X_{ii}$ by its real part $R(X_{ii})$.

We consider the class of matrices for which $X^{**}$ is positive dominant diagonal. For real matrices, of course, this reduces to the usual class of positive dominant diagonal matrices. Since stable Metzler matrices have a negative dominant diagonal, their negatives form a subclass; it is the last set which was studied by Enthoven and Arrow [2].

Since $|X_{ii}| \geqq R(X_{ii}) = X_{ii}^{**}$, while $X_{ij}^{*} = X_{ij}$ for $i \neq j$, it is obvious that if $X^{**}$ has a dominant diagonal, then so has $X$, and therefore every principal minor of a matrix in this class is nonsingular.

It remains to show that if $X$ belongs to the class under consideration, so does $Y = X + iE + aI$; then, as in the case of Hermitian matrices, we will have verified that the class is a subset of that specified in Theorem 9. But obviously $Y_{ij}^{**} = X_{ij} = X_{ij}^{**}$ for $i \neq j$, since $iE + aI$ is a diagonal matrix; while $Y_{ii}^{**} = X_{ii}^{**} + a \geqq X_{ii}^{**}$. Hence if $X^{**}$ has a positive dominant diagonal, so has $Y^{**}$.

**Corollary 8.3**  If $X^{**}$ (obtained from $X$ by replacing the diagonal elements by their real parts) has a positive dominant diagonal, then in $DX =$ in $D$ for all rdm's $D$.

For the record, we state a generalization of Theorem 8, corresponding to the generalization from Theorem 6 to Theorem 7. The proof completely parallels that of Theorem 8 and is omitted.

**Theorem 9**  Let $A$ be a class of rdm's, and let $X$ have the property that $X_{SS} + iE + aI$ is nonsingular for every $a \geq 0$ and every $S$ and $E$ for which $E \in dk(A_S^{-1})$. Then in $DX =$ in $D$ for all $D \in A$.

**Corollary 9**  If $X + iE + aI$ is nonsingular for every $a \geq 0$ and every one-signed rdm $E$, then $X$ is $D$ stable.

We may conclude with one tiny generalization, which nevertheless gives rise to a new stability result.

**Theorem 10**  If in $DX =$ in $D$ for all rdm's $D$ and if $P$ is positive diagonal, then in $DPX =$ in $D$ for all rdm's $D$.

*Proof*  Since $DP$ is a rdm, it follows immediately from the hypothesis that in $DPX =$ in $DP$. But, for each $i$, the sign of $d_{ii}p_{ii}$ is the same as that of $d_{ii}$. Since the characteristic roots of $D$ are the numbers $d_{ii}$ and those of $DP$ are the numbers $d_{ii}p_{ii}$, we clearly have in $DP =$ in $D$.

In conjunction with Corollary 8.1, we then see:

**Corollary 10**  If $X$ is Hermitian and $P$ positive diagonal, then in $DPX =$ in $D$ for all rdm's $D$.

Thus, $PX$ is $D$ stable for positive diagonal $P$ and Hermitian (e.g., quasi-definite) $X$, a result which, though obvious once stated, seems not to have been noticed in stability theory.

No similar generalization can be derived from Corollary 8.3; if a matrix of the class defined there is premultiplied by a positive diagonal matrix, another matrix of the same class results.

### ACKNOWLEDGMENT

I am very grateful to John S. Chipman for his comments, which have markedly improved the exposition.

### REFERENCES

1. Arrow, K. J., and McManus, M., "A Note on Dynamic Stability," *Econometrica* **26** (1958), 448–454.
2. Enthoven, A. C., and Arrow, K. J., "A Theorem on Expectations and the Stability of Equilibrium," *Econometrica* **24** (1956), 288–293.
3. Fiedler, M., and Pták, V., "Some Generalizations of Positive Definiteness and Stability," *Numerische Mathematik* **9** (1966), 163–172.
4. Gale, D., and Nikaidô, H., "The Jacobian Matrix and Global Univalence of Mappings," *Mathematische Annalen* **159** (1965), 159–183.
5. Hicks, J. R., *Value and Capital*. London and New York: Oxford Univ. (Clarendon) Press, 1939.
6. Lange, O., *Price Flexibility and Employment*. Bloomington, Indiana: Principia Press, 1944.

7. Metzler, L. A., "Stability of Multiple Markets: The Hicks Conditions," *Econometrica* **13** (1945), 277–292.
8. Samuelson, P. A., "The Stability of Equilibrium: Comparative Statics and Dynamics," *Econometrica* **9** (1941), 97–120.
9. Samuelson, P. A., "The Relation between Hicksian Stability and True Dynamic Stability," *Econometrica* **12** (1944), 256–257.

# A CLASS OF GENERALIZED METZLERIAN MATRICES

*James P. Quirk*

*California Institute of Technology*

## I

This chapter returns to a problem concerning the relationship between dynamic stability and Hicksian stability raised by Metzler more than 25 years ago [10]. The present chapter identifies a class of matrices which has the property that dynamic stability implies Hicksian stability, as in the gross substitute or "Metzlerian" case. Further, as in the Metzlerian case, such matrices are specified in terms of their qualitative properties, i.e., their sign pattern configurations. Some links between this class of matrices and Samuelson's correspondence principle are also indicated.

## II

It might be in order to give a brief review of work that has been done on Metzlerian matrices and variants of this class of matrices. In *Value and Capital*, Hicks' treatment of the competitive economy centered attention on two special cases: (a) the case where all commodities are gross substitutes, and (b) the case where all commodities obey the rules "substitutes of substitutes and complements of complements are substitutes and complements of substitutes and substitutes of complements are complements," all commodities being assumed to obey the law of demand in both cases. Hicks' analysis showed that, in small dimension cases at least, the assumption of Hicksian perfect stability [all $i$th order principal minors have sign$(-1)^i$] implied certain comparative statics properties for the competitive economy. In particular, he asserted the famous Hicksian laws for the gross substitute economy, i.e., that an increase in demand for good $i$ at expense of the *numéraire* (i) increased all equilibrium prices; (ii) increased the price of good $i$ proportionately more than other prices. The proof of the proposition for many goods relied on the properties of composite commodities. Mosak [13] then presented a formal proof for the case of many goods using matrix analysis. Following this, Samuelson [16] raised the issue of the relationship between Hicksian and dynamic stability in the general case. Metzler's article [10] was addressed to Samuelson's question, and contains a number of important propositions concerning dynamic stability and Hicksian stability. First, in a concise and brilliant argument, Metzler established that in the gross substitute case, Hicksian and dynamic stability are equivalent. Secondly, by use of counter-examples, Metzler showed that in the general case, Hicksian stability is neither necessary nor sufficient for dynamic stability. Finally, Metzler proved in what is now known as the case of "total stability," i.e., dynamic stability of any isolated subset of markets under any positive speeds of adjustment of prices, Hicksian stability characterizes the system of adjustment equations.

The next important breakthrough concerning the link between dynamic stability and Hicksian stability was given by Morishima [11], who showed that Hicks' case (b) also had the property that dynamic stability is equivalent to Hicksian stability; in addition, Morishima derived a more general set of Hicksian laws of comparative statics to cover the presence of complements in the economy. One of the intriguing aspects of the work by Metzler and Morishima is that these results were obtained by economists unfamiliar with the Perron–Frobenius theorem, and in fact represented extensions of this classical mathematical tool. Debreu and Herstein [5] summarized earlier findings concerning the Frobenius problem, and indicated generalizations and applications of particular interest to economists.

In the mid-1950's, Arrow and McManus [3] studied variants of the total stability problem posed by Metzler, with particular emphasis on the problem of $D$ stability, i.e., stability under all positive speeds of adjustment of markets. It might be mentioned that despite extended work on the problem of invariance of stability, the derivation of equivalent conditions for total stability and $D$ stability remains an unsolved problem.

Finally, Arrow and Hurwicz [2] and Arrow *et al.* [1] in their treatment of stability of the competitive equilibrium introduced the properties of excess demand functions (homogeneity of degree zero in prices, Walras' law, continuity, and nonsatiation) directly into the analysis of stability, obtaining as a major result the proof that under the gross substitutability assumptions, the competitive equilibrium is globally stable. McKenzie [9] provided an alternative proof of global stability in the gross substitute case, introducing the concept of a dominant diagonal matrix, a tool of central importance in a number of economic models. Morishima [12] extended the local Hicksian laws of comparative statics in the gross substitute case to global laws, under conditions guaranteeing global stability of the competitive economy.

## III

The central concepts of this chapter are the following. Given a real matrix $A$ of dimension $n \times n$, we say that $A$ is *Hicksian* (or *Hicksian stable*) if every $i$th-order principal minor of $A$ has sign $(-1)^i$, $i = 1, \ldots, n$. Then $A$ is said to be a *stable* matrix if every characteristic root of $A$ has its real part negative. The basic question we are concerned with is that of identifying classes of matrices such that if a member of the class is stable, then the matrix is Hicksian as well. Beyond the interest in this question simply as an issue in the history of economic thought, there is the fact that while stability of $A$ is the relevant property while analyzing convergence of an economic model, Hicksian stability is considerably more useful from the point of view of comparative statics analysis, and links between the results to be derived here and Samuelson's "correspondence principle" are also noted.

Among the many results relating to Hicksian and dynamic stability, the following may be noted.[1]

(1) If $A$ is a symmetric matrix, then $A$ is stable if and only if $A$ is Hicksian [12].

(2) If $A$ is quasi-negative definite, then $A$ is stable and $A$ is Hicksian [12].

(3) If $A$ is totally stable, then $A$ is Hicksian [10].

(4) If $A$ is Hicksian, then there exists a diagonal matrix $D$ with diagonal elements positive such that $DA$ is stable [6].

(5) If $A$ is $D$ stable, then $A$ is "almost" Hicksian, i.e., every $i$th order principal minor of $A$ has sign$(-1)^i$ or 0, with at least one principal minor of every order nonzero [15].

(6) In general, $A$ Hicksian does not imply $A$ is stable nor does $A$ stable imply that $A$ is Hicksian [10].

Historically, of particular interest to economists has been the analysis of stability and Hicksian stability in qualitatively specified matrices. The most important of these are Metzlerian matrices and Morishima matrices. For

---

[1] $A$ is quasi-negative definite if $x'Ax < 0$ for $x \neq 0$ ($A$ not necessarily symmetric). $A$ is $D$ stable if $DA$ is a stable matrix for every diagonal matrix $D$ with diagonal elements positive. $A$ is totally stable if every principal submatrix of $A$ is $D$ stable.

purposes of this chapter, we define a *Metzlerian* matrix as a matrix $A$ such that $a_{ii} < 0$, $i = 1, \ldots, n$, and $a_{ij} \geqq 0$, $i \neq j$, , $i, j = 1, \ldots, n$. A *Morishima* matrix $A$ is a square matrix which can be permuted into the form

$$A = \begin{bmatrix} A_{11} & A_{12} \\ \hline A_{21} & A_{22} \end{bmatrix}$$

where $A_{11}$ and $A_{22}$ are Metzlerian matrices and $A_{12} \leqq 0$, $A_{21} \leqq 0$.

To further characterize a Morishima matrix, we use the concept of a *cycle* in a matrix [7, 8]. By a *cycle in A* (of length $r$) we mean a product of elements of $A$ of the form $a_{i_1 i_2} a_{i_2 i_3} \cdots a_{i_{r-1} i_r} a_{i_r i_1}$ where all indices $i_1, \ldots, i_r$ are distinct. As a matter of convention, diagonal elements in $A$ are regarded as cycles in $A$ of length one. We also define a *chain in A* (of length $r - 1$) as a product of elements of $A$ of the form $a_{i_1 i_2} a_{i_2 i_3} \cdots a_{i_{r-1} i_r}$, where all indices $i_1, \ldots, i_r$ are distinct. We use the notation $a(i_1 \rightarrow i_r)$ to denote a chain from $i_1$ to $i_r$ so that a cycle containing the indices $i_1, i_r$ can be written as $a(i_r \rightarrow i_1) a(i_1 \rightarrow i_r)$. The importance of cycles in the analysis of stability (and Hicksian stability) of $A$ stems from the determinantal formula developed by Maybee [7], which establishes that negative cycles of length $r$ enter into the principal minor of order $r$ with $\text{sign}(-1)^r$ while positive cycles of length $r$ enter into the principal minor with $\text{sign}(-1)^{r+1}$.[2]

A link between cyclic analysis and Morishima matrices is the following. For $A$ indecomposable, $A$ is a *Morishima* matrix if and only if $A$ satisfies (i) $a_{ii} < 0$, $i = 1, \ldots, n$ and (ii) every cycle in $A$ of length greater than one is nonnegative [4].[3] Clearly a Morishima matrix is a generalized version

---

    [2] For completeness, we summarize Maybee's determinantal formula to show that negative cycles enter into the expansion of principal minors with "correct" sign.

    Let $S = \{1, \ldots, n\}$ and let $\alpha(r, S)$ denote the set of all strictly increasing multi-indices of length $r$ in $S$. Thus, if $H \in \alpha(r, S)$, $H = \{h_1, h_2, \ldots, h_r)\}$, where $1 \leqq h_1 \cdots < h_r \leqq n$. Similarly, $\alpha(p, H)$ is the set of all strictly increasing multi-indices of length $p$ in $H$. Let $A_H$ denote the principal minor of $A$ with index set $H$ and let $A_{(H)}$ denote the sum of all cycles of length $r$ in $H$. Then, given a fixed $K \in \alpha(n-1, S)$, the determinantal formula is given by

$$|A| = a_{k'k'} A_K + \sum_{r=0}^{n-1} (-1)^{n+1-r} \sum_{H \in \alpha(r, K)} A_H A_{(H')}$$

where $a_{k'k'}$ is the diagonal element in $A$ with index not contained in $K$ and $H'$ is the complement of $H$ in $S$, and $A_\phi = 1$. Clearly negative cycles of length $n$ enter into $|A|$ with $\text{sign}(-1)^n$. Applying the same formula to a principal minor of $A$ of order $r$ then leads to the conclusion that negative cycles of length $r$ enter such principal minors with $\text{sign}(-1)^r$.

    [3] When $A$ is decomposable, the cyclic characterization of a Morishima matrix does not necessarily correspond to the definition of a Morishima matrix given earlier. Thus

$$\begin{bmatrix} - & + & 0 \\ + & - & 0 \\ + & - & - \end{bmatrix}$$

has all cycles of length greater than one nonnegative and yet is not a Morishima matrix.

of a Metzlerian matrix in the sense that every Metzlerian matrix is also a Morishima matrix. Then the following results hold.

(7) If $A$ is a Metzlerian matrix, then $A$ is stable if and only if $A$ is Hicksian [10].

(8) If $A$ is a Morishima matrix, then $A$ is stable if and only if $A$ is Hicksian [11, 4].

Here we introduce a further generalization of Metzlerian (and Morishima) matrices that seems particularly appropriate for qualitatively specified economic models. We define a *generalized Metzlerian* (GM) matrix as follows.

Let $I = (i_1, \ldots, i_r)$ denote the index set of a negative cycle in an $n \times n$ real matrix $A$ and let $J = (j_1, \ldots, j_s)$ denote the index set of a positive cycle in $A$. Then $A$ is said to be a generalized Metzlerian (GM) matrix if (i) $a_{ii} < 0$, $i = 1, \ldots, n$, and (ii) given any $I$ and $J$ as defined, either $I \cap J = \phi$ or $I \subseteq J$.

The concept of a GM matrix can be illustrated by the following examples.

$$
1 \quad
\begin{bmatrix}
- & + & + & + & + \\
+ & - & + & + & + \\
+ & + & - & + & + \\
+ & + & + & - & + \\
+ & + & + & + & -
\end{bmatrix}, \quad
2 \quad
\begin{bmatrix}
- & + & - & - & - \\
+ & - & - & - & - \\
- & - & - & + & + \\
- & - & + & - & + \\
- & - & + & + & -
\end{bmatrix},
$$

$$
3 \quad
\begin{bmatrix}
- & + & 0 & 0 & 0 \\
- & - & - & 0 & 0 \\
0 & + & - & - & 0 \\
0 & 0 & + & - & - \\
0 & 0 & 0 & + & -
\end{bmatrix}, \quad
4 \quad
\begin{bmatrix}
- & - & + & + & + \\
+ & - & 0 & 0 & 0 \\
0 & + & - & + & + \\
0 & + & + & - & + \\
0 & + & + & + & -
\end{bmatrix},
$$

$$
5 \quad
\begin{bmatrix}
- & + & 0 & 0 & 0 \\
0 & - & + & 0 & 0 \\
0 & 0 & - & + & 0 \\
0 & 0 & 0 & - & + \\
- & 0 & 0 & 0 & -
\end{bmatrix}, \quad
6 \quad
\begin{bmatrix}
- & + & 0 & 0 & 0 \\
- & - & + & 0 & 0 \\
0 & 0 & - & - & 0 \\
0 & 0 & 0 & - & - \\
+ & 0 & - & 0 & -
\end{bmatrix}.
$$

Example 1 is a Metzlerian matrix, while example 2 is a Morishima matrix. Since neither matrix contains any negative cycles of length greater than one, the GM conditions follow immediately. Example 3 is a "sign stable" matrix, i.e., one such that any matrix of this sign pattern is stable [15]. Such a matrix contains only negative cycles, hence is a member of the GM class. Example 4 is a nontrivial extension of the Metzlerian matrix, since $a_{12} a_{21}$ forms a negative cycle, with all other cycles in the matrix of length greater than one positive. Example 5 contains only negative cycles. In example 6, there is only one positive cycle, namely, $a_{12} a_{23} a_{34} a_{45} a_{51}$; hence the GM conditions are satisfied.

Because we will be dealing extensively with index sets and with cycles in the rest of this chapter, the following notation is introduced. We use the symbol $J$ or $I$ to denote the set of indices appearing in a cycle without regard to the order of such indices. $\mathbf{J}$ or $\mathbf{I}$ will be used to refer to the ordered set of indices in a cycle. Thus the cycle $a_{23}a_{31}a_{12}$ has an index set $J = (1, 2, 3)$ with ordered index set $\mathbf{J} = (2, 3, 1)$. The cycle $a_{13}a_{32}a_{21}$ then has an index set $I = (1, 2, 3)$ with ordered index set $\mathbf{I} = (1, 3, 2)$, so that $J = I$ but $\mathbf{J} \neq \mathbf{I}$. We will use interchangeably the terms "the cycle $\mathbf{I}$" and "the cycle $a_{i_1 i_2} a(i_2 \to i_1)$" when $\mathbf{I} = (i_1, i_2, \dots)$.

# IV

Because of the results derived by Metzler and Morishima, we know that for Metzlerian and Morishima matrices as special classes of GM matrices, stability implies Hicksian stability. This section is concerned with identifying other classes of GM matrices for which this proposition is true. An immediate result is the following theorem.

*Theorem 1* Let $A$ be an indecomposable GM matrix satisfying either (i) all cycles in $A$ of length greater than one are nonnegative; or (ii) all cycles in $A$ are nonpositive. Then $A$ stable implies that $A$ is Hicksian.

*Proof.* The proof of (i) is well known [4]; in fact in this case $A$ stable is equivalent to $A$ Hicksian. To prove (ii) we use Maybee's determinantal formula. Negative cycles of length $r$ enter into the expansion of principal minors of order $r$ with sign $(-1)^r$; hence, if $A$ is GM with all cycles nonpositive, then every term in the expansion of an $r$th order principal minor has sign $(-1)^r$ or 0. Further, $A$ a GM matrix implies that diagonal elements in $A$ are negative, so that there exists a nonzero term in every principal minor in $A$; hence $A$ is Hicksian.

So long as $A$ contains no negative cycles of length greater than one or so long as $A$ contains no positive cycles, under indecomposability the GM conditions guarantee that $A$ stable implies that $A$ is Hicksian. Theorem 2 proves the proposition for a special case in which $A$ contains both positive and negative cycles of length greater than one. We first state several lemmas.

*Lemma 1* Let $A$ be an $n \times n$ GM matrix containing no positive cycles of length less than $n$. Then $A$ stable implies that $A$ is Hicksian.

*Proof* By the Routh–Hurwitz conditions, $A$ stable implies sign $|A| = (-1)^n$. Cycles of length $n$ enter into the expansion of no principal minor of order less than $n$, and since all cycles of length less than $n$ are nonpositive, all terms in any principal minor of order $i$, $i = 1, \dots, n - 1$, have sign $(-1)^i$ or 0.

By the GM conditions, diagonal elements in $A$ are negative, so that every $i$th-order principal minor of $A$ contains a term in its expansion of sign$(-1)^i$, from which the lemma follows.

**Lemma 2** Let $A$ be an $n \times n$ indecomposable GM matrix. Let $I$ be the index set of a negative cycle in $A$ and let $J$ be the index set of a positive cycle in $A$ where $I \cap J \neq \phi$. Then if $I = J$, $J = S$ where $S = \{1, \ldots, n\}$, and all positive cycles in $A$ are of length $n$.

*Proof* Let $I = J = \{1, \ldots, s\}$ so that **I** and **J** are permutations of the first $s$ integers, $s < n$. Without loss of generality reindex the negative cycle into $a_{12} a_{23} \ldots a_{s1}$. Since $A$ is a GM matrix, every positive cycle containing an index from $I$ must contain all indices from $I$; hence every positive cycle in the principal submatrix with index set $I = J$ is of length $s$. $A$ indecomposable means that given any $i \neq j$, $i, j = 1 \ldots, n$, there exists a nonzero chain $a(i \to j)$ in $A$. There exists $a_{ij} \neq 0$ for some $i \in J$, $j \in S \backslash J$. Then $A$ indecomposable implies that there exists a nonzero cycle $a_{ij} a(j \to i)$ with index set $K$. This cycle cannot be negative since $K \cap J \neq \phi$ but $K \nsubseteq J$. If the cycle were negative, the GM conditions would be violated. Assume then that the cycle is positive. Since $I \cap K \neq \phi$, then $I \subseteq K$, i.e., the positive cycle contains all indices, $1, \ldots, s$. Without loss of generality one can assume that this cycle contains the element $a_{1s+1}$, so we can write the positive cycle as $a_{1s+1} a(s + 1 \to j^*) a(j^* \to 1)$ where $j^*$ is the first index (following 1) in the cycle which also appears in $I$. We first prove that $j^* = 2$. This is established as follows.

First, $j^* \neq 1$ since then the positive cycle could be written as $a_{1s+1} a(s + 1 \to 1)$ with $1 \in K$ but $I \nsubseteq K$. If $j^* > 2$, then consider the cycle $a_{1s+1} a(s + 1 \to j^*) a_{j^* j^*+1} \cdots a_{s1}$. This cycle does not contain the index 2. If this cycle is negative, then it violates the GM conditions since it has indices in common with $J$ but its index set is not contained in $J$. On the other hand, if the cycle is positive, then again the GM conditions are violated since the cycle contains some but not all indices from $I$. It follows that $j^* = 2$, so that the positive cycle with index set $K$ can be written as $a_{1, s+1} a(s + 1 \to 2) a(2 \to 1)$.

Next write the positive cycle with index set $J$ as $b(1 \to 2) b(2 \to 1)$. Thus a cycle is formed by $a_{1, s+1} a(s + 1 \to 2) b(2 \to 1)$. Since $s + 1$ appears in this cycle it cannot be negative by the GM condition. If the cycle is positive it must contain all indices from $I$ by the GM conditions, which means that $b(2 \to 1)$ contains all indices from $I$. This means that $a_{12}$ is an element both in the positive cycle with index set $J$ and the negative cycle with index set $I$. Thus, sign $a_{23} \cdots a_{s1}$ is opposite to that of $b(2 \to 1)$. But now the cycle $a_{1, s+1} a(s + 1 \to 2) a_{23} \cdots a_{s1}$ must be negative, which violates the GM condition. It follows that $J = S$ and hence every positive cycle in $A$ is of length $n$.

**Theorem 2**  Let $A$ be an $n \times n$ indecomposable GM matrix. Let $I$ be the index set of a negative cycle in $A$ and let $J$ be the index set of a positive cycle in $A$. If $I = J$, then $A$ stable implies that $A$ is Hicksian.

*Proof*  From Lemma 2, every positive cycle in $A$ is of length $n$, which by Lemma 1 establishes the theorem.

Certain other special cases of interest in economics follow from the preceding argument, including the case where $A$ is "sign symmetric" (sign $a_{ij} =$ sign $a_{ji}$, $i \neq j$, where 0 is treated as a sign) and the case where $A$ contains no zero entries.

**Theorem 3**  Let $A$ be an $n \times n$ indecomposable GM matrix, satisfying sign symmetry. Then $A$ is either a Metzler or a Morishima matrix; hence $A$ is stable if and only if $A$ is Hicksian.

*Proof*  Sign $a_{ij} =$ sign $a_{ji}$, $i \neq j$; hence every nonzero cycle in $A$ of length two is positive. Since every index $i$, $i \in \{1, \ldots, n\}$, appears in a nonzero cycle, every index appears in some positive cycle of length two. It immediately follows that $A$ can contain no negative cycles of length greater than one under the GM conditions. Indecomposability, together with the condition that all cycles of length greater than one are nonnegative, establishes the result.

**Theorem 4**  Let $A$ be an $n \times n$ GM matrix satisfying $a_{ij} \neq 0$ for every $i, j = 1, \ldots, n$. Then $A$ stable implies $A$ is Hicksian.

*Proof*  If $A$ contains no negative cycle of length greater than one, then the result follows from Theorem 1. Hence assume $A$ contains a negative cycle of length greater than one. First assume $A$ has no negative cycles of length greater than two and reindex a negative cycle into $a_{12}a_{21} < 0$. If $n = 2$ the theorem is immediate. If $n > 2$, then $a_{12}a_{23}a_{31} > 0$ and $a_{21}a_{32}a_{13} > 0$ which implies in turn either that $a_{23}a_{32} < 0$ and $a_{13}a_{31} > 0$ or $a_{23}a_{32} > 0$ and $a_{13}a_{31} < 0$. In either case the GM conditions are violated, so that $A$ must contain a negative cycle of length greater than two. Reindex such a cycle into $a_{12}a_{23} \cdots a_{r1} < 0$. By the GM conditions, $a_{ij}a_{ji} < 0$ for $a_{ij}$ in this cycle. If $r$ is odd, it follows that $a_{1r}a_{r,r-1} \cdots a_{21} > 0$; hence by Theorem 2, $A$ stable implies $A$ is Hicksian. If $r$ is even, consider $a_{12}a_{23} \cdots a_{r-2,r-1}a_{r-1,1}$. By the GM conditions this cycle must be negative. But $r - 1$ is odd, hence $a_{1r-1}a_{r-1,r-2} \cdots a_{21}$ is positive and again Theorem 2 applies, establishing the present theorem. (Note that Theorem 4 is vacuous except for $n \leq 3$ or when $A$ contains no negative cycles of length greater than one.)

Examples of GM matrices satisfying the conditions of Theorems 2–4 include

$$
\begin{bmatrix}
- & - & 0 & 0 & + \\
+ & - & - & 0 & 0 \\
0 & + & - & - & 0 \\
0 & 0 & + & - & - \\
- & 0 & 0 & + & -
\end{bmatrix},
\qquad
\begin{bmatrix}
- & + & - & 0 & 0 \\
+ & - & 0 & 0 & 0 \\
- & 0 & - & + & 0 \\
0 & 0 & + & - & + \\
0 & 0 & 0 & + & -
\end{bmatrix},
\qquad
\begin{bmatrix}
- & - & + \\
+ & - & - \\
- & + & -
\end{bmatrix}.
$$

Theorem 2              Theorem 3              Theorems 2 and 4

We next characterize GM matrices containing both positive cycles and negative cycles of length greater than one. Of interest is the following basic result concerning matrices and cycles.

**Lemma 3** [4]   Let $A$ be an $n \times n$ indecomposable matrix containing both negative and positive cycles of length greater than one. Then there exists at least one index common to both a negative cycle of length greater than one and a positive cycle of length greater than one.

Under the GM conditions, this result can be sharpened considerably.

**Lemma 4**   Let $A$ be an $n \times n$ indecomposable GM matrix. If $A$ contains a positive cycle, then every index $i$, $i \in \{1, \ldots, n\}$ appears in a positive cycle in $A$.

*Proof* Indecomposability requires that every index appears in some non-zero cycle of length greater than one. Suppose some index, say 1, appears only in a negative cycle. Denote the index set of the negative cycle by $I_1$. By indecomposability there exists $a_{ij} \neq 0$, $i \in I_1$, $j \notin I_1$, with associated non-zero cycle $a_{ij} a(j \to i)$ and index set $I_2$. If this cycle is positive, then by the GM conditions $I_1 \subseteq I_2$; hence the index 1 appears in a positive cycle. If the cycle is negative, then again by indecomposability there exists a nonzero cycle with index set $I_3$ such that $(I_1 \cup I_2) \cap I_3 \neq \phi$. If this cycle is positive, then either $I_1 \cap I_3 \neq \phi$ or $I_2 \cap I_3 \neq \phi$ implies by the GM conditions that either $I_1 \subseteq I_3$ or $I_2 \subseteq I_3$. But since $I_1 \cap I_2 \neq \phi$ by hypothesis, either case leads to the conclusion that $(I_1 \cup I_2) \subseteq I_3$; hence $1 \in I_3$. A continuation of this procedure until all indices in $A$ are exhausted thus leads to the conclusion that $A$ can contain no positive cycles if the index 1 appears only in a negative cycle, which leads to the desired contradiction.

Consider a GM matrix of the type

$$
\begin{bmatrix}
- & - & 0 & + & + & + \\
0 & - & + & 0 & 0 & 0 \\
+ & 0 & - & 0 & 0 & 0 \\
0 & + & 0 & - & + & + \\
0 & + & 0 & + & - & + \\
0 & + & 0 & + & + & -
\end{bmatrix}.
$$

One of the peculiarities of this matrix is that any positive cycle having an index in common with the negative cycle $a_{12} a_{23} a_{31}$ also contains the elements $a_{23} a_{31}$; e.g., $a_{14} a_{42} a_{23} a_{31}$, $a_{15} a_{56} a_{64} a_{42} a_{23} a_{31}$, etc. This property is in fact a distinguishing characteristic of indecomposable GM matrices, as indicated in Lemma 5.

**Lemma 5** Let $A$ be an $n \times n$ indecomposable GM matrix. Let $I$ be the index set of a negative cycle in $A$ of length $r$, $r > 1$, and let $J$ be the index set of a positive cycle in $A$ of length $s$, $s < n$. If $I \cap J \neq \phi$ but $I \neq J$, then every positive cycle of length less than $n$ in $A$ with an index in common with $I$ has $r - 1$ *elements* in common with the negative cycle, each such positive cycle having the same elements in common.

*Proof* Let $\mathbf{I}$ and $\mathbf{J}$ be the ordered index sets of negative and positive cycles such that $I \cap J \neq \phi$, $I \neq J$, where, without loss of generality, $\mathbf{I} = \{1, 2, \ldots, r\}$, $r > 1$, so that the negative cycle may be written as $a_{12} a_{23} \cdots a_{r1}$. Again without loss of generality let $a_{1, r+1}$ be an element in the positive cycle assumed to be of length $s < n$. We will show that under the conditions of the lemma, every positive cycle of length less than $n$ with an index belonging to $I$ contains the elements $a_{23}, \ldots, a_{r1}$. We begin by writing the positive cycle $\mathbf{J}$ as $a_{1, r+1} a(r + 1 \to j^*) a(j^* \to 1)$ where $j^*$ is the first index (following 1) in the cycle which also appears in $I$.

The idea of the proof is the following. In Step 1, we show that $j^* = 2$. Step 1a shows that if $j^* > 2$ then for any $i \in J \setminus I$, there exists a negative cycle $a(i \to j) a(j \to i)$ containing some but not all indices in $I$. Step 1b shows that $j^* > 2$ implies that every positive cycle with index set contained in $J$ has the index set $J$. Step 1c then establishes that $j^* > 2$ implies either that $A$ is decomposable or $J = S$, where $S = \{1, \ldots, n\}$. Step 2 shows that the cycle $a_{1, r+1} a(r + 1 \to 2) a_{23} \cdots a_{r1}$ is a positive cycle, where $a(r + 1 \to 2)$ is the chain $a(r + 1 \to j^*)$ appearing in $\mathbf{J}$. Step 3 then shows that any positive cycle of length less than $n$ with an index in common with $I$ contains the elements $a_{23}, \ldots, a_{r1}$.

*Step 1.* $j^* = 2$.

The positive cycle $\mathbf{J}$ is written as $a_{1, r+1} a(r + 1 \to j^*) a(j^* \to 1)$ where $j^*$ is the first index (following 1) in the cycle which also appears in $I$. Clearly $j^* \neq 1$ since then $I \cap J \neq 0$ but $I \nsubseteq J$. Hence assume $j^* > 2$.

*1a.* $j^* > 2$ implies that for any $i \in J \setminus I$ there exists a negative cycle $a(i \to j) a(j \to i)$ containing some but not all indices in $I$.

If $j^* > 2$ then a nonzero cycle is formed by $a_{1, r+1} a(r + 1 \to j^*) a_{j^* j^* + 1} \cdots a_{r1}$. Since the index 2 does not appear in this cycle, by the GM condition the cycle must be negative. Consider next the product $a_{12} \cdots a_{j*-1,j*}a(j* \rightarrow 1)$. This product is not a cycle since $a(j* \rightarrow 1)$ must contain every index in $I$. Any product of this type which forms a closed loop can be factored into the product of cycles. (Note that all indices in the set $\{1, \ldots, j* - 1\}$ are repeated and that all other indices appearing in the product are distinct.) Write $a(j* \rightarrow 1)$ as $a(j* \rightarrow k_1*)a(k_1* \rightarrow k_2*) \cdots a(k_{j*-1}^* \rightarrow 1)$ where $k_1*$, $k_2*$, $\ldots$, $k_{j*-1}^*$ are distinct indices from the set $\{1, 2, \ldots, j* - 1\}$. Each of these chains appears in a cycle within the product $a_{12} \cdots a_{j*-1,j*}a(j* \rightarrow 1)$. Since $j* > 2$, it follows that none of these cycles contains all indices from $I$, since in particular the index 1 appears only in cycles involving $a_{12}$ and $a(k_{j*-1}^* \rightarrow 1)$ and any such cycle does not contain all indices from $I$. Hence, by the GM conditions, each such cycle is negative. It thus follows that if $j* > 2$, then given any index $i \in J\backslash I$, there exists a negative cycle $a(i \rightarrow j)a(j \rightarrow i)$, where each such cycle contains some but not all indices from $I$.

*1b.* $j* > 2$ implies that every positive cycle with index set $K$, $K \subseteq J$, satisfies $K = J$.

Assume that there is a positive cycle with index set $K$ such that $K \subseteq J$, $K \neq J$. If there exists an index $i \in I \cap K$, then $K = J$ since every index in $J\backslash I$ appears in a negative cycle containing indices from $I$ (and $I \subseteq K$ by the GM conditions). On the other hand, if $K$ contains any indices from $J\backslash I$, then by the same argument $I \subseteq K$ so that $K = J$.

*1c.* $j* > 2$ implies that $J = S$, where $S = \{1, \ldots, n\}$, or $A$ is decomposable.

Suppose $J$ contains $s$ indices where $s < n$. By indecomposability there exists $a_{ij} \neq 0$, $i \in J$, $j \in S\backslash J$ with associated nonzero cycle $a_{ij}a(j \rightarrow i)$. Write this cycle as $a_{ij}a(j \rightarrow k*)a(k* \rightarrow i)$ where $k*$ is the first index (following $i$) in the cycle which also appears in $J$. Any such cycle cannot be negative by the GM conditions since it includes indices from $J$, the index set of a positive cycle, as well as indices distinct from $J$. Further, if the cycle is positive, it must contain all indices from $J$ since every index in $J$ also appears in a negative cycle in the principal submatrix with index set $J$. If $i \in I$, $k* \in I$, then $a_{ij}a(j \rightarrow k*)a_{k*,k*+1} \cdots a_{i-1,i}$ forms a cycle which does not contain all indices from $J$; hence it violates the GM conditions. If $i \in I$, $k* \in J\backslash I$, then, since there exists a nonzero chain $a(k* \rightarrow i)$ not containing all indices from $I$, again the cycle $a_{ij}a(j \rightarrow k*)a(k* \rightarrow i)$ does not include all indices from $J$ and violates the GM conditions. Note finally that every index in $J\backslash I$ appears in a negative cycle; hence the two cases considered prove the assertion for $i \in J\backslash I$, $k* \in J\backslash I$ and $i \in J\backslash I$, $k* \in I$. Hence $A$ is decomposable and the principal submatrix with index set $J$ has no positive cycles of length less than $s$.

This completes the proof that under the conditions of the lemma, the positive cycle $\mathbf{J}$ written as $a_{1,r+1}a(r + 1 \rightarrow j*)a(j* \rightarrow 1)$ satisfies $j* = 2$.

*Step 2.* $a_{1,r+1}a(r+1 \to 2)a_{23} \cdots a_{r1}$ is a positive cycle, where $a(r+1 \to 2)$ is the chain $a(r+1 \to j^*)$ appearing in the cycle **J**.

The nonzero cycle $a_{1,r+1}a(r+1 \to 2)a_{23} \cdots a_{r1}$ contains all indices from $I$. Suppose that this cycle were negative. The positive cycle **J** is written as $a_{1,r+1}a(r+1 \to 2)a(2 \to 1)$. Then $a_{12}a(2 \to 1)$ forms a cycle. Since $a_{12}a_{23} \cdots a_{r1} < 0$ and $a_{1,r+1}a(r+1 \to 2)a(2 \to 1) > 0$, while by hypothesis $a_{1,r+1}a(r+1 \to 2)a_{23} \cdots a_{r1} < 0$, it follows that $a_{12}a(2 \to 1) > 0$.

But this contradicts the GM conditions since the index $r+1$ does not appear in the cycle $a_{12}a(2 \to 1)$. Hence $a_{1,r+1}a(r+1 \to 2)a_{23} \cdots a_{r1} > 0$.

*Step 3.* $j^* = 2$ implies that every positive cycle of length less than $n$ with an index in common with $I$ may be written as $a_{1k}a(k \to 2)a_{23} \cdots a_{r1}$, where $k \notin I$.

*3a.* $a_{1,r+1}a(r+1 \to 2)a(2 \to 1)$ has the property that the ordered index set of $a(2 \to 1)$ is a permutation of the set $I = (1, \ldots, r)$.

$a_{1,r+1}a(r+1 \to 2)a(2 \to 1) > 0$ by hypothesis, while $a_{1,r+1}a(r+1 \to 2)a_{23} \cdots a_{r1} > 0$ by Step 2. Since $a_{12}a_{23} \cdots a_{r1} < 0$, this implies $a_{12}a(2 \to 1) < 0$. Since $a_{12}a(2 \to 1)$ includes all indices from $I$, its index set must be contained in the index set of $a_{1,r+1}a(r+1 \to 2)a_{23} \cdots a_{r1}$. But $a_{12}a(2 \to 1)$ containing an index $k \notin I$ is consistent with its index set being contained in that of $a_{1,r+1}a(r+1 \to 2)a_{23} \cdots a_{r1}$ only if $k$ is in the index set of $a(r+1 \to 2)$. But this in turn implies that $a_{1,r+1}a(r+1 \to 2)a(2 \to 1)$ is not a cycle. Hence the ordered index set of $a(2 \to 1)$ is a permutation of the set $I$.

Note that any positive cycle of length less than $n$ having an index in common with $I$ can be written as $a_{ij}a(j \to i+1)a(i+1 \to i)$, $i \in I$, $j \notin I$, where $i+1$ is the first index (following $i$) in the cycle that appears in $I$. (This holds if $i \in \{1, \ldots, r-1\}$. If $i = r$, then $i+1$ is replaced by the index 1.) It is also immediate from Steps 2 and 3a that $a_{ij}a(j \to i+1)a_{i+1,i+2} \cdots a_{i-1,i} > 0$ and $a(i+1 \to i)$ has an ordered index set that is a permutation of $I$.

*3b.* In any positive cycle of length less than $n$, $a_{1k}a(k \to 2)a(2 \to 1)$, where $k \notin I$, the ordered index set of $a(2 \to 1)$ is the set $(2, 3, \ldots, r, 1)$, i.e., $a(2 \to 1) = a_{23}a_{34} \cdots a_{r1}$.

From Step 3a, the ordered index set of $a(2 \to 1)$ is a permutation of the set $I$. To satisfy the GM conditions any such permutation must preserve the following properties of the principal submatrix with index set $I$.

(i) All nonzero chains $b(2 \to 1)$ in the principal submatrix of length less than $r - 1$ have sign opposite to that of $a_{23} \cdots a_{r1}$; and

(ii) Every cycle in the principal submatrix is negative.

Consider a permutation of $I$ so that the ordered index set of $a(2 \to 1)$ is not equal to $(2, 3, \ldots, r, 1)$. Then there exists a nonzero element $a_{ij}$, $i$, $j \in I$ such that $j > i + 1$.

Then by (i) $\text{sign}(a_{23} \cdots a_{i-1,i} a_{ij} a_{j,j+1} \cdots a_{r1}) \neq \text{sign}(a_{23} \cdots a_{r1})$, which implies $\text{sign } a_{ij} \neq \text{sign } a_{i,i+1} \cdots a_{j-1,j}$. On the other hand, by (ii) $a_{ij} a_{j,j+1} \cdots a_{i-1,i} < 0$. But $a_{i,i+1} \cdots a_{j-1,j} a_{j,j+1} \cdots a_{i-1,i} < 0$. This contradiction establishes that $a(2 \to 1) = a_{23} \cdots a_{r1}$.

*3c.* Let $K$ denote the index set of a positive cycle of length less than $n$, $a_{ij} a(j \to i + 1) a(i + 1 \to i)$, $i \in I$, $j \notin I$. Then $i \neq 1$ implies $K = J$ and every index in $J$ appears in a negative cycle in the principal submatrix with index set $J$.

Form the product

$$a_{ij} a_K(j \to i + 1) a_{i+1,i+2} \cdots a_{r1} a_{1,r+1} a_J(r + 1 \to 2) a_{23} \cdots a_{i-1,i}$$

where $a_K(j \to i + 1)$ is the chain $a(j \to i + 1)$ from the ordered index set $\mathbf{K}$ and $a_J(r + 1 \to 2)$ is the chain $a(r + 1 \to 2)$ from the ordered index set $\mathbf{J}$. This product is negative, since $\text{sign } a_{ij} a_K(j \to i + 1) \neq \text{sign } a_{i,i+1}$, and $\text{sign } a_{1,r+1} a_J(r + 1 \to 2) \neq \text{sign } a_{12}$ while $a_{12} a_{23} \cdots a_{r1} < 0$. If no index in $a_K(j \to i + 1)$ appears in $a_J(r + 1 \to 2)$, then the product is a negative cycle containing some but not all indices from $J$, thus violating the GM conditions. Hence there exists $p_1$ such that the product can be written as

$$a_{ij} a_K(j \to p_1) a_K(p_1 \to i + 1) a_{i+1,i+2} \cdots$$
$$a_{1,r+1} a_J(r + 1 \to p_1) a_J(p_1 \to 2) a_{23} \cdots a_{i-1,i}.$$

The cycle $a_K(p_1 \to i + 1) a_{i+1,i+2} \cdots a_{1,r+1} a_J(r + 1 \to p_1)$, if positive, violates the GM conditions. If negative, then all indices in $a_K(p_1 \to i + 1)$ must appear in $J$ and all indices in $a_J(r + 1 \to p_1)$ must appear in $K$. If the cycle is negative, then

$$a_{ij} a_K(j \to p_1) a_J(p_1 \to 2) a_{23} \cdots a_{i-1,i} > 0;$$

hence this is not a cycle. This implies that the product can be written

$$a_{ij} a_K(j \to p_2) a_K(p_2 \to p_1) a_J(p_1 \to p_2) a_J(p_2 \to 2) a_{23} \cdots a_{i-1,i}.$$

Then $a_K(p_2 \to p_1) a_J(p_1 \to p_2) < 0$ since $p_1$ appears in a negative cycle, and the same argument can be applied so that every index in $a_K(p_2 \to p_1)$ appears in $J$, and every index in $a_J(p_2 \to p_1)$ appears in $K$. Clearly, a continuation of this procedure establishes the desired result.

*3d.* In the positive cycle, $a_{ij} a(j \to i + 1) a(i + 1 \to i)$, $i = 1$.

If $i \neq 1$, then by Step 3c, all positive cycles with length less than $n$ and an index in common with $I$ have the index set $J$. Further, every index in $J$ appears in a negative cycle of length greater than one in the principal submatrix with index set $J$.

Since $A$ is indecomposable, there exists a nonzero cycle $a_{pq}a(q \rightarrow p)$, $p \in J$, $q \notin J$. This cycle must be a positive cycle of length $n$; if negative, it violates the GM conditions, while if of length less than $n$, it has no indices outside of $J$.

Given any element $a_{uv}$ from the cycle $a_{1,r+1}a(r + 1 \rightarrow 2)a(2 \rightarrow 1)$, form the product

$$a_{pg}a(q \rightarrow u)a_{uv}a(v \rightarrow p).$$

If this is not a cycle then there exists a cycle of length less than $n$ involving $a_{pq}$. It it is a cycle, $a_{uv}$ belongs to the cycle $a_{pq}a(q \rightarrow p)$. Since this holds for every element in $a_{1,r+1}a(r + 1 \rightarrow 2)a(2 \rightarrow 1)$, $a_{pq}a(q \rightarrow p)$ cannot be a cycle of length $n$. Hence $i = 1$.

This completes the proof of the lemma.[4]

This lengthy and cumbersome proof, for which I apologize, not only provides a characterization of GM matrices, but also leads to several other cases where the GM conditions lead to the conclusion that stability of $A$ implies that $A$ is Hicksian. These cases again involve matrices that contain positive cycles as well as negative cycles of length greater than one.

***Theorem 5***    Let $A$ be an indecomposable GM matrix such that $A$ contains a positive cycle of length greater than one, and no positive cycles in $A$ are disjoint, i.e., if $J_1$ and $J_2$ are the index sets of two positive cycles in $A$, the $J_1 \cap J_2 \neq \phi$. Then $A$ stable implies that $A$ is Hicksian.

*Proof*    Assume that $A$ is stable but that $A$ contains a principal minor of order $i$ with sign $(-1)^{i+1}$. This principal minor must contain a positive cycle by Theorem 1. Then there exists within the principal minor a principal minor of order $k$, $k \leq i$, with sign$(-1)^{k+1}$, containing positive cycles only of length $k$. Denote the index set of this $k$th-order principal minor by $K$. Because no

---

[4] To illustrate the role played by indecomposability in Lemma 5, consider the following example:

$$\begin{bmatrix} - & - & 0 & + & 0 & + \\ 0 & - & - & 0 & 0 & + \\ - & 0 & - & 0 & + & + \\ - & 0 & 0 & - & + & + \\ 0 & + & 0 & - & - & + \\ 0 & 0 & 0 & 0 & 0 & - \end{bmatrix}.$$

The matrix contains two positive cycles, $a_{14}a_{45}a_{52}a_{23}a_{31}$ and $a_{35}a_{54}a_{41}a_{12}a_{23}$. All other nonzero cycles are negative and the lemma fails because of decomposability.

positive cycles in $A$ are disjoint, the complementary principal minor in A of order $n - k$ contains no positive cycles; hence its sign is $(-1)^{n-k}$. In the expansion of $|A|$, we thus have the product of these two principal minors entering with $\text{sign}(-1)^{n+1}$ plus terms representing products of cycles with principal minors, the cycles being of the form $a_{ij}a(j \to i)i \in K$, $j \notin K$. Each such cycle must be nonnegative by the GM conditions, since every index in $K$ appears in a positive cycle. No principal minor multiplying such a cycle can contain a positive cycle since positive cycles are not disjoint. Hence every term in the expansion of $|A|$ has $\text{sign}(-1)^{n+1}$ or 0. On the other hand, stability of $A$ implies that $\text{sign}|A| = (-1)^n$. An identical argument holds for the case where $A$ contains a principal minor which is zero, so that the theorem follows.

An example of a matrix satisfying the conditions of Theorem 5 is

$$\begin{bmatrix} - & - & + & 0 \\ + & - & 0 & 0 \\ 0 & + & - & + \\ 0 & + & - & - \end{bmatrix}.$$

Finally, we consider the case of combinatorially symmetric matrices. An $n \times n$ real matrix $A$ is *combinatorially symmetric* if $a_{ij} \neq 0$ implies $a_{ji} \neq 0$, $i, j = 1, \ldots, n$.

**Theorem 6**  Let $A$ be an $n \times n$ indecomposable GM matrix which is combinatorially symmetric. Then **A** stable implies $A$ is Hicksian.

*Proof*  We first show that if $A$ contains both negative cycles of length greater than one and positive cycles, then no positive cycle of length less than $n$ has an index in common with such a negative cycle.

*Step 1.*  Assume that $A$ contains a negative cycle of length greater than one with an index in common with a positive cycle of length less than $n$. Write the negative cycle as $a_{12}a_{23} \cdots a_{r1}$. Then by Lemma 5, the positive cycle may be written as $a_{1,r+1}a(r + 1 \to 2)a_{23} \cdots a_{r1}$. By combinatorial symmetry, $a_{1r}a_{r,r-1} \cdots a_{21}$ forms a nonzero cycle which is negative by Lemma 2. Further $a_{ij}a_{ji} < 0$ for each term $a_{ij}$ in this cycle.

Similarly, by combinatorial symmetry, $a_{r+1,1} \neq 0$ and $a_{1,r+1}a_{r+1,1} < 0$, while $a_{ij}a_{ji} < 0$ for every element $a_{ij}$ appearing in the chain $a(r + 1 \to 2)$.

Let $a(2 \to r + 1)$ represent the chain formed by the elements $a_{ji}$ where $a_{ij}$ is an element in $a(2 \to r + 1)$. Then $a(2 \to r + 1)a_{r+1,1}a_{1r}a_{r,r-1} \cdots a_{32}$ forms a cycle. Note that $a_{1r}a_{r,r-1} \cdots a_{32}a_{21} < 0$ and $a_{1r}a_{r,r-1} \cdots a_{32}a_{12} > 0$. Hence $\text{sign } a(2 \to r + 1)a_{r+1,1} \cdots a_{32} = \text{sign } a(2 \to r + 1)a_{r+1,1}a_{12}$. Thus if $a(2 \to r + 1)a_{r+1,1} \cdots a_{32} > 0$, the GM conditions are violated by the cycle $a(2 \to r + 1)a_{r+1,1}a_{12} > 0$. If the cycle is negative, then $A$ is decomposable by Lemma 2. Hence no negative cycle in $A$ of length greater than one has an index in common with a positive cycle of length less than $n$.

*Step 2.* If $A$ contains a positive cycle of length $n$, and a negative cycle of length greater than one, then some element $a_{ij}$ in the positive cycle has the index $j$ in common with the negative cycle. Then by the GM conditions $a_{ij}a_{ji} < 0$ for any such element. But $a_{ij}$ appearing in a negative cycle, $a_{jk}$ also in the cycle of length $n$ implies $a_{jk}a_{kj} < 0$, so that $a_{rs}a_{sr} < 0$ for every element $a_{rs}$ in the positive cycle. This implies in turn by Step 1 that $A$ contains no positive cycles of length less than $n$, hence by Theorem 2, $A$ stable implies $A$ is Hicksian.

It has not yet been possible to prove the following conjecture.

*Conjecture*   Let $A$ be an $n \times n$ indecomposable GM matrix. Then $A$ stable implies that $A$ is Hicksian.

Extensive work on this conjecture indicates that the key to establishing the conjecture might lie in matrices of type 4 depicted on page 207. For small-dimension cases, the conjecture holds for such matrices, but the extension to $n$ large has not been accomplished. Thus, for $n = 3$, the conjecture follows immediately. For $n = 4$, consider a matrix with sign pattern given by

$$
\begin{bmatrix}
- & - & + & + \\
+ & - & 0 & 0 \\
0 & + & - & + \\
0 & + & + & -
\end{bmatrix}.
$$

Then $|A|$ may be written as

$$
|A| = (a_{11}a_{22} - a_{12}a_{21})(a_{33}a_{44} - a_{34}a_{43}) - a_{21}a_{13}a_{34}a_{42} - a_{21}a_{14}a_{43}a_{23}
$$
$$
+ a_{44}(a_{21}a_{13}a_{32}) + a_{33}(a_{21}a_{14}a_{42}).
$$

Since all nonzero cycles of length three and four are positive, the stability condition $|A| > 0$ implies that $a_{33}a_{44} - a_{34}a_{43} > 0$; hence all $2 \times 2$ principal minors are positive. This implies in turn that the only $3 \times 3$ principal minors which might be positive are those with indices $(1, 2, 3)$ or indices $(1, 2, 4)$. Let $\Delta_{123}$ denote the principal minor with indices $1, 2, 3$. Then

$$
|A| = a_{44}\Delta_{123} - a_{34}a_{43}(a_{11}a_{22} - a_{12}a_{21}) - a_{21}a_{13}a_{34}a_{42}
$$
$$
- a_{21}a_{14}a_{43}a_{32} + a_{33}(a_{21}a_{14}a_{42}).
$$

If $\Delta_{123} \geq 0$, then every term in this expansion of $|A|$ is nonpositive, which violates $|A| > 0$. A similar argument proves that $\Delta_{124} < 0$; hence $A$ stable implies that $A$ is Hicksian.

## V

To indicate the relevance of the GM class for comparative statics analysis, assume that an economic model is specified in terms of variables $x_1, \ldots, x_n$, parameters $\alpha_1, \ldots, \alpha_n$ and functional relations $f_i(x_1, \ldots, x_n; \alpha_1, \ldots, \alpha_n)$, $i = 1, \ldots, n$. For given values $\alpha_1^0, \ldots, \alpha_n^0$ of the parameters, an equilibrium of the model is defined as a vector $(\bar{x}_1, \ldots, \bar{x}_n)$ such that

$$f_i(\bar{x}_1, \ldots, \bar{x}_n; \alpha_1^0, \ldots, \alpha_n^0) = 0, \qquad i = 1, \ldots, n.$$

Given a change in the $j$th parameter, the resulting changes in the equilibrium values of the variables are obtained by solving the system

$$\sum_{k=1}^{n} \partial f_i/\partial x_k \; d\bar{x}_k \,/\, d\alpha_j = -\partial f_i/\partial\alpha_j, \qquad i = 1, \ldots, n.$$

Suppose that $\partial f_i/\partial\alpha_j = 0$ for $j \neq i$, so that each functional relation has associated with it its "own" parameter only. Then $d\bar{x}_i/d\alpha_i$ is of known sign for $i = 1, \ldots, n$ if and only if in the matrix $[\partial f_i/\partial x_k]$ the determinant of this matrix and all $n - 1 \times n - 1$ principal minors of the matrix are of known sign.

In particular, assume that only the signs of the entries in $[\partial f_i/\partial x_k]$ are known (with diagonal elements negative). Then the postulate of stability of this matrix implies through the "correspondence principle" that the signs $d\bar{x}_i/d\alpha_i$ are known for $i = 1, \ldots, n$ only if $[\partial f_i/\partial x_k]$ is a Hicksian matrix; further, for the special cases taken up in Section IV, it is known that the GM conditions are sufficient for signing $d\bar{x}_i/d\alpha_i$, $i = 1, \ldots, n$, under stability.

### ACKNOWLEDGMENTS

I would like to thank Dan McFadden for his many comments, criticisms, and suggestions on an earlier draft of this paper. John Maybee's comments have also been extremely helpful. Errors that remain are my own.

### REFERENCES

1. Arrow, K., Block, H. D., and Hurwicz, L., "On the Stability of the Competitive Equilibrium, II," *Econometrica* 27 (1959), 82–109.
2. Arrow, K., and Hurwicz, L., "On the Stability of the Competitive Equilibrium, I," *Econometrica* 26 (1958), 522–552.
3. Arrow, K., and McManus, M., "A Note on Dynamic Stability," *Econometrica* 26 (1958), 448–454.
4. Bassett, L., Maybee, J., and Quirk, J., "Qualitative Economics and the Scope of the Correspondence Principle," *Econometrica* 36 (1968), 544–563.
5. Debreu, G., and Herstein, I. N., "Non-Negative Square Matrices," *Econometrica* 21 (1953), 597–607.

6. Fuller, A., and Fisher, M., "On the Stabilization of Matrices and the Convergence of Linear Iterative Processes," *Proceedings of the Cambridge Philosophical Society* **54** (1958), 417–425.

7. Maybee, J., "New Generalizations of Jacobi Matrices," *SIAM Journal of Applied Mathematics* **14** (1966), 1032–1037.

8. Maybee, J., and Quirk, J., "Qualitative Problems in Matrix Theory," *SIAM Review* **11** (1969), 30–51.

9. McKenzie, L., "The Matrix with Dominant Diagonal and Economic Theory," in *Mathematical Methods in the Social Sciences* (K. Arrow, S. Karlin, and H. Scarf, eds.). (Stanford, California: Stanford Univ. Press, 1960).

10. Metzler, L., "Stability of Multiple Markets: The Hicks Conditions," *Econometrica* **13** (1945), 277–292.

11. Morishima, M., "On the Laws of Change of the Price System in an Economy Which Contains Complementary Commodities," *Osaka Economic Papers* **1** (1952), 101–113.

12. Morishima, M., *Equilibrium, Stability and Growth*. London and New York: Oxford Univ. (Clarendon) Press, 1964.

13. Mosak, J., *General Equilibrium Theory and International Trade*. Bloomington, Indiana: The Principia Press, 1944.

14. Ohyama, M., "On the Stability of Generalized Metzlerian Systems," *Review of Economic Studies* **39** (1972), 193–204.

15. Quirk, J., and Ruppert, R., "Qualitative Economics and the Stability of Equilibrium," *Review of Economic Studies* **32** (1965), 311–326.

16. Samuelson, P., *Foundations of Economic Analysis*. Cambridge, Massachusetts: Harvard Univ. Press, 1947.

# HYSTERESIS OF LONG-RUN EQUILIBRIUM
# FROM REALISTIC ADJUSTMENT COSTS

*Murray C. Kemp*

*University of New South Wales*

*Henry Y. Wan, Jr.*

*Cornell University*
*and*
*Academia Sinica*

## I. Introduction

Much of the economic literature concerns problems of adjustment. Sometimes the adjustment process is assumed to be costless and of infinite speed (as, e.g., in the "Metzler effect"). Sometimes the lag-structure plays a crucial role (as, e.g., in the Laursen–Metzler theorem and in the Metzler models of transfer effects, inventory cycles, and multiple market stability). More recently, partly as an outgrowth of the lagged adjustment literature, the speed of adjustment has been assumed to be consciously chosen by firms and households in the light of the cost of adjustment.

It is now known that many traditional propositions concerning the behavior of individual firms must be either abandoned or substantially revised when costs of adjustment are allowed for.[1] In the present chapter we ask the obvious next question: How does a whole economy of rationally adjusting firms behave?

Perhaps our most interesting conclusion concerns the possible multiplicity of long-run equilibria. If, as we suppose, adjustment costs depend on the speed of adjustment, and at the origin the derivative is discontinuous,

[1] See, for example, refs. [2], [4–6], and [8–12].

then under positive time preference the position of long-run equilibrium depends crucially on initial conditions—a dramatic example of hysteresis (like that in physics associated with standing friction as distinct from well-behaved viscous friction).

An example from trade theory will suggest the essential point. Labor moves from Europe to America in search of higher wages. With time preference and interest rates zero, the migration of infinitely long-lived workers will continue until real wages are equal, whatever the cost of migration. But suppose that time preference or interest rates are positive. Then migration must cease unless the present discounted value of the perpetual wage differential exceeds the costs of migration. The result is that a whole range of geographical equilibria can prevail, depending on initial locations; the range of indeterminacy shrinks to zero as the interest rates fall to zero.

A less novel but perhaps no less interesting finding of ours is that causal indeterminacy may arise under quite varied assumptions (just as in the case of two-sector growth models). Alternative means to handle causal indeterminacy, i.e., the contingent differential equation approach and the branch-continuity approach, are proposed and explored to some extent. Since the presence of causal indeterminacy affects the predictive power of any dynamic economic model, the relevance of such discussions is not limited to the adjustment cost problem.

Other novelties of this chapter include the "resource bounds" on the speed of adjustment, speculative pricing, and rational adjustment under perfect foresight. To our knowledge, none of these has been explicitly analyzed before.

Our analysis is in terms of three special examples.[2] Section II contains a detailed statement of assumptions, notation, and conclusions. In Sections III–V the examples are examined in detail, and Section VI contains some miscellaneous remarks concerning possible modifications of the examples.

## II. Assumptions, Notation, Conclusions

We consider a closed economy with two industries, each producing one final good with the aid of one mobile factor, labor (and any number of invisible immobile factors). The supply of labor is completely inelastic and constant through time; units are chosen so that the aggregate supply is equal to one. Within each industry all firms have access to the same diminishing-returns technology and share the same expectations concerning future wage rates and commodity prices. However, the form of the production functions is complicated by the fact that labor is the subject of hiring and

---

[2] More general formulations may be found in the paper by Kemp and Wan [7].

firing operations which are costly in terms of labor. Let $Q_i$ be the output of the $i$th industry and $L_i$ the employment of labor by the $i$th industry. It is assumed that when $L_i$ changes, the $i$th industry incurs adjustment costs equal to $|\dot{L}_i|$, where $\dot{L}_i \equiv dL/dt$. Production functions are assumed to be quadratic; specifically,

$$Q_i = (L_i - |\dot{L}_i|) - \tfrac{1}{2}(L_i - |\dot{L}_i|)^2 \tag{1}$$

so that when production is completely specialized, the marginal product of labor is zero in the active industry.[3]

It is supposed that at each moment of time firms seek to maximize their expected quasi rents or profits. We work with two alternative polar assumptions concerning expectations. The first and second of our examples are based on the assumption of static expectations, while in the third example we switch to the assumption of perfect foresight.

Suppose that prices and wages are not expected to change. Let $p_i$ be the price of the $i$th commodity, $w$ the wage rate, and $r \geq 0$ the rate of interest.[4] The problem facing firms in the $i$th industry at time 0 is to find the maximum of [5]

$$\int_0^\infty (p_i Q_i - wL_i) \exp(-rt)\, dt. \tag{2}$$

On the demand side, the community is supposed to behave either as though it were maximizing the utility function,

$$U(d_1, d_2) = kd_1 + (1 - k)d_2, \qquad 0 < k < 1 \tag{3a}$$

(Example 1), or as though it were maximizing

$$U(d_1, d_2) = d_1^{1/3} d_2^{2/3} \tag{3b}$$

(Example 2) where $d_i$ is the aggregate consumption of the $i$th commodity. Finally, at each moment prices and wages settle at market-clearing levels.

[3] Some of the complications of our analysis and the novelty of our conclusions stem from the nonsmoothness of our cost-of-adjustment function at the origin. We believe that in this respect our assumptions are realistic. Smoothness of the cost-of-adjustment function at the origin requires that both the marginal hiring cost and the marginal firing cost approach zero at the origin. There is no evidence that these conditions hold in reality. In their pioneering study of adjustment costs, Holt et al. recognized that a realistic cost-of-adjustment function might be nonsmooth and introduced a smooth function solely for ease of computation [6, pp. 52–53].

[4] There is no investment in either of our examples. However, pure consumption loans are not ruled out; hence there is no difficulty in postulating a rate of interest.

[5] If $r = 0$, the integral may not converge. However, one may adopt the familiar Ramsey device to render the problem valuation-finite (see Brock and Gale [1]).

Suppose alternatively that prices and wages are foreseen with perfect accuracy. An economy with demands derived from the utility function $U(d_1, d_2)$ then behaves as though it were guided by a Ramsey planner seeking to maximize the integral of discounted aggregate utility. In our third example we consider the Ramsey path of the economy under the assumption that the utility function is of the Mill–Graham type $U(d_1, d_2) = d_1^a d_2^{1-a}$.

On the basis of our first two examples, which incorporate the assumption of static expectations, we are able to state the following propositions (starred statements hold only when $r > 0$).

(a) The value of the marginal product of labor may differ from industry to industry (i) during a transient phase and (ii)* in a steady state.

(b) In any particular industry, the wage rate and the value of the marginal product of labor may differ (i) during a transient phase and (ii)* in a steady state.

(c)* For given commodity prices, there may exist a continuum of neutral steady state configurations of inputs, outputs, and wage rates. Any sufficiently small displacement of an interior steady state position of this type results neither in a return to the initial position nor in a centrifugal movement away from it.

(d) (i) The short-run supply curve for each commodity is backward-bending; (ii)* at the maximum output there may be a perfectly inelastic range.

(e) General-equilibrium models with rationally adjusting firms may be infected by causal indeterminacy: there may exist allocations of labor to each of which there correspond several distinct market-clearing commodity prices, with each price determining a different rate of labor reallocation (it is even possible that different prices determine different directions of labor reallocation). We have not been able to find plausible conditions which, if satisfied, rule out indeterminacy.

From our third example, which incorporates the assumption of perfect foresight, we are able to derive the following propositions.

(α) The (shadow and market) value of the marginal product of labor may differ from industry to industry (i) during a transient phase and (ii)* in a steady state.

(β) The hysteresis of long-run equilibrium still persists if $r > 0$.

## III. Example 1

In this section we consider the system (1), (2), (3a) under the restriction that prices are constant, with $p_1 = k$ and $p_2 = 1 - k$. That restriction is relaxed in Appendix B.

We begin by studying the decision problem of the individual firm. Since the hiring cost increases monotonically with hiring rate, we may define the "intensity of hiring activity" $u_i$ as the portion of labor force diverted for hiring operations. Defining the "intensity of firing" in the same manner and treating it as negative hiring intensity, we have the following formulas for $u_i$:

$$\dot{L}_i > 0, \quad u_i = g_i(\dot{L}_i)/L_i$$
$$\dot{L}_i = 0, \quad u_i = 0$$
$$\dot{L}_i < 0, \quad u_i = -g_i(\dot{L}_i)/L_i$$

where $g_i(\dot{L}_i)$ is the adjustment cost function in labor terms. Simplifying, we obtain

$$u_i = (\text{sign } \dot{L}_i)(g_i(\dot{L}_i)/L_i).$$

In our case, $g_i(\dot{L}_i) = |\dot{L}_i|$, so $u_i = \dot{L}_i/L_i$. Since $g_i(\dot{L}_i)$ can never exceed $L_i$, we obtain the "resource bounds" on the intensity of adjustment: $|u_i| \leq 1$. Defining $\omega_i = w/p_i$, the problem is to find

$$\max_{u_i} \int_0^\infty [(1 - |u_i|)L_i - \tfrac{1}{2}(1 - |u_i|)^2 L_i^2 - \omega_i L_i] \exp(-rt) \, dt, \qquad 0 \leq r < 1, \tag{4}$$

subject to $\dot{L}_i = u_i L_i$ and $-1 \leq u_i \leq 1$. The Hamiltonian is

$$\bar{H}_i = [(1 - |u_i|)L_i - \tfrac{1}{2}(1 - |u_i|)^2 L_i^2 - \omega_i L_i] \exp(-rt) + \bar{\mu}_i u_i L_i. \tag{5}$$

The modified or "present-value" Hamiltonian is then

$$H_i \equiv \bar{H}_i \exp(rt)$$
$$= (1 - |u_i|)L_i - \tfrac{1}{2}(1 - |u_i|)^2 L_i^2 - \omega_i L_i + \mu_i u_i L_i, \qquad \mu_i = \bar{\mu}_i \exp(rt), \tag{5'}$$

and among the necessary conditions for a maximum we have

$$\dot{\mu}_i = (r\bar{\mu}_i + \dot{\bar{\mu}}_i) \exp(rt) = r\mu_i - (\partial H_i/\partial L_i)$$
$$= r\mu_i - [(1 - |u_i|) + \mu_i u_i - \omega_i] + (1 - |u_i|)^2 L_i \tag{6a}$$

$$\dot{L}_i = \partial H_i/\partial \mu_i = u_i L_i \tag{6b}$$

$$H_i(L_i, \mu_i, u_i^*) \geq H_i(L_i, \mu_i, u_i) \qquad \text{for all} \quad u_i \in [-1, 1] \quad \text{and} \quad t \geq 0 \tag{6c}$$

where $u_i^*(t)$ is the optimal value of the control $u_i$ at time $t$. We calculate that

$$\partial H_i/\partial u_i = L_i[\mu_i - (1 - L_i)(\partial |u_i|/\partial u_i) - u_i L_i], \qquad u_i \neq 0, \tag{7}$$

the graph of which is displayed in Fig. 1, and that

$$\partial^2 H_i/\partial u_i^2 = -L_i^2 < 0, \qquad u_i \neq 0. \tag{8}$$

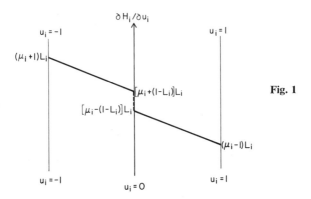

**Fig. 1**

Thus

$$
u_i^*(L_i, \mu_i) = \begin{cases}
-1 & \text{when} \quad \mu_i \leqq -1 \\
(\mu_i + 1 - L_i)/L_i & \text{when} \quad -1 \leqq \mu_i \leqq -(1 - L_i) \\
0 & \text{when} \quad -(1 - L_i) \leqq \mu_i \leqq 1 - L_i \quad (9) \\
(\mu_i - 1 + L_i)/L_i & \text{when} \quad 1 - L_i \leqq \mu_i \leqq 1 \\
1 & \text{when} \quad \mu_i \geqq 1.
\end{cases}
$$

Applying (9) to (6a) and (6b), we obtain the arrow scheme of Fig. 2. In Appendix A it is shown that the optimal trajectory consists of the stable arm $A'A$ of the saddle centered on $A$, the stable arm $B'B$ of the saddle centered on $B$, and the set of stationary points $AB$. It is also shown in Appendix A that, for $L_i(0) \geqq (1 - r - \omega_i)/(2 - r)$,

$$
L_i(t) = \begin{cases}
\left[L_i(0) - \left(1 - \dfrac{\omega_i}{1 - r}\right)\right] \exp[-(1 - r)t] + \left(1 - \dfrac{\omega_i}{1 - r}\right) \\
\qquad \text{if} \quad L_i(t) < 1 - \dfrac{\omega_i}{1 - r} \\[2mm]
\left[L_i(0) - \left(1 - \dfrac{\omega_i}{1 + r}\right)\right] \exp(-t) + \left(1 - \dfrac{\omega_i}{1 + r}\right) \qquad (10) \\
\qquad \text{if} \quad L_i(t) > 1 - \dfrac{\omega_i}{1 + r} \\[2mm]
L_i(0) \qquad \text{if} \quad 1 - \dfrac{\omega_i}{1 - r} \leqq L_i(t) \leqq 1 - \dfrac{\omega_i}{1 + r}
\end{cases}
$$

where $L_i(0)$ is the initial labor allocation. If $L_i(0) < (1 - r - \omega_i)/(2 - r)$, then $\dot{L}_i = L_i$ and $L_i(t) = L_i(0)e^t$ until $t = t'$, where $L_i(t') = (1 - r - \omega_i)/(2 - r)$. For $t > t'$, (10) takes over, with $L_i(0)$ replaced by $L_i(t')$ and $t$ by $t - t'$.

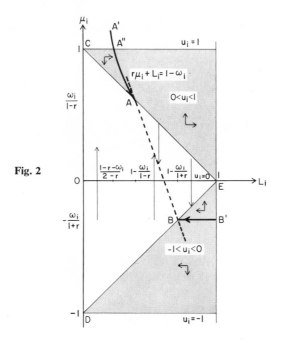

Fig. 2

Given the labor allocation $L_i$ and commodity prices $p_i$, an increase in the wage rate reduces the return to hiring and increases the return to firing. There is therefore a monotonic relationship between the increase in labor requirements and the wage rate. Moreover, $\dot{L}_i = 0$ if

$$1 - [w/p_i(1 - r)] \leqq L_i \leqq 1 - [w/p_i(1 + r)].$$

This "interval of hysteresis" shrinks to the single point $1 - (w/p_i)$ when $r$ decreases to zero. This information is summarized in Fig. 3a. We may call $p_i(1 - r)(1 - L_i)$ the (maximum) hiring wage and $p_i(1 + r)(1 - L_i)$ the (minimum) firing wage.

Moving beyond the individual firm and industry, we may redraft Fig. 3a with two curves, one for each industry, as in Figs. 3b and 3c. Then we can see that an equilibrium wage rate always exists. The set of equilibrium wage rates forms a closed interval which may degenerate to a single point (as in Fig. 3b). If in equilibrium hiring and firing take place or if $r = 0$ (so that the horizontal sections of the curves disappear), the equilibrium wage rate is unique. If the equilibrium wage rate is not unique, net hiring and firing are zero in each industry, as in Fig. 3c.

The adjoint variable $\mu_i$ is the shadow price of the marginal unit of labor $L_i$, measured by variations in the optimal value of the integral (2). If something is being produced, optimality requires that $|\mu_i|$ be equal to the

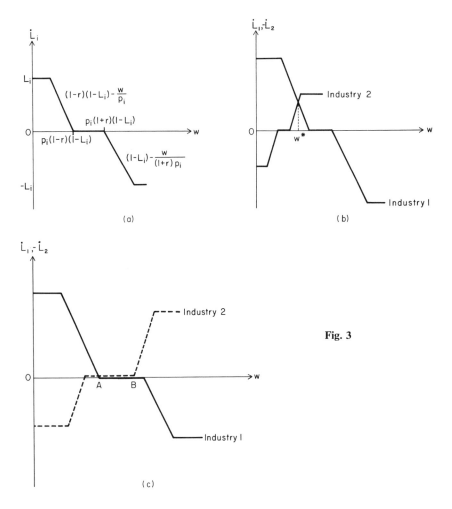

Fig. 3

marginal product of labor; otherwise, equality is replaced by a sort of Kuhn–Tucker inequality, with $\mu_i \geqq$ (marginal product) $= 1.$[6] Hence (see Fig. 2), if the economy is still in transition, the marginal product of labor in the hiring industry must be greater than the real wage rate $\omega_i$, so that the value of the marginal product of labor must be greater than the wage rate,[7] and the value of the marginal product of labor in the firing industry must be not greater (less, if $r > 0$) than the wage rate. Thus propositions (a)(i) and (b)(i)

[6] Notice that while $u^*$ may be $+1$, it can never be $-1$; that is, it may be optimal for a firm or industry to stop producing for purposes of rapid hiring but not for purposes of firing.

[7] In Fig. 2, along $A'A$, marginal product $= \min(\mu_i, 1) > \omega_i/(1 - r) > \omega_i$.

are established. From Fig. 2 we may also infer propositions (a)(ii) and (b)(ii). Proposition (c) follows from Fig. 3c.

Through time the curve in Fig. 3a moves to the left (right) if the industry is a hirer (firer) and the economy asymptotically approaches a unique stationary equilibrium in which the hiring wage of one industry is equal to the firing wage of the other. During the transition the wage rate steadily rises, for, at a given wage rate, the rate of hiring tapers off more slowly than the firing rate [see (10)] and the curve of Fig. 3a is downward sloping in the relevant ranges of $w$.

From (10) we can compute the "productive" labor force $x_i \equiv L_i - |\dot{L}_i|$:

$$
x_i(t) = \begin{cases}
1 - (2 - r)L_i(t) + (w/p_i) \\
\quad \text{when} \quad L_i(t) < 1 - [w/(1 - r)p_i] \\
1 - [w/(1 + r)p_i] \\
\quad \text{when} \quad L_i(t) > 1 - [w/(1 + r)p_i] \\
L_i(t) \quad \text{when} \quad 1 - [w/(1 - r)p_i] \leq L_i(t) \leq 1 - [w/(1 + r)p_i].
\end{cases}
\tag{11}
$$

The backward-bending form of the short-run supply curve is obvious. If $p_i$ steadily increases, then beginning at some level below $w/(1 + r)(1 - L_i)$ the productive labor force (and therefore output) at first increases, reache as plateau at $p_i = w/(1 + r)(1 - L_i)$, and begins to fall at $p_i = w/(1 - r)(1 - L_i)$.

## IV. Example 2

We turn to the system (1), (2), (3b). To eliminate some nonessential complications we assume $r = 0$. Prices are normalized so that $p_1 + p_2 = 1$. We define $p_1 = p$, so that $p_2 = 1 - p$, and $L_1 = L$, so that $L_2 = 1 - L$.

We must now face up to the problems posed by variable prices. From (10) the fact that $|u_i| \leq 1$ and the equilibrium condition $\sum \dot{L}_i = 0$, we find that, if $r = 0$,

$$
\dot{L}(t) = \begin{cases}
\min[p(t) - L(t), L(t), 1 - L(t)] & \text{if} \quad p(t) \geq L(t) \\
-\min[L(t) - p(t), L(t), 1 - L(t)] & \text{if} \quad L(t) \geq p(t)
\end{cases}
$$
$$
= f(L, p), \quad \text{say.}^8
\tag{12}
$$

---

[8] Equation (10) implies that, for $L(t) < 1 - (w/p)$, $\dot{L}(t) = [1 - (w/p)] - L(t)$; also,

$$
0 = \dot{L}(t) + \overline{(1 - L(t))} = \left[\left(1 - \frac{w}{p}\right) - L(t)\right] + \left[\left(1 - \frac{w}{1 - p}\right) - (1 - L(t))\right];
$$

hence $w = p(1 - p)$. Thus $\dot{L}(t) = p - L(t)$. The case of $L(t) > 1 - (w/p)$ can be similarly analyzed.

TABLE 1

| Zone | $\dot{L}$ | $x_1 \equiv L - |\dot{L}|$ | $x_2 \equiv 1 - L - |\dot{L}|$ | $Q_1$ |
|------|-----------|----------------------------|--------------------------------|-------|
| $1 \geq p \geq 2L$ | $L$ | $0$ | $1 - 2L$ | $0$ |
| $2L \geq p \geq L$ | $p - L \geq 0$ | $2L - p$ | $1 - p$ | $(2L - p) - \frac{1}{2}(2L - p)^2$ |
| $L \geq p \geq 2L - 1$ | $p - L \leq 0$ | $p$ | $1 + p - 2L$ | $p - \frac{1}{2}p^2$ |
| $2L - 1 \geq p \geq 0$ | $L - 1$ | $2L - 1$ | $0$ | $(2L - 1) - \frac{1}{2}(2L - 1)^2$ |

For given $p(t)$, this relation is depicted in Fig. 4a. Alternatively, we may consider Fig. 4b, a contour map for $\dot{L}$ values. In Fig. 4b the lines $p = 2L$, $p = L$, and $p = 2L - 1$ divide the unit square into four zones. Between $p = 2L$ and $p = 2L - 1$, $\dot{L} = p - L$. Outside these two boundary lines, $\dot{L} = L$ or $\dot{L} = 1 - L$, depending on which constraint is binding.

Table 1 contains the essential data for the present example. All entries except those in the last column follow from (12) and the definitions of $x_i$ and $Q_i$. It remains to obtain the equilibrium condition for each zone. Invoking the special properties of Mill–Graham demand functions, we have

$$pQ_1 = \tfrac{1}{3}[pQ_1 + (1 - p)Q_2] = \tfrac{1}{2}(\tfrac{2}{3})[pQ_1 + (1 - p)Q_2] = \tfrac{1}{2}(1 - p)Q_2 \quad (13)$$

where $pQ_1 + (1 - p)Q_2$ is the value of national income, of which a proportion $(i/3)$ is spent on the $i$th commodity. For (13) to be satisfied in the zone $1 \geq p \geq 2L$, it is necessary that $p \cdot 0 = 0 = (1 - p)Q_2$ and, since $Q_2 > 0$,

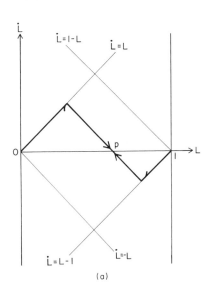

(a)

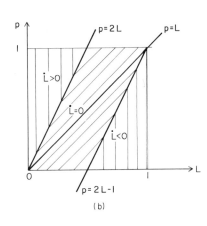

(b)

Fig. 4

| Zone | $Q_2$ | Equilibrium condition |
|---|---|---|
| $1 \geq p \geq 2L$ | $(1 - 2L) - \frac{1}{2}(1 - 2L)^2$ | $p = 1$ |
| $2L \geq p \geq L$ | $(1 - p) - \frac{1}{2}(1 - p)^2$ | $L = \frac{1}{2}\{1 + p - [2 - (1/p) + p - p^2]^{1/2}\}$ |
| $L \geq p \geq 2L - 1$ | $(1 + p - 2L) - \frac{1}{2}(1 + p - 2L)^2$ | $L = \frac{1}{2}\{p + [1 - p^2(2 - p)/(1 - p)]^{1/2}\}$ |
| $2L - 1 \geq p \geq 0$ | $0$ | $p = 0$ |

that $p = 1$. Similarly, for (13) to hold in the zone $2L - 1 \geq p \geq 0$, it is necessary that $p = 0$. In these zones, the nonproduced commodity is so urgently desired that consumers are willing to pay any price. However, the backward-bending property of short-run supply ensures that an infinite relative price serves to retard rather than stimulate the momentary production of the good in question. Turning to the remaining two zones, we have, from (13) and Table 1,

$$x_1^2 - 2x_1 + ((1/p) - 1 - p + p^2) = 0 \quad \text{if} \quad 2L \geq p \geq L$$
$$x_2^2 - 2x_2 + p^2(2 - p)/(1 - p) = 0 \quad \text{if} \quad L \geq p \geq 2L - 1. \tag{14}$$

Completing the squares and noting that $x_i \leq 1$, we obtain

$$x_1 = 1 - [1 - ((1/p) - 1 - p + p^2)]^{1/2} = 2L - p \quad \text{if} \quad 2L \geq p \geq L$$
$$x_2 = 1 - [1 - p^2(2 - p)/(1 - p)]^{1/2} = 1 + p - 2L \quad \text{if} \quad L \geq p \geq 2L - 1. \tag{15}$$

Solving (15) for $L$ we obtain the remaining entries in Table 1.

As Table 1 makes clear, the equilibrium $\dot{L}$ may not be unique, that is, the system is causally indeterminate. Can nothing be said about the evolution of the economy? Let $P(L)$ be the set of $p$ in pairs $(p, L)$ which satisfy the equilibrium conditions of Table 1; and let $S(L)$ be the set of $\dot{L} = f(L, p)$ for some $p$ in $P(L)$. Then all available information about the evolution of the economy is summarized in the "contingent equation"[9]

$$\dot{L} \in S(L). \tag{16}$$

(If the correspondence is single-valued for all $L$, (16) reduces to a differential equation.) The graph of $S(L)$ is displayed in Fig. 5a, which differs from the usual phase diagram in that to all $L$, $\underline{L} \leq L \leq \bar{L}$, there corresponds more than one value of $\dot{L}$. Suppose that $0 < L(0) < \underline{L}$. Then the evolution of the system is as shown in Fig. 5b. Starting at $L(0)$, the system reaches $\underline{L}$ within a definite

---

[9] The term comes from Castain [3].

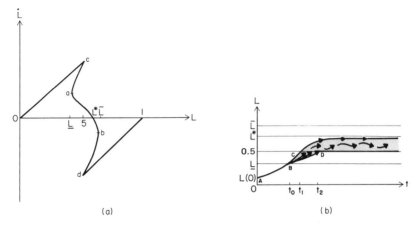

Fig. 5

time period. It then moves to $L = 0.5$, arriving not before $t_1$ and not after $t_2$. After that, we can say only that $L(t) \in (0.5, L^*)$ for $t > t_2$.[10]

## V. Example 3

We turn to an example involving perfect foresight. The problem now is to find the allocation of labor resources through time which maximizes the integral of discounted Mill–Graham utility,

$$\int_0^\infty e^{-rt} d_1^a d_2^{1-a} \, dt,$$

subject to the production relationships (1), the resource constraint $L_1 + L_2 = 1$ and some obvious nonnegativity restrictions. After some simplification, the problem is to find

$$J = \max_{v(t)} \int_0^\infty e^{-rt} [(L - |v|) - \tfrac{1}{2}(L - |v|)^2]^a [(1 - L - |v|)$$
$$- \tfrac{1}{2}(1 - L - |v|)^2]^{1-a} \, dt, \qquad 0 < a < 1, \qquad (17)$$

[10] By means of additional market–institutional assumptions it is possible to eliminate most, but not necessarily all, of the indeterminacy. Consider again Fig. 5a. From any initial point between $a$ and $b$ the assumption of "branch continuity" [i.e., $\dot{L}(t)$ is continuous in $t$] ensures that the system will move to the stationary point $(L^*, 0)$. However, for any other initial point other than $a$ and $b$, branch continuity answers only that the system will move continuously to $c$ or $d$. When one of those points is reached, a jump is inevitable. At points $a$ and $b$, indeterminacy remains.

subject to

$$\dot{L} = v \tag{18}$$

$$-\min(L, 1 - L) \leqq v \leqq \min(L, 1 - L) \tag{19}$$

$$0 \leqq L(0) \quad \text{given.} \tag{20}$$

Suppose $J$ exists. Then we may write $J = J(L(0))$. It is easy to show that $J(L(0))$ reaches its maximum on the closed interval $0 \leqq L(0) \leqq 1$ at the unique point $L(0) = L^{**}$ where

$$a(1 - L^{**})/[L^{**} - \tfrac{1}{2}(L^{**})^2] = (1 - a)L^{**}/[(1 - L^{**}) - \tfrac{1}{2}(1 - L^{**})^2]. \tag{21}$$

Suppose without loss of generality that $L(0) \leqq L^{**}$. Then clearly the optimal value of $L(t)$ can never exceed $L^{**}$. [If for some $t$, say $t'$, $L(t) = L^{**}$, to later overshoot $L^{**}$ is to leave the feasible path which, from $t'$ on, dominates all other feasible paths.] Next, we note that the path of optimal $L(t)$ must be monotonic (to move in a circle is to needlessly dissipate effective labor in costly hiring and firing activities) and that the feasible path $L(t) \equiv L(0)$ dominates any feasible path $L(t) \leqq L(0)$, with $L(t) < L(0)$ for some $t$ [to let $L$ fall below $L(0)$ at, say, $t = t'$ is to use up labor in "unproductive" hiring and firing and, in addition, to endow the economy with a less-preferred initial value of $L$ vis-à-vis the period beginning at $t'$], and infer that the optimal $v(t)$ is nonnegative. Thus the optimal $L(t)$ is monotonic and not greater than $L^{**}$.

We can now distinguish the three cases of Fig. 6.

*Case 1* After dropping the redundant constraint, the problem (17)–(20) reduces to

$$\max_{u'(t)} \int_0^\infty e^{-rt}[(1 - u')L - \tfrac{1}{2}(1 - u')^2 L^2]^a$$
$$\times [(1 - (1 + u')L) - \tfrac{1}{2}(1 - (1 + u')L)^2]^{1-a} \, dt, \tag{22}$$

subject to

$$\dot{L} = u'L \tag{23}$$

$$0 \leqq u' \leqq 1. \tag{24}$$

*Case 2* Again after dropping a redundant constraint, the problem reduces to

$$\max_{u''(t)} \int_0^\infty e^{-rt}[((1 + u'')L - u'') - \tfrac{1}{2}((1 + u'')L - u'')^2]^a$$
$$\times [(1 - u'')(1 - L) - \tfrac{1}{2}(1 - u'')^2(1 - L)^2]^{1-a} \, dt, \tag{25}$$

subject to

$$\dot{L} = u''(1 - L) \tag{26}$$

$$0 \leqq u'' \leqq 1. \tag{27}$$

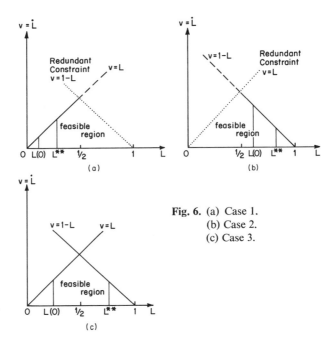

Fig. 6. (a) Case 1.
        (b) Case 2.
        (c) Case 3.

*Case 3* The problem does not simplify in this case. If in the solution to (22)–(24) with $L^{**} > \frac{1}{2}$, it turns out that the limit, as $t \to \infty$, of optimal $L(t)$ is not greater than $\frac{1}{2}$, then we need go no further. But if opt $L(\infty) > \frac{1}{2}$, then we must seek

$$J(L(0)) = \max_{u'(t),T} \left\{ \int_0^T e^{-rt}[(1 - u')L - \tfrac{1}{2}(1 - u')^2L^2]^a[(1 - (1 - u')L) \right.$$
$$\left. - \tfrac{1}{2}(1 - (1 - u')L)^2]^{1-a} \, dt + J(L(T))e^{-rT} \right\} \qquad (28)$$

where $L(T) = \frac{1}{2}$. That is, the planner must solve an infinite-horizon problem of type (25)–(27), with an initial value $L = \frac{1}{2}$, and another finite-horizon problem of type (22)–(24) with $L(T) = \frac{1}{2}$.

Since the integrand is a concave function of $L$ and $v$, the solution is in each case unique.

Let us now return to propositions ($\alpha$) and ($\beta$) of Section II, in particular to ($\alpha$)(ii) and ($\beta$). It suffices to concentrate on Case 1; the other cases can be handled in the same way, with the same conclusions. For problem (22)–(24) the Hamiltonian is

$$H = V(L, u') + \mu u'L$$

where

$$V(L, u') = [(1 - u')L - \tfrac{1}{2}(1 - u')^2 L^2]^a$$
$$\times [(1 - (1 + u')L) - \tfrac{1}{2}(1 - (1 + u')L)^2]^{1-a}.$$

As necessary conditions for an optimum we have

$$\dot{\mu} = r\mu - (\partial V/\partial L) - \mu u' \tag{29}$$

$$0 = \partial H/\partial u' = \partial V/\partial u' + \mu L. \tag{30}$$

In a steady state, by definition,

$$\dot{\mu} = 0 = \dot{L} = u'L. \tag{31}$$

Combining (29)–(31), we obtain

$$-L^{-1} \, \partial V/\partial u'|_{(L(\infty), \, 0)} = r^{-1} \, \partial V/\partial L|_{(L(\infty), \, 0)} \tag{32}$$

where the subscript indicates the point at which the partial derivatives are to be evaluated. The left-hand side of (32) represents the onceover cost of adjustment; the right-hand side represents the capitalized gain to be derived from the transfer of a unit of labor into the first industry; that is, the excess shadow value of the marginal product of labor in the first industry over that of the second industry. For $r > 0$, the two values of the marginal product of labor remain unequal, costs of adjustment making it suboptimal to ever realize the potential gain from labor reallocation. Thus, neither standing friction nor persistent differences in labor productivity go away when the assumption of static expectations is replaced with that of perfect foresight. Again the "interval of hysteresis" shrinks to a single point if $r$ decreases to zero.

In the example just studied the time path of the economy was causally determined. However, it would be a mistake to infer that perfect foresight is inconsistent with casual indeterminacy. To avail ourselves of the device of the Ramsey planner it was necessary to assume that aggregate demand could be generated by a single well-behaved utility index. However, if there exist several types of consumer, each with its own peculiar utility index, causal indeterminacy may reappear even under conditions of perfect foresight. To see this we need only recall that in a simple exchange economy with just two consumers and two goods there may be multiple equilibria, and then reflect that one good may be interpreted as present resources, the other as future resources. Perfect foresight is shown here as nothing but unanimous, self-validating predictions. If a bank cannot survive panic withdrawals but will thrive otherwise, then both the predictions that the same bank will be safe and will go bankrupt may qualify as perfect foresight! If we postulate a price-making auctioneer who maximizes the value of excess demand (over semipositive price vectors summing to one), causal indeterminacy under perfect foresight is equivalent to the multiplicity of Nash equilibria in a noncooperative game.

## VI. Final Remarks

On the basis of special examples, we have established the possibility of interindustrial wage and marginal productivity differences and of the hysteresis of long-run equilibrium. As may be obvious to the reader, these phenomena emerge in more general models than those presented here. Specifically, hysteresis depends on the nondifferentiability at the origin of the cost-of-adjustment functions but does not depend on the special "absolute value" form assumed in our examples. Hysteresis cannot be excluded for any production function $Q_i = F_i(L_i - g_i(\dot{L}_i))$ with appropriate concavity and nondifferentiability-at-the-origin properties for $F_i$ and $g_i$, respectively. It can be shown that $\dot{L}_i = 0$ over the "interval of hysteresis":

$$\left[ F_i'^{-1}\left\{\frac{\omega_i}{1 - |g_i'(0+)|r}\right\}, F_i'^{-1}\left\{\frac{\omega_i}{1 + |g_i'(0-)|r}\right\}\right];$$

also the marginal product of labor approaches

$$\frac{\omega_i}{1 - |g_i'(0+)|r} \left(\frac{\omega_i}{1 + |g_i'(0-)|r}\right)$$

for the hiring (firing) sector.

We have assumed that the cost of adjustment is related to the rate of *net* hiring or firing. Alternatively, and perhaps more realistically, we might have related the cost of adjustment to gross hiring or firing; that is, to the rate of labor turnover. Now if the cost of adjustment is related to turnover, a firm in transition will never find it optimal to hire and fire simultaneously. Thus in periods of transition the net and gross formulations amount to the same thing. In stationary equilibrium, however, this is not so. Consider Fig. 3c. There is a range $AB$ of (stationary) equilibrium wage rates. Moreover, if costs of adjustment are related to turnover, there is no reason for the same wage rate to prevail in both industries. If $w_1$, the wage rate prevailing in the first industry, is greater than $w_2$, the wage rate prevailing in the second industry, workers in the second industry will attempt to transfer to the first industry, offering to take a wage less than $w_1$. Firms in the first industry, however, have no incentive to accept their offers, for the cost of adjustment exceeds the present value of the reduction in the wage bill.

One can hope that models of rational adjustment will eventually throw light on puzzling phenomena which in the past have been ascribed to institutional factors or to irrationality. The institutional wage rate of dualistic growth theory and the interindustrial wage gaps of the Hagen–Prebisch variety of protectionist argument come to mind.

## Appendix A. Derivation of Optimal Trajectories for Individual Firm or Industry

Throughout this appendix we drop industry subscripts.

We begin by noting that the polygonal line $CABE$ (on which $\dot{L} = 0 = \dot{\mu}$) in Fig. 2 forms a barrier to any trajectory satisfying (6a) and (6b). Thus, on any path, either $\mu > 0$, $\dot{L} \geq 0$ or $\mu < 0$, $\dot{L} \leq 0$; that is, under static expectations, no producer will plan to first hire (fire) and later fire (hire).

To pin down the optimal trajectory, it is necessary to establish the appropriate transversality conditions. To this end we partition all trajectories into seven classes (see Fig. 2).

1. The arc $A'A$. This is a stable arm of the saddle centered on $A$.
2. The arc $BB'$. This is a stable arm of the saddle $B$.
3. The degenerate stationary trajectories on the heavy dotted line $AB$.
4. Arcs to the right of $A'A$ with $\dot{L} > 0$.
5. Arcs to the left of $A'A$ with $\dot{L} > 0$.
6. Arcs which cross the line $L = 1 - [\omega/(1 - r)]$ and on which $\dot{L} < 0$.
7. Arcs other than $BB'$ which do not cross the line $L = 1 - [\omega/(1 - r)]$ and on which $\dot{L} < 0$.

Now all trajectories in class 4 cross a vertical line $L = \hat{L} \equiv 1 - [\omega/(1 + r)] + \Delta$ for some $\Delta$, $\omega/(1 + r) > \Delta \geq 0$. But then $\omega > 1 - L$, that is, the value of the marginal product of labor, with no labor diverted to hiring or firing, is already less than the wage rate. Nevertheless, hiring continues. Hence all such trajectories are nonoptimal. Formally, on any trajectory in class 4,

$$[(\hat{L} - \tfrac{1}{2}\hat{L}^2) - \omega\hat{L}] > [(L - \tfrac{1}{2}L^2) - \omega L] \geq [(1 - |u|)L$$
$$- \tfrac{1}{2}(1 - |u|)^2 L^2] - \omega L \qquad \text{for} \quad L > \hat{L}.$$

Hence, for $L > \hat{L}$, that trajectory is dominated by a feasible path $L \equiv \hat{L}$. Since any subtrajectory of an optimal trajectory is optimal with respect to its initial state, the trajectory is nonoptimal.

Similarly, all trajectories in class 6 are nonoptimal. For each such trajectory crosses a vertical line $L = \check{L} \equiv 1 - [\omega/(1 - r)] - \Delta$ for some $\Delta$, $1 - [\omega/(1 - r)] > \Delta \geq 0$, and the subsequent subtrajectory is dominated by the feasible path $L \equiv \check{L}$.

To rule out trajectories in classes 5 and 7, a more elaborate calculation is needed. Members of class 5 (class 7) will be compared with the trajectory $A'A$ (respectively, $B'B$). For the time being, as far as class 5 is concerned, we restrict our attention to those trajectories for which $(1 - r - \omega)/(2 - r) \leq L(0) \leq 1 - [\omega/(1 - r)]$, and compare members of this subclass with the trajectory $A''A$. We note that on $A''A$ and $B'B$, $u$ never changes sign and $\lim_{t \to \infty} \dot{\mu}(t) = 0$ ($A$ and $B$ are saddle points which can be approached only asymptotically); and that, on the other hand, trajectories in classes 5 and 7 reach constant levels in finite time. Now let $(L^0, \mu^0)$ be the trajectory $A''A$ or $B'B$ and $(L, \mu)$ any trajectory in class 5 [with $L(0)$ satisfying the above inequalities] or class 7, respectively. We shall show that $(L^0, \mu^0)$ dominates $(L, \mu)$. Set

$$D \equiv \int_0^\infty \exp(-rt)[(L^0 - |\dot{L}^0|) - \tfrac{1}{2}(L^0 - |\dot{L}^0|)^2 - \omega L^0]\, dt$$

$$- \int_0^\infty \exp(-rt)[(L - |\dot{L}|) - \tfrac{1}{2}(L - |\dot{L}|)^2 - \omega L]\, dt$$

$$+ \int_0^\infty \exp(-rt)\mu^0[(u^0 L^0 - uL) - (\dot{L}^0 - \dot{L})]\, dt$$

$$= \int_0^\infty \exp(-rt)\{[(L^0 - |\dot{L}^0|) - \tfrac{1}{2}(L^0 - |\dot{L}^0|)^2] - [(L - |\dot{L}|) - \tfrac{1}{2}(L - |\dot{L}|)^2]$$

$$+ \mu^0(\dot{L}^0 - \dot{L})\}\, dt - \int_0^\infty \mu^0 \exp(-rt)(\dot{L}^0 - \dot{L})\, dt$$

$$- \omega \int_0^\infty \exp(-rt)(L^0 - L)\, dt.$$

The concavity of $(x - \tfrac{1}{2}x^2)$ allows us to approximate the difference between the first two terms under the first integral above. Moreover, for classes 1, 2, 5, and 7, sign $\dot{L}^0 = $ sign $\dot{L} = $ sign $\mu^0$, thus $\mu^0 \dot{L}^0 = |\mu^0||\dot{L}^0|$ and $\mu^0 \dot{L} = |\mu^0||\dot{L}|$. Hence,

$$D > \int_0^\infty \exp(-rt)\{[1 - (L^0 - |\dot{L}^0|)][(L^0 - |\dot{L}^0|) - (L - |\dot{L}|)]$$

$$+ |\mu^0|(|\dot{L}^0| - |\dot{L}|)\}\, dt$$

$$- \int_0^\infty \mu^0 \exp(-rt)(\dot{L}^0 - \dot{L})\, dt - \omega \int_0^\infty \exp(-rt)(L^0 - L)\, dt$$

$$= D_1, \text{ say.}$$

Along $A''A$ or $B'B$, $|\mu^0| = 1 - (L^0 - |\dot{L}^0|)$. Making substitution accordingly in $D_1$ and computing the middle integral by parts,

$$D_1 \geq \int_0^\infty \exp(-rt)(|\mu^0| - \omega)(L^0 - L)\, dt$$

$$- \left\{ \lim_{t \to \infty} [\mu^0(t)\exp(-rt)] \left[ \limsup_{t \to \infty} L^0(t) - \liminf_{t \to \infty} L(t) \right] \right.$$

$$\left. - \mu^0(0)[L^0(0) - L(0)] - \int_0^\infty (L^0 - L)(\dot{\mu}^0 - r\mu^0)\exp(-rt)\, dt \right\}$$

$$= D_2, \quad \text{say.}$$

Noting that $L^0(0) = L(0)$, that $\lim_{t \to \infty}[\mu^0(t)\exp(-rt)] = [\omega/(r \pm 1)](0) = 0$ for all $r > 0$, and that $|[\lim_{t \to \infty} \sup L^0(t) - \lim_{t \to \infty} \inf L(t)]| \leq 1$ since $0 \leq L^0, L \leq 1$, we obtain

$$D_2 = \int_0^\infty \exp(-rt)(L^0 - L)(\dot{\mu}^0 - (\omega + r\mu^0 - |\mu^0|)]\, dt.$$

Since $\dot{\mu}^0 = \omega + r\mu^0 - |\mu^0|$ along $A''A$ or $B'B$, $0 = D_2 \leq D_1 < D$.

This proves that class 7 and one subclass of class 5 are not optimal. It remains to consider the other subclass of trajectories in class 5, with $0 < L(0) < (1 - r - \omega)/(2 - r)$. We know that for the subclass $L(0) \geq (1 - r - \omega)/(2 - r)$, $A''A$ is optimal. Since any subarc of an optimal trajectory is optimal with respect to its initial state, any optimal trajectory must contain $A''A$ as a subarc. But for $L(0) < (1 - r - \omega)/(2 - r)$, only the $A'A''$ arc can reach $A$; hence $A'A$ is the only optimal trajectory and the entire class 5 cannot be optimal.

The complete optimal trajectory is therefore given by the heavy line $A'AB'B$ of Fig. 2.

Finally, from (6a), (6b) and (9), making use of the initial condition $L(0) = L_0$ and the transversality conditions $\dot{\mu}(\infty) = 0 = \dot{L}(\infty)$, we obtain the explicit solution for $L(t)$:

$$L(t) = \begin{cases} \left[ L(0) - \left(1 - \dfrac{\omega}{1 - r}\right) \right]\exp[-(1 - r)t] + \left(1 - \dfrac{\omega}{1 - r}\right) \\ \qquad \text{when} \quad \dot{L} > 0 \\[2ex] \left[ L(0) - \left(1 - \dfrac{\omega}{1 + r}\right) \right]\exp(-t) + \left(1 - \dfrac{\omega}{1 + r}\right) \\ \qquad \text{when} \quad \dot{L} < 0 \\[2ex] L(0) \qquad \text{when} \quad \dot{L} = 0. \end{cases}$$

## Appendix B.  Speculative Pricing

If in any particular industry hiring takes place at the maximum rate, so that nothing is produced and nothing consumed, we cannot rely on the slope of the indifference curves of Example 1 to determine prices. For example, if nothing is produced of the first commodity we can say only that $p_1 \geqq k$. In Section III we simply assumed that $p_1 = k$ whether or not something is produced of each commodity. Here we complete our analysis of Example 1 by relaxing that assumption.

Suppose that unspecified speculative forces set $p_1 \geqq k$ and that $L_1(0) < [1 - r - (w/p_1)]/(2 - r)$. To eliminate irrelevant complications, we assume $r = 0$, so that

$$L_1(0) < \tfrac{1}{2}[1 - (w/p_1)]. \tag{B.1}$$

Differentiating the first two entries of (10) at $t = 0$ and adding, we obtain

$$0 = \sum_i \dot{L}_i = -\left[L_1(0) - \left(1 - \frac{w}{p_1}\right)\right] - \left[L_2(0) - \left(1 - \frac{w}{1 - p_1}\right)\right]$$

so that, when both goods are produced,

$$w = p_1(1 - p_1). \tag{B.2}$$

Combining (B.1) and (B.2), we obtain $L_1(0) < \tfrac{1}{2}(p_1)$.[11] Thus we have the case

$$p_1 \geqq k, \qquad L_1(0) < \tfrac{1}{2}(p_1).$$

In fact it suffices to consider the more restricted case in which

$$p_1 > k, \qquad L_1(0) < \tfrac{1}{2}k. \tag{B.3}$$

Discussion of this case will be conducted in terms of Fig. 7, which is a specialization of Fig. 2, with $r = 0$. If $p_1 = k$, the optimal path is $A''_\alpha A_\alpha' A$, with full-speed or maximum hiring (and zero output) until $A_\alpha'$ is reached and reduced-speed hiring thereafter. If $2k \geqq p_1 > k$, the optimal path is $A''_\beta A_\beta' A_\beta{}^0 A$, with maximum hiring until $A_\beta'$ is reached followed by the collapse of $p_1$ to $k$ and abruptly reduced hiring thereafter. If $p_1 > 2k$, the optimal path is $A''_\gamma A_\gamma' B_\gamma{}^0 B$. In this case the industry overshoots its long-run equilibrium and must later tack back, steadily divesting itself of its surplus labor.

We have supposed that $p_1$ is *constant* at some value not less than $k$ until it collapses to that value. Once the assumption of constancy is relaxed, $p_1$ may jump erratically and anything may happen. For example, in Fig. 7, the trajectory may oscillate between the $A_\varsigma A_\gamma'$ branch and the $B_\gamma{}^0 B$ branch forever without ever reaching $B$.

---

[11] From Fig. 3b we see that, when only one good is produced, the wage is lower than indicated by (B.2). However, this is irrelevant in arriving at the inequality just stated.

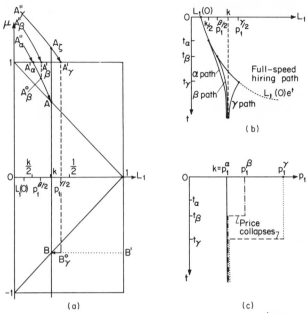

**Fig. 7.** (a) Phase diagram, $\alpha$ path: $A_\alpha''A_\alpha'A$; $\beta$ path: $A_\beta''A_\beta' \xrightarrow{\text{jump}} A_\beta{}^0 A$; $\gamma$ path: $A_\gamma''A_\gamma' \xrightarrow{\text{jump}} B_\gamma{}^0 B$. (b) Labor paths. (c) Price paths.

## ACKNOWLEDGMENTS

We are grateful to Paul Samuelson and to Avinash Dixit for many constructive suggestions. In particular, we owe to Professor Samuelson the suggestion that we treat the case of perfect foresight and that we handle it by the device of the Ramsey planner. From him we also have our title.

## REFERENCES

1. Brock, W. A., and Gale, D., "Optimal Growth under Factor Augmenting Progress," *Journal of Economic Theory* **1**, No. 3 (October 1969), 229–243.
2. Burton, E. T., III, "The Development Process in a Dual Economy," Working Paper No. 20, Dept. of Economics, Cornell Univ., 1971.
3. Castain, C., "Some Theorems in Measure Theory and Generalized Dynamic Systems Defined by Contingency Equations," in *Mathematical Systems Theory and Economics* (H. W. Kuhn and G. P. Szego, eds.), Vol. II, pp. 319–328. New York: Springer-Verlag, 1969.
4. Eisner, R., and R. Strotz, "Determinants of Business Investment," in *Impacts of Monetary Policy*. Englewood Cliffs, New Jersey: Prentice-Hall, 1963.
5. Gould, J. P., "Adjustment Costs in the Theory of Investment of the Firm," *Review of Economic Studies* **35** (1), No. 101 (January 1968), 47–56.
6. Holt, C. C., Modigliani, F., Muth, J. F., and Simon, H. A., *Planning Production Inventories and Work Force*. Englewood Cliffs, New Jersey: Prentice-Hall, 1960.

7. Kemp, M. C., and Wan, H. Y., Jr., "Competitive Equilibrium with Rationally Adjusting Firms," Working Paper No. 8, Dept. of Economics, Cornell Univ., 1970.
8. Lucas, R., "Optimum Investment Policy and the Flexible Accelerator," *International Economic Review* **8** (February 1967), 78–85.
9. Rothchild, M., "On the Cost of Adjustment," *The Quarterly Journal of Economics* **85**, No. 4 (November 1971), 605–622.
10. Solow, R. M., "Short-run Adjustment of Employment to Output," in *Value, Capital and Growth: Papers in Honor of Sir John Hicks* (J. N. Wolfe, ed.), pp. 481–484. Edinburgh: Edinburgh Univ. Press, 1968.
11. Treadway, A. B., "On Rational Entrepreneurial Behavior and the Demand for Investment," *Review of Economic Studies* **36** (2), No. 106 (April 1969), 227–239.
12. Treadway, A. B., "Adjustment Costs and Variable Inputs in the Theory of the Competitive Firm," *Journal of Economic Theory* **2**, No. 1 (March 1970), 329–347.

# STABILITY IN AN ECONOMY WITH PRODUCTION

*Anjan Mukherji*

*University of Rochester*
 *and*
*Jawaharlal Nehru University, New Delhi*

## I. Production and Gross Substitutes

The usual framework within which the stability of competitive equilibrium is demonstrated is that of an exchange economy, so that production decisions have no role to play. There are only a few exceptions to this, namely, the contributions by Morishima [8], Rader [11], and the recent discussions by Arrow and Hahn [2]. Now, the most important result in stability analysis has been the recognition of the fact that in a gross substitute economy, global stability prevails; this result is attributed to Arrow *et al.*, [1]. The most general form of the adjustment process in such a framework has been the one employed by McKenzie [5]. The gross substitute condition, however, was introduced into this area by Metzler [6] and has since been taken to be the principal condition for the stability of competitive equilibrium. The difficulty with this condition lies in the regrettable but unavoidable fact that if production conditions are normal, some factor inputs are complementary to one another (Rader [12]). Thus the condition of gross substitution will

243

usually not be applicable to a production model, and hence the demonstration of the stability of equilibrium may turn out to be difficult, to say the least.

To put this chapter in the proper perspective, let us briefly review the results that are available for application to a production economy. Any condition for stability which allows for complementarity would be such a result. For instance, McKenzie [5], Morishima [7], Rader [11], Ohyama [10], and Mukherji [9] are examples of such results. Arrow and Hahn [2] argue, on the other hand, for the case of small income effects. All of the results mentioned so far are local results. We shall deduce in Section III a condition for stabilizing income effects which will guarantee local stability (Theorem 1). In contrast to the results mentioned above, this condition is based on the assumption that the net sellers' income effect is weaker that the net buyers' income effect. However, as will be obvious, stabilizing income effects are difficult to guarantee. Thus it seems that we shall have to look for conditions under which the income effects are outweighed by substitution effects.

A feature of the gross substitute case is that the own price effect dominates. This has led to the formulation of a separate condition: the case where the Jacobian of the excess demand functions has a dominant diagonal. The condition that the weights yielding the dominant diagonal be the same for all prices has been used by Arrow *et al.* [1]; Arrow and Hahn [2, p. 294] look at the case where the weights are the prices. In Section IV we generalize these conditions to look at a situation where the weights are arbitrary functions of prices, and further, these weights are also taken to be the variable speeds of adjustment. A global stability result is seen to follow (Theorem 2). The only difficulty in this context turns out to be ensuring the boundedness of the solution path.

In the preceding discussion the existence of a unique supply response at each price is assumed. Thus the important case of a constant returns-to-scale economy has not been considered. The existing results in this area are those due to Morishima [8] and Arrow and Hahn [2]. In the final section we shall consider a particularly simple constant returns-to-scale economy, one with a single primary factor. The result claimed in this context by Arrow and Hahn [2] is then correctly demonstrated (Theorem 3).

This chapter thus relates quite closely to the treatment of Arrow and Hahn [2]. Our Theorem 1 proposes a way to get stability from income effects—a method only hinted at in ref. [2]. Theorem 2 proves a conjecture made in ref. [2], whereas in Theorem 3 we correct an error in the proof provided in ref. [2]. However, the nature of the preference and endowment patterns which guarantee the conditions of Theorems 1 and 2 remain unclear. Theorem 3 is the most general in this respect; the restriction in this case appears on the production side.

## II. The Economy

There are two classes of economic agents: *competitive firms* and *individuals*. Individuals are indexed by $k$, firms by $r$. Each individual possesses an initial endowment of resources $w^k$, where we include quantities of goods as well as factors. The $k$th individual maximizes a strictly increasing quasi-concave utility function subject to a budget constraint, given prices $p' = (p_1, p_2, \ldots, p_n)$ to derive his demand $d_i^k$ for the $i$th commodity, $i = 1, 2, \ldots, n$. The $d_i^k - w_i^k > 0$ would signify that $k$ is a net demander, whereas $d_i^k - w_i^k < 0$ would signify that $k$ is a net supplier of the commodity $i$. We shall assume that each individual $k$ has an income $I^k$ obtained from the sale of the initial endowment and from his participation in the profits of the firms, and this constitutes his budget constraint. The share of the profits will be explained later. The *net market demand* for commodity $i$ is given by $D_i - w_i = \sum (d_i^k - w_i^k)$, where $D_i = \sum d_i^k$, $w_i = \sum w_i^k$. For the demand functions:

**(A1)** $d_i^k(p_1, p_2, \ldots, p_n)$ is assumed to be single valued and continuous with continuous partial derivatives for all $p > 0$, for all $i$, and for all $k$. Also the demand functions are homogeneous functions of degree zero in the prices. All these properties obtain for the aggregate demand functions $D_i(\ )$.

There are $l$ firms. For a given firm, a production specification is a specification of all inputs required and the outputs produced; the outputs are distinguished by a positive sign, whereas inputs are associated with a negative sign. The collection of such input–output vectors constitutes the production possibility set $Y_r$ for the $r$th firm. Given a price vector $p$, the $r$th firm chooses $s_r$ such that $s_r$ maximizes profits; i.e., $s_r$ solves the maximum problem

$$\max \quad p'y \qquad \text{subject to} \quad y \in Y_r.$$

Thus $s_r = s_r(p)$ denotes the supply of the $r$th firm. We suppose that $Y_r$ is closed convex and bounded; also $Y_r$ contains the origin. $Y_r$ need not, in general, be bounded. However, we may restrict ourselves to a compact subset $Y_r' \subseteq Y_r$. The $Y_r'$ is the attainable production set of $r$, within which each firm is restricted due to a lack of available resources (see, for instance, Debreu [3, pp. 44–49]). The above problem, therefore, yields a solution $s_r(p)$ for each $r$, given $p$. We also insist that the supply response $s_r(p)$ be uniquely determined, given $p$. See, for instance, Arrow and Hahn [2, pp. 69–72] for a detailed investigation of the conditions under which this is possible. The total supply of the economy is defined to be $S(p) = \sum s_r(p)$. Then, it is well known that:

**Lemma 1** $S(p)$ maximizes $p'y$ for $y \in Y = \sum Y_r$.

As will be obvious soon, the uniqueness of the supply response $S(p)$ is essential for our purpose. Writing $S(p) = (S_j(p))$, we shall assume:

**(A2)**   $S_j(p)$ is continuous for $p > 0$ (i.e., $p_i > 0$ for all $i = 1, 2, \ldots, n$) with continuous partial derivatives for all $j$; further, $S_j(p)$ is homogeneous of degree zero in the prices.

Under these conditions, if production occurs, firms will make profits: the $k$th individual owns $\alpha_{kr} p's_r$ of the profits of the $r$th firm, where $\alpha_{kr} > 0$ and $\sum_k \alpha_{kr} = 1$ for each $r$. This completes the description of the model. As should be apparent, this is a stricter version of Debreu's model [3]—stricter in the sense that we insist on demand and supply functions rather than on correspondences. This is made possible by some assumptions of strict convexity on individual preferences and the individual production set (see Arrow and Hahn [2, pp. 69–72, 100–105]). Hence we will assume that there exists $p^*$ such that

$$D(p^*) - w = \sum_k (d^k(p^*) - w^k) = \sum_r s_r(p^*) = S(p^*) \tag{1}$$

which is thus the equilibrium price.

A few properties of the model may be noted for easy reference. At any price $p \neq p^*$, the state of excess demand or supply in the markets may be denoted by $Z(p) = D(p) - S(p) - w$. An easy check enables us to confirm that

$$p'Z(p) = p'(D(p) - w) - p'S(p) = 0. \tag{2}$$

This, of course, is the well-known Walras' law. At an equilibrium price, $p^*$, we have by (1), $Z(p^*) = 0$. The following properties of the supply functions $S(p)$ may also be noted:

**Lemma 2**   $(S_{ij}) = (\partial S_i / \partial p_j)$ exists almost everywhere and the matrix is positive semidefinite.

*Proof*   See Arrow and Hahn [2, p. 72], for instance.

Also, from (A2),

$$(S_{ij}(p)) \, p = 0. \tag{3}$$

using the homogeneity property. We also require that the following holds:

**(A3)**   A change in relative prices must alter supplies.

In terms of the usual notion of the transformation locus, the above is an assumption on the shape and smoothness of this locus. This allows us to prove:

**Lemma 3**   The rank of the matrix $(S_{ij})$ is $n - 1$.

*Proof*   By (3) the required rank is $\leq (n - 1)$. Suppose that the strict inequality holds. Then the set of solutions to $(S_{ij})x = 0$ is spanned by a set of at least two linearly independent vectors. Thus there is $q \neq \lambda p$, such that

$(S_{ij})q = 0$. In other words, if the prices are changed so that $dp_j = q_j$, then the relative prices change, but $dS_i = \sum_j S_{ij}q_j = 0$, which contradicts (A3). Therefore the assertion follows.

## III. Stabilizing Income Effects

At each price $p$, which is not an equilibrium price, there are excess demands and excess supplies as represented by $Z(p)$. We suppose that the price adjustment rule is

(A4)        $\dot{p}_j = Z_j(p), \qquad j = 1, 2, \ldots, n,$

which is the usual version of the Walrasian *tâtonnement*. By virtue of (A1) and (A2), $Z_j(p)$ is continuous with continuous first-order partial derivatives and hence, there is a solution $p(t) = p(t; p^0)$, which is unique and continuous with respect to the initial point $p^0 > 0$. To guarantee that $p(t) > 0$ for all $t$, given $p^0 > 0$, we assume:

(A5)    There is $e > 0$ corresponding to $\delta > 0$, such that $\| p \| \geq \delta$ and $p_j \leq e$ implies $Z_j(p) > 0$.

Note that the solution to (A4) remains bounded over time; in fact:

**Lemma 4**    $\| p(t; p^0) \| = \| p^0 \|$ for all $t$, where $\| p \|^2 = \sum p_j^2$.

*Proof*

$$\frac{d}{dt}(\| p(t; p^0) \|^2) = \frac{d}{dt}\sum p_j^2(t) = 2\sum p_j Z_j(p(t)) \qquad \text{by (A4)}$$

$$= 0 \qquad \text{by Walras' law.}$$

Define $V(p(t)) = \frac{1}{2}\sum Z_j^2(p(t))$. Then:

**Lemma 5**    $V(p) = 0$ if and only if $p \in E$, the set of equilibrium price vectors; $V(p) > 0$ otherwise. Further, $\dot{V}(p(t))$ exists.

*Proof* Immediate.

From the definition of $Z(p)$, it follows that

$$Z_{ij} = D_{ij} - S_{ij}. \tag{4}$$

Also $D_{ij} = \sum_k d_{ij}^k$, by definition. From the usual Slutsky relation (see Hicks [4]),

$$d_{ij}^k = c_{ij}^k - \left(d_j^k - w_j^k - \sum_r \alpha_{kr}s_{rj}\right)d_{iI}^k \tag{5}$$

where $c_{ij}^k$ is the pure substitution term and $z_j^k = d_j^k - w_j^k - \sum_r \alpha_{kr}s_{kr}$, say, may be interpreted as the net demand for good $j$ by individual $k$; also $d_{iI}^k$

is the marginal propensity to consume good $i$ by individual $k$. The income term may be written $z_j^k d_{iI}^k$. Income effects are defined to be stabilizing, provided they help decrease $V(t)$ over time; i.e.,

$$Z'\left(\sum_k z_j^k d_{iI}^k\right)Z \geq 0.$$

**Lemma 6**  Income effects are stabilizing implies that $\dot{V}(t) < 0$ for $p(t) \notin E$.

*Proof*  Note that

$$\dot{V}(p(t)) = \sum_i \sum_j Z_i Z_{ij} Z_j \qquad \text{by (A4)}$$

$$= \sum_i \sum_j Z_i \left(\sum_k c_{ij}^k\right) Z_j - \sum_i \sum_j Z_i \left(\sum_k z_j^k d_{iI}^k\right) Z_j - \sum_i \sum_j Z_i S_{ij} Z_j$$

by virtue of (4) and (5).

From the properties of the substitution terms, $Z'(c_{ij}^k)Z \leq 0$ for each $k$. Also from Lemma 2, $Z'(S_{ij})Z \geq 0$ and stabilizing income effects yield $Z'(\sum_k z_j^k d_{iI}^k)Z \geq 0$.

Consider the matrix $(c_{ij}^k)$: it is the Jacobian of the compensated demand function for the individual $k$. The uniqueness of demand functions imply that rank$(c_{ij}^k) = n - 1$. Thus $Z'(c_{ij}^k)Z < 0$ unless $Z = p$,[1] but $Z = p$ is impossible, since $Z$ denotes excess demands at prices $p > 0$, and consists of positive and negative elements. Thus $Z'(c_{ij}^k)Z < 0$ for all $k$. A similar argument and Lemma 3 imply that $Z'(S_{ij})Z > 0$. Thus $\dot{V}(p(t)) < 0$ provided $Z(p(t)) \neq 0$ or $p(t) \notin E$.

Finally, to complete the argument, one must show that the solution path $p(t; p^0)$ to (A4) does converge to the set of equilibrium price vectors, under the conditions of Lemma 6. Actually:

**Lemma 7**  Every limiting point to the solution path $p(t; p^0)$ is an equilibrium price vector.[2]

---

[1] Let $C = (c_{ij}^k)$. Then $C$ is negative semidefinite. Suppose that $Z'CZ = 0$ but $Z'C \neq 0$. For any vector $y$ and any scalar $t$, we have: $0 \geq (y + tZ)'C(y + tZ) = y'Cy + 2tZ'Cy + t^2 Z'CZ = y'Cy + 2tZ'Cy$. Since $Z'C \neq 0$, choose $y$ such that $y' = Z'C$ and $t$ very large and positive; then $0 \geq y'Cy + 2ty'y > 0$: a contradiction. Thus $Z'CZ = 0$ implies $Z'C = 0$.

[2] Although this result is widely used, there seems to be some confusion regarding the proof and what is required to yield convergence. For instance, ". . .the path $p(t, p^0)$ is bounded so, since $V(\ )$ is taken as continuous, it too is bounded" [2, p. 273]. This does not give the true role of the bounded path. The boundedness of $V(\ )$ is guaranteed by definition where $V(p(t)) > 0$, and this is the only bound required since $V(p(t))$ is usually shown to be monotonic decreasing. The boundedness of the solution path is needed to guarantee the existence of limit points.

*Proof* See Uzawa [13]. Briefly, the proof is as follows. Under the conditions of Lemma 6, $V(t)$ is decreasing and bounded below by 0. Hence $\lim V(t)$ exists and is, say, $V^*$. By Lemma 4 the solution path $p(t; p^0)$ is bounded, and thus convergent subsequences exist. Let $p(t_s)$ be one such with $p^*$ as the limit point. Consider $p(t; p^*)$, the solution path with $p^*$ as the initial point. Then

$$V^* = \lim_{s \to \infty} V(t_s) = \lim_{s \to \infty} V(p(t_s; p^0)) = \lim_{s \to \infty} V(p(t + t_s; p^0))$$

$$= \lim_{s \to \infty} V(p(t; p(t_s; p^0)))$$

$$= V(p(t; p^*)) \qquad \text{for any} \quad t > 0.$$

Thus along the path $p(t; p^*)$, $V$ remains constant at $V^*$; consequently, $\dot{V}(p^*) = 0$ or $p^*$ must be an equilibrium, and this proves the assertion.

We have assumed that income effects are stabilizing; we next deduce conditions under which this is true. These conditions will then guarantee the stability of equilibrium. Note that the supply functions of the producers provide no problems; it is the income effects which have to be well behaved for the stability result to follow. We limit our aim to the consideration of local stability; as will be obvious, this is difficult enough to guarantee.

For local stability, the matrix $(Z_{ij})$ will be evaluated at an equilibrium $p^*$. We are therefore searching for conditions under which

$$Z'(I_{ij})Z \geq 0 \qquad \text{where} \qquad I_{ij} = \sum_k z_j^{\,k}(p^*)d_{iI}^k(p^*).$$

We first look at a case suggested by Hicks [4], where at equilibrium, everyone has the same propensity to consume each commodity $i$. In other words,

$$d_{iI}^k = d_{iI}^m = \cdots = d_{iI} \qquad \text{for all} \quad k, m, \ldots . \tag{H}$$

Under (H),

$$I_{ij} = \sum_k z_j^{\,k}(p^*)d_{iI}$$

$$= d_{iI} \sum z_j^{\,k}(p^*) = d_{iI} Z_j(p^*) = 0 \qquad \text{for all } i, j.$$

Thus, income effects vanish in the aggregate. We have, therefore:

**Lemma 8** If every individual has the same propensity to consume each commodity $i$ at equilibrium, then (A4) is locally stable.

The quantitative restrictions we have on the matrix $(I_{ij})$ may be summed up in Lemma 9.

**Lemma 9** $p^{*\prime}(I_{ij}) = (I_{ij})p^* = 0.$

*Proof* From Walras' law $p'Z(p) = 0$; or, differentiating with respect to $p_j$, $\sum_i p_i Z_{ij} + Z_j = 0$. Evaluation at $p^*$ yields $p^{*\prime}(Z_{ij}) = 0$, and hence from

(4), $p^{*\prime}(D_{ij}) - p^{*\prime}(S_{ij}) = 0$; or, $p^{*\prime}(\sum_k c_{ij}^k) - p^{*\prime}(I_{ij}) = 0$ since $p^{*\prime}(S_{ij}) = 0$. Hence, from the property of the compensated terms, $p^{*\prime}(I_{ij}) = 0$. Similarly, from the homogeneity of the excess demands, $(Z_{ij})p^* = 0$; and as above, one may conclude $(I_{ij})p^* = 0$.

Lemma 8 dealt with the case of symmetric income effects. However, even if income effects are asymmetric, one might obtain stabilizing income effects, as we propose to show. For each commodity $j$, consider the set $B_j = \{k/z_j^k(p^*) > 0\}$, the net buyers of the commodity $j$. Note that it is not the case that for all $j$ that $B_j = \phi$; and for each $j$, there is $k \notin B_j$. This follows, since $\sum_k z_j^k(p^*) = 0$. Individuals not in $B_j$ may be treated as net sellers of the commodity $j$. Now,

$$I_{jj} = \sum_{k \in B_j} z_j^k d_{jI}^k + \sum_{k \notin B_j} z_j^k d_{jI}^k = \sum_{k \in B_j} z_j^k d_{jI}^k - \sum_{k \notin B_j} (-z_j^k) d_{jI}^k. \tag{6}$$

The first term in (6) may be identified as the net buyers' income effect and the second term as the net sellers' income effect. Consider an asymmetric situation where the net buyers' income effect is not weaker than the net sellers' income effect, so that from (6),

$$I_{jj} \geq 0, \qquad j = 1, 2, \ldots, n. \tag{J}$$

Even if (J) holds, and there are more than two goods, stabilizing income effects are not achieved. If there are two goods, then (J) together with Lemma 9 implies $I_{ij} \leq 0$, $i \neq j$, and stabilizing income effects follow. However, with more than two goods, this does not hold, Writing out the term $I_{ij}$, $i \neq j$, as

$$I_{ij} = \sum_{k \in B_j} z_j^k d_{iI}^k + \sum_{k \notin B_j} z_j^k d_{iI}^k,$$

we may suppose that the net buyers of a commodity $j$ have a relatively low propensity to consume commodity $i \neq j$; given this, one would be led to assume that

$$I_{ij} \leq 0 \qquad \text{for} \quad i \neq j. \tag{J'}$$

Thus (J') is an added restriction when there are more than two goods, and (J) together with (J') yields stabilizing income effects, as we shall show.

Let $M = \{j/I_{jj} = 0\}$. Then if $M \neq \phi$, Lemma 9 and (J') imply that $I_{kj} = I_{jk} = 0$ for all $k, j \in M$. Let $I = (I_{ij})_{\sim M}$; i.e., $i \notin M, j \notin M$. Then $Z'(I_{ij})Z = Z_{\sim M}IZ_{\sim M}$. In particular, let $I = (I_{ij})_1^r$, $r \leq n$ (that is, $I$ is the leading principal submatrix of $(I_{ij})$ of order $r$), and assume that $I$ is indecomposable. Then $p_{\sim M}^{*\prime}I = Ip_{\sim M}^* = 0$, by Lemma 9. Hence $I^* = (I_{ij})_1^{r-1}$ and $I^{*\prime}$ both have dominant positive diagonals, so that $I^* + I^{*\prime}$ has a dominant positive diagonal. Hence $x'(I^* + I^{*\prime})x \geq 0$, with equality only if $x = p_{\sim M}^*$. Thus $Z'(I_{ij})Z = Z_{\sim M}'I^*Z_{\sim M} \geq 0$, and stabilizing income effects obtain. Thus:

***Theorem 1*** If the net buyers' income effect is not weaker than the net sellers' income effect (J), and further, if the net buyers of a commodity $j$ are likely to have a small marginal propensity to consume the commodity $i \neq j$, so that (J') holds, then (A4) is locally stable.

The above perhaps indicates the difficulty of obtaining income effects that are stabilizing. Stabilizing income effects is too strong a condition to insist. on. In case we have $Z'(C_{ij} - I_{ij} - S_{ij})Z < 0$, stability would be guaranteed. Thus it seems better to seek conditions under which the income effects are outweighed by substitution effects.

## IV. On an Arrow–Hahn Conjecture

One well-known method of allowing for income effects is to assume that the Jacobian of the excess demand functions has a dominant negative diagonal. "The kind of result we need here is one that would allow us to deduce global stability from the postulate that the Jacobian of the excess supplies has everywhere $DD$. No such result is available ..." [2, p. 295]. We report in this section partial success in demonstrating the kind of result referred to above. We claim only partial success since, in assuming the most general form of the dominant diagonal hypothesis, the price adjustment rule had to be specialized somewhat. Alternatively we may interpret the result of this section as the study of a case where the variable speeds of adjustment yield dominant diagonals. Also an additional assumption is needed to bound the solution path. In addition to (A1) and (A2), we assume:

**(A4')** The price adjustment rule:

$$\dot{p}_j = h_j(p)Z_j(p), \qquad j = 2, \ldots, n$$
$$p_1 = 1$$

where $h_j(\ ) > 0$ for $p > 0$ and possesses continuous partial derivatives of the first order for all $j = 2, \ldots, n$.

**(A5')** There is $e > 0$ such that $\|p\| \geq 1$ and $p_j \leq e$ implies $Z_j(p) > 0$.

**(A6)** (i) $Z_{jj}(p) < 0, j = 2, \ldots, n$ for all $p > 0$.
(ii) $h_j(p)|Z_{jj}(p)| > \sum_{1 < k \neq j} h_k(p)|Z_{jk}(p)|, j = 2, \ldots, n$ for all $p > 0$.

(ii) guarantees that the Jacobian of the excess demand functions without the numéraire row and column has a dominant negative [by (i)] diagonal. Note that the weights are allowed to vary with the prices. This therefore describes a general form of the dominant diagonal hypothesis. In fact, if we choose to define $h_j(\ )$ by (A6)(ii), then this would be the most general form of the dominant diagonal hypothesis; but then the price adjustment rule would be somewhat special, as we indicated earlier.

**(A7)**  If $\|p\| \to \infty$ with $p_1 = 1$, then $Z_1(p) \to \infty$.

**(A8)**  There are functions $K_j(\|p\|, Z_j)$ and $D_j(\|p\|, Z_j)$ such that

$$D_j(\|p\|, Z_j) \leq h_j(p)/p_j \leq K_j(\|p\|, Z_j)$$

for all $j = 2, \ldots, n$ and $\|p\| > M$, a given positive number $Z_j > 0$ implies $K_j(\ ) \leq 1$ whereas $\|p\| > M$, $Z_j < 0$ implies $D_j(\ ) \geq 1$.

Assumptions (A7) and (A8) require special comment. (A7) is the so-called numéraire assumption [2, p. 208]. (A8) is crucial to the boundedness of the solution path to (A4'), as we shall see; that is satisfied by the case studied in ref. [2, p. 293]. Thus, if prices are large enough, then the speeds of adjustment $h_j(\ )$ must be *at least* as large as $p_j$ if the $j$th commodity is in excess supply, and *at most* as large as $p_j$ if the $j$th commodity is in excess demand. This is thus the second restriction that must be placed on the variable speeds of adjustment, the first being that they yield (A6).

We begin by noting that under our assumptions, there is a solution $p(t) = p(t; p^0)$ to (A4') which is unique and continuous with respect to the initial point $p^0 > 0$.

Define

$$V(p(t)) = V(t) = \max_{k \neq 1} |Z_k(p(t))| = |Z_j(p(t))|. \tag{7}$$

If there is only one $J$ satisfying (6), then derivatives exist and

$$\dot{V}(t) = (\operatorname{sgn} Z_j) \sum_k Z_{Jk} h_k Z_k \qquad \text{by (A4').} \tag{8}$$

At this stage we may indicate a result due to Arrow and Hahn [2, p. 234] which asserts that under (A6) and (A7) there is a unique equilibrium price $p^*$. We are now ready for:

**Lemma 10**  $p(t) \neq p^*$ implies $\dot{V}(t) < 0$ provided derivatives exist.

*Proof*  Suppose $p(t) \neq p^*$ and let $Z_J(p(t)) > 0$. If possible, let

$$\sum_k Z_{Jk} h_k Z_k \geq 0.$$

Then by (A6)(i),

$$|Z_{JJ} h_J Z_J| \leq |\sum_{1 < k \neq J} Z_{Jk} h_k Z_k| \leq \sum_{1 < k \neq J} |Z_{Jk}| |h_k Z_k| \leq |Z_J| \sum_{1 < k \neq J} |Z_{Jk}| h_k$$

or $|Z_{JJ}| h_J \leq \sum_{1 < k \neq J} |Z_{Jk}| h_k$, which contradicts (A6)(ii) for $j = J$. Thus $Z_J > 0$ implies $\sum_k Z_{Jk} h_k Z_k < 0$. Similarly, $Z_J < 0$ implies $\sum_k Z_{Jk} h_k Z_k > 0$. Hence the conclusion follows, by virtue of (8).

**Lemma 11**  $V(t)$ is monotone decreasing if $p(t) \neq p^*$.

*Proof* If derivatives exist, then the assertion follows from Lemma 10. If derivatives do not exist, then there is a set $S(t)$, such that $S(t) = \{j/V(t) = |Z_j(p(t))|\}$ and there are $j$, $k$ $j \neq k$, but $j$, $k \in S(t)$. This is the only case when derivatives may not exist. Now for $h > 0$ and small, $S(t + h) \subseteq S(t)$. Thus let $J$ be such that $V(t + h) = |Z_J(t + h)|$; hence $J \in S(t + h)$. But for $h > 0$ and sufficiently small, $J \in S(t)$. Hence

$$\lim_{h \to +0} \frac{V(t + h) - V(t)}{h} = \lim_{h \to +0} \frac{|Z_J(t + h)| - |Z_J(t)|}{h}$$

$$= \frac{d}{dt}(|Z_J(t)|) \qquad \text{for some } J \in S(t)$$

$$< 0 \qquad \qquad \text{by Lemma 10.}$$

Consequently, $V(t + h) < V(t)$ for $h > 0$ and sufficiently small. However, $V(t)$ is continuous in $t$; and so $V(t + h) < V(t)$ for any $h > 0$ and the assertion follows.

As things stand, the next step would be to demonstrate the boundedness of the solution path. Since we shall show that the equilibrium is a limit point of the solution path, an argument to guarantee the boundedness of the solution path becomes necessary. The crucial nature of (A7) and (A8) will now be made clear.

**Lemma 12** Under (A7) and (A8), the solution path $p(t, p^0)$ to (A4′) is bounded.

*Proof* Under (A5′), we may note that $p_j(t) \geq e > 0$ for all $j$, for all $t$. If possible, let $\|p(t)\| \to \infty$ as $t \to \infty$ with $p_1 = 1$. Then $p(t) \geq M$ for all $t > T(M)$. Hence,

$$\Sigma \dot{p}_j = \sum h_j(p)Z_j(p)$$
$$\leq \sum p_j Z_j(p) \qquad \text{by (A8)}$$
$$= -Z_1(p) \qquad \text{by Walras' law}$$
$$< 0 \qquad \text{by (A7),}$$

so that $\sum \dot{p}_j(t) < 0$ for all $t > T(M)$. Since $p(t) > 0$, this contradicts the fact that $\|p(t)\| \to \infty$ as $t \to \infty$.

Now, since limit points exist (Lemma 12) and since $V(t)$ is monotone decreasing and bounded below, one may use the argument in the proof of Lemma 7 and conclude that every limit point is an equilibrium. Recall, however, that there is a unique equilibrium under these assumptions. We have therefore demonstrated the validity of:

***Theorem 2*** Under (A1), (A2), (A5′), (A6), (A7), and (A8) the adjustment mechanism (A4′) is globally stable.

A special case of this result occurs when $h_j(p) = p_j, j = 2, \ldots, n$. We would like at this stage to comment on the special diagonal dominance used in ref. [2, p. 295]. The condition termed $D^*D^*$ says that

$$
\begin{aligned}
& e_{ii}(p) < 0, & i = 2, \ldots, n, \quad p > 0 \\
& |e_{ii}(p)| > \sum_{1 < j \neq i} |e_{ij}(p)|, & i = 2, \ldots, n
\end{aligned}
\tag{10}
$$

where $e_{ij}(p) = p_j D_{ij}/D_i$, and $D_i(p) > 0$ is the market demand for the good $i$ at prices $p$. The model under consideration is one of pure exchange. It is clear that in a pure exchange model

$$
\text{(A6) with } h_j(p) = p_j \Leftrightarrow \text{(10)}.
$$

However, for a production model, $Z_{ij} \neq D_{ij}$. To extend (10) to a production model, the authors consider the following added restriction: "The numéraire good does not enter into production, nor is it produced; also $S_{ij}(p) < 0$, $i \neq j$, for all $p > 0$" [2, p. 294]. Thus, Arrow and Hahn have two sets of assumptions: (10) for the demand side, and the above for the production side. Note that the production side assumption is like assuming gross substitutes in production. In our scheme, we assume that the $DD$ hypothesis is satisfied by the entire system. It is an easy exercise to check that (10) together with the latter Arrow and Hahn assumption implies (A6) with $h_j(p) = p_j$. It is weaker, therefore, to assume that (A6) holds.

Finally, we may conclude by summarizing the result of this section in the following manner.

If prices adjust according to

$$
\begin{aligned}
\dot{p}_j &= h_j(p)Z_j(p), & j = 2, \ldots, n \\
p_1 &= 1
\end{aligned}
$$

where the speeds of adjustment $h_j(p)$ in general depend on $p$ and are such that the dominant diagonal conditions are satisfied with the $h_j(p)$'s as weights, then the unique competitive equilibrium is globally stable, provided the solution path is bounded. Boundedness may be ensured by an assumption like (A8).

## V. The Leontief Model

In the preceding sections we used the assumptions of strictly decreasing returns to scale in production. If one had constant returns to scale, the above framework would be inapplicable since then the supply functions are not well defined. A treatment of such a case is given by Morishima [8] and Arrow and

Hahn [2]. In the latter the authors consider a particularly simple model of this type: one with a single primary factor. Whereas Morishima followed Walras [14] in restricting the tâtonnement to the market for factors, Arrow and Hahn consider an adjustment in the market for goods.[3] In a later model, Morishima [8] does consider simultaneous tâtonnement in the factor and goods markets where the prices in the goods market adjust according to the level of excess demand. Let us first introduce the assumptions of the model we are about to study:

(A9)   If $y_j \in Y_j \le R_{n+1}$, then $ky_j \in Y_j$ for any $k > 0$, $j = 1, 2, \ldots, n$.

(A10)   $y_j \in Y_j$ implies that $y_{jj} \ge 0$, $y_{rj} \le 0$, $y_{0j} < 0$, $r \ne j$.

(A11)   For each $j$ there is $y_j \in Y_j$ such that $\sum_{r \ne 0} y_{rj} > 0$.

(A12)   Households supply labor only; this is the only primary factor, labeled 0. All households have a demand function $d^h(p) = d^h(p_0, p_1, \ldots, p_n)$ which is homogeneous of degree zero in the prices.

We may explain the above in the following terms. The $Y_j$ denotes the production possibility set for the $j$th sector which produces good $j$. (A9) guarantees constant returns to scale in production. (A10) ensures that there is no joint production and that some labor is necessary to operate any process. (A11) may be interpreted as ensuring that the model is productive. Note that by virtue of (A9) we may so choose $y_j \in Y_j$ that $y_{jj} = 1$; i.e., one unit of good $j$ is produced by each process $y_j$. This has usually been defined to be the Leontief model in the literature. Define $C_j(p) = p_j - p'y_j$, $j = 1, 2, \ldots, n$. We further require that (see [2, p. 41]):

(A13)   (a)   For every $p > 0$, there is $y_j(p) \in Y_j$ such that

$$C_j^*(p) = p_j - p'y_j(p) \le p_j - p'y_j \quad \text{for all} \quad y_j, Y_j.$$

$C_j^*(p)$ is the minimum unit production cost for the good $j$ at prices $p$.

(b)   $C_j^*(p)$ is continuous for $p > 0$ for all $j = 1, 2, \ldots, n$.

(c)   There is no production at a negative profit and profits are zero in equilibrium:

(i)   $p_j \le C_j^*(p)$
(ii)   $p_j y_{jj} = C_j^*(p)y_{jj}$.

---

[3] Whereas Morishima [8] assumes fixed proportions in production, i.e., there is a single process for the production of each good, Arrow and Hahn [2] allow for many processes which operate under constant returns to scale. The two differ further in that, whereas Morishima allows for many primary factors, Arrow and Hahn limit considerations to the case where there is a single primary factor.

Under (A9)–(A13) there is a unique equilibrium price $p^* > 0$: for a proof of this result, see Arrow and Hahn [2, p. 236]. In the framework of this model, the following adjustment process is considered in [2]:[4]

(A14)
$$p_0 = 1$$
$$\dot{p}_j = H_j(C_j^*(p) - p_j), \quad j = 1, 2, \ldots, n$$

where $H_j(\ )$ is a sign-preserving continuous function with continuous partial derivatives.[5]

In ref. [2, p. 316], the argument goes as follows:

Let $m(p) = \max p_i/p_i^* = p_r/p_r^*$; then $p_r = m(p)p_r^* = C_r^*(m(p)p^*)$ from the homogeneity of the unit cost functions. *"To pass from $m(p)p^*$ to $p$, at least one price, namely that of the nonproduced input, must be lowered, so certainly $p_r = C_r^*(m(p)p^*) > C_r^*(p)$* [italics mine]."

The above argument is correct, provided we consider $m(p) = \max p_i/p_i^*$, $i = 0, 1, \ldots, n$; but $p_r/p_r^* = p_0/p_0^*$ is possible and then the analysis in ref. [2] falls through since the adjustment only occurs on $p_j$ for $j \neq 0$. Alternatively, if the maximum is taken only over the nonnuméraire goods, then the conclusion (see the italicized portion) does not hold. However, it is possible to correct the proof and this is what we do next.

Let

$$m(p) = \max_{i \neq 0} p_i/p_i^* = p_r/p_r^* \quad \text{and} \quad n(p) = \min_{i \neq 0} p_i/p_i^* = p_s/p_s^*.$$

Suppose $m(p) > 1$. Then $p_j \leq m(p)p_j^*, j = 1, 2, \ldots, n$, and since $p_0 = p_0^* = 1$ $p_0 < m(p)p_0^*$. Thus $p \leq m(p)p^*$ and hence,

$$C_r^*(p) < C_r^*(m(p)p^*) = m(p)p_r^* = p_r$$

---

[4] The adjustment is the same as the one used in ref. [9]. However, in ref. [9, p. 65, Assumption 9], the adjustment is taken to be instantaneous. In a fixed-coefficients model, where we have an indecomposable nonnegative matrix $A$ of material input coefficients and $w$ is the vector of labor requirements—i.e., $A = (a_{ij})$, $a_{ij}$ denotes the quantity of good $i$ used to produce one unit of the good $j$, and $w = (w_j)$, where $w_j$ is the labor requirement for the $j$th industry to produce 1 unit of the $j$th good—the adjustment mechanism reduces to

$$\dot{p} = H(p'(I - A) - w).$$

This type of mechanism makes sense only if the auctioneer has no knowledge of the matrix $A$ and the vector $w$. For if the auctioneer knows these quantities, then solving for the equilibrium price is a relatively straightforward matter. The point to be noted is that even if there is one with complete information about these coefficients, the economy is able to attain the equilibrium price by following the above process, where each sector revises prices in the manner indicated.

[5] Note that the solution to the system (A14) exists and is unique and continuous with respect to the initial point. Also note that the solution remains positive over time, since $p_j = 0$ implies $\dot{p}_j > 0$.

so that $\dot{p}_r < 0$. Note the dependence of this result on $m(p) > 1$. Next, let $m(p) \leq 1$. Then $n(p) \leq m(p) \leq 1$. We may exclude the case where $n(p) = m(p) = 1$, since then $p = p^*$. Hence $n(p) < 1$. Now, $p_j > n(p)p_j^*$, $j = 1, 2, \ldots, n$, and $p_0 > n(p)p_0^*$. Hence,

$$C_s^*(p) > C_s^*(n(p)p^*) = n(p)p_s^* = p_s$$

so that $\dot{p}_s > 0$. Now, let $V(p(t)) = \max_{i \neq 0} |(p_i/p_i^*) - 1|$. For simplicity, suppose that $\dot{V}$ exists; then

$$\dot{V} = \text{sgn}(p_j/p_j^* - 1)\dot{p}_j/\dot{p}_j^*.$$

If $p_j/p_j^* > 1$, then $j = r$ and $m(p) > 1$ so that $\dot{V} < 0$; if $p_j/p_j^* < 1$, then $j = s$ and $n(p) < 1$ so that $\dot{V} < 0$. Thus, provided derivatives exist, $\dot{V} < 0$ at disequilibrium, with $\dot{V} = 0$ only at equilibrium.

It now remains to consider the case when derivatives do not exist. The only case where this might happen is if the maximum does not occur for a single $j$. Then, as in Section IV, one may show that $V(t + h) < V(t)$ for $h > 0$ and small, and then use the continuity of $V(t)$ to conclude that $V(t)$ is monotonically decreasing at disequilibrium. Note that the solution remains bounded [for, if not, then some $p_j(t) \to \infty$ and hence $m(p(t)) = p_j/p_j^* > 1$ for $t$ large, and then $\dot{p}_j < 0$]. We may now use an argument similar to Lemma 7 and, noting the uniqueness of prices in this case, conclude that:

**Theorem 3** For the Leontief model, the unique equilibrium price is globally stable under an adjustment of the form (A14).

As noted earlier, this is the result that Arrow and Hahn [2] claim. We see now that their claim was justified. However, the validity of (A14) as a true explanation of how prices are formed depends crucially on there being only one nonproduced input. If we believe this to be the case, then in (A14) we have the rudiments of a markup theory of price formation, as Arrow and Hahn [2, p. 316] note.

### ACKNOWLEDGMENTS

I am deeply indebted to Professor Lionel W. McKenzie for guidance, to Professor Henry Y. Wan, Jr., for helpful comments, and to the Woodrow Wilson National Fellowship Foundation for financial support. This chapter forms a part of my thesis submitted to the University of Rochester in Spring 1973.

### REFERENCES

1. Arrow, K. J., Block, H. D., and Hurwicz, L., "On the Stability of the Competitive Equilibrium, II," *Econometrica* **27** (January 1959), 82–110.
2. Arrow, K. J., and Hahn, F. H., *General Competitive Analysis*. San Francisco: Holden-Day, 1971.

3. Debreu, G., *Theory of Value*. New York: Wiley, 1959.
4. Hicks, J. R., *Value and Capital* (2nd ed.). London and New York: Oxford Univ. Press, 1946.
5. McKenzie, L. W., " Stability of Equilibrium and the Value of Positive Excess Demand," *Econometrica* **28** (July 1960), 606–617.
6. Metzler, L. A., "Stability of Multiple Markets: The Hicks Conditions," *Econometrica* **13** (October 1945), 277–293.
7. Morishima, M., " A Generalization of the Gross Substitute System," *Review of Economic Studies* **37** (April 1970), 177–187.
8. Morishima, M., " A Reconsideration of the Walras–Cassel–Leontief Model of General Equilibrium," in *Mathematical Methods in Social Sciences* (K. Arrow, S. Karlin, and H. Scarf, eds.). Stanford, California: Stanford Univ. Press, 1959.
9. Mukherji, A., "On Complementarity and Stability," *Journal of Economic Theory* **4** (June 1972), 442–458.
10. Ohyama, M., " On the Stability of Generalized Metzlerian Stability," *Review of Economic Studies* **39** (April 1972), 193–205.
11. Rader, T., "General Equilibrium Theory with Complementary Factors," *Journal of Economic Theory.* **4**, (June, 1972), 372–31.
12. Rader, T., " Normally, Factor Inputs Are Never Gross Substitutes," *Journal of Political Economy* **76** (January/February, 1968), 38–43.
13. Uzawa H., "The Stability of Dynamic Economic Processes," *Econometrica* **29** (October 1961), 617–632.
14. Walras, L., *Elements of Pure Economics* (W. Jaffe, transl.). London: Allen and Unwin, 1954.

# STABILITY OF MARKETS WITH PUBLIC GOODS

*A Case of Gross Substitutability*

*Takashi Negishi*

*University of Tokyo*

## I

One of the most important contributions to mathematical economics made by Metzler is the study of the stability of multiple markets under the assumption of gross substitutability. Following the argument of Samuelson [15] to the effect that the Hicksian stability condition is, in general, neither necessary nor sufficient for true dynamic stability, Metzler [10] skillfully proved that the Hicksian perfect stability condition is necessary and sufficient for dynamic stability in the small if all the commodities are gross substitutes. This achievement in 1945 was the starting point for many mathematical economists when they began to study the stability problem in the late 1950's. First, it was proved that gross substitutability is sufficient for Hicksian perfect stability and, therefore, for local dynamic stability. Secondly, such stability ensured by gross substitutability was shown to be unaffected by the introduction of certain expectations of future prices as well as trading out of equilibrium (see Negishi [12]).

Apart from attempts to introduce money into the model (e.g., Arrow and Hahn [2]), one of the problems of current interest in the study of stability of multiple markets is the introduction of public goods—in particular, whether their supply is optimal at the resulting equilibrium.[1] One may consider, for example, the stability of the adjustment process in which the planning agency decides the amount of public goods to be supplied. The agency considers the marginal valuations of those goods as reported by consumers and firms, on the one hand, and the marginal production costs, on the other, while simultaneously the markets for private goods are adjusted by price changes according to excess demands. If consumers and firms reveal their valuation of public goods honestly, the supply of public goods can be Pareto optimal at the resulting equilibrium, with the sum of individual marginal valuations being equal to the marginal cost. Because of nonexcludability, however, rational individuals will understate their preferences for public goods. Furthermore, there is no clear incentive for, or pressure on, the planning agency to supply the optimal amount of public goods, even if individual preferences are honestly revealed.[2]

In the case of local public goods, however, individuals will voluntarily reveal their preferences for public goods by moving to the community whose local government best satisfies their demands [17]. As for the criterion of local governments' policy, the principle of fiscal profitability is suggested [9]. In our opinion, the incentive to adopt this principle should be found not in the maximum profit to the local treasury but in the maximum benefit to the local taxpayers. Perhaps it should be pointed out that the principle, as such, is logically independent of the movement of individuals among districts, i.e., voting with one's feet. As a matter of fact, it holds even for a single-district economy. Local governments are induced to follow the principle of fiscal profitability, not directly by the voting of people moving with their feet but by the political pressure of local taxpayers who do not move among districts.

In ref. [14] we analyzed a model of interaction among local districts through the movement of consumers and firms (voting with one's feet) and in which the local government's decision was based on fiscal profitability under the pressure of local taxpayers. Pareto optimality of the supply of public goods was demonstrated under the assumptions that (i) individual preferences for local public goods are revealed through demand for the services of land in the same local district, (ii) local taxes to cover the cost of public goods are proportional to the value of land so as to make local governments adopt the fiscal profitability principle, and (iii) local governments consider, as a rule of thumb, the average and marginal effects of their decisions to be identical. The stability of

---

[1] For literature on the stability of tâtonnement with public goods, see Malinvaud [8].
[2] Downs [4] and Negishi [13] emphasized this point.

adjustment processes was proved in ref. [14] only in the case of identical consumers.[3]

The aim of this chapter is to consider the stability of the adjustment process of the supplies of local public goods determined by voting with one's feet and fiscal profitability under alternative conditions, viz., gross substitutability. Assuming that private goods are gross substitutes and the markets for those goods are stable for any given amount of public goods, stability will be shown to be unaffected by the introduction of the adjustment of public goods to the optimal equilibrium amount. Section II will summarize the model of the adjustment of the supply of local public goods as considered in ref. [14]. After some theorems on stability and gross substitutability are introduced in Section III, extensions are attempted to cover the case of an economy with public goods as developed in Section II. Local stability is proved in Section IV, while global stability is considered in Section V.

## II

Let us sketch the model of an economy with localized public goods determined by voting with one's feet and fiscal profitability, as considered in ref. [14].

The utility of the $i$th consumer is assumed to be given by a continuously differentiable function

$$U_i = U_i(x_i, l_i, t_{i1}G_1, \ldots, t_{in}G_n),\tag{1}$$

and the production function of the $j$th firm is assumed to be a continuously differentiable function

$$x_j' = F_j(l_j', t_{j1}'G_1, \ldots, t_{jn}'G_n)\tag{2}$$

where $x_i$, $l_i$, and $t_{ik}$, are, respectively, the quantity of the private good produced, labor services (including leisure), and the services of land in the $k$th local district—all consumed by the $i$th consumer; $x_j'$, $l_j'$, and $t_{jk}'$ are, in turn, the amount of the private good produced, labor services used, and the services of land in the $k$th local district—all used by the $j$th firm; and $G_k$ is the quantity of the public good supplied in the $k$th district. Private-sector competitive behavior implies:

---

[3] It was also proved in the case of identical and homogeneous utility functions for all consumers, which is formally identical with the case of identical consumers, i.e., identical tastes and budget.

*Assumption 1*

$$(\partial U_i/\partial G_k)/(\partial U_i/\partial t_{ik}) = t_{ik}/G_k, \qquad (\partial F_j/\partial G_k)/(\partial F_j/\partial t'_{jk}) = t'_{jk}/G_k.$$

This assumption implies that the amount of improved land in terms of efficiency units is proportional to the amount of public expenditure on land, and that land, as such, stripped of all social overhead capital, is of no use in consumption and production. Alternatively, one can say that the benefits of public goods one can enjoy are proportional to the amount of land services purchased in the district where the good is supplied. Assumption 1 enables consumers and firms to reveal their valuation of public goods through their demand for the services of land, i.e., voting with one's feet.

The production function of the public good in the $k$th district is denoted by a continuously differentiable function

$$G_k = f_k(l''_k) \tag{3}$$

where $l''_k$ is the amount of labor service used in its production.

Both consumers and firms are assumed to be competitive. The $j$th firm maximizes its profit

$$px_j' - wl_j' - \sum_k r_k t'_{jk}$$

with respect to $x_j'$, $l_j'$, and $t'_{jk}$, given the production function (2), where $p$, $w$, and $r_k$ are, respectively, the price of the produced private good, the wage rate, and rent in the $k$th district. Profits are exhaustively distributed to consumers in a specified way.

The $i$th consumer maximizes utility (1) with respect to $x_i$, $l_i$, and $t_{ik}$ subject to

$$px_i + wl_i + \sum_k r_k t_{ik} = Q_i + w\bar{l}_i + \sum_k r_k \bar{l}_{ik} - \sum_k (\bar{l}_{ik}/\sum_i \bar{l}_{ik})wl''_k \tag{4}$$

where $Q_i$, $\bar{l}_i$, and $\bar{l}_{ik}$ are, respectively, the $i$th consumer's receipt of firms' profits, his initial endowment of labor, and his initial endowment of land in the $k$th district. The last term on the right-hand side of (4) signifies the land tax imposed on the $i$th consumer so as to cover the cost of public goods.

*Assumption 2*   Local public expenditures are financed by proportional taxes on land.

The implication of this assumption for the decision making of local governments is that they try to maximize the total net value of land after deducting the land tax to cover the cost of public goods. This is the principle of fiscal profitability, i.e., the maximization of the benefit of local taxpayers. Therefore, subject to the production function (3),

$$V_k(G_k) - wl''_k \tag{5}$$

must be maximized, where $V_k$ signifies the total value of land in the $k$th district, perceived by the $k$th local government as a function of public expenditure.

*Assumption 3* $\partial V_k/\partial G_k$ is estimated, as a rule of thumb, by $r_k \sum_i \bar{t}_{ik}/G_k$ by the $k$th local government.

Then we have

$$r_k \sum_i t_{ik}/G_k = w/(\partial f_k/\partial l_k'') \tag{6}$$

from the maximization of (5).

Competitive behavior of consumers and firms, coupled with the local governments' policy based on fiscal profitability, determines the excess demands for the produced private good, labor services, and services of land in each district as functions of $p$, $w$, and $r_k$; i.e.,

$$X(p, w, r_1, \ldots, r_n, G_1(r_1, w), \ldots, G_n(r_n, w)) \equiv \sum_i x_i - \sum_j x_j'$$

$$L(p, w, r_1, \ldots, r_n, G_1(r_1, w), \ldots, G_n(r_n, w)) \equiv \sum_i l_i + \sum_j l_j' + \sum_k l_k'' - \sum_i \bar{l}_i$$

$$T_k(p, w, r_1, \ldots, r_n, G_1(r_1, w), \ldots, G_n(r_n, w)) \equiv \sum_i t_i + \sum_j t_{jk}' - \sum_i \bar{t}_{ik}$$

$$k = 1, \ldots, n, \tag{7}$$

where $G_k(r_k, w)$ signifies the quantity of public goods supplied in the $k$th district.

Equilibrium $(p, w, r_1, \ldots, r_n)$ is defined by

$$X(p, w, r_1, \ldots, r_n, G_1(r_1, w), \ldots, G_n(r_n, w)) = 0$$

$$L(p, w, r_1, \ldots, r_n, G_1(r_1, w), \ldots, G_n(r_n, w)) = 0$$

$$T_k(p, w, r_1, \ldots, r_n, G_1(r_1, w), \ldots, G_n(r_n, w)) = 0, \qquad k = 1, \ldots, n.$$

It can easily be shown that conditions for Pareto optimality are satisfied in equilibrium. In particular, the optimal condition for the supply of public goods derived by Samuelson [16] and Kaizuka [7], viz., the sum of the individual marginal rates of substitution between public and private goods is equal to the marginal rate of transformation between these goods, is obtained by the use of Assumption 1 and Eq. (6) (see Negishi [14]).

## III

Before we discuss the stability of equilibrium just defined, i.e., the convergence of the adjustment process to equilibrium, it may be convenient to summarize some of the results so far established in the case of gross substitutability.

Consider the following adjustment process:

$$dp_i/dt = E_i(p_1, \ldots, p_n), \qquad i = 1, \ldots, n-1,$$
$$p_n \equiv 1$$
(8)

where $p_i$ and $E_i$ signify the price and excess demand, respectively, of the $i$th good at time $t$.

The assumption of gross substitutability is:

**Assumption 4**  Either $\partial E_i/\partial p_j > 0$, $i \neq j$, $i = 1, \ldots, n$, $j = 1, \ldots, n-1$, or $\partial E_i/\partial p_j > 0$, $i \neq j$, $i = 1, \ldots, n-1$, $j = 1, \ldots, n$.

The first lemma we have is the one on local stability, i.e., the convergence of the solution of (8) to equilibrium prices such that all $E_i = 0$ when starting from a sufficiently small neighborhood of equilibrium:

**Lemma 1**  If the $E_i$'s are homogeneous functions of degree zero and Walras' law $\sum_i p_i E_i \equiv 0$ is satisfied, then solutions of (8) are locally stable under Assumption 4 (gross substitutability) [5, 11, 3].

To prove the global stability of solutions of (8), it is sufficient to show that the domain of $p_i$'s is bounded and that there exists a continuous function of $p_i$'s which decreases through time [6]. Among many proofs of global stability, we have in particular:

**Lemma 2**  If the $E_i$'s are homogeneous functions of degree zero and Walras' law holds, solutions of (8) are globally stable under Assumption 4 [1].

## IV

Equilibrium $(p, w, r_1, \ldots, r_n)$ defined in Section II may be established through the following adjustment process of prices:

$$dp/dt = X(p, l, r_1, \ldots, r_n, G_1(r_1, l), \ldots, G_n(r_n, l))$$
$$dr_k/dt = T_k(p, l, r_1, \ldots, r_n, G_1(r_1, l), \ldots, G_n(r_n, l)), \qquad k = 1, \ldots, n.$$
(9)

Since $G_k$, $X$, $L$, and $T_k$ are homogeneous functions of degree zero and Walras' law $(pX + wL + \sum_k r_k T_k \equiv 0)$ is satisfied, prices can be normalized so as to make $w \equiv 1$.

Let us assume quasi-gross substitutability, i.e.:

**Assumption 5**  For any given constant $G_1, \ldots, G_n$, $\partial X/\partial r_k > 0$, $k = 1, \ldots, n$, $\partial T_k/\partial r_s > 0$, $s = 1, \ldots, n$, $k = 1, \ldots, n$, $s \neq k$, $\partial T_k/\partial p > 0$, and either $\partial X/\partial w > 0$, $\partial T_k/\partial w > 0$, $k = 1, \ldots, n$, or $\partial L/\partial p > 0$, $\partial L/\partial r_k > 0$, $k = 1, \ldots, n$.

Then, by the use of Lemma 1, we can have the local stability of solutions of (9) if $G_k(r_k, l)$, $k = 1, \ldots, n$, are replaced by some constant $G_k$'s, say equilibrium values of $G_k$'s. Therefore, to prove the local stability of solutions of

(9), we have to show that gross substitutability is unaffected by the introduction of changes of $G_k$'s due to the changes of $r_k$'s.

First, consider the changes of $G_k$ induced by changes of $r_k$. Differentiating (6) with respect to $r_k$, we have

$$\frac{dG_k}{dr_k} = \frac{f_k' \overline{T}_k}{G_k[(r_k \overline{T}_k/G_k^2)f_k' - (w/(f_k')^2)f_k'']} = \frac{G_k/r_k}{[(1 - (r_k \overline{T}_k)^2)/G_k]f_k''} \tag{10}$$

where $\overline{T}_k = \sum_i \overline{t}_{ik}$ and $f_k' = \partial f_k/\partial l_k''$, and the like. Assuming $f_k' > 0$, $f_k'' < 0$, we see from (10) that

$$dG_k/dr_k > 0, \qquad dG_k/dr_k < G_k/r_k. \tag{11}$$

Then, we can show that the sign of the changes of $X$, $T_k$, and $L$ due to the changes of $r_k$, as assumed in Assumption 5, are unchanged even if $G_k$'s are allowed to change as $r_k$'s change. To see this, we must check the changes of individual components (like $x_i$, $x_j'$, $t_{ik}$, $t_{jk}'$, $l_i$, $l_j'$, $l_k''$) of $X$, $T_k$, and $L$, which are defined in (7).

For example, consider the case of $t_{jk}'$. This is determined by the maximization of profit subject to the production function (2). Since proportional changes of $G_s$ and $r_s$ do not change the equilibrium values of $G_s t_{js}'$, $t_{jk}'$, $k \neq s$, $x_j'$, and $l_j'$,[4] we have

$$-(\partial t_{jk}'/\partial r_s)_{G=c}/(\partial t_{jk}'/\partial G_s) = G_s/r_s$$

where $G = C$ signifies the constant $G_s$. Therefore, the change of $t_{jk}'$ when $G_s$ is allowed to change is

$$\partial t_{jk}'/\partial r_s = (\partial t_{jk}'/\partial r_s)_{G=c} + (\partial t_{jk}'/\partial G_s)(dG_s/dr_s)$$
$$= (\partial t_{jk}'/\partial r_s)_{G=c}\{1 - (r_s/G_s)(dG_s/dr_s)\},$$

which must be positive in view of Assumption 5 and (11). A similar relation is derived for the changes of $x_j'$ and $l_j'$. The ratio of changes with constant $G_s$ and variable $G_s$ is always

$$\{1 - (r_s/G_s)(dG_s/dr_s)\} > 0.$$

In the case of $t_{ik}$, which is determined by the maximization of utility (1) subject to the budget restraint (4), we note first that proportional changes of $G_s$ and $r_s$ do not change the value of the right-hand side of (4) if the changes are infinitesimal. This is because the $Q_i$ remain constant and, in view of (6), the change of the last term due to the change of $G_s$ is equal to the change of the next-to-the-last term due to the change of $r_s$. Then it is easy to see that

---

[4] Therefore $r_s t_{is}'$ and the profit of firms are also unchanged.

equilibrium values of $G_s t_{is}$, $t_{ik}$, $k \neq s$, $x_i$, $l_i$ are unchanged by proportional changes of $G_s$ and $r_s$.[5] Therefore we have

$$-(\partial t_{ik}/\partial r_s)_{G=c}/(\partial t_{ik}/\partial G_s) = G_s/r_s$$

and the ratio of the changes with constant $G_s$ and variable $G_s$ is again $\{1 - (r_s/G_s)(dG_s/dr_s)\}$. This is also true in the case of $x_i$ and $l_i$.

Collecting changes of all the individual components, we have

$$\partial X/\partial r_s = (\partial X/\partial r_s)_{G=c}\{1 - (r_s/G_s)(dG_s/dr_s)\} > 0$$
$$\partial T_k/\partial r_s = (\partial T_k/\partial r_s)_{G=c}\{1 - (r_s/G_s)(dG_s/dr_s)\} > 0 \qquad (12)$$
$$\partial L/\partial r_s = (\partial L/\partial r_s)_{G=c}\{1 - (r_s/G_s)(dG_s/dr_s)\} + (\partial l_s''/\partial r_s) > 0$$

from Assumption 5, since $\partial l_s''/\partial r_s > 0$ is derived by the differentiation of (6), taking note of $f_s' > 0, f_s'' < 0$. Therefore, gross substitutability (Assumption 4) is obtained with respect to (9), and applying Lemma 1, we have the following theorem.

***Theorem 1*** Solutions of (9) are locally stable under Assumption 5.

## V

To consider the global stability of (9) by the use of Lemma 2, we wish to know, in addition to (12), whether the gross substitutability of $X$ and the $T_k$'s with respect to $w$ hold even after adjustment of the quantities of the $G_k$'s due to the change of $w$.

Since $G_k(r_k, w)$ is a homogeneous function of degree zero, we have

$$\partial G_k/\partial w = -(r_k/w)(\partial G_k/\partial r_k)$$

and from (11)

$$dG_k/dw < 0. \qquad (13)$$

Therefore,

$$\partial X/\partial w = (\partial X/\partial w)_{G=c} + \sum_k (\partial X/\partial G_k)(dG_k/dw)$$
$$= (\partial X/\partial w)_{G=c} - \sum_k (\partial X/\partial r_k)_{G=c}(r_k/G_k)(dG_k/dw) > 0 \qquad (14)$$

in view of the arguments in the previous section and Assumption 5. Similarly, we have for $k \neq s$,

$$(\partial T_k/\partial G_s)(\partial G_s/\partial w) = -(\partial T_k/\partial r_s)_{G=c}(r_s/G_s)(dG_s/dw) > 0. \qquad (15)$$

---

[5] Therefore $r_s t_{is}$ and the value of consumer's expenditure [the left-hand side of (4)] remain unchanged.

In view of (12), (14), (15) and Assumption 5, which hold for any levels of the $G_k(r_k, l)$, we can conclude that the excess demand functions satisfy gross substitutability even after being adjusted for the changes of the quantities of public goods. Therefore, Lemma 2 implies global stability.

**Theorem 2**  Solutions of (9) are globally stable under Assumption 5.

Global stability of (9) implies local stability since equilibrium is unique under gross substitutability. As is well known, however, local stability obtained by the use of Lemma 1 actually implies the stability of a linearly approximated version of (9), which is not necessary, though sufficient, for the local stability of (9). Separate statement of the two theorems may thus be of some interest.

ACKNOWLEDGMENTS

The author is grateful to Professor Daniel McFadden and Mr. Osamu Ichioka for valuable comments.

REFERENCES

1. Arrow, K. J., Block, H. D., and Hurwicz, L., "On the Stability of the Competitive Equilibrium, II," *Econometrica* **26** (1959), 82–109.
2. Arrow, K. J., and Hahn, F. H., *General Competitive Analysis*. San Francisco: Holden-Day, 1971.
3. Arrow, K. J., and Hurwicz, L., "On the Stability of the Competitive Equilibrium, I.," *Econometrica* **26** (1958), 522–552.
4. Downs, A., *An Economic Theory of Democracy*. New York: Harper, 1957.
5. Hahn, F. H., "Gross Substitutes and the Dynamic Stability of General Equilibrium," *Econometrica* **26** (1958), 169–170.
6. Hahn, W., *Theorie und Anwendung der Direkten Methode von Lyapunov*. Berlin: Springer-Verlag, 1959.
7. Kaizuka, K., "Public Goods and Decentralization of Production," *Review of Economics and Statistics* **47** (1965), 118–120.
8. Malinvaud, E., "A Planning Approach to the Public Good Problem," *Swedish Journal of Economics* **73** (1971), 96–112.
9. Margolis, J., "The Demand for Urban Public Services," in *Issues in Urban Economics* (H. S. Perloff and L. Wingo, eds.). Baltimore: Johns Hopkins Press, 1968.
10. Metzler, L. A., "Stability of Multiple Markets: The Hicks Conditions," *Econometrica* **13** (1945), 277–292.
11. Negishi, T., "A Note on the Stability of An Economy Where All Goods Are Gross Substitutes," *Econometrica* **26** (1958), 445–447.
12. Negishi, T., "The Stability of a Competitive Economy: A Survey Article," *Econometrica* **30** (1962), 635–669.
13. Negishi, T., "Dynamics of the Public Expenditure in a Two-Party System," *Zeitschrift für Nationalökonomie* **31** (1971), 323–330.

14. Negishi, T., "Public Expenditure Determined by Voting with One's Feet and Fiscal Profitability," *Swedish Journal of Economics* **74** (1972), 452–458.
15. Samuelson, P. A., "The Stability of Equilibrium: Comparative Statics and Dynamics," *Econometrica* **9** (1941), 97–120.
16. Samuelson, P. A., "The Pure Theory of Public Expenditure," *Review of Economics and Statistics* **36** (1954), 387–389.
17. Tiebout, C., "The Pure Theory of Local Expenditure," *Journal of Political Economy* **64** (1956), 416–424.

# MARX AS MATHEMATICAL ECONOMIST

## Steady-State and Exponential Growth Equilibrium

Paul A. Samuelson

Massachusetts Institute of Technology

## Introduction

What do Marx and Metzler and Markov have in common? The German radical in London exile, the small-town Kansas boy, and the Petersburg aristocrat all worked with matrices of nonnegative elements.

So important are these in varied branches of science that we could speak of Marx–Leontief–Sraffa input–output matrices; of Metzler–Keynes–Chipman–Goodwin–Machlup–Johnson many-country multiplier matrices; of Metzler–Hicks–Mosak–Arrow–Hurwicz gross-substitutes matrices; of Markov–Frechet–Feller–Champernowne–Solow transition-probability matrices; and in pure mathematics itself, of Perron–Frobenius–Minkowski matrices $a$, with nonnegative elements, and the related $(I - a)^{-1}$ matrices with either positive or nonnegative elements. Or, divorcing them from any one application, we could call them Morishima–Solow–Dosso–McKenzie–Kemp matrices, after writers who explicated their general properties and applications. I am sure that I have omitted some important names and some important fields of application.[1]

---

[1] I vaguely recall that these matrices arose a century ago in connection with electric network theory.

Just when the New Left seems beginning to lose interest in the mature Marxism of *Das Kapital*—in favor of the *Grundrisse* and early philosophical writings of the Young Marx (alienation and all that)—the Leontief–Sraffa analytical literature is beginning to pay deserved homage to Marx's seminal contribution to the study of "simple reproduction" and "extended reproduction."

Tongue somewhat in cheek, I once referred to Karl Marx as "...from the viewpoint of pure economic theory...a minor Post-Ricardian...a not uninteresting precursor of Leontief's input–output of circular independence..." [1]. This is a bit less fulsome than Professor Morishima's recent evaluation: "...economists are in the wrong...in undervaluing Marx, who should in my opinion be ranked as high as Walras in the history of mathematical economics."[2] I do not know where Professor Morishima's tongue was when his quill penned these lines, but one can hope that the truth will eventually be found within these valid bounds!

Ignoring the fact that Marx is an important ideological figure, I propose in this essay to explore the nature of Marx's key analytical contribution to economic theory—one that links him directly with Leontief and modern Harrod–Robinson–Solow growth theory, and links him indirectly with Keynes, Metzler, Hicks, and the rest.

## I. Two Claims to Fame

I agree with Morishima (and I think, with Joan Robinson and Nicholas Kaldor) that Marx's Volume II models of simple and extended reproduction have in them the important germ of general equilibrium, static and dynamic. If Schumpeter reckoned Quesnay, by virtue of his *Tableau Économique*, among the four greatest economists of all time,[3] Marx's advance on Quesnay's *Tableau* should win him a place inside the Pantheon.

One's respect for Friedrich Engels as an editor goes up when one wades through Marx's Volume II, made up as it was of incomplete, overlapping, and tedious manuscripts and notes written at different times. However, by going three-quarters of the way through the book and singling out the tableau of simple reproduction found there (Tableau 1), one can claim immortal fame for Marx. This was presumably arrived at by Marx in the 1860's.

Before reviewing the meaning of the symbols, we may consolidate Marx's right to fame by adding his tableau of extended reproduction (Tableau 2),

---

[2] Morishima [2]. I salute this valuable work, and respect its differences of conclusions from my own. The quotation is from p. 1.

[3] After Walras, and along with Cournot and either Smith or Marshall (from his 1935–1936 Harvard lectures; I cannot remember which one of the last two).

TABLEAU 1

SIMPLE REPRODUCTION

---

Department I,
   Capital goods:     4000 of $c_1$ + **1000** of $v_1$ + **1000** of $s_1$ = 6000 total
Department II,
   Consumption goods: **2000** of $c_2$ +  500 of $v_2$ +  500 of $s_2$ = 3000 total

---

TABLEAU 2

EXPANDING REPRODUCTION
(at 10% Rate per Period)

---

Present period

   I:   4400 of $c_1$ + 1100 of $v_1$ + 1100 of $s_1$ = 6600

   II:  1600 of $c_2$ +  800 of $v_2$ +  800 of $s_2$ = 3200

Next period

   I:   4840 of $c_1$ + 1210 of $v_1$ + 1210 of $s_1$ = 7260 = $(1 + \tfrac{1}{10})$6600

   II:  1760 of $c_2$ +  880 of $v_2$ +  880 of $s_2$ = 3520 = $(1 + \tfrac{1}{10})$3200

---

taken almost from the book's end. This seems to come from the 1870's; and from the internal evidence of Marx's expositions, one senses that he had not mastered the intricacies of the extended reproduction case in quite the way he had that of simple reproduction.[4]

[4] These tableaux are taken, in trivially modified notations, from Volume II, Part III, Chapter XX, Section 11 (p. 459 of the 1909 Kerr edition), Chapter XXI, Section III (pp. 598 and 599). We might have been able to avoid some sterile disputes over Marx's "transformation" of his notions of "values" into his Volume III discussion of bourgeois prices if Marx had carried through a straightforward conversion of his p. 459 simple reproduction example, with its equal-organic composition or direct-labor intensity property, into the following alternative to his quoted p. 598 examples, recorded here for future reference.

TABLEAU 1*

---

   I:   4400 of $c_1$ + 1100 of $v_1$ + 1100 of $s_1$ = 6600
   II:  1600 of $c_2$ +  400 of $v_2$ +  400 of $s_2$ = 2400

---

This preserves the technology and initial labor supply of his simple reproduction example, but displays balanced growth of 10% per period. Thus in the following period 4400 would be replaced by 4400(1 + 0.1), and all entries would be amplified by the same (1 + 0.1) factor.

## II. Simple Reproduction

We may quickly explain Marx's terminology. Society is split into two industries or departments:

Department I, which produces a capital good—to keep notions simple, suppose it to be a raw material such as coal.

Department II, which produces a consumption good—corn for simplicity, to be consumed by workers for their needed sustenance and reproduction and by capitalists for their luxurious spending of surplus value or profit.

It will simplify exposition *not* to regard each department as the consolidation of several different capital-goods and consumption-goods industries. Though it would not be hard to replace coal by a durable machine, we avoid all problems of depreciation and periods of turnover by sticking with a raw material (such as coal) consumed completely in each production use.

Technically, corn is produced by labor and by coal. There is no great novelty here. But coal is produced by labor and by *itself*—a great leap out of what came to be known as the Ricardo–Austrian world (with "triangular hierarchy" of earlier and later stages of production) and into the Leontief–Sraffa world of circularly interdependent input–output.

### A. Explanation of Symbols

The $v_1$ and $v_2$ in Tableau 1 represent the 1000 and 500 of direct wage costs—"variable capitals" in standard Marx terminology. The $c_1$ and $c_2$ represent the 4000 and 2000 of raw material costs for coal—"constant capitals."

Marx assumes that "surplus" or capitalists' profit happens to be equal to the wage cost in each industry. As we would say, half of *all* values added goes to property and half to labor, with Net National Product happening to be distributed in equal shares.[5]

---

[5] Incidentally, Marx's long quibble with Adam Smith over Smith's assertion that "...the price of every commodity finally dissolves into one or another of these...parts (wages, profit, ...)" which "...are the final...sources of all income as well as exchange value" is refuted after all by Marx's own analysis! When Smith resolves price into $\sum (s + v)$, he obviously is referring to summed value added, even being quoted by Marx on p. 427 to say: "The value which laborers add to the material resolves itself...," Marx nodded, and failed to point out that Net National Product = 3000 of Department II's final corn; and *not* the gross total 6000 + 3000 of I and II together, since Smith would have agreed with Marx that it would involve double counting to count in the labor needed to produce corn's needed net coal *along* with that of coal itself. (I return to this dispute in footnote 12.)

Modern economists, Smith, and Marx would today agree that Net National Product equals both the sum of values added and the flow of *final* products:

$$\text{NNP} = \sum_{1}^{2} (v_j + s_j) = \sum_{1}^{2} \{(c_j + v_j + s_j) - c_j\}.$$

## B. Equal Rates of Surplus Value and of Profit

Because of the happy accident that this first example of Marx chances to involve equal "organic compositions of capital" in all departments (i.e., equal fractions of total cost in the form of direct wages, or equal $v_i/c_i$), we can luckily have equality in all industries of *both* the rates of surplus value $s_i/v_i$ and the usual bourgeois rates of profit or interest $s_i/(c_i + v_i)$—at 100% and 20%, respectively. That is, in Tableau 1,

$$1000/1000 = s_1/v_1 = 1.00 = \text{uniform } s/v = s_2/v_2 = 500/500 \quad (1a)$$

$$1000/(4000 + 1000) = s_1/(c_1 + v_1)$$

$$= 0.20 = \text{uniform } s/(c + v)$$

$$= s_2/(c_2 + v_2) = 500/(2000 + 500). \quad (1b)$$

## C. Zero Saving

The wage half of NNP, $\sum v_i$, goes to buy half of Department II's corn output for needed real-wage subsistence. Since there is no accumulation in simple reproduction, capitalists spend all their incomes, $\sum s_i$, on the other half of the corn, performing zero net saving. Hence,

$$\sum_1^2 (v_i + s_i) = c_2 + v_2 + s_2. \quad (2)$$

It follows then, by arithmetic tautology, that the total of coal used up in all industries, $\sum c_i$, must just equal all of Department I's coal production. Or (2) implies

$$\sum_1^2 c_i = c_1 + v_1 + s_1, \quad (3)$$

since by definition

$$\sum_1^2 (v_i + s_i) + \sum_1^2 c_i \equiv \sum_1^2 (c_i + v_i + s_i). \quad (4)$$

---

Ricardo, the Physiocrats, and other classical economists would, in certain moods, regard subsistence wages as a cost not unlike that involved for coal; hence, they would subtract from NNP labor-subsistence costs, $\sum v_i$, to get Neat Product, *Produit Net*, or Net–Net National Product:

$$\text{NNNP} = \sum_1^2 s_j = \sum (\{(c_j + v_j + s_j) - c_j\} - \sum v_j).$$

Fortunately, Marx's vendetta with Smith and his predecessors led him, in this case, to the pure gold of simple and extended reproduction.

Marx clearly sees, and somewhat belabors, a further implication of either (2) or (3): namely, simple reproduction requires

$$c_2 = v_1 + s_1. \tag{5}$$

That is why in Tableau 1 I wrote these numbers in boldface, so that the reader could see their equivalence. Since the sum of the first column equals the sum of the first row's terms, striking out the upper-left-hand element shared in common by the row and column, $4000 = c_1$, gives us this equivalence.

### D. CHANGING THE RATE OF "EXPLOITATION"

Suppose that, by some mechanism (not well explained by Marx), workers are now to get a lower subsistence wage. Then there must result a higher rate of surplus value and of profit—even if technology remains unchanged.

Thus, suppose the same laborers can now be made to work for wages low enough to give them only 1200 rather than 1500 of the producible corn. Then we must now have a rate of surplus value of 150% rather than 100%. Similarly, with *fully* as much insight, we can say that the rate of profit must now be 25% rather than 20%. To see this, calculate

$$(3000 - 1200)/1200 = 1.50 > 1.00 = 1500/1500$$
$$(3000 - 1200)/(6000 + 1200) = 0.25 > 0.20 = 1500/(6000 + 1500).$$

In this special case of equal organic compositions of capital, the price ratio of a ton of coal relative to a bushel of corn will be unaffected by a change in the profit rate. If, instead, corn were more labor intensive than coal (as in Marx's Tableau 2, where $v_2/c_2 > v_1/c_1$), a rise in the rate of profit would raise the market price of coal relative to that of corn. But in no case could a change in the real wage and a rise in (the equalized-across-industries) rate of surplus value alter in any way the ratio of corn's Volume I "value" to coal's "value." This ratio will still remain equal to the ratio of embodied total labor contents ("direct" and "indirect") of the two goods.

I recall no evidence that Marx ever knew how to calculate the infinite-term matrix series that decomposes each good into its total labor content—namely, the matrix series

$$a_0 + a_0 a + a_0 a^2 + \cdots$$

where $a_0$ is the row vector of direct labor requirements and $a$ is the square matrix of input–output coefficients. (See footnote 12 that comments further on his quarrel with Adam Smith.)

However, he could in principle have calculated the total labor requirement of the simple reproduction 3000 corn by replacing *all* $(v_i + s_i)$ by a new equivalent $(v_i{}^* + 0)$. Then $\sum (v_i{}^* + 0)$ is the total labor cost of the corn. And to get the total labor cost of each unit of *net* coal, or of the $6000 - 4000 = 2000$ *net* coal, he had only to reckon the $v_1{}^* + 0$ total.

## E. The Three-Sector Model

I leave mathematical analysis of simple reproduction until after extended reproduction is discussed. But, in concluding the zero-growth case, we may notice that Marx could treat capitalists' consumption of luxury corn as a separate luxury Department III. Now Tableau 1 takes the form given in Tableau 3.

TABLEAU 3

| | |
|---|---|
| I:   4000 of $c_1$ + 1000 of $v_1$ + 1000 of $s_1 = 6000$ | Capital goods |
| II:   1000 of $c_2$ +   250 of $v_2$ +   250 of $s_2 = 1500$ | Subsistence goods |
| III:   1000 of $c_3$ +   250 of $v_3$ +   250 of $s_3 = 1500$ | Luxury goods |

This is a familiar three-sector model in the Marxian literature. And for it we have obvious equalities between respective rows and columns:

$$c_1 + c_2 + c_3 = c_1 + v_1 + s_1$$
$$v_1 + v_2 + v_3 = c_2 + v_2 + s_2 \qquad (6)$$
$$s_1 + s_2 + s_3 = c_3 + v_3 + s_3.$$

And, corresponding to (5), we have the equivalent three-sector relation

$$c_2 + c_3 = v_1 + s_1 \qquad (5')$$

with numerous similar implications of (6). Note that any two of (6)'s three relations implies the remaining third one, as well as implying (5').

## F. Changed Pattern of Luxury Consumptions

What if capitalists chose to spend one-third of their incomes on coal, and only two-thirds rather than three-thirds on corn? At least in this simple case, Marx could probably arrive at the correct new form of the two-sector model of simple reproduction (Tableau 4). No longer is $c_2 = v_1 + s_1$, now that Department I is providing *more* coal than the system *uses up as intermediate* $\sum c_j$.

Note that Tableau 4 is in fact identical to footnote 4's extended reproduction variant of Marx's first simple reproduction tableau (Tableau 1), namely, the footnote's Tableau 1*. That is why I decided to pick this numerical amount of luxury coal consumption—to prepare the way for exponential-growth equilibrium.

TABLEAU 4

Simple Reproduction
($\frac{1}{3}$ Luxury Spending on Coal, $\frac{2}{3}$ on Corn, Zero Saving)

---

I:   4400 of $c_1$ + 1100 of $v_1$ + 1100 of $s_1$ = 6600

II:   1600 of $c_2$ +   400 of $v_2$ +   400 of $s_2$ = 2400

---

## III. Balanced Expanding Reproduction

A gap of years separated Marx's writing on simple and extended reproduction. Perhaps this explains why he did not proceed directly from his original simple reproduction example of Tableau 1 to Tableau 1*, its new equilibrium configuration when capitalists accumulate part of their incomes to finance golden-age exponential growth of all parts of the system, including the labor supply.

Thus, let capitalists save half their $\sum s_j$ incomes. With a uniform profit rate assumed to remain at 20%, we know from modern Kalecki–Robinson–Kaldor tautologies that a balanced growth rate of 10% per period is then implied.[6] If coal production is, like everything else, to rise at this rate, our new tableau must have coal output available for next period, $c_1 + v_1 + s_1$, equal to $\frac{11}{10}$ of the total used up, $\sum c_j$, of this period. With the same initial labor supply of Tableau 1, we have our new Tableau 1* (which is not in *Das Kapital*).

To explain the interrelations of Tableau 1*, note that the half of 1500 of $\sum s_j$ saved comes to 750; this total of net saving is exactly enough to match the increment of capital between the two periods. Thus, we have the saving-investment identity

$$0.5 \sum s_j = 750 = S = I = \{6600 \text{ of coal produced} - 600 \text{ of coal used up}\}$$
$$+ \{1650 \text{ of new corn-wage outlay}$$
$$- 1500 \text{ of old corn-wage outlay}\}$$
$$= \{600\} + \{150\} = 750. \quad \text{Q.E.D.}$$

A three-sector rearrangement of Tableau 1* can illuminate how $\sum v_j$, $\sum s_j$, and $\sum c_j$ get "spent" (see Tableau 1**).

---

[6] In Marx's own extended reproduction case (Table 2), this tautology would not be available—since, with unequal organic compositions of capital and insistence on uniform rates of surplus value, we encounter unequal rates of profit and inapplicability of the tautology. See Morishima [2, Chapter 12] on the "dynamic" transformation problem, for demonstration of the greater complexity of the relationship between the rates of growth, saving, and uniform surplus value, in comparison with the first two and the rate of uniform profit.

TABLEAU 1*

EXTENDED REPRODUCTION
(10% Growth Rate; 0.5 Saving Rate Out of Profits)

First period

I: $\quad 4400$ of $c_1 + 1100$ of $v_1 + 1100$ of $s_1 = 6600$

II: $\quad 1600$ of $c_2 + \quad 400$ of $v_2 + \quad 400$ of $s_2 = 2400$

| 6000 | 1500 | 1500 | 9000 |

Next period

I: $\quad 4800$ of $c_1 + 1210$ of $v_1 + 1210$ of $s_1 = 7260 = 6600(1 + 0.1)$

II: $\quad 1760$ of $c_2 + \quad 440$ of $v_2 + \quad 440$ of $s_2 = 2640 = 2400(1 + 0.1)$

| 6600 | 1650 | 1650 | 9900 | 9000(1 + 0.1) |

Etc.

TABLEAU 1**

EXTENDED REPRODUCTION
(10% Growth Rate; 0.5 Saving Rate of Profits)

I**: $\quad 4000$ of $c_1 + 1000$ of $v_1 + 1000 s_i = 6000$ of "nonfinal" coal

II**: $\quad 1000$ of $c_2 + \quad 250$ of $v_2 + \quad 250 s_2 = 1500$ of "subsistence" corn wages

III**: $\quad \left.\begin{matrix} a \\ b \\ c \end{matrix}\right\}$ : $\quad \left.\begin{matrix} 500 \\ 400 \\ 100 \end{matrix}\right.$ of $c_3 + \left.\begin{matrix} 125 \\ 100 \\ 25 \end{matrix}\right\}$ of $v_3 + \left.\begin{matrix} 125 \\ 100 \\ 25 \end{matrix}\right\}$ of $s_3 = 1500 = \left\{\begin{matrix} 750 \text{ of luxury corn} \\ \quad \text{consumption} \\ 600 \text{ of new coal} \\ \quad \text{inventory} \\ 150 \text{ of new corn} \\ \quad \text{inventory for} \\ \quad \text{wage "advances"} \end{matrix}\right.$

Note that in this rearrangement[7] the sum of the columns do match the sum of the respective rows. Again verify that the two final columns of "values added" and the final two rows of "flow of *final* products (consumption + net capital formation)" do each equal Net National Product or National Income. I see no reason to doubt that both Adam Smith and Marx could agree on this.

[7] If corn and coal have unequal organic composition, in any model with uniform profit rates, the aggregation in Department III** of diverse $(c_i, v_i, s_i)$ magnitudes would make the resulting totals sensitive to the weightings of the various subaggregates. By contrast, using Volume I's regime of equalized rates of surplus value would leave the breakdown between aggregate $v_3$ and $s_3$ invariant; moreover, a mere change in the rate of surplus value would not affect the relative size of $c_3$ to $v_3 + s_3$. This simplification of analysis is not matched by real-world simplification.

A. COMPARATIVE EXPONENTIAL-GROWTH STATES

When we "go" from the simple reproduction of Tableau 1 to the extended reproduction of Tableau 1**, we are not describing an actual transition process that takes place in the real world. All we are doing is comparing (a) an equilibrium system that has always been, and will always be, in no-growth balance with (b) an equilibrium system that has always been, and will always be, in 10%-growth balance. Marx seems to understand this, as suggested by his shrewd observation (p. 572):† "It is further assumed that production on an enlarged scale has actually been in process previously."

Yet in some of Marx's attempts to compute a valid extended reproduction Tableau, he begins with a no-growth configuration and goes through an algorithm designed to end him with a balanced-growth equilibrium. Morishima [2, pp. 117–122] nicely clears up the steps in Marx's algorithm. As Morishima observes (p. 118):

> Marx then introduced his very peculiar investment [saving] function, such that (i) capitalists of Department I devoted a constant proportion of their surplus value to accumulation. . .[whereas] (iii) capitalists of Department II adjusted their investment [behavior] so as to maintain the balance between the supply and demand for capital goods.

Morishima shows that Marx's algorithm, whatever you or I may think of its illogical split in capitalists' behavior, does converge in two periods to an admissible configuration of true balanced growth. And (on p. 120) Morishima contrasts this exact two-period convergence of Marx with the disappointingly slow rate of convergence to balanced-growth golden-age states of neoclassical growth models.

Such a pejorative comparison seems odd. Marx presumably is not purporting to describe a real-life transition. The algorithm does not take place in the capitalist marketplace, but rather at Marx's desk in the British Museum. There are an infinite number of alternative unrealistic algorithms that could also be conjured up. For that matter, once we permit ourselves unrealistic saving behavior, why not pick on one of the infinite number of alternative models each with the property of converging in *one* step from simple reproduction.[8]

---

† All page references to Marx's *Capital* are to the 1909 Kerr edition.

[8] Thus, start with Tableau 1. Let the 6000 of coal be diverted, not 4000 to Department I and 2000 to Department II, but 4400 to I and 600 to II. And let all capitalists still save nothing for this initial period. Then Tableau 1 goes in one step to the first state of Tableau 1*; and forever after all capitalists can save half their incomes and have the system grow at 10% per period bringing 10% more labor into the system in each period. When organic compositions are unequal, one of course cannot keep, in the one-stage transition to the expanding model, both the labor total and the coal-input total the same as in the steady state. "Putty–clay" models, as against "putty–putty" models, become even more complicated.

This would be an arbitrary scenario, but neither more nor less arbitrary than Marx's suggested algorithm.

## IV. A Digression on Morishima's Alternative to Marx

Morishima [2, pp. 122–126] proposes to replace Marx's admittedly "unnatural" behavior equations by what he hopes will be more reasonable assumptions about saving behavior. He ends with the matrix difference equations for the two departments' values, $y(t)$, of the form $y(t) = My(t + 1)$, where $M$ is a positive matrix with characteristic roots less than unity in absolute value. [The coefficients of $M$ depend on the $(a_0, a)$ technical coefficients, and on the consumption propensities of the classes: if the technology satisfies Hawkins–Simon conditions for productivity of a net surplus above subsistence requirements, and if the percent saved from profits cannot exceed unity, $M$ should be well behaved.] As is well known from the work of Jorgenson [3] Solow [4], Morishima [5], Dorfman–Samuelson–Solow [6], and others, such a "backward-defined" difference equation must be damped moving *backward* in time, and antidamped or explosive as we follow it forward in time. One wonders then why Professor Morishima wishes to propose it as the "fundamental equation of the theory of reproduction."

Actually, it is expecting too much of a pioneer like Marx that he should solve adequately the non-steady state behavior of a system. This problem taxes modern ingenuity. Indeed, we have here the indeterminacy of the famous Hahn problem, on which Hahn [7], Stiglitz [8], Shell [8, 9], Samuelson [10], Burmeister [11], and many others have written much in the last decade. Whatever the ultimate solution of the Hahn problem—i.e., the problem of how a *heterogeneous*-capital *many*-sector model can be expected to develop under competition when *overall* saving propensities are *alone* given—the Morishima proposal seems not to constitute a "self-warranting" permanent time solution. His variant of what Dorfman–Samuelson–Solow [6] called a "Leontief trajectory" (defined as a path that *insists on the equalities*, and rules out the feasible inequalities, of the dynamic relations) will necessarily become self-contradictory, generating negative physical quantities and ultimately in effect recognizing bankruptcy.

To see that static equalities cannot hold on a consistent self-warranting solution, consider the easier case of a Ramsey-planned Marxian system that acts to maximize, say, $\sum_0^\infty (1 + \rho)^{-t} \log x_t y_t$, where $x_t$ and $y_t$ are per capita corn and coal consumptions, $\rho$ is a planner rate of time preference equal to (1 + profit rate of 20%)/(1 + growth rate of 10%), available labor supply grows at 10% per period, Marx's implicit technology prevails, and we begin with prescribed initial stocks of corn and coal appropriate to an outmoded simple reproduction state. Then it can be shown that the system will

asymptotically change itself optimally into the extended reproduction configuration proportional to Tableaux like my earlier Tableaux 2 or 4. In the
transition, the dual variables of price will *not* have the steady state values that
the system both begins and ends with and which Marx and Morishima seem
implicitly to use. One sees heuristically (the Furuya–Inada theorem generalized)
that, if there is a self-warranting (perfect-futures market!) path consistent with
strictly constant fractions of profit saved, it must asymptotically approach
the golden-age state and not explode away from it in the Morishima manner.
[For certain special utility functions, such as $U = \log x_t y_t$ or $(x_t y_t)^\gamma / \gamma$, constant average saving propensies may hold.]

I dare not state arguments as heuristic as these except with the greatest
diffidence and absence of self-confidence.

## V. Marx as Advancer of Mainstream-Economics Analytical Technique

First, let us observe that there is nothing "radical" or "leftish" about
these tableaux—even for the mid-nineteenth century. On the contrary, they
could be used to convey a 1931 Hayek message[9] that the Douglas Social
Credit cranks are wrong in believing that there is a necessary flaw in the
circulation system that must lead to underconsumption and unemployment.
Indeed, in some moods, Engels and Marx wrote with scorn of Rodbertus's
naive underconsumptionist views. And, after the turn of the century, Tugan–
Baronowsky or a Domar could use these compound-interest models of Marx
to refute a crude Luxemburg–Hobson thesis of *necessary*-and-*inevitable*
eventual underconsumption in a closed capitalistic system.[10]

Second, careful examination of Marx's analysis will show that, despite his
frequently reiterated belief that he is correcting this or that contemporary
vulgar economist or earlier bourgeois writer, there is no sense in which these
tableaux, properly understood, *refute* earlier mainstream writers. Merely one
case in point is the one already mentioned, in which Marx thought he was correcting Smith's erroneous belief[10a] that wages and profit (rent being ignored)

---

[9] See, for example, Hayek [12], where the easier Austrian case is shown to have identity
between total value added and flow of final product.

[10] Not too much should be read into this last sentence. We must remember that the
Harrod–Domar "warranted rate of growth" that Marx is anticipating need not be equal
to the "natural rate of growth of the labor supply" in a realistic not-necessarily-Marxist
model of actual population and labor-price growth. We must remember too the "instability" or knife-edge property of the warranted rate in a fixed-coefficient technology. And,
finally, we must remember the possible indeterminacy of the Hahn problem of heterogeneous-capital's dynamic behavior when only *aggregate* saving propensities are hypothesized.

[10a] In private correspondence, Professor William Baumol has expressed the view that
Marx's only, or main, difference with Smith's view of price as equal to wages plus profits

form the "components" of price; but, as seen, once the straightforward differentiation between gross and net totals is respected, Marx's own analysis serves to confirm Smith's formulation. Indeed Marx deserves high praise for demonstrating this formulation in the important and novel "non-Austrian" case of circular interdependence. In summary, Marx's tableaux of simple and extended reproduction constitute an important extension and generalization—to the case of circular interdependence—of the orthodox techniques of equilibrium analysis employed by Smith, Ricardo, or Mill.

## VI. Living in Marx's Skin: Numerical Examples Generalized

It is a somewhat odd feeling to immerse one's self in the numerical-example world of an earlier writer like Marx. Perhaps only by doing so can one infer how he arrived at his insights, and recognize the limitations of his perceptions. Nor will it do, when you are reading the gropings, backslidings, and discoverings of a Kepler, to become irritated and wish to clap him on the shoulder and say—from the vantage point of post-Newtonian celestial mechanics—"Why can't you see this and that?"

### A. Possible Class of Numerical Tables of Simple Reproduction

One expects pioneering work to be somewhat rough. Elegance can come later after genius encounters diminishing returns in new insights. Having no students, no colleagues, and no readers, Marx understandably wanders a bit in his derivations. Let us stand back and see the general rules that one can follow to generate *any* tableau of simple reproduction and of extended reproduction.

It simplifies things to begin by combining all value-added terms: work with two $(v_i + s_i)$ terms rather than four such terms; call them $d_i = v_i + s_i$ for short. So long as we stick with Marx's value formulation, where $d_i$ is always broken up into the same proportional fraction, only the $(c_i, d_i)$ totals need be considered.

*Not* any four positive numbers $\begin{bmatrix} c_1 & d_1 \\ c_2 & d_2 \end{bmatrix}$ can provide a tableau of simple reproduction. Only those with column sums equal to respective row sums can serve. This makes the off-diagonal elements equal, $c_2 = d_1$, and leaves us with only three arbitrary degrees of freedom. Since mere scale does not matter, we are free to set column 2's total value added or NNP equal to unity, leaving us with only two degrees of freedom. We may select the two elements of the

---

was that this was only a superficial surface relation (as indeed it is). Baumol may be right; but the reader should review the thousands of words on Smith in Volume II and decide whether that is *all* Marx finds wrong with Smith's view.

main diagonal arbitrarily: thus every admissible tableau comes from picking for $d_2$ an arbitrary fraction, and for $c_1$ an arbitrary positive number.

Suppose we consider the narrower case of equal organic compositions of capital, not for its realism but because the simplicities of algebra that Marx employed turn out to be legitimate for it. Then we have only one degree of freedom left, since the rows (or columns) must be proportional. Instead of the general simple reproduction case

$$\begin{bmatrix} c_1 & 1 - d_2 \\ 1 - d_2 & d_2 \end{bmatrix},$$

we have

$$\begin{bmatrix} (1 - d_2)^2/d_2 & 1 - d_2 \\ 1 - d_2 & d_2 \end{bmatrix},$$

as for example, $\begin{vmatrix} 4/3 & 2/3 \\ 2/3 & 1/3 \end{vmatrix}$, that corresponds to Marx's Tableau 1 (p. 271).

As we will see, for fixed technology, it will not be the case that the $(c_i, d_i)$ preserve the same magnitudes when the real subsistence wage changes, changing the uniform rate of profit with it. Only in the equal-organic-composition case will this be true—for the reason that only in such a case will equalized-profit-rates be compatible with the alternative of equalized-rate-of-surplus-value model (in which it must be always true that the $c_i$ and $d_i$ breakdowns are invariant to changes in the real wage).

B. POSSIBLE TABLEAUX OF EXTENDED REPRODUCTION

Actually, a square array of *any* four positive numbers is admissible to define such a growth tableau, since no longer do respective column and row sums have to correspond. The ratio $(c_1 + d_1)/(c_1 + c_2)$ defines a growth rate, $1 + g$, whether it be greater or less than unity. However, since scale does not matter, we have only three degrees of freedom once we fix column 2's NNP or total value added at unity. Two arbitrary elements of the first column plus an arbitary fraction for one element of the second column define an admissible extended reproduction tableau. For example,

$$\begin{bmatrix} c_1 & 1 - d_2 \\ c_2 & d_2 \end{bmatrix} \quad \text{or} \quad \begin{bmatrix} c_1 & 1 - d_2 \\ (1 - d_2 - c_1 g)/(1 + g) & d_2 \end{bmatrix},$$

as in Table 2's $\begin{bmatrix} 22/19 & 11/19 \\ 8/19 & 8/19 \end{bmatrix}$.

Turn now to the singular case of equal organic compositions of capital, where a change in the profit rate within fixed technology leaves invariant the expanded reproduction $(c_i, d_i)$ tableau for a given balanced-growth rate (it being understood that the saving ratio changes appropriately and scale is immaterial). Since now the columns and rows must be proportional, we lose one of our three degrees of freedom. Now instead of the general case of three arbitrary elements, such as $(g, c_1, d_2)$ only $(g, d_2)$ are assignable: e.g.,

$$\begin{bmatrix} (1 - d_2)^2/(g + d_2) & 1 - d_2 \\ (1 - d_2)d_2/(g + d_2) & d_2 \end{bmatrix},$$

as in $\begin{bmatrix} 44/30 & 22/30 \\ 16/30 & 8/30 \end{bmatrix}$ of Tableau 1*, that corresponds to Marx's Tableau 1 modified to grow at 10% per period.

## VII. Handling Marx's Underlying Technology

As far as I have been able to discover, Marx apparently never pierced below the veil of his pound, franc, or labor-hour tableaux to their underlying technology. This was not so much fetishism on his part, as that the implied problem may not have occurred to him or may have seemed to him to be too hard algebraically. That it was probably not the latter reason is suggested by the fact that it apparently never occurred to him to master even that one case where the algebra would have been easy to handle—namely, the Ricardo–Austrian case where the coal that labor needs to produce corn is itself producible by labor *alone*. Let us shift to this simple case for expository clarity.

### A. The "Triangular" Ricardo–Austrian Hierarchy

Let us suppose 1 labor in Department I produces 1 coal. And, in Department II, $\frac{1}{2}$ labor plus $\frac{1}{2}$ corn produces 1 corn. Then coal and corn each have total labor requirements (direct plus indirect) of 1.

### B. Bourgeois Pricing Regime

Using capital letters $(C_i, V_i, S_i)$ for equalized-profit-rate regimes, the correct simple reproduction tableaux at zero profit, 100%, and 200% profit rates are given in Tableau 5. Note that the $D_i/C_i$ or $(V_i + S_i)/C_i$ ratios are quite different depending on the real corn wage and corresponding profit rate: e.g., for the 100 and 200% profit rates of Tableau 5, we find $(0.5 + 1.5)/1 \neq (0.5 + 4.0)/1.5$.

A word of explanation of these tableaux may help. For simple reproduction, one-half of society's labor—the total of which can be taken as unity— must go to produce coal, all of which is used with the other half of labor to produce consumed corn. Nothing is saved out of profits (whose share of NNP depends on the posited rate of profit). This is the technocratic bedrock at the base of all examples.

At 100% profit rate, the 0.5 of labor used to produce 0.5 of coal gets marked up by 100%. So 0.5 coal costs 1.0 in all. Hence, the cost of corn is the sum of this 1.0 of coal plus 0.5 of labor, all marked up by 100%, until

TABLEAU 5

| Profit Rate | |
|---|---|
| 0% | $0$ of $C_1 + 0.5$ of $V_1 + 0$ of $S_1 = 0.5$ |
| | $0.5$ of $C_2 + 0.5$ of $V_2 + 0$ of $S_2 = 1$ |
| 100% | $0$ of $C_1 + 0.5$ of $V_1 + (1.0)(0 + 0.5) = 1.0$ |
| | $1$ of $C_2 + 0.5$ of $V_2 + (1.0)(1 + 0.5) = 3$ |
| 200% | $0$ of $C_1 + 0.5$ of $V_1 + (2.0)(0.5 + 0)\ \ = 1.5$ |
| | $1.5$ of $C_2 + 0.5$ of $V_2 + (2.0)(1.5 + 0.5) = 6$ |

corn ends costing 3.0 in all. Likewise a 200% profit markup on all $(C_i + V_i)$ outlays at every stage would lead to Department II's corn receipts of 6.0 in all.

To distinguish actual capitalistic pricing at uniform profit rates in all departments from Marx's Volume I regime of values reckoned at uniform rates of surplus value in all departments (i.e., uniform markups on direct labor alone), I have used capital letters, $C_i + V_i + S_i = C_i + V_i + R(C_i + V_i)$ against Marxian lower case letters, $c_i + v_i + s_i = c_i + v_i + r(v_i)$. A uniform rate of profit is written as $R$; a uniform rate of surplus value is written as $r$.

## C. "VALUES" REGIME

The "values" regimes alternative to the above "prices" regimes produce the corresponding three tableaux (given in Tableau 6) which at $r = 0, 2.0$, and 5.0, respectively, provide the comparable subsistence real wage in corn terms that was provided by $R = 0, 1.0$, and 2.0, respectively. If you calculate the three $(c_i, d_i = v_i + s_i)$ numbers for these three quite different distributions of incomes between laborers and capitalists, you find them all exactly the same

TABLEAU 6

| Rate of surplus value | |
|---|---|
| 0% | $0$ of $c_1 + 0.5$ of $v_1 + 0$ of $s_1 = 0.5$ |
| | $0.5$ of $c_2 + 0.5$ of $v_2 + 0$ of $0.s_2 = 1$ |
| 200% | $0$ of $c_1 + 0.5$ of $v_1 + (2.0)0.5$ of $s_1 = 1.5$ |
| | $1.5$ of $c_2 + 0.5$ of $v_2 + (2.0)0.5$ of $s_2 = 3$ |
| 500% | $0$ of $c_1 + 0.5$ of $v_1 + (5.0)0.5$ of $s_1 = 3$ |
| | $3.0$ of $c_2 + 0.5$ of $v_2 + (5.0)0.5$ of $s_2 = 6$ |

except for inessential scale, each being proportional to $\begin{bmatrix} 0 & 1/2 \\ 1/2 & 1/2 \end{bmatrix}$. That is definitely not at all the case for the $(C_i, D_i)$ numbers of realistic competitive pricings, which are respectively proportional to

$$\begin{bmatrix} 0 & \frac{1}{2} \\ \frac{1}{2} & \frac{1}{2} \end{bmatrix}, \quad \begin{bmatrix} 0 & \frac{1}{3} \\ \frac{1}{3} & \frac{2}{3} \end{bmatrix}, \quad \begin{bmatrix} 0 & \frac{1}{4} \\ \frac{1}{4} & \frac{3}{4} \end{bmatrix}.$$

## D. Extended Reproduction Alternatives

Now, in parallel, I show the way the tableaux must look at the same balanced growth rate of $100\%$ per period in the alternative prices and values regimes. All have to be generated by the same technology, in which $\frac{2}{3}$ of society's labor goes to Department I to produce twice as much coal as was produced in the previous period for use in this period's Department II corn production.

To these same physical labor-coal-corn magnitudes, I apply the respective "prices" and "values" appropriate to the stipulated ($R$ or $r$) rates, ($0\%$ or $0\%$), ($100\%$ or $200\%$), and ($200\%$ or $500\%$). This gives the first-period tableaux (Tableau 7) each with $1 + g = 1 + 1.0$, so that in the subsequent period each tableau will have all of its elements *double*.

TABLEAU 7

| $R$ | |
|---|---|
| $0\%$ | $0$ of $C_1 + \frac{2}{3}$ of $V_1 + 0$ of $S_1 = \frac{2}{3}$ |
| | $\frac{1}{3}$ of $C_2 + \frac{1}{3}$ of $V_2 + 0$ of $S_2 = \frac{2}{3}$ |
| $100\%$ | $0$ of $C_1 + \frac{2}{3}$ of $V_1 + (1.0)\frac{2}{3}$ of $S_1 = \frac{4}{3}$ |
| | $\frac{2}{3}$ of $C_2 + \frac{1}{3}$ of $V_2 + 1.0(\frac{2}{3} + \frac{1}{3})$ of $S_2 = \frac{6}{3}$ |
| $200\%$ | $0$ of $C_1 + \frac{2}{3}$ of $V_1 + 2.0(0 + \frac{2}{3})$ of $S_1 = \frac{6}{3}$ |
| | $\frac{3}{3}$ of $C_2 + \frac{1}{3}$ of $V_2 + 2.0(\frac{3}{3} + \frac{1}{3})$ of $S_2 = \frac{12}{3}$ |

| $r$ | |
|---|---|
| $0\%$ | $0$ of $c_1 + \frac{2}{3}$ of $v_1 + 0$ of $s_1 = \frac{2}{3}$ |
| | $\frac{1}{3}$ of $c_2 + \frac{1}{3}$ of $v_2 + 0$ of $s_2 = \frac{2}{3}$ |
| $200\%$ | $0$ of $c_1 + \frac{2}{3}$ of $v_1 + (2.0)\frac{2}{3}$ of $s_1 = \frac{6}{3}$ |
| | $\frac{3}{3}$ of $c_2 + \frac{1}{3}$ of $v_2 + (2.0)\frac{1}{3}$ of $s_2 = \frac{6}{3}$ |
| $500\%$ | $0$ of $c_1 + \frac{2}{3}$ of $v_1 + (5.0)\frac{2}{3}$ of $s_1 = \frac{12}{3}$ |
| | $\frac{6}{3}$ of $c_2 + \frac{1}{3}$ of $v_2 + (5.0)(\frac{1}{3})$ of $s_2 = \frac{12}{3}$ |

The substantial differences between the Tableau 5 price regimes and the Tableau 6 value regimes are obvious. The greater algebraic simplicity of the market-unrealistic right-hand-side tableaux is also apparent. All three of the right-hand value tableaux are, except for scale,[11] identical in everything but the three uniform fractional allocations of the $d_i$ of value added between wages and surplus, $v_i$ and $s_i$.

## VIII. Indeterminacy of Wage and Distributive Shares?

Suppose any of the preceding elementary relationships not fully understood by Marx were explained to him. What difference would it make to his *Weltanschauung* and fundamental vision about capitalist development? Quite possibly none of importance.

### A. ROOTS OF THE POLEMIC AGAINST SMITH'S VIEW OF PRICE OR WAGES-PLUS-PROFITS

Marx might concede that some of his strictures against Smith's formulation of price as composed of wage-plus-profit components would have to be withdrawn or reworded.[12] But I think his animus against Smith's "explanation" of price as wage-cost-plus-profit goes deeper. Putting things this way, he

---

[11] These scale changes arise from my choice of normalizing the elements of the tableaux by conveniently stating the $V_i$ and $v_i$ elements in terms of actual labor-hour allocations.

[12] In Volume II, Part III, Chapter XIX, Section II, 3, fourth paragraph of the section, pp. 431–432, Marx comes close to admitting that Smith is correct in decomposing price into all the values added, $v + s$, of all the earlier stages—provided we stay in a Ricardo–Austrian triangular hierarchy of production (where everything can be "ultimately" produced out of labor above). But he denies that this will work in the case of circular interdependence, where without initial raw materials production can never get off the ground: so, in effect, he is missing the fact that the multiplier chain already referred to, $a_0(I + a + \cdots + a^t + \cdots)$, is a *convergent* infinite series. Had he constructed the tableaux of Section VII and compared them with his general case, he would still have avoided all error and realized that *final* product, or NNP, can be taxonomically split up into its $V_i + S_i$ or $v_i + s_i$ components (*pace* Sraffa [30]). The cited passage where Marx comes near to clearing up his own confusion bears quoting:

> Smith...admits...that the price of corn does not only consist of $v$ plus $s$, but contains also the price of the means of production consumed in the production of corn.... But, says he, the prices of all these means of production likewise resolve themselves into $v$ plus $s$.... He forgets, however, ...that they also contain the prices of the means of production consumed in their production. He refers us from one line of production to another, and from that to a third. The contention that the entire price of commodities resolves itself "immediately" or "ultimately" into $v$ plus $s$ would not be a specious subterfuge in the sole [!] case that the product...[depends ultimately on] products ...which are themselves produced by the investment of mere variable capital, by a mere investment in labor-power [i.e., what I here dub the Ricardo–Austrian hierarchy of non-circularly-dependent production] [Volume II, p. 431].

might legitimately have felt, tends to *justify* the state of affairs in which capitalists get much of what might otherwise go to labor.

Marx is here revealing more than a value judgment against unearned property incomes. He seems also to be stressing that there is nothing inevitable, nothing determined by lasting economic principle, in an existing share of profit in price formation. There is an implicit prediction by Marx that, by power or otherwise, labor could *alter* the status quo of high profits and low wages.

But there is also more here than a value judgment, and a hortatory call to action on the part of the proletariat. There is, I think, a perception by Marx that NNP $= \sum v + \sum s$ (or price equals the sum of wages and surplus) is, by itself, an indeterminate system. The economic system of his predecessors, he feels, lacks the conditions needed to determine whether 4 is $2 + 2$, or $1 + 3$, or $4 + 0$.

## B. MARX'S ANTICIPATION OF ROBINSONIAN CRITIQUE?

This perception strikes a resonant response in our own age. Joan Robinson, building on Sraffa's work and her own earlier writings, says as much: Microeconomists lack an equation to determine the profit rate and profit share.[13] Their's is an *indeterminate system*—once microeconomists' fanciful marginal-productivity conditions are denied by virtue of (a) heterogeneity of capital goods, and (b) fixity of input proportions in nonsmooth production functions.[14]

[13] Of course, one might supply the missing link from a Kalecki–Kaldor–Robinson–Pasinetti long-run tautology of macroeconomic theory. But that is another story, and not one easily found in Smith, Ricardo, Marshall, or Walras—or, for that matter, in Marx.

[14] In order to achieve clarity on exact differences of opinion between different modern schools, it would be well to ignore smooth neoclassical production functions in any Department. But one might still stipulate, as being realistic or interesting, that in Tableaux 1 or 2, there are many alternative ways of producing coal and corn out of labor and raw materials. Thus, in Department I, along with $(a_{01}, a_{11})$ coefficients of $\frac{2}{3}$ coal needed to produce 1 of coal, along with say $\frac{1}{3}$ labor, we might have the alternative technical options $(\frac{1}{3}, \frac{2}{3})$, $(\sqrt{2}/3, \sqrt{2}/3)$, $(\frac{1}{30}, \frac{20}{3})$ and $(\frac{20}{3}$ and $\frac{1}{30})$. And, at the same time, we might have in Department II, a half-dozen equally varied technical options: i.e., varied "pages" in Joan Robinson's book of technical blueprints.

As a matter of logical clarity, it would be useful to know whether those who dislike Cobb–Douglas and other simplified Clarkian production functions would agree or disagree with the proposition that this sheaf-of-varied-option cases produces pretty much the same results as would two Clarkian functions of coal and labor inputs for Departments I and II. Thus, a Ramsey planner with low time preference in $\sum (1 + \lambda)^{-t} V[c_t]$ would give up corn consumption in the present in order to build up coal stocks for greater future efficiency in producing corn, etc., etc.—much as in the Clarkian case. If this is not a bone of contention, its conclusion perhaps need not be—namely, that in the Marxian system, the inherited stock of coal per capita (or the amount accumulated at the expense of current consuming) will be an important factor bearing on whether it is likely to involve a high or low trend for the profit rate.

From the side of Böhm–Fisher time preference, the missing equation for the steady state profit rate might be sought; but to do so would not be to incur the pleasure and approval of the Cambridge–Italian school, or of Karl Marx.

I do not wish to pronounce any opinion at this time on whether Marx was insightful or obtuse in regarding the profit component of price and NNP as being undetermined by mainstream bourgeois political economy. I merely wish to advance the hypothesis that we understand much of Marx's *Weltanschauung* if we employ this interpretive hypothesis. And we understand better why he was attracted to a subsistence-wage hypothesis (however far-fetched, empirically and analytically, such an hypothesis appeared to his critics).

### IX. The Number One Issue in Appraising Karl Marx's Theoretical Innovations

I leave to the Appendix the Leontief–Sraffa–Metzler elucidation of Marx's models of simple and extended reproduction. But we must not let a preoccupation with Marx as a *mathematical* economist divert us from trying to form a just opinion of how novel and fundamental was what he and Engels and Lenin regarded as his most innovative and insightful contribution to political economy—namely, Marx's way of handling "surplus value."

What Marx claimed as most originally his is also precisely that which mainstream economists have been most unanimous in rejecting. It is precisely Marx's models in Volume I and Volume II of equalized-rates-of-positive-surplus-value-markups-on-direct-wages-alone that have seemed bizarre to most non-Marxian economists. "Reactionaries" like Pareto or "liberals" like Wicksteed, as well as pedants like Böhm–Bawerk, are only the most dramatic examples of the near-universal rejection by non-Marxian political economists of these Volume I and Volume II paradigms as (a) gratuitously unrealistic, (b) an unnecessary *detour* from which Marx in Volume III had to beat a return, even though a return he was too stubborn or too unperceptive or too unscientific to admit.

This, I think, has been the Number One issue in the debates about Marxian economics throughout the years of my professional life as an economist and indeed both before and after the 1894 posthumous appearance of *Capital's* Volume III.

Failure to recognize and focus on this clearly defined question seems to me to account for a good deal of the confusion and cross-talk in pro-Marxian and anti-Marxian economics debate. What is less important, some of the misinterpretation of my own Marxian analyses (commented on in footnote 24 in the Appendix) seem to me to stem from a failure to realize that it was this issue that has motivated my own exploration in understanding, appraising, and developing Marxian analyses. And it is on this key issue that two such different people as Joan Robinson and I have been so singularly in agreement.

The issue, to repeat, is this:

What are the merits or disadvantages of hypothesizing models of (a) uniform $s_i/v_i$ mark-ups, alongside of, or as against, models of (b) uniform $S_i/(C_i + V_i)$ markups? What, if any, are the advantages of equalized-rates-of-surplus-value regimes, in comparison with the regimes of Marx's predecessors, contemporaries, and successors, which stipulate that competitive arbitrage enforces equalized-rates-of-profit by industries? What valid insights come from a macroeconomic ratio, $\sum s_j/\sum v_j$ or $\sum S_j/\sum V_j$, that are not already (better?) contained in a $\sum S_j/\sum (C_j + V_j)$ ratio?

To guide the reader in more rapid understanding of my argument, let me state at once that I have arrived at a definite view as to how this Number One question should be answered. On the basis of much reflection and analysis of the problem, and after a valiant attempt to read every Marxian and non-Marxian argument that bears on the issue, here is my own opinion.

Save as only an admitted first approximation, justifiable for dramatic emphasis and hortatory persuasiveness or defended because of its obvious greater simplicity of algebraic structure, the paradigm of equalized-rates-of-surplus-values is an unnecessary detour from the alternative paradigm of equalized-rate-of-profit that Marx and mainstream economists inherited from Ricardo and earlier writers. This digressing Marxian alternative paradigm not only lacks empirical realism as applied to competitive arbitrage governing capital flows among industries and competitive price relations of different goods and services, but also it is a detour and a digression to the would-be student of monopolistic and imperfect competition, to the would-be student of socialism, to the would-be student of the modern mixed economy and its laws of motion, to the would-be student of the historic laws of motion of historic capitalism (including, be it stressed, of earlier golden or nongolden ages of precommodity exchanges among artisans and farmers).

Specifically, logical analysis—like that here, and enumerated at greater length in my 1971 discussion [13][15] of the Marxian "transformation problem"—will *refute* the more sophisticated notion[16] that, although the equal-rates-of-profit behavior equations are indeed

---

[15] See also refs. [14] and [15], and my two replies [16, 17]. See also Samuelson [18] which carries further the Weizsäcker–Samuelson demonstration that, even in a planned socialist society, uniform $R^* = S_j/(C_j + V_j)$, rather than $r^* = s_j/v_j$, would be needed for efficient dynamic asymptotes. My earlier articles on Marx and Ricardo are also relevant [19–22]. The elements of Marxian analysis are given in my *Economics* [23].

[16] This point, which I argue is not valid, is perhaps most clearly made by Meek [24]. In ref. [13], p. 417], my parody tries to make the point that the macroeconomic total of profit does not (repeat not) require or benefit from any $s/v$ analysis. The present chapter spells out my arguments for this thesis. I have tried to appraise impartially Meek's thesis [24, p. 95]: "For, according to him [Marx], the profit which the capitalists receive in each branch of industry must be conceived of as accruing to them by virtue of a sort of a redivision of the aggregate surplus value produced over the economy as a whole." And my findings are as adverse to this as they are to Marx's contention (Volume I, Chapter IX, Section 1, p. 239, n. 2): "We shall see, in Book III, that the rate of profit is no mystery, so soon as we know the laws of surplus-value. If we reverse the process, we cannot comprehend either the one or the other." A careful search of Marx's earlier and later writings does not produce any evidence that he was able to make good on this claim in the eyes of a competent analyst who understands all the issues—pro-Marxian and anti-Marxian. A referee has also made this point. Baumol [25] has made a similiar claim for Marx, and in [31] I have assayed to refute the cogency of the line of argument Baumol attributes to Marx.

more valid *micro*economically (to parcel out the *macro*economic *total* of surplus among the different subaggregate departments), nonetheless the insights of the $s/v$ or $\sum s/\sum v$ Marxian paradigm are crucial (or at least "useful") in "explaining" and "understanding" how the total of social product gets divided into paid labor and the exploiter's surplus in the years of developing capitalism. To repeat, there is no validity to this doctrine of surplus-value-paradigm-needed-macroeconomically-to-determine-the-rate-of-profit-that-microeconomically-partitions-out-the-surplus.

This is not the place to provide a comprehensive analysis of the pros and cons of these issues, as discussed by Marx, Hilferding, Dobb, Sweezy, Mandel, Meek, and many others. What is appropriate in this discussion of Marx as mathematical economist is to take notice of writings of Bortkiewicz, Sraffa, Robinson, Okishio,[17] Bródy,[18] Johansen,[19] and, most of all, Morishima.

From the standpoint of this Number One question I have scrutinized each page of Morishima's *Marx's Economics: A Dual Theory of Growth* [2], and each equation and footnote. My resulting judgment is that there is no reason given there that leads me to want to weaken the above view on the Number One question.[20]

---

[17] Okishio [26]. If I had known of the article earlier, I would have referred to it in the bibliography of my 1971 paper. Its views essentially coincide with my own (although I do not think its attempt to resolve differences in labor qualities into differences in producible education does justice to the empirical complexity of realistic "primary" factors).

[18] Bródy [27] provides a valuable and original analysis of Marx along general Leontief lines.

[19] To my 1971 bibliography should now be added the article by Johansen [28].

[20] Volume I's discussion can make this clear. Since in that volume, Marx talks repeatedly of successive stages of production, such as the spinning of yarn and the weaving of it into cloth, he is evidently already in what Leontief, Sraffa, and Böhm would dub a more-than-one-department world. But, even without the mathematics given in the Appendix, we can easily jot down a truly one-department-model—to see whether I am right in denying that $S/V$ reveals some insight that conventional $S/(C+V)$ analysis deceptively conceals.

Suppose to produce 1 corn at the end of a period, it takes at the beginning of the period, $a_0 = \frac{1}{2}$ of labor along with $\frac{1}{2}$ of corn as raw material or seed. Then if labor can be reproduced instantly for less than 1 corn, an exploitative positive rate of profit is deducible. Thus, if subsistence corn per unit of $L$ is $m = \frac{1}{3}$ corn, the competent reader can verify that $R^*$ is 50%. He can verify that half the gross product goes for raw materials. Of the remaining half of Net National Product, one-third goes to labor and two-thirds goes to profit receivers (to consume now in simple reproduction cases; or, in extended reproduction cases, to consume a fixed fraction and plow back into extensive growth of the system the remaining fraction saved).

We have full insight into the problem, by mainstream economic concepts that are Ricardian (i.e., pre-Marxian), Millian (i.e., contemporaneous with Marx), Wicksellian, or Sraffian (i.e., post-Marxian). We know: At any profit rate $R$ higher than $R^*$, workers will get too low a real wage to reproduce themselves; at any profit rate lower than $R^*$, there would be opportunity for infinite-sure-thing arbitrage—in which I borrow to buy corn, pay workers with it, and use it as raw material, then sell the product at a return greater than what I have to pay as interest, and without risk, make as much as I like. So we see, from capitalist pricing and accounting and avaricious arbitrage exactly how and why exploitation takes place.

If we want to write down a $C + V + S = C + V + R^*(C + V)$ tableau, here is how it would read for each unit of steady state labor:

> 1 of corn as raw material $+ \frac{1}{3}$ of corn as subsistence wage $+ 0.5(1 + \frac{1}{3})$ of corn profit
>
> $= 2$ of corn produced gross (of which the 1 of NNP is seen to be divided up into $\frac{1}{3}$ for labor and $\frac{2}{3}$ for exploiter).

Thus, we know all there is to know both in pecuniary and physical terms.

Now, is there any *new insight* possible from concentrating on the ratio of surplus to wages alone, $S/V$? Since with only one department there cannot be differing organic compositions of capital, we know from the beginning that the surplus-value innovations of Volume I must give us exactly the same answer as mainstream economics. So, was that trip really necessary? Or somehow desirable? Surely, on reflection, one will see that in this case, where it does no harm and requires no transformation algorithm, it also does not one iota of extra good. One might as usefully squander one's time in considering still a third regime in which we concentrate on $S/C$ ratios.

To be sure, one can describe the same degenerate 1-department tableau by saying that the rate of surplus value is 200%: i.e., $r^* = 2.00$. Admittedly, a 200% rate *sounds* more exploitative than a 50% rate. But that is only for illiterates, since (as Marx clearly points out) the 200% of $S/V$ is the same absolute loot for the exploiter merely expressed as a fraction of the smaller base $V$, rather than the base $(C + V)$.

But have we not added the vital fact that "living labor" is the true source of all product and *a fortiori* exploitative profits? No; conventional analysis tells us that without labor, there is no product at all. And it tells us that, without beginning-of-the-period raw material, there is also no product. That is not an apologetic for profit; it is a technical fact: mainstream economics fully recognizes that, if the $m$ minimum of subsistence goes up, $R^*$ will fall; and if the workers—by power or education—insist on an $m$ up to 1, they can get all the NNP and bring $R^*$ to zero. But, you may say, there may be strong political reasons why workers will not succeed in doing this or will be prevented from organizing to raise $m$ and their real wage. You may be right. But you will be equally right or wrong or insightful in terms of $R^*$ analysis as in parallel $r^*$ analysis. And further, you will be able with $R^*$ to understand the Sraffa dated-labor resolution, à la Adam Smith, of price into wages and profit in all the (infinite but converging) earlier stages of production—namely

$$P = a_0(1 + R^*) + a_0 a(1 + R^*)^2 + \cdots + a_0 a^{t-1}(1 + R^*)^t + \cdots$$
$$= a_0(1 + R^*)/[1 - a(1 + R^*)]$$

which Marx, throughout all his jousting with Adam Smith, was never able to get straight when $R > 0$. [Indeed, this makes one wonder whether he actually ever was able to rigorously perceive that, for $R^* = 0$, price does indeed equal total embodied labor content (direct plus indirect).] Now try to make that same correct resolution in the surplus-value $r^*$ regime, with its gratuitous neglect of compound interest, and its quite unmerited belief that only the last-stage's direct labor contributes to profit. Tell that to a capitalist who hires a worker to plant a 10-year rather than a 5-year tree. On these workers' "live labor," will the exploiters' profit end up the same? Of course not.

I have discussed elsewhere the views of others of these writers. Specifically, I wish to iterate that my view on these matters is quite divorced from the disputes over the inadequacies of neoclassicism. I would be quite content to call my position on this Number One question Sraffian, or Robinsonian, or Ricardian, or Passinettian, or Leontiefian. (For example, in a regime of values, with uniform rates of surplus value, the realistic possibility of reswitching could not logically occur: The technique that minimizes "values" at $r = 0$ will minimize them for all $r$'s—a shortcoming of the "values" model.)

## X. Final Summing Up

The preceding analysis does demonstrate that Karl Marx deserves an honored place among economic pioneers of steady state and balanced growth equilibrium. What is valid in this seminal contribution is in no sense contrary to mainstream economics of Marx's predecessors, contemporaries, or successors. Even if we end with the view that Marx was not so much a mathematical economist as "merely" a great economist, this recognition of his analytical abilities in no sense diminishes our appreciation of him as an original and creative shaper of the science of political economy. In science, your ultimate grade depends on the best performance you achieve, and not on your worst or even average performance.

I leave to the Appendix the more rigorous summarizing of these models, and discussion of Morishima's criticism of my Marxian writings.

## Appendix

### 1. TECHNICAL COEFFICIENTS OF PRODUCTION

Let $X_{ij}$ be the amount of the $i$th good used as input for the industry producing the $j$th nonnegative output, $X_j$; let $L_j$ be the direct labor used by the $j$th industry. All these are nonnegative. Then $a = [a_{ij}] = [X_{ij}/X_j]$ represents the nonnegative Marx–Markov–Metzler–Leontief matrix, and $a_0 = [L_j/X_j]$ represents the row vector of direct labor requirements.

### 2. EXAMPLES

Some possible cases are the following.

$$\begin{bmatrix} a_0 \\ \cdots \\ a \end{bmatrix} = \begin{bmatrix} 1 & 1 \\ \cdots & \cdots \\ 0 & 0 \\ 0 & 0 \end{bmatrix}, \quad \text{Smith's deer–beaver case}; \qquad (2.1)$$

$$\begin{bmatrix} a_0 \\ \cdots \\ a \end{bmatrix} = \begin{bmatrix} 1 & \frac{1}{2} \\ \cdots & \cdots \\ 0 & \frac{1}{2} \\ 0 & 0 \end{bmatrix}, \qquad \text{the Ricardo–Austrian coal–corn case of my six tableaux;} \qquad (2.2)$$

$$\begin{bmatrix} a_0 \\ \cdots \\ a \end{bmatrix} = \begin{bmatrix} \alpha & \beta \\ \cdots & \cdots \\ 1-\alpha & 1-\beta \\ 0 & 0 \end{bmatrix}, \qquad \begin{array}{l} \text{Marx's tableaux of corn–coal:} \\ \alpha = \beta \text{ as in Tableau 1,} \\ \alpha < \beta \text{ as in Tableau 2;} \end{array} \qquad (2.3)$$

$$\begin{bmatrix} a_0 \\ \cdots \\ a \end{bmatrix} = \begin{bmatrix} 1-\alpha_1-\beta_1 & 1-\alpha_2-\beta_2 \\ \cdots & \cdots \\ \alpha_1 & \alpha_2 \\ \beta_1 & \beta_2 \end{bmatrix}, \qquad \text{the general two-department case.} \qquad (2.4)$$

In every case, I have followed the convention of selecting units so that "total" labor requirements ("direct" plus "indirect") are unity.

## 3. Admissible Cases

In case (2.4) we could have $1 - \alpha_2 - \beta_2 = 0$; but in order that every good require, directly or indirectly, some labor input, we could *not* then also have either $\alpha_2$ or $1 - \alpha_1 - \beta_1$ zero. Sraffa chooses to require that there exist at least one good (a basic) that is directly or indirectly required by all goods (including itself). But there seems no reason to rule out cases (2.1) and (2.2).

The simplest case to talk about is where $a_0$ and $a$ have strictly positive elements: $a_0 > 0$, $a > 0$. But it is almost as simple if nonnegative $a$ is "indecomposable" and at least one element of $a_0$ is positive. (Indecomposability is verified when $(I + a + \cdots + a^{n-1})$ is strictly positive.) Ricardo and Marx often adjoined to "necessary" goods a set of "luxury" goods, i.e., goods which are not themselves needed as inputs for the necessary goods. This gives

$$\begin{bmatrix} a_0 \\ \cdots \\ a \end{bmatrix} = \begin{bmatrix} a_{0,I} & a_{0,II} \\ \cdots & \cdots \\ a_{I,I} & a_{I,II} \\ 0 & a_{II,II} \end{bmatrix}.$$

Here $a_{I,I}$ must be nonnegative and indecomposable and at least one element of $a_{0,I}$ must be positive. Columns of $a_{I,II}$ must have a positive element. The subscript $I$ refers to necessary goods; the subscript $II$, to "luxury" goods (which must be understood to be able to include a wage-subsistence good such as corn).

## 4. GENERAL TIME-PHASED SYSTEM

These input–output relations are the steady state plateaux of the actual time-phased technology and allocation relations.

$$X_j(t + 1) = F_j[L_j(t), X_{1j}(t), \ldots, X_{nj}(t)] \qquad (j = 1, \ldots, n) \qquad (4.1)$$

$$= \text{Min}[L_j(t)/a_{0j}, X_{1j}^{(t)}/a_{1j}, \ldots, X_{nj}^{(t)}/a_{nj}] \qquad (4.1')$$

$$X_j(t) = X_{j1}(t) + \cdots + X_{jn}(t) + B_j(t) \qquad (4.2)$$

where $B_j(t)$ is the nonnegative "final consumption" in the $t$th period of the $j$th good. (Whenever an $a_{ij}$ is zero rather than positive, we can follow the convention of disregarding its $X_{ij}/a_{ij}$ term.)

In (4.1) we can have *any* continuous production function (not necessarily possessing well-defined partial derivatives of marginal productivity). Only joint production and externalities are ruled out.

However, much of the Marx and Leontief literature chooses to concentrate on the single-fixed-technology case shown in (4.1'). It is well to notice that in (4.1') any pattern of nonnegative $a$'s and $a_0$'s are permitted, provided only that every good requires directly or indirectly some positive labor. In short, the so-called Hawkins–Simon conditions—that are necessary and sufficient if something of every good is to be producible for *steady* net consumption— need *not* be stipulated to hold in general. (It is worth pointing out that the belated discovery of the H–S conditions came out of Hawkins' study of a dynamic *Marxian* system!)

## 5. STEADY STATE PLATEAUX

For steady states, we equate variables at all times:

$$\begin{aligned}
X_j(t) &= X_j(t + 1) = \cdots = X_j \\
X_{ij}(t) &= X_{ij}(t + 1) = \cdots = X_{ij} \\
L_j(t) &= L_j(t + 1) = \cdots = L_j \\
B_j(t) &= B_j(t + 1) = \cdots = B_j .
\end{aligned} \qquad (5.1)$$

If the consumption $[B_j]$ are to be capable of taking on all-positive values, we must be able to satisfy the steady state form of (4.1') and (4.2).

$$\begin{aligned}
L_1 + \cdots + L_n = L > 0, \qquad X_{ij} \geqq 0 \\
X_i - (X_{i1} + \cdots + X_{in}) = B_i > 0 \qquad (i = 1, \ldots, n)
\end{aligned} \qquad (5.2)$$

$$\begin{aligned}
a_{01} X_1 + \cdots + a_{0n} X_n = L > 0 \\
X_i - (a_{i1} X_1 + \cdots + a_{in} X_n) - B_i > 0 \qquad (i = 1, \ldots, n)
\end{aligned} \qquad (5.2')$$

or, in matrix terms,

$$\begin{bmatrix} a_0 \\ \hline I-a \end{bmatrix} X = \begin{bmatrix} L \\ \hline B \end{bmatrix} > 0. \tag{5.3'}$$

## 6. Hawkins–Simon Conditions for Positive Steady State Consumptions

Suppose nonnegative $a$ can be rearranged by renumbering of corresponding rows and columns into the partitioned form

$$\begin{bmatrix} A_{0,I} & A_{0,II} & \cdots & A_{0,N} \\ \hline A_{I,I} & A_{I,II} & \cdots & A_{I,N} \\ 0 & A_{II,II} & \cdots & A_{II,N} \\ \hline 0 & 0 & \cdots & A_{N,N} \end{bmatrix} \tag{6.1}$$

where each diagonal $A_{I,I}, \ldots, A_{N,N}$ matrix is indecomposable, except possibly the last, but where elements above this diagonal can be zero (provided, of course, that every indecomposable set is tied directly or indirectly to a positive $A_0$ element). [Examples would be (2.4) with $(\beta_1, \alpha_2)$ the only vanishing elements; or with $\beta_1$ and $1 - \alpha_2 - \beta_2$ the only vanishing elements.]

Then the Hawkins–Simon conditions say: "It is necessary and sufficient for producible steady state production of any one consumption good (and of all such) that every principal-minor subsystem of $I - a$ (and of $I - A_{J,J}$) have a positive determinant."

Our examples (2.1)–(2.4), because of their normalized-to-unity form automatically satisfy the H–S conditions for a "steady state surplus economy." This is so because the condition

$$\sum_{j=1}^{n} a_{ij} < 1 \qquad (i = 1, \ldots, n) \tag{6.2}$$

is a sufficient condition for H–S. It is of course not necessary, since changing units of goods can always destroy it; but H–S holds, if and only if, for *some* choice of units, *every* diagonal matrix in (6.1) can be made to have its row sums satisfy

$$a_{0i} = 1 - \sum_{j} a_{ij} \geq 0 \tag{6.3}$$

with the strong inequality holding for at least one of its columns. Clearly, (6.2) is an overly strong case of (6.3).

## 7. Subsistence-Wage Theory of Labor's Cost of Reproduction

We must now introduce the Marx-like notion that labor itself has a cost of production and reproduction. If $L(t + 1)$ satisfied equations like those satisfied by $X_j(t + 1)$ in (4.1), we would have a von Neumann system in which labor could be treated like any other "nonprimary" input. But Marx never quite articulated that case.

Marx failed to develop in detail his subsistence-wage process. Perhaps the simplest version is to assume that, from the reserve army of unemployed or the countryside, the system can always get the $L(t) = \sum_{j=1}^{n} L_j(t)$ it needs *now* at the beginning of the period's production process. It gets each such unit of $L(t)$ by providing it with the column vector of subsistence-goods requirements $[m_i]$, where one or more of these nonnegative elements is strictly positive. (In the typical Marxian model, when workers consume different goods from those used as inputs, the only positive $m_i$ elements belong to rows of $A_{NN}$ in (6.1) that consist exclusively of zeros. If capitalists' luxury consumption items are different from those of workers' subsistence consumption, there may be still other rows of $A_{NN}$ in which the elements are zero.[21] But the results would be essentially similar if $m_i$ were positive for *all i*).

## 8. TECHNOCRATIC SUBSISTENCE-WAGE MODEL

Without using Marx's "value" concepts or (as yet) those of bourgeois prices, I review the familiar Leontief–Sraffa technocratic formulation of a steady state, where workers get subsistence wage consumption $mL$, or $M$ for short, and capitalists get the rest, $B - M$. We have, from (5.3′):

$$X = aX + B = (I - a)^{-1}B$$
$$a_0 X = a_0(I - a)^{-1}B = L > 0 \qquad\qquad (8.1)$$
$$a_0(I - a)^{-1}(B - M) = L - a_0(I - a)^{-1}mL.$$

Here the row vector $a_0(I - a)^{-1}$ represents the total technocratic labor requirements (direct plus indirect) required in the steady state to produce unit amounts of the respective goods. If $B - M = 0$, so that the system is just producing needed wage subsistence, and "exploitation" were zero, goods

---

[21] By Seton's 1957 device of "feeding coefficients," we could handle subsistence wages by adding to each original $a_{ij}$ the new requirement $a_{0j}m_i$. Or, in the case where a unit of work in each $j$th industry requires a different amount of subsistence to be paid at the beginning of the period, namely, $m_{ij}$, we add to $a_{ij}$ the term $a_{0j}m_{ij} = k_{ij}$. Here I shall not make $m_i$ depend on $j$, and shall not employ the feeding-coefficient notation even though it has its advantages. Thus, let $[a_{ij} + k_{ij}]$ be indecomposable. Then positive principal minors of $[I - a_{ij} - k_{ij}]$ is the *strengthened* Hawkins–Simon condition that guarantees not merely the producibility of positive $B$, but also that enough be producible to leave something over for employers' positive profit. In our notation, this is equivalent to $a_0[I - a]^{-1}m < 1$, so that $a_0(1 + R)[I - a(1 + R)]^{-1}m = 1$ have a positive $R$ root for the profit rate. The reader of Morishima will note that there is no need to *duplicate* this condition by an *equivalent* requirement that $a_0(1 + r)[I - a]^{-1}m = 1$ have a positive $r$ root for the "rate of surplus value." This last adds (and subtracts) nothing to the analysis of realistic competitive equilibrium. (For simplicity, I posit length of working day constant.)

might actually be priced (relative to the wage) at these undiluted-labor-theory-of-value $a_0(I - a)^{-1}$ levels.

## 9. Coefficient of "Exploitation"

We could for any system calculate as a measure of exploiters' "share" in social production:

$$\rho \overset{\text{def}}{=} a_0(I - a)^{-1}(B - M)/a_0(I - a)^{-1}M \geq 0. \tag{9.1}$$

(This is sometimes given the Marxian name, ratio of "unpaid" to "paid" labor.) Under the rude undiluted labor theory of value, we would have $\rho$ and $B - M$ zero rather than positive. This $\rho$ coefficient has the pleasant property that changes in capitalists' tastes among different $B - M$ consumption will not affect the magnitude of $\rho$. However, as we should expect, changes in the consumption of subsistence $m$ or $M$ requirements, like changes in any $a_{0j}$ or $a_{ij}$, will change $\rho$. For example, reducing any one $m_i$, or any one $a_{0j}$ needed for some $m$'s production, will necessarily raise $\rho$.

## 10. Exploitation Pricing

To verify that there is never an advantage, save to those of limited algebraic ability, in *ever* considering Marx's regime of equalized-positive-rates-of-surplus value, I proceed on conventional bourgeois Ricardo–Sraffa–Leontief lines. For each uniform profit rate $R$, the row vector of prices (relative to the wage numéraire), written as $P[1 + R]$, will consist of monotone-increasing functions of $R$, $P_j[1 + R]$, satisfying competitive-arbitrage steady state pricing

$$P_j[1 + R] = \left\{ a_{0j} + \sum_{i=1}^{n} P_i[1 + R]a_{ij} \right\}(1 + R) \qquad (j = 1, \ldots, n). \tag{10.1}$$

In matrix terms

$$\begin{aligned} P[1 + R] &= a_0(1 + R) + P[1 + R]a(1 + R) \\ &= a_0(1 + R)[I - a(1 + R)]^{-1} > 0. \end{aligned} \tag{10.1'}$$

## 11. Effect of Varying Level for Exploitative Profit Rate on Relative Prices.

Generally, as $R$ increases from 0 to its maximum value at which $[I - a(1 + R)]^{-1}$ remains finite, $R = R_{\max} \leq \infty$, the $P_j[1 + R]$ prices will grow at *unequal* percentage rates. Hence, the ratio $P_{1+j}[1 + R]/P_1[1 + R]$ can rise, or can fall, or in general can both rise and then later fall. However, Marx realized that in the case he called "equal organic composition of capital," such price ratios could never change. We may express this in the following propositions.

**Marx–Sraffa Theorem**   If, and only if,

$$a_{0j}(1 + R)/P_j[1 + R] \equiv a_{01}(1 + R)/P_1[1 + R] \qquad (j = 2, \ldots, n) \quad (11.1)$$

for *some* nonnegative $R$, will this identity be true for *all* admissible $R$. And, in that case, for an observed equilibrium profit rate, $R = R^*$:

$$P_j[1 + R^*] \equiv P_j[1](1 + \rho) \tag{11.2}$$

where $\rho$ is the exploitation coefficient of Section 9, which can be defined, as we will see in the next section, once the subsistence-requirement vector is known, as a unique function of the $R = R^*$ profit rate that is implied by the condition of a real wage rate at the subsistence level.

## 12. Defining the Subsistence-Theory's Equilibrium Profit Rate

The equilibrium profit rate is defined as the unique $R = R^*$ level at which

$$P[1 + R]m = 1 \tag{12.1}$$

where

$$1/P[1 + R]m = W[R] \tag{12.2}$$

defines the "factor-price tradeoff frontier" linking the real wage and the profit rate. Because $P_j'[1 + R] > 0$, necessarily $W'[R] < 0$.

## 13. "Exploitative Rate" Greater than Profit Rate

An easy Marx-like tautology is that, for equilibrium $R$ positive

$$\rho > R \tag{13.1}$$

provided only that some one positive intermediate input $a_{ij}$ is needed to produce the subsistence-wage basket.[22]

## 14. The Equal-Organic Case of Constant Relative Prices

When all $a_{0j}(1 + R)/P_j[1 + R]$ have uniform values $\alpha[R]$, as in (11.1), each price takes on the special simple form of (11.2):

$$P_j[1 + R] = (1 + \rho[R])P_j[1] \tag{14.1}$$

---

[22] To see this, define the monotone-increasing function

$$g[R_2] = a_0[I - a(1 + R_2)]^{-1}m = P[1 + R_2]m/(1 + R_2).$$

By definition of $R^*$ and $\rho^*$,

$$1 = P[1 + R^*]m = g[R^*](1 + R^*) = P[1](1 + \rho^*)m = g[0](1 + \rho^*).$$

For $R^* > 0$, $g[R^*] > g[0]$ and hence $r^* > R^*$, the final proof that the defined exploitation rate $\rho$ exceeds the profit rate numerically. This tautology has no empirical content (and no empirical relevance or insight).

where the monotone function $\rho[R]$ is defined in terms of $\alpha[0] = \alpha$ by

$$\rho[R] = R/[1 - (1 - \alpha)(1 + R)] > R, \qquad 0 < R \leq R_{max} = \alpha/(1 - \alpha). \quad (14.2)$$

This follows from easy substitution into (10.1). As a convenient check, we note that the exploitation rate $\rho$ corresponding to the positive subsistence-equilibrium profit rate $R^*$ is given as

$$\rho = \rho[R^*] = (L - P[1]M)/P[1]M = (P[1]m)^{-1} - 1. \quad (14.3)$$

## 15. SIMPLE REPRODUCTION TABLEAU

$L$ is given. It produces steady state gross outputs $(X_i)$, which, at the equilibrium profit rate $R^*$ sell at $P_j[1 + R^*]$. The revenues of each $j$th industry $P_j[1 + R^*]X_j$ are equal to costs of production defined by

$$P_j[1 + R^*]X_j = \{a_{0j}X_j\} + \left(\sum_{i=1}^{n} P_i[1 + R^*]a_{ij}X_j\right)$$

$$+ R^*\left\{a_{0j}X_j + \sum_{i=1}^{n} P_i[1 + R^*]a_{ij}X_j\right\} \qquad (j = 1, \ldots, n).$$

$$(15.1)$$

This can be rearranged into my text's $C + V + S$ arrangement:

$$\left\{\sum_{i=1}^{n} P_i[1 + R^*]a_{ij}X_j\right\} + \{a_{0j}X_j\} + R^*\left\{\sum_{i=1}^{n} P_i[1 + R^*]a_{ij}X_j + a_{0j}X_j\right\}$$

$$\equiv \{C_j\} + \{V_j\} + R^*\{C_j + V_j\} = C_j + V_j + S_j \qquad (j = 1, \ldots, n). \quad (15.1')$$

The prime cause of stumbling (and sterility) in the usual $C + V + S$ analysis is the failure to relate these magnitudes to the underlying technology, and the related failure to break down $C_j$ into its price and quantity factors. These capital letters, note, represent the bourgeois pricing regime in which

$$S_1/(C_1 + V_1) = S_2/(C_2 + V_2) = \cdots = R^* \quad (15.2)$$

where $R^*$ is the equilibrium profit rate.

In matrix terms, by the usual transposition of the row vectors of (15.1'), we get the simple reproduction tableau,

$$P[1 + R^*]aX + a_0 X + R^*\{P[1 + R^*]aX + a_0 X\} = P[1 + R^*]X \quad (15.1'')$$

where the composition of $X$ is determined by the $B - M$ selected by the capitalists subject to the simple reproduction no-saving condition

$$P[1 + R^*](B - M) = \sum_{j=1}^{n} S_j. \quad (15.3)$$

Except for the usual transposition of row and column, we then have the well-defined tableau of simple reproduction[23]

$$P[1 + R^*]a(I - a)^{-1}B + a_0(I - a)^{-1}B$$
$$+ R^*\{(P[1 + R^*]a + a_0)(I - a)^{-1}B\} = P[1 + R^*]X. \quad (15.4)$$

## 16. EXTENDED REPRODUCTION

Now, what about the case of extended reproduction, with growth rate $g = $ (saving rate out of profits)$/R^*$? Then we must have dynamically

$$aX(t + 1) \leq X(t) - B(t), \qquad a_0 X(t + 1) \leq L(t). \quad (16.1)$$

For $L(t) \equiv L_0(1 + g)^t$ and *all* variables growing in proportion

$$X(t) = (1 + g)^t X, \qquad B(t) = (1 + g)^t B, \qquad M(t) = (1 + g)^t mL_0. \quad (16.2)$$

Then (16.1) becomes

$$a(1 + g)X = X - B, \qquad a_0(1 + g)X = L_0. \quad (16.3)$$

Evidently (16.3) relating the coefficients of the $(1 + g)^t$ expression is just like (5.3), but with all $(a_0, a)$ coefficients blown up by $(1 + g)$ to allow for "widening" of capital goods.

As before, $B(t)$ gets split up into $M(t)$ and capitalists' expenditures for consumption, an amount determined by that part of their profit income which they do not invest. But as final product, we now have added to consumption $B$ the vector of net capital formation $gX$.

---

[23] I have qualms about calling $\rho$ by the commonly met Marxian expression "the ratio of 'unpaid labor' [which workers perform for the exploiting employers' ultimate benefit] to 'paid labor' [which workers do for themselves]." This expression tempts one to think that $\rho$ is an indicator of "profit share in NNP $\div$ labor share in NNP." But, in a general competitive regime, such an identification is not valid. Actually, a shift in employer's tastes toward consumption goods with low $a_{0j}/P_j[1]$ will raise profit's NNP share to its upper limit; conversely, a shift to high $a_{0j}/P_j[1]$ will depress it to its lower limit; yet $\rho$ itself remains constant between these limits independently of how, at the fixed profit rate $R^*$, capitalists select their luxury consumption. Although

$$\text{Min}[S_j/V_j] \leq \rho \leq \text{Max}[S_j/V_j],$$

it will generally *not* be the case that, "in the aggregate,"

$$\rho = \sum_j S_j / \sum_j V_j.$$

Only for the uninteresting lowercase "values" definition of $s_j/v_j$ will each of these equal $\rho$. But my defined $\rho$ *never* has need for any $s_1/v_1 = s_2/v_2$ concepts.

Applying prices $P[1 + R^*]$ to (16.3), we get the extended reproduction tableau for the system at time $t = 0$, namely,

$$\left\{\sum_{i=1}^{n} P_i[1 + R^*]a_{ij} X_j\right\} + \{a_{0j} X_j\} + R^*\left\{\sum_{i=1}^{n} P_i[1 + R^*]a_{ij} X_j + a_{0j} X_j\right\}$$

$$= P_j[1 + R^*]X_j + \sum_{i=1}^{n} P_i[1 + R^*]a_{ij} g X_j \qquad (j = 1, \ldots, n). \qquad (16.4)$$

The last term on the right, involving $gX_j$, represents net capital formation needed for widening of capital.

The left-hand side of (16.4) can be rewritten in the familiar form

$$C_j + V_j + R^*\{C_j + V_j\} \qquad (i = 1, \ldots, n)$$

of the extended reproduction tableaux—as in my text's equal-profit-rate tableaux.

## 17. The Alternative "Values" Regime of Marx

Now we must jettison Sections 10–16. ("Erase and replace." Or "Consider a dual accounting system.") I have argued that there is no good reason for a person well versed in algebra and logic to waste a moment on this alternative regime. (It is not a "dual" regime in the usual sense of dual—as for example Peter's game strategy as compared to Paul's dual strategy; or the primal linear programming maximum problem and its *dual* minimum problem; or the conjugate variables of coordinates and *dual* momenta in mechanics; or the point–line dualities of projective geometries; or the production function and its *dual* minimum unit cost of production; or optimal-control variables and their Pontryagin *dual* shadow prices; or of the duality theorem relating $P[1]X$ from (10.1) to $a_0(I - a)X^{-1}X$ of (8.1) and also discussed in Morishima's first chapter.

Still, this final section may be useful to those of us who wish, if only for antiquarian reasons, to be clear on the logical differences between the concepts involved in Marx's detour and those involved in a regime of ruthless competition.

The same subsistence wage defines, in the "values" regime, not "prices" written in capital letters, $P$, but "values," written as $(p_1, \ldots, p_n) = p$. It is understood that, as a useful convention, these prices are expressed in wage-numéraire units. They are defined in terms of a parameter $r$, the rate of equalized markups on direct wages alone and are written as $p_j[1 + r]$. Alternatively to the behavior equation of arbitrage in (10.1), we now *arbitrarily* postulate with Marx

$$p_j[1 + r] = a_{0j} + \sum_{i=1}^{n} p_i[1 + r]a_{ij} + ra_{0j} \qquad (j = 1, \ldots, n). \qquad (17.1)$$

In matrix terms this gives

$$p[1 + r] = a_0 + p[1 + r]a + ra_0 = a_0(I - a)^{-1}(1 + r)$$
$$= p[1](1 + r) = P[1](1 + r). \qquad (17.2)$$

Note that, for $r = 0$ and no exploitation, we do not get something *better* than our bourgeois $P[1]$ of embodied labors. Actually, we get the *identical* technocratic total labor requirements (direct plus indirect) of the undiluted labor theory of value, namely, $p[1] \equiv P[1]$. However, once workers do not get all the product, it is false in logic and in history (century by century) that there was ever a time when (17.2) could have been expected to prevail under the unequal organic composition of capital.

The equilibrium rate of surplus value, $r = r^*$, set by the minimum subsistence postulate of each laborer's consumption being $m$, is determined as the unique root of

$$p[1 + r]m = 1 = p[1]m(1 + r), \qquad r^* = (p[1]m)^{-1} - 1. \qquad (17.3)$$

It is an easy exercise, along the lines of footnote 22, to prove that the technocratically defined exploitative coefficient, $\rho$ of (4.1), must equal $r^*$:

$$r^* = \rho = P[1](B - mL)/P[1]mL = p[1](B - mL)/p[1]mL. \qquad (17.4)$$

When we apply the $X$ terms of (5.3') or (16.3) to (17.2), we get the simple reproduction or extended reproduction tableaux of Marx's "values" regimes (as in Volume II of *Capital*). Thus, in matrix terms

$$\{c\} + \{v\} + \{s\} = \{c\} + \{v\} + r\{v\} = \{p[1 + r^*]aX\} + \{a_0 X\} + r\{a_0 X\} \quad (17.5)$$

as in my text's simple and extended reproduction "values" tableaux.

Of course, by the stated Marx–Sraffa theorem, if $a_{0j}/P_j[1]$ are the same $\alpha$ for all industries, the two alternative regimes coincide, with

$$p_j[1 + \rho[R]] \equiv P_j[1 + R] \qquad (j = 1, \ldots, n)$$

and where $\rho[R]$ is defined as in (14.2).

In general, the "transformation problem" consists of the procedure that relates $r^*$ to $R^*$ taking into account the common subsistence-wage basket imposed on the alternative regimes. (Morishima uses the name "dynamic transformation problem" for discussion that relates "the saving rate out of profit" to "the saving rate out of surplus values," at a common growth rate imposed on the alternative regimes.)

How can one describe the greater algebraic simplicity of the values regime in comparison with the prices regime? Chiefly in three aspects:

$$\frac{p_j[1 + r]}{p_1[1 + r]} \equiv \frac{p_j[1](1 + r)}{p_1[1](1 + r)} = \frac{p_j[1]}{p_1[1]} \qquad \text{for all } r. \qquad (17.6)$$

No similar relation holds for general $P_j[1 + R]/P_1[1 + r]$.

Instead of having to solve an $n$th degree polynomial for the subsistence-wage profit rate $R^*$, as in (12.1), in (17.3) we need solve only a *linear* equation

$$1 = (p[1]m)(1 + r) \qquad (17.7')$$

for $r^*$!

Finally, suppose we have a reproduction tableau

$$c + v + s$$

for one real wage and $r^*$. Suppose there is now a change in $r^*$, but (for some odd reason) the capitalists spend on consumption goods in the same proportion that the workers spend. (Neither Marxians nor non-Marxians vouch for realism in this.) Then, by dropping our no-longer-useful convention of measuring always in wage-numéraire units, we can immediately write down the new reproduction tableau as equal to, or proportional to,

$$\{c'\} + \{v'\} + \{s'\} = \{c\} + \{\beta(v + s)\} + \{(1 - \beta)(v + s)\}.$$

That is, we simply repartition the total $v + s$ of each industry into new proportionate parts as between wages and surplus, leaving their $c$ and $v + s$ unchanged. This simplicity explains how Marx could consider a variety of cases without having to know how to handle his tableaux in detail.

Have I omitted an advantage for "values" when it comes to aggregating into more manageable subaggregates? Yes, deliberately. For I perceive no such advantages in the $p[1 + r]$ or $p[1]$ weights over the $P[1 + R^*]$ or $P[1 + R]$ weights. Since $R$, empirically, is poorly approximated by the biased value of $R = 0$, the $p[\cdot]$ values weights are unnecessarily biased. Apparently, Professor Morishima and I have not reached agreement on this point, since his case for values seems in significant part to hinge on this dubious aggregation question. (I like his generalization of the Marx–Sraffa theorem, but I think it is *better* stated in $P_j[1 + R]$ terms.)

Have I omitted an advantage for the $s_1/v_1 = s_2/v_2$ values regime when it comes to computing "employment multipliers" in the $L = \sum A_{0j} B_j = a_0(I - a)^{-1} B$ relation for societies' net-production-possibility frontier?[24] Yes, deliberately. For, *all* we need is $P[1] = a_0(I - a)^{-1}$ concepts of the *bourgeois* analysis for the $R^* = 0$ case.

---

[24] I owe to an unpublished review by von Weizsäcker [29] a similar point. Also for the point that $P_j[1]$, $p_j[1]$, or $p_j[1 + r]$ weights are worse than $P_j[1 + R]$ weights would be for some positive $R$ provides a more realistic approximation than $R = 0$. Arguing that $P_j[1]$ weights are more fixed than $P_j[1 + R]$ weights when $R$ is changing is like arguing that a frozen weather vane is less capricious than one which is changed by the wind!

## 18. Conclusion

I append in a terse footnote my elucidation of positions that Morishima has taken explicit exception to.[25] But I believe that this Appendix could be expanded to show that there is never macroeconomic or microeconomic advantage in rate-of-surplus-value analysis.

[25] The Morishima index has 16 references to me by name. Some, like those referring to pp. 29, 56, 140, 181, and 185 contain citations that represent no disagreements. Those on pp. 70 and 78 point out that the equal-internal-organic-composition of capitals case of Section VII of my 1971 *JEL* paper [13] is, for more-than-two department systems, a sufficient but not necessary condition—to which I gladly agree and authorize the reader to go through an "erase-and-replace" algorithm: *erase* the section's first word "The" and *replace* it by "A." And I agree that this singular case is not empirically realistic or even admissible for those Marx models in which wage goods are not used for production and other goods are: I never thought otherwise. All that I wished to do was show that Marx's algorithm need not always be wrong; but that *even* where it is not, his claim that we need "value" systems to reveal active exploitation processes is completely unfounded, *logically* and *empirically*, *macro*economically and microeconomically. [Although Morishima thinks that the issue of these two pages are relevant to his criticisms on other pages, I believe that once misunderstandings of my arguments are cleared away, such issues as whether $C_j + V_j = c_j + v_j$ (or, for Morishima's notation, $C_j^p + V_j^p = C^j + V^j$) are quite irrelevant and uninteresting.]

On p. 129 Morishima argues that Marx would have rejected the Neumann–Malthus model of Section IV of my *JEL* paper. That is no point against me (even *if* one argues that the logic of the passages Morishima quotes are relevant and cogent to the issue). I tried to fill the lacunae in Marx's models with possible realistic demographic and migration patterns. And, as a special limiting case of that model, I was able to generate exactly his exploitation conditions and to do it without departing from bourgeois competitive conditions.

On p. 115, Morishima somehow thinks that Dorfman–Samuelson–Solow (1958) [6] fall into the error of believing that competition requires profit to be zero. On pp. 224, 227, and 229 of Chapter 9 of ref. [6] where $P[1] = a_0 + P[1]a$, the authors are obviously dealing with the statical, instantaneous, or time-satiated Leontief system—as the chapter's beginning warns in its early statement: "Subsequent chapters will deal with dynamic models involving time and stock of capital, and also more general models...of Leon Walras and J. B. Clark," I, for one, regret that we did not explicitly deal with the special steady state case $P[1 + R] = \{a_0 + P[1 + R]\}(1 + R)$ in the book, but the very fact that all three of us in those same years were writing papers with $R > 0$ should have prevented any such odd interpretation of our view of the real competitive world. (In the same 1958 year, my *QJE* papers on Ricardo appeared [21, 22] with pre-Sraffa models of exactly this type, with or without joint production.) Making a Marx versus no-Marx issue on this is straining.

Most of the rest of the references—as for example, on pp. 39, 46–47, 59–61, 72, 74, and 85—involve the same set of misunderstandings, in which I (either alone, or in the good company of Marx, or of Paul Sweezy or Joan Robinson) am supposed to have made misleading assertions. Here is a typical sentence of mine, quoted no less than three times (pp. 47, 59, 74): "Volume I's first approximation of equal positive rates of surplus value, $S_j/V_j$, is not a simplifying assumption but rather—to the extent it contradicts equal profit rates $S_i/(V_i + C_i)$—a complicating detour." That sentence, the reader can confirm in context, purports to say precisely this:

## ACKNOWLEDGMENTS

I owe thanks to the National Science Foundation for financial aid, and to Norma Wasser for editorial assistance. I have also benefited from helpful comments by Professor Edward Ames of Stony Brook.

## REFERENCES

1. Samuelson, P. A., "Economists and the History of Ideas (Presidential Address)," *American Economic Review* **52** (March 1962), 1–18, reproduced as Chapter 113 in my *Collected Scientific Papers*, Volume II. Cambridge, Massachusetts: MIT Press, 1966. The quotation appears on p. 12 of the former, or p. 1510 of the latter.
2. Morishima, M., *Marx's Economics; A Dual Theory of Growth.* London and New York: Cambridge Univ. Press, 1973.
3. Jorgenson, D. W., "Stability of a Dynamic Input-Output System," *Review of Economic Studies* **28** (February 1961), 105–116.
4. Solow, R. M., "Competitive Valuation in a Dynamic Input-Output System," *Econometrica* **27** (January 1959), 30–53.

---

If, as generally holds, $C_i/(C_i + V_i) \neq C_j/(C_j + V_j)$, where these refer to an actual competitive system, then the $S_i/(C_i + V_i) = S_j/(C_j + V_j)$ real-world arbitrage equivalences imply $S_i/V_i \neq S_j/V_j$, except as an unuseful first approximation; and any alternative model or accounting regime, where by definition uniform $s_i/v_i$ rates are postulated and equal $s_i/(v_i + c_i)$ rates denied, represents an unuseful detour.

Now that is what is said. It could be right or wrong; the reader must weigh my many arguments, here and elsewhere, on this; and he may read the Morishima book line for line for light it throws on this Number One question.

But now see what interpretations are put on the quotation. It is supposed to overlook that $C_i + V_i \equiv c_i + v_i$ equivalences may not hold [and why should they?]. It is supposed to fail to see that $s_i/v_i = s_j/v_j$ is no logical contradiction to $S_i/V_i \neq S_j/V_j$. Perhaps when different writers use different letters for similar things, such misinterpretations are unavoidable. But no one who reads this paper and Morishima's book need be left with the view that we disagree on all the things his text thought we did.

Morishima's transformation algorithm is isomorphic to that of Seton [32] (and for that matter 1907 Bortkiewicz). So is mine. So *if* mine is [and it is] an "erase and replace algorithm," so must be his. To speak of a "dual accounting system" is to be isomorphic with what my *JEL* paper [13] said. If one reads the remaining dissents with quoted positions of mine, they are generally of the type, "Samuelson doesn't recognize that Marx is trying to reveal the deceptiveness of capitalist accounting in terms of price," to explain and uncover the divergences between what is written here as $P_j[1 + R]$'s and $p_j[1 + r]$'s or $p_j[1]$'s, or $(P_j[1 + R]m)^{-1}$ and $(P_j[1]m)^{-1}$, to illuminate exploitation, to show how profit has its source in living labor, etc. Of course I recognize that Marx was trying to do that (he said so repeatedly), and thought he had. But why should Morishima and I believe that he had *succeeded* in such a useful program? That is the Number One question, and I could not find a single theorem in the Morishima book that predisposes one toward a favorable verdict on the question. (This includes the more-than-one proposition awarded the adjective "fundamental.")

Space does not here permit the more detailed evaluation of Morishima's criticisms that one could make, nor the explicit singling out for praise of his many novel contributions.

5. Morishima, M., "Prices, Interest and Profits in a Dynamic Leontief System," *Econometrica* **26** (July 1958), 358–380; *Equilibrium, Stability and Growth*. London and New York: Oxford Univ. Press, 1964.

6. Dorfman, R., Samuelson, P., and Solow, R., *Linear Programming and Economic Analysis*, Chapter 11, pp. 283–300. New York: McGraw-Hill, 1959.

7. Hahn, F. H., "Equilibrium Dynamics with Heterogeneous Capital Goods," *Quarterly Journal of Economics* **80** (November 1966), 633–646.

8. Shell, K., and Stiglitz, J. E., "The Allocation of Investment in a Dynamic Economy," *Quarterly Journal of Economics* **8** (1967), 592–609.

9. Caton, C., and Shell, K., "An Exercise in the Theory of Heterogeneous Capital Accumulation," *Review of Economic Studies* **38** (January 1971), 13–22.

10. Samuelson, P. A., "Indeterminacy of Development in a Heterogeneous-Capital Model with Constant Saving Propensity," in *Essays in the Theory of Optimal Growth* (K. Shell, ed.). Cambridge, Massachusetts: MIT Press, 1967.

11. Burmeister, E., Caton, C., Dobell, A. R., and Ross, S., "The 'Saddlepoint Property' and the Structure of Dynamic Heterogeneous Capital Good Models," *Econometrica* **39** (January 1973).

12. Hayek, F. A., "The 'Paradox' of Saving," *Economica* **11** (May 1931), 125–169.

13. Samuelson, P. A., "Understanding the Marxian Notion of Exploitation: A Summary of the So-Called Transformation Problem between Marxian Values and Competitive Prices," *Journal of Economic Literature* **9** (June 1971), 399–431. Reproduced as Chapter 153, pp. 276–308, of my *Collected Scientific Papers* (hereafter *CSP*), Volume III. Cambridge, Massachusetts: MIT Press, 1972).

14. Samuelson, P. A., "The 'Transformation' from Marxian 'Value' to 'Competitive' Prices: A Process of Replacement and Rejection," *Proceedings of the National Academy of Sciences* **67** (September 1970), 423–425 (*CSP*, Volume III, Chapter 152, pp. 268–275).

15. Samuelson, P. A., and von Weizsäcker, C. C., "A New Labor Theory of Value for Rational Planning through Use of the Bourgeois Profit Rate," *Proceedings of the National Academy of Sciences* **68** (June 1971), 1192–1194 (*CSP*, Volume III, Chapter 155, pp. 312–136).

16. Samuelson, P. A., "The Economics of Marx: An Ecumenical Reply," *Journal of Economic Theory* **10** (March 1972), 51–56.

17. Samuelson, P. A., "Samuelson's 'Reply on Marxian Matters'," *Journal of Economic Theory* **11** (March 1973), 64–67.

18. Samuelson, P. A., "The Optimality of Profit-Inducing Prices under Ideal Planning," *Proceedings of the National Academy of Sciences* **70**, No. 7 (July 1973), 2109–2111.

19. Samuelson, P. A., "Wages and Interest: A Modern Dissection of Marxian Economic Models," *American Economic Review* **47** (December 1957), 884–912 (*CSP*, Volume I, Chapter 29, pp. 341–369).

20. Samuelson, P. A., "Reply," *American Economic Review* **50** (September 1960), 719–721 (*CSP*, Volume I, Chapter 30, pp. 370–372).

21. Samuelson, P. A., "A Modern Treatment of the Ricardian Economy: I. The Pricing of Goods and of Labor and Land Services," *Quarterly Journal of Economics* **73** (February 1959), 1–35 (*CSP*, Volume I, Chapter 31, pp. 373–407).

22. Samuelson, P. A., "A Modern Treatment of the Ricardian Economy: II. Capital and Interest Aspects of the Pricing Process," *Quarterly Journal of Economics* **73** (May 1959), pp. 217–231 (*CSP*, Volume 1, Chapter 32, pp. 408–422).

23. Samuelson, P. A., *Economics*, 9th ed., Chapter 42 Appendix. New York: McGraw-Hill, 1973.

24. Meek, R., "Some Notes on the Transformation Problem," *Economic Journal* **66** (March 1956), 94–107 (reprinted in Meek, R., *Economics and Ideology and Other Essays*, pp. 143–157. London: Chapman and Hall, 1967.

25. Baumol, W., "Values versus Prices, What Marx 'Really' Meant," *Journal of Economic Literature* **11** (December 1973).

26. Okishio, N., "A Mathematical Note on Marxian Theorems," *Weltwirtschaftliches Archiv* **2** (1963), 297–298.

27. Bródy, A., *Proportion, Prices and Planning: A Mathematical Restatement of the Labor Theory of Value*. Budapest: Akadémie Kiadó, and Amsterdam: North-Holland *Publ.*, 1970.

28. Johansen, L., "Labour Theory of Value and Marginal Utilities," *Economics of Planning* **3** No. 2 (September 1963).

29. von Weizsäcker, C. C., "Morishima on Marx" (Working Paper No. 7, Institute of Mathematical Economics, University of Bielefeld), 1972.

30. Sraffa, P., *Production of Commodities by Means of Commodities*, Appendix D, 3, 94. London and New York: Cambridge Univ. Press, 1960.

31. Samuelson, P. A., "Insight and Detour in the Theory of Exploitation: A Reply to Baumol," *Journal of Economic Literature* **11** (March 1974).

32. Seton, F., "The 'Transformation Problem'," *Review of Economic Studies* **25** (June 1957), 149–160.

*Part III*

# INVENTORY FLUCTUATIONS

# AGGREGATE INVENTORY BEHAVIOR

## A Critical Study of a Class of Models

John A. Carlson        William E. Wehrs

Purdue University      University of Wisconsin
                       La Crosse

## Introduction

The potential contribution of inventory investment to fluctuations in the level of national income was dramatized by Metzler in his article "The Nature and Stability of Inventory Cycles" [19]. He showed that interactions between adjustments in firms' expected demand, accelerator effects on planned inventory investment, and a multiplier impact on demand can, for a seemingly plausible range of parameter estimates, produce unstable cycles in economic activity.[1]

Subsequently, with the development of high-speed computing facilities, a number of economists have attempted to estimate some of the key parameters in equations that purport to explain variations in manufacturers' reported inventories. By the mid to late 1960's a consensus developed about how to interpret the results, at least for a relatively simple class of models. However, a few doubts have persisted as to the believability of the estimates.

---

[1] When an adaptive-expectations hypothesis is substituted for the extrapolative-expectations hypothesis used by Metzler, the region of instability in the parameter space appears to be reduced but by no means eliminated. See Carlson [4].

When in doubt there are at least two courses of action. One way is to "push on." Add new explanatory variables and see how this changes the estimated relationships. This, we venture to say, has been the typical procedure in econometric work.

Another way is to go back and critically examine the underlying model. If possible, formulate a decision problem to see if the solution is consistent with the available evidence. We propose to pursue this latter approach in connection with some simple models of finished-goods inventory investment that are direct descendents of the Metzler model. In this article any reference to the term "inventories" should be interpreted as inventories of finished goods.

Section I sketches the development of an equation that represents a flexible accelerator model modified to allow for plan revision. We then raise an objection that is most readily spelled out in conjunction with this simple model, although the same objection could be extended to more complex versions. It is known intuitively that two coefficients should be related, but there is no basis for judging the plausibility of a set of empirical estimates so long as time aggregation is treated implicitly.

Section II presents an optimizing model that allows time aggregation to enter explicitly. This enables us to specify a link between the typical empirical results and the parameters of the optimizing problem. Section III describes how we chose to limit the admissible parameter values. We find that there is an admissible subset of the parameter space consistent with some empirical results.

Section IV examines more closely the parameter values associated with the industries for which the estimates were obtained and reaches a somewhat negative conclusion. The flexible accelerator model, as presented here, does not seem to be an acceptable explanation for observed movements of finished goods inventories. At this stage we can only speculate about the most promising directions to pursue. The main point of the exercise, however, is to show that a decision-theoretic approach can be used to reconstitute implicit models in explicit form and thus move toward genuine tests of the models. The applicability of the procedure is not limited to inventory investment problems.

## I. The Basic Model

An important feature of many of these models is that they have been developed by what Theil calls the analogy approach [27, p. 6]. Hypotheses about relationships between aggregates and/or index numbers are formulated by analogy to the relationships that theory indicates for the microeconomic level. More specifically in the context of our problem, the analogy approach will be taken to mean viewing aggregate production as if it were the result of plans formed by a single decision maker. This approach might be defended as a "useful fiction" if there were no reason to doubt the validity of the ensuing results. Perhaps, more honestly, it is a "convenient fiction" when we do not know what else to do. We shall carry it along here because it characterizes all the models that fall into the class we are considering.

The Metzler model is formulated as one in period analysis. Time is divided into a sequence of periods. At the beginning of each period the decision makers form their notion of expected sales and then plan production levels. Actual sales are revealed during the period but production plans are not revised until the beginning of the next period. According to Metzler [18, p.10], "The only indispensable assumption in the theory of inventory cycles is that businessmen do not immediately adapt their production plan to a change in sales."

One of the potentially destabilizing elements in Metzler's model is the assumption that business seeks to maintain a constant ratio of inventories to expected sales. A simple alternative, often used in econometric work, is that businesses try to maintain inventories as a linear function of expected sales. The effect is qualitatively the same. The change in the "desired" stock of inventories is proportional to the change in expected sales.

It is not clear what length of time is the appropriate one for these decision periods. If the period is not very long and there are costs of adjusting the level of production, then it may be prudent for firms to adjust only part of the way from the current to the desired level of inventories. These considerations have led to the introduction of the flexible accelerator, proposed by Goodwin [9] for fixed investment, into models of inventory investment.

We can state more formally the elements of the model introduced so far. Assume that sales anticipations for period $t$ are formulated at the beginning of the period and that these anticipations can be represented by a single number which will be denoted $S_t^e$. At the beginning of the period, there is also assumed to be a desired level of inventories which, if costs of adjusting production are ignored, depend on the level of expected sales. If this is a linear function,

$$H_t^d = \alpha + \beta S_t^e, \qquad \beta > 0, \quad \alpha \geqq 0, \tag{1}$$

where $H_t^d$ is the so-called desired stock of inventories.

The flexible accelerator allows planned investment in inventories during a period to be some fraction of the difference between the actual stock at the end of period $t - 1$ and the desired stock. Let $\Delta H_t^p$ denote planned investment in inventories. Then

$$\Delta H_t^p = \delta(H_t^d - H_{t-1}), \qquad 0 < \delta \leqq 1, \tag{2}$$

where $\delta$ is the *planned partial-adjustment coefficient*.

Let $Q_t$ denote the quantity of finished goods produced during period $t$. If firms intend to meet expected sales and also adjust inventories as planned,

$$Q_t = S_t^e + \Delta H_t^p.$$

The actual change in inventories of finished goods $\Delta H_t = H_t - H_{t-1}$ will then be the difference between production of finished goods and the quantity sold $S_t$, i.e.,

$$\Delta H_t = Q_t - S_t$$

or substituting for $Q_t$

$$\Delta H_t = \Delta H_t^p + (S_t^e - S_t)$$

and for $\Delta H_t^p$ from (2):

$$\Delta H_t = \delta(H_t^d - H_{t-1}) + (S_t^e - S_t). \tag{3}$$

In this form, actual investment in inventory is partitioned into two parts, a planned component and an unplanned component that arises from forecasting errors. If $H_t^d$ is eliminated by using Eq. (1), the flexible-accelerator equation for inventory investment becomes

$$\Delta H_t = \delta\alpha + (1 + \delta\beta)S_t^e - S_t - \delta H_{t-1}. \tag{4}$$

Actual investment in finished-goods inventory can thus be written as a linear function of expected sales $S_t^e$, actual sales $S_t$, and stock of inventory at the end of the previous period $H_{t-1}$.

Since a number of surveys have collected data on businessmen's expectations of sales on a quarterly basis, it is tempting to assume that the period is a quarter of a year and try to estimate the parameters in Eq. (4). Suppose we have the following regression equation:

$$\Delta H_t = b_0 + b_1 S_t^e + b_2 S_t + b_3 H_{t-1} + u_t \tag{5}$$

where $u_t$ is an assumed random variation of $\Delta H_t$ around the linear function of the three variables $S_t^e$, $S_t$, and $H_{t-1}$. If there is a one-to-one correspondence between the $b_i$ coefficients in (5) and the coefficients in (4), one would expect to find $b_1$ greater than 1 and $b_2$ equal to $-1$. No sensible manipulation of these quarterly data are capable of producing coefficients of this sort. There is a ready explanation.

The decision period is generally believed to be considerably shorter than a quarter. Therefore, within a quarter, production plans can be adjusted to information about actual sales. Refer back to Eq. (3). There, actual investment in inventory differs from planned investment by the difference between expected and actual sales. Once it is recognized that production plans may be changed within the period, the discrepancy between actual and planned investment may be much less than that implied by (3). One way to allow for flexibility of production within the accounting period is to hypothesize:

$$\Delta H_t = \delta(H_t^{\,d} - H_{t-1}) + \gamma(S_t^{\,e} - S_t), \qquad -\delta\beta \leqq \gamma \leqq 1. \qquad (6)$$

This sort of equation has been used by Lovell [16], Orr [24], and Courchene [7] in econometric studies of inventory–investment equations. We shall call $\gamma$ the *production adaptation coefficient*. A positive $\gamma$ implies that inventory investment differs from the level originally planned by some proportion of the difference between expected and actual sales. When $\gamma$ is at its upper limit of 1, Eq. (6) reduces to Eq. (3). If $\gamma$ equals 0, the interpretation is that firms are able to carry out original investment plans $\Delta H_t^{\,p}$ and to adjust production to meet any sales not correctly anticipated. Finally, if within a data period firms revise planned investment, $\gamma$ may even be negative. The lower bound of $-\delta\beta$ allows for the possibility that actual investment might equal the hypothesized level that would have been planned if actual sales had been correctly forecast.

Other ways of allowing for within-period production flexibility can be found in studies by Modigliani and Weingartner [21], Pashigian [25], Lovell [17], Orr [23], and Modigliani and Sauerlander [20]. However, in the simple structure we are considering here, all of the different formulations result in the same regression equation and can be shown to be equivalent models.[2]

Substituting for $H_t^{\,d}$ in Eq. (6) leads to the equation

$$\Delta H_t = \delta\alpha + (\gamma + \delta\beta)S_t^{\,e} - \gamma S_t - \delta H_{t-1}. \qquad (7)$$

A comparison of coefficients in Eq. (7) with those in the regression equation (5) suggests that estimates of the structural parameters may be obtained from estimates of the $b_i$. Thus, $\gamma = -b_2$ and $\delta = -b_3$ if coefficients are equated. Adding a production adaptation coefficient to the flexible accelerator model means that a much wider range of $b_i$ coefficients may be interpreted as consistent with the model. In the terminology of hypothesis testing, for a given probability of a Type I error, this change increases the acceptable region in the sample space and makes the critical region smaller.

Despite a variety of data sources and differing estimation techniques, very similar interpretations have emerged from the studies of inventory investment. A set of representative estimates are arrayed in Table 1.

The consensus is that $\delta$ is small and $\gamma$ is very small. We shall characterize the typical empirical result as one in which $\delta \leqq 0.5$ and $\gamma \leqq 0.1$. These results are consistent with the class of models as specified and yet there remain suspicions that $\gamma$ may be "too low." See for example Lovell [16, p. 195].

---

[2] The details of this link are spelled out in an unpublished manuscript by J. A. Carlson, "Aggregative Inventory Investment and Anticipations" (June 1968).

TABLE 1

ESTIMATED VALUES OF $\delta$ AND $\gamma$

| References[a] | Total manufacturing | | Durable manufacturing | | Nondurable manufacturing | |
|---|---|---|---|---|---|---|
| | $\hat{\delta}$ | $\hat{\gamma}$ | $\hat{\delta}$ | $\hat{\gamma}$ | $\hat{\delta}$ | $\hat{\gamma}$ |
| Pashigian [25]– Orr [23] | 0.29 | −0.02 | 0.34 | 0.02 | 0.10 | 0.02 |
| Lovell [16] | 0.24 | 0.05 | 0.31 | 0.03 | 0.12 | 0.07 |
| Lovell [17] | | | 0.33 | −0.03 | 0.46 | 0.02 |
| Modigliani and Sauerlander [20] | | | | | 0.47 | −0.06 |

[a] A description of the data, estimation techniques, and derivation of the structural parameters is given by Wehrs [29, Appendix A].

Before he had a statistical estimate, Lovell [15, p. 307] expressed a belief that $\gamma = 0.5$ is "presumably a low value for a three-month planning period."

Another author, Orr [23, p. 372], finds these results "rather surprising" because the interpretation is that firms plan over a full quarter of a year to adjust less than half of the discrepancy between desired and actual stocks ($\delta \leq 0.5$), while during the quarter virtually all unplanned inventory investment arising as a result of forecast errors is eliminated ($\gamma \leq 0.1$). This is a puzzling position. Either the results are consistent with a proffered model and are not surprising, or else they are not consistent with the model and hence are surprising to anyone who tentatively believed the model.

The problem here is one of implicit theorizing, discussed years ago by Leontief [14]. Instead of deriving a parameter such as $\gamma$ from a "fundamental set of primary assumptions," many authors define it implicitly in terms of what would be found if the logical implications of aggregation over time were fully worked out in conjunction with the available data on inventory movements. As Leontief points out [14, p. 345]: "The main difficulty in dealing with implicit theorizing is that it is impervious to logical criticism. The weakness of its short-cut methods consists not in formal mistakes but rather in the irrelevance and unconclusiveness of the results obtained." The advantage of having a surprising result is that it helps draw attention to the existence of the implicit theorizing and to the need to undertake "the onerous task of explicit interpretations."

The class of models takes production as the only instrument. Unexpected changes in demand must then be met either by a change in the rate of production or by a change in the discrepancy between actual and desired stocks of inventory or by both. A small value of $\delta$ implies relatively slow adjustments in production rates and a small value of $\gamma$ implies relatively great flexibility in adjusting production. Both parameters should therefore not be too low at the same time. But what constitutes too low? To answer this sort of question we must develop a more complete model capable of being used to examine whether or not empirical evidence is consistent with attempts by business to achieve a specified set of objectives.

## II. A More Complete Model

The period over which data are collected will be called the *data period*, which, in many of the studies already cited, is a quarter of a year. The production adaptation coefficient was presumably introduced because of a belief that the decision period postulated in Metzler-type models is considerably shorter than the typical data period. We would like to retain most features of the basic model but introduce an explicit objective function and formally recognize the time aggregation involved in having several decision periods within a data period.

For simplicity and in order to maintain conformability with the basic model, variables other than production that firms in an industry might manipulate, such as prices and advertising expenses, have been ruled out of consideration here. Thus, demand is treated as exogenous to the model, and the appropriate objective is one of expected cost minimization over several periods into the future. Since the basic model has linear equations, we shall postulate a quadratic cost function.

While the planning horizon may carry well into the future, it is often necessary to make only one decision at a time with tentative plans for the future. The next decision may differ from the tentative plan if new information, which becomes available in the interim, calls for a revision of plans. Therefore, our model will be a sequential decision process in which production is determined for one decision period at a time, but plans are always tentatively formulated for future periods.

Despite the fact that the problem is formulated under conditions of risk, it may be treated as if it were formulated under certainty with the random variables in the problem replaced by their respective expected values. This means that future values of noncontrolled variables may be replaced by their conditional expectations, a result of Simon's [26] and Theil's [28] theorems on first-period certainty equivalence when there is a quadratic objective function subject to linear constraints. Consequently, the resulting first-period decision rules are not only linear, but also depend only on initial conditions and the first moment of the conditional distributions of future noncontrolled variables.

These advantages have been exploited by several economists in order to derive hypotheses regarding the behavior of production, price, finished-goods inventory, and unfilled orders at the industry level of aggregation. Belsley [2] considered production and finished inventories as decision variables and emphasized Abramovitz' [1] distinction between industries producing to stock and those producing to order. Childs [6] introduced a separate decision rule for the backlog of unfilled orders maintained by industries producing to order. More recently, Hay [11] has extended the analysis to include output price as a decision variable.

In his survey article on distributed lags, Griliches [10, p. 43] states that the basic premise of the *flexible* accelerator model is "the existence of some kind of costs of adjustment which in turn justify the observed inertia in the responsiveness of entrepreneurs . . . to economic stimuli." Eisner and Strotz [8] have shown that the linear flexible accelerator model can be derived from a cost situation in which a firm balances costs which increase as a quadratic function of the rate of investment or disinvestment, against quadratic costs of operating away from an ideal capital stock. In general, such a model requires two types of costs: the first a cost of being out of equilibrium, and the second a cost of change.

With desired inventory stock treated as an equilibrium concept, the "out of equilibrium" cost is the cost of deviation from the desired inventory level; and, in our model, the cost of change must be related to changes in the rate of production. Therefore, the following expected cost function is specified for a given period $i$ in an $I$ period planning horizon:

$$C_i = (a/2)p_{0,i}^2 + (b/2)(h_{0,i} - h_{0,i}^{\mathrm{m}})^2, \qquad a, b > 0, \tag{8}$$

where $p_{0,i}$ is the rate of production planned for decision period $i$, $h_{0,i}$ the stock of finished goods planned for the close of decision period $i$, and $h_{0,i}^{\mathrm{m}}$ the minimum-expected-cost level of finished-goods inventory at the close of decision period $i$.

The subscripts 0 denote that the expectations and plans are formulated at time 0. As a general convention, when there are two subscripts, the first denotes the time *at* which plans or expectations are formed and the second, when added to the first, gives the period *to* which the plans or expectations refer. Constant and linear terms are omitted from (8) for the sake of simplicity since they have no bearing on coefficients in the associated decision rule other than the intercept term.

The cost of adjustment in the rate of production is viewed as a smoothing cost and is represented by the parameter $a$. Each period in the planning horizon the marginal cost of production increases with the rate of production in that period. Such a specification is intended to reflect increasing inefficiencies as production is increased relative to current capacity. Unevenness in the rate of production is penalized.

The other term in (8) is a device for penalizing deviations from an assumed least-cost level of inventories $h_{0,i}^m$. The costs are proportional to the square of the deviation. We shall assume, as Belsley [2] has, that a quadratic function is a good approximation of stock costs within the range observed. The parameter $b > 0$ reflects an increasing marginal cost of deviating from the desired level. The primary objective of these assumptions is to obtain linear relationships as were postulated for the basic model.

Minimum-cost inventory is assumed to be related to anticipated sales as follows:

$$h_{0,i}^m = \alpha + \beta s_{0,i}^a, \qquad i = 1, 2, \ldots, I, \tag{9}$$

where $s_{0,i}^a$ is the anticipated sales for decision period $i$ with the anticipations formed at the start of the first period of an $I$-period planning horizon.

This specification of minimum-cost inventory is similar to the corresponding assumption, Eq. (1), of the basic model. The parameter $\beta$ is like Metzler's accelerator coefficient. An increment in future anticipated sales increases the least-cost, or "desired," stocks by $\beta$ times the change in $s_{0,i}^a$.

In lieu of actual data, there will need to be some mechanism by which anticipated sales can be revised between decision periods within a data period. The appropriate choice, of course, depends on the planners' perception of the process by which the sales data are generated. For purposes of working out precise links between structural parameters and regression parameters, assume that sales in each decision period are generated by a stochastic process proposed by Muth [22] or else follow what Box and Jenkins [3] call an ARIMA $(0, 1, 1)$ process. In either case, the forecasts that minimize the mean square error have two properties. The first is that anticipations are adaptive:

$$s_{j,1}^a = \omega s_j + (1 - \omega)s_{j-1,1}^a. \tag{10a}$$

The interpretation of (10a) is that the one-period-ahead forecast is a weighted average of the most recently observed $s_j$ and the one-period forecast made a period earlier.

The second property is that the forecasts for all other periods into the future are the same as the one-period forecasts, i.e.,

$$s_{j,i}^a = s_{j,1}^a \qquad \text{for} \quad i = 2, 3, \ldots, I. \tag{10b}$$

We could introduce a known or assumed trend in sales in a way that affects only the constant term in the final relationship, but to avoid cluttering the algebra, the model will be worked out with stochastic processes that call for forecasts shown by Eqs. (10a) and (10b).

By virtue of (10b), the minimum-cost level of inventories will be the same for all future decision periods until new information becomes available, i.e.,

$$h_{0,I}^{m} = h_{0,i}^{m}, \qquad i = 1, \ldots, I - 1.$$

Thus $h_{0,I}^{m}$ may be substituted for $h_{0,i}^{m}$ in the cost functions represented by $C_i$ in Eq. (8).

The planning objective will be to minimize the summation of $C_i$ from $i = 1$ to $I$, subject to the constraint that expected inventories of finished goods at the end of decision period $i$ equal expected inventories at the end of the previous period plus planned production minus expected sales during period $i$:

$$h_{0,i} = h_{0,i-1} + p_{0,i} - s_{0,i}^{a}, \qquad i = 1, \ldots, I, \tag{11}$$

and $h_{0,0}$ is the known initial stock $h_0$.

If projections are made for anticipated sales over the planning horizon and an interior solution is assumed, then the first-order conditions can be solved for production in the first decision period:

$$p_1 = p_{0,1} = \sum_{i=1}^{I} k_{I,i} s_{0,i}^{a} - k_{I,1}(h_0 - h_{0,I}^{m}). \tag{12}$$

The $k_{I,i}$ terms are relatively complicated functions of $I$ and the ratio $b/a$ but can be computed by a simple recursive relationship.[3]

Since $k_{I,1}$ is important in determining the partial adjustment coefficient, it is wise to consider why the length of the planning horizon has an influence. Suppose $h_0$ is less than $h_{0,I}^{m}$. There will be anticipated stock cost savings if $p_1$ is raised above anticipated sales $s_{0,1}^{a}$; but if sales are expected to stay at about that level, it may prove more costly to have a very large $p_1$ and plan to cut back production abruptly than it is to smooth production by keeping it slightly above sales and build up inventories gradually. The more periods there are in the planning horizon, the greater the perceived savings in stock costs if inventories can be quickly adjusted to $h_{0,i}^{m}$, and hence the larger will be the initial increase in production. Similar considerations apply to the situation where $h_0$ is above the minimum-cost level and a temporary cut in production is contemplated. Thus, $k_{I,1}$ will be greater, the longer the planning horizon $I$.

---

[3] The relationships between $k_{I,i}$ and the parameters $b/a$ and $I$ are developed by Wehrs [29]. The formula is

$$k_{I,i} = (b/a) d_{I,i}/[1 + (b/a) d_{I,i}]$$

where

$$
\begin{aligned}
d_{1,1} &\equiv 1 \\
d_{I,1} &\equiv 1 + (1 - k_{I-1,1}) d_{I-1,1} && \text{for } I = 2, 3, 4, \ldots \\
d_{I,i} &\equiv d_{I-1,i-1} - k_{I-1,i-1} d_{I-1,1} && \text{for } i = 2, \ldots, I \text{ and } I = 2, 3, 4, \ldots.
\end{aligned}
$$

The foregoing remarks indicate why the plan for $p_1$ depends on the planning horizon, but as the planning horizon is extended, $p_1$ converges to a finite value.[4] Thus, changes in $p_1$ associated with extensions in $I$ will eventually become smaller and smaller. The expression $|p_1^{I+1} - p_1^I|/p_1^I$ denotes the percentage change in $p_1$ that results from an increase of the planning horizon from $I$ to $I + 1$. Define an *effective planning horizon* $I^*$ as the minimum $I$ for which this percentage change in $p_1$ is less than some $\varepsilon$ for all $I \geq I^*$. We have taken the idea of defining an effective planning horizon in this way from Kunreuther [13]. For purposes of computing an $I^*$ from $\varepsilon$, we shall assume that sales expectations are stationary and that initial stocks are at their least cost level. $I^*$ then becomes a function only of $\varepsilon$ and $b/a$. For later reference, Table 2 shows some values of $I^*$ for a selected set of values of $\varepsilon$ and $b/a$.

TABLE 2

NUMBER OF DECISION PERIODS IN AN EFFECTIVE PLANNING HORIZON FOR ALTERNATIVE VALUES OF $b/a$ AND $\varepsilon$

| $\varepsilon$ | $b/a$ | | | | | | |
|---|---|---|---|---|---|---|---|
| | 0.0001 | 0.001 | 0.01 | 0.1 | 1.0 | 10.0 | 100.0 |
| 0.01 | 122 | 65 | 30 | 13 | 5 | 2 | 1 |
| 0.05 | 38 | 29 | 17 | 8 | 4 | 2 | 1 |
| 0.10 | 20 | 18 | 12 | 6 | 3 | 1 | 1 |
| 0.15 | 14 | 13 | 10 | 5 | 3 | 1 | 1 |
| 0.20 | 10 | 10 | 8 | 5 | 2 | 1 | 1 |
| 0.25 | 8 | 8 | 7 | 4 | 2 | 1 | 1 |

Presumably the determination of the appropriate $\varepsilon$ could also be formulated as a decision involving cost tradeoffs. There is a cost of not projecting demand any further into the future and a cost of making additional projections. A formal model incorporating these features is not presented here. The parameter $\varepsilon$ is treated as if it were exogenously determined, and in what follows the planning horizon is assumed to be of length $I^*$. This means that the decision-rule coefficients $k_{I,i}$ can now be treated as functions of $\varepsilon$ and $b/a$.

We are assuming that the level of production $p_1$ planned at time 0 for decision period 1 can be realized during that period. At the time that $p_1$ is determined, the cost minimization solution yields a tentative production plan: $p_{0,2}, \ldots, p_{0,I}$. However, before the plan for period 2 needs to be carried out,

---

[4] The structure of the problem assures this convergence. A discussion of such problems is contained in an unpublished paper by J. A. Carlson, "On Solving a Class of Economic Planning Problems" (June 1972).

the planner has information about $s_1$ and is free to revise his expectations of future sales and his production plans for decision period 2. The revised sales anticipations are to be in accordance with Eqs. (10a) and (10b).

With revised anticipations and new desired stock, the same sort of first-period production is determined for period 2, then for period 3, and so on. Let there be $T$ decision periods in the data period so that production for each of the decision periods is given by the formula

$$p_j = p_{j-1,1} = \sum_{i=1}^{I^*} k_{I,i} s_{j-1,i}^a - k_{I,1}(h_{j-1} - h_{j-1,1}^m), \qquad j = 1, 2, \dots, T.$$

(13)

Equation (13) becomes Eq. (12) when $j = 1$. The level of inventories $h_j$ at the end of period $j$ is given by

$$h_j = h_{j-1} + p_j - s_j.$$

(14)

After $p_T$ has been determined and $s_T$ is known, the actual inventory investment in terms of actual sales, initial expected sales, and initial inventories for data period $t$ can be found from $\Delta H_t = h_T - h_0$ by successively substituting for all other variables. The resulting linear equation may be written

$$\Delta H_t = b_0 + \sum_{i=1}^{I^*} b_{1,i} s_{0,i}^a + \sum_{j=1}^{T} b_{2,j} s_j + b_3 h_0.$$

(15)

The $b$ coefficients are functions of the parameters of the more complete model. See Wehrs [29] for more details. Of particular interest, $b_3$ is a function of the parameters $b/a$, $T$, and $\varepsilon$ while the $b_{2,j}$ coefficients depend not only on $b/a$, $T$, and $\varepsilon$, but also on $\omega$ and $\beta$. These latter effects arise because $s_j$ represents information that is not available at the beginning of the data period. As the $s_j$ become known, their influence on actual investment in inventory depends (1) on how much $s_j$ influences anticipated sales (the $\omega$ parameter) and (2) on how much a change in anticipated sales changes the hypothesized desired inventory (the $\beta$ parameter).

We would now like to link Eq. (15) from the more complete model to the regression equation (5) used in conjunction with the basic model. In Eq. (5), $S_t^e$ denotes sales anticipated for the data period $t$ with the anticipations formed at the beginning of the data period. In terms of the anticipations allocated to each decision period,

$$S_t^e = \sum_{i=1}^{T} s_{0,i}^a.$$

If there is no expected trend in anticipated sales over the planning horizon, then by (10b) it is possible to write

$$\sum_{i=1}^{I^*} b_{1,i} s^a_{0,i} = b_1' S_t^e \tag{16}$$

where $b_1' = (1/T) \sum_{i=1}^{I^*} b_{1,i}$.

The next step is to relate the $b_{2,j}$ coefficients in (15) to the $b_2$ coefficient in (5). Sales for data period $t$ are $S_t = \sum_{j=1}^{T} s_j$. This, of course, is after the data period is completed. Since the $s_j$ cannot be known with certainty in advance, it is useful to treat them as random variables with an expected value $s$, i.e.,

$$E(s_j) = s \quad \text{for} \quad j = 1, 2, \ldots, T. \tag{17}$$

Then let

$$b_2' = (1/T) \sum_{i=1}^{T} b_{2,j}. \tag{18}$$

Now add and subtract $b_2' S_t$ on the right-hand side of (15) as well as substituting for the $s^a_{0,i}$ from (16). The resulting equation is

$$\Delta H_t = b_0 + b_1' S_t^e + b_2' S_t + b_3 h_0 + u_t \tag{19}$$

where $u_t = \sum_{j=1}^{T} (b_{2,j} - b_2') s_j$ and $u_t$ is a random variable because $s_j$ is a random variable. Furthermore, the common assumption for a regression equation that the expected value of $u_t$ be zero is satisfied by virtue of (17) and (18).

There is now a term-by-term correspondence between (19) and the flexible accelerator model modified for production adaptation. If coefficients are equated, $\gamma = -b_2'$, $\delta = -b_3$. By design this is the same sort of correspondence used by other authors with the basic model. The difference is that with the more complete model the coefficients relate to a set of structural parameters that enter a specified decision model.[5] They can therefore be used to identify tradeoffs between $\gamma$ and $\delta$ and hence to determine the plausibility of the typical empirical result.

[5] The correspondence takes the form

$$\gamma = T^{-1} \left\{ \frac{1 - (1 - k_{I,1})^T}{k_{I,1}} - \omega \left[ \sum_{i=1}^{I} k_{I,i} + \beta k_{I,1} \right] \left[ \frac{\sum_{i=1}^{T-1} (1 - k_{I,1})^i - \sum_{i=1}^{T-1} (1 - \omega)^i}{\omega - k_{I,1}} \right] \right\}$$

and

$$\delta = 1 - (1 - k_{I,1})^T$$

where the $k_{I,i}$ are defined in footnote 4.

### III. A Preliminary Test for Consistency

The regression coefficients of particular interest in this paper are functions of five structural parameters in the more complete model, but the functions are too messy to evaluate analytically. In order to determine the relationship between $\gamma$ and $\delta$, we need to conduct a search over the space of the structural parameters. This requires specifying *a priori* restrictions to be imposed on the range of each of the parameters $(T, \beta, \omega, \varepsilon, b/a)$.

($T$) The parameter $T$ is the number of decision periods within a data period, which will be taken to be a quarter of a year. We lack direct information about what values of $T$ would be appropriate in various manufacturing industries and must rely on indirect considerations. Carlson [5] has shown that it is possible to use accounting data to obtain rough estimates of how long on the average it takes to produce items in different industries. Call this the *production period*. In all two-digit industries the production period appears to be less than a quarter, and in two-thirds of them it is less than a month. Fifteen of the 19 industries had estimated production periods of six weeks or less. The lowest was about one week. Our model assumes that by the end of a decision period, planned production can be realized. This suggests that if the decision period is less than the production period, plans must be formulated over more than one production period. While there is no reason to doubt that the model could be reformulated to handle such cases, the gain in additional flexibility in planning at more frequent intervals is at least partially offset by the rigidity of having a time-to-completion-of-production that extends over several decision periods. We therefore contend that the set

$$T \in \{1, 2, 3, 4, 6, 12\}$$

will span most cases of frequency of plan revision.

These values for $T$ correspond to decision periods of twelve weeks ($T = 1$), six weeks ($T = 2$), four weeks ($T = 3$), three weeks ($T = 4$), two weeks ($T = 6$), and one week ($T = 12$).

($\beta$) In Eq. (9) the parameters $\alpha$ and $\beta$ serve to link the desired inventory level with anticipated sales. We have assumed that $\alpha$ is restricted to nonnegative values and $\beta$ to positive values. It would be desirable if $\beta$ could be further restricted.

If $\alpha = 0$, $\beta$ denotes a desired-inventory/anticipated-sales ratio, and rough estimates may be obtained by initially calculating $\beta_Q$, the inventory/quarterly sales ratios. Since inventory in the numerator is a stock variable (and hence invariant with respect to the length of the period), while sales in the denominator is a flow variable, an estimate of $\beta$ pertaining to a decision period will be directly proportional to the number of decision periods $(T)$ in the data period, i.e., $\beta = \beta_Q T$.

Examination of quarterly finished-goods-inventory/shipments ratios indicates that for manufacturing industries this ratio rarely exceeds a value of unity. If $\alpha > 0$, the implied marginal inventory/sales ratio is reduced. Therefore, $\beta_Q$ will be restricted as $0 < \beta_Q \leq 1$.

($\omega$) The adaptive anticipations hypothesis, Eq. (10a), depicts a type of error-correcting behavior. This hypothesis may be expressed in the form

$$s^a_{j, 1} = s^a_{j-1, 1} + \omega(s_j - s^a_{j-1, 1}).$$

Future anticipations are revised in proportion to the most recent anticipation error. If $\omega = 0$, the forecast is the same as in previous periods and no account is taken of error. If $\omega = 1$, the forecast is a simple projection of the most recent realization of the variable being forecast. For a stochastic process of the sort postulated by Muth [22], $\omega$ should lie in the interval from zero to one. Therefore, $\omega$ will be restricted as $0 \leq \omega \leq 1$.

($\varepsilon$) An effective planning horizon $(I^*)$ is defined so that the absolute percentage change in first-period production, when the horizon is extended one period beyond the effective length, is small to a specified degree. The $\varepsilon$ denotes the upper bound allowed on this percentage change in first-period production. In the absence of any prior knowledge as to feasible values for $\varepsilon$, this parameter will be restricted to values between 1 and 25% and only a discrete set of values will be considered, i.e.,

$$\varepsilon \in \{0.01, 0.05, 0.10, 0.15, 0.20, 0.25\}.$$

The upper bound on $\varepsilon$ may be implausibly high. It implies that a one-period extension of the horizon could change planned production by about 25%.

($b/a$) Both the cost parameters $b$ and $a$ in (8) are restricted to positive values in order to ensure a strictly convex cost equation. In the absence of any knowledge as to feasible values for their ratio, the following restriction will be imposed: $b/a > 0$.

Having tentatively limited the domain of the functions determining $\delta$ and $\gamma$, it is of interest to determine how changes in individual parameters from the more complete model affect the theoretical values of $\delta$ and $\gamma$. Knowledge of the partial derivatives of these functions with respect to each of their arguments would provide the necessary information. However, it has not proved possible to determine the partial derivatives of these functions analytically.

Instead, a numerical analysis of the response of the functions to variations in the parameters of the more complete model has been conducted over a wide range of values in the domain of the functions. The $b/a$ assumed values between 0.0001 and 100.0; $T$ and $\varepsilon$ assumed all six values in their respective admissible set, and both $\beta_Q$ and $\omega$ assumed values between 0.1 and 1.0. The results of this analysis indicate that if the partial derivatives could be analytically determined, the signs would be as follows:[6]

$$\frac{\partial \delta}{\partial(b/a)} > 0, \qquad \frac{\partial \delta}{\partial T} > 0, \qquad \frac{\partial \delta}{\partial \varepsilon} < 0,$$

$$\frac{\partial \gamma}{\partial(b/a)} < 0, \qquad \frac{\partial \gamma}{\partial T} < 0, \qquad \frac{\partial \gamma}{\partial \varepsilon} > 0, \qquad \frac{\partial \gamma}{\partial \omega} < 0, \qquad \frac{\partial \gamma}{\partial \beta} < 0.$$

The parameter $\delta$, it will be recalled, indicates the degree of influence of the initial deviation between actual and desired stocks on the actual change in inventories over a data period. It has been called the planned partial adjustment coefficient. The $\gamma$ indicates the influence of the discrepancy between anticipated and actual sales on the change in inventories and has been called the production adaptation coefficient. The partials with respect to $b/a$, $T$, and $\varepsilon$ emphasize the inverse relationship between $\delta$ and $\gamma$ and can be used to offer explicit explanations for the hither-to ad hoc idea that anything that increases $\delta$ ought to decrease $\gamma$.

Consider first $b/a$. The cost function was set up so that the parameter $b$ influences the cost of being out of equilibrium and the parameter $a$ influences the cost of change. Thus, the higher the ratio $b/a$, the faster will be the planned adjustment toward the desired stock. In terms of $\delta$ and $\gamma$, the higher is $b/a$, the more of the discrepancy between actual and desired stocks will be planned to be removed over the data period (higher $\delta$) and the less of an influence will a deviation of actual and expected sales have on inventory investment (lower $\gamma$).

The effect of a change in $T$ is similar. Other things, including $b/a$, held constant, a larger $T$ allows more periods in which to remove the discrepancy between actual and desired stocks (higher $\delta$) and to correct for sales surprises during the data period (smaller $\gamma$).

A lower value of $\varepsilon$ implies a longer planning horizon. See Table 2. The longer the planning horizon, the more the present benefit of adjusting production early in order to avoid future stock costs in subsequent periods, since

---

[6] The concept of a derivative is used here strictly as an expository device. The complexity of the functions involved precludes an investigation as to whether or not the functions are in general differentiable in the given domain. However, the numerical analysis does indicate that the direction of change in function values is consistent in all cases.

more periods are taken into account in the objective function. This means that a lower $\varepsilon$ calls for a higher $\delta$ and lower $\gamma$.

The effects of $\omega$ and $\beta$ were anticipated in our discussion above of Eq. (15). They do not influence $\delta$ since $\delta$ is determined at the beginning of the data period. $\beta$ influences desired stocks but not the optimal rate of approach. Both $\omega$ and $\beta$, however, do influence the extent of the unplanned (as of the beginning of the data period) adjustment to new information. The more weight put on current information in forming expectations (higher $\omega$), the less influence will the discrepancy between sales anticipated at the beginning of the data period and actual sales have on inventory investment ($\partial\gamma/\partial\omega < 0$). $\beta$ determines the marginal response in desired inventory to revised sales anticipations. Anything in this model that increases the production response to information obtained during the data period lessens the influence of the discrepancy between anticipated and actual sales. Hence $\partial\gamma/\partial\beta < 0$.

We are now ready to consider the following question. Is there a subset of the admissible region from the parameter space of the more complete model that corresponds to the typical empirical result ($\delta \leq 0.5$, $\gamma \leq 0.1$)? To answer this question a search procedure has been devised.

The parameters $\varepsilon$ and $T$ have each been limited to six possible values. It is feasible to search over all 36 pairs. For each ($\varepsilon$, $T$) pair there will be a range of values of $b/a$ such that $\delta \leq 0.5$. From the partial derivative $\partial\gamma/\partial(b/a) < 0$, an increase in $b/a$ will decrease $\gamma$. Since the problem will be to find very low values of $\gamma$, the largest value of $b/a$ was chosen such that $\delta \leq 0.5$. These values of $b/a$ are arrayed in Table 3 beside a value for $T$ within a section corresponding to a value of $\varepsilon$. For example, with $\varepsilon = 0.01$ and $T = 4$, $\delta \leq 0.5$ when $b/a \leq 0.007$.

The next step was to consider what values of $\beta_Q$ and $\omega$ will also satisfy the restriction $\gamma \leq 0.1$ given $\varepsilon$, $T$, and $b/a$. To limit the search, values of $\beta_Q$ were introduced in increments of 0.1 from 0.1 to 1.0. Since an increase in $\omega$ decreases $\gamma$, the smallest $\omega \leq 1.0$ such that $\gamma \leq 0.1$ were found. A blank space in Table 3 means that no such $\omega \leq 1.0$ could be found. Other entries imply that a subset of the parameter space as initially restricted does exist such that the typical empirical result can be expected to hold. Only results for $\varepsilon = 0.01$, 0.05, and 0.10 are shown in Table 3. The table would be completely empty for $\varepsilon = 0.25$ and there would be only two or three nonempty entries when $\varepsilon = 0.15$ and 0.20, all with $\beta_Q = 0.9$ or 1.0.

For what follows in the next section, we should emphasize one other way of looking at the nonblank entries in Table 3. For any set of values of $\varepsilon$, $T$, and $b/a$ such that $\delta \leq 0.5$, there is a lowest value of $\beta_Q$ that satisfies the constraints $\gamma \leq 0.1$ and $\omega \leq 1.0$. For example, with $(\varepsilon, T, b/a) = (0.01, 4, 0.007)$, the lowest value of $\beta_Q$ (to the nearest 0.1) consistent with the constraints can be found in Table 3 to be 0.3.

# TABLE 3

COMPUTER SEARCH OF THE PARAMETER SPACE: MINIMUM ADMISSIBLE VALUES OF $\omega^a$

| $T$ | $b/a^b$ | $\beta_Q = 0.1$ | $\beta_Q = 0.2$ | $\beta_Q = 0.3$ | $\beta_Q = 0.4$ | $\beta_Q = 0.5$ | $\beta_Q = 0.6$ | $\beta_Q = 0.7$ | $\beta_Q = 0.8$ | $\beta_Q = 0.9$ | $\beta_Q = 1.0$ |
|---|---|---|---|---|---|---|---|---|---|---|---|
| | | | | | | $\varepsilon = 0.01$ | | | | | |
| 1 | 0.09 | | | | | | | | | | |
| 2 | 0.02 | | | | | | | | | | |
| 3 | 0.01 | | | | | 0.94 | 0.87 | 0.81 | 0.76 | 0.71 | 0.67 |
| 4 | 0.007 | | | 0.85 | 0.74 | 0.66 | 0.60 | 0.56 | 0.52 | 0.48 | 0.45 |
| 6 | 0.003 | | 0.81 | 0.65 | 0.55 | 0.48 | 0.54 | 0.39 | 0.36 | 0.34 | 0.31 |
| 12 | 0.0009 | | 0.57 | 0.40 | 0.32 | 0.27 | 0.24 | 0.21 | 0.19 | 0.17 | 0.16 |
| | | | | | | $\varepsilon = 0.05$ | | | | | |
| 1 | 0.09 | | | | | | | | | | |
| 2 | 0.05 | | | | | | | | | | |
| 3 | 0.02 | | | | | | | 0.95 | 0.87 | 0.80 | 0.75 |
| 4 | 0.01 | | | | | | | 0.97 | 0.85 | 0.76 | 0.69 |
| 6 | 0.007 | | | | | 0.85 | 0.66 | 0.55 | 0.48 | 0.43 | 0.39 |
| 12 | 0.002 | | | | | | | | 0.56 | 0.41 | 0.33 |
| | | | | | | $\varepsilon = 0.1$ | | | | | |
| 1 | 0.09 | | | | | | | | | | |
| 2 | 0.07 | | | | | | | | | | |
| 3 | 0.03 | | | | | | | | | | 0.93 |
| 4 | 0.01 | | | | | | | | | | |
| 6 | 0.01 | | | | | | | | | 0.70 | 0.50 |
| 12 | 0.004 | | | | | | | 0.92 | 0.70 | 0.58 | 0.44 |

[a] Given $\varepsilon$, $T$, $b/a$, and $\beta_Q$, the value shown is the smallest $\omega$ such that $\gamma \leqq 0.10$.

[b] Given $\varepsilon$ and $T$, the value shown is the largest $b/a$ such that $\delta \leqq 0.50$.

## IV. Conclusion

Without looking further at the parameter restrictions, one can say that it may not be surprising to obtain the typical empirical result. With low values of $b/a$ and $\varepsilon$ and with high values of $T$, $\omega$, $\beta_Q$, it is possible to have small values of $\delta$ and very small values of $\gamma$. The main question to answer now is: For the industries from which the empirical results were obtained, can the structural parameters be expected to fall within the necessary ranges?

Consider, in particular, $\beta_Q$. In the discussion above on parameter restrictions, it was pointed out that with $\alpha \geq 0$, the upper bound for $\beta_Q$ may be approximated by the actual inventory/shipments ratio. For the aggregate industries reported in Table 1, we have prepared Table 4 to show the cor-

TABLE 4

SAMPLE MEAN AND STANDARD DEVIATION OF FINISHED-GOODS-INVENTORY/QUARTERLY-SHIPMENTS RATIOS: I 1961–I 1968

|  | Mean | Standard deviation |
|---|---|---|
| Total manufacturing | 0.190 | 0.009 |
| Durable manufacturing | 0.174 | 0.013 |
| Nondurable manufacturing | 0.209 | 0.005 |

responding finished-goods-inventory/quarterly-shipments ratio. For these aggregate industries, the ratios are all close to 0.2. If $\beta_Q$ is limited to 0.2 or below and we refer to Table 3 to find nonempty entries that correspond to such a restriction, we need to consider only the pairs $(\varepsilon, T) = (0.01, 6)$ and $(0.01, 12)$.

Using an estimation procedure for the production period of the sort employed by Carlson [5], we find that the elements of our set $T$ that come closest to the estimates for the production periods in the corresponding industries are: total manufacturing, $\hat{T} = 3$; durable manufacturing, $\hat{T} = 2$; nondurable manufacturing, $\hat{T} = 6$.

Only for nondurables is there *any* overlap with a region of the parameter space consistent with the typical empirical result.[7] But even this is tenuous. In Table 1, many of the estimates of $\delta$ are well below 0.5 and many of the

[7] In correspondence, Gerald Childs has made the following interesting point. When firms produce to order, as they do in many durable-goods industries, shipments are not exogenous. Therefore, it may not be surprising that only for nondurables is there possible conformity with the underlying production-to-stock model.

estimates of $\gamma$ are below 0.1. For smaller values of $\delta$, the $b/a$ entries in Table 3 would have to be smaller. This further restricts the range in the $(\omega, \beta)$ parameter space such that $\gamma \leqq 0.1$. Then if $\gamma$ is believed to be some number less than 0.1, the parameter space consistent with the estimates is restricted to still higher ranges of $\omega$ and $\beta$, so that the overlap becomes even less likely.

Furthermore, when $\varepsilon = 0.01$ and $T = 6$, the upper bound on $b/a$ is 0.003 if $\delta$ is as large as 0.5. The combinations of $\varepsilon = 0.01$ and $b/a = 0.003$ implies an effective planning horizon $I^*$ of 42 decision periods! With $T = 6$, plans are revised every 2 weeks. The model then calls for an average horizon in calendar time of 84 weeks, or more than $1\frac{1}{2}$ years.

In our more complete model, the typical empirical result requires small values of $b/a$. A lower $b/a$ implies that the out-of-equilibrium costs are considered less important relative to the production-smoothing costs. This is what generates a slow stock adjustment and may account for the relatively low estimates of $\delta$. At this point we have no evidence that would rule out very low values of $b/a$, so long as they are positive.

The idea of quick plan revision, incorporated in the low estimates of the parameter $\gamma$, then requires a large number of periods in the planning horizon (high $I^*$ or low $\varepsilon$), a relatively high accelerator coefficient $\beta$, a responsive adjustment of expectations (high $\omega$), and a relatively large number of decision periods ($T$) per data period. Our examination of industry data leads us to the conclusion that, along these dimensions, the evidence is against the hypothesis that this model adequately explains the observed patterns of inventory movements.

The model was designed primarily to fill in the time aggregation relationships left implicit in the literature. Several possibilities come to mind as to why the simple model is unacceptable. In fact, every assumption made could be modified. As mentioned earlier, some authors have already considered added dimensions to the decision problem, such as including unfilled orders and price in the objective function and/or the constraints. There is the possibility, introduced by Childs in this volume, of allowing the adjustment parameters to vary with business conditions. There may also be a need to recognize more explicitly the effect of aggregating over firms as well as over time.[8] Whatever directions are pursued, we challenge others to propose explanations for inventory movements that can withstand critical scrutiny and to demonstrate convincingly the acceptability of their models.

---

[8] There is evidence that substantial estimation bias may occur when there is firm as well as time aggregation, whereas relatively little bias has been found because of time aggregation alone within the relevant parameter ranges of our more complete model. See Wehrs [30].

## REFERENCES

1. Abramovitz, M., *Inventories and Business Cycles*. New York: National Bureau of Economic Research, 1950.
2. Belsley, D. A., *Industry Production Behavior: The Order-Stock Distinction*. Amsterdam: North-Holland Publ., 1969.
3. Box, G. E. P., and Jenkins, G. M., *Time Series Analysis: Forecasting and Control*. San Francisco: Holden-Day, 1970.
4. Carlson, J. A., " Forecasting Errors and Business Cycles," *American Economic Review* **57**, No. 3 (June 1967), 462–481.
5. Carlson, J. A., "The Production Lag," *American Economic Review* **63**, No. 1 (March 1973), 73–86.
6. Childs, G. L., *Unfilled Orders and Inventories: A Structural Analysis*. Amsterdam: North-Holland Publ., 1967.
7. Courchene, T., "Inventory Behavior and the Stock-Order Distinction: An Analysis by Industry and Stage of Fabrication with Empirical Application to the Canadian Manufacturing Sector," *Canadian Journal of Economics and Political Science* **33** (August 1967), 325–357.
8. Eisner, R., and Strotz, R., "Determinants of Business Investment," in *Impacts of Monetary Policy* (a series of research studies prepared for the Commission on Money and Credit), pp. 61–337. Englewood Cliffs, New Jersey: Prentice-Hall, 1963.
9. Goodwin, R., "Secular and Cyclical Aspects of the Multiplier and the Accelerator," in *Income, Employment and Public Policy: Essays in Honor of Alvin H. Hansen*. New York: Norton, 1948.
10. Griliches, Z., "Distributed Lags: A Survey," *Econometrica* **35**, No. 1 (January 1967), 16–49.
11. Hay, G. A., "Production, Price, and Inventory Theory," *American Economic Review* **60**, No. 4 (September 1970), 531–545.
12. Holt, C., and Modigliani, F., "Firm Cost Structures and the Dynamic Responses of Inventories, Production, Work Force, and Orders to Sales Fluctuations," In Joint Economic Committee of the U.S., 87th Congress, 1st Session, 1961. *Inventory Fluctuations and Economic Stabilization*, Part II, pp. 3–55. Washington, D.C.: U.S. Govt. Printing Office, 1961.
13. Kunreuther, H., "Determining Planning Horizons for Quadratic Production and Inventory Costs," Center for Mathematical Studies in Business and Economics Rep. No. 7025, Univ. of Chicago (June 1970).
14. Leontief, W., "Implicit Theorizing: A Methodological Criticism of the Neo-Cambridge School," *Quarterly Journal of Economics* **51** (February 1937), 337–351.
15. Lovell, M. G., "Manufacturers' Inventories, Sales Expectations, and the Acceleration Principle," *Econometrica* **29**, No. 3 (July 1961), 293–314.
16. Lovell, M. G., "Determinants of Inventory Investment," in National Bureau of Economic Research, *Models of Income Determination* (Studies in Income and Wealth, Vol. 28), pp. 177–244. Princeton, New Jersey: Princeton Univ. Press, 1964.
17. Lovell, M. G., "Sales Anticipations, Planned Inventory Investment, and Realizations," in National Bureau of Economic Research, *Determinants of Investment Behavior*, pp. 537–580. New York: Columbia Univ. Press, 1967.
18. Metzler, L., "Factors Governing the Length of Inventory Cycles," *The Review of Economic Statistics* **29**, No. 1 (February 1947), 1–14.
19. Metzler, L., "The Nature and Stability of Inventory Cycles," *The Review of Economic Statistics* **23**, No. 1 (February 1941), 113–129.

20. Modigliani, F., and Sauerlander, O., "Economic Expectations and Plans of Firms in Relation to Short-term Forecasting," *in* National Bureau of Economic Research, *Short-Term Economic Forecasting* (Studies in Income and Wealth, Vol. 17), pp. 261–351. Princeton, New Jersey: Princeton Univ. Press, 1955.

21. Modigliani, F., and Weingartner, H. M., "Forecasting Uses of Anticipatory Data on Investment and Sales," *Quarterly Journal of Economics* **72**, No. 1 (February 1958), 23–54.

22. Muth, J. F., "Optimal Properties of Exponentially Weighted Forecasts," *Journal of the American Statistical Association* **55**, No. 290 (June 1960), 299–306.

23. Orr, L., "A Comment on Sales Anticipations and Inventory Investment," *The International Economic Review* **8**, No. 3 (October 1967), 368–373.

24. Orr, L., "Expected Sales, Actual Sales, and Inventory–Investment Realization," *The Journal of Political Economy* **74**, No. 1 (February 1966), 46–54.

25. Pashigian, B. P., "The Relevance of Sales Anticipatory Data in Explaining Inventory Investment," *The International Economic Review* **6**, No. 1 (January 1965), 65–91.

26. Simon, H., "Dynamic Programming under Uncertainty with a Quadratic Criterion Function," *Econometrica* **24**, No. 1 (January 1956), 74–81.

27. Theil, H., *Linear Aggregation of Economic Relations*. Amsterdam: North-Holland Publ., 1954.

28. Theil, H., "A Note on Certainty Equivalence in Dynamic Planning," *Econometrica* **25**, No. 2 (April 1957), 346–349.

29. Wehrs, W. E., "Incomplete Specification and Aggregation in a Class of Econometric Inventory Investment Models," Unpublished Ph.D. dissertation, Purdue Univ., (1972).

30. Wehrs, W. E., "Aggregation and a Class of Inventory Investment Models," presented at Midwest Econ. Assoc. Mtg., Chicago (April 1973).

# INVENTORIES AND THE GENERALIZED ACCELERATOR

*Gerald L. Childs*

*Rutgers University*

## I. Introduction

Metzler's seminal article of 1941 [18] stimulated further research on inventory behavior and the acceleration principle. Among the best known extensions and applications of the inventory accelerator are the work of Darling and Lovell [4–6, 14]. In the early 1960's Eisner and Strotz [8] derived the flexible input accelerator hypothesis from a (present value of) profit maximization specification; Holt *et al.* [12] derived a generalized flexible inventory accelerator decision rule for buffer stocks by minimizing the (present value of) costs of adjusting to demand fluctuations. The Eisner–Strotz result was generalized by Lucas [15], whose work was extended and applied by Gould [9], Nadiri and Rosen [20], and Taubman and Wilkinson [21], among others. Some extensions of the Holt *et al.* model may be found in the work of Belsley [1], Childs [3], and Hay [10].

Theoretically and empirically the input accelerator has been utilized to explain the conomic behavior and impact of fixed capital investment. Yet, the generalized input accelerator is applicable to any input stock, provided that when changing the stock level the firm encounters costs that are independent of input flow costs (factor payments). Inventories of materials satisfy this condition but have seldom if ever been empirically subjected to the input

333

accelerator model.[1] One objective of this study is to provide such an experiment. Therefore, the buffer stock model is applied to inventory investment in finished and semifinished[2] goods; the input stock model is assumed to describe planned investment in materials. If this approach is correct, it has certain implications for aggregate (all stages of fabrication) inventory equations. For example, output and input prices enter the planned stock equations in both accelerator formulations. But we should not expect buffer stocks and materials stocks to react identically to those prices; i.e., an equation for aggregate inventory investment which includes output prices and wages is likely to hide the differential impacts hypothesized by the different accelerator models.

My second objective is an empirical test of the hypothesis that the firm does not absorb a fixed proportion of forecast errors with buffer stocks. Metzler, by a priori model restrictions, assumed that buffer stocks absorb all such errors. In the 1941 model he (1) ruled out price changes, (2) implicitly assumed production to stock, and (3) assumed that production plans are unchanged after being initially set to satisfy expected demand and inventory deficiencies, the latter arising from forecast errors of the preceding period. In ensuing inventory research it became customary to assume either (a) a fixed fraction of the forecast error is absorbed by buffer stocks or (b) the estimated residual of the buffer stock equation represents unintended inventory investment resulting, presumably, from forecast errors. If the reaction by firms to forecast errors takes the form of a period-by-period behavioral decision, assumption (a) is incorrect and assumption (b) is of no help in describing and anticipating that behavior. Furthermore, (b) implies the complementary assumption that the investigator's equation correctly specifies *planned* inventory investment. Few, if any, economists having had research experience in this field would dare to make so bold a claim!

Dispensing with Metzler's first two assumptions has obvious implications for a buffer stock model. But dropping the third assumption—production plans for a period are unchanged during that period—affects materials stocks as well as buffer stocks. The input accelerator model yields an equation for *planned* investment. It does not explicitly incorporate responses to forecast errors.

Let IN and OUT, respectively, represent inflows and outflows. The change in any stock during a period is

$$\Delta \text{STOCK} = \text{IN} - \text{OUT}. \tag{1}$$

[1] An exception is a recent Ph.D. dissertation by John Keith: "Inventory Investment, The Generalized Flexible Accelerator and Interrelated Factor Demand" (University of California, Berkeley, 1972). But Keith's approach is somewhat different. He attempts to incorporate labor, fixed capital, and inventory decisions at *all* stages of fabrication into a unified decision model.

[2] Justification for including goods-in process is given in Section IV.

Let superscripts p and e stand for planned and expected. We may write

$$\Delta \text{STOCK}^{\text{p}} = \text{IN}^{\text{e}} - \text{OUT}^{\text{e}}. \tag{2}$$

Subtracting (2) from (1) yields

$$\Delta \text{STOCK} = \Delta \text{STOCK}^{\text{p}} + (\text{IN} - \text{IN}^{\text{e}}) - (\text{OUT} - \text{OUT}^{\text{e}}). \tag{3}$$

If one assumes that planned production will equal actual production, $X^{\text{p}} = X$, then (a) for finished goods inventories $\text{IN} = \text{IN}^{\text{e}}$, and the difference between actual and planned investment is a direct consequence of the error in forecasting shipments; (b) for materials and supplies $\text{OUT} = \text{OUT}^{\text{e}}$, and the difference between actual and planned investment is the error in forecasting receipts from suppliers.

We will see that there is some evidence to question the assumption $X^{\text{p}} = X$. For example, the rate of capacity utilization appears to influence the degree to which buffer stocks absorb demand forecast errors.

## II. Data

It would undoubtedly be of some interest to use data that are not seasonally adjusted to measure the response of firms to predicted and surprise seasonal, as well as cyclical, fluctuations of demand. But I have chosen to abstract from the seasonal fluctuations in order to study cyclical behavior. Since seasonal adjustment smooths the data, it, hopefully, removes some observational errors. A 1 % error in the published inventory stock series can correspond to a 50 % (or greater) error in investment. Whether or not seasonal adjustment mitigates these errors, it is likely that considerable random noise remains.

The seasonally adjusted and deflated data we will need for estimation may be readily constructed from OBE, national income account, BLS, and Federal Reserve System sources. The flow and stock series requiring deflation are inventories, unfilled orders, new orders, Department of Defense prime contract awards, fixed capital stock, and sales. The wholesale price index (durables or nondurables) WPI is used as a measure of output price and as the deflator for buffer inventories, unfilled orders, new orders, and sales. The WPI for intermediate materials (durables or nondurables) is the measure of materials prices and the deflator for materials stocks. Since the vintage distributions of inventories and unfilled orders are unknown, any approximate method of deflation will have flaws.

Prime contract awards are deflated by the WPI for all manufacturing. The implicit GNP deflator for nonresidential fixed investment represents the price of fixed capital goods and the deflator for gross investment in plant and equipment. After deflation, the latter is accumulated to arrive at a fixed capital stock series, assuming an initial stock of zero at the end of 1946/IV, straight-line-depreciation, and a five-year useful equipment life.

The rate of output is measured by the Federal Reserve Board Index, the stock of labor by production workers employed in the appropriate manufacturing sector, and wages by average hourly earnings of those production workers. The calculation of demand forecasts requires a separate section.

## III. Demand Forecasts

In their study of sales forecasting by firms, Hirsch and Lovell [11] tested two structural forecasting hypotheses: extrapolative and adaptive expectations. Their results were not decisive. For short-term forecasts they could not choose between extrapolative and adaptive structures. For longer-term forecasts the adaptive model seemed to dominate.

Implicit expectations, at best a quasi-structural hypothesis, scored at least as well as the other two. The implicit model depicts the forecast as somewhere on the line between naive and perfect. For seasonally adjusted data the extrapolative forecast is a linear combination of (1) the actual figure of four quarters ago and (2) the change in actual sales between $t - 1$ and $t - 5$. Metzler [18] employed an extrapolative relationship between periods $t$, $t - 1$, and the change from $t - 2$ to $t - 1$. The adaptive forecast is a geometric distributed lag of past sales. Abstracting from intercept terms, the implicit and adaptive models are one-parameter specifications; the extrapolative is a two-parameter structure.

The three forecasting techniques for new orders ($O$) yield the following expectations and forecast errors ($\varphi$), omitting random disturbance terms:

Implicit: $\quad O_t^e = \rho O_{t-1} + (1 - \rho)O_t = O_t - \rho \Delta O, \qquad 0 \leqq \rho \leqq 1,$

$\qquad \qquad \varphi_t = O_t - O_t^e = \rho \Delta O_t;$

Extrapolative: $\quad O_t^e = \beta O_{t-4} + \gamma(O_{t-1} - O_{t-5}),$

$\qquad \qquad \varphi_t = O_t - \beta O_{t-4} - \gamma(O_{t-1} - O_{t-5});$

Adaptive: $\quad O_t^e = \lambda O_{t-1}^e + (1 - \lambda)O_{t-1} = (1 - \lambda) \sum_0^\infty \lambda^i O_{t-1-i},$

$\qquad \qquad \qquad \qquad \qquad \qquad \qquad \qquad \qquad \qquad 0 \leqq \lambda < 1,$

$$\varphi_t = \sum_0^\infty \lambda^i \Delta O_{t-i}.$$

The decisions for the coming period should be conditional upon expectations of demand in the future as well as the current period. This is precisely the specification of linear decision rules for demand buffers that I will employ in Section IV. However, a linear combination of future forecasts, as required by the buffer model, presents some empirical difficulties. If $O_{t+j}^e$ depends on $O_{t+i}$ for $j \geqq i > 0$, we should substitute $O_{t+i}^e$ for the latter. Under this scheme,

(1) the implicit expectations model breaks down unless we are willing to include actual orders for $t + 1$, $t + 2$, ..., $t + n$ in the equation; (2) the extrapolative form yields a distributed lag on past orders for $t - 1$ through $t - 5$ with weights dependent on (a) the parameters of the cost structure or profit function (that gives rise to the linear decision rule) and (b) the parameters $\beta$ and $\gamma$ of the anticipations model; (3) adaptive expectations leads to $O_{t+j}^e = O_t^e$ (e.g., $O_{t+1}^e = \lambda O_t^e + (1 - \lambda)O_t$ and substitution of $O_t^e$ for $O_t$ results in $O_{t+1}^e = O_t^e$), so that $\sum_0^n w_i O_{t+1}^e$ collapses to $O_t^e \sum_{i=0}^n w_i = wO_t^e$.

Given these considerations I employed only $O_t^e$, with one exception. For durable manufacturing I estimated a buffer stock equation for the case of extrapolative expectations that includes a polynomial distributed lag of five quarters ($O_{t-1}$ to $O_{t-5}$). There is no a priori reason to prefer one weight distribution over any other since the cost parameters are unknown.

In the implicit model the regression coefficients yield the value of $\rho$ directly. For the extrapolative model I avoided a two-parameter search for $\beta$ and $\gamma$ by adopting the Hirsch–Lovell estimates of $(\beta, \gamma) = (0.5, 0.4)$ for durable manufacturing and $(1.0, 0.6)$ for nondurables. For statistical and casual empirical reasons I used a truncated form of the adaptive model, cutting off the geometric lag after eight terms. This is tantamount to invoking an initial condition for $O_{t-8}^e$ which will not affect the results. As $\lambda$ falls, the omission becomes less serious since the coefficient of $O_{t-8}^e$ in the adaptive scheme is the eighth power of $\lambda$. The truncation permits one to calculate a series for $O_t^e$, avoiding the introduction of serial correlation into the residual of the inventory equation by a Koyck-type of tranformation. In addition, I find it difficult to believe that any demand forecaster bases his forecast on the distant past, a notion consistent with, but not identical to, a small value of $\lambda$.

## IV. Buffer Stocks

Anticipated demand fluctuations may be absorbed by assorted means. The extent to which inventories play a part depends on the initial values of all the buffers (decision variables) and the cost of changes in them. In the linear decision rule model, costs are reflected in the coefficients of (1) the initial values of the alternative decision variables and (2) forecasted demand.

A decision rule for inventories of finished goods that incorporates production, unfilled orders, and prices as alternative buffers is derived by Hay [10] by maximizing the following present value of profits:

$$G = \sum_{t=1}^n k^{t-1}\{P_t O_t - C_1(U_t) - C_2(H_t) - C_3(\Delta X_t) - C_4[\Delta(P_t - V_t)] - V_t X_t\}$$

subject to the constraints

$$O_t - S_t = \Delta U_t \quad \text{and} \quad X_t - S_t = \Delta H_t \quad \text{for all } t$$

where the demand function is assumed to be $O_t = Q_t - bP_t$ and the variables are defined as $O_t$, new orders; $P_t$, price of output; $U_t$, unfilled orders, end of $t$; $H_t$, finished goods inventory, end of $t$; $V_t$, direct unit production costs; $S_t$, shipments; $X_t$, output; $k$, discount rate; $Q_t$, an exogenous time-dependent intercept; and $C_i$, quadratic cost functions.

The cost associated with $U_t$ is assumed to vary directly with the squared deviation of unfilled orders from the least-cost stock size $U_t^*$. The cost of $H_t$ depends on $(H_t - H_t^*)^2$. The $U_t^*$ is specified as a linear function of current output; $H_t^*$ is a linear function of current shipments. The cost of $\Delta X_t$ is proportional to $(\Delta X_t)^2$; the cost of $\Delta(P_t - V_t)$ is proportional to $[\Delta(P_t - V_t)]^2$.

The variables $V_t$, $Q_t$, and consequently $O_t$, are assumed exogenous. Lacking observations on $Q_t$, Hay substitutes the demand function for $Q_t$ and obtains the decision rule

$$\Delta H_t = f(X_{t-1}, P_{t-1}, H_{t-1}, U_{t-1}, V_{t-1}; O_{t+\tau}^e; V_{t+\tau}^e)$$

where $O_{t+\tau}^e$ and $V_{t+\tau}^e$ represent vectors of expected value forecasts for $\tau = 0, 1, 2, \ldots$, and $f$ is a linear function. Variation of each of the cost parameters in a reasonable range yielded the result that the a priori signs of the decision rule coefficients are ambiguous, with the following exceptions:

(1)   the coefficient of $X_{t-1}$ is positive,
(2)   the coefficient of $H_{t-1}$ is negative,
(3)   the coefficients of $P_{t-1}$ and $V_{t-1}$ are equal but of opposite sign (since they enter the cost function symmetrically).

If we adopt the above linear decision rule as our specification of the desired or planned investment in stocks of finished goods, but the data report actual stocks, we must add an explanation of the buffer role played by $H_t$ in absorbing forecast errors. Noting that the maximization of the profit function leads to similar decision rules for prices, production, and unfilled orders, it is natural to ask if the distribution of the absorption of forecast errors should be identical to that of anticipated values of new orders. I think the answer is no. The reaction to expected orders is planned at the beginning of a period. Adjustments to forecast errors as they become manifest are midcourse corrections to optimally set plans. One would expect the relevant cost structures in these instances to differ.

To simplify matters[3] let the cost of absorbing forecast errors be

$$C = b_1(X - X^p)^2 + b_2(U - U^p)^2 + b_4(H - H^p)^2$$

---

[3] Price may be added as an additional buffer. The implied symmetry of response for over- and underforecasting both here and in what follows is assumed to be a reasonable approximation.

where the superscript p indicates planned, $t$ subscripts are omitted, and the $b$'s are functions of predetermined or exogenous variables.[4] Minimization of $C$ subject to the constraint[5] $O_t = X_t - \Delta H_t + \Delta U_t$ yields

$$H = H^p - (m)(O - O^e) \qquad \text{or equivalently} \qquad \Delta H = \Delta H^p - (m)(O - O^e)$$

with $m > O$, $\partial m/\partial b_1 > O$, $\partial m/\partial b_2 > O$, $\partial m/\partial b_4 < O$ where $O^e = X^p - \Delta H^p + \Delta U^p$.

Since $m$ is the fraction of the forecast error absorbed by buffer stocks, we have the obvious result that given the forecast error in a period, inventories shoulder more of the burden the higher the costs of $X - X^p$ and $U - U^p$ relative to that of $H - H^p$. Similar conclusions are obtained regarding rules for forecast-error adjustments in unfilled orders and output. We shall make use of those latter adjustments in Section V on materials stocks.

Incorporation of forecast error adjustments requires specification of the functions $b_i$, or, alternatively, $m = m(b_1, b_2, b_4)$. Although $m$ is nonlinear, I assume the linear approximation

$$m_t = r_1 UCAP_{t-1} + r_2[U_{t-1}/(X_{t-1}/UCAP_{t-1})] + r_3(\Delta P_{t-1}/P_{t-2})$$
$$+ r_4(H_{t-1}/S_{t-1}), \qquad r_i > O, \quad i = 1, 2, 3, 4.$$

Call the four right-hand variables in this equation $R1$, $R2$, $R3$, and $R4$, respectively. They are assumed to comprise the arguments of the corresponding $b_i$ functions; $b_3$ represents the cost of changing prices.

$R1$ is assumed to govern the cost of $X - X^p$. The closer is last period's output to capacity, the more expensive it is to raise output above the planned rate to meet forecast errors.[6]

$R2$ embodies the assumption that the longer the minimum lead time at the start of the period, the more costly it is to backlog more orders in response to forecasting errors.

---

[4] A more rigorous way to handle forecast error adjustments is to incorporate them in the original profit function. For example, the cost functions associated with inventories, unfilled orders, etc., can include other variables—current or lagged endogenous or exogenous—with expectations entered directly into the profit function. The length of the decision period can be an argument of those cost functions as well. Such a respecification is beyond the intended scope of this study. The approach I have taken here is an admittedly simpler and more *ad hoc* type of alternative than the kind of rigorous derivation described above.

[5] Obtained by eliminating $S$ from (a) $O - S = \Delta U$ and (b) $X - S = \Delta H$.

[6] In another chapter in this volume, Carlson and Wehrs, assuming that only production and inventories buffer demand, find that inventories should absorb less and production more of the forecast error the higher the cost of deviating from desired stocks relative to production change costs. In their model the cost of changing production is equivalent to the steepness of the marginal cost curve.

$R3$ is added to reflect the cost of raising price if orders exceed expected orders. I assume that this cost is proportional to the percentage price increase of last period.

Finally, $R4$ represents the cost of buffering forecast errors with finished goods inventories. The higher the initial inventory-to-sales ratio, the *lower* the cost of reducing inventories below the planned level, so that $r_4$ is assumed to be positive.

Let $\varphi = O - O^e$. Our equation for the change in buffer stocks is now

$$\Delta H = \Delta H^p - r_1\varphi \cdot R1 - r_2\varphi \cdot R2 - r_3\varphi \cdot R3 - r_4\varphi \cdot R4.$$

Since all $r_i$'s are assumed to be positive, the regression coefficients of all four $\varphi \cdot R$ terms should be negative.

As we shall see, the empirical success of this specification of $m$ is somewhat mixed, but I think sufficiently interesting to warrant future experimentation. It can be argued that, although I have used predetermined variables to express the cost of adjusting to forecast errors, there may remain some double counting of components of the cost function specified for the determination of optimal plans. As examples, for the cost function, $U_t^*$ is assumed to depend on production (but not capacity output) and $H_t^*$ depends on shipments (but not the initial ratio of $H$ to $S$; see footnote 4).

Before presenting my results I must justify a few deviations from Hay's specification of planned buffer inventory investment.

The most significant change is to define buffer stocks as finished goods plus goods-in-process. The structural equations are estimated with quarterly data for the aggregate manufacturing sectors, durables and nondurables. Within each sector there is production both to order and to stock, but the data are not conveniently disaggregated to enable separate treatment of these two types of order–production–shipment processes. If production is to order, unfilled orders play a buffer role similar to finished-goods stocks in production to stock. However, in the former case, inventories of goods-in-process may be expected to absorb some demand fluctuations, depending on how far production may proceed before features specific to the particular customer must be added. That is, the product may be standardized until some point in the production process, after which it becomes specialized. Until that point goods-in-process may assume a buffer role comparable to that of finished goods in production to stock. Therefore, if the data combine production to order with production to stock, it is meaningful to define buffer stocks as finished goods plus goods-in-process.[7] This definition of buffer stocks is more defensible for

---

[7] In addition there is reason to believe that some firms in reporting their inventories associate the stage of fabrication with the location of the item in the plant. A semifinished product stored in a warehouse may be counted as a finished good.

durable than nondurable manufacturing because a relatively small proportion of nondurable goods is produced to order. For that reason I estimated two sets of equations for nondurables. In Table 2 are regression estimates using the combined production-to-order and to-stock model in which $H$ is everywhere replaced by $H + IP$ (finished goods plus goods-in-process) and exogenous demand is measured by new orders. In Table 3 are estimates assuming production to stock: buffer stocks are finished goods, exogenous demand is shipments, and unfilled orders are omitted (both $U_{t-1}$ and $R2$).

There are other theoretical omissions and substitutions in the estimated equations. (1) I omitted expected orders for future periods with the exception of the fourth equation in Table 1. This was discussed in Section III. (2) Lagged average hourly earnings of production workers (AHE) is substituted for lagged unit costs of production. (3) I omitted forecasts of unit costs. These forecasts are probably partially reflected in (perhaps offsetting the effects of) lagged AHE and may help to explain the relatively poor results for that variable in all but one equation—adaptive expectations for durables. (4) Lagged prime contract awards are added to measure the differential influence of defense orders.

Tables 1–3 contain quarterly estimates of the buffer-stock investment equation parameters for durable and nondurable manufacturing. The sample period is 1955/I–1971/II. Three assumptions are employed regarding the structure of anticipations—implicit, extrapolative, and adaptive. In the case of adaptive expectations the best equation (in my judgment) for values of $\lambda = 0.1, 0.2, \ldots, 0.9$, is presented with the corresponding value of $\lambda$, although the results were not especially sensitive to the value of $\lambda$ shown, plus or minus 0.2.

Immediately below each estimated regression coefficient is its absolute $t$ value. For testing the null hypothesis that a coefficient is zero the appropriate rejection region is two-tailed, if no a priori signs are specified, but one-tailed if definite signs are predicted by the underlying theoretical structure. The appropriate $t$ values for a 5% rejection region are 2.01 and 1.67 for two-tailed and one-tailed regions, respectively. A complete list of definitions of variables is offered in the Appendix.

For durables, the adaptive model is most appealing. The null hypothesis of zero is rejected in favor of the alternative theoretical prescription, with the appropriate 5% rejection region, for all but two coefficients—those of $\varphi^* R2$ and $\varphi^* R4$. The polynomial lag specification seems to improve somewhat the extrapolative model. The results for implicit expectations imply a negative effect of expected orders on buffer stocks and a value of $\rho > 1$.

The adaptive model supports the generalized accelerator formulation for *planned* buffer stocks. The significant negative coefficients of $\varphi^* R1$ and $\varphi^* R3$ support the hypothesis that buffer stocks do not absorb a fixed

TABLE 1

QUARTERLY ESTIMATES OF BUFFER-STOCK INVESTMENT EQUATION PARAMETERS, DURABLES: $\Delta(H + IP)$

| | Implicit | Extrapolative | Adaptive | Extrapolative–polynomial lag[a] |
|---|---|---|---|---|
| Constant | −1.2271 | 1.0227 | −4.8035 | 0.8067 |
| | (0.73) | (0.46) | (2.72) | (0.37) |
| $(H + IP)(-1)$ | −0.2718 | −0.5546 | −0.1282 | −0.5661 |
| | (4.65) | (5.29) | (2.96) | (5.83) |
| $X(-1)$ | 9.3924 | 22.9964 | 4.1080 | 29.1563 |
| | (5.75) | (4.52) | (2.53) | (5.94) |
| $U(-1)$ | 0.0256 | −0.0097 | −0.0511 | −0.0936 |
| | (1.60) | (0.29) | (2.96) | (2.68) |
| WPI$(-1)$ | −0.7352 | −1.4128 | 13.3536 | 0.5915 |
| | (0.18) | (0.31) | (3.32) | (0.14) |
| AHE$(-1)$ | 0.9388 | −0.7725 | −4.9988 | −2.1722 |
| | (0.65) | (0.61) | (3.62) | (1.52) |
| PCA$(-2)$ | 0.0276 | 0.0151 | 0.0161 | 0.0131 |
| | (3.52) | (1.73) | (1.82) | (1.64) |
| $O$ | −0.0094 | — | — | — |
| | (1.41) | | | |
| $\Delta O$ | 0.0992 | — | — | — |
| | (0.78) | | | |
| $O^e$ | — | 0.0041 | 0.0381 | 0.0123[b] |
| | | (0.46) | (3.81) | |
| $\varphi^* R1$ | −0.1296 | −0.0862 | −0.1288 | −0.1287 |
| | (1.44) | (3.19) | (3.62) | (5.33) |
| $\varphi^* R2$ | −0.0001 | 0.0002 | 0.0007 | 0.0007 |
| | (0.21) | (0.98) | (3.08) | (3.24) |
| $\varphi^* R3$ | −0.9637 | −0.0239 | −0.7685 | 0.0704 |
| | (1.38) | (0.29) | (1.69) | (0.91) |
| $\varphi^* R4$ | 0.3170 | 0.5144 | 0.6243 | 0.5662 |
| | (0.59) | (4.46) | (3.36) | (5.08) |
| $\bar{R}^2$ | 0.7313 | 0.7195 | 0.7330 | 0.7658 |
| $s_e$ | 0.2561 | 0.2617 | 0.2553 | 0.2454 |
| DW | 1.31 | 1.51 | 1.55 | 1.74 |
| df | 53 | 54 | 54 | 55 |
| $\lambda$ | — | — | 0.7 | — |

[a] Estimated over the sample period 55/I–71/IV.
[b] Sum of the weights −0.0008, 0.0023, 0.0039, 0.0041 and 0.0028 for $t - 1$ through $t - 5$; second-degree polynomial constrained to zero at $t - 6$.

TABLE 2

QUARTERLY ESTIMATES OF BUFFER-STOCK INVESTMENT EQUATION
PARAMETERS, NONDURABLES; PRODUCTION-TO-ORDER AND
TO-STOCK: $\Delta(H + IP)$

|  | Implicit | Extrapolative | Adaptive |
|---|---|---|---|
| Constant | −0.6337 | −0.8336 | 0.5334 |
|  | (0.42) | (0.49) | (0.30) |
| $(H + IP)(-1)$ | −0.1326 | −0.0961 | −0.0667 |
|  | (1.70) | (1.50) | (1.03) |
| $X(-1)$ | 1.0954 | 0.9758 | 2.8186 |
|  | (0.58) | (0.39) | (1.10) |
| $U(-1)$ | 0.0772 | 0.1064 | 0.1015 |
|  | (0.85) | (1.30) | (1.23) |
| $WPI(-1)$ | 0.4947 | 0.6247 | −0.7382 |
|  | (0.26) | (0.32) | (0.37) |
| $AHE(-1)$ | 0.3533 | 0.2005 | 0.7710 |
|  | (0.63) | (0.33) | (1.08) |
| $PCA(-2)$ | 0.0079 | 0.0083 | 0.0091 |
|  | (1.61) | (1.54) | (1.71) |
| $O$ | 0.0005 | — | — |
|  | (0.05) |  |  |
| $\Delta O$ | −0.3864 | — | — |
|  | (0.97) |  |  |
| $O^e$ | — | −0.0001 | −0.0156 |
|  |  | (0.01) | (0.98) |
| $\varphi^* R1$ | 0.2019 | 0.0867 | 0.1094 |
|  | (1.32) | (0.80) | (1.04) |
| $\varphi^* R2$ | 0.0008 | −0.0030 | 0.0006 |
|  | (0.11) | (0.60) | (0.11) |
| $\varphi^* R3$ | −1.1075 | −0.6115 | −0.0187 |
|  | (0.87) | (0.66) | (0.02) |
| $\varphi^* R4$ | 3.1408 | −08.690 | −1.3335 |
|  | (0.71) | (0.69) | (1.07) |
| $\bar{R}^2$ | 0.1436 | 0.1272 | 0.1475 |
| $s_e$ | 0.1508 | 0.1523 | 0.1505 |
| DW | 1.82 | 1.63 | 1.81 |
| df | 53 | 54 | 54 |
| $\lambda$ | — | — | 0.5 |

TABLE 3

QUARTERLY ESTIMATES OF BUFFER-STOCK INVESTMENT EQUA-
TION PARAMETERS, NONDURABLES; PRODUCTION-TO-STOCK:
$\Delta H$

|  | Implicit | Extrapolative | Adaptive |
|---|---|---|---|
| Constant | −0.4798 | −0.2845 | 1.1107 |
|  | (0.35) | (0.19) | (0.75) |
| $H(-1)$ | −0.1551 | −0.0909 | −0.0296 |
|  | (2.10) | (1.40) | (0.41) |
| $X(-1)$ | 0.4396 | −0.2014 | 2.2323 |
|  | (0.25) | (0.09) | (0.95) |
| WPI($-1$) | 0.5474 | 0.1268 | −1.0944 |
|  | (0.34) | (0.08) | (0.65) |
| AHE($-1$) | 0.5223 | 0.4458 | 1.0724 |
|  | (1.08) | (0.84) | (1.57) |
| PCA($-2$) | 0.0054 | 0.0069 | 0.0076 |
|  | (1.34) | (1.64) | (1.70) |
| $S$ | 0.0006 | — | — |
|  | (0.06) |  |  |
| $\Delta S$ | −0.4870 | — | — |
|  | (1.84) |  |  |
| $S^e$ | — | 0.0012 | −0.0203 |
|  |  | (0.10) | (1.26) |
| $\varphi^*R1$ | 0.2878 | 0.1515 | 0.1296 |
|  | (2.24) | (1.67) | (1.57) |
| $\varphi^*R3$ | −0.8050 | 0.1475 | 0.1990 |
|  | (0.77) | (0.20) | (0.38) |
| $\varphi^*R4$ | 4.6108 | −2.4837 | −2.1642 |
|  | (1.23) | (1.72) | (1.63) |
| $\bar{R}^2$ | 0.1423 | 0.1253 | 0.1263 |
| $s_e$ | 0.1283 | 0.1296 | 0.1295 |
| DW | 1.57 | 1.29 | 1.45 |
| df | 55 | 56 | 56 |
| $\lambda$ | — | — | 0.7 |

proportion of the forecast error. Bosworth [2] used a variable similar to $\varphi^*R1$ in his total inventory investment equation for durable manufacturing. His variable is a distributed lag on $\Delta O^*UCAP$. Bosworth gives no a priori reason for the inclusion of this distributed lag, but suggests three reasons, ex post, for its negative effect. His second reason is tantamount to my hypothesis.

The variables $\varphi^*R2$ and $\varphi^*R4$ have perverse coefficients. Although I think this indicates that the costs of varying unfilled orders and buffer stocks for the purpose of absorbing forecast errors have been misspecified (perhaps by doublecounting as explained earlier), the preferred adaptive as well as the polynomial lag model exhibit high $t$ ratios for those coefficients. The null hypothesis of a zero value would be rejected in a two-tailed test in both cases. If those variables do not measure what they are intended to measure, what do they reflect? I offer the following explanations. The positive coefficient of $\varphi^*R2$ may indicate a buildup of semifinished stocks as a consequence of raising output in response to lengthening lead times. The coefficient of $\varphi^*R4$ may reflect first and second-order serial correlation. Since the Durbin–Watson statistic is biased toward 2.0, with $(H + IP)(-1)$ as a regressor, we cannot use it to test for autocorrelated residuals. The economic meaning of this explanation is that adjustment responses to past period increases (decreases) and underforecasts (overforecasts) of demand take place over several periods; e.g., the attempt to increase buffer stocks in response to a faster than anticipated growth in demand is a multiperiod process.

The results for nondurables are consistently very poor. The production-to-stock model (Table 3) is, perhaps, slightly better than the mixed model (Table 2). The only bright spot is the correct negative sign for the coefficient of $\varphi^*R4$ in the cases of extrapolative and adaptive expectations. On the basis of these results we cannot, for nondurable manufacturing, support the generalized accelerator formulation and we can, at best, be skeptical about the behavioral hypothesis regarding the absorption of forecast errors. However, we shall see in Section V that the results for materials stocks tend to corroborate the latter hypothesis.

## V. Materials and Supplies

In his generalization of the input accelerator, Lucas [15] worked with a production function that expressed output as dependent on a vector of "variable inputs" and one of "stock inputs." The stock inputs have usually been identified with plant and equipment but need not be so limited. Output depends directly on input flows rather than on (perhaps partially idle) stocks. Every input flow may be considered the product of a rate of utilization and a stock. The Nadiri–Rosen [20] and Taubman–Wilkinson [21] studies explicitly incorporated utilization rates, the former utilizing a stock of labor as well as a stock of capital. If there are costs associated with changes in a particular stock that are independent of input–flow charges, the stock in question will conform to the Lucas mold; i.e., demand for that stock will be a function of the gaps between "desired" and on-hand stock levels for every such input stock. The desired stock levels are obtained from the optimal short-run solution for the variable inputs, which may be interpreted as rates of utilization. Desired stocks, for a competitive firm, depend upon ratios of input to output prices. Therefore planned stock changes depend upon these price ratios as well as the levels of all on-hand stocks.

There are distinct stock-change costs associated with labor and materials, as well as capital. For labor there are hiring, training, and firing costs. For materials, firms incur storage and finance charges for increases in stocks, and costly risks associated with production delays for reductions in stocks if new orders for materials encounter shipment delays.

Application of the generalized flexible-input accelerator to planned change in materials stocks results in

$$\Delta M_t^{\,p} = g(M_{t-1}, \text{EP}_{t-1}, K_{t-1}, \text{PMAT}_t/\text{WPI}_t, \text{AHE}_t/\text{WPI}_t, \text{PK}_t/\text{WPI}_t),$$

in which $\text{PMAT}_t$ is the wholesale price index for intermediate materials (price of materials); $M_t$ the stock of materials, end of $t$; $\text{EP}_t$ the stock of labor (employed production workers), end of $t$; $K_t$ the stock of manufacturers' plant and equipment, end of $t$; $\text{WPI}_t$ the wholesale price index (output price); $\text{AHE}_t$ the average hourly earnings of production workers; and $\text{PK}_t$ the implicit GNP deflator for nonresidential fixed investment goods (price of capital goods). Assuming a linear form for $g$, the coefficients of $M_{t-1}$ and $\text{PMAT}_t/\text{WPI}_t$ should be negative, but there are no a priori model predictions concerning the other coefficients.

As with buffer stocks, actual $\Delta M$ may differ from planned investment because of forecast errors. A demand forecast error may result in a midcourse correction of production plans with a consequent change in $M$ in the opposite direction. I assume the same model for forecast error absorbtion as in Section IV. Recalling that

$$\varphi_t = O_t - O_t^{\,e}, \qquad R1 = \text{UCAP}_{t-1}, \qquad R2 = U_{t-1}/(X_{t-1}/\text{UCAP}_{t-1}),$$
$$R3 = (\Delta P_{t-1}/P_{t-2}), \qquad R4 = (H_{t-1}/S_{t-1}),$$

the equation for $\Delta M$ (omitting subscript $t$) is

$$\Delta M = \Delta M^{\,p} + a_1\varphi \cdot R1 + a_2\varphi \cdot R2 + a_3\varphi \cdot R3 + a_4\varphi \cdot R4.$$

We expect $a_1 > 0$, $a_2 < 0$, $a_3 < 0$, $a_4 > 0$.

But a second forecast error should be considered, namely, the error arising from unanticipated delivery delays for items ordered from suppliers. To represent this error I added to the above equation: (1) man-days-idle in excess of 10 million (MDI) to measure the impact of severe work stoppages; and (2) $(U_t + U_{t-1})/X_t$, or average lead time during period $t$. Both variables should have negative coefficients. It should be noted that if data on unfilled purchase orders were available, we could use Ruth Mack's [16, 17] suggested decision variable, materials on stock plus on-order, and dispense with these two delivery-delay variables.

Lucas [15] derived the generalized input-accelerator for a perfectly competitive firm. As an alternative to the competitive model, I estimated equations having expected new orders as an additional exogenous variable.

Inclusion of quantity demanded as well as output price permits imperfectly competitive elements to enter the model.

The estimated quarterly equations are presented in Tables 4–6. The sample period is 1955/I–1971/II. Addition of forecasted demand improves the fit for durables but not for nondurables. Two sets of results are given for nondurables—production to both order and stock (Table 5) and production to stock only (Table 6).

Let us first consider the accelerator hypothesis, incorporating the variables $M(-1)$, EP($-1$), AHE/WPI, PMAT/WPI, $K(-1)$, PK/WPI, and demand forecasts. Generally, these variables appear to exert a significant influence on both manufacturing sectors, although the coefficient signs for the two sectors differ for AHE/WPI and $K(-1)$. For durables the coefficients for these variables are negative and positive, respectively, with the reverse being true for nondurables. For durables the introduction of expected demand enhances the significance of real wages and price of capital, but has the opposite effect on the lagged stock of labor. The regression coefficients of the nondurable equations are, by comparison, relatively insensitive to the inclusion of expected demand, with the exception of a few isolated cases.

Many reasonable explanations for the apparent success of this model can be given, one of which incorporates complementarity and rivalry between factors in the sense of a microeconomic production function. (1) Firms may react to relative increases in materials prices by factor substitution designed to minimize waste by recycling or more sophisticated preparation and handling of materials. (2) Changes in product mix may be induced by relative input-price changes. (3) A short-run flow of funds constraint may force rational reallocation of expenditures to various input stocks. In any case, the implication cannot unambiguously be drawn that more or less materials will be used per unit of output for a given product in response to changes in the explanatory variables. We can say only that materials *stocks* will be higher or lower. Substitution may be in terms of stocks rather than flows. That is, if we view excess stocks of all inputs as elements of excess capacity, the rational firm may be expected to redistribute its expenditures on these elements in response to economic conditions.

Next, how does the demand forecast-error hypothesis fare? The expected signs of the relevant coefficients are positive for $\varphi^* R1$ and $\varphi^* R4$, negative for $\varphi^* R2$ and $\varphi^* R3$. The coefficient of $\varphi^* R1$ is positive and significant for nondurables, but negative and statistically weaker for durables. In the latter case the negative coefficient may simply reflect a reduction in materials stocks due to an increase in output, however small, in response to underforecasting. In the durables equations the coefficient of $\varphi^* R2$ is positive, those of $\varphi^* R3$ and $\varphi^* R4$ change signs from one equation to the next. For nondurables the coefficients of $\varphi^* R3$ and $\varphi^* R4$ are consistently negative, that of $\varphi^* R2$ is negative

TABLE 4

QUARTERLY ESTIMATES OF MATERIALS-STOCK INVESTMENT EQUATION PARAMETERS, DURABLES: $\Delta M$

|  | Implicit | Implicit | Extrapolative | Extrapolative | Adaptive | Adaptive | Adaptive |
|---|---|---|---|---|---|---|---|
| Constant | 6.9826 | 11.0196 | 4.6071 | 5.3917 | 1.6801 | 11.9758 | 17.9727 |
|  | (0.86) | (1.72) | (0.74) | (0.94) | (0.22) | (1.86) | (2.25) |
| $M(-1)$ | −0.4996 | −0.4613 | −0.4532 | −0.4935 | −0.4824 | −0.4915 | −0.5450 |
|  | (3.62) | (3.99) | (4.31) | (5.09) | (3.79) | (4.58) | (4.72) |
| $EP(-1)$ | 0.7197 | 0.1764 | 0.2857 | 0.2426 | 0.7382 | 0.1188 | 0.1060 |
|  | (3.07) | (0.84) | (1.23) | (1.14) | (3.81) | (0.55) | (0.42) |
| AHE/WPI | 1.2678 | −3.9665 | −1.0062 | −3.7741 | −1.2636 | −4.5038 | −5.5969 |
|  | (1.47) | (3.50) | (1.20) | (3.35) | (1.30) | (3.86) | (3.82) |
| PMAT/WPI | −11.5818 | −13.9905 | −13.5354 | −14.6003 | −12.8298 | −14.1567 | −15.6663 |
|  | (2.22) | (3.39) | (3.34) | (3.92) | (2.78) | (3.47) | (3.66) |
| $[U + U(-1)]/X$ | 0.0021 | −0.0035 | −0.0170 | −0.0167 | 0.0016 | −0.0044 | −0.0098 |
|  | (0.54) | (1.11) | (3.13) | (3.35) | (0.44) | (1.42) | (2.48) |
| MDI | −0.0099 | −0.0158 | −0.0094 | −0.0139 | −0.0167 | −0.0194 | −0.0144 |
|  | (1.02) | (1.88) | (1.24) | (1.96) | (1.91) | (2.50) | (1.83) |
| $K(-1)$ | 0.0581 | 0.0826 | 0.1108 | 0.0964 | 0.0928 | 0.0887 | 0.0839 |
|  | (1.93) | (3.27) | (3.77) | (3.53) | (3.12) | (3.72) | (3.33) |
| PK/WPI | −0.0965 | 10.5384 | 12.9478 | 18.3367 | 10.6868 | 11.2293 | 9.8583 |
|  | (0.02) | (2.03) | (2.44) | (3.58) | (1.62) | (2.16) | (1.67) |
| $\varphi*R1$ | −0.0143 | −0.0504 | −0.0130 | −0.0148 | −0.0058 | −0.0150 | −0.0443 |
|  | (0.28) | (0.56) | (1.34) | (1.67) | (0.30) | (0.39) | (1.53) |
| $\varphi*R2$ | 0.0001 | 0.000003 | 0.0004 | 0.0003 | 0.0002 | 0.0001 | 0.0004 |
|  | (0.16) | (0.01) | (4.36) | (3.35) | (1.12) | (0.63) | (2.06) |
| $\varphi*R3$ | −0.0281 | 0.2636 | 0.1209 | 0.0968 | −0.3849 | 0.0777 | −0.3426 |
|  | (0.04) | (0.43) | (1.70) | (1.48) | (1.16) | (0.13) | (0.77) |
| $\varphi*R4$ | 0.0622 | −0.2813 | −0.1699 | −0.0494 | 0.0325 | 0.0525 | 0.1747 |
|  | (0.27) | (0.50) | (3.55) | (0.87) | (0.30) | (0.29) | (1.22) |
| O | — | 0.0190 | — | — | — | — | — |
|  |  | (5.86) |  |  |  |  |  |
| $\Delta O$ | — | 0.0581 | — | — | — | — | — |
|  |  | (0.43) |  |  |  |  |  |
| $O^e$ | — | — | — | 0.0217 | — | — | — |
|  |  |  |  | (3.36) |  |  |  |
| $\bar{R}^2$ | 0.1806 | 0.4946 | 0.5121 | 0.5916 | 0.3566 | 0.5085 | 0.4709 |
| $s_e$ | 0.2844 | 0.2234 | 0.2195 | 0.2008 | 0.2521 | 0.2203 | 0.2286 |
| DW | 1.23 | 1.68 | 1.68 | 1.61 | 1.59 | 1.64 | 1.56 |
| df | 53 | 51 | 53 | 52 | 53 | 52 | 52 |
| $\lambda$ | — | — | — | — | 0.9 | 0.2 | 0.7 |

TABLE 5

QUARTERLY ESTIMATES OF MATERIALS-STOCK INVESTMENT EQUATION PARAMETERS, NONDURABLES; PRODUCTION-TO-ORDER AND -TO-STOCK: $\Delta M$

| | Implicit | Implicit | Extrapolative | Extrapolative | Adaptive | Adaptive |
|---|---|---|---|---|---|---|
| Constant | 4.0387 | 6.1471 | 5.3389 | 6.3284 | 6.7147 | 7.4479 |
| | (1.72) | (2.43) | (2.12) | (2.39) | (2.73) | (3.19) |
| $M(-1)$ | −0.2709 | −0.3191 | −0.3640 | −0.3704 | −0.3498 | −0.3809 |
| | (2.78) | (3.23) | (3.64) | (3.72) | (3.68) | (3.88) |
| $EP(-1)$ | 0.5378 | 0.3189 | 0.7056 | 0.6089 | 0.6730 | 0.8474 |
| | (1.71) | (0.96) | (2.13) | (1.79) | (2.09) | (2.61) |
| AHE/WPI | 0.7394 | −0.2185 | 0.9478 | 0.3227 | 0.7069 | 1.0923 |
| | (1.68) | (0.32) | (2.08) | (0.46) | (1.49) | (1.43) |
| PMAT/WPI | −6.4876 | −7.4495 | −8.1953 | −8.6684 | −10.0774 | −11.6197 |
| | (3.09) | (3.48) | (3.55) | (3.72) | (4.34) | (4.45) |
| $[U + U(-1)]/X$ | 0.0233 | 0.0299 | 0.0251 | 0.0321 | 0.0422 | 0.0331 |
| | (0.90) | (1.16) | (0.84) | (1.06) | (1.16) | (0.63) |
| MDI | −0.0001 | −0.0012 | −0.0002 | 0.0001 | −0.0009 | −0.0010 |
| | (0.02) | (0.31) | (0.05) | (0.03) | (0.23) | (0.25) |
| $K(-1)$ | −0.0308 | −0.0310 | −0.0376 | −0.0419 | −0.0437 | −0.0452 |
| | (1.76) | (1.73) | (2.12) | (2.32) | (2.64) | (2.52) |
| PK/WPI | 1.5356 | 2.5711 | 1.7251 | 2.1616 | 2.8671 | 3.3285 |
| | (1.02) | (1.62) | (1.09) | (1.33) | (1.74) | (2.11) |
| $\varphi*R1$ | 0.2480 | 0.3714 | 0.2143 | 0.1913 | 0.2337 | 0.1831 |
| | (3.03) | (3.03) | (2.59) | (2.26) | (3.33) | (2.81) |
| $\varphi*R2$ | −0.0003 | 0.0013 | −0.0043 | −0.0053 | −0.0045 | −0.0029 |
| | (0.05) | (0.20) | (0.94) | (1.15) | (0.82) | (0.53) |
| $\varphi*R3$ | −0.9237 | −1.1058 | −0.8827 | −1.0454 | −0.7091 | −0.4941 |
| | (1.01) | (1.21) | (1.31) | (1.53) | (1.39) | (1.39) |
| $\varphi*R4$ | −2.8215 | 2.5875 | −2.2624 | −1.9042 | −2.4623 | −1.9654 |
| | (2.98) | (0.81) | (2.38) | (1.92) | (3.11) | (2.62) |
| $O$ | — | 0.0078 | — | — | — | — |
| | | (1.75) | | | | |
| $\Delta O$ | — | −0.4934 | — | — | — | — |
| | | (1.67) | | | | |
| $O^e$ | — | — | — | 0.0056 | — | −0.0064 |
| | | | | (1.19) | | (0.75) |
| $\bar{R}^2$ | 0.2450 | 0.2734 | 0.2066 | 0.2127 | 0.2939 | 0.2743 |
| $s_e$ | 1.1074 | 1.1053 | 0.1101 | 0.1096 | 0.1038 | 0.1053 |
| DW | 1.77 | 1.82 | 1.93 | 1.97 | 2.01 | 2.07 |
| df | 53 | 51 | 53 | 52 | 53 | 52 |
| $\lambda$ | — | — | — | — | 0.6 | 0.8 |

TABLE 6

Quarterly Estimates of Materials-Stock Investment Equation Parameters, Nondurables; Production-to-Stock: $\Delta M$

|  | Implicit | Implicit | Extrapolative | Extrapolative | Adaptive | Adaptive |
|---|---|---|---|---|---|---|
| Constant | 3.7003 | 4.4773 | 4.1094 | 4.2923 | 7.6652 | 8.1637 |
|  | (2.00) | (2.13) | (2.21) | (2.20) | (3.40) | (3.58) |
| $M(-1)$ | −0.3043 | −0.3286 | −0.3498 | −0.3542 | −0.4014 | −0.3930 |
|  | (3.52) | (3.57) | (4.00) | (3.97) | (4.31) | (4.23) |
| $EP(-1)$ | 0.7138 | 0.6572 | 0.8600 | 0.8432 | 0.7996 | 0.8514 |
|  | (2.84) | (2.42) | (3.39) | (3.23) | (3.30) | (3.47) |
| AHE/WPI | 0.6635 | 0.1711 | 0.6429 | 0.4646 | 0.5411 | 1.2532 |
|  | (1.73) | (0.25) | (1.65) | (0.70) | (1.34) | (1.77) |
| PMAT/WPI | −6.6006 | −6.9734 | −7.9392 | −7.9946 | −10.4758 | −11.4097 |
|  | (3.33) | (3.41) | (3.83) | (3.82) | (4.36) | (4.54) |
| $K(-1)$ | −0.0357 | −0.0370 | −0.0438 | −0.0447 | −0.0428 | −0.0384 |
|  | (2.21) | (2.17) | (2.69) | (2.68) | (2.69) | (2.36) |
| PK/WPI | 1.8512 | 2.3110 | 2.7239 | 2.8441 | 2.7909 | 2.6861 |
|  | (1.39) | (1.59) | (1.94) | (1.95) | (2.02) | (1.95) |
| $\varphi{}^{*}R1$ | 0.2208 | 0.2372 | 0.2049 | 0.1948 | 0.0906 | 0.1199 |
|  | (3.57) | (2.20) | (3.41) | (2.88) | (3.28) | (3.29) |
| $\varphi{}^{*}R3$ | −1.0236 | −1.2379 | −0.6991 | −0.7313 | −0.4629 | −0.3627 |
|  | (1.30) | (1.47) | (1.21) | (1.24) | (2.03) | (1.50) |
| $\varphi{}^{*}R4$ | −3.2714 | −1.5268 | −3.0778 | −2.9039 | −1.2987 | −1.7952 |
|  | (3.33) | (0.47) | (3.22) | (2.65) | (2.82) | (2.93) |
| $S$ | — | 0.0041 | — | — | — | — |
|  |  | (0.87) |  |  |  |  |
| $\Delta S$ | — | −0.1084 | — | — | — | — |
|  |  | (0.47) |  |  |  |  |
| $S^{e}$ | — | — | — | 0.0016 | — | −0.0137 |
|  |  |  |  | (0.33) |  | (1.23) |
| $\bar{R}^{2}$ | 0.2965 | 0.2807 | 0.2876 | 0.2761 | 0.3051 | 0.3113 |
| $s_{e}$ | 0.1036 | 0.1048 | 0.1043 | 0.1051 | 0.1030 | 0.1025 |
| DW | 1.74 | 1.77 | 1.85 | 1.85 | 2.08 | 2.1 |
| df | 56 | 54 | 56 | 55 | 56 | 55 |
| $\lambda$ | — | — | — | — | 0.9 | 0.9 |

350

but would survive neither a one- nor two-tailed 5% rejection-region test. This could be interpreted as some evidence in support of the production to stock model. The only perverse result for nondurables, then, is the coefficient of $\varphi^*R4$. It may reflect a response to $H/S$ regardless of forecast errors—an increase in this ratio signals a reduction of, at least, the rate of increase of output and, consequently, the desire to reduce $\Delta M$. For durables, positive signs for the coefficients of $\varphi^*R2$ and $\varphi^*R3$ could be explained by the ability of firms to change materials inventories in response to fluctuating demand with much more rapidity than is presumed by the model structure. I believe there is some support here for the proposition that the burden of forecast errors is distributed to many alternative buffers in variable proportions, but much more experimentation is required for the proper specification of this hypothesis. The determinants of midcourse correction costs must be investigated, as well as asymmetries dictated by the differences between production to order and to stock.

The "bottleneck" variables, MDI and average lead time, perform as expected for durable goods with demand forecasts included. For nondurables they are not significant and are omitted from the second set of equations (Table 6). The MDI is dominated by strikes in the steel and automobile industries; unfilled orders are relatively unimportant for the nondurable sector.

In terms of explanatory power, extrapolative expectations with $O^e$ included is best for durables; adaptive expectations has a slight edge for nondurables.

The effect of varying the parameter $\lambda$ of the adaptive structure was relatively nil for nondurables for $0.5 \leq \lambda \leq 0.9$. For durables with $O^e$ included, the results are slightly more sensitive—as $\lambda$ declines, the $t$ ratios of the coefficients of the $\varphi^*R$ variables and average lead time become smaller, while those of MDI and PK/WPI become larger. The only sign change is for $\varphi^*R3$—$\lambda = 0.2$ and $0.1$. For durables with $O^e$ omitted, (1) $\bar{R}^2$ declines monotonically with reductions in $\lambda$; (2) for $0.3 \leq \lambda \leq 0.7$ the coefficient of $\varphi^*R2$ is negative, but not significant; (3) for $\lambda \leq 0.6$ the coefficient of AHE/WPI is positive, its $t$ ratio increasing from 0.19 to 1.34 with smaller values of $\lambda$; (4) for $0.2 \leq \lambda \leq 0.6$ the coefficient of $\varphi^*R3$ is positive with a $t$ ratio smaller than 0.11.

Most readers will have noted the absence of interest rates in this study. Investigators who have obtained significant negative interest rate coefficients are members of a very small minority of economists working in this field. Bosworth, in a recent study [2, p. 218], states "no direct role for monetary variables could be identified .... Such measures as the bank loan rate, interest rate differentials, and rates of change of the monetary base were tested—all without success." Positive significant coefficients have been estimated for inventory investment in interest rate equations. Such evidence implies either (1) an, as yet, unresolved identification problem or (2) the rate of return for proper inventory policy has exceeded the cost of borrowing during a sufficiently large subsample of our observations to yield a negligible interest elasticity of demand for inventory investment.

I would like to conclude this section by reporting the results of an experiment that has, I think, some implications for future study of material inventory investment. As an alternative to the bottleneck variables, I attempted to capture receipts of materials through the proxies, imports and manufacturing "sales of other materials and supplies and intermediate products" (SOMSI). My definition for SOMSI was intended to exclude from total manufacturing sales items that are not likely to become part of any manufacturing firm's inventory of materials. However, it is not the best measure possible because it does not consist only of those sales for which both supplier and demander are manufacturing firms. SOMSI equals all manufacturing sales less (1) home goods and apparel, (2) consumer staples, (3) equipment and defense products, (4) automotive equipment, and (5) construction materials, supplies, and intermediate products. By including imports and SOMSI, I was able to raise $\bar{R}^2$ by about 0.2 for both durables and nondurables. Both variables had positive and significant coefficients in equations similar to the ones reported. I abstracted from both variables in this study because their inclusion would very likely introduce simultaneous-equations bias. I think the lesson of this experiment is the need for either (1) simultaneous determination of supply, demand, and price of materials or (2) incorporation in our $\Delta M$ equation of the influence of the demand for materials in one, or (for durable produced-to-order materials) even two, previous periods.

## VI. Conclusions

In this study I have tested two hypotheses: (1) the generalized input accelerator applies to materials stocks; (2) errors in forecasting are absorbed by several means and in variable proportions from period to period. The errors-in-forecasting model was appended to the materials stock equation and the buffer inventory accelerator model for inventories of finished and semi-finished goods.

The data for durable manufacturing supported both accelerator formulations, although Table 1 reveals that the parameters of the buffer stock model are sensitive to the assumed structure of anticipations. The estimated nondurable equations exhibited strong support for the input accelerator model for materials, but none for the buffer stock model. The results for the forecast-error hypothesis were mixed, but seemed to indicate that production plans are subject to mid-period correction. Despite likely misspecifications of the arguments of the cost functions for varying buffer stocks, production, prices, and unfilled orders in response to forecast errors, the results are sufficiently suggestive to warrant additional study.

A consequence of the success of the input accelerator model for materials is that inventory studies should disaggregate by stage of fabrication.

## Appendix. Definition of Variables

The following is a definition of variables in the regressions in their order of appearance with $t$ subscripts omitted. Construction and deflation of data are discussed in Sections II and III.

| | |
|---|---|
| $H$ | Stock of finished goods, end of period |
| IP | Stock of goods-in-process, end of period |
| $X$ | Production during period |
| $U$ | Unfilled orders, end of period |
| WPI | Output price |
| AHE | Wage rate |
| PCA | Department of Defense prime contract awards during period |
| $O$ | Net new orders during period |
| $O^e$ | Forecast of new orders during period |
| $\varphi$ | $= O - O^e$ |
| $R1$ | Utilization of capacity in manufacturing (FRB) in $t-1 = \text{UCAP}(-1)$ |
| $R2$ | Minimum lead time, end of preceding period, $= U(-1)/[X(-1)/\text{UCAP}(-1)]$ |
| $R3$ | Lagged percent change in output price, $= \Delta\text{WPI}(-1)/\text{WPI}(-2)$ |
| $R4$ | Ratio of buffer stocks to sales, end of preceding period |
| $S$ | Shipments during period |
| $S^e$ | Forecast of shipments during period |
| $M$ | Stock of materials and supplies, end of period |
| EP | Number of employed production workers, end of period |
| PMAT | Price of materials |
| MDI | Man-days idle in excess of 10 million during period |
| $K$ | Stock of fixed capital, end of period |
| PK | Price of fixed capital goods |

## REFERENCES

1. Belsley, D. A., *Industry Production Behavior: The Order-Stock Distinction.* Amsterdam: North-Holland Publ., 1969.
2. Bosworth, B., "Analysing Inventory Investment," *Brookings Papers on Economic Activity* **1**, 2, (1970).
3. Childs, G. L., *Unfilled Orders and Inventories: A Structural Analysis.* Amsterdam: North-Holland Publ., 1967.
4. Darling, P. G., "Manufacturers Inventory Investment, 1947–58: An Application of Accelerator Analysis," *American Economic Review* **40**, 5 (December 1959), 950–962.
5. Darling, P. G., "Inventory Fluctuations and Economic Instability: An Analysis Based on the Postwar Economy," in *Inventory Fluctuations and Economic Stabilization, Part III.* Washington, D.C.: Joint Economic Committee of the U.S., 87th Congress, 1st Session, 1961.

6. Darling, P. G., and Lovell, M., "Factors Influencing Investment in Inventories," in *The Brookings Quarterly Econometric Model of the United States*, Chapter 4 (J. S. Duesenberry *et al.*, eds.),. Chicago: Rand-McNally, 1965.

7. Eckstein, O., and Fromm, G., "The Price Equation," *American Economic Review* **58**, 5 (December 1968), 1159–1183.

8. Eisner, R., and Strotz, R. H., "Determinants of Business Investment" in Commission on Money and Credit, *Impacts of Monetary Policy*. Englewood Cliffs, New Jersey: Prentice-Hall, 1963.

9. Gould, J. P., "Adjustment Costs in the Theory of Investment of the Firm," *Review of Economic Studies* **35**, 1 (January 1968), 47–55.

10. Hay, G., "Production, Price and Inventory Theory," *American Economic Review* **60**, 4 (September 1970), 531–545.

11. Hirsch, A., and Lovell, M., *Sales Anticipations and Inventory Behavior*. New York: Wiley, 1969.

12. Holt, C., Modigliani, F., Muth, J., and Simon, J., *Planning Production, Inventories, and Work Force*. Englewood Cliffs, New Jersey: Prentice-Hall, 1960.

13. Holt, C., and Modigliani, F., "Firm Cost Structures and the Dynamic Responses of Inventories, Production, Work Force, and Orders to Sales Fluctuations," in *Inventory Fluctuations and Economic Stabilization*, Part II. Washington, D.C.: Joint Economic Committee of the U.S., 87th Congress, 1st Session, 1961.

14. Lovell, M., "Manufacturers' Inventories, Sales Expectations, and the Acceleration Principle," *Econometrica* **29**, 3 (July 1961), 276–297.

15. Lucas, R. E., Jr., "Optimal Investment Policy and the Flexible Accelerator," *International Economic Review* **8**, 1 (February 1967), 78–85.

16. Mack, R., "Changes in Ownership of Purchased Materials," in *Inventory Fluctuations and Economic Stabilization*, Part II, Washington, D.C.: Joint Economic Committee of the U.S., 87th Congress, 1st Session, 1961.

17. Mack, R., *Information, Expectations, and Inventory Fluctuations: A Study of Materials Stock on Hand and on Order*. New York: National Bureau of Economic Research, Columbia Univ. Press, 1967.

18. Metzler, L., "Nature and Stability of Inventory Cycles," *Review of Economics and Statistics* **23**, 3 (August 1941), 113–129.

19. Mills, E., *Price, Output, and Inventory Policy*. New York: Wiley, 1962.

20. Nadiri, M. I., and Rosen, S., "Interrelated Factor Demand Functions," *American Economic Review* **59**, 4, Part I (September 1969), 457–471.

21. Taubman, P., and Wilkinson, M., "User Cost, Capital Utilization and Investment Theory." *International Economic Review* **2**, 2 (June 1970), 209–215.

# MONETARY POLICY AND THE INVENTORY CYCLE

---

*Michael C. Lovell*

*Wesleyan University*

## Introduction

Metzler's [17] analysis of the inventory cycle, published on the eve of American involvement in World War II, deviated in a number of important respects from earlier studies of how fluctuations in inventory investment contribute to economic instability. Hawtrey [5, 6] and Keynes [11] had stressed the role of inventories in the cycle, but they did not study inventory behavior within the context of a carefully articulated model. Metzler's contribution built on the achievements of Lundberg [15], Frisch [4], and Samuelson [21]. While Lundberg had illustrated with numerical examples certain dynamic sequences involving inventory investment, he had not studied their dynamic properties analytically. Frisch and Samuelson both investigated the dynamic properties of their cycle models analytically, but their models were simplified to the point where inventory movements were entirely neglected. Metzler's contribution was to develop stability conditions for a dynamic model involving inventory investment and an equation explaining the generation of expected sales.

In concentrating attention on the effect of errors made by firms in forecasting demand, Metzler suppressed entirely the effect of changing interest rates

355

on the desired stock of inventories. In this respect his "real" model of the inventory cycle stands in marked contrast to the earlier work of such writers as Hawtrey, who had argued that it was the inventory investment component of total demand which provides the fulcrum by which monetary policy has its primary impact on the pace of economic activity. This Chapter will introduce monetary complications into Metzler's model of the inventory cycle.[1] The model developed in Section I is constructed in the spirit of Metzler's analysis, but with the desired stock of inventories depending on the rate of interest as well as the level of economic activity. Numerical examples presented in Section II illustrate how a quite simple type of monetary policy can contribute to economic stability. Section III determines within the context of an elementary family of monetary rules the type of central bank response which serves to maximize the speed with which the economy converges to equilibrium. Stochastic complications are considered in Section IV.

## I. The Model

The desired (equilibrium) stock of end-of-period inventories will be assumed to be linearly related to anticipated sales $\hat{X}_t$ and the rate of interest $r_t$:

$$H_t^d = a_0 + a_1 \hat{X}_t - a_2 r_t. \tag{1}$$

But planned stocks $H_t^p$ deviate from the desired level because costs of adjustment make it advisable to attempt only a partial adjustment toward this long-run target during the current production period. That is, planned inventory investment is

$$H_t^p - H_{t-1} = \delta(H_t^d - H_{t-1}), \qquad 0 < \delta \leqq 1. \tag{2}$$

Because the production plan cannot be revised in the light of developments during the production period, realized stocks will deviate from the planned level by the amount of the gap between anticipated versus realized sales:

$$H_t - H_t^p = \hat{X}_t - X_t. \tag{3}$$

Letting $a = 1 + \delta a_1$ for notational convenience, these assumptions yield inventory stock of

$$H_t = \delta a_0 + a\hat{X}_t - \delta a_2 r_t + (1 - \delta)H_{t-1} - X_t. \tag{4}$$

[1] A similar approach was used by Lovell and Prescott [14] to introduce monetary variables into the Samuelson multiplier–accelerator model.

Hence, the flow of inventory investment is

$$I_t = H_t - H_{t-1} = a(\hat{X}_t - \hat{X}_{t-1}) - \delta a_2(r_t - r_{t-1}) + (1 - \delta)I_{t-1} - (X_t - X_{t-1}).$$
(5)

This reduces to the Metzler hypothesis when $a_2 = 0$ and $\delta = 1$.[2]

Depending on the sign of inventory investment, sales volume $X_t$ may either exceed or fall short of output $Y_t$; that is,

$$I_t = Y_t - X_t.$$
(6)

Further, sales meet consumption plus exogenous demand $G_t$ (government spending and fixed investment),

$$X_t = C_t + G_t.$$
(7)

Since consumption is assumed to be proportionate to output,[3]

$$C_t = bY_t, \qquad 0 < b < 1,$$
(8)

we have

$$Y_t = (X_t - G_t)/b$$
(9)

and

$$I_t = (1 - b)Y_t - G_t.$$
(10)

With the aid of (5), (6), and (9), we obtain

$$Y_t = a(\hat{X}_t - \hat{X}_{t-1}) - \delta a_2(r_t - r_{t-1}) + [1 - \delta(1-b)]Y_{t-1} + \delta G_{t-1}.$$
(11)

Suppose equilibrium is defined as a steady state in which $Y_t^e = Y_t = Y_{t-1}$, $r_t = r_{t-1}$, and $\hat{X}_t = \hat{X}_{t-1}$; then equilibrium output is

$$Y_t^e = (1 - b)^{-1}G_{t-1}.$$
(12)

Just as with Metzler's model, equilibrium output is determined by the simple multiplier; it is unaffected by the level of expected sales or the rate of interest; further, investment spending is zero in equilibrium for the stock of

[2] That this type of linear decision rule is compatible with the assumption of profit maximization is well known; see, for example, Holt and Modigliani [9, p. 13], who derive the Metzler inventory decision rule from a quadratic cost function. However, the quadratic-cost-function approach does not justify an equation of form (5) when $a_2 \neq 0$, for changes in the rate of interest constitute an adjustment in carrying cost which influences the coefficients of the linear decision rule; but see Trivedi [23].

[3] Tax policy will influence $b$, for it is the marginal propensity to consume out of gross output rather than disposable income.

inventories is at the desired level. However, in equilibrium $H_t^d$ and $H_t$ would be influenced by the rate of interest and any persistent discrepancy between $X_t$ and $\hat{X}_t$.

Before the dynamic properties of the inventory cycle model can be analyzed it is necessary to explain the behavior of expectations and interest rates. For expectations, we begin with a rather general statement

$$\hat{X}_t = \eta_0 + \eta_1 X_t + \eta_2 X_{t-1} + \eta_3 X_{t-2}. \tag{13}$$

Metzler analyzed a specific form of this expression; specifically, for Metzler's expectations we set $\eta_0 = \eta_1 = 0$, $\eta_2 = 1 + \eta_m$, and $\eta_3 = -\eta_m$, where $\eta_m$ is Metzler's coefficient of expectations; thus for Metzler[4]

$$\hat{X}_t = X_{t-1} + \eta_m(X_{t-1} - X_{t-2}). \tag{13a}$$

A particularly convenient simplification, stressed by Metzler, is the case of static expectations, which is obtained by setting $\eta_m = 0$:

$$\hat{X}_t = X_{t-1}. \tag{13b}$$

In an imaginative empirical investigation Ferber [3] found that a model of anticipations formation which was very similar to Metzler's proved quite helpful in explaining anticipations, but Ferber was surprised to find that expectations have a tendency to regress back toward prior experience ($\eta_m < 0$), rather than extrapolate recent changes into the future.

An alternative approach, often used in empirical studies of the production decision and finished goods inventory behavior, is to postulate perfect forecasting; from (13) one obtains

$$\hat{X}_t = X_t, \tag{13c}$$

by setting $\eta_1 = 1$ and $\eta_0 = \eta_2 = \eta_3 = 0$. Although entrepreneurs are obviously not clairvoyant, the dynamic implications of perfect forecasting may be of interest for two reasons. First of all, much recent empirical work on inventory behavior and the production decision has been based on the hypothesis that anticipations are randomly distributed about the actual realization; second, if we are interested in whether forecast errors play a causal role in generating the cycle, we must ask how the dynamic properties of the economy would be affected if expectational errors made by firms when planning production were eliminated. Still another hypothesis concerning expectations formation is obtained by setting $\eta' = \eta_1 = (1 - \eta_2)$ and $\eta_0 = \eta_3 = 0$:

$$\hat{X}_t = \eta' X_t + (1 - \eta') X_{t-1}. \tag{13d}$$

---

[4] This expression deviates from Metzler's approach in one major respect; Metzler presumed that firms made errors in forecasting only consumer sales; the present formulation allows for errors in forecasting total sales, including government demand.

The hypothesis that expectations are a blend of static and perfect forecasts was invoked by Lovell [13] in an empirical study of inventory behavior. Hirsch and Lovell [7] found in an empirical study of manufacturers' short run expectations that an intermediate value of $\eta'$ dominated both perfect and static expectations; indeed, it proved somewhat stronger than the Metzler–Ferber hypothesis that entreprenuers extrapolate from the past. Finally, a fourth special case of (13) involves exogenous expectations; setting $\eta_1 = \eta_2 = \eta_3 = 0$ will reveal the implications for stability when expectations are completely insensitive to current economic developments.

Substituting Eq. (13) into (11) yields, with the aid of (9), a third-order difference equation in output:

$$Y_t = \frac{a(\eta_2 - \eta_1)b + 1 - \delta(1 - b)}{1 - a\eta_1 b} Y_{t-1}$$

$$+ \frac{a(\eta_3 - \eta_2)b}{1 - a\eta_1 b} Y_{t-2} - \frac{a\eta_3 b}{1 - a\eta_1 b} Y_{t-3} - \frac{\delta a_2}{1 - a\eta_1 b}(r_t - r_{t-1}) + G_t^*$$

$$(14)$$

where

$$G_t^* = \{\delta G_{t-1} + a[\eta_1 G_t + (\eta_2 - \eta_1)G_{t-1}$$
$$+ (\eta_3 - \eta_2)G_{t-2} - \eta_3 G_{t-3}]\}/(1 - a\eta_1 b).$$

## II. Dynamic Properties of the Deterministic Model

An example of the type of behavior generated by the model is illustrated in Table 1. An initial equilibrium is disturbed in 1972(3) by a step increase in government spending from 500 to 600. Because business firms did not anticipate the stepup in demand when setting the current level of output, the increased spending has to be met by an initial reduction in inventories of 100 units in 1972(3). Output expands in the next quarter in an attempt to replenish depleted stocks and meet the projected increase in demand. And the rise in output itself stimulates additional consumption and a higher desired inventory level; realized sales again exceed anticipations. But the high output cannot be sustained indefinitely, for once inventory stocks are replenished the inventory component of effective demand vanishes. While output peaks in 1973(2), the system continues to fluctuate, and output will ultimately converge for the specified parameter values to an equilibrium output of 1200. This is an example of the "real cycle"; since the interest rate has not been allowed to fluctuate, the movement in the desired inventory stock responds only to changes in the pace of economic activity.

TABLE 1

THE INVENTORY CYCLE[a]

| Year and quarter | | $Y$ | $C$ | $I$ | $G$ | $X$ | $\hat{X}$ | $H$ | $H^d$ | $r$ |
|---|---|---|---|---|---|---|---|---|---|---|
| 1972 | 1 | 1000.0 | 500.0 | 0.0 | 500.0 | 1000.0 | 1000.0 | 300.0 | 300.0 | 5.0 |
| | 2 | 1000.0 | 500.0 | 0.0 | 500.0 | 1000.0 | 1000.0 | 300.0 | 300.0 | 5.0 |
| | 3 | 1000.0 | 500.0 | −100.0 | 600.0 | 1100.0 | 1000.0 | 300.0 | 200.0 | 5.0 |
| | 4 | 1175.0 | 587.5 | −12.5 | 600.0 | 1187.5 | 1050.0 | 325.0 | 187.5 | 5.0 |
| 1973 | 1 | 1328.1 | 664.1 | 64.1 | 600.0 | 1264.1 | 1143.8 | 371.9 | 251.6 | 5.0 |
| | 2 | 1387.1 | 693.6 | 93.6 | 600.0 | 1293.6 | 1225.8 | 412.9 | 345.1 | 5.0 |
| | 3 | 1373.1 | 686.5 | 86.5 | 600.0 | 1286.5 | 1278.8 | 439.4 | 431.7 | 5.0 |
| | 4 | 1303.4 | 651.7 | 51.7 | 600.0 | 1251.7 | 1290.1 | 445.0 | 483.4 | 5.0 |
| 1974 | 1 | 1220.3 | 610.2 | 10.2 | 600.0 | 1210.2 | 1269.1 | 434.6 | 493.5 | 5.0 |
| | 2 | 1152.9 | 576.4 | −23.6 | 600.0 | 1176.4 | 1230.9 | 415.5 | 470.0 | 5.0 |
| | 3 | 1120.0 | 560.0 | −40.0 | 600.0 | 1160.0 | 1193.3 | 396.6 | 430.0 | 5.0 |
| | 4 | 1122.4 | 561.2 | −38.8 | 600.0 | 1161.2 | 1168.2 | 384.1 | 391.1 | 5.0 |
| 1975 | 1 | 1149.7 | 574.9 | −25.1 | 600.0 | 1174.9 | 1160.6 | 380.3 | 366.0 | 5.0 |
| | 2 | 1186.0 | 593.0 | −7.0 | 600.0 | 1193.0 | 1168.0 | 384.0 | 359.0 | 5.0 |
| | 3 | 1216.9 | 608.4 | 8.4 | 600.0 | 1208.4 | 1183.9 | 392.0 | 367.5 | 5.0 |
| | 4 | 1233.6 | 616.8 | 16.8 | 600.0 | 1216.8 | 1200.7 | 400.4 | 384.3 | 5.0 |
| 1976 | 1 | 1234.7 | 617.3 | 17.3 | 600.0 | 1217.3 | 1212.6 | 406.3 | 401.6 | 5.0 |
| | 2 | 1224.0 | 612.0 | 12.0 | 600.0 | 1212.0 | 1217.1 | 408.5 | 413.6 | 5.0 |
| | 3 | 1208.4 | 604.2 | 4.2 | 600.0 | 1204.2 | 1214.7 | 407.3 | 417.8 | 5.0 |
| | 4 | 1194.3 | 597.2 | −2.8 | 600.0 | 1197.2 | 1208.1 | 404.0 | 415.0 | 5.0 |

[a] The data for this simulation were generated with the following parameter values: $b = 0.5$, $a_0 = 50$, $a_1 = 0.5$, $a_2 = 50.$, $\delta = 1.$, $\eta_1 = 0$, $\eta_2 = \eta_3 = 0.5$.

How the cycle may be influenced by monetary complications is illustrated on Table 2. As income climbs, the monetary authorities respond by allowing interest rates to rise. As a result, the tendency for rising output to increase the desired inventory stock is partially offset, inventory investment is less volatile, and the path of output has been smoothed; in this simulation a policy of "leaning against the wind" has contributed to economic stability.[5]

Government spending and the interest rate constitute alternative control variables which can be manipulated in an attempt to stabilize output. With perfect knowledge of the parameters and the predetermined variables, either

[5] The precise way in which the interest rate response was generated will be explained later.

the rate of interest or government spending can be manipulated in order to achieve promptly the desired level of output. However, the optimal policy mix is hardly immaterial, for the authorities are unlikely to be indifferent concerning the level of the control variables and the magnitude of the capital stock. If the time path of government spending is determined by policy needs deemed of paramount importance (e.g., defense), the interest rate might still be manipulated in order to promptly adjust the system to its new equilibrium; all this is clear from Eq. (14). However, there may be penalties for adjusting either output or the rate of interest too abruptly; then an optimal strategy may involve only an asymptotic movement toward the output target. For an appropriately specified quadratic loss function and known parameter values the optimal stabilization strategy involves linear decision rules similar to those

TABLE 2

INTEREST RATES AND THE INVENTORY CYCLE[a]

| Year and quarter | | $Y$ | $C$ | $I$ | $G$ | $X$ | $\hat{X}$ | $H$ | $H^d$ | $r$ |
|---|---|---|---|---|---|---|---|---|---|---|
| 1972 | 1 | 1000.0 | 500.0 | 0.0 | 500.0 | 1000.0 | 1000.0 | 300.0 | 300.0 | 5.0 |
| | 2 | 1000.0 | 500.0 | 0.0 | 500.0 | 1000 0 | 1000.0 | 300.0 | 300.0 | 5.0 |
| | 3 | 1000.0 | 500.0 | −100.0 | 600.0 | 1100.0 | 1000.0 | 300.0 | 200.0 | 5.0 |
| | 4 | 1175.0 | 587.5 | −12.5 | 600.0 | 1187.5 | 1050.0 | 325.0 | 187.5 | 5.0 |
| 1973 | 1 | 1288.8 | 644.4 | 44.4 | 600.0 | 1244.4 | 1143.8 | 332.5 | 231.9 | 5.8 |
| | 2 | 1327.1 | 663.5 | 63.5 | 600.0 | 1263.5 | 1215.9 | 343.0 | 295.4 | 6.3 |
| | 3 | 1311.9 | 656.0 | 56.0 | 600.0 | 1256.0 | 1254.0 | 353.4 | 351.4 | 6.5 |
| | 4 | 1268.1 | 634.0 | 34.0 | 600.0 | 1234.0 | 1259.7 | 359.7 | 385.4 | 6.4 |
| 1974 | 1 | 1221.8 | 610.9 | 10.9 | 600.0 | 1210.9 | 1245.0 | 362.2 | 396.3 | 6.2 |
| | 2 | 1187.5 | 593.7 | −6.3 | 600.0 | 1193.7 | 1222.5 | 361.3 | 390.0 | 6.0 |
| | 3 | 1171.2 | 585.6 | −14.4 | 600.0 | 1185.6 | 1202.3 | 359.0 | 375.7 | 5.8 |
| | 4 | 1170.3 | 585.2 | −14.8 | 600.0 | 1185.2 | 1189.7 | 356.3 | 360.8 | 5.8 |
| 1975 | 1 | 1178.9 | 589.5 | −10.5 | 600.0 | 1189.5 | 1185.4 | 354.4 | 350.3 | 5.8 |
| | 2 | 1190.4 | 595.2 | −4.8 | 600.0 | 1195.2 | 1187.3 | 353.4 | 345.5 | 5.8 |
| | 3 | 1200.2 | 600.1 | 0.1 | 600.0 | 1200.1 | 1192.3 | 353.3 | 345.6 | 5.9 |
| | 4 | 1205.8 | 602.9 | 2.9 | 600.0 | 1202.9 | 1197.6 | 353.8 | 348.5 | 5.9 |
| 1976 | 1 | 1207.4 | 603.7 | 3.7 | 600.0 | 1203.7 | 1201.5 | 354.4 | 352.2 | 5.9 |
| | 2 | 1206.1 | 603.0 | 3.0 | 600.0 | 1203.0 | 1203.3 | 355.0 | 355.3 | 5.9 |
| | 3 | 1203.4 | 601.7 | 1.7 | 600.0 | 1201.7 | 1203.4 | 355.3 | 357.0 | 5.9 |
| | 4 | 1200.8 | 600.4 | 0.4 | 600.0 | 1200.4 | 1202.4 | 355.4 | 357.4 | 5.9 |

[a] The data for this simulation were generated with the following parameter values: $b = 0.5$, $a_0 = 50.$, $a_1 = 0.5$, $a_2 = 50.$, $\delta = 1.$, $\eta_1 = 0$, $\eta_2 = \eta_3 = 0.5$.

calculated by Holt [8] in his classic analysis of the multiplier–accelerator model. In practice, however, the parameters are not likely to be known precisely, and a wise policy maker will recognize that how well the economy will fare over the entire planning horizon depends in part upon how much the current decision contributes to an improved understanding of the economy's structure; that learning possibilities are a difficult complication involving elements of experimental design has been demonstrated by Prescott [20]; see also the discussion by Zellner [26, Chapter 11].

Although the optimal policy is of obvious relevance for policy markers, it is interesting when working with a model designed to explain certain aspects of our historical business cycle experience to suppose that interest rates have been governed by an equation representing an adaptive rule-of-thumb response by the central bank to changing economic conditions. And this approach facilitates a comparison of certain rules of behavior that have been advocated by many economists critical of the achievements of central bankers. As a rough approximation it is convenient to suppose that the monetary authorities allow a departure from a long-run target or neutral rate $(r^n)$ whenever output has departed from its target $Y^*$. That is

$$r_t - r^n = \pi(Y_{t-1} - Y^*). \tag{15}$$

If, as in the war years subsequent to the publication of Metzler's paper, the rate of interest is kept more or less constant, we have $\pi = 0$. Precisely this condition was illustrated in Table 1. When the FED deliberately "leans against the wind" by raising interest rates in periods of excessive boom and reducing them in recession, we have $\pi > 0$. A positive value of the policy parameter, $\pi = 0.0045$, was employed in generating Table 2.[6]

In effecting the interest rate policy implied by (15) the central bank has to manipulate the money supply appropriately. Precisely how the money supply must be manipulated in order to achieve the desired interest rate movements depends on liquidity preference; for example, if the demand for money function has the form

$$M_d = m_0 + m_1 Y - m_2 r, \tag{16}$$

the central bank can execute the interest rate policy prescribed by (15) by adjusting the money supply as follows:

$$\begin{aligned} M_s &= m_0 + m_1 Y - m_2[\pi(Y_{t-1} - Y^*) + r^n] \\ &= m_0 + m_2(\pi Y^* - r^n) + (m_1 - m_2\pi)Y_{t-1}. \end{aligned} \tag{17}$$

[6] Students studying macroeconomics at Wesleyan University run time-sharing simulations of this model on the DEC-10 computer; their task is to set the interest rate each quarter in an attempt to move the economy as rapidly as possible to equilibrium. Practice is required by the typical student before he can do better than rule (15).

While this equation is obtained by substituting (15) into (16), the central bank does not have to know the precise magnitude of the parameters of the liquidity preference function; after all, the FED maintained a rigid bill rate during World War II without such knowledge. The central bank executes the policy prescribed by (15) by buying government securities when the interest rate starts to rise above the prescribed level and selling when it falls below the target rate. And whether a specific value of $\pi$ implies that the money supply moves cyclically or countercyclically depends primarily on the parameters of the demand for money equation. Conversely, a policy formulated in terms of the money supply may be translatable into interest rate terms; for example, successful insulation of the money supply from fluctuations in output requires that $\pi$ be sufficiently large to ensure that the transaction demand for money generated by booming output is precisely offset by a rise in the rate of interest; specifically, we must have $\pi = m_1/m_2$, as may be seen from Eq. (17).[7]

## III. The Optimal Simple Rule: Deterministic Case

As a first step toward determining how the value of $\pi$ influences the inventory cycle, substitute (15) into (14), obtaining the fundamental difference equation

$$Y_t + \beta Y_{t-1} + \gamma Y_{t-2} + \rho Y_{t-3} = G^* \tag{18a}$$

where

$$\beta = [\delta(1 - b) - 1 + a(\eta_1 - \eta_2)b + \delta a_2 \pi]/(1 - a\eta_1 b) \tag{18b}$$

$$\gamma = [a(\eta_2 - \eta_3)b - \delta a_2 \pi]/(1 - a\eta_1 b) \tag{18c}$$

$$\rho = a\eta_3 b/(1 - a\eta_1 b). \tag{18d}$$

Equation (18) is a third-order linear difference equation whose dynamic properties depend on the roots of the cubic

$$\lambda^3 + \beta \lambda^2 + \gamma \lambda + \rho = 0. \tag{19}$$

Specifically the system converges to equilibrium if and only if all three roots of (19) are less than unity in absolute value; further, oscillatory movements will be generated if two of the roots are complex numbers, while sawtooth fluctuations can occur if there is a negative real root. That nonconvergence

---

[7] If prices tend to rise *pari passu* with output (in accordance with both classical and Keynesian theory), a somewhat larger value of $\pi$ will be required in order to keep the *nominal* money supply insulated from fluctuations in output.

is a distinct possibility can be easily recognized on the basis of the following conditions on the roots of the cubic:[8]

$$-\beta = \lambda_1 + \lambda_2 + \lambda_3 \tag{20a}$$

$$\gamma = \lambda_1\lambda_2 + \lambda_1\lambda_3 + \lambda_2\lambda_3 \tag{20b}$$

$$-\rho = \lambda_1\lambda_2\lambda_3. \tag{20c}$$

Clearly, stability requires

$$|\beta| < 3, \qquad |\gamma| < 3, \qquad |\sigma| < 1. \tag{21}$$

It can be shown that the following conditions are necessary and sufficient for stability:[9]

$$1 + \beta + \gamma + \rho = \frac{\delta(1 - b)}{1 - a\eta_1 b} > 0 \tag{22a}$$

$$1 - \beta + \gamma - \rho = \frac{2 - \delta(1 - b) - 2\delta a_2\pi - 2a(\eta_1 - \eta_2 + \eta_3)b}{1 - a\eta_1 b} > 0 \tag{22b}$$

$$|\rho| = \left| \frac{a\eta_3 b}{1 - a\eta_1 b} \right| < 1 \tag{22c}$$

$$\rho(\beta - \rho) - \gamma + 1 = \frac{a\eta_3 b[\delta(1 - b) - 1 + a(\eta_1 - \eta_2 - \eta_3)b + \delta a_2\pi]}{(1 - a\eta_1 b)^2}$$

$$+ \frac{\delta a_2\pi - a(\eta_2 - \eta_3)b}{1 - a\eta_1 b} + 1 > 0. \tag{22d}$$

The fact that $\delta(1 - b) > 0$, together with conditions (22a) and (22c), yields the following restrictions on the expectations coefficients:

$$\eta_1 < 1/ab, \qquad \eta_1 + \eta_3 < 1/ab, \qquad \eta_1 - \eta_3 < 1/ab. \tag{23}$$

In particular, for the type of expectations considered by Metzler ($\eta_0 = \eta_1 = 0$; $\eta_2 = 1 + \eta_m$; $\eta_3 = -\eta_m$), stability requires

$$-1/ab < \eta_m < 1/ab. \tag{23a}$$

Regardless of the magnitude of $\pi$, the monetary policy coefficient, the system

---

[8] These conditions arise from the theory of symmetric functions; see, for example, Turnbull [24, p. 67].

[9] These inequality conditions on the coefficients of the difference equation are stated by Samuelson [22, p. 437]. Note that the substitution of $\lambda = 1$ and $\lambda = -1$ in (19) would yield exact equalities in (22a) and (22b), respectively. See also Carlson [1] and Jury [10, p. 93].

will be unstable if these conditions are violated.[10] But even when the preceding conditions are satisfied, the system will be unstable unless $\pi$ satisfied two restrictions. Specifically, inequality (22b) yields an upper bound on $\pi$:

$$\pi < \frac{2 - \delta(1 - b) - 2a(\eta_1 - \eta_2 + \eta_3)b}{2\,\delta a_2}. \tag{24}$$

Thus, if monetary policy is too responsive, the system will be destabilized. And (22d) yields a lower bound on the policy coefficient:

$$\pi > \frac{[a(\eta_2 - \eta_3)b - \delta(1 - b)]a\eta_3 b - [1 - a(\eta_1 - \eta_2)b](1 - a\eta_1 b)}{\delta a_2[1 - a(\eta_1 - \eta_2)b]}. \tag{25}$$

The third-order system is of such complexity as to make the determination of the *optimal* value of $\pi$ an extremely difficult task. However, it is possible to specify precisely how changes in $\pi$ affect the stability of a restricted form of the model obtained when $\eta_3 = 0$, for then difference equation (18) reduces to the second order and stability conditions (22) require that the point $\langle \beta, \gamma \rangle$ lie inside the stability triangle illustrated on Fig. 1. In order to explore the options open to the monetary authorities in setting the policy coefficient,

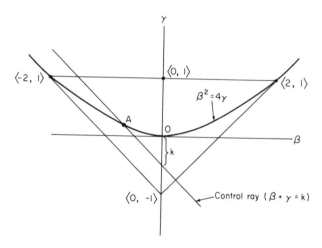

**Fig. 1.** Isostability triangle.

[10] These conditions, based on a macromodel without consideration of aggregation problems, are much weaker than those obtained by Lovell [13] within the context of a multisector dynamic model of the inventory cycle. In particular, a multisector model is prone to instability when $\eta_1 \neq 0$. It is interesting to note that condition (23a) is neutral with regard to the issue of whether expectations are regressive or extrapolative.

we first note that regardless of $\pi$ the two difference equation coefficients sum to a constant:

$$k = \beta + \gamma = [\delta(1 - b)/(1 - a\eta_1 b)] - 1. \tag{26}$$

This yields the "control ray" with slope minus one on Fig. 1 illustrating combinations of $\beta$ and $\gamma$ attainable by manipulating $\pi$. It is possible for the monetary authorities to obtain stability with an appropriately selected $\pi$ if, as in the case illustrated in Fig. 1,[11] a portion of the control ray lies within the triangle; this controllability condition involves $-1 < k < 3$ or

$$\delta(1 - b) < 4(1 - a\eta_1 b). \tag{27}$$

Note that this condition is necessarily satisfied for the type of expectations structure considered by Metzler, for he presumed $\eta_1 = 0$; that is to say, monetary policy is always capable of stabilizing the second-order Metzler inventory cycle model if the influence of interest rates on the desired inventory stock is admitted. But the smaller $|k|$, the faster the best attainable speed of convergence.

If the optimal value of the policy coefficient is defined as that which maximizes the speed of convergence, we must seek min max($|\lambda_1|$, $|\lambda_2|$). This involves equal real roots at the point $A$ where the control ray crosses the parabola labeled $\beta^2 = r\gamma$.[12] From (20) we observe that with equal real roots $k + 1 = \beta + \gamma + 1 = \lambda^2 - 2\lambda + 1 = (\lambda - 1)^2$; hence the optimal obtainable point, where

$$\lambda_1 = \lambda_2 = 1 - (1 + k)^{1/2} = 1 - [\delta(1 - b)/(1 - a\eta_1 b)]^{1/2} = -\beta/2 = \gamma^{1/2}, \tag{28}$$

is obtained by setting

$$\pi^0 = \frac{2[\delta(1 - b)(1 - a\eta_1 b)]^{1/2} + a(\eta_1 + \eta_2)b - 1 - \delta(1 - b)}{\delta a_2}. \tag{29}$$

If, as in the situation considered by Metzler, $k$ is negative, both roots should be positive and output should converge monotonically to equilibrium. The fact that cycles have been observed in practice could result from the pursuit by the central bank of a monetary policy involving a nonoptimal $\pi$; but it is also

---

[11] In Fig. 1, $k$ is negative, as must be the case in the situation Metzler analyzed ($\eta_1 = 0$).

[12] First of all, any attainable imaginary root on the control ray lies northwest of $A$; from (20b) we note that such a root has modulus $\gamma$, which is clearly worse than $A$. With real roots we have $k = \lambda_1\lambda_2 - \lambda_1 - \lambda_2$, and minimizing the largest root obviously requires $\lambda_1 = \lambda_2$.

conceivable that the historical cycle departs from this form because of stochastic disturbances; this possibility warrants consideration because it will turn out that with stochastic shocks a more responsive monetary policy— a larger $\pi$—is to be recommended.

## IV. Stochastic Complications

The inventory cycle model under consideration can converge to equilibrium over a wide range of values of the policy parameter $\pi$, yet the business cycle persists. The continuance of the cycle, Frisch [4, p. 178] argued long ago, may be explained by erratic shocks; he suggested:

> [It is] particularly fruitful and promising . . . to study what would become of the solution of a deterministic dynamic system if it was exposed to a stream of erratic shocks that constantly upset the continuous evolution, and by so doing introduced into the system the energy necessary to maintain the swings.

Let us consider the stochastic inventory cycle model obtained by adding a random disturbance to Eq. (18).[13] We shall show that the value of the policy parameter serving to minimize the variance of output is not identical to the value $\pi^0$ that served to maximize the rate of convergence of the deterministic model.

The analysis will be simplified by again restricting attention to the second order case obtained when $\eta_3 = 0$, so we may write

$$Y_t = -\beta Y_{t-1} - \gamma Y_{t-2} + \varepsilon_t + G^*. \tag{30}$$

The variance of output will be finite if and only if the deterministic counterpart previously considered is stable; i.e., the point $\langle \beta, \gamma \rangle$ must be inside the stability triangle (see Mann and Wald [16]).

As a first step toward determining the value of the policy parameter $\pi_s^0$ serving to minimize $\sigma_Y^2$, given the other parameters of the model, note immediately that under stationarity

$$\sigma_Y^2 = (\beta^2 + \gamma^2)\sigma_Y^2 + 2\beta\gamma \, \text{cov}(Y, Y_{-1}) + \sigma_\varepsilon^2. \tag{31}$$

Furthermore, we evaluate the covariance term by noting that if we take the expected value of (30), after multiplying both sides by $Y_{t-1}$, we obtain

$$(1 + \gamma) \, \text{cov}(Y, Y_{-1}) + \beta\sigma_Y^2 = \text{cov}(\varepsilon, Y_{-1}).$$

---

[13] We shall assume for simplicity that the disturbance is free of autocorrelation. This precludes random variation in government spending, for example, as may be seen from the expression for $G^*$ in (14). A moving average disturbance generates a higher order stochastic process less amenable to qualitative analysis.

But $\mathrm{cov}(\varepsilon, Y_{-1}) = 0$; therefore,

$$\mathrm{cov}(Y, Y_{-1}) = -\beta \sigma_Y^2 / (1 + \gamma). \tag{32}$$

Substituting back into (31) yields the fundamental equation

$$\sigma_Y^2 = \{1 - \gamma^2 - \beta^2 [(1 - \gamma)/(1 + \gamma)]\}^{-1} \sigma_\varepsilon^2. \tag{33}$$

Note that this expression is symmetric in $\beta$, as illustrated by the "isovariance" curves plotted on Fig. 2.

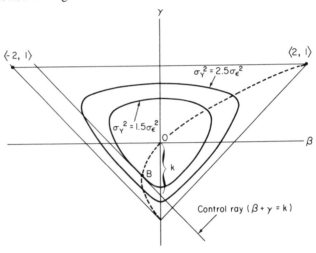

Fig. 2. Isovariance curves.

Although $\sigma_\varepsilon^2$ must be taken as a fact of life that cannot be influenced by monetary policy, $\sigma_Y^2$ is subject to manipulation because it is sensitive to variations in $\beta$ and $\gamma$. Tangency point $B$ reveals the point on the control ray yielding minimum $\sigma_Y^2$. Recalling from (23) that the sum $\beta + \gamma$ is a constant regardless of $\pi$, differentiation of (33) with respect to $\gamma$ after eliminating $\beta$ now yields a condition for an extremum:

$$(k - \gamma)[(1 - \gamma)/(1 + \gamma)] - \gamma + [(k - \gamma)/(1 + \gamma)]^2 = 0,$$

which vanishes when

$$\gamma = (1 + k)^{\frac{1}{2}} - 1. \tag{34}$$

The dotted line in Fig. 2 reveals these possible tangency points. Substituting from (34) with (26) into (18c) yields that value of policy parameter serving to minimize $\sigma_Y^2$ for given $k$:

$$\pi_s^0 = (1/\delta a_2)\{1 - a(\eta_1 - \eta_2)b - [(1 - a\eta_1 b)\,\delta(1 - b)]^{1/2}\}. \tag{35}$$

For negative $k$, the case Metzler considered, this involves a somewhat larger value of the policy coefficient than does a policy coefficient maximizing the speed of convergence of the deterministic model. Returning to Eq. (17), we see that the money supply *should* move countercyclically, contracting in boom and expanding in recession, if $\pi_s^0 > m_1/m_2$. Thus a central bank concerned with minimizing the variance of income is more likely to want a countercyclically moving money supply; still, for certain values of the model's parameters it might be better to have the money supply expanding in booms and contracting in recession.

## V. Summary and Conclusions

In this chapter the Metzler inventory cycle model has been modified to allow for the influence of the rate of interest on desired inventories. It was shown [condition (23a)] that unless the expectations coefficient is large, the Metzler inventory cycle model can always be stabilized by the monetary authorities, and this is so even if the central bank considers only a quite simple type of response to cyclical disturbances. However, for a more complicated structure of expectations than originally considered by Metzler, instability may be inevitable regardless of how abruptly the monetary authorities adjust interest rates in response to changes in output. The system appears particularly prone to instability when expectations are related to realized output [$\eta_1 \neq 0$ in Eq. (13)]. Furthermore, short sawtooth cycles are likely to be generated if expectations are regressive.

Monetary policy can be either too vigorous or too conservative, and the appropriate stabilization strategy cannot be determined by the monetary authorities without detailed knowledge of the magnitude of the parameters of the model. If the interest rate is raised too abruptly in response to upswings in economic activity, the rush to liquidate inventory stocks may cause the system to flutter rather than converge to equilibrium.[14] On the other hand, too timid a response of leaning against the wind with inadequate force may not suffice to stabilize an economy prone to instability. Unfortunately, there exists no simple rule that can be relied upon either in judging the historical performance of the central bank or in formulating current policy. If the demand for money were insensitive to the rate of interest [$m_2 = 0$ in (16)], the quantity of money should not be allowed to expand in boom and contract in recession. But once the influence of the rate of interest on the demand for money is admitted, the question of whether a money supply contracting in

---

[14] Precisely this type of behavior was observed by Liu [12] in certain simulations with his quarterly econometric model.

boom and expanding in recession would contribute to economic stability cannot be resolved without knowledge of the magnitude of all the parameters of the model, including the coefficients of the demand for money equation.

## ACKNOWLEDGMENTS

I am indebted to John A. Carlson, Jon M. Joyce, Edward C. Prescott, and Thomson M. Whitin for helpful comments on an earlier draft of this paper. Research time has been supported by Wesleyan University and National Science Foundation Grant GS 2903.

## REFERENCES

1. Carlson, J. A., "Forecasting Errors and Business Cycles," *American Economic Review*, (June 1967).
2. Chiang, A. C., *Fundamental Methods of Mathematical Economics*. New York: Mc-Graw-Hill, 1967.
3. Ferber, R., *The Railroad Shippers' Forecasts*. Urbana: Bureau of Economic and Business Research, Univ. of Illinois Press, 1953.
4. Frisch, R., "Propagation Problems and Impulse Problems in Dynamic Economics," from *Economic Essays in Honor of Gustav Cassel* (1933), as reprinted in *American Economic Association Readings in Business Cycles* (R. Gordon and L. Klein, eds.), 1965.
5. Hawtrey, R. G., *Trade and Credit*. London: Longmans, Green, 1928.
6. Hawtrey, R. G., *Capital and Employment*. London: Longmans, Green, 1937.
7. Hirsch, A. A., and Lovell, M. C., *Sales Anticipations and Inventory Behavior*. New York: Wiley, 1969.
8. Holt, C. C., "Linear Decision Rules for Economic Stabilization and Growth," *Quarterly Journal of Economics* (1962), 20–45.
9. Holt, C., and Modigliani, F., "Firm Cost Structures and the Dynamic Responses of Inventories, Production, Work Force and Orders to Sales Fluctuations," in *Inventory Fluctuations and Economic Stabilization*, Part II. Joint Economic Congress, 87th Congress, 1st Session, 1961.
10. Jury, E. I., *Theory of Application of the z-Transform Method*. New York: Wiley, 1964.
11. Keynes, J. M., *General Theory of Employment, Interest and Money*. New York: Harcourt, 1936.
12. Liu, T.-C., "An Exploratory Quarterly Econometric Model of Effective Demand in the Postwar U.S. Economy," *Econometrica* (July 1963).
13. Lovell, M. C., "Buffer Stocks, Sales Expectations, and Stability: A Multi-Sector Analysis of the Inventory Cycle," *Econometrica* (April, 1962).
14. Lovell, M. C., and Prescott, E., "Money, Multiplier Accelerator Interaction and the Business Cycle," *Southern Economic Journal* (1968), 60–72.
15. Lundberg, E., *Studies in the Theory of Economic Expansion*. London: King, 1937. Reprinted New York: Kelley and Millman, 1955.
16. Mann, H. B., and Wald, A., "On the Statistical Treatment of Linear Stochastic Difference Equations," *Econometrica* (July–October, 1943), 173–220.
17. Metzler, L. A., "The Nature and Stability of Inventory Cycles," *Review of Economics and Statistics* (August 1941), 138–149.
18. Metzler, L. A., "Factors Governing the Length of Inventory Cycles," *Review of Economics and Statistics* (November 1947), 1–15.

19. Phillips, A. W., "Stabilization Policy and the Time-Forms of Lagged Responses, *Economic Journal* (1957), 265–277.

20. Prescott, E. C., *Adaptive Decision Rules for Macro Economic Planning*. Unpublished doctoral dissertation, Graduate School of Industrial Administration, Carnegie-Mellon Univ. (1967).

21. Samuelson, P. A., "Interactions between the Multiplier Analysis and the Principle of Acceleration," *Review of Economics and Statistics* (1939), 75–78.

22. Samuelson, P. A., *Foundations of Economic Analysis*. Cambridge, Massachusetts: Harvard Univ. Press, 1947.

23. Trivedi, P. K., "Inventory Behaviour in U.K. Manufacturing, 1956–67," *The Review of Economic Studies* (October, 1970).

24. Turnbull, H. W., *Theory of Equations*. Edinburgh: Oliver and Boyd, 1939.

25. Uspensky, J. V., *Theory of Equations*. New York: McGraw-Hill, 1948.

26. Zellner, A., *An Introduction to Bayesian Inference in Econometrics*. New York: Wiley, 1971.

*Part IV*

# MACROMONETARY THEORY

# IS–LM AS A DYNAMIC FRAMEWORK

*Patric H. Hendershott and George Horwich*

*Purdue University*

## Introduction

The IS–LM schedules of Hicks have enjoyed unprecedented rule as the framework of modern macrotheory. Today, almost four decades after their introduction, they remain surprisingly useful tools of comparative-static analysis. However, a basic limitation of the schedules is their inability to describe the process or path connecting different points of equilibrium. IS–LM completely suppresses the fundamental financial force propelling the macroeconomic system from one position to another, and it precludes the possibility of disequilibrium in the output market by failing to distinguish between aggregate supply and demand.[1]

---

[1] The IS–LM diagram has been criticized in recent years as a very inadequate summary of the main contribution of Keynes' *General Theory* [9]. The typical user of the diagram treats it as a generalization of Keynes, but Leijonhufvud, in particular, has stressed the failure of IS–LM, as traditionally set forth, to capture the Keynesian market dynamics and dynamic process in general. See Leijonhufvud [10, p. 401; 11, pp. 4, 31, 63, 182, 213]. Minsky [14, p. 225] sees IS–LM as missing the essential elements of Keynes: the role of financial factors in economic fluctuations and of uncertainty in the management of assets. For a specific attempt to incorporate into IS–LM some Keynesian views on the financial character of saving and investment, see Horwich [6, pp. 428–429 and Appendix to chapter 10]. A recent effort to construct an enriched macromodel containing financial markets is that of Brunner and Meltzer [1]. However, they feature their model as an alternative to the IS–LM framework. We offer our analysis in the present essay as a development within the basic IS–LM relationships.

Various writers, including Hicks, have suggested or hinted at possible dynamic interpretations that might be placed upon the movement from one IS–LM equilibrium to another, but no one has seriously attempted to construct the dynamic framework for use within the Hicksian diagram.[2] That is our objective here. In order to carry it out, we first specify the link between IS–LM and the financial markets. Following the example of Metzler [13], the securities market is divided into stock and flow segments, which, since the flows are generated by saving and investment, are also linked to the real expenditure functions of the economy. The underlying adjustment mechanism by which investment–saving gaps are financed is then developed. Finally, the mechanism is translated into the IS–LM framework under varying assumptions as to the elasticity of output supply.

## I. The Hicksian IS–LM Analysis

Hicks [5, p. 153] derives the IS schedule as the locus of interest rates $r$ and real income levels $y$ that produce saving–investment equilibrium.[3] This is the same as equilibrium in the commodity markets, since income expenditures equal the sum of consumption and investment outlays, and saving is defined as income received less consumption. In the first instance Hicks takes investment $I$ to be determined by the marginal efficiency of capital; $I$ is thereby an inverse relation between the rate of investment spending and the rate of interest. Saving $S$ is simply a positive function of income. Given the

---

[2] Hicks [4, Chapter 11] develops a "cobweb" dynamics in the IS–LM space by simply postulating certain arbitrary lags in the adjustment of both income and the rate of interest. At any interest rate off the IS curve, income moves gradually toward IS along a horizontal vector, which reflects infinite elasticity of the stock of money and thus constancy of the rate of interest in the short run. Once on IS, the interest rate moves vertically to the longer-run (upward-sloping) LM schedule, and thence horizontally to IS, and so on. This pattern, together with the implicit assumption of a constant price level and infinite elasticity of the supply of output, generates counterclockwise linear cobwebs. But Hicks provides neither a general dynamic framework independent of special behavioral assumptions nor an explanation of how and why disequilibrium between saving and investment leads to the indicated movements of income.

Later writers have followed Hicks in failing to specify the relation between saving, investment, and the change in income. But they have introduced other arbitrary assumptions relative to LM. Conard [2, pp. 281–282] and Dernburg and Dernburg [3, pp. 229–231] assume that money market equilibrium is constantly maintained along the given (rising) LM schedule. The path to an IS–LM intersection point thus lies along LM. Siegel [18, p. 217] describes an initial movement to equilibrium as a horizontal path away from LM, followed by a vertical path back to LM, and so on along a resulting step function. See footnote 26 for a further comment on this interpretation.

[3] Hicks does not identify income as being real rather than nominal, but his analysis clearly implies that real income is the relevant variable. See p. 377.

rate of interest and the level of investment, "the multiplier tells us what level of income will be necessary to make savings equal to that value of investment" [5, p. 153]. Without further explanation, Hicks constructs the IS schedule as the familiar inverse relation between $r$ and $y$. The implied basis for the downward slope is that a reduction in $r$ raises investment and requires a higher income to bring saving to the greater investment level.

Several pages later in a more "general" version [5, pp. 156–157], Hicks allows saving to depend also on the rate of interest, and investment to vary also with income, both variables entering their respective functions positively. Then, in a diagram showing saving and investment rising and falling, respectively, with the rate of interest, a rise in income shifts both curves to the right. $S$ shifts more than $I$, lowering the equilibrium rate of interest. IS again is downward sloping.

In the money market the demand for money $L$ is a positive function of income and a negative function of the rate of interest. The money stock $M$ is initially an exogenously determined constant. With reference to an equation stating the equality of $M$ and $L$, Hicks derives the LM schedule, a positive relation between $r$ and $y$ "since an increase in income tends to raise the demand for money, and an increase in the rate of interest tends to lower it" [5, p. 153]. Hicks might well have added the all but obvious conclusion, "thereby maintaining the equality between $L$ and $M$." Later he relaxes the assumption of a fixed money stock, incorporating in LM a rising relationship between the rate of interest and the stock of money created by the "monetary authorities" [5, (p. 157)]. This reduces the slope of LM.

Hicks does not say explicitly that income is in general a real variable. However, near the close of the article he observes, "If there is 'full employment' in the sense that any rise in income immediately brings forth a rise in money wage rates; then it is *possible* that the CC [investment] and SS [saving] curves may be moved to the right to exactly the same extent, so that IS is horizontal" [5, p. 158].[4] Clearly, since IS is otherwise downward sloping, his earlier use of "income" must have referred to a real magnitude. Moreover, since Hicks at no time introduces the price level into his analysis, we are justified in concluding that he considered commodity prices to be constant, equal movements along the income axis thereby representing equal increments of real income.

Hicks' justification for including income as a determinant of investment is that "an increase in the demand for consumers' goods, arising from an

---

[4] Hicks goes on to qualify the possibility of the horizontal IS schedule by saying that the rise of wages may generate expectations of further rises. This could lead to a greater shift of $I$ than $S$ and create thereby an upward sloping IS curve. However, this would be at most a temporary outcome, since the movement of wages and prices is once-for-all, rather than continuing. Eventually the horizontal IS should prevail.

increase in employment, will often directly stimulate an increase in investment..." [5, p. 156]. This is a reference to the accelerator relation, according
to which $\Delta y$, not $y$, should be entered in the investment function. While
investment is often related to the *level* of income on the grounds that $y$ is a
proxy for profits, we reject this as an acceptable formulation of a *flow* investment function.[5]

## II. Financial Underpinnings

Perhaps the most serious shortcoming of Hicks' analysis is that the equilibrium rate of interest, given by the intersection of IS and LM, is derived
without once referring to the market in which it is directly determined, the
market for securities. It is true that if two of three markets are in equilibrium,
Walras' law can be invoked (as we do later) to show that the third is in
equilibrium. Thus the IS–LM determination is valid. But the dynamics of
interest rate determination are much more readily discernible in terms of the
securities market, and we shall turn to it in our description of the path between
IS–LM equilibrium points.

Our basic model contains one commodity, which serves both as a consumption and capital good, and two financial assets: real balances and an equity
(common stock) security. The primary advantage of an equity instrument is
that its real value is independent of the price level.[6] While those who want
this feature in a model generally obtain it from a constant purchasing power
bond, the latter fails to account for ownership of the capital stock.[7] The
earnings on the security are fully paid out as dividends and the market rate
of interest is thus the dividend–security price ratio. Given the real dividend
payment, the rate of interest is determined by the real price of securities.

There are two sectors: households and firms. For simplicity, firms are
assumed to hold the entire physical capital stock $K$, which is owned by
households. The equity securities, which are held only by households,
constitute the ownership claim. Both firms and households hold nominal
money balances $M$. The constraint on real asset demands of households is
real wealth:

$$L_h + D^E = W \tag{1}$$

[5] See the succinct comments to this effect by Pigou [17, pp. 55–56].

[6] Metzler [13, p. 99] is the first modern writer to see the usefulness of an equity security
as the sole nonmonetary financial asset.

[7] Patinkin [15, p. 217] uses a bond whose quantity is arbitrarily altered with movements
in the price level. It is thus effectively a purchasing power bond and, since no analysis of
an ownership claim is offered, serves much the same role that an equity instrument would.

where $L_h$ denotes household demand for real balances, $D^E$ is the real household existing demand for securities, and $W$ is real household wealth. The latter is defined as

$$W = S^E + M_h/P \tag{2}$$

where $S^E$ is the real value of the existing stock of securities and $M_h/P$ is the nominal stock of household balances divided by the general price level $P$.

We assume the following demand-for-money functions for households and firms, respectively:

$$L_h = L_h(y, r), \qquad \partial L_h/\partial y > 0, \quad \partial L_h/\partial r < 0 \tag{3}$$

$$L_f = L_f(y), \qquad \partial L_f/\partial y > 0. \tag{4}$$

We omit wealth from $L_h$ and $L_f$, and the rate of interest from $L_f$, in order to simplify the subsequent analysis. Wealth changes thus fall entirely on the demand for securities, and only households alter their money holdings when the rate of interest moves.[8]

The total stock of money is exogenous:

$$M = M'. \tag{5}$$

The value of the existing stock of securities is the capitalized value of the expected future dividends per share multiplied by the number of shares outstanding, $S_q$:

$$S^E = (d/r)S_q. \tag{6}$$

The dividend per share, $d$, is the aggregate return on capital and firm real balances divided by the number of shares:

$$d = [\rho K + r(M_f/P)]/S_q \tag{7}$$

where $\rho$ is the net real income produced by each unit of capital, and firm balances yield an implicit return equal to the rate of interest.[9] While $d$ is clearly subject to variation because of its variable components, we assume that shareholders expect the dividend payment to be constant in all future periods. Moreover, while we are concerned with changes in its components,

---

[8] See Horwich [6, pp. 32–33] for a rationalization of the assumption that wealth changes fall largely on the existing demand for securities, rather than the demand for real balances.

[9] Our assumption below of complete forced saving in disequilibrium processes implies that $\rho$ and $r$ are continuously equal. We recognize their equality in equilibrium situations, but ignore the movement of $\rho$ during the actual adjustment. For a detailed analysis that considers the impact of variations in $\rho$ in forced-saving adjustments, see Horwich [6, pp. 149–167].

we do not take account of changes in $d$ itself. Given households' expectations of constancy, the movements of $d$ have no particular bearing on our later analysis.

Substituting (7) in (6) and the result, (6'), in (2), yields alternative expressions for $S^E$ and $W$:

$$S^E = (\rho/r)K + M_f/P, \qquad \partial S^E/\partial r = -(\rho/r^2)K \qquad (6')$$

$$W = (\rho/r)K + M/P \qquad (2')$$

where $M/P$ is the sum of household and firm balances. In equilibrium, $\rho = r$ and $W = K + M/P$. An expression for $D^E$ is obtained by combining (1)–(3) and (6'):

$$D^E = (\rho/r)K + M/P - L_h(y, r)$$

$$\partial D^E/\partial r = -(\rho/r^2)K - \partial L_h/\partial r \gtreqless 0 \qquad (1')$$

$$\partial D^E/\partial y = -\partial L_h/\partial y < 0.$$

Because the sign of $\partial D^E/\partial r$ is uncertain and of no particular significance for our analysis, we shall draw the $D^E$ schedule as independent of the rate of interest in the figures below.[10]

A first step toward understanding the IS–LM analysis is recognizing the relationship between the money equilibrium curve (LM) and the existing securities market (Metzler [13, p. 104]). Walras' law for the existing asset market,[11] as applied to households, is derived by equating (1) and (2):

$$D^E - S^E + L_h - M_h/P = 0. \qquad (1'')$$

We assume that equilibrium holds continuously in the existing securities market:

$$S^E = D^E, \qquad (8)$$

which, from (1''), implies $L_h = M_h/P$. There is no impediment to the movement of security prices, and thus of the market or prevailing rate of interest, that would prevent the existing securities market from clearing immediately.

---

[10] $D^E$ indicates the real value, as opposed to the quantity, of securities households wish to hold. Thus the partial derivative of $D^E$ with respect to the interest rate varies with the interest elasticity of the underlying security *quantity* demand. See Horwich [6, pp. 25–32, 452–456, 460] for a discussion of these relationships.

[11] See May [12] on the importance of distinguishing between Walras' law as applied to stocks, on the one hand, and flows on the other. By discriminating between the old and the new security markets, Metzler's analysis [13, p. 102] implicitly embodies the same spirit of stock-flow separation in the application of Walras' law. A rigorous statement and explicit derivation of the two varieties of Walras' law was provided independently by Perg [16]. See the chapter by Perg in this volume, based on this source.

For firms, Walras' law for the existing asset market is

$$K^d - K + L_f - M_f/P = 0. \tag{9}$$

We assume that firms are always holding their desired capital:[12]

$$K^d = K \tag{10}$$

and thus $L_f = M_f/P$. Since the sectoral money demands are equal to their respective supplies, we have $L = M/P$, where $L = L_h + L_f$. Equation (10), together with (8), thus provides for equilibrium in the total money market, as well as in the existing securities market, at the prevailing rate of interest. A further implication of (10) is that disequilibrium in the commodities market is resolved *ex post* in favor of firms. Whenever excess commodity demand or supply exists, the invariable outcome for households is complete forced saving and dissaving, respectively.

A second step in understanding IS–LM is specifying the link between saving and investment (IS) and the securities market. The implicit assumption underlying IS is that all of saving is directed to the purchase of securities and all of investment is financed by the issuance of securities.[13] If this were true, it could be said that the equilibrium rate of interest (and its corresponding security price) is determined by equality of saving and investment. If savers direct a portion of saving to the acquisition of cash balances, or investing units use part of the proceeds of new security sales to accumulate balances, these are disturbances that are reflected in shifts of liquidity preference and the LM schedule. As permanent features of the model, they complicate, without significantly qualifying, any static or dynamic use of IS-LM. We therefore assume explicitly that saving is wholly a flow demand for securities $D^f$ and investment is a continuing (flow) supply of securities $S^f$. The converse statements are also true, except that the issuance of securities may secure funds that are temporarily held, prior to expenditure on investment. A summary of our behavioral assumptions as to saving and investment, and thus the flow security schedules, follows:

$$S = S(y, W) = D^f, \qquad \partial S/\partial y > 0, \quad \partial S/\partial W < 0^{14} \tag{11}$$

$$I = I(r) = S^f, \qquad \partial I/\partial r < 0. \tag{12}$$

---

[12] This assumption may seem to imply a zero or infinite rate of investment. However, we believe that a true flow investment function is generated only in a growth context, as reflected in positive and finite time derivatives of $K^d$ and $K$. For the implicit growth framework of our model and IS–LM, see pp. 383–384.

[13] This assumption is consistent with Metzler [13, p. 102], who identifies equality of saving and investment with equality between the demand and supply of new securities. Note that the assumption with respect to investment does not preclude the use of retained earnings, which are an implicit equity security issue.

[14] Since $C = y - S$, $C = C(y, W)$, where $\partial C/\partial y = 1 - \partial S/\partial y$ and $\partial C/\partial W = -\partial S/\partial W$.

Combining (11) and (12) yields Walras' law for the flow functions of the model:

$$S - I + S^f - D^f = 0.^{15} \qquad (13)$$

In equilibrium, $S = I$ and thus $S^f = D^f$.

Because saving can be either positively or negatively related to the rate of interest, for convenience we take the saving schedule, and thus $D^f$, to be independent of it. This specification of $D^f$ is consistent with that of $D^E$. Finally, since firms retain no earnings, we note that saving is performed by households only; and since firms hold the capital stock, they alone undertake investment.

In the spirit of IS–LM we do not write an explicit production function. Instead, we generally assume that the supply of output is either fixed or infinitely elastic at the going price level.

The merging of the flow and existing securities markets is shown in Fig. 1.[16] The investment and saving schedules, now denoted by $S^f$ and $D^f$, are drawn in Fig. 1a. $D^f$ and $S^f$ are drawn for a given level of income and capital stock, respectively, and are assumed to be constant functions recurring each period exactly as they appear in Fig. 1a. The interest rate at which they intersect is labeled $r_N$, the natural or equilibrium rate of interest. If income were higher, $D^f$ (and saving) would be drawn farther to the right, meeting $S^f$ (and investment) at a lower natural rate, as indicated by a downward IS relation.[17]

---

[15] Patinkin argues [15, pp. 272–273] that "the identity of saving with the demand for bonds [i.e., securities], and investment with their supply" implies an indeterminate price level and is thus inconsistent with "the very existence of a money economy." Indeed, since the excess of investment over saving equals the excess demand for commodities, and, in his full employment model, the sum of the excess demands for money, bonds, and commodities is zero, the assumption that $I - S$ equals the excess supply of bonds leaves the excess demand for money identically zero (and the price level indeterminate). However, in our model (and Metzler's, by implication) the existence of separate Walras' laws for stocks and flows enables $I - S$ to be purely an excess (flow) supply of securities without affecting the excess (stock) demand for money in any way. The way in which an excess demand for commodities (excess flow supply of securities) generates a nonzero excess demand for money is somewhat indirect and is described in Section III.

[16] This is perhaps the key difference between our model and Metzler's [13]. We combine the stock and flow components of the securities market (as in Figs. 1 and 2). Metzler, while recognizing the stock and flow distinction, ruled out the possibility of their integration on the grounds that the new (flow) component is too small to influence the price of securities (and the rate of interest) in any relevant time period [13, pp. 102, 115]. For a rebuttal to this argument, see Horwich [6, pp. 423–426].

[17] There is no presumption here that the natural rate is the equilibrium rate for full employment income only. At any level of income, the natural rate is simply the rate at

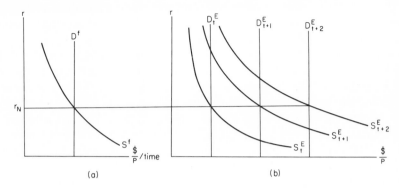

**Fig. 1.** Flow, stock, and total (combined) security markets in full equilibrium.

The existing securities market is pictured in Fig. 1b. Time subscripts have been attached to the $S^E$ and $D^E$ schedules because they shift through time as the flow supply and demand are added to them. The flow schedules in the left panel are added horizontally to the beginning-period existing schedules in the right panel to obtain the total schedules of the current period, which are also the opening schedules of the next period. Thus $D^E_{t+1} = D_t^E + D^f$ and $D^E_{t+2} = D^E_{t+1} + D^f$, and similarly for supply. The interest rate at which $S^E$ and $D^E$ intersect is the actually prevailing or market rate of interest $r_M$. Since the natural rate in Fig. 1b is equal to the market rate, equal quantities of flow supply and demand are added to the existing security schedules and the market rate is constant through time. While $D^E$ and $S^E$ are increasing each period, the $D^f$ (saving) and $S^f$ (investment) functions and hence the IS schedule are constant. Also, given a fixed price level, stock of money, and $L$ function, LM is also constant. The "moving" security–market equilibrium in Fig. 1 corresponds to a fixed intersection point between given IS and LM schedules.

It is now clear how equality of the demand and existing stock of money combined with equality of saving and investment determines the equilibrium rate of interest. The former equality coincides with equilibrium in the existing securities market and the latter implies equilibrium in the flow securities market. Simultaneous equilibrium in both markets is total equilibrium for the system.

Before proceeding to the disequilibrium process, our view of growth, from which the model and IS–LM abstract, should be made explicit. It may seem contradictory to hold income, the capital stock, and the price level constant

---

which the resulting *ex ante* saving and investment schedules are equal. IS is thus the locus of natural rates.

at the IS–LM intersection while allowing the existing securities market to increase over time. In fact, in equilibrium all behavioral schedules, along with income, capital, and wealth, increase at the given growth rate of the economy. Not only $S^E$ and $D^E$, but $S$, $I$, $L$, and $M/P$ (owing to reductions in $P$) shift to the right at the constant rate. Thus only the differences between the logarithms of the diagrammed saving and investment (flow securities) schedules and each pair of existing asset functions are constant, and fixity (or one-time increments) of $y$, $K$, and $P$ refers to behavior relative to trend. These qualifications will have no bearing on the analysis of disequilibrium in Section III, since the adjustment is caused purely by the interaction of excess demand functions that share the common growth factor. Our reason for making the movement of the existing security schedules explicit is that they are the focus of the dynamic analysis.

### III. Disequilibrium in the Financial Markets

We turn now to the merging of the stock (existing) and flow securities markets when they are not in full equilibrium and the market and natural rates differ. The process by which the two interest rates are brought together and income is changed is the basic adjustment mechanism. Although our functions and the adjustment are continuous over time, we shall analyze the process as a sequence of very brief, discrete intervals.

Since the IS–LM schedules are highly aggregative market-equilibrium curves, they are not very useful in the analysis of the adjustment. We therefore turn to an examination of behavior in the underlying markets. To keep the analysis familiar, the investment and saving schedules will be employed, but the reader should always bear in mind that they are really standing in for the flow securities schedules. Because the mechanism is somewhat complex when viewed in the money market, the securities market is considered first.

In Fig. 2 the investment–saving and existing securities markets are initially in full equilibrium at an interest rate $r_N'$. A disturbance occurs at the opening instant of an interval $t$. The investment schedule shifts spontaneously from $I'$ to $I''$, raising the natural rate from $r_N'$ to $r_N''$. The latter is above the initial market rate $r_M' = r_N'$, which, for the moment, still prevails. During the interval the stock and flow markets merge with the addition of $I''$ to $S_{t-1}^E$ and $S'$ to $D_{t-1}^E$. The merger raises the market rate because at the beginning interest rate $I'' > S'$ corresponds to an excess of securities being issued by firms over those that households wish to purchase with current saving. This excess supply of securities depresses the price of securities, raising the market rate of interest. The rise in the market rate creates an excess demand for securities on the part of existing asset-holders and continues until the excess

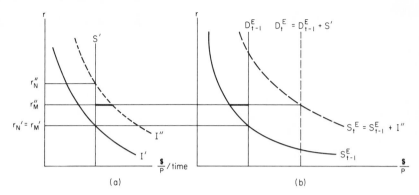

**Fig. 2.** The interaction of stock and flow security markets following an increase in investment.

existing demand is exactly equal to the excess flow supply. Thus, at the close of the interval, the interest rate $r_M''$ is one at which $I'' - S' = D_{t-1}^E - S_{t-1}^E$, as shown in Fig. 2 by the equal boldface horizontal segments.

The excess demand for securities by existing security holders is simultaneously an equal negative excess demand for money, as shown previously in the application of Walras' law to the existing wealth market [Eq. (1″)]. Households' de facto holdings of money are reduced by the desired amount when, during the merger process, the excess balances are spent on the excess new security supply. The money is thereby transferred to firms, who have now obtained financing for their intended higher investment outlays.

We shall describe the events occurring in the money market in more detail. But notice first that the market rate of interest has risen prior to any increase in income or the price level. Only a portfolio adjustment has occurred, with firms offering additional securities at a lower price and higher yield, inducing households to buy the securities in exchange for cash balances, which firms now hold in anticipation of additional investment expenditure.

Figures 3a and 3b picture the demands for real balances by households and firms, respectively, and the real stocks held by each. Firm demand is a vertical schedule coinciding with the line representing firm holdings of real balances. The sectoral demand schedules are summed to form the total demand in Fig. 3c. The initial values of the interest rate, the price level, and real income are $r_N'$, $P'$, and $y'$, respectively. At these levels the quantity of real balances demanded by households is $M_h'/P'$, the quantity demanded by firms is $M_f'/P'$, and the total quantity demanded is $M'/P'$, where $M' = M_h' + M_f'$. The initial points of equilibrium in the respective panels are denoted by the letters $A$, $B$, and $C$.

During the first adjustment period the interest rate rose to $r_M''$ as firms issued securities to finance additional investment. We assume that when firms

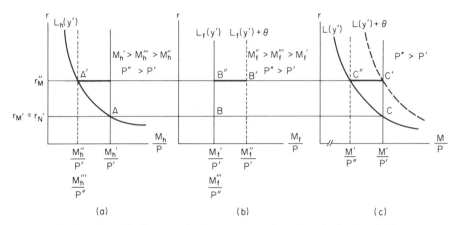

**Fig. 3.** The first-interval adjustment in the money market; the price level variable, output fixed: (a) households, (b) firms, (c) total.

plan new expenditures, they temporarily raise their demand for money from $L_f(y')$ to $L_f(y') + \theta$.[18] The quantity $\theta$ is equal to the anticipated investment increase and to the sectoral transfer of balances from households to firms:

$$\theta = I''(r_M'') - S'(r_M'') = M_h'/P' - M_h''/P' = M_f''/P' - M_f'/P'.$$

In Fig. 3a the household equilibrium point moves along the demand schedule $L_h(y')$ from $A$ to $A'$, and in Fig. 3b the firms' point moves from $B$ to the momentary equilibrium at $B'$. The increase of the $L_f$ schedule is reflected in Fig. 3c as an equal shift of the total demand from $L(y')$ to $L(y') + \theta$, the point of equilibrium moving vertically from $C$ to $C'$. The total stock of real balances $M'/P'$ is, of course, unchanged. The quantity $\theta$ appears in each figure as the boldface horizontal segment.

Firms are assumed to carry out their investment expenditure in the instant following the first adjustment interval. We shall describe the investment and induced household consumption response in more detail in Section IV, where we discuss IS–LM dynamics. In the present analysis of the existing asset markets, the investment expenditure is adequately summarized as a direct shift from money into commodities. The shift is reflected in our money market panels in a tendency for the firm demand for balances to return to its original position and for nominal balances to be restored to households as factor payments. The net movement of these variables and the general impact of the additional investment outlay depends on the degree to which the expenditure raises prices and total output.

Suppose first that the impact of investment is on the price level only, output

---

[18] The $\theta$ shift can be interpreted as reflecting the operation of the Keynesian finance motive, whereby firms' demand for money temporarily increases prior to an additional investment outlay. See Keynes [8].

remaining constant while $P$ rises from $P'$ to $P''$. In this case $L_f$ in Fig. 3b returns exactly to its initial position, since $\theta$ goes to zero and $y$ is unchanged at $y'$. But not all of the nominal balances received through the excess security issues are returned to households, since firm *nominal* demand for money rises along with the price level. While at the new equilibrium point $B''$, firms' *real* holdings $M_f'''/P'' = M_f'/P'$, the closing nominal balances stand in the relation $M_f' < M_f''' < M_f''$. Meanwhile, household real balances in Fig. 3a are unchanged at the level $M_h'''/P'' = M_h''/P'$, since, with output fixed, any balances received by households as income stimulate a proportionate (and presumably immediate) rise in the price level.[19] The equilibrium point remains $A'$. In the total money market in Fig. 3c the shift of $L_f$, as investment is undertaken, is reflected in an equal leftward shift of the total demand schedule from $L(y') + \theta$ back to $L(y')$. Since household real balances are constant during the investment expenditure, total real balances are reduced by an amount equal to the reduction of firm balances: $M'/P' - M'/P' = M_f'/P' - M_f'''/P''$. From an aggregate point of view, one can simply say that in the money market the investment outlay by firms—the movement from money into commodities—is manifested in an equal leftward shift of the demand for, and the stock of, total real balances. The reduction in the real stock is caused directly by the reduction in the demand for the stock, with the result that the components fall equally and synchronously and thereby provide no tendency to alter the market rate of interest. The money–market equilibrium point moves horizontally from $C'$ to $C''$.

The case where prices are constant at $P'$ and output rises from $y'$ to $y''$ is illustrated in Fig. 4.[20] The reversal of the temporary rise in firm demand for real balances again tends to shift $L_f$ back to its original position. But now the rise in real income raises both the firm and household demand for money. Instead of describing the individual sectors first, it is more convenient to begin with the total money market in Fig. 4c. Here we see readily that since prices and real balances are assumed to remain constant, the abscissa of the point generated by the investment expenditure, $C''$, must be $M'/P'$, the same as that of points $C$ and $C'$. Thus the shift of $L$ to the left as $\theta$ becomes zero is met by a shift to the right as $y$ increases, producing a final schedule, $L(y'')$,

---

[19] The expenditure response of households to additional real balances is, of course, the operation of the real-balance effect. See Patinkin [15, pp. 19–20, 236 ff.] for the definitive analysis of this effect.

[20] Our assumption $K^d = K$ [Eq. (10)] implies that there is no unintended reduction of inventories, so that additional output is an increase in net national product. This implies, within our short-run horizon, that firms produce the additional output by hiring unemployed resources. Whether they hire idle capital or labor, the expected dividend stream will increase and $S^E$ will shift to the right of $S_t^E$ in Fig. 2. On the assumption that wealth changes fall entirely on the demand for securities [Eq. (1')], $D^E$ and $S^E$ will shift equally and the market rate will remain at its prevailing level.

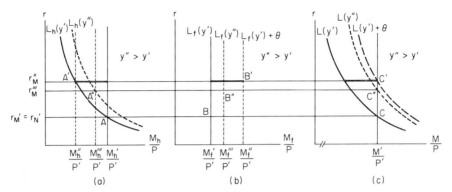

**Fig. 4.** The first-interval adjustment in the money market; the price level fixed, output variable: (a) households, (b) firms, (c) total.

intersecting $M'/P'$ at $C''$. The interest rate is now $r_M'''$, which, given that $L$ responds positively to income, is above the beginning yield $r_M'$. But it is likely to be below $r_M''$, the yield created during the transfer process. This is a fact best explained by reference to the securities market.

The transfer of real balances to households is an increase in wealth equal to the increment in new capital goods, which is also the rise in real output.[21] While the existing demand for securities rises equally with wealth, it falls with increases in output as the household transactions demand for money rises [see Eq. (1')]. Since the wealth increase and the increment to output are equal, $D^E$ will rise, be constant, or fall depending on whether $\partial L_h/\partial y \lesseqgtr 1$. It seems plausible to us that the partial derivative is less than unity[22] and thus that $D^E$ will rise and the market rate will fall.[23]

[21] From an aggregate point of view, the increase in wealth is due to the increase in the capital stock [Eq. (2')]. But, from the viewpoint of households, the rise in wealth appears as an increase in their real balances [Eq. (2)]. Initially households give up balances in exchange for excess new securities, wealth remaining constant. When firms buy investment goods, the increase in capital merely compensates for the decrease of firm balances and prevents the value of securities from falling [Eq. (6')]. Households thus experience a *net* wealth gain only when the balances are returned to them.

[22] The value of $\partial L_h/\partial y$ depends on the time period considered, since the numerator is a stock and the denominator a flow. In this process analysis the relevant period is the average income interval. We assume that $\partial L_h/\partial y$ is less than unity on the casual observation that during the income period households typically: (a) spend some portion of any increment to income receipts, thereby reducing the addition to the average level of balances held (and desired) during the interval *below* the increment to income that the balances represent; (b) do not liquidate existing securities or incur fresh debt for the purpose of making net additions to cash balances that exceed the income increment.

[23] An opposite effect on the rate of interest, but of negligible importance, arises because firms, unlike households, cannot draw on current income receipts for additional transactions balances and must obtain them from the securities market. This causes $S^E$ to shift to the right and the rate of interest to rise.

We complete our description of the first adjustment interval by allocating the net increase of $L$, relative to its starting position, to the sectoral demands for money. The sectoral schedules respond to the increase in output in accordance with their respective income coefficients. In the firm sector, in Fig. 4b, the final demand schedule is $L_f(y'')$, lying between $L_f(y') + \theta$ and $L_f(y')$. Thus as firms apply the $\theta$ quantity of real balances to investment expenditure, the resulting rise of aggregate output raises their demand for balances. This increment to demand is financed by additional security sales (see footnote 23). The final quantity of nominal balances is the indicated amount $M_f'''$. The closing point of the interval, at the interest rate $r_M'''$, is $B''$. Households, in Fig. 4a, complete the interval with balances, including those received as incremental factor income, equal to $M_h'''$, a quantity intermediate between beginning and post-transfer amounts. The final point $A''$ lies on the greater demand schedule $L_h(y'')$. The sectoral supplies and demands sum to the totals already described in Fig. 4c.

The changes in output and wealth, including both the capital stock and, when prices rise, real balances, change the level of saving and thereby the natural rate of interest. These tendencies are discussed in Section IV. Meanwhile, as long as the natural rate remains above the market rate, the events of the first interval are repeated in subsequent periods. Excess flow security supply drives the market rate upward and, by providing financing for greater investment expenditures, results in a rise in the price level, output, or both. When output rises, the concurrent rise in capital and wealth partially reverses the earlier rise in the market rate. As the investment–saving gap diminishes with the gradual approach of the market to the natural rate, all variables converge to new equilibrium levels.

## IV. IS–LM Dynamics

The IS–LM schedules cannot provide a framework for dynamic analysis because they implicitly assume that total income supplied and demanded are always equal. In order to translate the dynamic adjustment of Section III into the Hicksian diagram, real income must perform a dual role as both a supply and demand quantity. For this purpose we let $y_s$ be the supply and $y_d$ the demand for real income or output. Discrepancies between $y_s$ and $y_d$, as evoked by differences between the market and natural rates of interest, are the direct cause of the movements in prices and income described in Section III.

The derivation of IS–LM in Section I implicitly involved real income in its supply-of-output role. In tracing the response of both saving and the demand for real balances to changes in income, the relevant variable was the receipt of income, equal to the de facto real output of the economy. Incorporating the equilibrium assumption that $y_d = y_s$, IS–LM has thus provided a useful

comparative-static analysis of disturbances to the system, but has indicated
nothing of the process by which aggregate supply and demand interact to
determine the macroequilibrium.

For dynamic analysis the "effective" demand for output is defined as the
sum of real consumption and investment expenditures per period. We assume
that consumption is financed out of current income receipts or wealth; there is
no consumer borrowing. The letter $C$, real *ex ante* consumption, symbolizes
both desired and de facto consumption outlays, which are always equal. $C$ is
assumed to be independent of the rate of interest and to vary positively with
the level of wealth, as well as income (see footnote 14).

Desired investment expenditures $I$, an inverse function of the rate of interest, are financed wholly by the issuance of securities [see Eq. (12)]. Thus the
level of actual or effective investment spending $I_e(r_M)$ depends on the extent
to which firms are able to market their securities. When the market and
natural rates are the same, desired saving and investment are equal and
investment expenditures are equal to all of flow security supply. However,
when the market rate is below the natural rate, desired investment exceeds
saving and $S^f$ is greater than $D^f$. The ability of firms to sell securities at any
given *level* of the market rate is limited to the purchases of savers. During the
stock-flow security market process described in Section III, the resulting *rise*
of the market rate induced wealth holders to purchase the excess flow supply
of securities, $S^f - D^f$, by drawing down cash balances. Thus when $r_M < r_N$
and the market rate is rising, the total sale of securities and effective investment
demand are again equal to all of desired flow security supply.

The interaction of effective demand and the supply of output is shown
graphically in Fig. 5, an IS–LM diagram in which the IS schedule has just
shifted upward from $IS_1$ to $IS_2$ owing to an increase in investment demand
from $I'$ to $I''$. The highest schedule in Fig. 5, $IS_n$, prevails at the close of the
adjustment process and will be described. The parenthetical terms designating
each IS curve include, in addition to the relevant investment symbol, the
existing wealth levels [Eq. (2')]. At the predisturbance equilibrium, point $A$,
the natural and market rates were both equal to $r_N'$. For the present, and
prior to the adjustment, $r_M' = r_N'$ continues to be the market rate and $LM_1$
the prevailing LM schedule. The level of effective demand, $y_d' = C' + I_e(r_M')$,
remains equal to the supply of output $y_s'$.

The merger of stock and flow security markets in an ensuing period $t$, as
described in Section III, raises the market rate of interest to $r_M''$. Excess
investment, equal to the excess flow supply of securities, is financed when the
rise in the market rate induces a transfer of real balances from households to
firms in the amount of $\theta = M_h'/P' - M_h''/P' = M_f''/P' - M_f'/P'$ (see Figs.
3a and 3b). When these balances are spent, $y_d$ rises from $y_d'$ to $y_d''$, made
up of an unchanged volume of real consumption outlays $C'$, plus all of
the desired investment spending, $I(r_M'') = I_e(r_M'')$, at the interest rate $r_M''$.

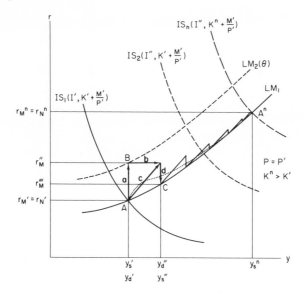

**Fig. 5.** Aggregate supply and demand in the IS–LM diagram; the supply of output variable, prices fixed.

This movement in effective demand is plotted in Fig. 5 as two connected vectors. The initial one, **a**, is vertical, reflecting the merger of security markets and the rise in the market rate. Effective demand remains $y_d'$ during this phase, but climbs vertically along the line at the output level $y_s'$ to the height $r_M''$. As the $\theta$ component of the demand for money goes to zero, $y_d$ rises to $y_d''$ along a horizontal rightward vector **b**. We summarize the initial interest rate and demand changes of the first interval by a northeast vector **c**, which emanates from point $A$ in Fig. 5 and is the resultant of **a** and the investment expenditure segment **b**.

While **c** rises in the same direction as the initial LM schedule, the two do not and, in general, will not coincide. Recall that LM is the locus of interest rates that clear the real balances and existing securities markets for different levels of $y_s$. In contrast, **c** is drawn for the initial level of $y_s = y_s'$. Moreover, while LM is independent of IS or its components, **c** contains effective investment, which depends critically on the size of the investment–saving gap at the given levels of $y_s$ and $r_M$. A flatter IS curve due, say, to a more interest-elastic $I$ schedule would imply a greater $I$–$S$ gap and a longer **c** vector at any preinterval market rate below the initially higher natural rate. The *slope* of **c**, on the other hand, depends only on the interest elasticity of the demand for money, reflecting the willingness of households to dishoard as interest rates rise. This is shown in the Appendix, which also compares the slopes of LM and **c**. Assuming that $\partial L/\partial y_s$ is less than unity, **c** will lie to the left of $LM_1$, as drawn in Fig. 5.

The expenditure of a $y_d''$ rate of total demand against the output level $y_s'$ occurs at the closing instant of $t$. Since the supply of output is less than $y_d''$, the expenditure tends to raise the price level and the quantity of output. We assume that these responses are lagged momentarily behind the excess effective demand. This assumption is designed to separate the various forces operating in the output market. It does not reflect any market imperfections in the model by which commodity prices or supply, within any period, adjust only gradually to discrepancies between effective demand and output.

Consider first a completely elastic response in output, prices remaining constant. This is the most common assumption underlying the use of IS–LM. Additional output, in the form of investment goods, thus raises $y_s$ to $y_s'' = y_d''$, while the capital stock rises equally to $K''$.[24] As noted in Section III (p. 388), the increase in capital raises household wealth and creates a net rise in the stock demand for securities. This lowers the market rate of interest from $r_M''$ to $r_M'''$. The movement appears in Fig. 5 as the downward vertical vector **d**, terminating at point $C$ on the $\text{LM}_1$ schedule. Point $C$ corresponds to the final money market equilibrium at $C''$ in Fig. 4c and is the closing point of the interval. Effective demand at point $C$ in Fig. 5 is still $y_d'' = y_s''$, but its composition is altered as demand moves along the **d** path. When the excess investment expenditure is completed at the end of the **b** vector (and a second round of financing has not yet occurred), effective investment falls, along **d**, to the level of voluntary saving. Simultaneously consumption rises in response to the increases in output and wealth. Since effective investment and saving along **d** are equal, total expenditures remain constant at $y_d'' = y_s''$.[25]

A second adjustment interval reenacts the events of the first. A monetary transfer raises the market rate, giving rise to a vertical movement analogous

[24] When resources are unemployed to the extent that increases in aggregate demand induce supply responses at a constant price level, it is somewhat difficult to imagine firms demanding new investment goods. Thus a shift in the investment schedule is an unlikely disturbance. However, the assumption of perfectly elastic output is intended to provide a polar case, which, together with the limiting case of fixed output and movements in prices only, will form the basis for the general and realistic intermediate case (pp. 396–397). Nevertheless, either of the following assumptions can be used to justify an investment shift under conditions of perfectly elastic output. First, the technology underlying the investment shift may be available only in new investment goods. Second, there may not be a secondary market for existing capital. If such were the case and if the increased demand for capital comes from firms in sectors where there is no excess capital, there will be a demand for new investment goods.

[25] At the end of the **b** vector and start of the **d** vector, $y_d'' = C(y_s', W') + I_e(r_M'')$. At the end of the **d** vector and close of the interval, $y_d = C(y_s'', W'') + S(y_s'', W'') = y_d''$ since $I_e(r_M''') = S(y_s'', W'')$. $W''$ incorporates the increase in the capital stock, but appears to households as an increase over $W'$ because of the receipt of additional real balances (see footnote 21). The latter, reflecting both additional real income and wealth, stimulate the additional consumption (see footnote 19).

to **a**. This is followed by a rightward horizontal vector analogous to **b**, which again is the excess of investment over saving that has been financed in the securities market. When the excess investment funds are spent, the sympathetic rise in the supply of output produces another downward vector similar to **d**. All three vectors in this interval, including a resultant northeast path analogous to **c**, would be smaller than those of the first interval. This is because the preceding rise in the market rate reduced the size of the investment–saving gap (and thus the horizontal vector), which is the direct cause of the current period's rise in the market rate (the vertical vector).

As long as the market rate is below the natural rate, desired investment exceeds saving and the events of the first two intervals are repeated. Security market stocks and flows interact to raise the market rate and finance excess investment expenditures, which, together, with investment financed by voluntary saving and increasing consumption outlays, raise the supply of output and the capital stock. In Fig. 5 the intervals beyond the first are summarized by vectors of the **c** and **d** varieties.[26] Each pair diminishes in size as the market rate rises and gradually closes the $I-S$ gap. The final equilibrium is reached in the $n$th interval at point $A^n$, the intersection of $LM_1$ and $IS_n(I'', K^n + M'/P')$.[27]

The parenthetical term designating $IS_n$ contains the wealth total prevailing in the new equilibrium. Each interval's increment to capital and wealth raises consumption and lowers the level of saving out of any given income. This raises the natural rate and the IS curve.[28] The rising demand–supply

---

[26] Siegel [18, p. 217] fails to allow the rise in the market rate to *precede* an increase in effective demand and the supply of output. He thus constructs the inflationary adjustment path below the LM curve rather than above it.

[27] This adjustment sequence between points $A$ and $A^n$ is nothing more than an enriched account of the traditional multiplier process. The analysis differs from the simple multiplier framework in that it describes the financing of expenditures and allows the interest rate to rise, choking off desired investment. It also permits consumption to respond to changes in wealth, as well as income.

[28] An alternative and possibly superior method of summarizing the response of IS to simultaneous changes in output and the capital stock is to build both responses into the IS function. In moving from one income level to a higher one, the simultaneous impact on saving of the associated increase in capital and wealth would be allowed to influence the movement of the natural rate and determine thereby the slope of IS. It is generally assumed that saving will rise, on net, in response to such changes (and IS will thus be downward sloping) because the positive income coefficient of saving is much greater than the negative wealth coefficient. However, the wealth change could be sufficiently greater in *magnitude* than the associated income change so that the wealth effect on saving would predominate and IS would thus slope upward. This promises to be a possibility when output is increased by rehiring unemployed capital, as contrasted with the purchase of new capital. While the net earnings from the capital are the same in either case, the holding of unemployed units entails negative earnings (interest payments, depreciation, property taxes). Thus when capital is reemployed, rather than newly purchased, the *increase* in earnings is greater, as is the wealth increment due to the capitalization of these earnings.

vectors thus pursue a constantly rising IS schedule, which they meet only if the system is stable.[29]

While the effective demand point reaches $IS_n$ only in the final equilibrium, it is always on LM schedules that move with the phases of the adjustment interval. The **a** movement of $y_d$ in Fig. 5 coincides with the temporary increase in the firm demand for real balances to $L_f(y_s') + \theta$ and thereby in the total demand for balances $L$. LM shifts responsively upward to the dashed curve $LM_2(\theta)$. In particular, at $y_s'$, $r_M''$ on $LM_2(\theta)$ is now the interest rate that clears the money and securities markets (see Fig. 4c). When $L^f$ and $L$ shift leftward during the investment outlay, $y_d$ moves to the right along **b** and LM shifts with it. The fact that the return path to $LM_1$ is **b** − **d**, instead of an instantaneous movement from point $B$ to $C$, reflects the implicit lag, noted earlier, in the response of $y_s$ to $y_d$ and thereby in the market rate of interest. In fact, such artificial lags, introduced for expository purposes, underly the entire adjustment process. Removing them would yield a smooth adjustment path above the $LM_1$ curve, such as the dotted line in Fig. 5.

Suppose, alternatively, that the level of real output is fixed during the adjustment process and only prices respond to the excess effective demand. Given a constant output, the capital stock must also be fixed.[30] Thus the component supplies of consumption and new capital goods are each completely inelastic with respect to their own price. The incremental investment expenditure of the first interval succeeds only in raising the price of new capital goods. This price movement reduces real investment and total effective demand to their respective supply quantities. In Fig. 6, which repeats the **a**, **b**, **c** demand vectors of Fig. 5 and adds a vertical supply-of-output schedule $y_s'$, the reduction of effective demand appears as a leftward horizontal vector coinciding with **b**. It is horizontal, since, in this fixed-output case, there is no tendency for the market rate to change during the expenditure phase (see p. 387).

When households receive the real balances as factor income, they apply them to additional consumption outlays. The latter are not, however, a net addition to total spending, for as consumption rises, real saving out of the given income, and thus investment, falls equally. Investment declines with saving since, in the aftermath of its first-round expenditure, it is constrained by the security purchases of savers (as it was in the variable-output case). With

---

[29] Another force tending to shift IS outward during the adjustment process is the investment accelerator. As the supply of output increases, investment rises because more capital is needed to produce the output. However, in the new equilibrium, output is constant (on its long-run growth path) and the investment schedule returns to its postdisturbance level $I''$.

[30] We could assume instead that some new capital is obtained by firms, but is not employed in the current production process. This would require that the present analysis be supplemented by a later description of a simultaneous increase in capital and output.

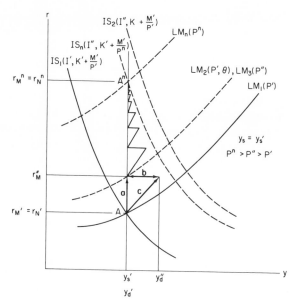

**Fig. 6.** Aggregate supply and demand in the IS–LM diagram; the supply of output fixed, prices variable.

total spending constant, the price level remains at the general level—say, $P''$—established by the interval's excess investment expenditure.

As in the fixed price-level case the LM schedule follows the $\mathbf{a} - \mathbf{b}$ and subsequent movements of effective demand. In Fig. 6 the beginning LM curve is $LM_1(P')$, where $P'$ is the initial price level. It is succeeded by $LM_2(P', \theta)$, for which the price level is unchanged, but $\theta$ has been added to the firm (and total) demand for money, pending the investment expenditure. The removal of $\theta$ again tends to shift LM back to the right, but the rise in the price level to $P''$ exerts a leftward force. Since the expenditure entails equal shifts in the demand for and stock of real balances, the excess demand for money is constant and $LM_3(P'')$, the final schedule of the interval, coincides with $LM_2(P', \theta)$. (Note that the same combination of variables $[y_s', r_M'']$ clears the money market both immediately before and after the investment expenditure.)

This pattern of rising prices and shifting LM continues through a succession of intervals similar to the first. In each one the market rate rises and an increase in aggregate demand is financed by a transfer of balances from households to firms. The price level rises in response to excess investment demand and is maintained by an induced rise in consumption. $y_d$ thus proceeds along an upward diminishing sequence of northeast–westward paths the right of the $y_s'$ schedule. After $n$ intervals the sequence converges on point $A''$, the intersection of $y_s'$ and $IS_n(I'', K' + M'/P'')$. The latter is the IS curve reflecting the increased propensity to invest and the reduced level of wealth due to the fall of real balances, while capital is fixed.[31] At the higher equilibrium price level $P^n$, $LM_n(P^n)$ also passes through the intersection at $A^n$.

In the intermediate and most general case, the supply of output is a rising function of the price level. We illustrate the resulting adjustment in Fig. 7, which reproduces the basic schedules and disturbance of Figs. 5 and 6. The initial supply-of-output schedule is $y_s(P')$, the quantity of output forthcoming at the beginning price level $P'$. Following the excess investment expenditure, prices rise to $P''$ and the vertical output line moves responsively to the right

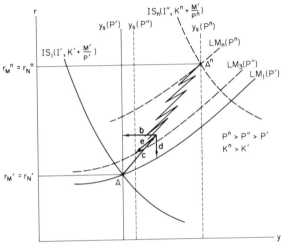

**Fig. 7.** Aggregate supply and demand in the IS–LM diagram; both the supply of output and prices variable.

[31] The shift of IS is not made during the course of the adjustment process because of our implicit assumption that households think the capital stock is growing so as to offset the decline in real balances. If households were immediately aware of the failure of firms to secure real capital, the market value of securities would fall equally with the increase in real balances received at the close of each interval. With wealth unchanged, and indeed identical to the preinterval portfolio in both quantity and composition, there would be no basis for a real-balance effect on consumption. Moreover, given unchanged preferences, households would apply the balances to securities, lowering the interest rate to its preinterval level.

If the failure to acquire real capital is disclosed after the new equilibrium is reached (via delayed publication of corporate earnings reports), the revealed loss in the value of securities will fall largely on the existing demand for securities, the interest rate remaining virtually constant. Expenditure responses would then take the form of the relatively small decrease in the rate of consumption due to a wealth decline. See Horwich [7, p. 720] for a discussion of the effects of wealth losses in the adjustment process and of the likelihood that disclosure will tend to be delayed.

to $y_s(P'')$. The reduction of demand to the new output level will be along a vector intermediate between **b** and **d**, the paths generated by fixed output and fixed prices, respectively. The new vector is the southwestwardly line **e** which lies inside the rectangle bounded by **b** and **d**. The greater is the elasticity of output, the more nearly will **e** coincide with **d**. The final LM schedule of the interval, $LM_3(P'')$, passes through the intersection of **e** and $y_s(P'')$. In future intervals the movement along northeastward **c**-type vectors, followed by a partial southwest return, generates a jagged northeast path to an equilibrium, such as $A''$ in Fig. 7. The equilibrium is determined by the intersection of an output supply schedule $y_s(P'')$ and $IS_n(I'', K'' + M'/P'')$, which reflects both the fall in real balances and the increase in the capital stock. $LM_n(P'')$ is also drawn through the final point.

## V. Summary

We have attempted to describe the dynamic paths between different points of equilibrium in the IS–LM diagram. In order to do so, it was necessary to specify the link between IS–LM and the securities market. In the money market (LM), household excess demand is equal and opposite to the excess existing demand for securities; firm excess demand equals the excess supply of capital. We assume that these excess demands are always zero. In the IS market, saving and investment are defined as a flow demand and supply, respectively, of securities. In full equilibrium, corresponding to a given IS–LM intersection point, the flow security demand and supply are added to the existing security schedules in a constantly recurring process over time. The market rate, which is determined in the existing market, is equal to the natural rate, the equilibrium of the flow market.

An increase in desired investment raises the flow supply of securities and the natural rate of interest. The resulting excess flow supply of securities raises the market rate and simultaneously induces a transfer of cash balances from households to firms. The additional firm balances finance an increase in investment expenditures, which raises the price level, output, or both.

The description of the dynamic process in the IS–LM diagram requires that the real output variable be interpreted as both a demand and supply quantity. The traditional IS–LM analysis treats output purely as a supply magnitude. We define the effective demand for output as the sum of consumption expenditures and desired investment which has been successfully financed in the securities market. During the stock-flow security market merger following the investment rise, the path of effective demand in the Hicksian diagram is a northeast vector to the left of the initial LM curve. Then, as the additional demand is applied to the supply of output, a perfectly elastic output response maintains effective demand at its higher level, but lowers the interest rate by creating a positive wealth effect in the securities market. This draws the demand vector vertically downward to the initial LM schedule. If only prices rise, demand is drawn horizontally leftward to the fixed output–supply schedule by a choking off of the excess investment demand. In general, with both prices and output rising, the demand path to a new equilibrium is a sequence of diminishing pairwise vectors, the first of which is northeast and the second, a smaller southwest return movement.

The demand paths are carried along by constantly shifting LM schedules. IS will shift in accordance with changes in wealth, consisting of increments of both the capital stock (positive) and real balances (negative).

## Appendix

The $c$ vector in Figs. 5–7 plots the relationship between effective demand $y_d$ and the rate of interest $r$. Effective demand equals consumption plus investment financed by the saving and dishoarding of households.[32] Dishoarding, as the market rate of interest moves from $r'$ to higher values, equals $L(r) - L(r')$. Thus when the market rate is below the natural rate, $c$ is defined by

$$y_d - C(y_s') - S(y_s') + [L(r) - L(r')] = 0. \qquad (A.1)$$

Its slope is $-(\partial c/\partial y_d)/(\partial c/\partial r) = -1/(\partial L/\partial r) > 0$.

The LM curve is the locus of $(r, y_s)$ points that equate the demand and existing stock of real balances. It is thus defined by

$$L(r, y_s) - (M'/P') = 0. \qquad (A.2)$$

Its slope is $-(\partial LM/\partial y_s)/(\partial LM/\partial r) = -(\partial L/\partial y_s)/(\partial L/\partial r) > 0$. Comparison of the expressions for the slopes reveals that the slope of $c$ will be greater than, equal to, or less than that of LM as $\partial L/\partial y_s \lessgtr 1$.

### ACKNOWLEDGMENTS

Support of the National Science Foundation is gratefully acknowledged. We have benefited from insightful comments by Thomas Mayer and Mathew Shane.

### REFERENCES

1. Brunner, K., and Meltzer, A. H., "Money, Debt, and Economic Activity," *Journal of Political Economy* **80** (September/October 1972), 951–977.
2. Conard, J. W., *An Introduction to the Theory of Interest*. Berkeley: Univ. of California Press, 1959.

---

[32] In the continuous case, when the market rate of interest is below the natural rate, $y_d = C + S - (\partial L/\partial r)(\partial r/\partial t)$.

3. Dernburg, T. F., and Dernburg, J. D., *Macroeconomic Analysis.* Reading, Massachusetts: Addison-Wesley, 1969.
4. Hicks, J. R., *A Contribution to the Theory of the Trade Cycle.* London and New York: Oxford Univ. Press, 1950.
5. Hicks, J. R., "Mr. Keynes and the 'Classics'; A Suggested Interpretation," *Econometrica* **5** (April 1937), 147–159.
6. Horwich, G., *Money, Capital, and Prices.* Homewood, Illinois: Irwin, 1964.
7. Horwich, G., "Real Assets and the Monetary–Interest Rate Mechanism: a Reply," *Journal of Political Economy* **75** (October 1967), 769–771.
8. Keynes, J. M., "Alternative Theories of the Rate of Interest," *Economic Journal* **47** (June 1937), 241–252.
9. Keynes, J. M., *The General Theory of Employment, Interest and Money.* New York: Harcourt, 1936.
10. Leijonhufvud, A., "Keynes and the Keynesians: A Suggested Interpretation," *American Economic Review* **57** (May 1967), 401–410.
11. Leijonhufvud, A., *On Keynesian Economics and the Economics of Keynes.* London and New York: Oxford Univ. Press, 1968.
12. May, J., "Period Analysis and Continuous Analysis in Patinkin's Macroeconomic Model," *Journal of Economic Theory* **2** (March 1970), 1–9.
13. Metzler, L. A., "Wealth, Saving, and the Rate of Interest," *Journal of Political Economy,* **59** (April 1951), 93–116.
14. Minsky, H. P., "Private Sector Asset Management and the Effectiveness of Monetary Policy: Theory and Practice," *Journal of Finance* **24** (May 1969), 223–238.
15. Patinkin, D., *Money, Interest, and Prices.* New York: Harper, 1965.
16. Perg. W. F., *Money and Macro Models.* Purdue Univ. dissertation, unpublished (1972).
17. Pigou, A. C., *Employment and Equilibrium.* New York: Macmillan, 1949.
18. Siegel, B. N., *Aggregate Economics and Public Policy.* Homewood, Illinois: Irwin, 1970.

# THE DYNAMICS OF INTEREST RATE
# ADJUSTMENT IN A KEYNESIAN MACROECONOMIC
# MODEL

*Wayne F. Perg**

*Board of Governors*
*of the Federal Reserve System*

## Introduction

Financial markets determine the rate of interest, but movements in the rate are affected by disequilibria elsewhere in the economy. This chapter explores the mechanism by which flows in the real sector influence interest rate movements. A dynamic model with variable output is developed for this purpose. It might quickly be described as a short-run Keynesian model with a stock-flow securities market. However, the structure of the model has some notable features. One is that the traditional form of Walras' law does not apply. Walras law applies only to the financial goods, securities and money. Therefore, although there are four markets (labor, commodities, securities, and money) determining three prices (the money wage, the price level, and the rate of interest), only one of two markets (securities or money) can be eliminated, instead of any one of the four as under the traditional form of Walras' law. A second feature of the model is *nontâtonnement* dynamics. A third, and most important feature, is the interest rate adjustment mechanism. Simply

---

* Present affiliation: Bowling Green State University.

401

stated, movements in the rate of interest are a function of the excess flow supply of securities.[1] This adjustment mechanism is the heart of the model. Saving and investment behavior, asset holdings, and portfolio choice are all brought together in the determination of security flows and interest rate movements.

These special features are logical consequences of two basic postulates of the model. The first postulate is the consumption function, viz., that consumption demand is a function of actual realized income. The second postulate is that the markets for financial goods are organized and those for existing capital goods and their services are not. An organized market matches buyers and sellers, determining a single price for all participants. Therefore the financial goods in the model (securities and money) are liquid—i.e., they can be sold quickly at an established market price at low cost—and capital goods are not. This second postulate is based on pragmatic empiricism and on the properties of financial goods in comparison to capital goods and their services. Organized markets exist generally for financial goods in the real world, but not for capital goods. Financial goods have properties favorable for organized markets—homogeneity, low information costs, and low transfer costs—and capital goods and their services do not.

Section I demonstrates the relationship between the two postulates, *nontâtonnement* dynamics, and Walras' law. The main emphasis here is on Walras' law because it is so strongly entrenched in the literature. Section II is concerned with the structure of the model. It derives the stock and flow functions of the financial sector, their interrelationships, and the interest rate adjustment mechanism. Section III derives the comparative-statics properties of the model, establishes its stability, and analyzes the dynamic interaction between changes in output and the rate of interest.

## I. The Postulates, *Nontâtonnement* Dynamics, and Walras' Law

The logical importance of the first postulate, the consumption function, has been brought out by Clower [1]. (See also Leijonhufvud [7, pp. 86–91] and Glustoff [2].) He demonstrated that the Keynesian consumption function is inconsistent with the *tâtonnement* adjustment process.[2] The

---

[1] See Horwich [4–6] for the early development of interest rate dynamics based on the flow security markets.

[2] Specifically this is the adjustment process in which the Walrasian auctioneer calls out a price vector, households and firms respond with their purchase and sale plans, the auctioneer adjusts the price vector in response to excess demand and calls out the new vector, etc., until an equilibrium set of prices is reached. Then and only then do actual trades, production, and consumption begin.

argument is simple and straightforward. Under *tâtonnement* all demand (and supply) functions have as their only argument the price vector called out by the auctioneer; the actual output that would occur at the resulting prices has no effect on consumption demand. Consumption as a function of de facto output, as described by Keynes, is thus incompatible with *tâtonnement*.

Clower also used the consumption function to attack the traditional form of Walras' law. The latter requires that an excess supply of labor be matched by an equivalent excess demand in some other market or markets. This balancing excess demand occurs because the income from the excess labor supply that households are offering, but businesses are not buying, is included in households' budget constraints. But this unrealized income drops out of the budget constraints when *tâtonnement* adjustment is dropped (as required by the consumption function), because actual labor sales equal only the amount demanded by businesses, and it is actual labor income that enters into households' budgets. Thus the balancing excess demand disappears.[3]

Walras' law[4] does not disappear as a result of the consumption-function postulate; it merely shrinks. Instead of applying to all markets, it applies to all but one—the labor market. It shrinks further—down to the markets for financial goods—when the second postulate is applied. This will be demonstrated later. An article by Patinkin [11][5] is drawn upon for a model in which the customary *tâtonnement* adjustment prevails and the traditional form of Walras' law is valid. Then, departing from Patinkin's analysis (which attacked as invalid the form of Walras' law that is established here), our two postulates are added, one at a time, changing the dynamics of the model and Walras' law.

A preliminary word on stocks and flows is in order. Our analysis will lead us to two distinct Walras' laws, one for stocks and one for flows. Walras' law for flows is derived from budget constraints because the latter have flow dimensions. Walras' law for stocks is derived from stock constraints. In Patinkin's model the stock constraint applies to the assets, bonds and money; capital goods are not included because he too does not incorporate a stock (existing) asset market for capital. Therefore, if we distinguish sharply between the time dimensions of stocks and flows, which Patinkin does

---

[3] This brief interpretation of Clower's long and rigorous argument has taken considerable liberties and should not be considered a summary.

[4] The definition of Walras' law is broadened in this chapter. Walras' law usually means that the sum of the excess demands in *all* markets must equal zero. We refer to this as the traditional form of Walras' law. Walras' law is expanded to apply to any subset (including the whole set) of excess demand functions that must always sum to zero.

[5] The liquidity preference versus loanable funds debate revolved around Walras' law. See Rose [13, 14] and Patinkin [12].

not,[6] we conclude that in his model Walras' law for stocks applies only to money and bonds while the one for flows applies to all four markets. This discrepancy will disappear after we add the two basic postulates to the model.

Patinkin's budget constraint for businesses is

*businesses* $\qquad N^d + R + D + I^d + \Delta M^b = C^s + I^s + B^s.$

Planned wage payments plus interest payments plus dividend payments plus Planned purchases of capital equipment plus planned net additions to cash balances (of businesses) equal planned sales of commodities to households plus planned sales of capital equipment plus planned net sales of bonds.

Patinkin's budget constraint for households is[7]

*households* $\qquad C^d + B^d + \Delta M^h = N^s + R + D.$

Planned purchases of commodities plus planned net purchases of bonds plus planned net additions to cash balances (of households) equal wage payments from planned sales of labor plus interest payments plus dividend payments.

Combining the budget constraints and rearranging terms, we obtain the traditional form of Walras' law:

*Walras' law* $\quad \Delta M^b + \Delta M^h = [N^s - N^d] + [(C^s + I^s) - (C^d + I^d)] + [B^s - B^d].$

The excess flow demand for money (equal to net planned additions to cash balances because there is no change in the money stock) equals the excess supply of labor plus the excess supply of commodities plus the excess flow supply of bonds.

---

[6] See May [8]. However, exact distinction between stocks and flows is not important for Patinkin's analysis. His use of *tâtonnement* adjustment precludes the stock-flow activity with which this chapter is concerned. In our model, disequilibrium flows move the stock markets from their temporary equilibria to their final (until another disturbance occurs) equilibria. Under *tâtonnement* no real economic activity occurs until everything—stocks and flows—is in equilibrium. Therefore, there are never any actual disequilibrium flows, and the final stock market equilibria hold from the beginning of actual activity because they are determined in the *tâtonnement*.

[7] In Patinkin's article $N^d$ replaced $N^s$ because the labor market is assumed to be in equilibrium. I have taken the liberty of restoring $N^s$ in order to emphasize that Patinkin advocates the traditional form of Walras' law. This substitution does not alter Patinkin's argument that it is invalid to require the excess demand for money to equal the excess supply of bonds. He argues this invalidity as follows: (1) the traditional form of Walras' law holds for all models; (2) its application to a model eliminates a market, bringing the number of markets into equality with the number of prices to be determined; (3) the requirement that the excess demand for money equal the excess supply of bonds eliminates a second market, rendering the model indeterminate because the number of markets is one less than the number of prices. Patinkin's logic is impeccable, but his first premise is wrong; the traditional form of Walras' law does not apply to *all* models. Therefore the argument is invalid.

In his analysis Patinkin did not specify whether he was speaking of the excess stock or the excess flow demands for money and bonds. He maintained strongly that the distinction was immaterial. He was correct, within the context of his *tâtonnement* model, but there are two caveats that make it important for our analysis to specify that they are excess *flow* demands. The first is that attention must be paid to the dates of stock excess demands, and the second is that units of measure differ for stocks and flows. The traditional form of Walras' law holds for excess stock demands, provided they are dated one time period in the future, but it does not hold for the current excess stock demands with which we are concerned. To show this, restate the preceding budget constraints in stock, rather than flow, units of measure and combine them. This yields: the excess stock demand for money at time $t + 1$ plus the excess stock demand for bonds at $t + 1$ equals the value of the amount of labor that households plan to sell during period $t$ minus the value of the amount that firms plan to buy plus the value of commodities that firms plan to sell during $t$ minus the value of commodities that households and firms plan to purchase during $t$. Note the date, $t + 1$, on the excess stock demands for money and bonds. If the time period is allowed to go to zero (see May [8], p. 4) in order to bring the excess stock demands at time $t + 1$ into equality with the current excess stock demands used in our analysis, the value of planned labor and commodity transactions during the period goes to zero, and we find that the current excess stock demand for money plus the current excess stock demand for bonds equal zero. Therefore it is important for us to specify the traditional form of Walras' law in terms of flows.

If Patinkin's model is changed in accordance with our first postulate, the traditional form of Walras' law no longer applies. The consumption function requires that $C^d$ depend on actual income. Therefore actual income must appear in the budget constraint for households, and actual labor income $N_A$ replaces $N^s$ in the household constraint. Since businesses know their actual purchases of labor, $N_A$ will also replace $N^d$. A combination of these new budget constraints produces a new form of Walras' law in which the labor market is missing. An excess supply of labor ($N^s > N_A$) does not produce a balancing net excess demand in the other markets because the new form of Walras' law, based on the constraint of actual income, requires net excess demand in these other markets to be zero.

The second of our two basic postulates, viz., that financial goods (money and securities) have organized stock markets while existing capital does not, is not really added to the model—it is activated. Patinkin, as noted, also assumes that there are organized stock markets for financial goods only, but this important assumption is not relevant for Walras' law (for flows) until *nontâtonnement* dynamics are used. The Keynesian consumption function activates the second postulate by forcing the model to operate out of equilibrium. With *actual* output being produced and consumed, inequality between planned sales of commodities by businesses to households and planned purchases of commodities by consumers causes actual money holdings of businesses and/or households to depart from desired levels. Under postulate two, there is no organized stock market for commodities. Thus commodities are illiquid. It would be time-consuming and expensive to adjust money holdings by means of commodity trade. However, there *is* an organized market in which bonds can be bought and sold quickly and at low cost. Therefore, taking actual commodity sales as given, businesses and households will revise their planned sales and purchases of bonds so as to bring money balances to desired levels. Thus actual sales of commodities, $C_A$ and $I_A$, replace $C^d$, $C^s$ and $I^d$, $I^s$, respectively, in the budget constraints, and Walras' law for flows shrinks to money and bonds. We show this in the context of the modified Patinkin model as follows.

The budget constraint for businesses is

*businesses*        $N_A + R + D + I_A + \Delta M_R^b = C_A + I_A + B_R^s.$

Actual wage payments plus interest payments plus dividend payments plus actual investment expenditures plus planned net changes in money balances (revised in accordance with actual transactions in the real sector) equal actual consumption expenditures plus actual investment expenditures plus planned net sales of bonds (revised in accordance with actual transactions in the real sector).

The budget constraint for households is

*households*        $C_A + B_R^d + \Delta M_R^h = N_A + R + D.$

Actual consumption plus net planned purchases of bonds and net planned changes in money balances (both revised in accordance with actual transactions in the real sector) equal actual wage payments plus interest payments plus dividend payments.

A combination of the budget constraints gives Walras' law for the modified Patinkin model:

*Walras' law*        $\Delta M_R^b + \Delta M_R^h = B_R^s - B_R^d.$

The excess flow demand for money equals the excess flow supply of bonds (both of which are *ex post* of actual transactions in the real sector). These excess flow demands are added to the stock markets for money and bonds, respectively, and a stock adjustment takes place.

The modifications in the Patinkin model associated with the two postulates produce results that are intuitively gratifying. Financial goods become more differentiated from commodities. Stock-flow relationships become more important and Walras' law for flows applies to the same markets as does Walras' law for stocks.

## II. Structure of the Model

Our model is one of continuous time with a single commodity. The assumption of a single commodity requires that the relative prices of capital and consumption goods be constant [3, p. 33], and this requires the limitation of organized markets to financial goods. For if there were an organized market for the stock of capital, a change in the rate of interest would change the yield on real capital and thereby the price of capital relative to consumption goods.[8]

Firms hold all capital,[9] the stock of which is fixed. There is a central bank, but the model has no government sector. The central bank pays out all of its earnings to households.

### A. THE REAL SECTOR

The real sector is based on a linear homogeneous production function with all of the usual properties. A simple Keynesian labor market is assumed. The demand for labor is a function of the real wage. The full-employment supply of labor is fixed. Money wages are inflexible downward, giving the model the desired variability in output.

The equations of the real sector are now presented. $X$ is the quantity of real output, $X_d$ the quantity demanded, and $X_s$ the quantity that firms desire to supply; $K$ is the stock of capital; $N$ is the amount of labor employed, $N_d$ the amount demanded, and $N_f$ the full-employment quantity; $C$ is realized, or actual, real consumption and $C_d$ is the quantity of real consumption demanded; $I$ is realized, or actual, real investment and $I_d$ is the quantity of real investment demanded; $P$ is the price level, $w$ the money wage,

---

[8] Alternatively one could force the price of consumption goods to follow the price of capital goods, keeping relative prices constant. However, there is no obvious economic rationale for this assumption and the resultant dynamics also seem strange. The constant real rate of interest means that the rate of inflation must adjust in order to produce the nominal rate of interest that equates the demand and supply of real balances. Thus the rate of change in the price level is determined by the money market rather than by the demand and supply of commodities. These are essentially the dynamics of the single-sector monetary growth models originated by Tobin, and these models have stability problems. See Nagatani [10] and Stein [15].

[9] The second postulate fits in with this assumption. Since there is no organized market for the services of capital goods, a marketing effort is required in order to make a capital good productive. In effect, a firm is formed; the firm owns the capital good and the household owns the firm, which includes both the capital good and marketing resources. In contrast, the mere ownership of a security gives households a claim on an income stream.

and $r$ the rate of interest; $F_N$ is the partial derivative of output with respect to labor and $e_K$ is the average real earnings of a unit of capital.

$$X = F(N, K), \quad K = \overline{K}, \quad \frac{\partial F}{\partial N} > 0, \quad \frac{\partial F}{\partial K} > 0, \quad \frac{\partial^2 F}{\partial N^2} < 0, \quad \frac{\partial^2 F}{\partial K^2} < 0. \quad (1)$$

$$N_d = N_d(w/P) \quad \text{such that} \quad w/P = F_N[N_d(w/P), \overline{K}]. \quad (2)$$

$$N_f = \overline{N}_f. \quad (3)$$

$$X_s = F(N_d, \overline{K}). \quad (4)$$

$$C_d = C_d(X), \quad 0 = dC_d/dX < 1. \quad (5)$$

$$I_d = I_d(r), \quad dI_d/dr < 0. \quad (6)$$

$$X_d = C_d + I_d. \quad (7)$$

$$e_K = [X - (w/P)N]/\overline{K}. \quad (8)$$

$$\dot{P}/P = \psi(X_d - X_s), \quad \psi > 0. \quad (9)$$

$$\dot{w}/w = \begin{cases} 0 & \text{if } N_d \leqq N_f \\ \lambda(N_d - N_f) & \text{if } N_d > N_f; \end{cases} \quad \lambda > 0. \quad (10)$$

$$C = C_d. \quad (11)$$

$$N = \begin{cases} N_d & \text{if } N_d \leqq N_f \\ N_f & \text{if } N_d > N_f. \end{cases} \quad (12)$$

The model has *nontâtonnement* dynamics, as required by the consumption function. Market disequilibria are resolved in accordance with (11) and (12). Since actual consumption always equals the quantity demanded (11), passive investment makes up the difference between output and demand ($I = I_d + X - X_d$). The amount of labor employed equals the amount demanded unless demand exceeds full employment, in which case the amount employed equals the full employment quantity (12).

## B. The Financial Sector

The model follows in the Metzler–Horwich [9, p. 99; 4, p. 20; 5, p. 629] tradition of choosing equities as the basic financial security of the economy. There are several advantages in choosing equities rather than bonds. The real value of equities is unaffected by changes in the price level. The total (net) earnings of capital go to the holders of equities,[10] whereas bond holders

---

[10] Retained earnings can be eliminated because holding shares in a firm that is retaining earnings is equivalent to receiving those retained earnings and using them to purchase new shares in the firm.

receive fixed money earnings, with the remainder of the earnings of capital going to the owners of firms. There are other important results. The wealth variable is changed significantly. Wealth equals the market value of firms plus real balances minus that part of the value of firms held by the central bank (following the Metzler–Horwich tradition of money creation by central bank open-market operations rather than by government deficits). If bonds are the basic security, there is no market determination of the value of firms. As a result, the value of firms is usually assumed to be constant, real balances become the only variable component of wealth, and the wealth effect becomes "the real balance effect" (as in Patinkin [16]).

## 1. *The Stock Functions*

The basis of Walras' law for stocks is the wealth constraint. Wealth equals the assets of households because they are the ultimate holders of all wealth. The assets consist of equities and real balances. Therefore wealth $W$ equals the real price of securities $P_E/P$ times the number of securities held by households $E^h$ plus their real balances:

$$W = (P_E/P)E^h + M^h/P. \tag{13}$$

The number of securities demanded by households $E_d^h$ times the real price of securities plus the amount of real balances demanded by households $L^h$ must equal the assets of households. Therefore Walras' law for stocks is

$$(P_E/P)E_d^h - (P_E/P)E^h + L^h - M^h/P = 0. \tag{14}$$

The household stock demand and supply of securities can be written in real-value terms as

$$D_E^h = (P_E/P)E_d^h \tag{15}$$

$$S_E^h = (P_E/P)E^h. \tag{16}$$

The household demand for real balances is given by liquidity preference:

$$L^h = L^h(r, X, W), \qquad \frac{\partial L^h}{\partial r} < 0, \qquad \frac{\partial L^h}{\partial X} > 0, \qquad 0 < \frac{\partial L^h}{\partial W} < 1. \tag{17}$$

By Walras' law for stocks,

$$D_E^h = S_E^h + M^h/P - L^h. \tag{18}$$

The organized stock markets for equities and real balances maintain continuous equilibrium,[11] determining a market rate of interest $r$ such that

$$D_E^h = S_E^h \quad \text{and} \quad L^h = M^h/P. \tag{19}$$

---

[11] The equities market must be in equilibrium in order to determine $P_E/P$.

The real price of an equity equals the expected earnings divided by the sum of the rate of interest and a risk discount. The expected earnings of an equity are assumed equal to current earnings, and the risk discount $d$ is assumed constant. Current earnings of an equity $e_E$ equal the earnings of firms (equal to the earnings of capital) divided by the number of equities $E$.

$$P_E/P = e_E/(r + d), \qquad d = \bar{d} \tag{20}$$

$$e_E = [X - (w/P)N]/E = e_K K/E. \tag{21}$$

Households and the central bank hold equities:

$$E = E^h + E^{cb}. \tag{22}$$

Households and firms hold real balances:

$$M/P = M^h/P + M^f/P. \tag{23}$$

The demand for real balances by firms may involve different parameters (e.g., the expected yield on capital goods) than does the demand for real balances by households. Rather than deriving such a function, we make the simplifying assumption of constant firm demand. The holdings of real balances by firms are kept equal to that demand:

$$M^f/P = L^f = \bar{L}^f. \tag{24}$$

## 2. The Flow Functions and Walras' Law for Flows

The flow supply of securities (in real value terms) equals the real price of securities times the rate at which firms are issuing securities:

$$S_{EF} = (P_E/P)\dot{E}. \tag{25}$$

The rate at which firms issue securities depends on the actual investment that they must finance and on their demand for money. Therefore the flow supply of securities must equal the rate of actual investment plus the rate at which price increases are reducing the stock of firms' real balances, if firms are to keep their balances equal to the desired constant amount as required by (24):

$$S_{EF} = I + (M^f/P)\dot{P}/P. \tag{26}$$

The real price of securities times the rate of change in the number of securities held by the central bank equals the rate at which the central bank is creating real balances. It is also equal to the flow demand for securities by the central bank:

$$(P_E/P)\dot{E}^{cb} = \dot{M}/P = D_{EF}^{cb}. \tag{27}$$

The flow supply of real balances equals the rate at which the central bank is creating real balances minus the rate at which price increases are reducing the stock of real balances:

$$(\dot{M}/P) = \dot{M}/P - (M/P)\dot{P}/P. \tag{28}$$

Because firms hold their stock of real balances constant, the rate of change in the stock of real balances held by households equals the flow supply of real balances:

$$(\dot{M^h}/P) = (\dot{M}/P). \tag{29}$$

The flow supply of securities to households equals the flow supply of securities issued by firms minus that part of the supply absorbed by the open market operations of the central bank:

$$S_{EF}^h = S_{EF} - D_{EF}^{cb} = I + (M^f/P)\dot{P}/P - \dot{M}/P. \tag{30}$$

The flow demands for securities and real balances by households are related to their respective stock demands. Period analysis is used for the derivation because stock adjustments can be clearly separated from flows. Given their saving, households will desire to purchase that number of equities and quantity of real balances that will maintain portfolio balance, given the current market rate of interest. These are the flow demands. If the number of securities that households desire to purchase differs from the number that firms create minus the number purchased by the central bank, the stock market for equities will be out of equilibrium and a stock adjustment will ensue, changing the market rate of interest. The total change in the stock demand for equities at the end of the period, $\Delta E_d{}^h$, equals the flow demand during the period plus the effect of the change in the rate of interest on the stock demand, $(\partial E_d{}^h/\partial r)\,\Delta r$. Let the time period go to zero, multiply by the real price of securities, and the flow demand for securities by households (in real value terms) is

$$D_{EF}^h = (P_E/P)\left[\dot{E}_d{}^h - \frac{\partial E_d{}^h}{\partial r}\,\dot{r}\right]. \tag{31}$$

Similarly, we can show that the flow demand for real balances by households equals the total change in the stock demand minus that part of the change due to the movement in the rate of interest as a result of the stock adjustment. Letting the time period go to zero, we obtain

$$L_F{}^h = \dot{L}^h - \frac{\partial L^h}{\partial r}\,\dot{r} = \frac{\partial L^h}{\partial X}\,\dot{X} + \frac{\partial L^h}{\partial W}\,\dot{W}. \tag{32}$$

$D_{EF}^h$ can be expressed in terms of $D_E{}^h$, using (31) and (15) and some mathematical manipulation:

$$D_{EF}^h = \dot{D}_E{}^h - \frac{\partial D_E{}^h}{\partial r} \dot{r} - \frac{D_E{}^h}{(P_E/P)} \left[ (\dot{P}_E/P) - \frac{\partial (P_E/P)}{\partial r} \dot{r} \right]. \tag{33}$$

There are two methods of deriving Walras' law for flows. One of them reinforces the view that Walras' law for flows is related to Walras' law for stocks and that they should apply to the same markets. This derivation is given in Appendix A, using the relationships between the flow and stock functions just derived, (32) and (33), and Walras' law for stocks, (14). The result is that the excess flow demand for securities by households plus their excess flow demand for real balances equals zero, and thus Walras' law for flows is

$$D_{EF}^h - S_{EF}^h + L_F{}^h - (M^{\dot{h}}/P) = 0. \tag{34}$$

A second method of proof is to combine the flow constraints of households, businesses, and the central bank. This follows.

The rate at which households can increase their holdings of equities and real balances equals their actual saving minus the rate at which price increases are reducing their stock of real balances. Therefore the flow constraint for households is

$$D_{EF}^h + L_F{}^h = S^h - (M^h/P)\dot{P}/P. \tag{35}$$

The flow constraint for businesses is (26) and the flow constraint for the central bank is (27). These two equations combine with (35) to form

$$D_{EF}^h + L_F{}^h = (S^h - I) + (S_{EF} - D_{EF}^{cb}) + \dot{M}/P - (M^f/P + M^h/P)\dot{P}/P. \tag{36}$$

$S^h - I = 0$ because it is the difference between *ex post* saving and investment, as required by *nontâtonnement* adjustment. By (30), $S_{EF} - D_{EF}^{cb} = S_{EF}^h$. By (28), $\dot{M}/P - (M^f/P + M^h/P)\dot{P}/P = (\dot{M}/P)$, and by (29), $(\dot{M}/P) = (M^{\dot{h}}/P)$. Therefore (36) reduces to (34).

## 3. The Interest Rate Adjustment Mechanism

Movements in the rate of interest are a function of the excess flow supply of securities. This is a gratifying result because it makes good intuitive sense. It is also an easily derived result. The markets for equities and real balances are continuously in equilibrium (19). Therefore $\dot{L}^h = (M^{\dot{h}}/P)$. Using (32) to substitute $L_F{}^h + (\partial L^h/\partial r)\dot{r}$ for $\dot{L}^h$ and then solving for $\dot{r}$, it follows that $\dot{r} = -[L_F{}^h - (M^{\dot{h}}/P)]/(\partial L^h/\partial r)$. Then, by Walras' law for flows,

$$\dot{r} = -(S_{EF}^h - D_{EF}^h) \bigg/ \frac{\partial L^h}{\partial r}. \tag{37}$$

## III. Comparative Statics, Stability, and Dynamics

### A. THE MARKETS

The four markets in the model determine three prices: the money wage, the price level, and the rate of interest. By Walras' law, one of two markets—the securities or money market—can be eliminated. Neither the labor nor the commodities market can be eliminated because they do not enter into Walras' law. Following conventional practice, the money market will be used in comparative-statics representations. However, in dynamic formulations the securities market is used because it is more informative.

Each of the three chosen markets is affected by the prices determined in the other markets. The price level affects the labor market, and the money wage and the rate of interest affect the commodities market in the usual manner. However, the effects of the money wage and the price level on the securities market are not obvious. The influence of $w$ and $P$ on the securities market is brought out by substituting into the interest rate adjustment mechanism (37) and solving for $\dot{r}$.[12] First substitute $L_F^h - (M^h/P)$ for $S_{EF}^h - D_{EF}^h$ (34). $L_F^h$ is a function of $\dot{X}$ and $\dot{W}$ (32). Solve $\dot{X}$ and $\dot{W}$ in terms of the excess demands for commodities and labor. Solve $(M^h/P)$ in terms of the excess demand for commodities and the effects of open-market operations [Eqs. (21), (28), and (29)]. Then solve for $\dot{r}$. Two different functions result, one for less than full employment and one for demand exceeding full employment. Only the less-than-full-employment function is used here:

$$\dot{r} = \frac{\psi(X_d - X_s)\left[\dfrac{\partial L^h}{\partial X}\left(\dfrac{-w^2}{P^2 F_{NN}}\right) + \dfrac{\partial L^h}{\partial W}\dfrac{E^h}{(r+d)}\dfrac{N}{E}\dfrac{w}{P} + \left(1 - \dfrac{\partial L^h}{\partial w}\right)\dfrac{M}{P}\right] - \left(1 - \dfrac{\partial L^h}{\partial W}\right)\dot{M}/P}{-\dfrac{\partial L^h}{\partial r} + \dfrac{S_E^h}{(r+d)}\dfrac{\partial L^h}{\partial W}}.$$

$$(38)$$

The signs of the coefficients in (38) are unambiguous. The coefficient on the excess demand for commodities, $X_d - X_s$, is always positive and the coefficient on open-market operations, $\dot{M}/P$, is always negative. The denominator is invariably positive. Therefore changes in $r$ are positively related to the excess demand for goods and negatively related to open-market purchases.

The relationship between the markets, and the markets themselves, can be better understood by graphing them as functions of their own prices. The

---

[12] See Appendix B for the full derivation of the $\dot{r}$ relation given in (38).

labor market is graphed in Fig. 1. The full-employment amount of labor $N_f$ is fixed. The demand for labor is a decreasing function of the real wage. Therefore, given $P$, $N_d$ is a decreasing function of the money wage $(\partial N_d/\partial w = 1/PF_{N_d N_d} < 0)$, and an increase in $P$ from $P_0$ to $P_f$ shifts the $N_d$ curve to the right. $P_f$ is the price level such that $N_d = N_f$, given $w = w_0$.

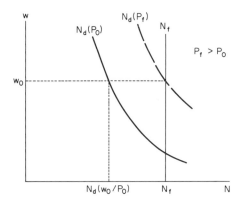

Fig. 1. The labor market.

The commodities market (Fig. 2) has three functions. $X_s$ is the amount that firms desire to produce: $X_s = F(N_d, \overline{K})$. Therefore, given $w = w_0$, $X_s$ is an increasing function of $P$ (i.e., $\partial X_s/\partial P = -w^2/P^3 F_{N_d N_d} > 0$). Actual output $X$ is identical to $X_s$ until $X$ equals full employment output, because $N = N_d$ for $N_d \leqq N_f$. The demand for commodities, $X_d$, is a function of $X$ and $r$. For $P < P_f(w_0)$, an increase in $P$ increases $X_d$ because $X$ increases. $X_d$ is constant for $P \geqq P_f(w_0)$ because $X$ is constant at $X_f$. A decrease in $r$ shifts the $X_d$ curve to the right. The $X_d$ cuts $X_s$ from below because $\partial X_d/\partial X < 1$ and

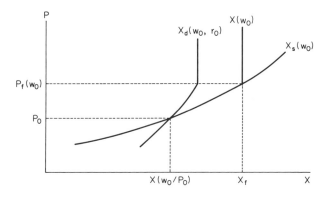

Fig. 2. The commodities market.

$\partial X/\partial P \leqq \partial X_s/\partial P$. Therefore the commodities market is stable in itself. An increase in $w$ rotates all of the curves upward. However, the output at which $X_d = X_s$ is unchanged.

Figure 3 shows the flow securities supply and demand and the saving schedule (the vertical line), all based on the prevailing real wage $w_0/P_0$. The central bank is assumed not to be conducting open-market operations; i.e., $\dot{M}/P = 0$. By (30), $S^h_{EF} = I + (M_f/P)\dot{P}/P - \dot{M}/P$. Then $I = S^h$ because *ex post* investment equals *ex post* saving. Therefore $S^h_{EF} = S^h$ and the $S^h_{EF}$ curve intersects the $S^h(w_0/P_0)$ line at a rate of interest $r^*$ at which $X_d = X_s$ and, by (21),

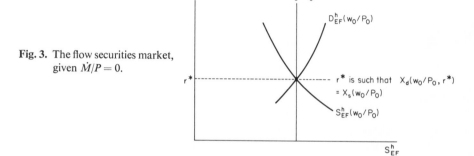

**Fig. 3.** The flow securities market, given $\dot{M}/P = 0$.

$\dot{P}/P = 0$. The slope of $S^h_{EF}$ is negative ($\partial S^h_{EF}/\partial r = (M^f/P)\psi \, \partial I_d/\partial r < 0$). From (35), $D^h_{EF} = S^h - (M^h/P)\dot{P}/P - L^h_f$. The value of $D^h_{EF}$ is dependent on $S^h_{EF}$ because $\dot{r}$ is an argument of $L^h_f$ and therefore of $D^h_{EF}$. However, (38) and (37) are used to show that $S^h_{EF} - D^h_{EF} \lessgtr 0$ for $r \gtrless r^*$. For $r \gtrless r^*$, $X_d - X_s \lessgtr 0$ and by (38), $\dot{r} \lessgtr 0$. Therefore, by (37), $S^h_{EF} - D^h_{EF} \lessgtr 0$ for $r \gtrless r^*$. The market is stable in itself.[13]

The flow demand and supply functions shift to the right and down if $w/P$ decreases. They shift to the right because the lower real wage increases output and saving. They shift down because higher saving lowers the rate of interest at which $X_d = X_s$.

---

[13] Although the slope of $D^h_{EF}$ is not necessarily positive, it will almost certainly be positive in the neighborhood of $r^*$. We have

$$\frac{\partial D^h_{EF}}{\partial r} = -\frac{\partial}{\partial r}(M^h/P)\dot{P}/P - \frac{\partial L^h_F}{\partial r}, \qquad -\frac{\partial}{\partial r}(M^h/P)\dot{P}/P = -(M^h/P)\psi\frac{\partial I_d}{\partial r} > 0$$

$$-\frac{\partial L^h}{\partial r} = -\frac{\partial L^h}{\partial X}\frac{\partial \dot{X}}{\partial r} - \dot{X}\frac{\partial^2 L^h}{\partial X\partial r} - \frac{\partial L^h}{\partial W}\frac{\partial \dot{W}}{\partial r} - \dot{W}\frac{\partial^2 L^h}{\partial W\partial r}, \qquad -\frac{\partial L^h}{\partial X}\frac{\partial \dot{X}}{\partial r} > 0.$$

$\dot{X}$ and $\dot{W}$ go to zero as $r$ approaches $r^*$. The sign of $-\partial L^h/\partial W \, \partial \dot{W}/\partial r$ is indeterminate.

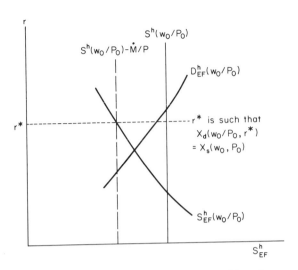

**Fig. 4.** The flow securities market, given $\dot{M}/P > 0$.

A flow open-market purchase (Fig. 4) directly affects the flow supply of securities to households and indirectly affects the flow demand for securities by households. The flow supply of securities to households is reduced by the central bank's rate of purchase. Therefore the $S_{EF}^h$ curve is shifted to the left by $\dot{M}/P$, intersecting the $S^h(w_0/P_0) - \dot{M}/P$ line at $r^*$. The $D_{EF}^h$ curve shifts slightly to the left because of the dampening effect exerted by $\dot{r}$ through the wealth term in $L_F^h$.[14] $L_F^h$ is not zero at $r^*$ because the open-market purchase makes $\dot{r} < 0$. Then $\dot{r} < 0$ creates $\dot{W} > 0$, which makes $L_F^h > 0$, and $D_{EF}^h$ shifts to the left by the increase in $L_F^h$. The shift in $D_{EF}^h$ is less than that of $S_{EF}^h$ because at $r^*$, $\dot{r} < 0$ requires that $D_{EF}^h - S_{EF}^h > 0$.

### B. Comparative Statics, Dynamics, and Stability

The comparative statics of the model are essentially those of a simple Keynesian model. Figure 5 shows the determination of the equilibrium $r$ and $P$, given $w$ and $M$. The $X_d = X_s$ curve is downward sloping with a kink at $P_f$. For $P < P_f$, an increase in $P$ increases $X_s$, $X$, and $X_d$. However, $\partial X_d/\partial X < 1$ and therefore $X_d$ increase less than do $X$ and $X_s$. Thus $r$ must fall in order to keep $X_d = X_s$. For $P \geq P_f$, an increase in $P$ increases $X_s$, but $X$ and $X_d$ are constant. Therefore $r$ must fall faster in order to keep $X_d = X_s$.

The $L^h = M^h/P$ curve is upward sloping because as $P$ increases, $M^h/P$ decreases, and the simultaneous increases in $X$ and $W$ act to increase $L^h$. There-

---

[14] It is from this dampening effect that the second term appears in the denominator of (38).

fore $r$ must increase in order to keep $L^h = M^h/P$. There is a kink at $P_f$ because $X$ is constant for $P > P_f$ and thus $L^h$ does not increase as quickly, slowing the increase in $r$.

The point $r^*$, $P^*$ in Fig. 5 is the equilibrium point for the economy. The labor market is in equilibrium because $P^* < P_f$ and thus $N_d < N_f$.[15] The commodities market is in equilibrium because $X_d = X_s$. The asset market is in both stock and flow equilibrium. For stock equilibrium, $L^h = M^h/P$. Flow equilibrium exists because by (38), $X_d = X_s$ implies $\dot{r} = 0$ provided that the central bank is not conducting open-market operations (and hence $\dot{M}/P = 0$), and, by (37), $\dot{r} = 0$ implies $S_{EF}^h = D_{EF}^h$.

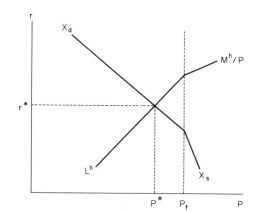

**Fig. 5.** Determination of equilibrium, given $w$ and $M$.

The slopes of the $X_d = X_s$ and $L^h = M^h/P$ curves determine the comparative-statics properties of the model. They are conventional. An open-market purchase (Fig. 6) increases $M$, shifting the $L^h = M^h/P$ curve to the right. Because the $X_d = X_s$ curve is downward sloping, the equilibrium rate of interest falls, while the equilibrium price level (and therefore equilibrium output and employment) rises. (The path indicated by the arrows will be discussed later.) A shift of the $C_d$ function to the right (Fig. 7), increasing commodity demand, shifts the $X_d = X_s$ function to the right. Because the $L^h = M^h/P$ curve is upward sloping, the equilibrium rate of interest and price level both increase.

The stability of the dynamic adjustment process is established with the help of (19), (38), and the comparative-statics diagrams. By (19), the prevailing $r$ and $P$ always lie on the $L^h = M^h/P$ curve. By (38) (and given $\dot{M}/P = 0$), $\dot{r}$ is $\gtreqless 0$ as $X_d \gtreqless X_s$. $X_d > X_s$ for all $r$, $P$ below the $X_d = X_s$ curve,

---

[15] The labor market is not actually in equilibrium, but acts as if it were, because, by (10), $\dot{w}/w = 0$.

and $X_d < X_s$ for all $r$, $P$ above the $X_d = X_s$ curve. The slope of the $X_d = X_s$ curve is negative and the slope of the $L^h = M^h/P$ curve is positive. Therefore $r$ and $P$ converge monotonically along the $L^h = M^h/P$ curve to their equilibrium values.

The little arrows show the path of dynamic adjustment in Figs. 6 and 7. In Fig. 6 the stock open-market purchase initially reduces $r$ to $r'$. Then the dynamic adjustment process of the model takes over, driving $r$ and $P$ up the $L^h = M^h/P$ curve until they reach $r^{**}$, $P^{**}$, at which point $\dot{r} = 0$ and the model is in equilibrium. In Fig. 7 it is the opening up of excess demand through the

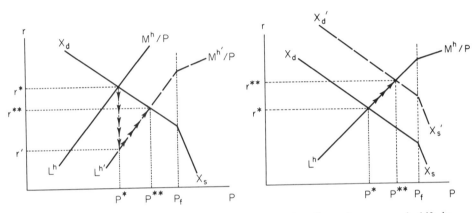

**Fig. 6.** The effect of an increase in the stock of money.

**Fig. 7.** The effect of an upward shift in consumption demand.

shift in $C_d$ that sets the adjustment process in motion. Excess demand for commodities corresponds to an excess flow supply of securities, driving $r$ and $P$ up the $L^h = M^h/P$ curve until equilibrium is reached at $r^{**}$, $P^{**}$.

Let us consider now the dynamic process in terms of behavior of the three underlying markets. For this purpose we utilize market diagrams of the kind drawn in Figs. 1–3. The analysis begins with the model in equilibrium.

A stock open-market purchase reduces the rate of interest from $r'$ to $r''$. In Fig. 8a the fall in the rate of interest shifts the $X_d$ curve from $X_d(w', r')$ to $X_d(w', r'')$. In Fig. 8c the initial path of the interest rate is downward and vertical, as shown by the arrows. The labor market is not affected. Therefore at $r''$ there is an excess demand for commodities, causing price and output to rise (Fig. 8a), and an excess flow supply of securities, causing the rate of interest to increase (Fig. 8c).

Increases in the rate of interest reduce the demand for investment and shift the $X_d$ curve in the upper diagram to the left. Thus the adjustment of the securities market reduces the rate of increase in the price level. Increases in the level of prices shift the $N_d$ curve in Fig. 8b to the right, increasing employment and output. Thus saving increases and the rate of interest at which $X_d = X_s$ falls, shifting the $D^h_{EF}$ and $S^h_{EF}$ curves (Fig. 8c) to the right and down. The adjustment in the commodities market thereby reduces the excess flow supply of securities, slowing the rate of increase in the rate of interest.

This process continues until the rate of interest rises to $r'''$ and the price level increases to $P'''$. At that point, $X_d(w', r''')$ equals $X_s(w')$ at $P'''$ and $D^h_{EF}(w'/P''')$ equals $S^h_{EF}(w'/P''')$ at $r'''$. The commodities market and the securities market are in equilibrium. They reach equilibrium at the same time because, by (38) and (37) (given $\dot{M}/P = 0$), the excess flow supply of securities is zero if and only if $X_d = X_s$. Thus overshooting does not occur, and since $P''' < P_f$, the demand for labor does not exceed full employment and the money wage is unchanged at $w'$. The arrows show the time paths of the variables.

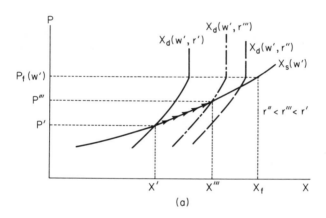

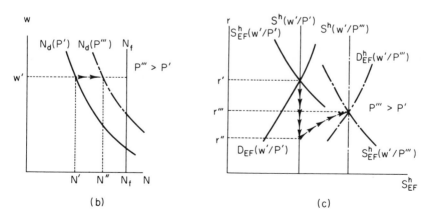

Fig. 8. A stock open-market purchase.

An upward shift in the consumption function shifts the $X_d$ curve in Fig. 9a from $X_d(w', r')$ to $X_d*(w', r')$, and the $D_{EF}^h$ and $S_{EF}^h$ curves in Fig. 9c to the left (as the $S^h$ line shifts from $S^h[w'/P']$ to $S^{h*}[w'/P']$) and up (as the rate of interest that equates $X_d$ and $X_s$ rises to $r*$). The new security schedules are $S_{EF}^{h*}(w'/P')$ and $D_{EF}^{h*}(w'/P')$. As a result of these shifts, there is an excess demand for commodities and an excess flow supply of securities. The price level and the rate of interest rise responsively. The rise in $P$ shifts the $N_d$ curve in Fig. 9b to the right, increasing employment and output, and it shifts the $S_{EF}^h$ and $D_{EF}^h$ curves in Fig. 9c to the right and down, slowing the rate of increase in the rate of interest. The rise in the rate of interest shifts the $X_d$ curve in the commodities diagram to the left, slowing the rate of increase in the price level. The rate of interest and the price level continue to increase until the

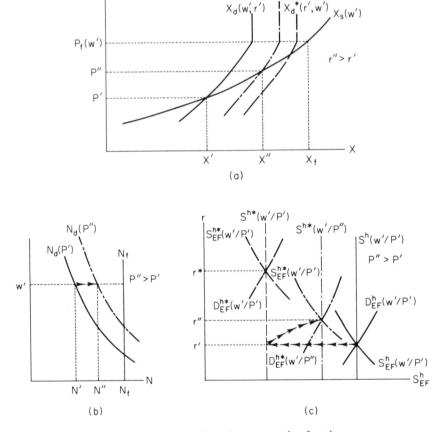

**Fig. 9.** An upward shift in the consumption function.

securities market and the commodities market simultaneously achieve equilibrium at $r''$ and $P''$, respectively. The money wage is unchanged at $w'$. The time paths are again indicated by arrows.

## IV. Summary

This chapter is a study of the dynamics of interest rate movements. The key result is that the rate of change in the interest rate is a function of the excess flow supply of securities. This follows from four structural characteristics of the model: (1) Walras' law for stocks, (2) Walras' law for flows, (3) continuous equilibrium in the markets for the financial goods, and (4) the relationships between the flow demands and supplies for financial goods and their respective stock demands and supplies. These four characteristics are logical consequences of two basic postulates of the model: (1) consumption demand is a function of actual, realized income, and (2) the markets for financial goods are organized and those for existing capital goods and their services are not.

Postulate One, that consumption demand is a function of realized income, requires the model to use *nontâtonnement* dynamics. It also changes the form of Walras' Law for flows, eliminating the labor market. Postulate Two, the limitation of organized markets to financial goods means that Walras' law for stocks applies only to financial goods. Given *nontâtonnement* dynamics this distinction between the markets for financial goods and for existing capital goods implies that Walras' law for flows is also limited to financial goods.

The markets for financial goods are in continuous equilibrium because an organized market matches buyers and sellers, determining a single price for all participants. The relationship between financial flows and their respective stock functions is also a result of the organized functioning of financial markets. In particular, because the stock demands for the two financial goods always equal their respective stock supplies, changes in the stock demands and supplies can be separated into shifts in the functions (flows) and changes in the relative price (i.e., the rate of interest).

The link between the real and financial sectors of the model is given by the real determinants of the financial flows. Financial flows are determined by actual saving and investment flows, by changes in the demand for real balances due to changes in output and wealth, and by the open-market operations of the central bank. Substituting the determinants of the model's financial flows into the interest rate adjustment mechanism shows that the rate of change in the rate of interest is a function of the excess demand for commodities and the open-market operations of the central bank. This relationship is used to demonstrate the dynamic properties and stability of the model.

## Appendix A. Walras' Law for Flows

By (33),

$$D_{EF}^h \equiv \dot{D}_E^h - \frac{\partial D_E^h}{\partial r}\,\dot{r} - \frac{D_E^h}{(P_E/P)}\left[(P_E/\dot{P}) - \frac{\partial(P_E/P)}{\partial r}\,\dot{r}\right].$$

Then $S_E^h = D_E^h$ always, by (19). Therefore $\dot{S}_E^h = \dot{D}_E^h$ always.
Substituting into the definition of $D_{EF}^h$, we get

$$D_{EF}^h \equiv \dot{S}_E^h - \frac{\partial D_E^h}{\partial r}\,\dot{r} - \frac{S_E^h}{(P_E/P)}\left[(P_E/\dot{P}) - \frac{\partial(P_E/P)}{\partial r}\,\dot{r}\right].$$

Then $S_E^h \equiv (P_E/P)E^h$ by (16). Therefore, $\dot{S}_E^h \equiv (P_E/P)\dot{E}^h + E^h(P_E/\dot{P})$.
Substituting into the expression for $D_{EF}^h$, we obtain

$$D_{EF}^h \equiv (P_E/P)\dot{E}^h + E^h(P_E/\dot{P}) - \frac{\partial D_E^h}{\partial r}\,\dot{r} - E^h\left[(P_E/\dot{P}) - \frac{\partial(P_E/P)}{\partial r}\,\dot{r}\right]$$

$$\equiv (P_E/P)\dot{E}^h - \frac{\partial D_E^h}{\partial r}\,\dot{r} + E^h\frac{\partial(P_E/P)}{\partial r}\,\dot{r}.$$

Thus, from (16),

$$E^h\frac{\partial(P_E/P)}{\partial r} = \frac{\partial S_E^h}{\partial r},$$

and by (31) and (27), $S_{EF}^h \equiv (P_E/P)\dot{E}^h$.
Substituting into the expression for $D_{EF}^h$, we have

$$D_{EF}^h \equiv S_{EF}^h - \frac{\partial D_E^h}{\partial r}\,\dot{r} + \frac{\partial S_E^h}{\partial r}\,\dot{r}.$$

Thus

$$\frac{\partial L^h}{\partial r} = \frac{\partial S_E^h}{\partial r} - \frac{\partial D_E^h}{\partial r}$$

follows from Walras' law for stocks (14). Therefore

$$D_{EF}^h \equiv S_{EF}^h + \frac{\partial L^h}{\partial r}\,\dot{r}.$$

By (32),

$$L_F^h \equiv \dot{L}^h - \frac{\partial L^h}{\partial r}\,\dot{r}.$$

Thus $\dot{L}^h = (\dot{M}^h/P)$ always by (19). Therefore

$$L_F{}^h \equiv (\dot{M}^h/P) - \frac{\partial L^h}{\partial r}\,\dot{r}.$$

Adding our expressions for $D_{EF}^h$ and $L_F{}^h$, we have

$$L_F{}^h + D_{EF}^h \equiv (\dot{M}^h/P) - \frac{\partial L^h}{\partial r}\,r + S_{EF}^h + \frac{\partial L^h}{\partial r}\,\dot{r}.$$

Therefore

$$L_F{}^h - (\dot{M}^h/P) + D_{EF}^h - S_{EF}^h \equiv 0.$$

## Appendix B. Derivation of Equation (38)

By (32),

$$L_F{}^h = \frac{\partial L^h}{\partial X}\dot{X} + \frac{\partial L^h}{\partial W}\,\dot{W}.$$

Because $N_d \leqq N_f$, we have $N = N_d$ and $\dot{w} = 0$. Therefore

$$\dot{X} = \frac{\partial X}{\partial P}\,\dot{P} = \frac{\partial X_s}{\partial P}\,\dot{P} = \frac{-w^2}{P^3 F_{NN}}\,\dot{P} = \frac{-w^2}{P^2 F_{NN}}\,\dot{P}/P.$$

Thus

$$\dot{W} = (\dot{M}^h/P) + \dot{S}_E{}^h = (\dot{M}/P) + E^h(P_E/P)^{16}$$

$$= \dot{M}/P - (M/P)\dot{P}/P + E^h\left[\frac{\dot{e}_E}{r+d} - \frac{e_E}{(r+d)^2}\,\dot{r}\right]$$

and

$$\dot{e}_E = \frac{K}{E}\,\dot{e}_K = \frac{K}{E}\left(\frac{\dot{X - (w/P)N}}{K}\right) = \frac{K}{E}\left[\frac{\dot{X}}{K} - \frac{(w/P)\dot{N}}{K} - \frac{N(w/P)}{K}\right]$$

$$= \frac{K}{E}\left[\frac{F_N \dot{N}}{K} - \frac{F_N \dot{N}}{K} - \frac{N\dot{w}/P}{K} + \frac{N(w/P)\dot{P}/P}{K}\right] = \frac{N(w/P)\dot{P}/P}{E}$$

because $\dot{w} = 0$.

[16] This is incorrect because $\dot{S}_E{}^h = E^h(P_E/P) + (P_E/P)\dot{E}^h$ and we know that $\dot{E}^h > 0$ if $I + (M^t/P)\dot{P}/P > 0$ (which will always be true in equilibrium with $I > 0$). It is, however, necessary to assume this incorrect statement (just as we assumed that $I > 0$ and $K$ is constant) in order for the model to achieve equilibrium at nonzero rates of investment. This is an inconsistency of short-run macromodels.

Since $\dot{P}/P = \psi(X_d - X_s)$,

$$L_F{}^h = \psi(X_d - X_s)\left[\frac{\partial L^h}{\partial X}\left(\frac{-w^2}{P^2 F_{NN}}\right) + \frac{\partial L^h}{\partial W}\left(\frac{-M}{P} + \frac{E^h}{(r+d)}\frac{N}{E}\frac{w}{P}\right)\right]$$

$$+ \frac{\partial L^h}{\partial W}\left(\dot{M}/P - \frac{E^h e_E}{(r+d)^2}\dot{r}\right).$$

By (37) and (34),

$$\dot{r} = -[L_F{}^h - (M^{\dot{h}}/P)]/\frac{\partial L^h}{\partial r},$$

and by (28) and (29),

$$(M^{\dot{h}}/P) = \dot{M}/P - (M/P)\dot{P}/P.$$

Solving for $\dot{r}$ we get (38).

## ACKNOWLEDGMENTS

The views expressed in this Chapter are personal and unofficial. I would like to thank John Carlson and Patric Hendershott for their helpful comments. Special thanks are due George Horwich for his extensive comments and invaluable editorial assistance.

## REFERENCES

1. Clower, R. W., "The Keynesian Counterrevolution: A Theoretical Appraisal," in *The Theory of Interest Rates* (F. H. Hahn and F. P. Brechling, eds.), pp. 103–125. New York: Macmillan, 1965.
2. Glustoff, E., "On the Existence of a Keynesian Equilibrium," *Review of Economic Studies* **35** (July 1968), 327–334.
3. Hicks, J. R., *Value and Capital*, 2nd ed. London and New York: Oxford Univ. Press, 1946.
4. Horwich, G., *Money, Capital, and Prices*. Homewood, Illinois: Irwin, 1964.
5. Horwich, G., "Money, Prices and the Theory of Interest Determination," *Economic Journal* **67** (December 1957), 625–643.
6. Horwich, G., "Open Market Operations, the Rate of Interest, and the Price Level," *Journal of Finance* **10** (December 1955), 508–509.
7. Leijonhufvud, A., *On Keynesian Economics and the Economics of Keynes*. London and New York: Oxford Univ. Press, 1968.
8. May, J., "Period Analysis and Continuous Analysis in Patinkin's Macreoeconomic Model," *Journal of Economic Theory* **2** (March 1970), 1–9.
9. Metzler, L., "Wealth, Saving, and the Rate of Interest," *Journal of Political Economy* **59** (April 1951), 93–116.
10. Nagatani, K., "A Note on Professor Tobin's 'Money and Economic Growth,'" *Econometrica* **38** (January 1970), 171–175.
11. Patinkin, D., "Liquidity Preference and Loanable Funds: Stock and Flow Analysis," *Economica* **25** (November 1958), 300–318.

12. Patinkin, D., "Reply to R. W. Clower and H. Rose," *Economica* **26** (August 1959), 253–255.
13. Rose, H., "Liquidity Preference and Loanable Funds," *Review of Economic Studies* **24** (February 1957), 111–119.
14. Rose, H., "The Rate of Interest and Walras' Law," *Economica* **26** (August 1959), 252–253.
15. Stein, J., "Monetary Growth Theory in Perspective," *American Economic Review* **60** (March 1970), 85–106.
16. Patinkin, D., *Money, Interest, and Prices*, 2nd ed. New York: Harper, 1965.

# THE THEORY OF MONEY AND INCOME
# CONSISTENT WITH ORTHODOX VALUE THEORY

*Earl A. Thompson*

*University of California*
*Los Angeles*

## Introduction

The challenge of Metzler's classic article, "Wealth, Saving, and the Rate of Interest" [17], has gone unanswered. The literature has remained without a model which captures the full logic of the classical theory of money and income. The main purpose of this chapter is not to specify such a model; it is to derive the theory of money and income that is consistent with orthodox value theory (i.e., Ricardian and neoclassical value theory and the competitive model of Arrow and Debreu). However, quite by accident, it turns out that any such theory of money and income must have all of the essential properties asserted by classical monetary economists.

The chapter proceeds as a development of the properties of any money economy which is constrained to be consistent with orthodox value theory, a theory which has a perfectly competitive, private supply of all goods. The central theoretical results are: (1) there is a money economy that is consistent with orthodox value theory, and (2) in any such economy, which we will call a "perfectly competitive money economy," there is: (a) a classical dichotomy between the real and monetary sectors, (b) an absence of real balance effects,

(c) an absence of effects of expected inflation on the real sector of the economy, and (d) an imperviousness of output prices and employment in a sticky-wage economy to shifts in capital productivity, thrift, liquidity preference, and the money supply of any individual.

These results are in sharp contrast to the central propositions of numerous modern monetary theorists. With respect to the first result, leading modern day authors have alleged an inconsistency between any money economy and orthodox value theory. Some of these authors (e.g., Friedman [8] and Pesek and Saving [22]) have claimed that money cannot attain a positive equilibrium value in an orthodox model in which nominal money is costless to create and competitively supplied. Since a good with a zero price cannot be used as a medium of exchange, this implies that the orthodox model cannot be extended to include money. Other authors (e.g., Marschak [15] and Radner [25]) have argued (each for a slightly different reason) that money, however supplied, would have a zero total value under the informational perfections of the standard competitive model. In working out the basic money model implied by the standard competitive model in Sections I.A and I.B, we shall see that these modern day authors have failed, each in his own way, to characterize accurately the information structure implicit in the standard competitive model. Section I.C then demonstrates the existence and Pareto optimality of an equilibrium consistent with orthodox value theory in which money emerges as an individually selected, specialized medium of exchange.

Regarding the second result, the set of properties we derive for any money economy consistent with orthodox value theory contains all of the properties that modern monetary theorists have represented as *logical* fallacies in the classical view of a money economy. Keynes in his *General Theory* [12], and all later writers of note, have considered the classical view of a money economy logically defective in that it does not allow shifts in capital productivity, thrift, and liquidity preference ever to affect prices or employment. As Metzler pointed out, Pigou [24] and others have implicitly *criticized* classical monetary theory by alleging that real cash balances have belonged in the excess demand functions for nonmonetary goods all along. Patinkin [21] has criticized classical monetary doctrine for having equilibrium relative prices between nonmonetary goods determined in the nonmoney markets and a unique level of equilibrium money prices determined in the money market. Friedman [7], Bailey [4], Marty [16], and Kessel and Alchian [11] have argued that shifts in the future money supplies, when prices are correctly anticipated and money is neutral, will generally have real effects on the economy, a fact which classical writers did not include in their theoretical discussions. Sections I.D and II.E show how each of these criticisms is inapplicable to a competitive money model and that the so-called fallacies in the classical view of a money economy are in fact necessary properties of any perfectly competitive money model.

Sections II.F and II.G specify the possible sources of involuntary unemployment in a perfectly competitive money economy and note the substantial evidence for the resulting theory of economic fluctuations in pre-1934 industrialized economies. Previous theories, by failing to specify the basic informational imperfection leading to involuntary unemployment, or by treating a Say's law economy [27] as if it were somehow immune to aggregate unemployment, have apparently failed to bring out the vulnerability of employment to certain shifts in technology and tastes in a classical money economy. As a result, previous theories have misled us as to the cause of the Great Depression, misled us into searching for Keynesian or Quantity Theory-type explanations. Correspondingly, we have been led away from understanding the fundamental change in the relevant macrotheory and the fundamental improvement in potential employment stability that occurred with the destruction of the fully convertible gold standard in 1934.

Section II.H shows the impossibility of *permanent* involuntary unemployment despite the absence of Pigou effects in a perfectly competitive money economy.

## I. The Theory of Money Consistent with Orthodox Value Theory

### A. Properties of Any Money Model Consistent with Orthodox Value Theory

The standard competitive model (e.g., Debreu [6]) specifies equilibrium allocations of real resources for given initial allocations. But it does not specify the *process* of achieving equilibrium allocations. Money is used as an intermediate good in transactions, achieving final allocations from initial ones. Therefore, since our model is a money model, our "equilibrium" necessarily specifies more information than the "equilibrium" of a standard competitive model. In particular, our equilibrium specifies a complete set of transactions in a private property system.

Despite the fact that our money model specifies more information than is provided by a standard competitive model, consistency with the standard competitive model implies a very special kind of money economy. First, in the standard competitive model, there are no transaction costs resulting from an equilibrium set of transactions. Equilibrium transactions leading to a standard competitive equilibrium's final allocations of resources must all be costless transactions. Transaction costs are dead-weight losses—losses due to imperfect contract information that an idealized central allocator could avoid. The laissez faire implication of the orthodox model, monetary or not, would not exist if transaction costs were to appear in achieving the equilibrium's final allocations of resources. (This is elaborated by Thompson [33].)

Second, in any economy with a determinate money, there are positive total transaction costs for some *conceivable* transaction sets. For if all *conceivable* transactions sets yielding the equilibrium's final allocations were totally costless, there would be no determinate money; one good could serve as a medium of exchange as well as any other, and no good would have to serve as money, which is defined as a specialized medium of exchange. However, no costly transaction set can be an *equilibrium* transaction set; the use of a particular asset as a specialized medium of exchange must be so efficient that it drives equilibrium transaction costs down to zero if the equilibrium is to contain a standard competitive equilibrium.

It is not correct to infer, as have several modern authors, from the fact that an economy with a determinate money implies informational imperfections for *some* sets of transactions, that an economy with a determinate money implies informational imperfections for *equilibrium* sets of transactions. A widespread argument, probably best developed by Marschak [15], goes: "No rational individual would hold a positive amount of money in the absence of transaction costs, for he would always prefer to buy, hold, and later sell an interest-bearing asset rather than hold onto barren money before his next ordinary purchase." But money need not be barren; indeed we shall find that in a money model consistent with orthodox value theory, money bears as much interest as the purchased asset. This, however, raises the objection: "If money bears interest, why should anyone, in the absence of transaction costs, hold anything but arbitrary amounts of their assets in the form of money, for they should be indifferent between (a) holding onto their money and (b) buying, holding onto, and later selling a different interest-bearing asset before their next ordinary purchase?" The answer to this, as we have seen, is that while there are zero costs of the monetary transactions that characterize the equilibrium set of transactions in a money economy consistent with orthodox value theory, there are positive costs of some unchosen, or disequilibrium, transactions.[1]

In a similar slip, Radner [25] argues that since a money economy implies an advantage to transactions in the future and therefore positive transaction costs in using only current transactions (including transactions in commodity futures) to allocate future resources, a money economy implies positive transaction costs, which is inconsistent with the standard competitive model. The error here is again the tacit neglect of the case in which the reliance on trans-

---

[1] Although not yet widely recognized, it is true of *any* model of orthodox value theory, monetary or not, that there are zero transactions costs in equilibrium and positive transactions costs in some disequilibria. This is developed by Thompson [33]. Transaction costs out of equilibrium are, for example, generally necessary to prevent the breakdown of decentralization by way of the monopolization of selling activities.

actions in the future, working through money, operates to remove the contract information costs from the equilibrium set of transactions.[2]

Since any real cost of providing the specialized services of a medium of exchange would be a transaction cost, a money model consistent with orthodox value theory has a zero cost of providing the services of the medium of exchange. We shall adopt the standard convention that money is paper, rather than commodity, money. (A rationalization of this assumption appears at the end of Section C.) Zero costs of providing the service of the medium of exchange therefore implies zero costs of creating and transferring the paper money.

A third property which characterizes orthodox value theory is that all assets are created according to a rule of wealth maximization for the price-taking creators, who receive all of the returns from their creation as long as the creation and sale does not reduce the property of others. Thus money is privately rather than "governmentally" produced. We shall hereafter refer to a money economy consistent with an orthodox value theory as a "perfectly competitive money economy."

## B. The Positivity of the Price of Money in a Perfectly Competitive Money Economy

A recent proposition regarding the production of money under competitive conditions is the following: "Since the cost of producing money is zero, the perfectly competitive real price of money is zero." (See, for example, Friedman [8] and Pesek and Saving [22].) Since an asset with a zero price cannot be used as a medium of exchange, the proposition implies the impossibility of a perfectly competitive money economy. But the proposition implies a violation of private property because the holders of one creator's money suffer a loss in utility from the reduction in their real cash balances occasioned by the supplies of the other money creators. To avoid these violations of private property, each money creator in the competitive model must be able to freely enforce his claim to issue money with a unique physical characteristic.[3] For

---

[2] Actually, Radner does not put his argument in terms of transaction costs, but rather in terms of uncertainty with respect to future demands under given future states of nature. While this uncertainty is neither necessary nor sufficient for markets in the future (see Thompson [33]), Radner infers both. We have therefore dealt with a repaired version of Radner's argument.

[3] My colleagues Armen Alchian and Benjamin Klein have independently uncovered this characterization of competitive money production (see Klein [13]). The difference between our analyses is that their argument has been that the appearance of "competing monies" or of "brand names" alters some models, while mine is the stronger claim that the conditions of the zero-price competitive money model represent a violation of the private property condition of orthodox value theory.

example, one money creator can obtain the sole right to issue blue money; others then must issue money of a different color. This prevents competitive sellers from depreciating the real product of one another. After a certain nominal money supply is produced, a seller's permanent doubling of his own produced money stock will simply halve the price of his money in terms of all other assets. Since the money creator's product is then the real balances he creates, he finds that to induce people to hold more of his product, he must make it more attractive. This is done—when direct interest is not paid on money—by committing himself to repurchasing some of the money with commodities (or other monies) at future dates, thereby decreasing his customer's cost of holding onto his money because of its subsequent real appreciation. Zero profits to a money creator will emerge once the principal and own interest on the asset initially obtained by selling money equals his corresponding future sales in the process of retiring his initially issued money. No money creator who offers a less generous repurchase plan can receive a positive price for his money. Although the return to the money holders comes in the indirect form of price-level deflation, the money creators are, in effect, paying real interest to the holders of their money at a rate equal to the own rate of interest on the assets initially sold to the money creators.

We now remove the artificial prohibition of the direct payment of interest on money. Our general argument becomes: Since it costs nothing to produce the nominal money, a competitive producer-seller will find that in order to sell it for a positive price—which is necessary for there to be any positive quantity of the money demanded—he must pay what amounts to real interest on the asset, devising through the tie-in sale of monetary services and commodity (or other money) interest, a salable money. Money, which yields the joint benefit to the buyer of real interest and monetary services, has a price which is equated in competitive equilibrium with the cost of providing the entire money asset. This cost, in an equilibrium without transaction costs, is the cost of the real interest payments on money. Thus, an equilibrium in a perfectly competitive money economy yields an allocation at which the marginal service value of money is zero. Many recent authors (e.g., Samuelson [26], Friedman [9], and Kessel and Alchian [11]) have conjectured that an equilibrium in a money economy (implicitly one with no transaction costs in equilibrium) is Pareto optimal only when the marginal service value of money is zero. But they have failed to see that the free market production of money achieves this condition. Pesek [23], for example, claims that competition cannot possibly achieve the optimum. He argues: Since an optimum requires a zero marginal use-value of monetary services, the price of money in this optimum would have to be zero. But we have seen that this does not hold when competitive interest is paid on money.

For the remainder of this chapter, we assume that our competitive money creators, rather than committing themselves to eventually retiring their issues, compete by offering direct interest on paper money (in the form of real commodities or the monies of other money creators) equivalent to the real return on a specified real good. This implies that money is "convertible" into the specified real good (or its value equivalent) at an intertemporally fixed rate. If the good into which money is explicitly convertible generates no commodity return, but only continual relative price inflation while it is serving to back money (e.g., noncoupon debt or undeveloped land), then there are no transactions representing interest payments on money even though direct real interest accrues on money equal to the real return on the specified real good. There appears to be a reasonable similarity between our competing money creators and bankers in the gold standard era; and we shall hereafter call our money creators "bankers."

## C. The Existence and Pareto Optimality of an Equilibrium in a Perfectly Competitive Money Economy

We can now prove that an equilibrium in a perfectly competitive money economy exists and is Pareto optimal. First consider final equilibrium allocations of real resources. Since the marginal service value of money is zero, money does not, in equilibrium, enter the wealth constraint, utility function, or feasible production set of any individual apart from its generating an interest return. The fact that a real interest return is the sole return provided on a nonreal asset makes the asset equivalent to a real bond in an orthodox model which contains real bonds as well as real assets. If the real bonds serving as money create individually nonoptimal intertemporal allocations, borrowing and lending through the nonmonetary bond market will reestablish the individual optima. A final equilibrium allocation of resources in such an environment, according to the well-known results of Arrow [2] and Debreu [6], exists and is Pareto optimal (assuming a finite horizon, no collective-type goods, positive wealth, continuous preference relations, nonsatiation, and closed, convex consumption and feasible production sets).

Now consider the equilibrium set of transactions.[4] We wish to show that an equilibrium set of transactions in a perfectly competitive money economy exists and achieves the final allocations of the standard competitive model. We shall do this for the following special case: We assume that there is a "natural" transaction process. In this process (a) following Ostroy [19], each individual meets separately with every other individual in sequential fashion

---

[4] The question of the existence of a competitive equilibrium set of transactions implying the existence of money is novel and our proof is rather technical. The novelty of the question perhaps indicates that most economists are willing to simply assume the existence of such an equilibrium. The reader so inclined is advised to skip the remainder of this subsection and proceed on to Section D.

during each trading period (which is of sufficiently short duration that no transaction costs arise due to delays in achieving the final commodity allocation of each period), and (b) following Starr [30], each individual transfers a good when and only when he has an excess supply of the good and his trading partner has an excess demand for the good.[5] These specifications imply, when "prices" are standard competitive equilibrium prices and there are no costs of any transaction in this "natural" exchange process, that once every individual has met with everyone else in a given period, he will have no excess demand for any commodity in that period.[6] (This is Ostroy's "Principal Proposition.")

We add to the natural transaction process that the asset which one receives in exchange for positive net commodity supplies is an IOU denominated in a specified good but payable in goods of the debtor's option at the time of repayment (where the relative values between these goods are the then-ruling relative prices). Once the period's final allocation of real resources is reached, an individual will still generally own some of these debts of others and owe some of these debts to others, although the *sum* of these positive and negative debts is zero for each individual (Starr [30, Theorem I], Ostroy [19, "Misleading Existence Theorem"]). The natural exchange process thus continues on into a second round after the final allocation of real commodities is reached, where now the bilateral exchanges are all exchanges of IOU's and each indi-

---

[5] Part (b) of the "natural" process is also a rational transaction strategy for individuals to adopt. This holds for the same reason that a bird in the hand is worth two in a bush. Given part (a) and assuming that an individual does not know his later transaction opportunities within the period, an individual is never assured of being able to reduce commodity excesses with later trading partners when he refuses the opportunity of reducing them in transactions with his current trading partner. On the other hand, as we shall note, by adopting the strategy in part (b) of the process, all excess commodity demands of all individuals at equilibrium prices will become zero. The "natural" transaction process is thus also an equilibrium process, given the assumption in part (a).

However, if other individuals do not adopt the strategy in part (b), then an individual who does adopt it will not generally be able to satisfy all of his excess commodity demands in the period. Then, if some goods are complements, an individual may be worse off by adopting the strategy in part (b). For his purchase of a left glove today is a loss if he cannot purchase a right glove tomorrow. Therefore, under such complementarities, there may be an *equilibrium* set of decentralized strategies which does not satisfy the conditions of a competitive equilibrium—it may pay to go without gloves rather than endure the risk of buying a right glove without being able to find a seller of a left one. To avoid these breakdowns in market communication, we would assume that each individual knows his future trading possibilities within the period. This assumption, which is implied by an alternative to the "natural" transaction process discussed later in this subsection, would make part (b) of the "natural transaction process" an arbitrary, but still rational, trading strategy.

[6] This result uses single-period budget constraints so that claims for delivery of assets in future periods are included as "commodities." This general definition of commodities is maintained throughout this chapter.

vidual *in turn* meets all of his creditors. The transactions in this round do not generally lengthen the previously specified trading period because such IOU's may be traded in the subsequent round of trading in commodities. A holder of a mature debt has an excess supply of the debt, and the debtor has an excess demand for the debt. For payment, creditors receive their own IOU's or the IOU's of third parties, which are acceptable because these third parties could not have already taken their turn at meeting all their creditors. No new debt is created, because each debtor owns sufficient IOU's of others. Each such trade therefore reduces the total stock of existing debts by at least the amount one party owes to the other. And since each debtor must meet all of his creditors in turn, no debts are outstanding at the end of this second round.

So our "natural" set of transactions in a world with no costs of the transactions in this set achieves competitive equilibrium allocations of resources without the appearance of any specialized medium of exchange. This is an apparently new, but rather trivial, result.

To move on to the possibility of a *competitive equilibrium* set of transactions, let us alter the hypothetical condition on transaction costs by assuming that IOU contracts of many—but not all—debtors are now costly to trade to third parties because third parties do not costlessly know the precise conditions and legal validity of these primary debt contracts or of contracts guaranteeing the default-risk status of the debtor. The *natural* transaction set now entails positive transaction costs. In the natural process, some individuals, those whose default-risk status and contractual debt obligations are now not costlessly recognizable by third parties, would have to pay a premium for some of their commodities to reflect the future costs to their commodity suppliers of verifying their default-risk status and contractual obligations to others. Such individuals will, before trading in commodities, *separately*, *rationally* trade debts with individuals whose default-risk status and contractual debt obligations are known by everyone. This begins a rational revision of the natural exchange process. In what was the first round and is now the second, individuals pay to their net suppliers of commodities debt obligations of the individuals whose default-risk status and contractual obligations are understood by everyone. The commodity suppliers in turn have no trouble purchasing goods with the costlessly recognizable debt. This debt is thus chosen as the common medium of exchange, so we may call it money and its creators, bankers. Our model is thus unique in that not only may it be efficient for a group of individuals to use a common medium of exchange, but the use of that medium of exchange results from the decentralized, rational decisions of the individuals in the model. On the third round of transactions, where debts are the only assets traded, first the nonbankers meet their creditor-bankers to pay off all of their bank debts. (This is possible because the value of each individual's accumulated intraperiod debt liabilities still equals the value of his accumulated intraperiod debt assets.) After that, the bankers meet one another for debt collection according to the natural process. The monies of third parties are accepted to clear debts between bankers, and the total debt of each banker to the others equals his total money holdings. Therefore, as above, once each of these debtors has met all of his creditors in turn, there is no longer any debt (money) outstanding. The rationally revised natural exchange process thus produces an equilibrium set of transactions which has zero transaction costs and achieves a standard competitive equilibrium.

In the above exchange process, money is serving only as a medium of exchange; it is not held for durations sufficient for time productivity or time preference to exist within holding periods. Consider, however, the possibility of borrowers' supplying longer-term debts to bankers. To guarantee that competitive bankers will make some such loans and still retain the zero-transaction-cost feature of the standard competitive model, assume that the demand for these longer-term loans exceeds the amount which nonbankers can supply at zero transaction costs, while bankers can always supply such loans at no transaction costs. The assumption is, in a sense, plausible because bankers, in contrast to nonbankers, make these loans by simply extending the maturities on existing loans. Since bankers now make loans maturing beyond the end of a trading period, they cannot pay off their current obligations with the repayments of their debtors. However, because profits to banking are zero in equilibrium, bankers must offer the interest they earn on their loans to the holders of their money; and an individual who, under zero lending costs, made loans now being made by bankers is now best off by accepting interest-bearing money in light of his preference for the future return and his positive costs of such lending. (An individual in the world without direct lending costs, who did not lend at maturities exceeding the end of the trading period, is faced with the same opportunities and will therefore still not hold any debt past the end of the trading period.) Consequently, we can specify a new competitive equilibrium set of money–commodity transactions, in a world in which there are positive lending costs to some individuals, but zero costs to others. It is the same equilibrium set of transactions as in the previous case, only with bankers now providing the loans which are now costly for some nonbankers to negotiate and providing these same individuals with a money which they will hold in place of their original loans because it bears the same interest as did those loans. Specifically, the transaction process proceeds as follows: First, bankers exchange their monies for personal debts maturing within the period. Second, all individuals meet one another sequentially to clear excess demands for all commodities (including bonds). Third, nonbankers other than those who wish loan extensions pay off their bank debts, leaving an outstanding aggregate money supply held by nonbankers at the end of the period equal to the aggregate monetary value of these loan extensions. Finally, each banker in turn meets all of the other bankers to exchange monies, paying his debts with his own interest-bearing money whenever he, because of his loan extensions, has insufficient receipts to cover current obligations, and the others, because their money is being held by nonbankers (i.e., the excreditors of the bank-debtors), have insufficient interest-bearing debt to meet their future obligations as bankers.

In this way a competitive equilibrium set of transactions with money is achieved out of a natural set of transactions by introducing certain transaction costs. While the particular description of the equilibrium set of transactions is dependent upon our description of a natural transaction process, none of our results will depend on the particular set of transactions representing the equilibrium set. It is only necessary that there exists a competitive equilibrium set of transactions in which money is employed to reach the real allocations described by a standard competitive equilibrium. We have shown that there is a model of the transaction process yielding such a solution set of transactions.

The model is based, however, on the thoroughly unrealistic assumption that each individual naturally meets separately with every other during each period. An alternative model, which does not contain this assumption, is provided by assuming, realistically, that whenever there is a change in the individuals who receive the benefits from real commodities, a technical transformation, including an act of transportation, is required. Then, since an individual cannot be in two places at the same time, deliveries from one individual to the others must be sequential. Since each delivery at a given time goes to a unique location, each delivery represents a different market. The transaction process in real commodities is then given by the optimal delivery pattern of real commodities determined in a standard competitive equilibrium.[7] Personal debts are, once again, used to match commodity deliveries. In some cases these debts may be repaid without a sale of the debts to third parties. But in an unrestricted technology, there are always cases in which these debts must be sold to third parties in order for the creditor to receive his efficient commodity return. Allowing, once again, the transaction costs of such sales to be positive for the debts of some individuals and zero for the debts of others, the latter debts are individually, rationally purchased with the former debts. The resulting monetary theory is not different than that developed above with respect to any of the properties of economies treated in this chapter.

---

[7] The problem with such a formulation is that the requirement of overhead transportation costs implies nonconvexities in production or preference sets and thus nonconvex demand or supply correspondences for some price vectors. Such nonconvexities may easily present situations in which no parametric prices can exist which equate quantities demanded and supplied.

We now proceed by deriving properties of a perfectly competitive money economy that distinguish it from the money economy described by modern monetary theorists.[8]

## D. The Validity of the "Invalid" Classical Dichotomy

Classical and neoclassical monetary theorists, as Patinkin [20] has stressed, assumed that equilibrium relative prices between real assets (including rights to future assets, or "bonds") were determined solely in the real asset markets. This, Patinkin claims to have shown, is consistent with a general equilibrium only if there is an "indeterminate" level of money prices regardless of the money supply. The now familiar argument can be paraphrased to read: "If equilibrium relative prices between real assets are determined in the markets for real assets (i.e., determined with Casselian demand and supply functions for real assets only), then, by Walras' law, the money market must be in equilibrium for such relative prices regardless of the level of money prices and the money supply. Thus the money price level under a classical dichotomy may be anything; it is arbitrary even for a fixed money supply."

But Patinkin's analysis implicitly requires all nonmonetary assets to generate real services (which include contractually specified future services). And this requirement is inconsistent with a money economy consistent with orthodox value theory because in such an economy some asset must yield current money-backing services, and these are obviously not part of the productive or consumptive services appearing in orthodox value theory.

Suppose, following Patinkin's standard example, we start out in an equilibrium in an economy admitting a classical dichotomy and then experimentally increase all money prices in the same proportion, keeping the money supply constant. In the absence of money illusion and distribution effects, the demand for nominal money increases. Patinkin claims that the resulting excess demand for money implies an inconsistency because an excess supply of real assets would then have to arise to satisfy Walras' law, but cannot because we have not altered relative prices. But an equivalent excess supply of *nonreal, nonmonetary* assets only need arise given that relative prices between nonmonetary assets have not changed. In fact, this is exactly what happens in a perfectly competitive money economy. The individuals who want more money necessarily plan to offer correspondingly more real goods to the money creators for money-backing purposes; and this *in itself* creates an excess supply of nonmonetary assets *equivalent* to the excess demand for money. And since the individuals will receive a return on their extra money equivalent to that which they received when they owned the real goods being sold to obtain the

---

[8] A mathematical development of the remainder of Section I is available (Thompson [34]). A mathematical development of Section II.A–E is also available (Thompson [35]).

money, the demand and supply relations for nonmonetary assets relevant for determining relative prices do not change. The point is that the real goods brought to the money creators now perform the *added* function of backing the medium of exchange. Before the excess demand for money appeared, these goods had only the potential of generating an asset that yielded money-backing services. The excess demand for money creates a nonmonetary asset. Thus, an equivalent excess supply of a nonmonetary asset, one providing backing services for a medium of exchange, is induced by the excess demand for money; the zero excess demand for those assets which appeared in the original equilibrium will remain. The market for money (and thus for money-backing services) can then be used to determine an equilibrium price level for a given money supply or, more descriptive of classical monetary analysis, an equilibrium money supply for a given price level.

Since the money-backing *services* of a good are provided free of cost, we might alternatively place a zero-price weight on the positive excess supply of the assets representing streams of money-backing services. But then, evaluating each asset at the price of its corresponding *service stream* and *not* at the price of the *good* generating the asset and its service stream, the original increase in demand for money would be a positive excess demand for a freely supplied service. So the excess demand for money services would also be of zero value. Either way, no positive excess supply of commodities would be implied by the excess demand for money in being consistent with Walras' law. Assuming that the increase in the price level represented an increase in the conversion rate of money into commodities, the excesses are cleared once the excess demand for monetary services induces the nominal money supply to increase to meet the higher demand. So, once again, we have a classical dichotomy and a determinate supply of real cash balances.

The classical dichotomy is easy to construct for a perfectly competitive money economy. Let the relative prices between real assets, and equilibrium in the real asset markets, be determined by the conventional method of orthodox value theory—without reference to money or any decentralized exchange process (e.g., Debreu [6]). Then impose transaction possibilities on the economy such that transaction costs are zero in achieving final, competitive allocations if and only if money is used in certain exchanges. At a given level of money prices, this implies that each individual has at least a certain nominal cash balance at each point in the transaction process. The balances comprise the money demands in the economy. Under perfectly competitive money supply conditions (described previously), these demands will be filled at no real cost. In this way, equilibrium money supplies, and thus real balances, are determined, but only after relative prices between nonmonetary assets have been determined in the real markets.

This construction implies the validity, in a perfectly competitive money economy, of Say's law [27], viz., that the aggregate value of the excess demands for all real goods is identically zero. Say's law is supposed by modern analysts to imply (1) an identically zero excess demand for money, (2) an indeterminate price level, and (3) the impossibility of recessionary forces in some industries without expansionary forces in others. We have seen that the first two supposed implications are false. The third supposed implication—which was also apparently held by classical writers—will be shown to be false in Section II.G.

## E. The Real Balance Effect

As noted in the Introduction, classical monetary theory has been implicitly criticized for failing to include the "real balance effect," i.e., an increase in aggregate wealth implied by a small drop in all commodity prices and a constant nominal money supply. There is no such effect in a perfectly competitive money economy with a money market initially in equilibrium, so that the classical theorists cannot be logically criticized for omitting it. This result is not entirely new; it is implied by Patinkin's claim that there is never any real balance effect in a model with only "inside," or privately produced, money [20]. While the argument of Patinkin has been shown to be incorrect by Pesek and Saving [22], we shall now see that there is a case in which the conclusion (but not the argument) holds, the case of a perfectly competitive money economy.

An overall price level reduction, i.e., a proportional reduction in all prices, for a given rate of conversion of money into a real asset, will create an arbitrage profit to the purchase of goods which back money, followed by their sale to the bankers at the conversion dates. The price level must return to its original level in order to restore equilibrium in the capital markets. But even if the real money supply were slightly increased, say by increasing the nominal money supply beyond its equilibrium level, there would be no increase in aggregate real wealth. This is simply because the increase in the real value of the monetary holdings of any individual is exactly matched by the increase in the real value of the debts that the bankers owe the individual as long as the competitive money market was initially in equilibrium.[9]

This result may be used to rationalize the absence of real balance effects in classical monetary discussions.

---

[9] In Section II.H we consider the closely related question of the presence of "Pigou effects," the effects on excess demands of changes in the general price level. Pigou effects follow almost immediately from real balance effects in a modern money economy, but in the perfectly competitive money economy the flexible money supply makes the two effects different in nature. Nevertheless, the magnitude of the Pigou effect in a perfectly competitive money economy will be seen to be the same as that of the real balance effect—zero.

## F. Effects of Anticipated Inflation

It has become standard, through the papers of Friedman [7], Bailey [4], Marty [16], and Kessel and Alchian [11], to argue that even if money is neutral, increases in *future* money supplies, for a given current money supply, do not merely increase *future* money prices in the same proportion when the future price increases are fully anticipated (and the demand for money is influenced by the cost of holding money). The reason is that the inflation will depreciate the real value of one's cash, thereby increasing the cost of holding cash relative to other assets in the current period. Switching into nonmonetary assets bids up the *current* price level and thereby lowers the current real cash balances in the system. The same effect is present in succeeding periods if the inflation is then expected to continue. The analysis makes the effects of inflation equivalent to the effects of a tax on money balances.

But, once again, the argument requires that competitive interest not be paid on money. When perfectly competitive interest is paid to the holders of money, bankers must pay interest on money equal in money value to the sum of the current rental and the expected price appreciation on the assets they obtain for their money. This sum would change with a change in expected future money supplies and proportionate change in future prices by an amount equal to the change in the expected inflation if no real effects were induced by the change in expected future prices and money supplies. But since the change in inflation would then not alter the return to holding *any* asset—including money —relative to any other asset, the hypothesized original allocation of real resources is an equilibrium allocation. So no real effects are induced by a change in expected inflation. A proportional increase in expected future prices and money supplies has no effect on the current price level. The returns and costs of holding money must change by the same amount when competitive interest is paid on money.

This result rationalizes the absence of distinctions between real and money interest rates and the absence of a monetary theory of interest in classical monetary theory, absences which are traditional bases for criticizing classical monetary theory.[10]

---

[10] While our results so far have displayed, and will continue to display, a detailed correspondence between the properties of a perfectly competitive money economy and the properties which most classical economists explicitly or implicitly believed to hold for a "laissez faire" money economy (see Schumpeter [28, pp. 729–731]), it is not clear that classical economists were considering a perfectly competitive money economy. However, these economists did uniformly assume fixed convertibility of bank notes into nonmonetary assets in their laissez faire systems. Under perfect competition, such assets would have to generate their valuable returns solely in terms of expected real price appreciation and not in terms of current services. This does correspond somewhat to the classical support of gold

## II. The Theory of Income Determination Consistent with Orthodox Value Theory

### A. THE PROBLEM

We now proceed to examine the short-period effects of various exogenous shifts on "involuntary unemployment" in a perfectly competitive money model. These effects are compared with the effects that emerge in a modern money model. We shall use the same theory of "temporary equilibrium" for both economies. (See Hicks [10] or Arrow and Hahn [3]). A temporary equilibrium is an equilibrium over an interval of time sufficiently small that expectations of all prices within the period are correct, while expectations of prices in trades in future periods are, in general, incorrect. All the properties of a perfectly competitive money economy which were developed previously (except for Pareto optimality) obviously hold for temporary as well as full equilibria. A temporary equilibrium containing "involuntary unemployment" is said to exist when the current-period supply curves of labor are based on incorrect perceptions of future wage offers or output prices and, as a result, laborers waste their current-period labor services on bargaining, searching, so adopting nonmarket vocations. We assume that a permanent reduction in the values of the marginal products of labor at the preshift, full-equilibrium quantities of labor will create involuntary unemployment. This amounts to assuming "sticky money wages."

Rudiments of a theory rationalizing this assumption are found in the book by Alchian and Allen [1]. We rationalize sticky money wages here with the hypothesis that some workers mistakenly regard reductions in their current wage offers as a result of their lower value productivities at those jobs *relative to* alternative jobs or the result of an attempt at tougher wage-bargaining by their employers. An economy which experiences no changes in technology or tastes and whose prices are not substantially bargained—i.e., the traditional

---

(which, during the classical era (ca. 1775–1850), significantly appreciated in real terms (see Viner [37].)) as backing for all note issues.

Furthermore, there is abundant evidence of the assumption by leading classical monetary economists of the applicability of much of modern monetary analysis in the presence of an inconvertible, government-supplied, paper money. One example is Thornton's famous analysis [36] of employment dynamics under inconvertible paper money. Another is Say's recognition of the fact that anticipated inflation with inconvertible paper money leads to increases in the transactions velocity of money (see Schumpeter [28, p. 710n]). Another prominent example is the analysis of Mill [18], which has deceived several modern authors not aware of the theoretical importance of convertibility into believing that Mill, and ergo the classical economists, were essentially modern monetary theorists (e.g., Becker and Baumol [5], Samuelson [26]).

underdeveloped economy—will experience no involuntary unemployment because workers there know from experience that lower money wage offers by their current employers are common to all employers. Involuntary unemployment can arise only in countries which have sufficient shifts in technology, tastes, or bargaining from one firm to another to lead some workers to confuse a shift down in the full equilibrium wage level with a shift in technology, etc., which is particular to only certain employers. The empirical presumption that business cycles containing substantial inefficient unemployment are a disease only of modern industrial societies is rather strong evidence in favor of the hypothesis we are using to rationalize sticky wages.

We shall first examine the effects on involuntary unemployment in a perfectly competitive money economy of those exogenous shifts which have long served to distinguish modern unemployment theory: shifts in the demand for money, the supply of money, the marginal efficiency of capital, and the propensity to consume. These effects are contrasted with those that arise in a modern, Keynes–Patinkin monetary environment. We then examine the effects of shifts in the marginal product of labor and input supplies. Finally, we complete a taxonomy of shifts by considering shifts which alter the relative prices between different outputs.

## B. Shifts in the Demand for Money

Suppose that transaction costs become positive in present exchanges of real assets occurring in an original equilibrium and that the extended use of money would obviate these costs. (For example, suppose the original equilibrium included present trades in which each of two capital owners accepted output futures from one of two producers, and now these trades become costly because each of the capital owners now plans to consume the future output of the producer who does not use his capital. And these producers and capital owners can, if they are given the extra money, costlessly adjust to the change by switching to present trades of capital for money and future trades of money for output.) This shift increases the demand for money at original equilibrium prices. Since bankers can supply the money at no real cost, we immediately arrive at a new equilibrium with no change in prices or the allocation of scarce resources. More money is demanded, more is supplied, and no utility or price is altered. (Completing the above example, in a perfectly competitive money economy the capital owners avoid transaction costs by first selling capital to a producer for a money on which he is paid the real return on the capital and then purchasing the output of the other producer at the end of the period; and each of the producers borrows the money from a banker to pay for their capital input, paying real interest on their loan, and finally repaying the principal at the end of the period with the proceeds from the sale of their capital outputs.)

This argument for the dynamical efficiency of an elastic free-market money supply was seen and emphasized by most classical writers, including Adam Smith and J. B. Say. But the argument has gradually fallen into ill-repute as it has come to be interpreted to mean that a money supply that does not bear *competitive interest* should expand (and contract) as aggregate money income expands (and contracts).[11]

In contrast to the perfectly competitive money model, the modern Keynes–Patinkin–Friedman money model has upward shifts in the demand for money (or increases in " liquidity preference ") recessionary in that the resulting excess demand for money can be cleared only through reductions in output prices and thus value marginal products and employment rather than through market-induced increases in the supply of money.

## C. Shifts in the Supply of Money

If there is an increase in the supply of money (without a corresponding change in the conversion price) in the original equilibrium of a perfectly competitive money model, it would represent an overissue and holders would, rather than trade it to nonbankers, hold it as a real asset or return such money to its creators. This effect was popularly emphasized by classical monetary writers, especially leaders of the " Banking School," such as Tooke and Fullarton, who had the support of the greater part of the scientific community, including Mill in the 1840's. (See Schumpeter [28].) Thus there is obviously no effect of changes in the supply of money on prices or employment in a perfectly competitive money economy as long as the conversion price of money is retained.

In a modern money model, money does not bear competitive interest, so an increase in supply is not held as if it were a real asset, and money cannot be simply returned to an issuer because of the finite elasticity of the money-supply function. Hence the money is spent and prices are bid up. The analysis is similar for reductions in the money supply.

## D. Shifts in the Marginal Efficiency of Capital

Suppose now that the perceived future productivity of currently produced assets shifts down. In a modern money economy, this shift results in a decrease in the return to capital and bonds relative to money and thus induces an excess

[11] The standard critique of the dynamics under the classical policy of a flexible private money supply has consequently been that under such a policy an increase (decrease) in the nominal prices of real assets generates an increase (decrease) in the nominal money supply, thus creating the possibility of procyclical variations in the money supply. The critique is obviously based on a failure to retain convertibility at a fixed rate as part of the set of all classical monetary institutions.

demand for money. The corresponding excess supply of nonmonetary goods implies a recession in the current period. But, in a perfectly competitive money economy, where perfectly competitive interest is paid on money, the decrease in the marginal efficiency of capital creates an equal decrease in yield to the competitive bankers, who therefore must react by lowering the yield they pay on money by an equal amount. This produces a situation in which money is no more attractive than before the shift. The drop in the marginal efficiency of capital therefore simply reduces the temporary equilibrium market rate of interest by the same amount, current investment remaining at its original level. (This ignores interest-induced shifts in consumption; we shall see later that no employment effects result from shifts in the propensity to consume in a perfectly competitive money economy.)

A lower real interest on money as well as other assets does not itself induce any involuntary unemployment, even though it lowers a worker's effective real wage. The reason for this is that the lower interest payment on money, unlike a lower nominal wage offer, is known by each money holder to apply to all money holders. The lower interest payment on money cannot be regarded by a rational worker as a reason for making the changes in search, nonmarket vocation, or bargaining that he would make (and regret) in the case of a small drop in nominal wages. That is, the decreased interest on his money wage cannot be rationally regarded by a worker as the result of his lower value productivity in his current job relative to alternative, future jobs or the result of an attempt at tougher labor bargaining by his employer. (This form of argument first appears in the book by Leijonhufvud [14].) The same argument applies to changes in a conversion price of money into capital, so that shifts in such a conversion price (such as those implied in Sections I.D–I.F) in a perfectly competitive money model also have no real effects.

Thus, the most distinguishing recessionary shift of the Keynesian model is ineffective in a classical economy because a decline in the marginal efficiency of capital implies an equal induced decline in the market rate of interest on money, so that no change in the relative cost of holding money occurs.

## E. Shifts in the Propensity to Consume

Suppose now there is a shift in plans so that current consumption decreases and planned future consumption increases. First assume it is a nonmonetary shift so that there is an equal increase in demand for investment goods in the form of bonds or real capital. Since there are as yet no alterations in the relative prices between consumption and capital goods, an assumption that serves to keep us in the environment of the standard income-expenditures model, the only possible effects of the shift on the aggregate demand for labor are through changes in bond prices. If bond prices are to remain the same, the increase in demand for bonds must be met by suppliers of bonds, who must

*pari passu* demand real capital. Under a constant cost of financial intermediation, this will occur and no recession will result. But if there is an increasing cost of such intermediation, a lower yield on bonds to consumers
and a higher borrowing cost to producers results. This induces an increase in
the demand for money and an equal reduction in factor demand by the producers, so a recession results. In an economy consistent with orthodox value
theory, there are no lending costs and thus no increasing spread between
borrowing and lending rates and no recession. The suppliers of bonds to the
consumers obtain their interest by lending to the producers at no transaction
costs; hence again there is no recession.[12]

Suppose now that the reduction in consumption represents a shift into
money. In a perfectly competitive money model the bankers, who must pay
real interest on the extra money that they supply, must *pari passu* provide the
intermediate demand for holding investment goods or bonds that the money
holders have now failed to provide. So there is no induced reduction in demand for real assets. In contrast, the bankers in the modern money model do
not have the flexibility to expand their money supplies and real asset demands. So a reduction in output prices and thus a recession obviously results
from the shift from consumption into money.

As a check of these results that the characteristic recession-creators in
modern monetary theory have no recessionary impact in a perfectly competitive money economy, we can reproduce them graphically or mathematically.
We can use a simple macromodel to describe the comparative static effects of
the above shifts, since they do not alter relative output prices. In particular,
we may use a model with only four markets: capital goods, money, and
capital and labor services for the upcoming period. (Bonds are perfect substitutes for capital goods in a standard Keynesian environment, so it is
redundant to include them in a separate market with a separate price.) Removing the market for capital goods with Walras' law, we can determine the
temporary equilibrium—the current price level, wage rate, and interest rate—
in the money and the two factor markets. This equilibrium can be constructed
graphically in price-interest rate space as follows: First find, for each price
level, the value of the marginal product of the fully employed capital that
results from the employment that equilibrates the competitive labor market
at that price level. Since the interest rate is the value of the marginal product

---

[12] However, even in an economy with positive costs of lending, if there is a competitive
supply of money and a positive, competitive interest rate paid on money, no recession results
from such a shift. (See Thompson [32].) The basic reason is that a reduction in the interest
paid on money equal to the higher marginal lending costs will simultaneously leave the
supply price of loans from the bank unaffected and leave the supply price of loans and
capital from the consumers unaffected by preventing the consumers from attempting to
substitute money for nonmonetary assets.

of capital plus the given, expected rate of price inflation divided by the price level, we have thereby determined, for each price level, the interest rate implied by equilibrium in the factor markets. Then find the interest rates that equate the demand and supply of money at each different price level. An intersection of these price-interest rate pairs determines a temporary equilibrium.[13] The difference between the two economies discussed in this chapter is that a perfectly competitive money model has its money supplies infinitely elastic at the price level established by convertibility, while a modern money model has a constant money supply (or a money supply function) and has a demand function for money in which the interest rate appears as the cost of holding money. Graphically, the curve showing equilibrium in the factor markets is the same in the two economies, but in the perfectly competitive money model the money-market-equilibrium curve is a straight line parallel to the interest rate axis at the fixed conversion price, while in a modern money economy the money equilibrium curve has a positive slope, as does the curve showing equilibrium in the factor markets. The manipulation of these models to obtain the preceding results is straightforward.[14]

We now examine the effects of the remaining possible shifts.

### F. Shifts in the Marginal Product and Supply of Labor

A shift in production functions generating a lower marginal physical product of labor or a shift out in the supply-of-labor curve in a modern money model will, of course, increase the temporary equilibrium rate of involuntary unemployment. The qualitative effects of these shifts are the same with classical, as with modern monetary institutions. Indeed, even the most classical of writers (i.e., Say [27, pp. 194–196]) admitted that unemployment resulted from such shifts.

In fact, still barring changes in relative output prices, it is only shifts in the marginal product or supply of labor that can alter the level of unemployment in a perfectly competitive money economy. This is easy to see: Unemployment in any temporary equilibrium can be altered only by altering the value of the marginal product curve or the money wage supply curve of labor. But since the money price of output is fixed by convertibility in a perfectly competitive money model, the only way to alter the temporary equilibrium unemployment rate is to shift the marginal physical product or real supply curve of labor.

---

[13] The above is the only atemporal model consistent with a Keynes–Patinkin environment. The standard Keynes–Patinkin model is internally inconsistent. For a verification of these propositions, and for an intertemporal model, see Thompson [34].

[14] One must note, however, that the only equilibria which count, i.e., which are stable, in a modern money model are those for which the interest rate that equilibrates the money market is more sensitive to a small change in price level than is the interest rate that equilibrates the factor markets.

With fully employed nonlabor inputs, we may conclude that the only way to change the rate of involuntary unemployment is to change input supplies or the rate of labor-favoring technical change. In fact, historical evidence (1860–1940) strongly suggests that the long (20-year) building business cycle—the largest and most widespread business cycle in modern history—has been due to a dynamic interaction between a kind of labor-favoring technical change and induced alterations in the supplies of certain inputs. (See Thompson [31].)

## G. Shifts Altering Relative Prices between Real Outputs

The preceding analysis in this section has treated all outputs as if they were physically homogeneous, so that relative output prices could not vary. As a consequence, the analysis could proceed in the same technological environment as the standard, income-expenditure model. Shifts in the demand for and supply of money, in real output, in the productivity of capital, and in the productivity and supply of labor exhaust the exogenous shifts possible in such a world.

Now we consider shifts in excess demands between the various real outputs and allow these shifts to alter relative output prices. We find—at long last—a shift for which the perfectly competitive money economy is clearly inferior to the modern money economy with respect to the magnitude of the induced alterations in involuntary unemployment. An example will suffice to show this. Suppose that an initial equilibrium in an economy with two real outputs is disturbed by a shift in demand between the outputs. The shift is toward the consumption good, which is produced only by capital, and away from the capital good, which is produced only by labor and under diminishing returns. First, consider the shift under perfectly competitive monetary institutions. Suppose that money is convertible into the consumption good.[15] Since the shift cannot raise the money price of the consumption good, there must be a fall in the money price of the capital good and a corresponding drop in employment. This drop in employment may easily be more severe than the corresponding drop in a modern money model. To see this, consider the same price and thus employment change in the latter model. The lower price of one output and the constant price of the other (together with the higher interest rate implied by the constant rental on capital and the lower capital price) implies a lower demand for money than before the shift (together with a higher demand for capital as a store of value than in the perfectly competitive money

---

[15] If money were convertible into capital in such a world, no shift in output demands could create any involuntary unemployment, because no shift could alter the price of capital and therefore employment. For the shift specified above, the price of consumption goods and rental on capital would simply climb sufficiently high that a new general equilibrium would be established.

economy.) Since the money supply in a modern money model does not fall with money demand, there is an excess supply of money (together with an excess demand for the capital output) in the modern money economy at the postshift, temporary equilibrium prices of the perfectly competitive money economy. Assuming that an increase in the consumption-good price does not reduce the demand for capital output,[16] clearing these excesses requires a higher price of capital and thus a lower rate of unemployment than in the perfectly competitive money economy.

More generally, any shift in demands that increases the relative price of the asset backing money relative to other, labor-using, outputs will obviously create involuntary unemployment starting from a full equilibrium in a perfectly competitive money economy.

There can be little doubt that classical monetary analysts, who were also inveterate policy advisors, put little or no weight on the recessionary significance of a rise in the relative demand for the asset backing money, i.e., gold.[17] The policy neglect of these shifts permitted a series of sharp recessions caused by sudden increases in the demand for gold throughout the history of Europe and the United States. This is abundantly clear from the statistical work of Warren and Pearson [38]. The last such recession was the Great Depression, which saw a five-year increase in the real price of gold (1929–1934) whose magnitude was unprecedented in recorded history [38], an increase resulting from the return to the gold standard from 1924 to 1928.[18] The free convertibility of money into gold was halted from 1931 to 1934 and replaced by what has become a system of government fiat money, a system represented in the modern money model.

---

[16] Alternatively, assume that consumers all have the same, constant marginal rate of substitution between consumption and investment goods after the shift has occurred. Then the price ratio between consumption and investment goods, as determined by this rate, is the same after the shift in both of the economies under discussion. Consequently, the excess supply of money in a modern money model at the temporary equilibrium prices of the perfectly competitive model implies proportionately higher prices of all outputs in achieving a temporary equilibrium in the modern money model.

[17] Even the leading employment pessimists of the classical era—the "general glut" theorists such as Malthus and Sismondi—had their recessions due only to shifts in the supply of labor. (See Sowell [29].)

[18] The move back to the gold standard and consequent increase in the real price of gold would probably not have created a depression if the countries had made a common decision to return to the gold standard at the same time. In such a case, the countries would probably have recognized the substantial effect that the return to the gold standard would have on the real value of gold and therefore would have returned at a much higher conversion rate of money into gold, a rate which would have reflected the substantial world inflation (33% in United States wholesale prices) that had occurred since the collapse of the international gold standard in 1914. In such a case, the increase in the real value of gold would have been immediate and would not have altered money wage or price levels.

The traditional disavowal by "respectable" economic theorists of the aggregative recessionary impact of an unexpected increase in the demand for the asset which backs money has been the argument that a rise in the demand for gold will simply expand output and employment in the gold industry, so that no aggregative recession results from the shift.[19] Such an argument is based on the absence of any formal theory of employment under a gold standard and a misunderstanding of the nature of the informational imperfection leading to involuntary unemployment. Formally, a pegged money price of gold and the fact that workers' temporary equilibrium supply curves are defined in terms of money wages prevent any expansion in the gold industry despite the fact that the real price of gold has risen. One economic rationale for the higher supply price of labor in terms of nongold commodities is that some workers simply do not know that the nongold price level has dropped and so require the same wages in terms of gold for the same employment. Another economic rationale is that other workers, who know the extent of the fall in the prices of nongold commodities, expect higher real wages in nongold commodities in the post-shift economy because they believe that the lower nongold prices are due to a higher-than-normal rate of technical progress in the nongold industries, when in fact there has been a shift in demand toward gold or a lower-than-normal rate of technical progress in the gold industry.[20]

## H. WAGE FLEXIBILITY AND THE POSSIBILITY OF PERMANENT INVOLUNTARY UNEMPLOYMENT

We have said nothing of the events that occur after market-learning by the unemployed lowers the future temporary equilibrium supply curves of labor. While we again cannot derive any general superiority of one of our monetary

---

[19] But perhaps the main reason for the academic neglect of employment fluctuations based on changes in the real value of gold was the development of central banking during the nineteenth and early twentieth centuries and the consequent development of numerous business cycle "models" in which central banking played a key role. While a central bank has no effect in a perfectly competitive money model, it has some effect in a competitive banking model with a positive transaction cost of bank lending; viz., the policies of the central bank affect the transaction cost of private lending at a given volume of total loans and hence affect the spread between borrowers' and lenders' rates of interest. While the fluctuation in central bank rates and bond purchases no doubt had some influence on the price of nongold durables and thus employment, the dominance of these fluctuations in pre-Keynesian business cycle theories obscured the causes of the larger economic fluctuations in economic history and has left us a legacy of "practical" men of affairs who believe that central banks affect our economies only through affecting the real cost of lending.

[20] A perfectly competitive money model relying solely on the latter type of rationale has some peculiar properties. First, it has the same temporary equilibria regardless of which good is used to back money. Second, all shifts which lead to contraction in some industries without expansion in others are shifts in demands or abnormal reductions in the rate of technical progress. Hence, under the latter rationale, money could indeed be called a "veil."

systems over the other, we can answer a related question. Namely, is permanent involuntary unemployment possible in our alternative monetary systems?

The answer to this question for the modern money model, as developed by Pigou [24], is well known: Permanent involuntary unemployment is impossible because the supply of real cash balances and therefore consumption demand would rise to infinity if wage reductions were to continually pull down output prices sufficiently to prevent the achievement of full employment. The argument, of course, employs a real balance effect. In a perfectly competitive money economy the supply of money changes with prices so as to retain equilibrium in the money market. Hence, even if price reductions for given money supplies generated real wealth increases in a perfectly competitive money economy (which they do not, as indicated in Section I.E), the induced reductions in the money supply would prevent real cash balances from rising during a deflation. The Pigou effect is absent in a perfectly competitive money economy.

However, while a perfectly competitive money economy lacks the anchor of a fixed money supply and real balance effect, it does have an anchor of its own—convertibility. Under convertibility at a fixed rate, when wages fall, it is impossible for all prices to fall in the same proportion. At least one price does not fall at all. In the simple case of a single output, into which money is convertible, a fall in wages produces a proportional fall in real wages because there is no change in the output price. In the general case, if we allow wage expectations and thus wages to fall continuously, adopting the macroeconomic convention that the disequilibrium is based upon incorrect wage expectations, we must, sooner or later, arrive at an equilibrium as long as one exists.

The preceding results lend rationale to the position of the classical economists that involuntary unemployment is only temporary and serve to rationalize the neglect by classical economists of Pigou and real balance effects.

## III. Conclusion

A money economy consistent with an orthodox value theory in which money is competitively supplied exists, and any such economy has just about all of the properties that modern monetary theorists claim to have proved to be classical fallacies. In particular: (1) Any perfectly competitive money economy has a classical dichotomy between the real and monetary sectors and yet a determinate equilibrium quantity of real cash balances. (2) Any perfectly competitive money economy has no real balance or Pigou effects but still has an impossibility of permanent, aggregate unemployment. (3) In any perfectly competitive money economy, equilibrium allocations of resources are never affected by anticipated inflation. (4) In any perfectly competitive money economy, aggregate output is never disturbed by Keynesian or Quantity Theory shifts—that is, by shifts in liquidity preference, the marginal efficiency of capital, the propensity to consume, or the money supply.

Despite the fact that Say's law holds for any money economy consistent with orthodox value theory, the level of aggregative involuntary unemployment in a temporary equilibrium of such an economy varies substantially with certain shifts which alter relative output prices, as well as with shifts in the marginal product and supply of labor. Indeed, such unemployment in a perfectly competitive money economy is *more* susceptible to some recessionary shifts—those which decrease the demand for money—than it is in a modern money economy. The historical accuracy of a perfectly competitive money model in explaining major business fluctuations prior to 1934 appears to be remarkable, and the model highlights the danger of returning to a fully convertible gold standard.

## ACKNOWLEDGMENTS

The author benefited from discussions with his colleagues, Armen Alchian, Benjamin Klein, Axel Leijonhufvud, and Joseph Ostroy. Helpful comments on an earlier draft were provided by Dan Benjamin and Robert Clower. Research support was provided by the Lilly Foundation Grant for the Study of Property Rights at UCLA. An earlier draft of this chapter, entitled "In Defense of the Classical Theory of Money and Income," was presented at the December 1969 meetings of the Econometric Society.

## REFERENCES

1. Alchian, A. A., and Allen, W. R., *University Economics*, 2nd ed., Chapter 25. Belmont, California: Wadsworth, 1967.
2. Arrow, K. J., "An Extension of the Basic Theorem of Classical Welfare Economics," *Proceedings of the Second Berkeley Symposium on Mathematical Statistics and Probability* (J. Neyman, ed.). Berkeley: Univ. of California Press, 1951.
3. Arrow, K. J., and Hahn, F., *General Competitive Analysis*, Chapter II. San Francisco: Holden-Day, 1971.
4. Bailey, M. J., "The Welfare Cost of Inflationary Finance," *Journal of Political Economy* **64** (April 1956), 93–110.
5. Becker, G. S., and Baumol, W. J., "The Classical Monetary Theory: The Outcome of the Discussion," in *Essays in Economic Thought* (J. Spengler and W. R. Allen, eds.), pp. 753–771. Chicago: Rand-McNally, 1960.
6. Debreu, G., *Theory of Value*. New York: Wiley, 1959.
7. Friedman, M., "Discussion of the Inflationary Gap," in *Essays in Positive Economics*, pp. 253–257. Chicago: Univ. of Chicago Press, 1953.
8. Friedman, M., *A Program for Monetary Stability*, p. 7. New York: Fordham Univ. Press, 1960.
9. Friedman, M., *The Optimum Quantity of Money and Other Essays*. Chicago: Aldine, 1969.
10. Hicks, J. R., *Capital and Growth*, Chapter VI. London and New York: Oxford Univ. Press, 1965.

11. Kessel, R. A., and Alchian, A. A., "Effects of Inflation," *Journal of Political Economy* **70** (December 1962), 521–537.
12. Keynes, J. M., *The General Theory of Employment, Interest and Money.* New York: Macmillan, 1936.
13. Klein, B., "The Competitive Supply of Money," *Journal of Money, Credit, and Banking.* (to be published).
14. Leijonhufvud, A., *On Keynesian Economics and the Economics of Keynes*, Chapter 2. London and New York: Oxford Univ. Press, 1968.
15. Marschak, J., "Rationale of the Demand for Money and of Money Illusion," *Metroeconomica* **2** (August 1950), 71–100.
16. Marty, A. L., "Gurley and Shaw on Money in a Theory of Finance," *Journal of Political Economy* **69** (February 1961), 57–58.
17. Metzler, L. A., "Wealth, Saving, and the Rate of Interest," *Journal of Political Economy* **59** (April 1951), 93–116.
18. Mill, J. S., *Principles of Political Economy* (W. J. Ashley, ed.), Book III. London: Longmans, Green, 1909.
19. Ostroy, J., "The Informational Efficiency of Monetary Exchange," *American Economic Review* (to be published).
20. Patinkin, D., *Money, Interest, and Prices*, 2nd ed. New York: Harper, 1965.
21. Patinkin, D., "The Indeterminacy of Absolute Prices in Classical Economic Theory," *Econometrica* **17** (January 1949), 1–27.
22. Pesek, B., and Saving, T., *Money, Wealth, and Economic Theory*, Part II. New York: Macmillan, 1967.
23. Pesek, B., "Comment," *Journal of Political Economy* **77**, Supplement (August 1969), 889.
24. Pigou, A. C., "The Classical Stationary State," *Economic Journal* **53** (December 1943), 342–351.
25. Radner, R., "Competitive Equilibrium under Uncertainty," *Econometrica* **36** (January 1968), 31–58.
26. Samuelson, P. A., "What Classical and Neoclassical Monetary Theory Really Was," *Canadian Journal of Economics* **1** (February 1968), 1–15.
27. Say, J. B., *Taite d'economie politique*, 5th ed., Vol. 1. Paris: Chez Rapilly, 1826.
28. Schumpeter, J. A., *The History of Economic Analysis*, Chapter 7. London and New York: Oxford Univ. Press, 1954.
29. Sowell, T., *Say's Law*, Chapters I–IV. Princeton, New Jersey: Princeton Univ. Press, to be published.
30. Starr, R., "The Structure of Exchange in Barter and Monetary Economies," *Quarterly Journal of Economics* **86** (May 1972), 290–302.
31. Thompson, E., "Technical Change, Its Measurement and Introduction into the Theory of the Firm with Special Application to the Explanation of the Building Cycle," Ph.D. Thesis, Harvard Univ. (1962).
32. Thompson, E., "An Optimal System of Property Rights for a General Money Economy," unpublished manuscript (1968).
33. Thompson, E., "A Reformulation of Orthodox Value Theory," manuscript (1971).
34. Thompson, E., "A Generalization of the Cassel–Patinkin Money Model," manuscript (1973).
35. Thompson, E., "A Reformulation of Macroeconomic Theory," manuscript (1973).
36. Thornton, H., *An Enquiry into the Nature and Effects of the Paper Credit of Great Britain*, reprint. London: 1939. Library of Economics.
37. Viner, J., *Studies in the Theory of International Trade*, Chapters IV and V. London: Allen and Unwin, 1955.
38. Warren, G. F., and Pearson, F. A., *Prices*, Chapter V. New York: Wiley, 1933.

# MONETARY THEORY AND ECONOMIC CONSOLIDATIONS

*Gerrit Bilkes\* and Edward Ames*

*State University of New York*
*Stony Brook*

## I

Monetary theory usually starts from a general equilibrium system involving *consumption, investment, government spending, labor services, bonds,* and *money.*[1] One of these variables can be suppressed by Walras' law. The remainder are then systematically analyzed. Usually no direct attention is paid to the institutional structure of the economy. Theorists, however, often do have an institutional specification in the backs of their minds. When different theorists have different specifications, it becomes hard to compare their work, and controversies arise. Much of the controversy around recent work by Gurley and Shaw [2], Pesek and Saving [3], Patinkin [4, 5], and Leijonhufvud [6] arises from a failure of these writers to specify clearly the institutional structure of the economies which they discuss. All their structures, however, can be derived from a single hypothetical six-sector economy which we shall introduce; we shall then present structures which can be found in the literature as appropriate consolidations of this basic structure.

---

\* Present affiliation: Laurentian University.
[1] See for example Patinkin [1, pp. 199–202]. There Patinkin groups consumption commodities, investment commodities, and commodities purchased by the government under the name "commodities."

We present the six-sector system in this first section. Section II considers various ways in which consolidated systems with fewer sectors can be constructed from the six-sector system, and presents definitions of money and the national product appropriate to a number of consolidations which have figured in recent economic literature. Section III discusses very simple economies of one and two sectors in which the money supply and household consumption are apt to disappear due to consolidation. Various "small" models in the literature are open to criticism, as they fail to make correct specifications of the variables which they could contain.

Macroeconomics is a simplification of general equilibrium theory made possible by lumping individuals and other economic units together into a small number of sectors. Macroeconomists assume that the behavior of the members of a sector is similar, while the behavior of different sectors is dissimilar, with reference to some phenomenon under study. As Tobin has said, each sector may be characterized by an income statement and a balance sheet [7]. The institutional structure of a macroeconomic (or monetary) model is given by a listing of the sectors and the names of the variables appearing in the income statements and balance sheets of each sector.

The simplest macroeconomics treats the economy as if it were a single sector. Many monetary models are one-sector models. Usually, however, theorists decide to use two- or three-sector models. They may use a two-sector model because they wish to show how one sector (e.g., consumers) interacts with the rest of the economy. This, for instance, was Patinkin's starting point when he wished to introduce the real-balance effect to his readers [1, pp. 202, 209, 288].[2]

The choice of a sectoral structure for a model depends on the problem under study. Writers dealing with the macroeconomics of developed economies, however, seem to agree that such economies consist of households, (nonfinancial) businesses, financial intermediaries, banks,[3] the central bank, and the government (as taxer, borrower, and spender). These six sectors are the finest breakdown of an economy which we require. The literature under discussion combines these six sectors in various ways to obtain economies with fewer than six sectors. This reduction in the number of sectors is achieved by consolidation, a well-known social accounting procedure.

---

[2] Here Patinkin distinguishes among households, firms and the government, stressing the partition between the private sector and the government.

[3] With Tobin, we distinguish between banks and other financial intermediaries chiefly on the basis of the presence and absence (respectively) of reserve requirements and interest rate ceilings established by the monetary authorities, and not on the basis of differences between bank liabilities and the liabilities of nonbank financial intermediaries. See Tobin [8].

Table 1 summarizes the accounts which would appear in our hypothetical six-sector economy. Each entry (account) would define a variable in a six-sector model. There are 65 accounts in all, and it is not surprising that economists might wish to simplify it somehow.

Table 1 is a compact way of representing the sectoral balance sheets and income statements of this economy. The accounts of a single sector are readily reconstructed from it. In the case of a balance sheet, the assets of a sector are found by reading down the appropriate column of Table 1a, and the liabilities of the sector are found by reading across the corresponding row. The physical assets and the "retained earnings" (accumulated saving or net worth) of the sector will appear in the diagonal boxes of Table 1a, since neither debts nor claims of other sectors are associated with these. In part, this is the case because it has been assumed that "bonds" are the only negotiable securities in the system. Likewise, in constructing sectoral income statements, one reads the sources of income for a sector from the columns in Table 1b, and the uses of the income from the corresponding row. Current saving and investment (additions to physical assets) of the sectors appear in the diagonal boxes of Table 1b.

The listing of accounts in Table 1 has been kept as simple as possible. Many items which everyone recognizes as heterogeneous (e.g., consumption, plant, bonds) are treated as homogeneous. Many possible transactions have been ignored, such as bank loans to financial intermediaries and consumer credit. The account structure used in the table facilitates our main argument; a more complicated one would not serve this purpose any better.

Take for example the banking sector. No items appear in the box in the fourth row and fourth column of Table 1a. All the items in the b column are therefore financial assets to the banking sector, and all the items in the b row are liabilities to the banking sector. The assets and liabilities of the banking sector would appear in a T account as shown in Table 2.

As a second example we shall construct the income statement of the household sector from Table 1b. Here there is an item in the box along the diagonal, $S_h^h$ (household saving). The other items are either expenditure flows (along the h row) or income flows (down the h column). The corresponding T account would be that shown in Table 3.

The remaining accounts of the six-sector structure of Table 1 can be constructed similarly. The advantage of the Table 1 presentation over ordinary T accounts lies in the fact that it brings out clearly and compactly the relationships among the accounts of the six sectors of the basic structure.

The net worth and saving items balance the balance sheets and income statements, respectively.[4] Consequently, we shall refer to the definition of net

---

[4] See footnote *b* to Table 1.

TABLE 1

A LIST OF VARIABLES REFLECTING THE ASSET–DEBT STRUCTURE AND THE INCOMES–EXPENDITURES STRUCTURE OF A HYPOTHETICAL SIX-SECTOR ECONOMY[a]

(a)  The Asset–Debt Structure[b]

Owed to

| Owed by | h | f | n | b | c | g |
|---|---|---|---|---|---|---|
| h (households) | $W_h^h, K_h^h$ | | $L_n^h$ | $L_b^h$ | | |
| f (businesses) | $B_{1h}^f, W_h^f$ | $W_f^f, K_f^f$ | $B_{1n}^f, L_n^f$ | $B_{1b}^f, L_b^f$ | | |
| n (financial institutions) | $W_h^n, M_{2h}^n, B_{2h}^n$ | $B_{2f}^n$ | | | | |
| b (banks) | $W_h^b, M_{2h}^b, M_{1h}^b$ | $M_{1f}^b$ | | | | |
| c (central bank) | $M_{1h}^c$ | $M_{1f}^c$ | $M_{1n}^c$ | $M_{1b}^c, M_{3b}^c$ | | $M_{1g}^c, W_g^c$ |
| g (government) | $M_{1h}^g, B_{1h}^g$ | $M_{1f}^g$ | $M_{1n}^g, B_{1n}^g$ | $M_{1b}^g, B_{1b}^g$ | $M_{1c}^g, B_{1c}^g, M_{4c}^g$ | $W_g^g, M_{5g}^g, K_g^g$ |

(b)  The Incomes–Expenditure Structure[c]

Paid to

| Paid by | h | f | n | b | c | g |
|---|---|---|---|---|---|---|
| h (households) | $S_h^h$ | $C_f^h$ | $R_n^h$ | $R_b^h$ | | $T_g^h$ |
| f (businesses) | $A_h^f, R_h^f, D_h^f$ | $S_f^f, I_f^f$ | $R_n^f$ | $R_b^f$ | | $T_g^f$ |
| n (financial institutions) | $R_h^n, D_h^n$ | | | | | |
| b (banks) | $R_h^b, D_h^b$ | | | | | |
| c (central bank) | | | | | | $D_g^c$ |
| g (government) | $A_h^g, R_h^g$ | $G_f^g$ | $R_n^g$ | $R_b^g$ | $R_c^g$ | $S_g^g$ |

worth (net worth = assets minus liabilities) and the definition of saving (saving = income minus expenditures) as accounting identities. A linkage identity will establish a definitional link between a balance sheet item and an income statement variable. Thus we shall define the investment of a sector to be equal to the change in its plant, equipment, and inventories during a given

FOOTNOTES TO TABLE 1

*a* Superscripts and subscripts on the symbols refer to the following sectors:

| h | households | b | banks |
|---|---|---|---|
| f | nonfinancial firms | c | central bank |
| n | nonbank financial intermediaries | g | government (the fiscal system) |

Capital letters refer to stock and flow accounts, as follows:

| $A$ | wages and salaries | $I$ | investment | $M_3$ | reserves |
|---|---|---|---|---|---|
| $B_1$ | bonds | $K$ | plant and equipment, | $M_4$ | gold certificates |
| $B_2$ | insurance claims | | inventories, property | $M_5$ | gold |
| $C$ | consumption | $L$ | loans | $R$ | interest |
| $D$ | dividends | $M_1$ | demand deposits, | $S$ | savings |
| $G$ | government spending | | notes and coins | $T$ | taxes |
| | | $M_2$ | savings deposits | | |

$W$   net worth (superscript and subscript identical)
     equities   (superscript and subscript different)

*b* As Table 1 is constructed, financial intermediaries, banks, and the central bank have zero net worth, and the net worth of nonfinancial businesses is interpreted as accumulated retained profit. We are thus treating equity securities as if they were bonds. Many subtle difficulties arise whenever macroeconomists need to discuss equity finance. We have not wanted to get involved in these difficulties, and recognize that our methods may contain errors. An alternative approach is to treat bonds as equities. This was done by Metzler [9] and subsequently by Horwich [10]. In their models, households hold money and/or equities, but never bonds.

*c* The term *aggregation* can be used in two ways. First, as noted previously, given a sectoral structure of an economy, it is possible to reduce (or increase) the number of variables in each sector's accounts by aggregating (or disaggregating) commodities. As indicated, this usage will not concern us. Second, given a set of variables in each sector's accounts, it is possible to reduce (or increase) the number of variables in an economic model by aggregating (or disaggregating) sectors. We are concerned with this latter meaning of *aggregation*. To avoid confusion, we shall, where possible, use the term *consolidation* (deconsolidation) in preference to *aggregation*.

---

period. And we shall define the saving of a sector during a given period to be equal to the change in its net worth over that period.

Each accounting identity and each linkage identity may be written as a linear function in some of the variables in the economy. A model of this economy must therefore take into consideration the linear dependencies introduced by the social accounting structure of the economy.

A standard notation is used, which may appear cumbersome at first, but which will be useful later on. Each symbol $V_j{}^i$ in Table 1 has both a superscript and a subscript. In a balance sheet $V_j{}^i$, $i \neq j$, refers to an *asset* of sector $j$ which is also a liability of sector $i$. No other sector has a direct claim on the asset in question, when $i = j$. In an income statement $V_j{}^i$, $i \neq j$, represents a

TABLE 2

BALANCE SHEET OF THE BANKING SECTOR

| | | | |
|---|---|---|---|
| $L_b^h$ | (loans to households) | $W_h^b$ | (bank equity held by households) |
| $B_{1b}^f$ | (business bonds) | $M_{2h}^b$ | (savings deposits held by households) |
| $L_b^f$ | (loans to businesses) | $M_{1h}^b$ | (demand deposits held by households) |
| $M_{1b}^c$ | (central bank notes) | $M_{1f}^b$ | (demand deposits held by businesses) |
| $M_{3b}^c$ | (reserves) | | |
| $M_{1b}^g$ | (government notes) | | |
| $B_{1b}^g$ | (government bonds) | | |

TABLE 3

INCOME STATEMENT OF THE HOUSEHOLD SECTOR

| | | | |
|---|---|---|---|
| $A_h^f$ | (wages from businesses) | $C_f^h$ | (consumption expenditures) |
| $R_h^f$ | (interest on business bonds) | $R_n^h$ | (interest on nonbank loans) |
| $D_h^f$ | (dividends on business equities) | $R_b^h$ | (interest on bank loans) |
| $R_h^n$ | (interest on savings deposits)[a] | $T_g^h$ | (taxes) |
| $D_h^n$ | (dividends on nonbank equities) | | |
| $R_h^b$ | (interest on savings deposits) | | |
| $D_h^b$ | (dividends on bank equities) | | |
| $A_h^g$ | (wages from government) | $S_h^h$ | (saving) |
| $R_h^g$ | (interest on government bonds) | | |

[a] Including payments on insurance policies.

payment by sector $i$ to sector $j$, and therefore a flow of goods or services from sector $j$ to sector $i$. $V_i^i$ (or $V_j^j$ for that matter) in an income statement is a form of investment (if it is viewed as an expenditure) or of saving (if it is viewed as an allocation of income) by sector $i$ (or sector $j$, as the case may be).

## II

A model of a 65-variable economy is bound to be messy. To simplify it, one could, of course, annihilate sectors by setting their assets and income equal to zero. But this form of simplification creates models which would be known, a priori, to differ from the economy we see around us, and invites the criticism that the models are irrelevant.

A second form of simplification would try to reduce the number of separate entries appearing in each sector's accounts, by "lumping" things together. This is what we did when we listed household consumption as a single entry in Table 1, even though households buy many kinds of goods. This lumping together of commodities is discussed in economic literature under the general heading of *aggregation*. We are not concerned with this subject.

Instead, we are concerned with simplification procedures which reduce the number of variables in a model by combining two or more sectors of the economy. Such combinations of sectors are called *consolidations*, and are the counterpart in social accounting of similar operations on the accounts of businesses. Consolidations simplify social accounts by suppressing information concerning the relations among the sectors being lumped together. We shall first discuss the simple technique of consolidation. Then we shall show that monetary economists have often failed to consider thoroughly the consequences of the consolidations which they have used.[5]

Our argument is simple: (i) writers may select any sectoral structure which is appropriate to the problem under study; (ii) they should, however, specify clearly the income and balance sheets of the sectors; (iii) if they have occasion to consolidate sectors for simplicity (or other reasons) they should follow normal accounting procedures. These "rules" are not based on elaborate methodological criteria, but are merely a plea for consistency and clarity. We shall discuss a number of cases violating the "rules." In one of them Patinkin consolidates the balance sheets of all sectors to obtain "total national assets," an argument of his demand function for goods. He fails, however, to consolidate sectoral income statements, and therefore fails to be consistent. In another case, Pesek and Saving try to talk about "the private sector," a consolidation of households, businesses, and banks. They also want to talk about deposits, which cannot appear on the "private sector" balance sheet (as we shall show). Their discussion, therefore, moves in a confusing way between the three-sector and the one-sector systems.

A consolidation transforms the social accounts of an economy having a given collection of sectors into a set of accounts of an economy having a smaller number of sectors. This transformation reduces the number of sectors by treating two or more sectors as if they were a single sector. Since transactions *inside* (among the members of) a sector are considered to involve accounting transfers rather than genuine acts of exchange, the consolidation reduces the number of kinds of transactions which can be observed and studied by a model.

Let us designate by $1, 2, \ldots, n$ the sectors of an economy, and by $[1, 2, \ldots, n]$ an economy consisting of these sectors. If sectors $i$ and $j$ are consolidated, a new sector $(i, j)$ is created. If sectors $i, j, k$ are consolidated, the sector $(i, j, k)$ is created. The operation of consolidation, designated Cons( ), is symmetric: $\text{Cons}(i, j) = \text{Cons}(j, i)$. It is also associative: $\text{Cons}(i, (j, k)) = \text{Cons}((i, j), k) = (i, j, k)$. Thus it does not matter in what order sectors are consolidated.

In the six-sector economy described by Table I, many consolidations of sectors are possible, and names can be given to many of the consolidations

---

[5] See footnote $c$ to Table 1.

which suggest contexts in which they might be discussed in economic literature. The sector $(b, c)$ is a "banking sector" combining the commercial banks and central bank. The sector $(h, f)$ is a "private nonfinancial" sector, $(n, b, c)$ a sector including banks and financial intermediaries, $(f, n, b)$ a "private business" sector, and so on.

Whenever the accounts of the economy $[1, 2, \ldots, n]$ are consolidated, a new structure $[a_1, a_2, \ldots, a_r]$ is defined. Each symbol $a_s$ stands for a consolidation of one or more sectors of $[1, 2, \ldots, n]$. Each of the original sectors $1, 2, \ldots, n$ is assigned to exactly one of the new sectors $a_1, a_2, \ldots, a_r$. Thus the new sectoral structure is associated with a partition of the sectors $1, 2, \ldots, n$, and there are as many consolidations of the original set of accounts as there are partitions of the original sectors. Some (though not all) of these partitions will be interesting to economists.

Each sector $1, 2, \ldots, n$ has a balance sheet and an income statement; these accounts can be summarized in a table having the general format of Table 1. Likewise, the consolidation having sectors $a_1, a_2, \ldots, a_r$ produces a new set of balance sheets and income statements derived from those of the original sectors. These, too, can be represented as in Table 1. The arithmetic of consolidation replaces entries $V_j^i$ with $i, j \in \{1, 2, \ldots, n\}$ by entries $V_{a_s}^{a_t}$ with $s, t \in \{1, 2, \ldots, r\}$. The rule used is a standard one in business and social accounting:

$$V_{a_s}^{a_t} = \sum_{i \in a_t} \sum_{j \in a_s} V_j^i.$$

Thus[6] if $V_j^i$ represents an asset of sector $j$ and a liability of sector $i$, then $V_j^i$ will be a component of $V_{a_s}^{a_t}$ whenever $i$ is consolidated into $a_t$ and $j$ is consolidated into a *different* sector $a_s$. But if sectors $i$ and $j$ are consolidated into a single sector, $V_j^i$ will disappear when the sectors are consolidated—the new sector owes $V_j^i$ to itself. Likewise if $V_j^i$ represents a payment by sector $i$ to sector $j$ for goods or services, and if $i$ and $j$ become parts of a new sector following a consolidation, then $V_j^i$ ceases to be an economic transaction and becomes a transfer within the (new) sector. Therefore $V_j^i$ will not appear in the accounts of the consolidated sector.

For example, if nonfinancial businesses and households are consolidated, wage payments by businesses and purchases of consumer goods will "disappear" from the social accounting system. If non-financial businesses and commercial banks are consolidated, business loans by banks and business bank deposits will "disappear" from the social accounts. We shall discuss this matter at greater length later. For the present, we note merely that con-

---

[6] We use $V$ to designate either the name of an account or the numerical value of the account. This procedure simplifies notation, and should not lead to confusion.

solidation of sectors reduces the number of sectors. It also reduces the number of variables in two ways: (a) some variables are added up, and only their sum remains in the consolidated account; (b) some variables disappear, because they become internal bookkeeping concerns of a sector, rather than representations of economic exchanges.

The six-sector economy [h, f, n, b, c, g] could be consolidated in many ways. Some of these would change the order of the six symbols. Thus [(h, c), f, n, b, g] is a mathematically possible consolidation of the household sector and the central bank. We have found no problem in which this consolidation would have economic meaning. Indeed, we think that all the economic structures which are consolidations of [h, f, n, b, c, g], and which have intuitive economic content, can be written down without changing the order of the six symbols. All the order-preserving consolidations of this six-sector economy are given in column 1 of Table 4.[7]

Table 4 in its entirety is concerned with showing the gain in simplicity which is attained by consolidations. Suppose that a model involving $n$ variables requires $n$ linearly independent equations. If the economist is to find a unique solution for the variables in the model or to derive a complete comparative statics analysis. Then column 5 of Table 4 will tell the economist the value of $n$ for a particular consolidation listed in column 1. This value is equal to 65 (which is the number of variables in the basic six-sector structure) minus the number of variables that disappear under the consolidation in question (column 4).

The theorist will not be unrestricted in his selection of the $n$ linearly independent equations. (a) For each sector there is an income statement and a balance sheet, each of which can be written as a linear equation (an identity). The number of such equations is given in column 6 of Table 4. (b) For certain sectors there will be one or more linkages between the balance sheet and the income statement, corresponding to the definitions of saving and investment. Column 7 of Table 4 gives the number of such linkage identities for the various consolidations listed in column 1.

Given the number of variables and the number of restrictions imposed by the restrictions (a) and (b), it is then possible to determine by subtraction the number of behavioral statements which must be introduced in order to eliminate the remaining degrees of freedom in the model and to obtain a unique solution (column 9 of Table 4).

[7] In this paragraph, and in much of the following text, commas appear between symbols designating sectors [3.g. in (h, c)]. Superscripts and subscripts will be written without commas [e.g., in $K_{cg}^{cg}$ in a balance sheet of the "Public Sector" (c, g) given below]. In our tables, moreover, commas are also omitted, to save space. The presence or absence of commas in structural specifications is determined solely by aesthetic considerations and has no substantive importance.

TABLE 4

CONSOLIDATIONS OF ADJACENT SECTORS OF THE ECONOMY [h, f, n, b, c, g]

| Consolidation | Number of variables | | | | Composition of accompanying models | | | |
|---|---|---|---|---|---|---|---|---|
| | Number of variables that disappear | | | Number of variables that remain | Number of accounting identities | Number of linkage identities | Total number of identities | Number of behavioral hypotheses needed |
| No. designation | Through elimination | Through combination | Total | | | | | |
| (1) | (2) | (3) | (4) | (5) | (6) | (7) | (8) | (9) |
| 1 [hfnbcg] | 0 | 0 | 0 | 65 | 12 | 4 | 16 | 49 |
| 2 [(hf)nbcg] | 6 | 12 | 18 | 47 | 10 | 3 | 13 | 34 |
| 3 [h(fn)bcg] | 4 | 5 | 9 | 56 | 10 | 4 | 14 | 42 |
| 4 [hf(nb)cg] | 0 | 13 | 13 | 52 | 10 | 4 | 14 | 38 |
| 5 [hfn(bc)g] | 2 | 5 | 7 | 58 | 10 | 4 | 14 | 44 |
| 6 [hfnb(cg)] | 7 | 4 | 11 | 54 | 10 | 4 | 14 | 40 |
| 7 [(hfn)bcg] | 17 | 13 | 30 | 35 | 8 | 3 | 11 | 24 |
| 8 [h(fnb)cg] | 8 | 15 | 23 | 42 | 8 | 4 | 12 | 30 |
| 9 [hf(nbc)g] | 3 | 17 | 20 | 45 | 8 | 4 | 12 | 33 |
| 10 [hfn(bcg)] | 12 | 6 | 18 | 47 | 8 | 4 | 12 | 35 |
| 11 [(hfnb)cg] | 28 | 11 | 39 | 26 | 6 | 3 | 9 | 17 |
| 12 [h(fnbc)g] | 12 | 17 | 29 | 36 | 6 | 4 | 10 | 26 |
| 13 [hf(nbcg)] | 16 | 14 | 30 | 35 | 6 | 4 | 10 | 25 |
| 14 [(hfnbc)g] | 33 | 14 | 47 | 18 | 4 | 3 | 7 | 11 |
| 15 [h(fnbcg)] | 28 | 17 | 45 | 20 | 4 | 3 | 7 | 13 |

| | | | | | | | | |
|---|---|---|---|---|---|---|---|---|
| 16 [(hfnbcg)] | 54 | 6 | 60 | 5 | 2 | 2 | 4 | 1 |
| 17 [(hf)(nbc)g] | 9 | 29 | 38 | 27 | 6 | 3 | 9 | 18 |
| 18 [(hf)n(bcg)] | 18 | 18 | 36 | 29 | 6 | 3 | 9 | 20 |
| 19 [h(fn)(bcg)] | 16 | 11 | 27 | 38 | 6 | 4 | 10 | 28 |
| 20 [(hfn)(bc)g] | 19 | 18 | 37 | 28 | 6 | 3 | 9 | 19 |
| 21 [(hfn)b(cg)] | 24 | 17 | 41 | 24 | 6 | 3 | 9 | 15 |
| 22 [h(fnb)(cg)] | 15 | 19 | 34 | 31 | 4 | 4 | 10 | 21 |
| 23 [(hf)(nbcg)] | 22 | 26 | 48 | 17 | 4 | 3 | 7 | 10 |
| 24 [(hfnb)(cg)] | 35 | 15 | 50 | 15 | 8 | 3 | 7 | 8 |
| 25 [(hf)(nb)cg] | 6 | 25 | 31 | 34 | 8 | 3 | 11 | 23 |
| 26 [(hf)nb(cg)] | 13 | 16 | 29 | 36 | 8 | 3 | 11 | 25 |
| 27 [hf(nb)(cg)] | 7 | 17 | 24 | 41 | 8 | 4 | 12 | 29 |
| 28 [h(fn)(bc)g] | 6 | 10 | 16 | 49 | 8 | 4 | 12 | 37 |
| 29 [(hf)n(bc)g] | 13 | 29 | 42 | 23 | 8 | 3 | 11 | 12 |
| 30 [h(fn)b(cg)] | 8 | 17 | 25 | 40 | 8 | 3 | 11 | 29 |
| 31 [(hf)(nb)(cg)] | 11 | 9 | 20 | 45 | 6 | 4 | 10 | 35 |
| 32 [(hfn)(bcg)] | 29 | 19 | 48 | 17 | 4 | 3 | 7 | 10 |

We may illustrate the reasoning underlying Table 4 by an example. It is chosen because it involves a two-sector model with relatively few variables. The more interesting cases are also more detailed and would require correspondingly more space.

Line 24 of Table 4 gives the consolidation [(h, f, n, b), (c, g)], which contains a private sector (h, f, n, b) and a public sector (c, g). Column 2 indicates that 35 variables are lost when the basic six-sector economy [h, f, n, b, c, g] is reduced to the consolidation [(h, f, n, b), (c, g)] through a process of elimination. One of these 35 variables, for example, is central bank holdings of government bonds ($B_{1c}^{g}$). Column 3 tells us that the number of variables is further reduced by 15 through the process of combination, which is implicit in the consolidation operation. For instance, $W_{h}^{h} + W_{f}^{f} = W_{hfnb}^{hfnb}$ (total net worth of the private sector hfnb), and $M_{1h}^{c} + M_{1h}^{g} + M_{1f}^{c} + M_{1f}^{g} + M_{1n}^{c} + M_{1n}^{g} + M_{1b}^{c} + M_{1b}^{g} = M_{1hfnb}^{cg}$ (the holdings of currency of the private sector hfnb). Only 15 variables remain under consolidation [(h, f, n, b), (c, g)]. This can be read in column 5. We shall list these 15 variables in the appropriate T accounts of the sectors (h, f, n, b) and (c, g) (Table 5).

It is obvious that from these four accounts we can obtain four accounting identities (column 6). Column 7 then indicates that the structure [(h, f, n, b), (c, g)] involves 3 linkage identities. They are

(i) $\quad S_{hfnb}^{hfnb} = \Delta W_{hfnb}^{hfnb}$ $\quad$ (saving of the private sector hfnb),

(ii) $\quad S_{cg}^{cg} = \Delta W_{cg}^{cg}$ $\quad$ (saving of the public sector cg), and

(iii) $\quad I_{hfnb}^{hfnb} = \Delta K_{hfnb}^{hfnb}$ $\quad$ (investment by the private sector hfnb).

TABLE 5

THE CONSOLIDATED ECONOMY [(h, f, n, b), (cg)]

**The Private Sector (h, f, n, b)**

| Balance Sheet | | | Income statement | |
|---|---|---|---|---|
| $M_{1hfnb}^{cg}$ (currency) | | | $A_{hfnb}^{cg}$ (wages | $T_{cg}^{hfnb}$ (taxes) |
| $B_{1hfnb}^{cg}$ (bonds) | | | $R_{hfnb}^{cg}$ (interest) | |
| $K_{hfnb}^{hfnb}$ (plant) | | | $I_{hfnb}^{hfnb}$ (investment) | |
| $M_{3hfnb}^{cg}$ (central bank reserves) | $W_{hfnb}^{hfnb}$ (net worth) | | $G_{hfnb}^{cg}$ (spending) | $S_{hfnb}^{hfnb}$ (saving) |

**The Private Sector (c, g)**

| Balance sheet | | | Income statement | |
|---|---|---|---|---|
| $M_{5cg}^{cg}$ (gold stock) | $M_{1hfnb}^{cg}$ (currency) | $T_{cg}^{hfnb}$ (taxes) | $A_{hfnb}^{cg}$ (wages) | |
| $K_{cg}^{cg}$ (property) | $M_{3hfnb}^{cg}$ (reserves) | | $R_{hfnb}^{cg}$ (interest) | |
| | $B_{1hfnb}^{cg}$ (bonds) | | $G_{hfnb}^{cg}$ (spending) | |
| | $W_{cg}^{cg}$ (net worth) | | $S_{cg}^{cg}$ (saving) | |

In all there are seven identities (column 8). Since there are 15 variables in this structure, the theorist must add eight more equations (column 9) to obtain a unique solution to his model. He will do so by making appropriate behavioral hypotheses.

Since the process of consolidation involves a linear transformation from a space of a certain dimension into a space of smaller dimension, there is no unique way to "deconsolidate" a given economy. Theorists prefer to start with a simple, and therefore highly consolidated model, and then to complicate it by considering its analogs in a less aggregated world. Patinkin, for instance, first talks about the economy [h, f, (n, b, c, g)] [4, p. 102] and later considers the economy [(h, f), (n, b, c, g)] [4, pp. 103–104]. Gurley and Shaw start from a three-sector economy [h, f, (n, b, c, g)] in chapter 2 [2, pp. 13–17, 57], give a four sector economy [h, f, n, (b, c, g)] in chapter 6 [2, pp. 192–193], and a five-sector economy [h, f, n, b, (c, g)] in chapter 7 [2, pp. 253, 257]. Pesek and Saving discuss a two-sector economy [(h, f, n, b), (c, g)] [3, p. 80] and then a three-sector economy [(h, f), (n, b), (c, g)] [3, pp. 80–94, 148–158]. The transition from one discussion to the next, in any of these works, would have been impossible if the authors had not initially constructed a "less consolidated system" such as we provided in Table 1.

The general problem discussed by monetary theorists concerns the connection between money (a collection of stocks) and income/output (a collection of flows). The two are linked by hypotheses which relate the demand for output to the stock of money (as in the quantity theory) or which relate the demand for money to the rate of output (as in the transactions motive). It has been recognized only tangentially that both the definition of money and the definition of the national product are materially affected by the degree of consolidation of the system.

Table 6 gives the definitions of the word *money* which are appropriate to Table 1 and to nine different consolidations of the six-sector model. (For later purposes, authors identified with each consolidation are noted.) The notation follows the conventions given previously. Table 6 elaborates a point made by Gurley and Shaw [2, pp. 135–140], who contrast the "net money" of a consolidated economy with the "gross money" of (say) the six-sector model. Their specific concern is with the effect of the consolidations (c, g) and (n, b, c, g) on the visible (nonconsolidated) stock of money. The former consolidation causes government deposits in the central bank and gold certificates to disappear. In an economy where open market operations are the main instruments of central bank policy, this consolidation may be an inconvenience, for it is no longer easy to distinguish between central bank sales of government securities and treasury borrowing to cover current spending. But this inconvenience does not extend to the concept of money per se. The second consolidation causes bank reserves and the cash assets of financial intermediaries to disappear. In this consolidation it is no longer possible to

TABLE 6

THE DEFINITIONS OF MONEY ASSOCIATED WITH VARIOUS CONSOLIDATIONS

| Sectors holding money | (line 16)[a] [(hfnbcg)] | Consolidation | | | |
|---|---|---|---|---|---|
| | | Leijonhufvud (line 15) [h(fnbcg)] | Patinkin–Gurley-S (line 13) [hf(nbcg)] | Gurley-Shaw (line 10) [hfn(bcg)] | Gurley-Shaw (line 6) [hfnb(cg)] |
| h | | $M_{1h}^{fnbcg} + M_{2h}^{fnbcg}$ | $M_{1h}^{nbcg} + M_{2h}^{nbcg}$ | $M_{1h}^{bcg} + M_{2h}^{bcg} + M_{2h}^{n}$ | $M_{2h}^{n} + M_{1h}^{b} + M_{2h}^{b} + M_{1h}^{cg}$ |
| f | | | $M_{1f}^{nbcg}$ | $M_{1f}^{bcg}$ | $M_{1f}^{b} + M_{1f}^{cg}$ |
| n | | | | $M_{1n}^{bcg}$ | $M_{1f}^{cg}$ |
| b | | | | | $M_{1b}^{cg} + M_{3b}^{cg}$ |
| c | | | | | |
| g | | | | | |
| cg | | | | | $M_{5cg}^{cg}$ |
| bcg | | | | $M_{5bcg}^{bcg}$ | |
| nbcg | | | $M_{5nbcg}^{nbcg}$ | | |
| fnbcg | | $M_{5fnbcg}^{fnbcg}$ | | | |
| hfnbcg | $M_{5hfnbcg}^{hfnbcg}$ | | | | |
| hf | | | | | |
| hfn | | | | | |
| hfnb | | | | | |
| nb | | | | | |

[a] The line numbers refer to lines in Table 4.

[b] Friedman and Schwartz [11, pp. 3–4, 776–780] refer to the sectors (h, f, n), b, and (cg) as respectively the "public," "banks," and the "monetary authorities." The distinction among these three sectors is based upon the roles that the sectors play as issuers of claims. The sector (cg) includes the Federal Reserve System as well as the Treasury (call this sub-sector $g_1$). But all local and state governments, federal government corporations, federal

| | | Consolidation | | |
|---|---|---|---|---|
| (line 1) [hfnbcg] | Patinkin (line 23) [(hf)(nbcg)] | Pesek–Saving (line 31) [(hf)(nb)(cg)] | Pesek–Saving (line 24) [(hfnb)(cg)] | Friedman[b] (line 21) [(hfn)b(cg)] |
| $M_{1h}^b + M_{1h}^c + M_{1h}^g + M_{2h}^n + M_{2h}^b$ | | | | |
| $M_{1f}^b + M_{1f}^c + M_{1f}^g$ | | | | |
| $M_{1n}^c + M_{1n}^g$ | | | | |
| $M_{3b}^c + M_{1b}^c + M_{1b}^g$ | | | | $M_{1b}^{cg} + M_{3b}^{cg}$ |
| $M_{1c}^g + M_{4c}^g$ | | | | |
| $M_{1g}^c + M_{5g}^c$ | | | | |
| | | $M_{5cg}^{cg}$ | $M_{5cg}^{cg}$ | $M_{5cg}^{cg}$ |
| | $M_{5nbcg}^{nbcg}$ | | | |
| | $M_{1hf}^{nbcg} + M_{2hf}^{nbcg}$ | $M_{1hf}^{cg} + M_{2hf}^{nb} + M_{1hf}^{nb}$ | | |
| | | | | $M_{1hfn}^{cg} + M_{1hfn}^b + M_{2hfn}^b$ |
| | | | $M_{1hfnb}^{cg} + M_{2hfnb}^{cg}$ | |
| | | $M_{1nb}^{cg} + M_{3nb}^{cg}$ | | |

credit agencies, foreign banks, nonbank foreigners, and foreign monetary authorities (let these be $g_2$) are included as part of the "public." A peculiarity of the consolidation [(h, f, n, $g_1$) b, (c, $g_2$)] used by Friedman and Schwartz is that certain payments among government agencies, usually considered transfers, now appear as payments between "the monetary authorities" and "the public"; while other payments by and to certain government agencies now disappear as transfers among "the public."

observe interactions among the commercial banks, the financial intermediaries, and the central bank. But if one considers that most interesting
monetary phenomena have to do with the cash assets of households and nonfinancial businesses, that objection will not be compelling.

In contrast, the consolidation [(h, f, n, b), (c, g)] used by Pesek and Saving
(second column from right in Table 6) completely eliminates all deposits of
households and businesses. The only "net money" in this case consists of the
liabilities of the central bank (bank reserves and the note issue). This consolidation eliminates most of what writers talk about when they speak of either the
quantity theory or the transactions motive, for these relate mainly to the cash
held by households and businesses. In a developed economy, this cash consists mainly of deposits.

The gross national product is also materially affected by the degree of
aggregation of the model, as Table 7 shows. The gross national product is
defined as sales of final output to the final consumers. Sales within a sector
are counted as intermediate output or as transfer payments. Consequently, if
the household and business sectors are consolidated, then consumption
(goods purchased from businesses by households) and personal income
earned by households in the business sector must vanish from the national
income and product, respectively. This circumstance seems not to have been
noticed either by Patinkin[8] or by Pesek and Saving.

TABLE 7

THE DEFINITIONS OF GROSS NATIONAL PRODUCT ASSOCIATED WITH
VARIOUS CONSOLIDATIONS

| Consolidation | Reference | Gross national product | | |
|---|---|---|---|---|
| [hfnbcg] | Starting point | $C_f^h$ | $+ I_f^f$ | $+ G_f^g$ |
| [hf(nbcg)] | Gurley–Shaw I | $C_f^h$ | $+ I_f^f$ | $+ G_f^{nbcg}$ |
| [hfn(bcg)] | Gurley–Shaw II | $C_f^h$ | $+ I_f^f$ | $+ G_f^{bcg}$ |
| [hfnb(cg)] | Gurley–Shaw III | $C_f^h$ | $+ I_f^f$ | $+ G_f^{cg}$ |
| [hf(nbcg)] | Patinkin I | $C_f^h$ | $+ I_f^f$ | $+ G_f^{nbcg}$ |
| [(hf)(nbcg)] | Patinkin II | | $I_{hf}^{hf}$ | $+ G_{hf}^{nbcg}$ |
| [(hfnb)(cg)] | Pesek–Saving I | | $I_{hfnb}^{hfnb}$ | $+ G_{hfnb}^{cg}$ |
| [(hf)(nb)(cg)] | Pesek–Saving II | | $I_{hf}^{hf}$ | $+ G_{hf}^{cg}$ |
| [h(fnbcg)] | Leijonhufvud | | $C_{fnbcg}^h$ | $+ I_{fnbcg}^{fnbcg}$ |

[8] When Patinkin consolidates the household and business sectors to determine the net
wealth of the private sector (which is important to the real balance effect), he simultaneously
consolidates out consumer expenditures (on which changes in real balances are said to have
an effect). In short, the real balance effect would apply to investment expenditures but not
to consumer expenditures. Neither would it apply to the demand for new business bonds,
since there would be government bonds only.

Symbols involving $C$, $I$, and $G$ appear with various superscripts and subscripts in Table 7. These correspond to the intuitive notions of consumption, investment, and government spending. But the exact empirical counterpart of one of these symbols in a particular model depends on the sectoral structure being used. Suppose, for instance, that financial intermediaries, or banks, or the central bank make purchases from nonfinancial businesses. Then $G_f^g$ would differ from $G_f^{cg}$, and these would differ from $G_f^{bcg}$ and from $G_f^{nbcg}$. The structure of accounts in Table 1 is not the only one which could be imagined and it is not necessarily to be defended on empirical grounds.

Thus, if an economist is theorizing on the basis of the consolidation [(h, f), (n, b, c, g)], the money stock includes deposits of households and businesses, but the national income/product includes neither personal consumption nor personal income earned in nonfinancial businesses. If he is theorizing on the basis of the consolidation [(h, f, n, b), (c, g)], the national income/product consists of investment and government spending, more or less as usually defined, while money consists of central bank liabilities. The most aggregated economy which retains personal consumption as part of the national product is Leijonhufvud's consolidation, [h, (f, n, b, c, g)], which is discussed in Section III. In this economy, however, government purchases of goods have vanished.

Indeed, by treating the banks as a single sector in Table 1, a class of deposits was eliminated: interbank. In certain kinds of questions, interbank deposits may be quite important. The Federal Funds market, for instance, is a market which cannot be analyzed unless a system of accounting *finer* than that of Table 1 is used. Interbank deposits are not important in every monetary problem, but if they are important in some problems, it would be necessary to have an accounting system fine enough to retain them.

The literature recognizes that the money stock is sensitive to the degree of consolidation in the model. Indeed, Gurley and Shaw contrast " gross " and " net " money [2, pp. 135–140] as defined in their two models. We would go further and point out that for each possible consolidation there is exactly one appropriate definition of the money stock.

It is not sufficient to note that the number of variables (and/or their meaning) differ from consolidation to consolidation. Behavioral hypotheses must be appropriate to a particular consolidation. The reason is that sectors are distinguished on the basis of individual behavior: whereas the behavior of units within a sector is thought to be similar, that of units belonging to different sectors is thought to be dissimilar. We can illustrate this problem by means of a hypothesis relating $Y$ (national product) and $M$ (the quantity of money). We write this hypothesis in the form $F(Y, M) = 0$. If this hypothesis holds, then there are two possible implicit functional relations. One of these is $Y = G(M)$, which links the aggregate demand for goods to the stock of money, as in Keynes' work in the 1920's. The other is $M = H(Y)$, which links the demand for money to the rate of current production, as in Keynes' work on the "transactions motive" in the 1930's. Either of these hypotheses is compatible with the hypothesis $F(Y, M) = 0$.

Suppose that the economy can be represented by an $n$-sector structure, and that this structure is then consolidated to $m$ sectors, with $m < n$. In each representation there will be suitable definitions of $Y$ and of $M$. We designate these by $Y_n$, $Y_m$, $M_n$, and $M_m$. We know that $Y_n \geqq Y_m$ and $M_n \geqq M_m$, since consolidation may cause some components of $Y_n$ and $M_n$ to disappear.

The monetary theorist may wish the hypothesis $F$ (or something like it) to appear in both the $n$-sector and the $m$-sector models. The functions $F_n$ and $F_m$ will not necessarily be the same.

Consider the two consolidations [(h, f), (n, b, c, g)] and [h, f, (n, b, c, g)]. In both economies, "money" consists of the currency and deposits held by households and nonfinancial businesses, plus gold and foreign exchange held by the banking system. But the national products are quite different. In the three-sector economy [h, f, (n, b, c, g)], consumption by households is a part of final demand. In the two-sector economy [(h, f), (n, b, c, g)], such consumption is internal to the "nonfinancial sector" (h, f) and is not part of final demand. (This case compares the two structures used by Patinkin.)

Consequently, a model of the three-sector economy includes the function $F_3(Y_3, M_3) = 0$, and a model of the two-sector economy includes the function $F_2(Y_2, M_2) = 0$. $M_3 = M_2$, but $Y_3 \neq Y_2$. Thus in general there is no function $F$ such that $F(Y_3, M_3) = F(Y_2, M_2) = 0$. And the process of consolidation would therefore mean that the forms of the function $Y = G(M)$ or of the function $M = H(Y)$ would have to be different in the two models.

Patinkin[9] provides a more subtle example in which two different consolidations appear in a single discussion. His three-sector model defines consumption and investment functions, which depend on "income" ($Y = C + I + G$) and the real balances (respectively) of the household and business sectors. A few pages later, he defines an "expenditure function" for a consolidated household-and-business sector. This function also depends on "income" and "real balances." Patinkin recognizes that the latter must be redefined. He continues, however, to use the symbol $Y$ for income, and treats it as if it were the same variable as in his first case. For this discussion to be correct, one would have to be able to consolidate the balance sheets of the household and business sectors without simultaneously consolidating the corresponding income statements. We assert that "income" should rather be defined as in Table 7 (under "Patinkin II").

Theorists cannot assume that a functional relation which holds among the

---

[9] Patinkin [4, p. 103; 1, pp. 200, 207, 285, 288]. See also Johnson [12].

variables appearing in one consolidation of an economy will also hold among correspondingly named variables in another consolidation of the same economy. It is clearly the theorist's privilege to select the consolidation he considers most convenient to study his problem, and the behavioral hypothesis he considers most interesting. However, the behavioral hypothesis must be appropriate to the selected consolidation. This is another way of saying that the theorist must select a consolidation which allows him to deal with the kind of behavior about which he wants to say something.

## III

We shall now consider three ways in which macroeconomists have tried to reduce complicated structures to simple ones. First, we consider Leijonhufvud, who has argued that Keynes' and Keynesian macroeconomic models involve only five variables, and has discussed systems of those five variables. Next, we consider the one-sector economy obtained by total consolidation of our initial six-sector model. We show that both "income" and "money" in this model must be defined in a way which greatly limits their relevance to the behavior which monetary theorists consider important. Finally, we consider the controversy between Patinkin and Pesek and Saving over proposed ways to retain a meaningful money account in a one-sector model, and conclude that while the account in question may be related to the stock of money, it is in general not equal to it.

Generally, the more variables in a model, the harder it is to make the model work nicely. The entire purpose of macroeconomics is to reduce an inordinately complicated world to manageable dimensions. Particularly if one is a monetarist, it seems important to develop an analysis which will permit simple explanations of what is taken to be something complex. Table 1 will therefore seem inordinately complicated to many macroeconomists, and it is natural to ask how simple a model can be constructed from the six-sector economy of Table 1.

Leijonhufvud [6, pp. 130–136], for example, claims that Keynesian models deal at most with five variables: labor services, consumer goods, capital goods, government debt, and money. We shall now see whether it is possible to select a consolidation of the six-sector economy [h, f, n, b, c, g] in such a way as to reduce it to a system with these five variables.

Any consolidation which is to retain consumer goods must have at least two sectors. From Table 4, we see that there are two three-sector consolidations in which households and (nonfinancial) businesses are in distinct sectors. These are [h, (f, n), (b, c, g)] with 38 variables; and [h, (f, n, b), (c, g)] with 31 variables. Clearly these consolidations have so many variables that if Leijonhufvud's reasoning were correct, he would have to use one commodity name to describe many different variables. We shall illustrate this proposition by considering a simpler consolidation, with only two sectors. This is [h, (f, n, b, c, g)] with "only" 20 variables. It is the only two-sector consolidation which retains consumer goods.

We shall proceed by reference to Table 8, which presents the social accounts of the consolidation under study according to the rules of Table 1. Wherever we list an account, we shall put next to the symbol designating it that commodity name from Leijonhufvud's list which seems best to fit it. By our choice of consolidations of sectors, we will make Leijonhufvud's defense against us as strong, and our criticism of it as weak as the rules of accounting permit.

The compression of 20 distinct variables into five commodity designations carried out in Table 8 takes several distinct forms. First, money must be listed as one variable, even though it is held separately by both sectors. Second, government debt must either be treated as "net" (after subtraction of household sector debts), or else as existing in positive and negative accounts. Third, interest payments would have to be regarded as a flow of government debt instruments (distinct from money), since interest is not listed among the commodities. Fourth, taxes must be considered to be negative labor services. Fifth, no distinction can be made between the stock of capital goods and the change in this stock (investment). Finally, there is no word which corresponds either to accumulated net worth, or to its change (saving). For operational purposes, it would be necessary to discard Leijonhufvud's terminology, if we are to analyze the workings of even a highly consolidated representation of a developed economy. The five-commodity classification which he presents is far too coarse to be usable. It is curious that we should reach this result, for Leijonhufvud cites with apparent approval [6, pp. 143–147] Tobin's paper [7] urging that macroeconomic and monetary models present explicit income and balance sheet accounts.

The second approach to constructing very simple models is the one-sector model,[10] which reduces the number of variables in the system as much as possible. It is impossible to reduce the six-sector economy of Table 1 any further than the one-sector model. A one-sector economy in the context of this chapter is the economy [(h, f, n, b, c, g)]. If it is isolated, so that it has no balance of payments, it can be represented by the set of accounts given in

[10] With the one-sector model we mean [(h, f, n, b, c, g)], because we started out with a six-sector model [h, f, n, b, c, g]. If we started out with a four-sector economy [h, f, n, b], then the one-sector model would have been [(h, f, n, b)]. Pesek and Saving [3, pp. 79–96] seem at times to deal with the latter one-sector model. However, they may have had a six-sector model in the back of their minds, and in that case they actually deal with the two-sector economy [(h, f, n, b), (c, g)]. Pesek and Saving are interested in the net wealth of the economy (or sector) [(h, f, n, b)]. But the one-sector economy [(h, f, n, b, c, g)] also has a net wealth. Just as gross (net) money is a relative concept, so is "net wealth."

TABLE 8

A List of Variables Reflecting the Asset–Debt Structure and the Income–Expenditure Structure of the Two-Sector Economy [h, (f, n, b, c, g)], together with the Corresponding Leijonhufvud Commodity Names

(a)  The Asset–Debt Structure

Owed to

| Owed by | Sector h | | Sector (f, n, b, c, g) | |
|---|---|---|---|---|
| | Our notation | Leijonhufvud's terminology | Our notation | Leijonhufvud's terminology |
| Sector h | $K_h^h$ $W_h^h$ | Capital goods ? | $L_{fnbcg}^h$ | Negative government debt |
| Sector (f, n, b, c, g) | $M_{1h}^{fnbcg}$ $M_{2h}^{fnbcg}$ $B_{1h}^{fnbcg}$ $B_{2h}^{fnbcg}$ $W_h^{fnbcg}$ | Money Positive government debt | $M_{5fnbcg}^{fnbcg}$ $K_{fnbcg}^{fnbcg}$ $W_{fnbcg}^{fnbcg}$ | Money Capital ? |

(b)  The Income–Expenditure Structure

Paid to

| Paid by | Sector h | | Sector (f, n, b, c, g) | |
|---|---|---|---|---|
| | Our notation | Leijonhufvud's terminology | Our notation | Leijonhufvud's terminology |
| Sector h | $S_h^h$ | ? | $R_{fnbcg}^h$ $C_{fnbcg}^h$ $T_{fnbcg}^h$ | Interest on negative government debt? Consumption goods Negative labor services? |
| Sector (f, n, b, c, g) | $R_h^{fnbcg}$ $D_h^{fnbcg}$ $A_h^{fnbcg}$ | Interest on positive government debt? Labor services | $I_{fnbcg}^{fnbcg}$ $S_{fnbcg}^{fnbcg}$ | Capital goods ? |

Table 9 (subscripts and superscripts having been dropped). Consumption disappears from view as a result of the consolidation of households and businesses into a single sector. Output is the sum of the investment of the various sectors. Income is the sum of their saving. Money consists of gold, foreign exchange (by hypothesis) being nonexistent.

TABLE 9

A ONE-SECTOR ECONOMY

| Balance Sheet | | Income statement | |
|---|---|---|---|
| Money  $M$  Capital  $K$ | Net worth  $W$ | Investment (output)  $I$ | Saving (income)  $S$ |

In this economy, if the usual linkage statements, $K = K_0 + I$ and $W = W_0 + S$, both hold, the stock of money must be fixed. This is because

$$W_0 + S = K_0 + I + M_0 + \Delta M$$
$$W_0 = K_0 + M_0$$
$$S = I$$
$$K_0 + M_0 + S = K_0 + M_0 + S + \Delta M$$
$$0 = \Delta M.$$

In this economy, output is the sum of the various kinds of investment. It would be possible to designate by the symbol $C$ some part of it—say investment by households. It would even be possible to assume that $C$ was some constant fraction of total output. This assumption, however, would mean a formal but not a substantive resemblance between this economy and the Keynesian hypothesis, $C = aY + b$, for Keynes was talking about consumption (as usually defined), not about a portion of investment.[11]

In this economy, it is possible for there to be a monetary theory. This theory might relate to portfolio analysis, if there was a connection between the desired stocks of money and of capital.[12] It might relate to the quantity theory if there was a connection between the stock of money and the demand

[11] Friedman [13, pp. 217–218] blurs the distinction between the household and business sectors (and the corresponding distinction between consumption and investment expenditures) by making the alternative distinction of spending conditional (C) on income versus spending independent (I) of income.

[12] Tobin has discussed a money versus capital model [7, pp. 31–34; 14]. But in these papers money is government debt, whereas in the one-sector model [(h, f, n, b, c, g)] money is gold (and perhaps foreign exchange). The money versus equities model of Metzler [9] requires a less consolidated structure, in which securities do not cancel out.

for current output. In any case, plant and output would change in response to changes in the appropriate behavioral function.

The trouble with such a monetary theory, applied to a developed economy, is this: gold is typically the property of the central bank, while other stocks and flows in the system are associated with other sectors of the economy. One can imagine the central bank influencing investment in response to its holdings of gold (and foreign exchange), but it is not easy to see why the demand for or the supply of investment goods should be influenced by the central bank's reserve position. Economists think they know enough about central banking to know that whatever may be the connection between central bank operations and the rate of investment, the mechanism involves many variables (including those of the securities markets) which simply do not appear in the one-sector model. Within the framework set forth here, there is no convincing way to link "money" and "output."

The one-sector model cannot cope with financial assets. These are owed by members of one sector to members of other sectors, and must all be "consolidated out" in an isolated one-sector economy. If the economy is not isolated, the system becomes a little more complicated. A foreign sector must be introduced. We designate it by superscripts and subscripts $\varphi$. (see Table 10.)

TABLE 10

A ONE-SECTOR ECONOMY WITH TRADE

| Balance sheet | | | | Income statement | | | |
|---|---|---|---|---|---|---|---|
| Money | $M$ | Bonds | $B_\varphi$ | Investment | $I$ | Saving | $S$ |
| Capital | $K$ | Net worth | $W$ | Exports | $Z^\varphi$ | Imports | $Z_\varphi$ |
| Bonds | $B^\varphi$ | | | | | | |

There are now foreign assets ($B^\varphi$), debts to foreigners ($B_\varphi$), and foreign trade. In this case, if one adds the two conditions, $K = K_0 + I$, $W = W_0 + S$, one can deduce the balance of payments:

$$\Delta M + \Delta B^\varphi + Z_\varphi = \Delta B_\varphi + Z^\varphi$$

and the amount of money can change. It would be plausible that exports and debts to foreigners be exogenous. Then four behavioral statements would be needed to close the model.

Since the model now includes money, capital goods, financial assets, and commodities, it comes close to meeting Leijonhufvud's specifications, and it is also much simpler than the two-sector model presented in Table 8. The resemblance is due to the fact that this model is now a two-sector model [(h, f, n, b, c, g), $\varphi$], and it is more superficial than real. The "money" is gold and foreign exchange, the "securities" are all owed by or to foreigners, the "goods" are imports or exports or investment goods. The phenomena accounted for by the one-sector model are thus fundamentally part of the international economy, most domestic matters having been consolidated away.

Writers like Patinkin and Pesek and Saving have paid little attention to the impact of consolidation on the national product, but they have recognized the impact on the money stock. Pesek and Saving have attempted to specify an economy in such a way that deposits and currency (or a quantity equal to deposits and currency) remains, even in the one-sector economy. There is a controversy about how (and whether) such a specification is to be accomplished.

Pesek and Saving [3, pp. 79–96] argue that "bank money" should really be viewed as part of the net worth of the private sector (h, f, n, b) in the consolidation [(h, f, n, b), (c, g)]. They set up an initial economy [(h, f), (n, b), (c, g)] in which "bank money" is an asset of (h, f) and part of the net worth of (n, b)—not a liability, as elementary textbooks tell us. Subsequent consolidation, then, leads to an economy [(h, f, n, b), (c, g)] in which money remains as an asset of (h, f, n, b), and in which the net worth of (h, f, n, b) has been correspondingly increased. This procedure violates the accounting convention that a given item appearing both as an asset account and as a liability account is to be removed from the books as an internal matter. Indeed, Patinkin [5] has disputed the Pesek and Saving procedure [3, pp. 79–96].

Patinkin and Pesek and Saving agree that the monetary system is in some sense an asset to an economy, but they disagree over the way this proposition is to be defended. To create a monetary system (says Patinkin), the "government," (c, g), gives individuals in (h, f) the right to set up banks. This right is a meaningful asset, and there is no reason why its value should not be included in the social accounts, if it can be determined. The right entails giving a windfall gain to certain people. Thus the net worth of the household sector increases by the value of the right. If the value of this right is equal to $X$, the balance sheet then changes from T diagram (i) to T diagram (ii) (Table 11). If (n, b) has no assets, (ii) will also represent the consolidated sector (h, f, n, b).

Patinkin then describes a "sequence of events" in which the banks acquire loan and deposit accounts.[13] He shows that after these events take

---

[13] The sequence of events is certainly implausible. Banks lend and people borrow, but the proceeds of the loan are never spent on productive assets (since plant remains constant). Moreover, to start off the story, it is supposed that there can be assets and income, but no credit money. We know of no historical economy which has not used credit and money. The hypothetical beginning is not a possible beginning. But if for "beginning" we read "consolidated sector (h, f, n, b)" and for "sequence of events" we read "verification of the conditions of deconsolidated sectors (h, f), (n, b)," then Patinkin's argument makes good sense.

TABLE 11

ACCOUNTING FOR THE RIGHT TO CREATE MONEY

| (i) Balance sheet of sector (h, f) | | (ii) Balance sheet of (h, f) having received rights $X$ | |
|---|---|---|---|
| $K$ (plant) | $W_{hf}^{hf}$ (net worth) | $K$ (plant) $X$ (rights) | $W_{hf}^{hf} + X$ (net worth) |

(iii)

| Balance sheet of the sector (h, f) subsequent to the establishment of the sector (n, b) | | Balance sheet of the newly established sector (n, b) | |
|---|---|---|---|
| $M$ (money) $K$ (plant) $W_{hb}^{nb}$ (bank equity) | $B$ (debts) $W_{hf}^{hf} + X$ (net worth) | $X$ (rights) $B$ (loans) | $M$ (deposits) $W_{hf}^{nb}$ (net worth) |

| Balance sheet of the consolidated sector (h, f, n, b) | |
|---|---|
| $K$ (plant) $X$ rights | $W_{hf}^{hf} + X \equiv W_{hfnb}^{hfnb}$ |

place, the balance sheet of (h, f, n, b) has the same form as (ii), even if (n, b) has assets, regardless of the amount of money actually created. He concludes that it is the right to create money, not money itself, which is an asset to the economy. Let us see why this assertion holds. In T diagram (iii), we consider the balance sheets of (h, f), of (n, b), and of the consolidated sector (h, f, n, b). It will be noted that we followed the rule book: for instance, $M$ cancels out, while $X$ does not. The first is true because deposits are simultaneously in the accounts of both sectors. But $X$ is the value of a right to have deposits. Physically, $X$ stands for a corporate charter, perhaps, or the text of a bank law, which belongs to a bank. This possession *does* increase the net worth of the banks from zero to $W_{hf}^{nb}$; this net worth *is* represented by capital stock which does belong to (h, f); and $W_{hf}^{nb}$ *does* cancel out when the sectors are consolidated. The consolidated sector (h, f, n, b) *does* have a balance sheet which is essentially like that of (h, f) in (ii)—if one can imagine an economy with productive assets and no money. We do not yet know what number $X$ may be, but whatever that number may be, it stands for an asset of (h, f, n, b). It is worth something to banks to be in business, and to their stockholders to own bank equities.

Pesek and Saving want to establish a connection between the numerical value of the rights $X$ and the money stock $M$, specifically the connection

$X = M$. They try, however, to assert that $X \equiv M$. They argue that money is "not really" a liability of the banking system, because indeed the only way that banks can earn more income is by creating more money. So (they say) money is "really" the main asset of the sector (n, b) "from an economic point of view," as well as an asset of the sector (h, f). This argument seems to us to be both unnecessary and incompatible with elementary bookkeeping. It is difficult to imagine how any double-entry bank bookkeeping system could avoid treating deposits as liabilities. An "economic" accounting system, such as that advocated by Pesek and Saving, would be fun to invent, and Pesek and Saving should be encouraged to persevere. But here we limit ourselves to double-entry.[14]

It is not out of place to remark here that we may relax the assumption made in footnote 13, namely that the proceeds of bank loans are never spent on productive assets. Suppose that the situation described in T account (iii) is immediately followed by such investment. In that case, the consolidated balance sheet of sector (h, f, n, b) would record plant equal to $(K + B)$, and a corresponding increase in net worth ($W_{hfnb}^{hfnb}$), since the investment would involve no further balance sheet entries.[15] In this sense, the banking system would be "worth" $B$ to the economy, even if the value, $X$, of the "right to create money" were zero. It is in this sense that all these writers can point to the value to an economy of its banking system.

It is useful, however, to consider further one point relating to the value $X$, of the "right to create money." We have concluded that $X \not\equiv M$. Let us consider the relation between $X$ and $M$. The banks make loans, and enter these at face value in their books. Simultaneously they create deposits, and enter these at face value in their books. In the present discussion, banks have no reserves with the central bank [for (c, g) has no assets] and there is no gold. Consequently $M = B$. If banks have no operating costs, if deposits are not interest-bearing, and if the credit market is in equilibrium, then $B$ is the present value of assets held by the banks. The $B$ is also the present value of the equities held by bank stockholders. Therefore $B = X$, and $M = X$.

If, however, these conditions are not all met, then $M > X$. Specifically:

(a)   If reserves are held in the central bank [so that the sector (c, g) has some assets], then the present value of bank credit, $B$, will be less than $M$.

(b)   If banks have operating costs, the present value of bank equities will be less than the present value of bank credit.

---

[14] More generally, we might use multiple-entry accounting. See Ijiri [15].

[15] A change in net worth is identified with saving. This particular form of increase can be thought of as a form of forced saving. To the extent that the demand for consumer goods or plant responds to such changes in net worth, this forced saving would bring about further adjustments in the entire economy. Limitations of space prevent us from doing more than allude to this complicated but interesting line of thought.

(c) If banks pay interest to some or all depositors, the present value of bank equities will be less than the present value of bank credit.

(d) If there is a difference between the risks of the banks and the risks of bank stockholders, then the present value of bank equities will differ from the present value of bank loans.

It is beyond the scope of this chapter to work out exact formulations for $X$. It is sufficient to indicate that $X$ and $M$ are both functions of the same variables, so that $X$ may be thought of as having an implicit functional relation to $M$.

If the economy [(h, f, n, b), (c, g)] is consolidated into [(h, f, n, b, c, g)], the value of the right appears in the balance sheet of the one-sector economy. This is the case, for the sector (c, g) incurs no liability by granting the banks the right to do business. In other words, the account $X$ remains as an asset of the one-sector economy. What we have said above remains valid: $X$ can probably be expressed as an implicit function of the quantity of money. It is probably misleading to write $X = X(M)$, however, and generally (though not always) incorrect to write $X = M$. It is always incorrect to write $X \equiv M$.

## IV

It is common for theorists to forget that when they move from a "simpler" to a "more complicated" economy they are simply moving back (in an accounting sense) to their starting point. A consequence of this lapse of memory is that writers confuse the separation of a financial sector, say (n, b), from a generalized business sector, say (f, n, b), with one of two quite different questions. Some writers say that the initial discussion of (f, n, b) relates to an economy with no banks, whereas the subsequent discussion of (f, n, b) relates to an economy with banks. This view of what they are doing is certainly incorrect, for the creation of a banking system in a previously bankless economy would certainly make more changes in economic life than they are prepared to discuss. The establishment of banks would alter the demand for physical assets, and for current output, for instance. One cannot imagine adding banks to an economy without *some* changes taking place in non-monetary variables. Other writers go further, and assert that they are characterizing (however briefly) an actual historical change from a system without banks to a system with banks. Such suggestions, viewed as history, are most doubtful, and it does not seem to be a fact that originally economies had one sector, then two sectors, then three sectors, and so on. Such suggestions have been made in otherwise serious work [2].

In our opinion, a considerable gain in clarity would result if monetary writers recognized explicitly that their natural tendency to move from simple to more complicated models is associated with a move from more consolidated to less consolidated sets of social accounts. The simple model is typically simple because it is either a one-sector or at most a two-sector model. We have shown that one-sector models must be " peculiar " because the variables remaining in them are not the variables which intuition would lead the economist to relate to each other. Two-sector models are more useful. For example Patinkin could explain the real balance effect using the economy [h, (f, n, b, c, g)].

To be more precise, in monetary literature, one finds a variety of statements connecting stocks of money to flows of goods. Among these are such familiar formulas as $MV = PT$, $M = L_1(Y) + L_2(r)$ and $C = C(Y, M/P)$. We have shown that the symbols $M$, $Y$, and $C$ have meanings which vary with the sectoral structure of the model. If the models are to be subject to empirical testing, it is important that the data used should conform to the specifications of the theory.

Consider again Leijonhufvud's classification of variables: money, government debt, capital goods, consumer goods, and labor services. Only two of these appear in a one-sector economy: money ("gold") and capital goods. Two sectors at least are needed to talk about any of the others, including nongold forms of money:

(1)   Most labor services are purchased by the business sector, and most consumption is purchased from the business sector. In any model trying to deal seriously with employment and consumer spending, including the real balance effect, the household and business sectors must be kept separate.

(2)   Much government debt is held by nonfinancial businesses, financial intermediaries, and banks. Unless these sectors are all separated from " government and the central bank," a large part of government debt does not show up, and cannot be dealt with.

(3)   Much money is held by nonfinancial businesses. Unless these businesses are kept separate from banks, this money disappears. In particular, econometric models which use United States Department of Commerce national product data are using data which consolidate (f, n, b). To be consistent, such models must replace " all demand deposits " and " all currency " by " demand deposits of households " and " currency held by households."

(4)   Many economists feel that investment by nonfinancial businesses is materially affected by conditions in securities markets and by bank credit markets. If this is the case, then certainly banks, and perhaps financial intermediaries, must be kept separate from businesses. If they are not, the only securities markets that can appear are markets in which households buy and sell business securities. When separation is made, however, the national product accounts of the Department of Commerce must be correspondingly disaggregated in empirical work.

## V

In our discussion, we have used only the most elementary of considerations: when sectors are consolidated, certain variables are suppressed and others are combined. We have found a common six-sector model which seems to underly a number of quite diverse papers. Our argument was based on the claim that each particular macroeconomic model deals with an economic structure consisting of one or more sectors, each with a balance sheet and an income statement. This sectoral composition may be selected by the theorist but once selected, its details are given by the properties of the (deconsolidated) economy and the rules of social accounting. There is nothing new about the ideas, but they have been applied more systematically than usual.

In particular, it has been argued that monetary economics has been involved in some unnecessary controversy because writers had not made clear the sectoral structures of the models they were using. It turned out that a single six-sector accounting structure could be used to derive a number of familiar systems, and in this sense to explain the reasons for differences among them.

Two defects have been found in the writing under discussion. In the first place some writers have assumed that it was possible to consolidate the balance sheets of various sectors without performing comparable consolidations of income statements. More effort has been devoted to the study of the way that the money stock is affected by consolidation than to the study of how the national product is affected. Specifically, one finds models in which balance sheets of households and businesses are consolidated, but in which consumption expenditures and income paid by businesses to households remain in the national income/product accounts. Such inconsistency seems to have been unnoticed by the writers under study, and it raises important questions about the validity of certain parts of the literature.[16]

A second defect arises because of a peculiarity of theoretical work. It is natural for a theorist to go from simple to more complicated models. Simple models involve few variables, and can therefore be associated with highly consolidated system. But more consolidated systems are constructed from less consolidated systems, and there is no well-defined inverse process of deconsolidation.

Ultimately, the purpose of monetary economics is to analyze more detailed systems, and we are at a loss to understand the insistence of theorists on very highly consolidated systems. As pedagogical exercises they might perhaps be

---

[16] One of the authors should henceforth practice what he preaches. Readers may test their understanding of this chapter by finding the inconsistency in the models presented by Ames [16].

justified. We have seen, however, that some writers seem to be unaware—when they construct highly consolidated models—that the variables they wish to analyze have been consolidated out of the system, and are no longer observable. We must therefore agree with Gurley and Shaw, who have said, "disaggregation [read deconsolidation] is the essence of monetary theory" [2, p. 140]. This proposition is all the stronger, because if one would deconsolidate, one must first have consolidated. The information one needs, then, about the structure of the "more complicated" economy is already at hand. The more consolidated the system, the less, quite literally, it can deal with. Surely one would wish for models which can explain more, rather than less.

## ACKNOWLEDGMENTS

The authors express their thanks to their colleague, H. O. Stekler, for numerous useful criticisms and suggestions. They have also more than the usual thanks to George Horwich for his careful editing, which led to the clarification of several parts of the text.

## REFERENCES

1. Patinkin, D., *Money, Interest, and Prices*, An Integration of Monetary and Value Theory, 2nd ed. New York: Harper, 1965.
2. Gurley, J. G., and Shaw, E. S., *Money in a Theory of Finance*. Washington, D.C.: The Brookings Inst., 1960.
3. Pesek, B. P., and Saving, T. R., *Money, Wealth, and Economic Theory*. New York: Macmillan, 1967.
4. Patinkin, D., "Financial Intermediaries and the Logical Structure of Monetary Theory, A Review Article," *American Economic Review* 51, No. 1 (March 1960), 95–116.
5. Patinkin, D., "Money and Wealth: A Review Article," *Journal of Economic Literature* 7, No. 4 (December 1969), 1140–1160.
6. Leijonhufvud, A., *On Keynesian Economics and the Economics of Keynes*, A Study in Monetary Theory. London and New York: Oxford Univ. Press, 1968.
7. Tobin, J., "Money, Capital, and Other Stores of Value," *American Economic Review*, Papers and Proceedings 51, No. 2 (May 1961) 26–37, especially p. 28.
8. Tobin, J., "Commercial Banks as Creators of 'Money'," in *Banking and Monetary Studies* (D. Carson, U.S. Treasury, ed.), pp. 408–419. Homewood, Illinois: Irwin, 1963.
9. Metzler, L. A., "Wealth, Saving, and the Rate of Interest," *The Journal of Political Economy* 59 (April 1951), 93–116.
10. Horwich, G., *Money, Capital, and Prices*. Homewood, Illinois: Irwin, 1964.
11. Friedman, M., and Schwartz, A. J., *A Monetary History of The United States* 1867–1960. Princeton, New Jersey: Princeton Univ. Press, 1963.
12. Johnson, H. G., "Monetary Theory and Policy," *American Economic Review* 52 (June 1962), 341.
13. Friedman, M., "A Theoretical Framework for Monetary Analysis," *Journal of Political Economy* 78, No. 2 (March/April 1970), 193–238.
14. Tobin, J., "A Dynamic Aggregative Model," *Journal of Political Economy* 63 (April 1955), 103–115.
15. Ijiri, Y., *The Foundations of Accounting Measurement*, A Mathematical, Economics and Behavioral Enquiry, pp. 105–108. Englewood Cliffs, New Jersey: Prentice-Hall, 1967.
16. Ames, E., *Income and Wealth*, Chapter 6. New York: Holt, 1969.

*Part V*

# GROWTH

# MONEY, GROWTH, AND THE PROPENSITY TO SAVE

## An Iconoclastic View

*Ronald I. McKinnon*
*Stanford University*

## Introduction

In his famous paper, "Wealth, Saving, and the Rate of Interest" [9], Metzler followed the classical tradition of Pigou in assuming that the stock of privately held wealth—an important part of which was real cash balances—was negatively correlated with the aggregate propensity to save. However, Metzler's model was mainly in the static Keynesian mold where the rate of growth did not enter explicitly, and a generation of graduate students has come to associate an increase in the net wealth of the household sector with an upward shift in the aggregate consumption function (unless the marginal propensity to save is arbitrarily assumed to be a fixed parameter). Indeed, the proposition must be true in certain disequilibrium situations where wealth holdings are deemed to be too large relative to current income flows, and individuals increase their current consumption in order to reduce stocks of money, bonds, or commodities to desired levels.

Once equilibrium growth is taken into account, however, there is an important sense in which this standard proposition drawn from static macroeconomic theory should be reversed. Instead, large holdings of private wealth,

487

particularly in the form of real cash balances, can increase the propensity to save when income itself is growing rapidly. Hence, monetary policy that induces individuals to increase their stock of financial assets, relative to the flow of current income, can encourage private saving and so increase the rate of accumulation of physical capital. On the one hand, a higher yield on liquid assets, including money, rewards saving directly while increasing desired stocks of financial assets.[1] On the other hand, the desire to maintain large stocks of assets in portfolio balance induces a further increment to saving once growth begins.

This latter "portfolio effect" of growth on the propensity to save is emphasized in this chapter, and related to the monetary system's role as a financial intermediary in the accumulation of physical capital. This portfolio effect can help explain the relationship between saving and financial structure in high growth economies such as Japan and Taiwan, both of which have unusually high saving rates and high money/GNP ratios for their level of development and per capita income. Elements of the model are also applicable to more mature economies, although the degree of applicability will have to be decided by each reader for himself, since this chapter is oriented toward the less-developed countries.

Metzler's remarkable contribution was written well over twenty years ago. Since then, there has been a plethora of articles, first on growth and accumulation alone, and then on money and growth, mainly within a neoclassical framework.[2] If real cash balances do indeed exert a strong positive influence on saving propensities and the accumulation of physical capital, as claimed here, should this portfolio effect not have been picked up in the literature now extant? Unfortunately, most contributors to the neoclassical literature on economic growth assume that the private propensity to save is fixed irrespective of the return on saving, the size of wealth holding, and the rate of growth; or they assume that real money balances, while useful as a means of facilitating current transactions, are substitutes for physical capital in the asset portfolios of the private sector. As we shall see, both of these neoclassical

---

[1] As is well known, this direct impact of higher interest rates is subject to an ambiguous income effect that makes it unclear theoretically as to whether current saving (and presumably stocks of financial assets) would actually increase. However, the present author has convinced himself [8, Chapter 8], that, as an empirical matter, stocks of financial assets can be expected to increase when the reward for holding them rises. If desired stocks of financial assets do not increase in response to interest rate stimuli, this does not invalidate my thesis about wealth effects in the presence of growth; but it does make the implications for economic policy considerably less interesting.

[2] Some principal authors in this monetary tradition are Friedman [2], Johnson [5], Levhari and Patinkin [7], Tobin [12], and Mundell [10].

postulates tend to vitiate one's understanding of the nexus between growth and the propensity to save—particularly in less-developed countries.

The neo-Keynesian approach to equilibrium growth is no better. For example, Williamson [13] specifies that monetary policies that increase desired real cash balances also shift the aggregate consumption function upward. In contrast, the model outlined herein is designed to avoid these pitfalls that seem to be inherent in the neoclassical and Keynesian approaches to monetary policy and the rate of accumulation. I hypothesize that large real cash balances, held in portfolio equilibrium, enhance rather than retard the rate of growth in physical capital over the time horizon relevant for economic development.

## I. Financial Structure and Monetary Policy

In analyzing poor countries, it is sometimes quite reasonable to suppose that "money," broadly defined to include time and savings deposits, is virtually the only financial asset available to savers that is at all liquid (see Goldsmith [3]). Open markets for primary securities such as bonds, mortgages, and common stock are usually quite moribund or very small. Hence there is no uniform rate of interest on "bonds" that represents the opportunity cost of holding money.

For analytical convenience, therefore, I assume that each saver can hold only money, whose return is heavily influenced by the State, or can hold physical commodities whose return will vary with the use that he himself in his household or firm can find for them.[3] Thus money has considerable importance as a store of value as well as a medium of exchange, and there is *no* market in primary securities for fully equalizing the returns on physical capital, much of which is self-financed. Private capital markets are highly imperfect.

A concomitant of restricting the asset portfolios of savers to money or commodities is that the role of the monetary system as a financial intermediary must be specified explicitly.[4] Here I assume that the net acquisition

---

[3] In contrast, the prevailing assumption in the neoclassical and Keynesian models is a "perfect" market in primary securities, so that a uniform rate of interest is established on "bonds" as well as on physical capital. This perfect capital-market assumption is no less extreme than to assume that individual savers simply do not have the chance of holding "bonds"—or indeed any primary security which is a claim on enterprises other than their own.

[4] With a perfect market for primary securities in the neoclassical world, the monetary system's role as a financial intermediary is redundant. Hence, money is usually created by "outside" means within traditional economic models, and the demand for money is justified purely on the grounds of improving the efficiency with which current transactions are conducted.

of real cash balances, $M/P$, by the private sector is channeled via bank credit either to industrial and agricultural borrowers, who wish to accumulate physical capital rather than consume, or to the government for current public consumption.[5] For simplicity, assume that the real rate of interest paid by private borrowers to the banking system fully reflects the scarcity value of total bank credit allocated to the private sector; and assume that the government consciously appropriates its own share of bank credit at a zero interest cost. In effect, the government determines the amount of seigniorage it wishes to extract from the monetary system, and the real bank credit remaining is allocated to the private sector at equilibrium rates of interest.[6]

For illustrative purposes, our model views the banking system—central bank, commercial banks, savings banks, and so on—as being completely integrated with only private depositors (inclusive of currency holders) on the liabilities side of its balance sheet (no bank ownership or equity capital), and the two classes of borrowers, private and public, on the asset side. Let $L$ be the loans outstanding to the private sector at high equilibrium rates of interest. Let us further suppose that seigniorage is appropriated through government sales of noninterest bearing securities, denoted by $S_g$, to the banking system in return for deposits that are immediately spent for current goods and services. The relevant $T$ account (balance sheet) for the banking system at any point in time is

Assets   Liabilities

$L$         $M$
$S_g$

To put the balance sheet in real terms, the *stocks* $L$, $S_g$, and $M$ can be divided through by $P$.

What then are the relevant instruments of monetary policy open to the authorities? In a relatively early paper [11], Tobin noted many of the subtle difficulties in using data on liquid assets—including real cash balances—as an "explanation" of consumption or spending behavior by economic units. As long as economic units attain portfolio equilibrium in the sense that they jointly determine both their average real cash balances and their level of consumption, cash balances cannot be used to "explain" consumption or

---

[5] Of course, there can also be real accumulation in the public sector or consumption loans in the private one. This sharp distinction is made for reasons of analytical convenience.

[6] The government can always allocate some of its seigniorage outside the public sector by designating certain private borrowers to receive low cost loans. Again, for simplicity, I omit this possibility because it does not affect the analysis in any essential way.

saving behavior. One must look for explanatory variables that are outside the direct control of households and firms, and in this chapter I focus on the real return on holding money as the control variable that may be manipulated by the monetary authority.

First let us define an appropriate time horizon. Only alternative "balanced-growth" paths will be considered. Along any such path, I assume that the holders of real cash balances (and the private recipients of bank credit) fully and accurately anticipate the actual percentage rate of inflation $\dot{P}$. The model is Fisherian in this respect. Now suppose that the composition of cash balances—various classes of deposits and currency—is determinate for given deposit rate(s) of interest and the relative liquidity values of hand-to-hand currency, demand deposits, and time deposits.[7] We can then define $d$ to be the *average nominal* interest rate on deposits and currency. Hence $d - \dot{P}$ is a primary determinant of the private sector's willingness to hold real money balances $M/P$. Insofar as government monetary policy operates on the private demand for real money balances at any given level of income $Y$, such policy must influence $d - \dot{P}$.

The demand for money that reflects these assumptions can then be written as a function of the real deposit rate $d - \dot{P}$ and real income $Y$:

$$M/P = f(d - \dot{P}, Y) \qquad \text{where} \quad f_1 > 0 \quad \text{and} \quad f_2 > 0. \tag{1}$$

Implicit in (1) would be the variance in future expectations regarding $\dot{P}$, and absent from (1) is a uniform market rate of interest on primary securities that simply does not exist in most of the underdeveloped world.

While the government cannot determine $d - \dot{P}$ directly, its own policies regarding the collection of seigniorage as related to the percentage rate of issue of nominal money $\dot{M}$ will eventually determine $d - \dot{P}$. For any nominal return $d$ to the holders of money, $\dot{M}$ will ultimately govern the percentage rate of change in the price level $\dot{P}$. In the neoclassical tradition, we are assuming that the price level rises at a rate equal to the rate of issue of nominal money less the rate of growth in the demand for real cash balances. Hence, by controlling $d$ and $\dot{M}$, the monetary authority ultimately controls $d - \dot{P}$, the real return on holding money. Accepting this, our principal task is to show how the selection of $d - \dot{P}$ is related to (or jointly determined with) seigniorage, investment in physical capital $I$, and the rate of growth in real output $\dot{Y}$.[8]

If $\dot{M}$ is increased while $d$ is fixed, higher price inflation ensues and the real return to the holders of money is decreased. They respond by reducing $M/P$,

---

[7] The problems involved in defining an optimal monetary portfolio are not pursued here. They have been discussed by Johnson [6].

[8] Throughout, the superscript dot is used to denote proportional growth. For example, $\dot{Y} = (dY/dt)/Y$.

and the economy moves to a new growth path with a higher rate of price inflation coupled with a *lower rate of investment*. This last effect is a direct consequence of the banking system's diminished role as a financial intermediary between private savers and private investors as $M/P$ declines. Essentially, the reduction in $d - \dot{P}$ associated with the increase in $\dot{M}$ (with $d$ fixed) has led to an increase in government seigniorage (real revenue from the banking system) which reduces and diverts private saving from investment in physical capital. Similar disintermediation would occur if $d$ were lowered when $\dot{M}$ was held constant.

To see the disintermediation effect of increasing $\dot{M}$ most clearly, let us start from a growth path in which the government extracts no explicit or implicit[9] seigniorage. Then the real return to the holders of money, $d - \dot{P}$, will fully reflect the returns on physical investment less the real costs of providing bank intermediation and transactions services. (The monetary system will be relatively large in real terms.) Consequently, any additions to the stock of real cash balances in the portfolios of private savers—due either to an increase in $d - \dot{P}$ or to an increase in income $Y$—will be fully reflected by the accumulation of a like amount of physical capital. Hence the government's budget must be balanced in the sense that it is not using the monetary system for financing unrequited deficits. There are an infinite number of combinations of $d$ and $\dot{P}$ (as determined by $\dot{M}$) that are consistent with this situation of no seigniorage.

Now suppose that the government runs a current account deficit for consumption, and finances it through the sale of interest-free securities to the banking system, causing $\dot{M}$ to rise. The $d$ is kept constant so that money holders are not compensated for the increased price inflation. The real return on holding money falls and disintermediation occurs. Two effects now operate so as to squeeze the flow of real bank credit to private investment. For a given flow of private saving and bank lending based on it, an increased share is appropriated by the government. But in addition, the fall in the real return to the holders of money causes a reduction in $M/P$, at any given level of income, that reduces the total flow of private saving and of real bank credit available to all borrowers. Hence, lending to the private sector for investment in physical capital will have fallen more than proportionately than real cash balances, once the new equilibrium growth path is achieved. The influence of bank disintermediation on investment can be very strong if private firms cannot sell their own primary securities to the general public because capital markets are imperfect.

---

[9] There are no usury restrictions and the banks are efficient and competitive—or at least simulate a competitive structure of interest rates for depositors and borrowers.

## II. The Saving Function

Corresponding to the simplified financial structure just sketched, there exists a social saving function that can be partitioned conveniently in the following manner:

$$s = \frac{\text{saving}}{Y} = \frac{d(M/P)/dt}{Y} - \frac{G}{Y} + s' \tag{2}$$

where $G$ is the real flow of government seigniorage and $s'$ is the ratio of self-financed investment to income. The $s$ is defined as the realized propensity to save socially, and need not be equal to the purely private propensity to save as long as opportunities exist for the government to extract seigniorage from the banking system. Our concern in this section is to show how monetary policy, as it operates through the government's choice of $d - \dot{P}$, influences $s$.

The first term in (2) is that portion of private saving that goes to acquire real cash balances; the remainder of private saving goes into self-financed investment as represented by $s'$. If we differentiate the money demand function (1) with respect to time, and remember that $d - \dot{P}$ must be constant on a balanced inflation path, then

$$d(M/P)/dt = f_2 \, dY/dt. \tag{3}$$

Substituting (3) back into the first term of (2) yields

$$s = f_2 \dot{Y} - (G/Y) + s'. \tag{4}$$

To demonstrate the positive influence of an increase in the real return from holding money on $s$, take the partial derivative of $s$ with respect to $d - \dot{P}$, with $\dot{Y}$ and $Y$ held constant, to yield

$$\frac{\partial s}{\partial(d - \dot{P})} > 0$$

because

$$f_{21} = \frac{\partial f_2}{\partial(d - \dot{P})} > 0, \qquad \dot{Y} > 0, \tag{5}$$

$$\frac{\partial(G/Y)}{\partial(d - \dot{P})} < 0, \tag{6}$$

and

$$\frac{\partial s'}{\partial(d - \dot{P})} \simeq 0. \tag{7}$$

Let us discuss in turn the economic rationale for the signs of each of the partial derivatives (5)–(7). Consider the importance of $f_{21}$. The positive coefficient $f_2$ of $\dot{Y}$ in (5) reflects the private incremental demand to hold money as income grows. This incremental demand will be higher, the higher are desired real cash balances at any given level of income as influenced positively by the real return on holding money, $d - \dot{P}$. Hence $f_{21} > 0$. Increases in $d - \dot{P}$ operate through the monetary system to stimulate greater private saving—an effect which is particularly important in a world where money is the only financial asset.

The other embodiment of private saving is the rate of self-financed investment in physical capital $s'$. What is the economic rationale for assuming that $\partial s'/\partial(d - \dot{P})$ is approximately zero? McKinnon [8] devotes a whole chapter to showing why real money balances $M/P$ and physical capital $K$ are likely to be complementary in private portfolios over some relevant ranges of $d - \dot{P}$, although the more conventional relationship of substitutability becomes important over other ranges. Since my principal concern is to demonstrate that $\partial s/\partial(d - \dot{P}) > 0$ in financially repressed economics, let me sketch briefly the rather unconventional argument that self-financed investment in physical capital might actually be augmented as the real return on holding money increases.

Since money is the only financial asset in our less-developed economy, self-financed investment is important. But the process of saving through time for internal investment is facilitated if real cash balances can be used as a convenient store of value. Then small enterprises will simply build up and then draw down their owned real cash balances as a means of "financing" their internal investments. But if real cash balances are unattractive to hold because $d - \dot{P}$ is, say, negative, such patterns of self-financed investment will be discouraged. That is, price inflation that heavily taxes holders of real cash balances also taxes the process of self-financed saving and investment. Therefore, if we begin from a situation where $d - \dot{P} < 0$, and the monetary authority takes steps to reduce $\dot{M}$ and raise $d - \dot{P}$, self-financed investment may well increase, i.e., $\partial s'/\partial(d - \dot{P}) > 0$.

Finally, the negative sign of the "seigniorage" term in our saving function needs justification. Equation (6) specifies that the flow of government seigniorage rises as $d - \dot{P}$ declines, which is consistent with the argument provided in Section I that extraction of seigniorage is associated with a decline in the real return to the holders of money.

We have, therefore, shown that $\partial s/\partial(d - \dot{P}) > 0$ in all three terms—(5), (6), and (7)—assuming that the economy moves from one equilibrium growth path to another when $d - \dot{P}$ is changed. If we also associate an increase in $M/P$—an endogenous variable—with a policy shift upward in $d - \dot{P}$, then investment in physical capital (realized social saving) and higher real cash balances are *positively* related. This is the "intermediation effect" of raising $d - \dot{P}$.

In the history of economic thinking on the subject, however, a *negative* wealth effect on saving has been posited (as in Metzler's "disequilibrium" static model [9]) in equilibrium growth theory in a Keynesian context as given by Williamson [13], and in the equilibrium neoclassical investment function as typified by Levhari and Patinkin [7]. Traditional theory ignores the intermediation role of the monetary system and essentially views real cash balances as competitive with, or a liquidity trap for, the accumulation of physical capital. This conventional approach is wanting generally, but it is peculiarly deceptive when applied to less-developed countries.

But there is another interesting aspect of our partitioned saving function as given by (4). From the first term $f_2 \dot{Y}$, we see that, *ceterus paribus*, an increase in the growth rate in real income will itself increase the private propensity to save, at least in the form of owned cash balances! For convenience, call the positive influence of an increased $\dot{Y}$ on $s$ the "portfolio effect" of growth on saving. The strength of this portfolio effect is also influenced by monetary policy because $f_2$ is derived from the money demand function and is positively related to $d - \dot{P}$. In contrast, the private propensity to save is usually specified independently of the rate of growth in both Keynesian and neoclassical models.

The economic rationale for this portfolio effect is simple enough. In an interdependent economy, an innovation that increases the aggregate rate of growth will spread its dividends to most firms and households—even those that were not directly affected by the initial innovation. Many workers find that their wages simply begin to grow fortuitously. But income and consumption cannot grow efficiently without asset accumulation. The "convenience" yield—transactions, liquidity and store-of-value services—of monetary assets induces firms and households to keep stocks of these assets in a certain balanced relationship with current income flows. Even households who are quite insensitive to interest rates find that they are induced to save—i.e., not to consume all their incremental income—in order that their stocks of money and commodities rise commensurately with their growing income. That is, $\partial s / \partial \dot{Y} > 0$ as we can see by noting that $f_2 > 0$ in Eq. (4).

This portfolio effect can be seen most clearly by starting from a stationary state where there is, by definition, no net saving. Now suppose there is continuous innovation that costlessly induces growth in aggregate income. Then individuals must begin to save to allow their net wealth—inclusive of $M/P$—to accumulate *pari passu* with $\dot{Y}$.[10] The propensity to save goes from zero

----

[10] There is a rather weak constraint that the desired net wealth position of the private sector rises with income. As a general proposition, I think this is empirically self-evident. But in the constrained world of imperfect capital markets used here, it would be virtually impossible for households or firms to issue primary securities so as to make their net wealth position negative.

to some positive number. But simply moving from a lower to a higher rate of growth will be sufficient for this portfolio effect to operate—an effect that will be accentuated the higher is the ratio of money to GNP. For example, suppose the desired money/GNP ratio is 0.5, and growth suddenly increases from 5 to 10% per year. Just to maintain their money/GNP ratios, individuals will have to increase their propensity to save out of current income from 2.5 to 5%. (Insofar as some physical assets also have a convenience yield to households, saving may rise even further to maintain portfolio balance.)

The preceding discussion of the intermediation and portfolio effects allows us to write down a more general and somewhat simpler version of the function describing the social propensity to save:

$$s = s(\dot{Y}; d - \dot{P}) \tag{8}$$

where

$$s_1 = \frac{\partial s}{\partial \dot{Y}} > 0 \quad \text{and} \quad s_2 = \frac{\partial s}{\partial(d - \dot{P})} > 0.$$

The real return on holding money, and the rate of growth itself, each influence positively the social propensity to save out of current income. This saving function, as described by (8), is the basis for the modified Harrod–Domar model developed in Section III within which $\dot{Y}$ is endogenously determined and $d - \dot{P}$ can be exogenously manipulated as the instrumental variable of monetary policy.

### III. A Harrod–Domar Growth Model with a Variable Propensity to Save

The original Harrod–Domar model [4, 1] made no reference to money and finance; and intended saving was automatically transformed into investment at a uniform rate of return along the equilibrium growth path. Correspondingly, the output/capital ratio—denoted by $\sigma$—was taken as given, and the aggregate production function was written as

$$Y = \sigma K \tag{9}$$

where $K$ is the stock of physical capital.

The omission from (9) of a separate labor constraint on aggregate output has been justified in two ways. Technical change is sufficiently labor augmenting so that the effective labor force grows at the same rate as aggregate output. Alternatively, one can assume the existence of a residual unemployed or underemployed labor force that requires new investment to bring it into "organized" economic activity. The former explanation applies mainly, although not exclusively, to mature economies; whereas the latter is more readily associated with less-developed countries.

Financial innovation could conceivably increase the output/capital ratio if new saving and investment were accompanied by increased intermediation through the monetary system. In the algebraic development to follow, however, I shall forgo this possibility and simply follow tradition by assuming that $\sigma$ is constant—that is, diminishing returns are absent. Furthermore, $M/P$ is omitted from the aggregate production function in order to emphasize the "intermediation" rather than the "transactions" role of money. Inclusion of real cash balances as a current factor of production in (9) would not alter the qualitative nature of any conclusions.

In the unmodified Harrod–Domar model, the propensity to save—as denoted by $s$—is simply a fixed proportion of income. Moreover, private saving is fully reflected in the accumulation of physical capital. That is,

$$I = dK/dt = sY. \tag{10}$$

Hence, one can easily solve (9) and (10) within the traditional framework to obtain the percentage rate of growth in aggregate income as simply the product of the output/capital ratio and the marginal propensity to save:

$$\dot{Y} = \sigma s. \tag{11}$$

Now, let us reinterpret $s$ as the social propensity to save—private saving minus government seigniorage—in the mode of our analysis of financial structure in Section II. Hence $s$ is now endogenous and is a function of the real return on holding money, $d - \dot{P}$, and the rate of growth itself, $\dot{Y}$. Combining Eqs. (8) and (11), we have $\dot{Y}$ defined by the implicit equation

$$\dot{Y} = \sigma s(\dot{Y}; d - \dot{P}) \tag{12}$$

where $d - \dot{P}$ is an exogenous variable under the policy control of the government.

The solution to (12) is portrayed graphically in Fig. 1 in a manner that visually distinguishes the intermediation effect from the portfolio effect on the variable saving propensity. In reading Fig. 1, the vertical axis should be interpreted as measuring the right-hand side of Eq. (12)—the product of the *ex ante* propensity to save $s$ and the constant output/capital ratio $\sigma$. The *actual* rate of growth is plotted on the horizontal axis. Hence equilibrium, where *ex ante* saving matches the rate of investment necessary to support the existing rate of growth, holds only along the 45° line from the origin.

*AB* and *CD* are alternative saving functions plotted so as to show saving increasing with $\dot{Y}$—their slopes representing the portfolio effect. (The saving function in the traditional Harrod–Domar model would simply be a fixed horizontal line.) By raising the real return on holding money, the monetary authority can raise the whole saving schedule from *AB* to *CD*—the shift representing the intermediation effect. The *AB* is associated with a "low" or

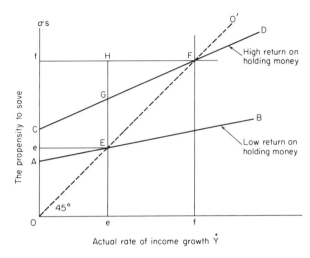

**Fig. 1.** The intermediation and portfolio effects of monetary policy.

negative return on money, and $CD$ is associated with a high positive return. Correspondingly, the equilibrium rate of growth increases from $E$ on $AB$ to $F$ on $CD$.

In Fig. 1, the buoyant impact of making money more attractive to hold by raising $d$ or reducing $\dot{M}$ can be partitioned into two stages. When $d - \dot{P}$ increases, but before growth in aggregate income responds, private saving moves upward from $E$ to $G$. Hence $EG$ measures the pure intermediation effect, which is the rise in the private propensity to save at a given rate of growth in aggregate income. However, aggregate income will be induced to grow faster as realized saving and investment rise. In order to maintain portfolio balance in the face of this general economic progress, individuals will be induced to save still more with a further impact on growth that is measured by the distance $GH$—the portfolio effect.[11] I hypothesize that the two effects together can be a powerful and positive influence on saving and growth.

Those with a penchant for pedantry will be worried, justifiably, about the stability of the model just outlined. Without pretending to specify completely the dynamics of adjustment, let us consider the case of the saving function $AB$ and the existence of the equilibrium position $E$. If the actual growth were "arbitrarily" set at zero so as to eliminate the portfolio effect, then the saving propensity would still be positive and equal to $OA$ (divided by $\sigma$). If these savings were successfully translated into net investment, the rate of growth would be driven upward toward $E$—as measured by $e$ on

---

[11] One should note that the upward slope of $CD$ is steeper than that of $AB$ because an increase in $M/P$ strengthens the influence of $\dot{Y}$ on the propensity to save.

either axis. However, to ensure that $AB$ intersects the 45° line so that an equilibrium such as point $E$ exists and the rate of growth does not become arbitrarily large, $AB$ must be constrained to having a slope of less than unity. That is, to prevent explosive growth in the context of the model it is necessary that

$$\partial s/\partial \dot{Y} < 1/\sigma. \tag{13}$$

Intuitively, it is easy to see that this last condition, which puts an upper bound on the portfolio effect, is not very stringent. Suppose that the output/capital ratio $\sigma$ is 1/3—a commonly assumed number. Then condition (13) implies that a one percentage point increase in $\dot{Y}$ can increase the propensity to save as much as three percentage points without inducing explosive growth. Hence, the portfolio effect of growth on saving can be quite large and still be consistent with the existence of equilibrium in our Harrod–Domar economy.

### IV. Concluding Notes and Empirical Observations

Across diverse countries, the observed high and positive correlation among saving propensities, stocks of monetary assets, and rates of growth must seem puzzling to economists steeped in the conventional theory that associates the real balance effect with a high social propensity to consume. Without pretending to be comprehensive empirically,[12] let me be merely provocative by providing fragmentary information on Taiwan and Japan, two countries that are well known to have experienced unusually high economic growth during the decade of the 1960's. Tables 1 and 2 display money/GNP ratios —where money is broadly defined to include time and saving deposits—for the benchmark years 1960, 1965, and 1970.

The data on Taiwan are presented together with a "peer" group of less-developed economies, which have per capita real incomes comparable to the Taiwanese, but rates of growth that are much lower. Similarly, the data on Japan are presented together with a peer group of developed industrial economies—although in this case the peer group had generally much higher per capita income, particularly in 1960. Comparing the two groups, per capita income is strongly related to financial maturity as measured by the money/GNP ratio.

For 1970, the relative size of the banking system in Taiwan was much higher, i.e., the money/GNP ratio was 0.46, than in the peer group of developing countries, where the average money/GNP ratio was 0.30. My

---

[12] An attempt to be somewhat more comprehensive can be found in the book by McKinnon [8, Chapter 8].

TABLE 1

THE RATIO OF MONEY ($M_2$) TO GNP IN SELECTED LESS-DEVELOPED COUNTRIES[a]

| Country | 1960 | 1965 | 1970 |
|---------|------|------|------|
| Taiwan | 0.20 | 0.36 | 0.46 |
| Argentina | 0.30 | 0.26 | 0.35 |
| Brazil | 0.31 | 0.26 | 0.32 |
| Chile | 0.12 | 0.16 | 0.18 |
| India | 0.23 | 0.25 | 0.25 |
| Ceylon | 0.30 | 0.34 | 0.29 |
| Turkey | 0.20 | 0.24 | 0.30 |
| Philippines | 0.23 | 0.24 | 0.32 |
| Colombia | 0.21 | 0.22 | 0.24[b] |

[a] Source: *International Financial Statistics*, published by the International Monetary Fund. $M_2$ is generally calculated from lines 34 and 35 of the *IFS*, unless additional data are available.

[b] Data for the year 1969 were used because data from 1970 were not available.

TABLE 2

THE RATIO OF MONEY ($M_2$) TO GNP IN SELECTED INDUSTRIAL COUNTRIES[a]

| Country | 1960 | 1965 | 1970 |
|---------|------|------|------|
| Japan | 0.88 | 0.98 | 0.97 |
| Belgium | 0.60 | 0.60 | 0.59 |
| France | 0.47 | 0.55 | 0.59 |
| Germany | 0.36 | 0.42 | 0.52 |
| United Kingdom | 0.52 | 0.50 | 0.56 |
| United States | 0.63 | 0.71 | 0.70 |

[a] Source: *International Financial Statistics* published by the International Monetary Fund. $M_2$ is generally calculated from lines 34 and 35 of the *IFS*, unless additional data are available.

theoretical model of equilibrium growth only compares economies along balanced growth paths after full adjustment to any discrete change in the real return on holding money has been made. Hence the model does not directly reflect the period of financial transition that Taiwan was going through in the 1960's, when the money/GNP ratio more than doubled—in large measure reflecting a dampening of inflationary expectations that had been built up in the 1950's. In a more general sense, however, the extraordinary growth in $M/P$ seems quite consistent with the high saving that one would expect from the intermediation and portfolio effects conceptualized in the theoretical model.

Japan is not so much of a transitional case because it had been maintaining a very high rate of growth for many years prior to 1960. Hence, it had already reached the level of monetary development associated with a high rate of saving and growth at the beginning of the 1960's. Still, the Japanese money/ GNP ratio moved up from 0.88 in 1960 to 0.97 in 1970, levels that were much higher than the average of 0.59 in the group of industrial countries (Table 2)—despite the greater wealth per capita of the peer group. Again, the Japanese data are consistent with my view of the importance of real cash balances for saving and growth, although the direction of causation can never be proved by simply observing statistical correlations.

The policy implications of the above theoretical and empirical analysis are obvious. Money and finance are important in the development process despite the short shrift they have been given in the development literature. Moreover, the extraction of seigniorage by inflation or other financial devices necessarily lowers the real return on holding money and shrinks the money/GNP ratio in a way which is very damaging to private saving and investment propensities. The traditional monetary literature, neoclassical or Keynesian, fails to reflect the extent of the damage because it is exclusively concerned with the transactions motive for holding money and assumes that private capital markets operate perfectly without bank intermediation.

## ACKNOWLEDGMENTS

I wish to thank Patric Hendershott and George Horwich for editing far beyond the call of duty, and significantly extending the logical structure of the manuscript.

## REFERENCES

1. Domar, E., "Capital Expansion, Rate of Growth, and Employment," *Econometrica* **14** (January 1946), 137–147; reprinted in *Growth Economics* (A. K. Sen, ed.). New York: Penguin, 1970.
2. Friedman, M., *The Optimum Quantity of Money and Other Essays*. Chicago: Aldine, 1969.
3. Goldsmith, R., *Financial Structure and Development*. New Haven, Connecticut: Yale Univ. Press, 1969.
4. Harrod, R. F., "An Essay in Dynamic Theory," *Economic Journal* **49** (March 1939), 14–33; reprinted in *Growth Economics* (A. K. Sen, ed.). New York: Penguin, 1970.
5. Johnson, H., "Money in a One-Sector Neoclassical Growth Model," in *Essays in Monetary Economics*. London and New York: Cambridge Univ. Press, 1967.
6. Johnson, H., "Problems of Efficiency in Monetary Management," *Journal of Political Economy* **76** (September/October 1968), 971–990.

7. Levhari, D., and Patinkin, D., "The Role of Money in a Simple Growth Model," *American Economic Review* **58** (September 1968), 713–753.

8. McKinnon, R. I., *Money and Capital in Economic Development*. Washington, D.C.: The Brookings Institution, 1973.

9. Metzler, L., "Wealth, Saving, and the Rate of Interest," *Journal of Political Economy* **59** (April 1951), 93–116.

10. Mundell, R., *Monetary Theory*. Pacific Palisades, California: Goodyear Publ., 1971.

11. Tobin, J., "Asset Holdings and Spending Decisions," *American Economic Review* **42** (May 1952), 109–133.

12. Tobin, J., "Money and Economic Growth," *Econometrica* **33** (October 1965), 671–684.

13. Williamson, J., "A Simple Neo-Keynesian Growth Model." *The Review of Economic Studies* **37** (April 1970), 157–171.

# ECONOMIC GROWTH AND STAGES OF THE BALANCE OF PAYMENTS

## A Theoretical Model

Stanley Fischer*

University of Chicago

Jacob A. Frenkel

University of Chicago
and
Tel-Aviv University

## Introduction

A well-known stylized fact in the theories of economic development and international trade is the notion that a country goes through a number of distinct balance of payments and balance of indebtedness stages in the process of growth. A typical classification defines four stages: young and growing debtor, mature debtor, young creditor, and mature creditor.[1]

A well-known model in the theory of international trade is the two-sector Heckscher–Ohlin model. The purpose of this chapter is to construct a formal model of a growing economy with a Metzleric wealth-saving relationship to be used in analyzing the structure and development of both the

---

* Present affiliation: Massachusetts Institute of Technology.

[1] See Samuelson [12, pp. 636–637]. See also Kindleberger [10, pp. 483–486]. The number of stages identified by various authors differs. For instance, Halevi [7] defines twelve stages; he also provides an empirical test of the hypothesis.

balance of payments and its components, and the balance of indebtedness, in the process of growth. To do so, we use the standard Heckscher–Ohlin model, modified to take account of asset flows. In Metzleric fashion, saving is identified with the flow demand for securities, and investment with the flow supply of securities (Metzler [11, p. 102]); their interaction generates the time paths that are the object of this analysis. It is shown that the model can indeed produce dynamic paths which are consistent with the stylized facts. The analysis is of further interest for its concentration on the qualitative properties of the time paths of endogenous variables in addition to their stability.[2]

Section I constructs the model and develops the production, consumption, and trade relationships of the economy. Section II discusses the existence and characteristics of the long-run steady state in production and consumption. Section III analyzes the dynamic behavior of the system and examines particularly the time path of the various international trading accounts and the implied stages of development. Section IV concludes the text. The Appendix provides the derivation of some propositions used in the chapter.

The analysis is confined throughout to the "small country" case, i.e., the case of a country whose terms of trade can be taken as fixed by the world market regardless of its growth. It is also assumed that the country does not specialize in the production of only one good in the course of its growth.

## I. The Production, Consumption, and Trade Relationships

Our model is that of a small, open, two-sector barter economy. Its basic elements are the production relationships of the two-sector growth model, the consumption function, and the trading assumptions.

It is assumed that there is international trade in consumption goods and in claims to income streams from capital equipment but not in capital goods themselves. Nonetheless, the "small country" assumption implies that the terms of trade between capital and consumption goods are fixed: any incipient deviation from the world terms of trade is eliminated by asset-holders who trade securities.[3]

The population (labor force) is growing at a constant rate $n$:

$$L(t) = L_0 e^{nt}. \tag{1}$$

Both consumption and investment goods are produced by constant returns-to-scale technologies, with production of the consumption good being more capital intensive than that of the investment good. The capital-intensity

---

[2] See Bhagwati [1, p. 62] and Caves [2, Chapter 9] for the comment that there are few genuinely dynamic analyses in the international trade literature.

[3] See the discussion following Eq. (4).

assumption is, as usual, important in that it is necessary for stability. The per capita output of each good depends on both the overall capital–labor ratio $k$ and the relative price of capital in terms of the consumption good $p_k$:

$$q_c = q_c(k, p_k), \qquad \partial q_c/\partial k > 0, \qquad \partial q_c/\partial p_k < 0 \qquad (2)$$

$$q_I = q_I(k, p_k), \qquad \partial q_I/\partial k < 0, \qquad \partial q_I/\partial p_k > 0 \qquad (3)$$

where $q_c$ and $q_I$ are, respectively, the per capita output of the consumption good and the investment good. The effects of increases in the per capita capital stock on output of the two sectors follows from the capital-intensity assumption, by the Rybczinski theorem.

The value of output is equal to the income of domestic factors:

$$q_c(k) + p_k q_I(k) = rk + v \qquad (4)$$

where $r$ is the rental rate on capital and $v$ the wage rate, each in terms of the consumption good numéraire. It can be shown that

$$\partial q_c/\partial k > r \qquad \text{and} \qquad \partial^2 q_c/\partial k^2 = 0$$

in the range of nonspecialization.

Using the "small country" assumption, we assume that the interest rate $i$ is fixed, since there is international trade in securities. This also fixes the price of capital $p_k$. To see this, consider the relationship between the rental rate on capital $r$, the interest rate $i$, and $p_k$. The interest rate is the return, valued in terms of consumption goods, obtained by investing resources (in either domestic capital or foreign securities) worth one unit of consumption goods. The rental rate $r$ is the return valued in terms of consumption goods, obtained by investing one unit of capital, costing $p_k$ in terms of consumption goods.

Now $i$, the interest rate, is given by the world market. Thus

$$r(p_k)/p_k = i \qquad (5)$$

is the condition which equalizes rates of return and determines $p_k$. Note that it is necessary to assume that no capital gains are expected on domestic capital in order for rate-of-return equalization to determine $p_k$ uniquely. This is an attractive assumption insofar as it is self-justifying; in fact, the path on which no capital gains are expected can be shown to be the only stable path on which expectations are fulfilled.

Given the constancy of $p_k$, we drop the explicit dependence of the supply functions (2) and (3) on $p_k$. Further, $v$, the wage rate, will also not change so long as $p_k$ is fixed. We are abstracting here from the possibility of improvements in the quality of the labor force through investment in human capital.

The per capita stock of capital changes through time as investment goods are produced:

$$\dot{k} = q_1 - nk. \tag{6}$$

Consumption is assumed to be an increasing function of permanent income, with the propensity to consume, $\gamma$, itself being an increasing function of permanent income. This latter assumption conforms with Metzler's wealth–saving relationship [11]. Thus[4]

$$c = \gamma(iw)iw, \qquad \gamma = \gamma(iw), \quad \gamma' > 0, \quad 2\gamma' + \gamma''iw > 0. \tag{7}$$

Per capita consumption and wealth are denoted by $c$ and $w$, respectively, $i$ is the interest rate, and $iw$ is permanent income (given that the rate of interest is expected to remain constant). It is assumed that there are low levels of permanent income at which saving takes place, i.e., at which $\gamma < 1$. Wealth consists of the value of the ownership of capital $p_k k$, net ownership of foreign securities $z$, and of human capital—the capitalized value of wage income $v/i$:

$$w = p_k k + z + (v/i). \tag{8}$$

Note that, with the constant interest rate, permanent income is equal to the actual income of domestic residents:

$$iw = ip_k k + iz + v = rk + v + iz. \tag{9}$$

The sum of the first two terms, $rk + v$, is equal to the value of domestic output, and $iz$ is income earned from net ownership of foreign securities. The consumption function is shown in Fig. 1. The propensity to consume may exceed unity.

Net purchases of foreign securities correspond to the deficit in the capital account. Denoting aggregate net purchases of foreign securities by $\dot{Z}$, we have

$$\dot{Z}/L = \dot{z} + nz = q_c(k) - \gamma(iw)iw + iz. \tag{10}$$

The interpretation of (10) follows, with all variables being per capita. The domestic output of the consumption good is $q_c(k)$ and domestic consumption is $\gamma(iw)iw$. The excess of domestic production over consumption of consumption goods is the surplus in the trade account. Debt is serviced by payments of consumption goods, and $iz$ is the surplus in the debt-service account. The sum of the surpluses in the trade and debt-service accounts is the current

---

[4] The restrictions imposed on $\gamma$ in Eq. (7) are consistent with the saving behavior implied by the consumer having a long-run desired wealth level. For derivation of a similar consumption function based on intertemporal optimization, see Uzawa [15]. We provide the solutions for the case of a constant saving rate in footnotes.

account surplus, which is identically equal to the capital account deficit $(\dot{z} + nz)$.

We shall sometimes use a different expression for the capital account deficit: inserting (4) in (10), using (9), and rearranging, we obtain

$$\dot{z} + nz = -p_k q_1(k) + iw[1 - \gamma(iw)].  \tag{10'}$$

Equation (10') states that the deficit on capital account is equal to the excess of saving [the second term on the right-hand side of (10')] over $p_k q_1(k)$, the value of investment, which is identified with the flow supply of securities [11, p. 102].

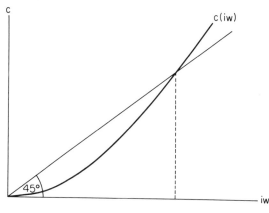

**Fig. 1**

## II. The Characteristics of the Steady State

The steady state in production occurs at that level of the capital stock at which $\dot{k} = 0$. Thus, from (6), the steady state capital stock $k^*$ is defined by[5]

$$q_1(k^*) = nk^*.  \tag{11}$$

The steady state in consumption is reached at that level of permanent income at which asset holders save exactly the amount needed to keep per capita wealth constant. Differentiating (8) with respect to time, and using (6) and (10'), we derive an expression for the rate of change of per capita wealth $\dot{w}$, which is identified with the flow demand for securities:

$$\dot{w} = iw[1 - \gamma(iw)] - n(w - v/i).  \tag{12}$$

---

[5] The steady state capital stock is, of course, a function of the price of capital; the higher $p_k$ is (equivalently, the lower the interest rate), the greater $k^*$ is.

Accordingly, the steady state level of per capita wealth $w^*$ is defined by[6]

$$iw^*[1 - \gamma(iw^*)] = n(w^* - v/i). \tag{13}$$

The left-hand side of (13) is per capita saving and the right-hand side is the amount of saving needed to provide newly born individuals with the existing per capita level of wealth.[7]

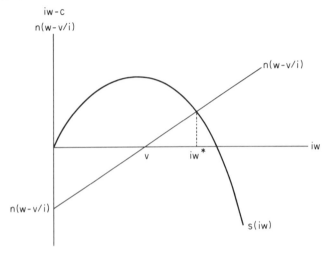

**Fig. 2**

Figure 2 is used in analyzing the steady state in wealth. The curve $s(iw)$ is per capita saving as a function of permanent income; in Fig. 1, saving, which is simply the excess of income over consumption, is the vertical distance between the consumption function and the 45° line. The straight line in Fig. 2 is the locus $n(w - v/i)$. The intersection of the two loci occurs at the steady state level of permanent income and so determines the steady state level of wealth. The existence of a steady state is guaranteed if the consumption function has the shape shown in Fig. 1, with saving (see Fig. 2) being zero at the

---

[6] The steady state level of per capita wealth is also a function of the price of capital (equivalently, of the interest rate). When there is no population growth, an increase in the price of capital results in a higher steady state level of wealth and the same steady state level of permanent income. The effects on steady state wealth of increases in the price of capital are ambiguous when there is population growth.

[7] Each individual is born with $v/i$ of wealth (his human capital), and there is no need to save to provide him with human capital—hence the $(w^* - v/i)$ term on the right-hand side of (13).

zero wealth level, increasing at low levels of permanent income, and then decreasing at an increasing rate at higher levels of permanent income.[8]

From (8), (11), and (13), steady state per capita net ownership of foreign securities is

$$z^* = w^* - p_k k^* - v/i. \tag{14}$$

It is clear from (14) that the country's steady state net debtor or creditor position depends on both its production technology and saving behavior. Given the rate of population growth, the higher $(w^* - v/i)$ is—the larger the value of per capita cumulative saving—the greater the net ownership of foreign securities in the steady state is. Similarly, the smaller $k^*$ is, the smaller must the cumulative supply of domestic securities have been, and thus the greater the value of $z^*$.

It follows from (11) that there is a unique positive $k^*$, from the discussion above that there is a unique $w^*$, and hence from (14) that there is a unique $z^*$ in the steady state.

## III. The Dynamic Behavior of the System

The behavior of capital and wealth through time is determined by (6) and (12), respectively, and we reproduce those equations for convenience:

$$\dot{k} = q_1(k) - nk \tag{6}$$

$$\dot{w} = iw[1 - \gamma(iw)] - n(w - v/i). \tag{12}$$

In Fig. 3 the rate of change of the capital stock (per capita) is plotted as a function of the capital stock (per capita). The relationship is linear because the output of investment goods is itself a linear function of the stock of capital, i.e., $\partial^2 q_1/\partial k^2 = 0$. When the capital stock is below $k^*$, the output of investment goods is greater than it is at $k^*$ and so the capital stock increases until $k^*$ is reached. Actually, the stock of capital grows according to a stock-adjustment equation.[9]

---

[8] Whether there is positive nonhuman wealth in the steady state depends on whether the intersection between the two loci in Fig. 2 occurs above the zero axis. We shall henceforth assume that the intersection occurs as in Fig. 2, with $iw^* > v$. As the rate of population growth changes, the saving curve in Fig. 2 does not shift and the $n(w - v/i)$ locus pivots about its intersection with the abscissa, and as $n \to \infty$, $iw^* \to v$. In the special case of a constant saving rate, the saving function in Fig. 2 becomes a straight line, and a necessary and sufficient condition for the existence of a positive $w^*$ is that $i(1 - \gamma) < n$. For an analysis of the case in which the saving rate is constant, see Frenkel and Fischer [6].

[9] Since $q_1(k)$ is a linear function of $k$, we can write $q_1(k) = a + (\partial q_1/\partial k)k$ and then $\dot{k} = a + (\partial q_1/\partial k - n)k$. Accordingly, $k^* = -a/(\partial q_1/\partial k - n)$ and $\dot{k} = (-\partial q_1/\partial k + n)(k^* - k)$.

In Fig. 4 the rate of change of per capita wealth is plotted as a function of the level of wealth. The locus in Fig. 4 is the vertical distance between the two curves in Fig. 2 at each level of wealth. (Since $i$ is constant, a rescaling of the $iw$ axis in Fig. 2 produces two curves which are functions of $w$ rather than $iw$.) It may have the shape of either the solid or the dotted line, depending on whether the slope of the saving locus at $w = 0$ exceeds or falls short of $n$. At any level of wealth below $w^*$, there is more saving than the amount required to keep the level of per capita wealth constant, and so per capita wealth rises until $w^*$ is reached.

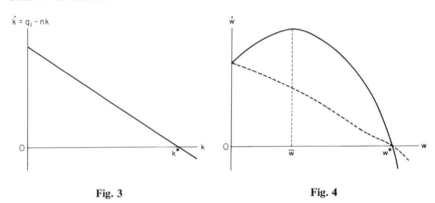

Fig. 3                                              Fig. 4

Thus the system is stable in $k$ and $w$ for $k_0 < k^*$; given any initial $k$ in the region of nonspecialization $(k_0 < k^*)$ and given initial wealth, each variable approaches its steady state level monotonically.

We are now in a position to investigate the behavior of the balance of payments and the balance of indebtedness through time. The per capita deficit in the capital account, as seen from (10), is $\dot{z} + nz$. The debt-service account surplus is $iz$. The trade account surplus[10] is, accordingly, $\dot{z} + (n - i)z$. It follows that once we know the time path of the balance of indebtedness $z$, we know the time paths of the three trading accounts. The dynamic behavior of these accounts is analyzed with the aid of Fig. 5, which is drawn in the $kw$ plane. The directions of the arrows in Fig. 5 are implied by the stability of the system in $k$ and $w$.

From the fact that $\dot{w} = p_k \dot{k} + \dot{z}$, we know that the rate of change of per capita holdings of foreign securities depends only on the rates of change of per capita wealth and capital stock. Thus at any point in Fig. 5, a particular behavior of $\dot{z}$ is implied. In particular, we show in Fig. 5 the locus $(\dot{z} = 0)$ along which net per capita holdings of foreign securities are constant.

---

[10] In the following, for the sake of brevity, we use the term "trade account" for the goods and services account where the latter excludes the debt-service account.

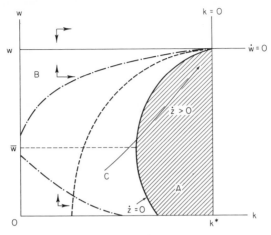

**Fig. 5**

The $\dot{z} = 0$ locus is alternatively described as consisting of those points at which the domestic per capita flow supply of securities is just sufficient to absorb the per capita flow demand for securities. Now the flow supply of securities $p_k \dot{k}$ can be read off Fig. 3, with suitable rescaling. The flow demand for securities, $\dot{w}$, can be read off Fig. 4. The $\dot{z} = 0$ locus is derived by plotting pairs of $k$ and $w$ at which the ordinates in Fig. 3 (appropriately rescaled) and Fig. 4 are equal.

Thus $(k^*, w^*)$ is a point on the $\dot{z} = 0$ locus. As wealth is reduced below $w^*$, $k$ too must fall to keep $\dot{z} = 0$. If the solid line in Fig. 4 applies, there may come a stage—namely, at $\bar{w}$—at which further reductions in wealth require increases in $k$ to maintain $\dot{z} = 0$. It is also possible that at the point of maximum rate of growth of per capita wealth, $\bar{w}$, there is no attainable level of the capital stock for which a sufficient domestic supply of securities is forthcoming to make $\dot{z} = 0$. The $\dot{z} = 0$ locus may accordingly have one of the four shapes shown in Fig. 5: it may be as shown by the solid line; it may consist of the two segments of the dot–dash line; it may consist only of the upper segment of the dot–dash line; or it may look like the dashed line. Despite this seeming complexity, we lose very little generality by working only with the solid line ($\dot{z} = 0$) locus.[11] This particular locus can apply only if the $s(iw)$ curve in Fig. 2

---

[11] In the special case of a constant average propensity to consume, the change in per capita wealth function in Fig. 4 must have the shape of the dotted line [the equation for $\dot{w}$ is $\dot{w} = (1 - \gamma)iw - n(w - v/i)$]. In this case the $\dot{z} = 0$ locus is a straight line with the slope

$$(dw/dk)_{\dot{z}=0} = [p_k(i-n) - \partial q_c/\partial k]/(i - n - \gamma i) > 0.$$

(The denominator is negative in order for $w^* > 0$ to exist; see footnote 8.)

has a steeper slope at the origin than the $n(w - v/i)$ curve, i.e., only if $i > n$. This is a reasonable case to investigate.

All points to the right of the $\dot{z} = 0$ locus are points at which the per capita flow supply of domestic securities is too low to absorb the per capita domestic saving required to keep $z$ unchanged, and $z$ is accordingly rising in that region. Thus $\dot{z} > 0$ in the shaded region of Fig. 5; similarly, $\dot{z}$ is negative in the unshaded region.

It follows from the fact that $k$ and $w$ converge to $k^*$ and $w^*$ that $z$—net per capita holdings of foreign securities—also converges to its steady state value. In what follows we assume that $z^* > 0$—that the country eventually becomes a net creditor—but this in no way affects the essentials of the analysis.

From Fig. 5 it may be seen that the time path of $z$ depends crucially on the initial endowments of wealth and capital. We consider only initial conditions in which both the capital stock and wealth are below their steady state levels—other cases can be readily investigated by the reader. Suppose, for instance, that the economy's initial endowment is at a point such as $A$, with low wealth but a capital stock close to its equilibrium level. Accordingly, $z$ too must be small and the economy is a net debtor. The approach to equilibrium is characterized by increasing $z$.

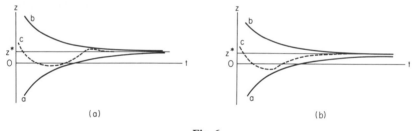

Fig. 6

Figures 6a and 6b describe possible paths of $z$. Paths "$a$" in both figures correspond to initial conditions such as $A$ in Fig. 5. On such paths very little investment in capital goods is taking place, but wealth is being accumulated: accordingly the flow demand for securities exceeds the domestic flow supply and holdings of foreign securities rise continuously. Suppose, alternatively, that the economy is initially at a position such as $B$ in Fig. 5, with large wealth and small $k$, and hence large $z$. Then the path to equilibrium will be characterized by high consumption and low saving and an excess flow supply of securities. In the process the net per capita ownership of foreign securities is reduced, the per capita capital stock is increased, and the economy may switch from being a net creditor to a net debtor. Paths "$b$" in Figs. 6a and 6b correspond to initial conditions such as $B$.

However, initial conditions such as those represented by both $A$ and $B$ are special, and it is not clear from Fig. 5 how $z$ will behave for initial conditions such as, say, $C$, where both $k$ and $w$ are low. One possible path is that shown, where $z$ initially falls as the country borrows to finance its investment, and then rises as the rate of investment falls off and wealth is accumulated. But one cannot, on the basis of Fig. 5 alone, rule out the possibility that the path to equilibrium could cross the $\dot{z} = 0$ locus an arbitrary number of times. This possibility is considered in detail in the Appendix where it is shown that in this model no path can cross the $\dot{z} = 0$ locus more than twice. Possible paths corresponding to initial conditions such as $C$ are shown by paths "$c$" in Figs. 6a and 6b.

It is shown in the Appendix that whether the $\dot{z} = 0$ locus can be crossed more than once depends on whether $\partial q_c / \partial k < p_k \, \partial c / \partial w$ (Fig. 6a) or whether $\partial q_c / \partial k > p_k \, \partial c / \partial w$ (Fig. 6b). It is clear from Fig. 5 that any path can enter the $\dot{z} > 0$ region. The question is whether, once $z$ starts rising, it can ever fall again. Consider now some path on which $\dot{z} > 0$: suppose that the path touches the $\dot{z} = 0$ locus. At that point we know that wealth is changing only through the accumulation of capital since net holdings of foreign securities are momentarily constant. The accumulation of capital increases the supply of consumption goods by $\partial q_c / \partial k$ and the demand for consumption goods by $p_k \, \partial c / \partial w$ since an increase in the capital stock of one unit increases wealth by $p_k$ units. If the increase in supply falls short of the increase in demand, i.e., if $\partial q_c / \partial k < p_k \, \partial c / \partial w$, then indeed $\dot{z}$ can become negative at that point and the path can leave the region in which $\dot{z} > 0$. On the other hand, if $\partial q_c / \partial k > p_k \, \partial c / \partial w$, then the path cannot leave the $\dot{z} > 0$ region once in it. These are the considerations on which the paths "$c$" are based.

Paths "$c$" are the paths most relevant to the analysis of the development of a poor country corresponding to a low level of wealth and a low level of capital. They are also the most complicated paths possible for the balance of indebtedness, where complications are measured by the number of turning points in the paths. Initially, since the levels of wealth and capital are relatively low, saving (the flow demand for securities) falls short of investment (the flow supply of securities); thus the economy becomes a net seller of securities, corresponding to a surplus in the capital account of the balance of payments and to an increase in the net debtor position. This process continues until the steady rise in wealth induces enough saving to match the flow supply of securities (which is declining through time as the capital stock is rising). At this point in time the capital account is balanced. As wealth continues to rise, saving exceeds the flow supply of securities and the economy becomes a net lender and thus reduces its net debtor position. For the case shown in Fig. 6b, any path approaching the steady state balance of indebtedness $z^*$ from below cannot cross the $z^*$ axis, i.e., it must approach it monotonically.

For the case shown in Fig. 6a, however, the economy may overshoot $z^*$ and then approach it from above. In other words, in the process of growth, cumulative net lending may exceed the steady state net creditor position and thus cause a new turning point as the economy lowers its net holdings of foreign securities which approach their steady state value $z^*$. It might be noted that the overshooting described above, though possible, does not necessarily occur. It should also be noted that the overshooting *cannot* occur if the saving rate is constant.[12]

The analysis of the time path of the balance of indebtedness as described in Figs. 6a and 6b also provides the time path of its counterpart in the balance of payments—the debt-service account. Since the latter is simply $iz$, it is obtained by rescaling the ordinates of Fig. 6 by multiplying by the rate of interest $i$.

As shown before, the deficit in the per capita capital account is $\dot{z} + nz$, the path of which can be determined given the initial conditions and the time path of $z$.

In Fig. 7 we draw the possible paths for the per capita deficit in the capital account corresponding to those of Fig. 6a, for which at equilibrium $\partial q_c/\partial k < p_k \, \partial c/\partial w$. The exact considerations on which these paths are based are dis-

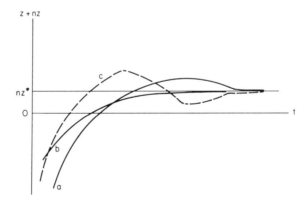

**Fig. 7**

---

[12] It may appear somewhat puzzling that although $k$ and $w$ proceed monotonically to $k^*$ and $w^*$, $z$ does not necessarily approach $z^*$ monotonically. The basic determinant of the time path of $z$ is differences in the rates of growth of the capital stock and wealth. When the capital stock grows more rapidly than wealth early in development, there will have to be foreign borrowing even though the steady state will be one in which the country is a net creditor. The reader may obtain an intuitive feeling for the possible paths of $z$ by examining the algebraic difference between the values of any two functions (in our case, $p_k k$ and $w$) approaching the asymptotes monotonically but at different speeds.

cussed and derived in the Appendix. Again the most complicated path is the one labeled "$c$," corresponding to initial condition $C$ in Fig. 5.

The path labeled "$c$" in Fig. 6 provides characteristics of the time path of the balance of indebtedness which are identical with the textbook version of the process as described by Kindleberger [10, p. 435, Fig. 25.4]. One could characterize path "$c$" in Fig. 6a as having four stages: up to the first turning point as "young and growing debtor"; from the first turning point to $z = 0$, as "mature debtor"; from the crossing of $z = 0$ to the next turning point, as "young creditor"; and the remainder of the path as "mature creditor." Any number of other classifications of stages, based on the direction of change of the balance of indebtedness, its relation to the steady state level, and the sign of the balance of indebtedness are possible. Obviously, such alternative possibilities arise whenever an attempt is made to describe a continuous path as consisting of a number of stages. But the important thing is that the qualitative characteristics of the path are consistent with the stylized facts of the "stages" hypothesis.[13]

## IV. Conclusions

The purpose of this chapter has been to construct a formal model which provides an economic rationale for the stylized facts of the balance of payments stages hypothesis. We have shown that the standard Heckscher–Ohlin model can generate time paths of the balance of payments which are consistent with the stages hypothesis. Necessary conditions for such a result are the strong factor-intensity assumption, initial conditions such that both the capital stock and wealth are below steady state levels, and a world interest rate exceeding the rate of population growth. The latter two conditions are eminently reasonable; the first less so. These conditions are not, however, sufficient: the model is consistent with the stages hypotheses but is also consistent with patterns of indebtedness in which debt increases or decreases monotonically over time.

Recent papers on the theory of economic growth and international trade have emphasized the structure of the balance of trade in the context of a two-sector model where both the consumption good and the investment good are internationally traded (e.g., Johnson [9] and Stiglitz [13]). In order to conduct an investigation into the development stages hypothesis, trade in debt which induces debt service had to be incorporated. Accordingly, the present chapter, while proceeding in the framework of a two-sector growth model, has allowed for trade in claims on income streams and has not allowed

---

[13] We have, available on request, an appendix in which we simulated the model, generating time paths such as those shown in Figs. 6 and 7.

trade of the capital goods themselves.[14] The model could be easily extended to a monetary economy by adding a portfolio relationship which in turn implies that part of the flow of saving manifests itself as a flow demand for money while the behavior of the monetary authority determines the flow supply of money. The essentials of the analysis, however, are unaffected.[15] Other extensions would consider models in which there is trade in both debt and machines and would also consider the stages hypothesis for a country which is not small.[16] In this chapter it has been shown that the process of economic development can indeed be characterized in terms of the various phases described in the literature, on the basis of a standard trade model.

### Appendix. Derivation of Time Paths of Net Holdings of Foreign Securities and the Capital Account

Here we study the time path of net holdings of foreign securities $z$ (and also the implied debt-service account) in more detail than was done in the text, and then proceed to an analysis of the time path of the capital account $\dot{z} + nz$.

Figure A.1, a phase diagram in $k$, $z$ space, is our basic diagram. It is derived from Fig. 5. The $\dot{z} = 0$ locus in Fig. 5 is derived from (10) of the text:

$$\dot{z} = q_c(k) - c + (i - n)z. \tag{A.1}$$

In deriving Fig. A.1 from Fig. 5 we note that $z = w - p_k k - v/i$ and that, accordingly, to transform the figure from $k$, $w$ to $k$, $z$ space, we have only to rotate and displace the ordinate appropriately. In what follows, to simplify the diagrammatic presentation we define units so that $p_k = 1$ and thus the appropriate rotation is through $-45°$. We examine explicitly only the case in which the $\dot{z} = 0$ locus in Fig. 5 is the solid line. Note also that isowealth lines can be drawn in Fig. A.1: they are lines with a slope of $-45°$. As usual, no significance attaches to the fact that $z^*$ is shown positive in Fig. A.1.

The slope of the $\dot{z} = 0$ locus in Fig. A.1 is, from (A.1),

$$\left(\frac{dz}{dk}\right)_{\dot{z}=0} = -\frac{(\partial q_c/\partial k) - p_k \, \partial c/\partial w}{i - n - \partial c/\partial w} = -\frac{\partial \dot{z}/\partial k}{\partial \dot{z}/\partial z}. \tag{A.2}$$

We know from Fig. 5 that the $\dot{z} = 0$ locus emerges from $k^*$, $z^*$ below the $w^*$ line. We do not, however, know whether it emerges with a positive or negative slope. Both possibilities are shown in Fig. A.1; by analogy with Fig. 5,

---

[14] For an analysis of trade in debt in a one-sector model, see Hamada [8].

[15] For an analysis along these lines, see Frenkel [5].

[16] We have extended the analysis to include these possibilities in Fischer and Frenkel [3, 4].

though, the $\dot{z} = 0$ locus does not necessarily have the negatively sloped portions at low levels of $z$ which we show in Fig. A.1.[17]

The direction of the horizontal arrows follows from Eq. (6). Anywhere to the right of and below the $\dot{z} = 0$ locus, the per capita flow supply of securities is too low to satisfy domestic demand and $\dot{z}$ is accordingly positive. To the left of and above the $\dot{z} = 0$ locus, $\dot{z}$ is negative, but we know that the economy is always moving in the direction of increasing wealth.

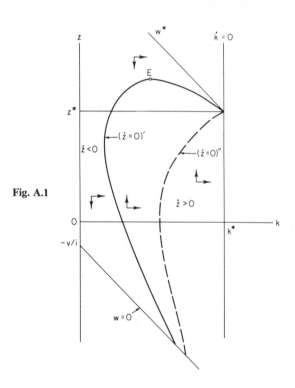

**Fig. A.1**

Now consider the number of times a path can cross the $\dot{z} = 0$ locus. Take first the $(\dot{z} = 0)'$ locus. Any path starting to the left of that locus and crossing it below $E$ cannot cross the locus again except beyond $E$: the reason is that any path touching the $(\dot{z} = 0)'$ locus to the left of $E$ has only horizontal motion to the right at that point. No path can cross the $(\dot{z} = 0)'$ locus beyond $E$ from above for a similar reason. Thus, for the locus $(\dot{z} = 0)'$, no path can

---

[17] Note that when $n = 0$, the $\dot{z} = 0$ locus must intersect the $w = 0$ line at $k = k^*$. Again, for the special case of a constant saving ratio, the $\dot{z} = 0$ locus is a straight line with the slope

$$(dz/dk)_{\dot{z}=0} = (p_k \gamma i - \partial q_c/\partial k)/(i - n - \gamma i) > 0.$$

cross the locus more than twice: any path crossing the locus twice must start from a region where $\dot{z} < 0$ and end in such a region; any path which starts with $\dot{z} > 0$ can go through $\dot{z} = 0$ at most once. However, a path in which $\dot{z} < 0$ initially may either fail to cross the $\dot{z} = 0$ locus or cross it only once, and a path on which $\dot{z} > 0$ initially may also not cross the $\dot{z} = 0$ locus.

Next consider the $(\dot{z} = 0)''$ locus. Using arguments similar to those of the preceding paragraph, it can be shown that the $(\dot{z} = 0)''$ locus can be crossed at most once and that by a path which starts with $\dot{z} < 0$.

We have not yet indicated the economic meaning of the differences between the two $\dot{z} = 0$ loci in Fig. A.1. The $(\dot{z} = 0)'$ locus is one on which, near the steady state, $\partial q_c/\partial k < p_k \, \partial c/\partial w$ and the $(\dot{z} = 0)''$ locus is one on which the reverse inequality holds. Consider a path on which $\dot{z} > 0$ near the steady state. At the same time, capital accumulation is taking place. If these increases in the capital stock increase the output of consumption goods less than they increase the demand for consumption goods ($\partial q_c/\partial k < p_k \, \partial c/\partial w$), then this accumulation induces an excess demand for the consumption good which will be financed by net sales of domestic securities; in other words, if the rise in the capital stock induces an excess supply of securities, then $\dot{z}$ can become negative and the path may accordingly cross the $\dot{z} = 0$ locus.

Notice also that initial endowments of both $k$ and $z$ play an important role in determining how many times the economy overshoots and undershoots the steady state value of per capita net holdings of foreign securities; i.e., the number of times the $\dot{z} = 0$ locus is crossed.

Once the path of $\dot{z}$ and the initial $z_0$ are known, the path of $z$ itself can be calculated. We assume, in plotting these possible paths of $z$ in Figs. 6a and 6b that the steady state $z^*$ is positive. Although we have shown $z^*$ positive in Fig. 6, it may be negative, and the appropriate time paths can be derived simply by raising the zero axis for $z$ above $z^*$ in Fig. 6.

The capital account deficit is $\dot{z} + nz$. Thus it is clear that asymptotically the capital account will be in deficit or surplus, depending only on whether $z^*$ is positive or negative.

To investigate the time path of the capital account, consider Fig. A.2 which reproduces the essentials of Fig. A.1 for the most general case, i.e., for the case in which the $(\dot{z} = 0)'$ locus applies. The locus for which $\dot{z} + nz = 0$ (balance in the capital account) must lie outside the $\dot{z} = 0$ locus for $z > 0$ and inside the $\dot{z} = 0$ locus for $z < 0$. In addition to the $\dot{z} + nz = 0$ locus, other isocapital account contours are drawn. In the nonspecialization region the slope of each contour depends only on $w$ and thus has the same slope as that of the balanced capital account locus along a given isowealth line. The deficit on capital account increases as movements from outer contours like $\alpha$ to inner contours like $\beta$ take place. For $z^* > 0$, the contour on which the deficit is $nz^*$ lies below the $\dot{z} = 0$ locus near the equilibrium. To facilitate the analysis we have drawn two isowealth lines: the first is $w = \hat{w}$, on which $\partial q_c / \partial k = p_k \, \partial c / \partial w$; and the second is $w = \overset{\scriptscriptstyle\circ}{w}$, on which $i = \partial c / \partial w$.

It may also be seen that we have divided the space in Fig. A.2 into six regions. Region I is the area below the $\overset{\scriptscriptstyle\circ}{w}$ line; II is the region between $\hat{w}$ and $\overset{\scriptscriptstyle\circ}{w}$ for which $\dot{z} < 0$; III is the region between $\hat{w}$ and $\overset{\scriptscriptstyle\circ}{w}$ for which $\dot{z} > 0$; IV is the region between $\hat{w}$ and $w^*$ for which $\dot{z} > 0$; V is the region between $\hat{w}$ and

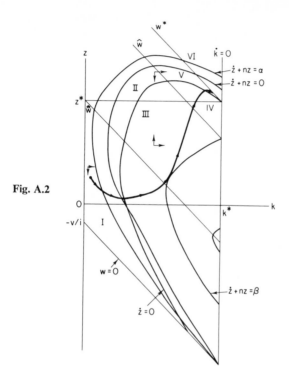

Fig. A.2

$w^*$ for which $\dot{z} < 0$; and VI is the region above $w^*$. This division into regions is made so that the path of the capital account can be examined in each region.[18]

In regions I and II the capital account deficit increases continuously since the slope of the path, namely,

$$\left(\frac{dz}{dk}\right)_{path} = \frac{\dot{z}}{\dot{k}} = -p_k + \frac{\dot{w}}{\dot{k}} = -p_k + \frac{iw - c - n(w - v/i)}{q_1(k) - nk} > -p_k \quad (A.3)$$

[18] As can be seen for the special case of a constant saving ratio, the only two possible regions are II and III.

is greater than the slope of the contours, which is

$$\left(\frac{dz}{dk}\right)_{CA} = -\frac{\partial q_c/\partial k - p_k\,\partial c/\partial w}{i - \partial c/\partial w} = -p_k\left[\frac{1/p_k\,\partial q_c/\partial k - \partial c/\partial w}{i - \partial c/\partial w}\right] < -p_k. \quad (A.4)$$

The CA in (A.4) stands for "capital account." Similarly, the capital account deficit decreases continuously in region IV and increases continuously in region VI.

In regions III and V, however, the capital account deficit increases at some points and decreases at others. We are able to establish that there can be at most one turning point in the capital account in region III, but we have not been able to do the same for region V—for which we assume there is only one turning point.[19] Consider now region III. The slope of the path increases continuously in region III, while the slope of the contours decreases. Specifically,

$$\left(\frac{d^2z}{dk^2}\right)_{path} = \frac{\dot{w}}{\dot{k}^2}\left[\frac{1}{p_k}\frac{\partial q_c}{\partial k} - \frac{\partial c}{\partial w}\right] > 0 \qquad \text{in region III} \qquad (A.5)$$

$$\left(\frac{d^2z}{dk^2}\right)_{CA} = \frac{\partial^2 c}{\partial w^2}\frac{[p_k i - \partial q_c/\partial k]^2}{[i - \partial c/\partial w]^3} < 0 \qquad \text{in region III.} \qquad (A.6)$$

It follows that there can at most be one tangency between the path and the contours in region III.

The path we have drawn in Fig. A.2 is that called "$c$" in Fig. 7 of the text.

## ACKNOWLEDGMENTS

We are grateful to T. N. Srinivasan and George Horwich for helpful comments. In addition, we are indebted to Rudiger Dornbusch, Harry G. Johnson, members of the International Economics Workshop at the University of Chicago, and members of the Faculty Seminar at Tel-Aviv University and the Hebrew University, Jerusalem, for their comments on an earlier draft.

## REFERENCES

1. Bhagwati, J., *Trade Tariffs and Growth*. Cambridge, Massachusetts: MIT Press, 1969.
2. Caves, R. E., *Trade and Economic Structure*. Cambridge, Massachusetts: Harvard Univ. Press, 1960.
3. Fischer, S., and J. A. Frenkel, "Investment, the Two-Sector Model and Trade in Debt and Capital Goods," *Journal of International Economics* 2 (August 1972), 211–233.

[19] Note, however, that as far as the trend is concerned, region V must be characterized as a region in which the per capita capital-account deficit initially falls and eventually increases.

4. Fischer, S., and Frenkel, J. A., " Interest Rate Equalization and Patterns of Production, Trade, and Consumption in a Two-Country Growth Model," Rep. No. 7340, Center for Mathematical Studies in Business and Economics, Univ. of Chicago, 1973.

5. Frenkel, J. A., "A Theory of Money, Trade and the Balance of Payments in a Model of Accumulation," *Journal of International Economics* **1** (May 1971), 159–187.

6. Frenkel, J. A., and S. Fischer, "International Capital Movements along Balanced Growth Paths: Comments and Extensions," *Economic Record* **48** (June 1972), 266–271.

7. Halevi, N., "An Empirical Test of the 'Balance of Payments Stages' Hypothesis," *Journal of International Economics* **1** (February 1971), 101–117.

8. Hamada, K., "Economic Growth and Long-Term International Capital Movements," *Yale Economic Essays* **6** (Spring 1966), 49–96.

9. Johnson, H. G., "Trade and Growth: A Geometrical Exposition," *Journal of International Economics* **1** (February 1971), 83–101.

10. Kindleberger, C. P., *International Economics*, 4th ed. Homewood, Illinois: Irwin, 1968.

11. Metzler, L. A., "Wealth, Saving, and the Rate of Interest," *Journal of Political Economy* **59** (April 1951), 93–116.

12. Samuelson, P. A., *Economics*, 8th ed. New York: McGraw-Hill, 1970.

13. Stiglitz, J. E., "Factor Price Equalization in a Dynamic Economy," *Journal of Political Economy* **78** (May/June 1970), 456–488.

14. Uzawa, H., "On a Two-Sector Model of Economic Growth II," *Review of Economic Studies* **30** (June 1963), 105–118.

15. Uzawa, H., "On a Neo-Classical Model of Economic Growth," *Economics Studies Quarterly* (September 1966), 1–14.

# ON THE DYNAMIC STABILITY OF ECONOMIC GROWTH

*The Neoclassical versus Keynesian Approaches*

---

*Hirofumi Uzawa*

*University of Tokyo*

## I. Introduction

Whether or not the dynamic allocation of scarce resources through the market mechanism can achieve stable economic growth is not simply a matter of theoretical interest, but also is indispensable in the consideration of the effects of public policy. However, there are two opposing approaches to the problem of the dynamic stability of the market mechanism. One approach bases its analysis on the neoclassical economic theory, the other considers the problem within the framework developed in Keynes' *General Theory*. The approach based on neoclassical theory concludes that the process of market growth is usually stable, and, but for exceptional situations, prices change stably and full-employment growth obtains. Keynesian theory, on the other hand, comes to the conclusion that the market allocation of scarce resources is an inherent cause of instability in a modern capitalistic system and that maintaining stable economic growth is akin to walking on the edge of a knife.

The primary purpose of this chapter is to examine the kind of assumptions on which these two conclusions concerning the stability of the growth process in a market economy are based, and, if possible, to ferret out some of the more fundamental differences between the neoclassical and Keynesian approaches.

## II. Basic Assumptions of the Neoclassical Growth Theory

The neoclassical theory of economic growth was first formulated in the works of Tobin [32], Solow [28], and Swan [31]. Although the theoretical background is much older and may be traced back to the early works of Jevons, Menger, and Walras, the models of Tobin, Solow, and Swan have put neoclassical theory into an even clearer form, and at the same time the limitations of the neoclassical framework have been more explicitly brought out.

Let us first consider the concept of capital which lies at the basis of neoclassical theory. Capital refers to the various factors of production which have been accumulated through refraining from past consumption. Added to capital are the variable factors of production, such as the labor employed through the labor market, and these are combined for the purposes of productive activity. However, the phenomenon of the fixity of capital has been ignored in neoclassical theory. It has been assumed that the market price of the stock of capital which is traded on the market is the same for newly produced capital goods and for existing capital goods which are the result of past investment. Entrepreneurs engage in productive activity either by purchasing capital goods or by renting the services of capital goods, and by employing variable factors of production. However, any individual may similarly engage in productive activity, resulting in the disappearance of the essential difference between consumers and producers.

This assumption has important implications for the portfolio behavior of each economic unit. Namely, various economic units may hold either physical capital or financial assets in whatever way they prefer. In order to examine in more detail the implications of the neoclassical hypothesis concerning the choice of assets, let us consider a simplified case in which physical capital and financial assets are each composed of a homogeneous type. Let us also assume that the goods produced are of one variety, identical with the capital assets.

Financial assets will be defined as fixed-interest bearing short-term securities. The holder of these assets can divide the total real amount $A$ between real capital $K$ and financial assets $B$:

$$A = K + B.$$

The holders of assets choose their portfolios in such a way as to maximize profits. If the real rate of interest of financial assets is $\rho$, the real amount of interest income becomes $\rho B$. Physical capital is used as a factor of production and, with the addition of various other factors, goods and services are produced. Assuming that labor is the only other factor besides physical capital, the production function is given by $F(K, N)$, where $K$ and $N$ stand for the amounts of physical capital and labor, respectively. In order to maximize profits, labor is employed at the level where the real wage rate $w$ is equal to the marginal product of labor $F_N$:

$$F_N(K, N) = w.$$

The net profit then becomes

$$F(K, N) - wN = rK$$

where $r$ is the marginal product of capital $F_K$.

Assuming a linear homogeneous production function, the marginal products of both labor and capital are determined solely by the labor/capital ratio $n = N/K$. For example, denoting the production function per unit of capital by

$$f(n) = F(1, n),$$

the marginal products of labor and capital become

$$F_N = f'(n), \qquad F_K = f(n) - nf'(n),$$

respectively.

In this way, the profit yielded by portfolio $(K, B)$ becomes

$$rK + \rho B.$$

If the profits from real capital and financial assets possess the same degree of uncertainty, it is easy to choose the portfolio which will maximize profits. When $r > \rho$, $K = A$ and $B = 0$; and when $r < \rho$, $K = 0$ and $B = A$. Both are held in positive amounts only when $r = \rho$.

Let us denote the economic units comprising the national economy by $j = 1, \ldots, J$, and the various physical capital and financial assets held at the beginning point in time by $K_j{}^0$, $B_j{}^0$. The amount of assets held by unit $j$, $A_j{}^0$, is

$$A_j{}^0 = K_j{}^0 + B_j{}^0.$$

The optimum portfolio $(K_j, B_j)$ is that which maximizes profits $rK_j + \rho B_j$ subject to

$$A_j{}^0 = K_j + B_j.$$

At the beginning of the period, the total amounts of physical capital and financial assets in the society are, respectively, given by

$$K^0 = \sum_j K_j{}^0, \qquad B^0 = \sum_j B_j{}^0.$$

Accordingly, in order for the supply and demand of physical capital and financial assets to be in equilibrium, we must have

$$K^0 = \sum_j K_j, \qquad B^0 = \sum_j B_j.$$

To realize these conditions, the marginal product of capital and the real rate of interest must be equal: $r = \rho$. The labor market attains a state of equilibrium when the real wage rate is at the level where demand equals supply. Hence,

$$w = f'(n^0), \qquad n^0 = N^0/K^0.$$

Now, if the labor possessed by economic unit $j$ at the beginning point of time is $N_j^0$,

$$N^0 = \sum_j N_j^0,$$

and the income of unit $j$ is given by

$$Y_j = rK_j + \rho B_j + wN_j^0,$$

then, in a state of equilibrium, the above can also be written

$$Y_j = rA_j^0 + wN_j^0.$$

Each economic unit determines consumption and saving not only according to present income, but also according to expectations of future income and future market conditions. If the expectations are static, i.e., if income is expected to remain at current levels and the rate of interest is not expected to change, consumption and saving will be determined by current income $Y_j$ and the current market rate of interest $\rho$. And if the subjective preference over consumption paths of each economic unit is homothetic, the consumption and saving functions take on the form

$$C_j = [1 - s(\rho)]Y_j, \qquad S_j = s(\rho)Y_j$$

where $s(\rho)$ is the average propensity to save, depending solely on the rate of interest $\rho$. As shown in ref. [36], $s(\rho)$ is in general an increasing function of $\rho$.

The aggregate consumption $C$ and saving $S$ of the national economy are given by

$$C = \sum_j C_j = [1 - s(\rho)]Y, \qquad S = \sum_j S_j = s(\rho)Y,$$

with $Y$ as the aggregate income:

$$Y = \sum_j Y_j = rK^0 + \rho B^0 + wN^0.$$

Hence,

$$Y = F(K^0, N^0) + \rho B^0.$$

If financial assets possessed and those issued by each economic unit cancel each other out, $B^0 = 0$. Hence,

$$Y = F(K^0, N^0).$$

Summarizing the above analysis, we derive the following prototype of the neoclassical model of economic growth.

The national economy is comprised of economic units $j = 1, \ldots, J$, and these units possess various quantities of physical capital $K_j$, financial assets $B_j$, and labor $N_j$. Aggregating the capital and labor, we get

$$K = \sum_j K_j, \qquad N = \sum_j N_j. \tag{1}$$

If we assume that there are no external assets, then

$$\sum_j B_j = 0. \tag{2}$$

Equilibrium of the assets market is established when the rate of interest and the marginal product of capital are equal:

$$\rho = r. \tag{3}$$

The marginal product of capital and the wage rate of labor are established in response to the conditions of full employment:

$$r = f(n) - nf'(n), \qquad w = f'(n), \tag{4}$$

with $n$ being the labor/capital ratio at the current point in time.

National income $Y$ equals the amount produced:

$$Y = F(K, N) = rK + wN, \tag{5}$$

and the levels of consumption and saving are given by

$$C = [1 - s(\rho)]Y, \qquad S = s(\rho)Y. \tag{6}$$

The accumulation of capital is determined by

$$\dot{K} = S, \tag{7}$$

while the rate of increase of the labor supply is exogenously given:

$$\dot{N}/N = v. \tag{8}$$

As shown in the dynamic equation (7), the saving of each economic unit automatically becomes investment and capital accumulation. This conclusion is derived naturally from the concept of capital in neoclassical theory. Based on the assumption that real capital and financial assets can both be freely traded in the same way on the market, each economic unit can at various points in time continuously put together a desirable portfolio of assets according to income and market conditions. Accordingly, each economic unit is always satisfied with the composition of its assets, and there is no incentive to change them. Saving—that is, the portion of income not consumed—is simply accumulated as capital.

## III. Dynamic Equilibrium of the Neoclassical Model

It is easy to prove the stability of the dynamic process of the neoclassical model. Define the variables per unit of real capital as

$$n = N/K, \quad \text{labor/capital ratio}$$
$$y = Y/K, \quad \text{income/capital ratio.}$$

The conditions of equilibrium and the dynamic equation can be simplified as

$$y = f(n) \tag{9}$$

$$\rho = r = f(n) - nf'(n), \qquad w = f'(n) \tag{10}$$

$$\dot{n}/n = v - sf(n) \tag{11}$$

where $s$ is the average propensity to save.

The neoclassical assumptions concerning the production functions and the average propensity to save are

$$f(0) = 0, \quad f(\infty) = \infty; \qquad f'(0) = \infty, \quad f'(\infty) = 0 \tag{12}$$

$$f'(n) > 0, \qquad f''(n) < 0 \tag{13}$$

$$s = s(\rho), \qquad s'(\rho) \geqq 0. \tag{14}$$

The right-hand side of the dynamic equation (11) decreases with increases in $n$. Accordingly, the stability of (11) may easily be shown, as illustrated in Fig. 1. The horizontal and vertical axes are the labor/capital ratio and the income/capital ratio, respectively. The production function $f(n)$ and the saving function $sf(n)$ are illustrated by curves $OA$ and $OB$, respectively. The labor supply is represented by the straight line $CC$ at height $v$. Taking $n^*$ as the labor/capital ratio corresponding to the intersection of curves $OB$ and $CC$, $n^*$ represents the state of long-term steady growth.

When $n$ is larger than $n^*$, the saving curve $OB$ is above the labor supply line $CC$. Hence, the rate of capital accumulation exceeds the rate of increase of the labor supply, and $n$ tends to decrease. In the same way, when $n$ is less than $n^*$, there is a tendency for $n$ to increase. That is, the labor/capital ratio tends to approach the long-run steady state with the passage of time. In other words, the process of economic growth in the neoclassical system is dynamically stable.

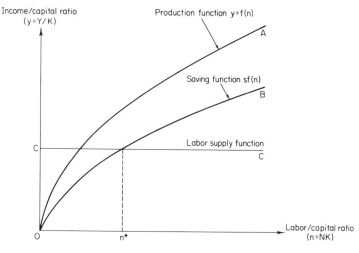

**Fig. 1**

## IV. The Neoclassical Theory of Monetary Growth

Attention up to this point has been paid to the real aspect of the neoclassical process of economic growth, in which money has not played any role. How is the process of growth, when money plays an essential role, formulated? Monetary growth in neoclassical theory has been treated by Tobin [32, 33], Sidrauski [27], Johnson [10], Levhari and Patinkin [15], and Uzawa [34], among others. Characteristic of the neoclassical theory of monetary growth is its hypothesis concerning the money supply. It ignores the institutional details of the money supply mechanism. The central bank, through transfer payments, distributes money to the economic units of the national economy. Money supplied in this way supplements each unit's income as transfer payments. In one formulation money performs the function of a consumer good which increases the level of utility for each individual; in another, it is a factor of production which is a substitute for labor and capital. Accordingly, it may be assumed that the demand for money depends on the market rate of interest and the level of income.

At a certain point of time, the physical capital held by each economic unit will be denoted by $K_j^0$ and the cash balance by $M_j^0$. If the market price of goods and services is taken as $P$, the real amount of assets is expressed by

$$A_j^0 = K_j^0 + (M_j^0/P).$$

The profit derived from real capital will be obtained in the same way as it was previously. When the real wage rate is given, the marginal product of capital which corresponds to it becomes the rate of profit. The gains derived from real cash balances $M_j/P$, as a consumption good, is in the form of marginal utility, and, as a production good, in the form of marginal product. If the rate of profit from real cash balances is taken as having no relation to capital, labor, and consumption levels, then, as shown in Fig. 2, the larger $M_j/P$ is (with quantities increasing to the left), the lower is the marginal product of real balances. In Fig. 2, $AB$ represents the real amount of total

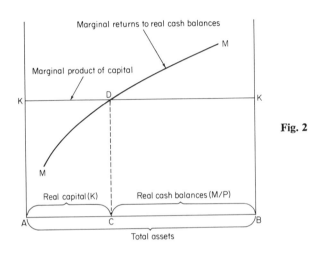

Fig. 2

assets held $A_j$, $AC = K$ is the quantity of real capital, and $CB = M_j/P$ is the amount of real balances held. The marginal products of real capital $KK$ and of real balances $MM$ are measured along the vertical axis. The optimum composition of capital is at point $C$, which corresponds to the intersection $D$ of the $KK$ and $MM$ curves.

Thus the optimum asset portfolio $(K_j, M_j/P)$ is related to the marginal product of capital.

The conditions of equilibrium of the stock of capital and money can be stated by

$$K_j = K^0 \ \left(\equiv \sum_j K_j{}^0\right), \qquad M_j = M^0 \ \left(\equiv \sum_j M_j{}^0\right).$$

The real wage rate is determined at the level at which demand and supply in the labor market are equal, and the marginal product of capital at full employment is given by

$$r = f(n^0) - n^0 f'(n^0), \qquad n^0 = N^0/K^0.$$

It follows from the preceding analysis that the aggregate demands for real capital and cash balances can both be regarded as being related to the price level $P$, and that the equilibrium price level is uniquely determined. It is also assumed that the market price $P$ of real capital determined through the process of equilibrium in the assets market can be regarded as the price of goods and services.

The increase in the money supply is included in income as a transfer payment; nominal income becomes

$$PF(K, N) + \dot{M}.$$

Now, if the expected rate of increase of the price level is given by

$$\pi^e = (\dot{P}/P)^e,$$

real income $Y$ is obtained by subtracting the depreciation of real cash balances from nominal income:

$$Y = F(K, N) + (\dot{M}/P) - \pi^e(M/P).$$

If the rate of increase in the money supply is denoted by

$$\mu = \dot{M}/M,$$

real income $Y$ may be expressed by

$$Y = F(K, N) + (\mu - \pi^e)(M/P).$$

Denoting the average propensity to consume by $1 - s$, consumption is $C = (1 - s)Y$, while the nominal amount of saving $S$ is given by

$$S = [PF(K, N) + \dot{M}] - PC$$

or

$$S = s[PF(K, N) + \mu M] + (1 - s)\pi^e M.$$

Saving is used either for the purchase of capital $P\dot{K}$ or for the increase in cash balances. Hence, the amount of new capital purchased may be written as

$$P\dot{K} = S - \mu M = sPF(K, N) - (1 - s)(\mu - \pi^e)M$$

or

$$\dot{K} = sF(K, N) - (1 - s)(\mu - \pi^e)M/P.$$

The rates of increase of the money supply and labor are exogenously given:

$$\dot{M}/M = \mu, \qquad \dot{N}/N = v.$$

If the portfolio preference is homothetic, the demand function for real cash balances may be given by

$$M/PK = \lambda(i, Y/K)$$

where $i$ is the nominal (or market) rate of interest, being the sum of the real rate of interest $\rho$ and the expected rate of price increase $\pi^e$: $i = \rho + \pi^e$.

It may be assumed that $\lambda(i, Y/K)$ is a decreasing function of $i$ and an increasing function of $Y/K$:

$$\frac{\partial \lambda}{\partial i} < 0, \qquad \frac{\partial \lambda}{\partial (Y/K)} > 0.$$

In order to analyze the model of neoclassical monetary growth formulated here, the following variables will be introduced:

$m = M/PK,$      real cash balances per unit of capital

$y = Y/K,$      income per unit of capital

$n = N/K,$      labor/capital ratio.

The short-run equilibrium conditions may be stated as

$$y = f(n) + (\mu - \pi^e)m \tag{15}$$

$$m = \lambda(i, y) \tag{16}$$

where

$$i = \rho + \pi^e, \qquad \rho = r = f(n) - nf'(n). \tag{17}$$

The basic dynamic equation becomes

$$\dot{n}/n = v - [f(n) - (1 - s)y]. \tag{18}$$

At each moment of time, $n$ and $\pi^e$ are given at the levels historically determined, while $\mu$ is a policy variable. Then $\rho$ and $m = M/PK$ are established so as to satisfy the equilibrium conditions (15) and (16), together with the equilibrium level of $n$. Finally, $\dot{n}/n$ is simply given by Eq. (18).

When the expected rate of price increase is inelastic, namely, $\pi^e$ is maintained at a fixed level, it can be shown that the dynamic equation (18) is stable. To prove this stability, Eqs. (15) and (16) may be rewritten as

$$y = (\mu - \pi^e)\lambda(i, y) + f(n). \tag{19}$$

For a given $n$, the $y$ satisfying Eq. (19) may be assumed to be uniquely determined. This is indeed the case if the following condition is satisfied:

$$(\mu - \pi^e)\frac{\partial \lambda}{\partial y} < 1.$$

Moreover, it may be assumed that when $n$ increases, the $y$ satisfying (19) also increases. This condition is met if either $\mu$ is less than $\pi^e$ or the elasticity of demand for real balances with respect to the rate of interest $i$ is relatively small.

The average propensity to save is in general a function of the expected real rate of interest. However, this dependency will be ignored in the following analysis, so that the average propensity to save is assumed to be constant, taking a value between 0 and 1. It is also easily seen that the right-hand side of the dynamic equation (18) is a decreasing function of the labor/capital ratio, provided the elasticity of demand for real balances with respect to the rate of interest is small relative both to $\mu - \pi^e$ and $s$. In this case, there is a uniquely determined long-run steady labor/capital ratio $n^*$ for which $\dot{n} = 0$. When the current $n$ is larger than $n^*$, $\dot{n} < 0$ and $n$ tends to decrease. On the other hand, when $n$ is less than $n^*$, $\dot{n} > 0$ and $n$ tends to increase. Thus the long-run steady state $n^*$ is dynamically stable.

It is not generally the case that the right-hand side of Eq. (18) is a decreasing function of $n$. However, in the general case the right side of (18) tends to be positive as $n$ tends to 0 and to be negative as $n$ tends to infinity. Hence, it can be shown that there exists at least one long-run steady labor/capital ratio $n^*$ and that any dynamic path satisfying (18) converges to a certain long-run steady state.

The dynamic stability shown above crucially depends on the assumption that the expected rate of price increase is inelastic. Let us assume instead that expectations are adjusted according to the adaptive expectation of the Cagan–Nerlove type ([1, 19]):

$$\dot{\pi}^e = \beta(\pi - \pi^e), \qquad \pi = \dot{P}/P \tag{20}$$

where $\beta$ is the speed of adjustment in expectations.

Equation (20) has the following meaning. When each economic unit chooses its asset portfolio, it does so not with reference to the current rate of price increase but rather to the expectations of the average rise in prices from now through the future. Moreover, when there is a discrepancy between $\pi$ and $\pi^e$, expectations are adjusted according to the difference between these two rates.

When $\beta$ is close to 0, the dynamic system (18) and (20) can be shown to be stable. One has only to note that the stability criterion obtained in the previous case remains valid because of a slight perturbation caused by the process of adaptive expectations for which the speed of adjustment is small.

However, $\beta$ is expected to be generally large within the framework of neoclassical theory. In order to explain why this is the case, let us note that the following reasons are offered to justify the use of the expected rate of price increase in choosing a portfolio. The real value of profits from various assets is affected by the rate of price increase; when choosing a portfolio at the current point in time, it is necessary to make choices according to the expectations of the price increase during the period that the portfolio is to be held. In neoclassical theory, it is assumed that the portfolio may be instantaneously and freely changed without incurring any costs of adjustment and without regard to whether the portfolio consists of real capital or financial assets. Hence, the expectation of price increases in the very near future may be regarded as relevant, and there is no need to anticipate the rate of price increase over a longer term because the portfolio can be rechosen at any time ·in the future. Thus it may be assumed that $\pi^e$ is either little different from that of the present or, if there is a difference, it is quickly adjusted to the current level. In other words, under the assumption of neoclassical theory, $\beta$ is expected to be large.

I should like to consider the limiting case in which the speed of adjustment is infinity and it is assumed that the expected rate of price increase coincides with the current rate of price increase:

$$\pi^e = \pi = \dot{P}/P.$$

The equilibrium conditions (15)–(17) may now be written as

$$y = f(n) + (\mu - \pi)m \tag{21}$$

$$m = \lambda(i, y) \tag{22}$$

$$i = \rho + \pi, \qquad \rho = r = f(n) - nf'(n). \tag{23}$$

At each moment of time, $n$ and $m$ are given, together with $\mu$. The level of real income per unit of capital and the rate of price increase are determined in such a way that equilibrium conditions (21) and (22) are both satisfied. Since, under (21), increases in $\pi$ have to be accompanied by decreases in $y$, the combinations of $\pi$ and $y$ for which (21) is satisfied may be described by a downward-sloping curve IS in Fig. 3. Similarly, the combinations of $\pi$ and $y$ for which (22) is satisfied may be described by an upward-sloping curve LM in Fig. 3. The equilibrium $(y, \pi)$ then is uniquely determined by the intersection of the IS and LM curves.

The dynamic path of such a monetary growth model then is described by the differential equations

$$\dot{n}/n = v - [f(n) - (1 - s)y] \tag{24}$$

$$\dot{m}/m = \mu - \pi - [f(n) - (1 - s)y]. \tag{25}$$

The long-run behavior of dynamic paths described by Eqs. (24) and (25) is not easy to analyze, particularly in view of ambiguities concerning the effects of changes in $n$ and $m$ on $\pi$. However, it can be shown that the solution paths

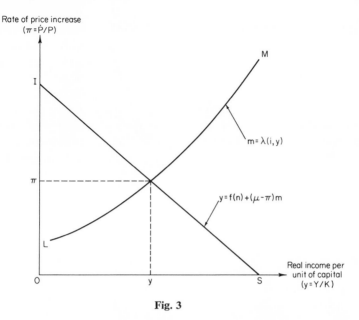

**Fig. 3**

to the dynamic system (24) and (25) either converge cyclically to, or approach a limit cycle around, the long-run steady state. This is due to the fact that solution paths are all bounded and that, in view of the Poincaré–Bendixon theorem on a pair of differential equations, any solution path has to converge to a singular point or to a limit cycle. The stability of typical solution paths is illustrated by the curves with arrows in Figs. 4 and 5. The cases illustrated assume that the $\dot{m} = 0$ curve $(AA)$ is steeper than the $\dot{n} = 0$ curve $(BB)$. The dynamic stability for other cases may be similarly illustrated.

The preceding was an attempt at considering the basic assumptions underlying neoclassical theory and analyzing the stability of the dynamic process of the neoclassical growth models developed by Tobin, Solow, and Swan. The model formulated here does not necessarily incorporate all the characteristic features of their model, but it does seem to describe essential aspects of neoclassical theory. Among them, the lack of a distinction between business firms and households as the basic units of the national economy; the assumption that real capital as a factor of production is simply the accumulation of invested goods; and the assumption that the assets market is perfectly competitive. Further, the assumption is made that the money supply mechanism simply distributes new money to each member as transfer payments. Within this framework, it has been shown that both the real and monetary growth processes are dynamically stable, provided certain qualifying constraints are satisfied.

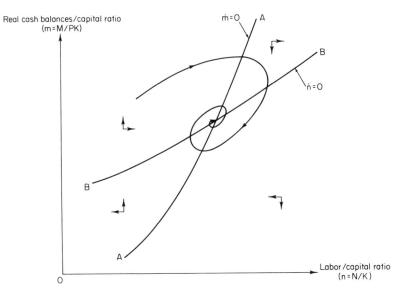

**Fig. 4**

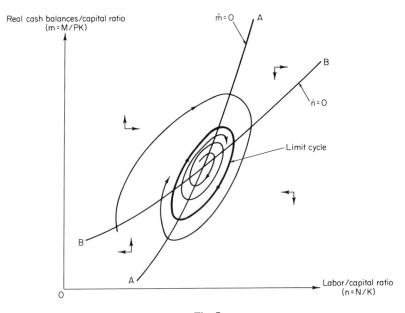

**Fig. 5**

## V. A Keynesian Theory of Economic Growth

In the previous sections, I presented a general view of the process of economic growth within the framework of neoclassical theory. Next I should like to consider the problem based on the theoretical framework of Keynes' *General Theory*.

Many economists have constructed what may be termed Keynesian growth models. Examples may be found in the works of Stein [29, 30], Hahn [3, 4], and Rose [21–23]. But these writers seem to have emphasized only certain aspects without touching on what seem to be the central features of the *General Theory*. They are based on the theoretical models developed by Hicks [8], Hansen [5], Lange [13], Modigliani [17, 18], and others, which have slightly different nuances than those originally intended by Keynes. The formulation commonly referred to as the income–expenditure approach seems, for the following reasons, not to be in accord with the theoretical framework of the *General Theory*.

The first point concerns the price mechanism of the goods and services market. The income–expenditure approach presupposes that the price level is fixed as long as there is involuntary unemployment. This assumption is difficult to reconcile with other aspects of the theory of effective demand, as discussed in detail by Sato [26], Saito [24, 25], Fujino [2], and Leijonhufvud [14].

The second point concerns the role of the market rate of interest in the process of investment determination. In the income–expenditure approach the premise is that the current level of investment is determined by the rate of interest and other factors concerning the expectations of future profits and costs. Recent empirical research on whether investment is flexible in relation to the market rate of interest seems to be not entirely consistent with the income–expenditure assumption. It would be more in accord with the *General Theory* to assume that investment behavior is based on expectations formed in the corporate sector concerning future profits and the rate of interest, as discussed by Inada and Uzawa [9] and Uzawa [37, 38], among others.

For purposes of developing a simplified Keynesian model, the national economy is viewed as consisting of business firms and households. Business firms employ labor and other factors of production and engage in production and sales; households own the primary factors of production and possess as assets securities issued by the firms.

Besides households and business firms, which make up the private sector, there is also a governmental sector. The latter provides various public goods and services which are financed through taxes or the issue of new money. New money is provided by the central bank and includes not only increases in the money supply to meet fiscal deficits, but also money issued through open market operations. It is assumed that governmental policies concerning expenditures and revenues, i.e., fiscal policy, and policies concerning the money supply, i.e., monetary policy, can be controlled independently. This assumption, of course, does not obtain in reality, but it is assumed here chiefly to bring out the crucial differences in the effects of the two policies on the working of the national economy.

An abstraction is also made concerning the market system. The market is broken down into three main divisions: the goods and services market, the labor market, and the financial market. The following simplified assumptions will be made about the mechanisms by which these markets are adjusted. First, in the goods and services market it is assumed that prices are always adjusted to equate supply with demand, and in the corporate sector production is always adjusted in response to changes in prices. In the labor market it is assumed that when the demand for labor exceeds supply, money wage rates are immediately increased and equilibrium is restored, but when the supply of labor exceeds demand, wage rates do not decline, resulting in involuntary unemployment. In the core of the financial market lies the money (short-term asset) market, which is highly organized and operates efficiently. It is assumed that money and short-term financial assets are transacted efficiently in the money market, but the price adjustment mechanism for long-term securities is not efficient and there is a time lag in the adjustment of securities prices.

The total amount of goods and services supplied by the whole corporate sector is determined by the scale of the production schedule of individual firms in response to market conditions. The productive capacity of various firms depends on the amounts of fixed factors of production accumulated through past investment. Assuming that labor is the only variable factor of production which can be obtained in the market, the production function of each firm may be expressed as

$$Q_j = F_j(N_j)$$

where $Q_j$ is the amount produced and $N_j$ is the amount of labor employed. It is assumed that only one kind of good is produced so that products of different firms may be measured by the same unit. The amount produced by firm $j$, $Q_j$, and the labor employment $N_j$ will be determined so as to maximize profits $PQ_j - WN_j$, where $P$ is the market price of the product and $W$ is the money wage rate. Profits are maximized when the marginal product of labor equals real wages:

$$F_j'(N_j) = W/P.$$

It must be kept in mind that this assumes that labor is a variable factor of production and that the firm can, at any point in time, freely increase or decrease its labor employment.

Now, by aggregating the amount of labor employed by each firm, the total amount of labor employed is

$$N = \sum_j N_j .$$

An increase in $W$ or a decrease in $P$ both increase real wages. The amount produced by firm $j$ is measured in terms of money wages:

$$P_W Q_j = PQ_j/W, \qquad P_W = P/W.$$

In this way the aggregate quantity $Z$ defined as

$$Z = \sum_j P_W Q_j$$

becomes what Keynes referred to as the aggregate supply price.

The aggregate supply price $Z$ corresponds to the goods and services produced by the corporate sector as measured in units of money wages. An increase in market price $P$ induces a decline in real wages $W/P$, increasing the amount of labor employed $N$ as well as the aggregate supply price $Z$. The relationship between $Z$ and $P$ is commonly shown in a curve such as $OZ$ in Fig. 6. An increase in money wages increases the real wage rate, resulting in a downward shift in the aggregate supply curve and the aggregate labor demand curve.

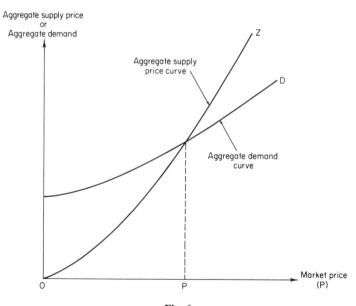

Fig. 6

In this way, the aggregate supply price can be explained by the productive capacity of the corporate sector as expressed by the production function and the maximizing behavior of business firms. On the other hand, aggregate demand is determined by the behavior of households, business firms, and government vis-à-vis consumption and investment.

First, consumption demand is determined by the way in which households choose to divide their income between consumption and saving. Household income consists of wages, dividends, and interest payments. Current consumption is determined by expected real income, which is based on long-term expectations concerning future wage rates and future earnings obtained from currently held financial assets.

Expressing real income measured in money wages as $Y_W$,

$$Y_W = N + \rho A_W$$

where $\rho$ is the real rate of interest (to be obtained by subtracting the rate of price increase $\pi$ from the market rate of interest $i$) and $A_W$ is the amount of assets measured in money wage units. Permanent income $Y_W^e$ is based on the expected real rate of interest and the expected increase in the wage rate.

Consumption demand $C_W$ is a function of the expected real rate of interest $\rho^e$ and permanent real income $Y_W^e$:

$$C_W = C_W(\rho^e, Y_W^e).$$

When the relationship of time preference which expresses subjective value judgments is homothetic, the elasticity of consumption demand with respect to permanent real income is 1 and the consumption function may be written as

$$C_W = [1 - s(\rho^e)] Y_W^e$$

where $s(\rho^e)$ is the average propensity to save (relative to the level of permanent real income). In what follows, the dependency of $s = s(\rho^e)$ on the expected real rate of interest will be mostly ignored.

Since consumption depends on permanent real income, increasing the money supply through open market operations can be seen to have the following effects on consumption demand. Permanent real income is defined as the level of real income which households expect to receive for the entire period of their lifetime, and it has to take into account the effects that fiscal and monetary policies may have on the financial situation of the private sector. Since an open market purchase of privately held securities tends to have a compensating effect on the future earnings of the private sector, it may be assumed that any change in the money supply does not induce private economic units to change their long-term expectations. This is related to the point mentioned by Metzler [16, p. 109, n. 16]. It will also be assumed that the expected real rate of interest $\rho^e$ is not affected by changes in the market rate of interest which accompany fluctuations in the money supply. However, $\rho^e$ is assumed to be adaptively adjusted over time; namely, $\rho^e$ is assumed to change according to the differential equation

$$\dot{\rho}^e = \beta(\rho - \rho^e), \tag{26}$$

with $\beta$ being the speed of adjustment.

Next let us consider the factors determining investment demand. First it is necessary to touch on the concept of capital in Keynes' theory. In neoclassical theory, capital has been merely understood as material factors of production, with little attention paid to its fixity. Only the demand and the market for capital goods as a stock are allowed for. Keynes' treatment differs from neoclassical theory on this point concerning the fixity of capital.

The firm carries on production with an assortment of fixed and variable factors of production. The management consists of various scarce resources which are employed for accomplishing certain specific goals. The firm tries to maximize profit by producing and selling goods and services, but to maximize the future flow, as well as the current level, of profits. For that purpose it not only employs variable factors, but accumulates fixed factors in order to produce efficiently in the future. The fixed factors are land, factories, machines, equipment, and other physical inputs, as well as technological, managerial, administrative, and other scarce resources. Moreover, once these scarce resources are accumulated in a firm they cannot be disposed of easily without sustaining a substantial loss. These fixed resources are not accumulated simply by being purchased on the market, but expenditures are needed for their installation as well.

What effect does the system of fixed factors of production have on the activities of the firm at different points in time? Two difficulties arise with respect to this problem. First, the fixed factors of a firm are of many different types and, moreover, they have been accumulated in the past when different market conditions prevailed. Accordingly, it is not always possible to quantify the role they play in the production process. This problem was avoided earlier in this chapter by assuming that all goods and services are of one kind. Whether or not a market price exists, the role of scarce resources in the production process is not reflected in the price when the factors are fixed. An evaluation of the accumulated fixed scarce resources of the firm must be related to the role these resources play in the production process. Because profits express the accomplishment of the firm, it is natural to measure its capacity by the ability to create profits. The index of the capacity of the firm at a point in time $t$, to be denoted by $K_t$, is defined as the ratio of the real profit $Q_t - wN_t$ at time $t$ over the real profit $Q_0 - wN_0$ at the standard time 0, with $w$ being the real wage rate. However, the index of a firm's capacity thus defined is related to the real wage. When a different real wage rate is used, the profit ratio will differ and the index of the firm's capacity will possibly change as well. Uzawa [35] avoided this difficulty by postulating that the profit ratio is determined independently of $w$. Based on this postulate, the production relation at time $t$ can be expressed in terms of $K_t$ and $N_t$:

$$Q_t = K_t f(N_t/K_t) \tag{27}$$

where $f(\ )$, the production function, is the same as that prevailing at the standard time 0.

The index of the firm's capacity derived in this manner expresses the role that accumulated fixed resources play in the firm's production process. It corresponds to the concept of real capital in neoclassical theory, and it will be referred to simply as real capital in the present context.

Real capital $K_t$ is increased by investment activity. What is referred to as investment activity means not only the accumulation of physical factors, such as the purchase of capital goods and construction, but also the accumulation of technology through research and development, as well as the accumulation of managerial and administrative resources.

How can the effect of fixed factors accumulated through the purchase of goods and services be measured? The effects of investment are measured by the extent to which the production function shifts as a result of investment. It is assumed that there is a fixed relationship between the real amount of investment $\Phi_t$ and the resulting increase in real capital $\dot{K}_t$. This relationship is determined by the scarce resources accumulated by the firm which are required for growth and expansion. Uzawa [35] called this the Penrose effect, associated with the pioneering work of Edith Penrose [20] on the theory of the growth of the firm. For the purposes of considering this problem from a general standpoint, it will simply be called the investment effect. The investment effect depends on the quantity of fixed factors accumulated for the purpose of growth and on the shift which accompanies changes in that quantity. Assuming that the index of a firm's capacity is proportional to the amount of scarce resources, the relationship between the rate of investment $\Phi_t/K_t$ and the resulting rate of increase of real capital $\dot{K}_t/K_t$ is expressed as

$$\Phi_t/K_t = \varphi(\dot{K}_t/K_t). \tag{28}$$

The effect of investment is governed by the investment-effect function $\varphi(\ )$, which is assumed to exhibit the features of diminishing returns to investment:

$$\varphi'(\alpha) > 0, \qquad \varphi''(\alpha) > 0. \tag{29}$$

As was touched on previously, real investment becomes an increase in real capital in neoclassical theory; namely, in neoclassical theory the investment-effect function is given by

$$\varphi(\alpha) = \alpha \qquad \text{or} \qquad I = \dot{K}. \tag{30}$$

The long-run behavior of the firm may be assumed to be described by the maximization of the discounted present value of future net cash flows. Let the real net cash flow at time $t$ be denoted by $\Gamma_t$, namely,

$$\Gamma_t = Q_t - w_t N_t - \Phi_t \tag{31}$$

where

$$Q_t = K_t f(N_t/K_t) \tag{32}$$

$$\Phi_t = K_t \varphi(\dot{K}_t/K_t). \tag{33}$$

The discount rate to be used to discount future real net cash flows is not simply the market rate of interest, but the real rate of interest expected to prevail in the future. The scarce resources which are accumulated through investment activity will become fixed factors of production not to be disposed of easily during their lifetime. Hence, the firm has to use the rate of discount which is expected to prevail during the period in which invested resources will last. The rate depends on the way in which the firm obtains its funds for investment, but the model being developed here ignores such aspects of the financial market.

It will be assumed that the expectations adjustment mechanisms concerning the real rate of interest are the same for the corporate sector as for the household sector. Accordingly, the discounted present value $V_0$ is given by

$$V_0 = \int_0^\infty \Gamma_t \exp(-\rho^e t)\, dt, \tag{34}$$

which is to be maximized subject to the investment and employment schedules (31)–(33) of the firm.

If the expectations of the real wage rate are assumed to be constant, the following conditions are established concerning the plan for which $V_0$ is maximized. First, the labor/capital ratio is a constant depending on the expected real wage rate only:

$$N_t/K_t = n \qquad \text{where} \quad f'(n) = w.$$

Moreover, the optimum rate of investment and the rate of growth are both constant over time:

$$\Phi_t/K_t = \varphi(\alpha), \qquad \dot{K}_t/K_t = \alpha.$$

Then the discounted present value simply becomes

$$V_0 = ([r - \varphi(\alpha)]/[\rho^e - \alpha])\, K_0 \tag{35}$$

where $r$ is the marginal product of capital corresponding to the labor/capital ratio $n$:

$$r = f(n) - nf'(n).$$

The rate of accumulation for which (35) is maximized is a function of $\rho^e$ and $r$:

$$\alpha = \alpha(\rho^e, r), \qquad \varphi = \varphi(\rho^e, r).$$

Both $\alpha$ and $\varphi$ are decreasing functions with respect to $\rho^e$, and increasing functions with respect to $r$.

From the preceding argument the investment function can be expressed as

$$\Phi = \varphi(\rho^e, r)K.$$

Government expenditures can be formulated in a variety of ways depending on how policy variables are used. Here, government expenditures are assumed to have a fixed ratio $g$ to national income, and taxation may be ignored. Government expenditures $G_W$ become

$$G_W = g Y_W \tag{36}$$

where $g$ is a policy variable.

The aggregate demand for goods and services is the sum of consumption demand, investment demand, and government expenditures:

$$D = C_W + \Phi_W + G_W$$

or

$$D = [1 - s] Y_W^e + P_W \varphi(\rho^e, r)K + g Y_W. \tag{37}$$

An increase in the price level measured in wage units $P_W$ is always accompanied by an increase in the level of labor employment, which in turn results in an increase in the rate of profit. Hence aggregate demand increases when the price level increases, provided the market rate of interest is kept constant and the expected real rate of interest remains fixed. As shown in Fig. 6, aggregate demand can be expressed by a curve having a slope less steep than the schedule of the aggregate supply function, given that the average propensity to save $s$ exceeds the governmental expenditure ratio $g$ and that permanent real income coincides with current income.

Equilibrium in the goods and services market is obtained when aggregate supply $Z$ equals aggregate demand $D$:

$$D = Z \tag{38}$$

or

$$(1 - s) Y_W^e + P_W \varphi(\rho^e, r)K + g Y_W = Y_W. \tag{39}$$

When (39) is measured not in money wage units, but in units of produced goods and services, we get

$$(\rho^e, r)K = (s - g)Q + (1 - s)(Y_W - Y_W^e)/P_W. \tag{40}$$

If expectations concerning the real wage rate are static, then

$$Y_W{}^e/P_W = wN + \rho^e A/P$$

where $A$ is evaluated according to the market price of assets in the private sector.

The aggregates in real capital units are defined as

$$f(n) = Q/K, \qquad\qquad \text{output/capital ratio}$$

$$a = A/PK = \frac{[r - \varphi(\alpha)]}{[\rho^e - \alpha]}, \qquad \text{assets/capital ratio.}$$

The condition of equilibrium for the goods and services market can be expressed by

$$\varphi(\rho^e, r) = (s - g)f(n) + (1 - s)(r - \rho^e a). \tag{41}$$

The price level $P$ and the corresponding labor/capital ratio are uniquely determined by

$$f'(N/K) = w = W/P. \tag{42}$$

The investment function $\varphi(\rho^e, r)$ may be assumed to be a decreasing function of $\rho^e$ and an increasing function of $r$. As was discussed in detail in ref. [36], these assumptions may be justified for a broad class of circumstances in which the schedule of the marginal efficiency of investment is subject to a diminishing rate of return. A simple calculation also shows that

$$\rho^e a = \rho^e [r - \varphi(\alpha)]/(\rho^e - \alpha)$$

is a decreasing function of $\rho^e$. Hence, a decrease in $\rho^e$ results in a decrease of the quantity on the left side of (41), while the quantity on the right side is increased. Hence, a decrease in $\rho^e$ (or similarly an increase in $r$) results in an increase in the demand for both investment and consumption, thus entailing an increase in the effective level of employment. The equilibrium relation between $\rho^e$ and $n$ can be seen in Eq. (41) and is plotted as the downward-sloping curve IS in Fig. 7.

The market rate of interest is related to the market price of securities, which in turn is related to the condition of portfolio demand. This makes it necessary to consider the factors which go into determining the portfolio of financial assets.

In the *General Theory*, a broad class of money was used including time deposits and short-term securities such as Treasury bills, thus justifying the focus on the analysis of speculative motives (see, e.g., Keynes [11, p. 167]). In this chapter, however, money is used in a narrower sense; it is comprised of cash and demand deposits, so that the motives for holding it are based mainly on transaction purposes, while speculative motives may be ignored.

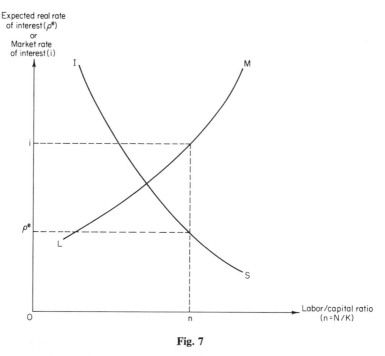

**Fig. 7**

The demand for money depends first on expectations of the aggregate amount of transactions. If the demand for real cash balances $L_W$ has unit elasticity and we let income stand in for total transactions, we may write

$$L_W = \lambda Y_W \tag{43}$$

where $L_W$ and $Y_W$ are measured in money wage units. The coefficient $\lambda$ is the demand for real cash balances per unit of income, corresponding to Marshall's $k$.

The demand for real balances depends not only on real income, but also on the opportunity costs of holding money or on the market rate of interest. When the rate of interest increases, it becomes desirable to possess securities and the demand for money per unit of income falls. Namely, $\lambda$ is a decreasing function of the market rate of interest:

$$\lambda = \lambda(i), \qquad \lambda'(i) < 0. \tag{44}$$

When the nominal quantity of money is determined by the central bank, the market rate of interest is determined by the equilibrium of the money market:

$$\lambda(i) Y_W = M_W \quad (\equiv M/W). \tag{45}$$

If the demand for money is less than the supply, i.e., if $\lambda(i)Y_W < M_W$, the demand for securities exceeds the supply and the price of securities increases, resulting in a decrease in the market rate of interest. In the opposite situation, there is an increase in the rate of interest; equilibrium is established in the money market only if (45) is satisfied. The LM curve in Fig. 7 expresses the combinations of $i$ and the labor/capital ratio $n$ for which the money market is in equilibrium. An increase in the aggregate level of labor employment or in $n$ shifts the demand schedule for real balances upward, entailing an increase in the equilibrium rate of interest. Hence, the LM curve has an upward-sloping shape as indicated in Fig. 7.

The determination of the short-run equilibrium in our model may be illustrated in terms of the IS and LM curves in Fig. 7. The level of the expected real rate of interest is historically given at $\rho^e$. Then the labor/capital ratio $n$ corresponding to the effective level of employment is determined by the IS schedule, as illustrated by a dotted line in Fig. 7. The market rate of interest $i$ for which the money market is in equilibrium then is determined by the LM schedule, as indicated again by a dotted line in Fig. 7.

A decrease in the expected real rate of interest $\rho^e$ increases effective demand, and the labor/capital ratio corresponding to the effective employment of labor is increased. At the same time, the demand for money shifts upward, resulting in an increase in the market rate of interest.

## VI. Keynesian Growth under Full Employment

In Section V we considered how employment, income, prices, and the market rate of interest are determined in a Keynesian system. Next, let us consider these variables under the conditions of full employment and continuous economic growth.

Let the rates of increase in money supply and labor supply both be exogenously given:

$$\dot{M}/M = \mu, \qquad \dot{N}/N = \nu.$$

When the conditions of full employment are satisfied, real national income per capita $\hat{y}$ becomes

$$\hat{y} = f(n)/n, \qquad n = N/K.$$

When economic growth is to continue under the conditions of full employment, the following conditions have to be satisfied. First, $\rho^e$ must be at a level where the aggregate demand it engenders is equal to the supply of goods and services. Given $\rho^e$ and the governmental expenditure coefficient $g$, the labor/capital ratio corresponding to effective demand can be expressed as

$n(\rho^e, g)$. The elasticity of the effective labor/capital ratio with respect to $\rho^e$ is denoted by $\eta$:

$$\eta = -\frac{1}{n}\frac{\partial n}{\partial \rho^e}.$$

The rate of change in $n$ under conditions of full employment is

$$\dot{n}/n = v - \alpha \tag{46}$$

where $\alpha$ is the rate of increase in real capital under the equilibrium conditions:

$$\dot{K}/K = \alpha = \alpha(\rho^e, r). \tag{47}$$

In order to maintain full-employment growth, the changes in $\rho^e$ must fulfill the conditions

$$\dot{\rho}^e = (1/\eta)(\alpha - v). \tag{48}$$

On the other hand, $\rho^e$ is assumed to be adaptively adjusted:

$$\dot{\rho}^e = \beta(\rho - \rho^e), \qquad \rho = i - \pi. \tag{49}$$

Hence, in order for changes in $\rho^e$ to satisfy the conditions of full employment, the market rate of interest $i$ and the rate of price increase $\pi$ simultaneously satisfying (48) and (49) must be realized. Therefore, the following relation exists between $i$ and $\pi$:

$$i - \pi = \rho = \rho^e + (1/\beta\eta)(\alpha - v)$$

or

$$\pi = i - \rho^e - (1/\beta\eta)(\alpha - v). \tag{50}$$

A necessary condition for full-employment growth is that the money wage rate change so as to establish the equality of supply and demand in the labor market. Since

$$f'(n) = W/P, \tag{51}$$

the required rate of increase $\omega = \dot{W}/W$ in the money wage rate satisfies the relation

$$\omega = \pi + \varepsilon(\alpha - v) \tag{52}$$

where $\varepsilon$ is the elasticity of the marginal product of labor,

$$\varepsilon = s_K/\sigma,$$

and $s_K$ is the relative share of capital and $\sigma$ is the elasticity of substitution between labor and capital.

Finally, it is necessary to maintain the market rate of interest at a level where the money market is continuously in equilibrium. The equilibrium of the money market was formulated in (45), and putting it into units of real capital we get

$$\lambda(i)f(n) = M/PK. \tag{53}$$

Since the rate of increase in the money supply is exogenously given through monetary policy,

$$\dot{M}/M = \mu, \tag{54}$$

the continuation of the equilibrium of the money market yields the condition

$$-\gamma \frac{di}{dt} + (1 - s_K)\frac{dn}{dt} = \mu - \pi - \alpha \tag{55}$$

where $\gamma$ is the elasticity of the demand for money with respect to the market rate of interest:

$$\gamma = -\frac{1}{\lambda}\frac{d\lambda}{di} > 0.$$

Equation (55) may be written as

$$\frac{di}{dt} = \frac{1}{\gamma}\left[\pi - (\mu - v) + s_K(\alpha - v)\right] \tag{56}$$

or, using (50),

$$\frac{di}{dt} = \frac{1}{\gamma}\left[i - \rho^e - (\mu - v) - \left(\frac{1}{\beta} - s_K\right)(\alpha - v)\right]. \tag{57}$$

For the rate of change of per capita real national income, we have

$$\frac{1}{\hat{y}}\frac{d\hat{y}}{dt} = s_K(\alpha - v). \tag{58}$$

When full-employment growth continues, the dynamic equations (57) and (58) have to prevail. These are the two basic equations in a Keynesian theory of growth.

To analyze this dynamic system, let us consider the changes in $\rho^e$ and $\alpha$ accompanying changes in $\hat{y}$. As seen from the definition of per capita income $\hat{y}$, an increase in $\hat{y}$ results in a decrease in $n$. Hence, the value of $\rho^e$ for which $n$ corresponds to equilibrium in the goods and services market has to be increased, entailing a decrease in the rate of capital accumulation $\alpha$. Thus, an increase in $\hat{y}$ is shown to result in a decrease in $\alpha$. Moreover, because $\alpha$ is not directly affected by changes in $i$, changes in $\hat{y}$ can be examined separately. The level $\hat{y}^*$ of per capita real income for which $\dot{\hat{y}} = 0$ is uniquely determined. Namely, there is a level $\hat{y}^*$ which corresponds to the condition of long-term equilibrium and it is easily shown that it is dynamically stable. The long-run steady level $\hat{y}^*$ of per capita real income is determined independently of monetary policy $\mu$ and is affected only by the government expenditure coefficient $g$. In Fig. 8, the straight line $AA$ is a distance $\hat{y}^*$ from the vertical axis.

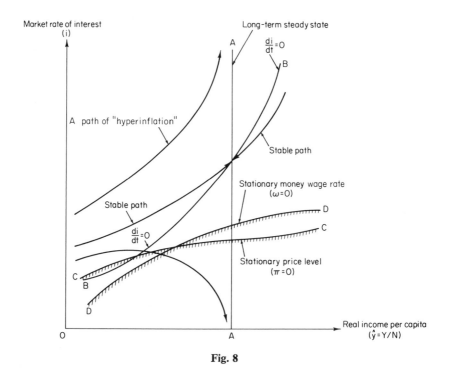

**Fig. 8**

Next let us consider the dynamic equation (57) concerning the market rate of interest $i$. For the market rate of interest $i$ to be maintained at a constant level, it is necessary for the right side of Eq. (57) to equal 0; namely,

$$i = \rho^e + (\mu - v) + [(1/\beta\eta) - s_K](\alpha - v). \qquad (59)$$

The right side of (59) is a function of $y$, and it can be typically expressed by the upward-sloping curve $BB$ in Fig. 8, where the market rate of interest $i$ is measured along the vertical axis and per capita real income $\hat{y}$ along the horizontal axis.

When the combination of $i$ and $\hat{y}$ is such that it lies on the $BB$ curve, the market rate of interest $i$ remains stationary over time. If it lies above the $BB$ curve, then $di/dt > 0$ and $i$ tends to increase. Conversely, if $i$ is lower than the level corresponding to the $BB$ curve, then $di/dt < 0$ and $i$ tends to decrease. Accordingly, the dynamic equation (57), which describes changes in the market rate of interest $i$, is unstable with respect to $i$.

Since the last term of the quantity on the right side of Eq. (59) disappears on the $AA$ line, it can be shown that the solution paths of the dynamic equations (57) and (58) may be represented in Fig. 8 by the cluster of curves with arrows. As indicated in Fig. 8, this system exhibits a kind of knife-edge instability. Namely, there are only two stable paths approaching long-term equilibrium states; for any other path the market rate of interest approaches either 0 or $\infty$.

In Fig. 8 there are two curves $CC$ and $DD$ which correspond to the conditions of stationary price level and stationary wage level, respectively. The $CC$ curve represents the combinations of $i$ and $y$ for which the price level remains stationary, i.e., $\pi = 0$. From Eq. (50), we can see that an increase in $y$ has to be associated with an increase in $i$ in order for $\pi$ to be 0, thus resulting in the upward-sloping curve $CC$. The rate of price increase is positive above the $CC$ curve. On the other hand, the $DD$ curve corresponds to the combinations of $i$ and $y$ for which the rate of money wage increase is 0, i.e., $\omega = 0$. Again we can show that the $DD$ curve has an upward slope, intersecting with the $DD$ curve as illustrated in Fig. 8. Below the $DD$ curve, the money wage rate has to decrease in order to maintain economic growth under the conditions of full employment. Hence, the phenomenon of involuntary unemployment occurs below the $DD$ curve.

For the general situation where the $BB$ curve is not necessarily rising to the right, it can be shown that the long-run steady state is uniquely determined. However, the saddle-point property of the long-run steady state may not necessarily be valid, and there exists a possibility that there is a class of solution paths to the dynamic system (57) and (58) which converges to the long-run steady state. Outside of such a class of solution paths, the asymptotic behavior of dynamic processes exhibits an unstable feature as already depicted.

Thus, it is very difficult to maintain a stable full-employment growth under the conditions of a constant rate of increase in the money supply. There are either unlimited increases in the rate of price increase, i.e., the state of hyperinflation, or there comes to be a state of involuntary unemployment. Economic growth displays the kind of knife-edge instability discussed by Harrod [6, 7]. To realize stable economic growth, it is necessary to have a flexible policy concerning the supply of money, e.g., that directed toward stabilization of the market rate of interest or the rate of price increase.

## VII. Concluding Remarks

In this chapter I have examined the various implications of the neoclassical and Keynesian approaches to the analysis of economic growth. The phenomenon of economic growth has been analyzed within an extremely simplified framework, and it is impossible to argue the general validity of the conclusions concerning the two approaches. However, the implications for the dynamic stability of the growth process seem to reflect the differences in the basic premises of each framework, suggesting that the implications may be generally applicable to a broader class of circumstances. In the neoclassical growth model, the path of economic growth is dynamically stable under fairly general assumptions, while, in the Keynesian theory, there is an intrinsic tendency for the growth process to be dynamically unstable unless certain stabilizing monetary and fiscal policies are adopted.

The two approaches have been discussed within a framework of dynamic equilibrium in which all markets are in equilibrium at each moment of time. It has not yet been possible to analyze the disequilibrium situation where all or some of the markets are not necessarily in equilibrium and changes in monetary and fiscal policies may bring about additional disequilibrating effects.

### ACKNOWLEDGMENTS

I should like to express my gratitude to Professors George Horwich and Akira Takayama for their comments and criticisms on an earlier version of this chapter.

### REFERENCES

1. Cagan, P., "The Monetary Dynamics of Hyperinflation," in *Studies in the Quantity Theory of Money* (M. Friedman, ed.), pp. 25–117. Chicago: Univ. of Chicago Press, 1956.
2. Fujino, S., "Keynesian Theory and the Determination of National Income," in *Keynes and Modern Economics* (R. Tachi, ed.), pp. 174–193. Tokyo: Univ. of Tokyo Press, 1968 (in Japanese).
3. Hahn, F. H., "The Stability of Growth Equilibrium," *Quarterly Journal of Economics* **74** (1960), 206–226.
4. Hahn, F. H., "On Money and Growth," *Journal of Money, Credit, and Banking* **1** (1969), 172–187.
5. Hansen, A. H., *Monetary Theory and Fiscal Policy.* New York: McGraw-Hill, 1949.
6. Harrod, R. F., "An Essay in Dynamic Theory," *Economic Journal* **64** (1939), 14–33.
7. Harrod, R. F., *Towards a Dynamic Economics.* New York: Macmillan, 1948.
8. Hicks, J. R., "Mr. Keynes and the 'Classics'; A Suggested Interpretation," *Econometrica* **5** (1937), 147–159.
9. Inada, K., and Uzawa, H., *Economic Development and Fluctuations,* particularly pp. 245–334. Tokyo: Iwanami, 1972 (in Japanese).
10. Johnson, H. G., "The Neo-Classical One-Sector Growth Model: A Geometric Exposition and Extension to a Monetary Economy," *Economica* **33** (1966), 265–287.
11. Keynes, J. M., *The General Theory of Employment, Interest and Money.* New York: Macmillan, 1936.
12. Klein, L. R., *The Keynesian Revolution.* New York: Macmillan, 1947.
13. Lange, O., *Price Flexibility and Employment.* Bloomington, Indiana: Principia Press, 1944.

14. Leijonhufvud, A., *On Keynesian Economics and the Economics of Keynes*. London and New York: Oxford Univ. Press, 1968.
15. Levhari, D., and Patinkin, D., "The Role of Money in a Simple Growth Model," *American Economic Review* **58** (1968), 713–753.
16. Metzler, L. A., "Wealth, Saving, and the Rate of Interest," *Journal of Political Economy* **59** (1951), 93–116.
17. Modigliani, F., "Liquidity Preference and the Theory of Interest and Money," *Econometrica* **12** (1944), 45–88.
18. Modigliani, F., "The Monetary Mechanism and Its Interaction with Real Variables," *Review of Economics and Statistics* **45** (1963), 79–107.
19. Nerlove, M., *Dynamics of Supply Estimation of Farmers' Response to Price*. Baltimore: Johns Hopkins Univ. Press, 1958.
20. Penrose, E. T., *The Theory of the Growth of the Firm*. Oxford: Blackwell, 1959.
21. Rose, H., "Unemployment in a Theory of Growth," *International Economic Review* **7** (1966), 260–282.
22. Rose, H., "On the Non-Linear Theory of the Employment Cycle," *Review of Economic Studies* **34** (1967), 153–173.
23. Rose, H., "Real and Monetary Factors in the Business Cycle," *Journal of Money, Credit, and Banking* **1** (1969), 138–152.
24. Saito, K., "On the Short-Run Mechanism of the Aggregate Income Distribution," *Shogaku Ronshu* **30** (1962), 1–44 (in Japanese).
25. Saito, K., "The Aggregate Supply Function and Macro-Economic Distribution," *Keizai Kenkyu* **13** (1962), 314–321 (in Japanese).
26. Sato, K., "On the Synthesis of Income Analysis and Price Theory: A Reconstruction of the Multiplier Theory," *Keizaigaku Kenkyu* **8** (1955), 51–88 (in Japanese).
27. Sidrauski, M., "Rational Choice and Pattern of Growth in a Monetary Economy," *American Economic Review, Proceedings* **57** (1967), 534–544.
28. Solow, R. M., "A Contribution to the Theory of Economic Growth," *Quarterly Journal of Economics* **70** (1956), 65–95.
29. Stein, J. L., "Money and Capacity Growth," *Journal of Political Economy* **74** (1966), 451–465.
30. Stein, J. L., "'Neoclassical' and 'Keynes–Wicksell' Monetary Growth Models," *Journal of Money, Credit, and Banking* **1** (1969), 153–171.
31. Swan, T. W., "Economic Growth and Capital Accumulation," *Economic Record* **32** (1956), 334–361.
32. Tobin, J., "A Dynamic Aggregative Model," *Journal of Political Economy* **63** (1955), 103–115.
33. Tobin, J., "Money and Economic Growth," *Econometrica* **33** (1965), 671–684.
34. Uzawa, H., "On a Neoclassical Model of Economic Growth," *Economic Studies Quarterly* **17** (1966), 1–15.
35. Uzawa, H., "The Penrose Effect and Optimum Growth," *Economic Studies Quarterly* **19** (1968), 1–14.
36. Uzawa, H., "Time Preference and the Penrose Effect in a Two-Class Model of Economic Growth," *Journal of Political Economy* **77** (1969), 628–652.
37. Uzawa, H., "Towards a Keynesian Model of Monetary Growth," *Proceedings of the International Economic Association Conference on the Theory of Economic Growth* (forthcoming).
38. Uzawa, H., "Diffusion of Inflationary Processes in a Dynamic Model of International Trade," *Economic Studies Quarterly* **22** (1971), 14–37.

# Author Index

Entries refer to authors designated by a numbered reference. Numbers in brackets are reference numbers and indicate that an author's work is referred to, although his name is not cited at that point in the text. Numbers in italics show the page on which the complete reference is listed.

## A

Abramovitz, M., 318, *331*
Aitken, A. C., 42, *75*
Alchian, A. A., 428, 432, 441, 442, *452,*
  *453*
Alexander, S. S., 130, *151*
Aliber, R. Z., 122, *126*
Allen, W. R., 442, *452*
Ames, E., 483, *484*
Arrow, K. J., 2, *75,* 184, 199, *201,* 204,
  *219,* 243, 244, 245, 246, 248[2],
  251[2], 252[2], 254, 255, 256, *257,*
  259, 264[1, 3], *267,* 433, 442, *452*

## B

Bagehot, W., 112, *126*
Bailey, M. J., 428, 441, *452*
Bassett, L., 206[4], 207[4], 208[4],
  211[4], *219*
Bastable, C. F., 22, *75*
Baumol, W., 289, *307,* 442, *452*
Becker, G. S., 442, *452*
Belsley, D. A., 318, 319, *331,* 333, *353*
Bhagwati, J. N., 14, *18,* 164, 165, 167,
  *177,* 504, *520*

Block, H. D., 69, *75,* 204[1], *219,* 244[1],
  *257,* 264[1], 265[1]
Bosworth, B., 351, *353*
Box, G. E. P., 319, *331*
Bresciani-Turroni, C., 23, *75*
Brock, W. A., 223, *241*
Bródy, A., 290, *307*
Brunner, K., 375, *398*
Burmeister, E., 279, *306*
Burton, E. T., III, 221[2], *241*

## C

Cagan, P., 533, *552*
Carlson, J. A., 311, 324, 329, *331,* 364,
  *370*
Cassel, G., 24, 25, *75*
Castain, C., 231, *241*
Caton, C., 279, *306*
Caves, R. E., 116, *126,* 504, *520*
Chiang, A. C., *370*
Childs, G. L., 318, *331,* 333, *353*
Chipman, J. S., 25, 28, 29, 31, 32, 38, 49,
  51, 52, 59, 66, 68, *75*
Claassen, E., 112, *126*
Clower, R. W., 402, *424*

554